3rd Edition

1999 - 2000

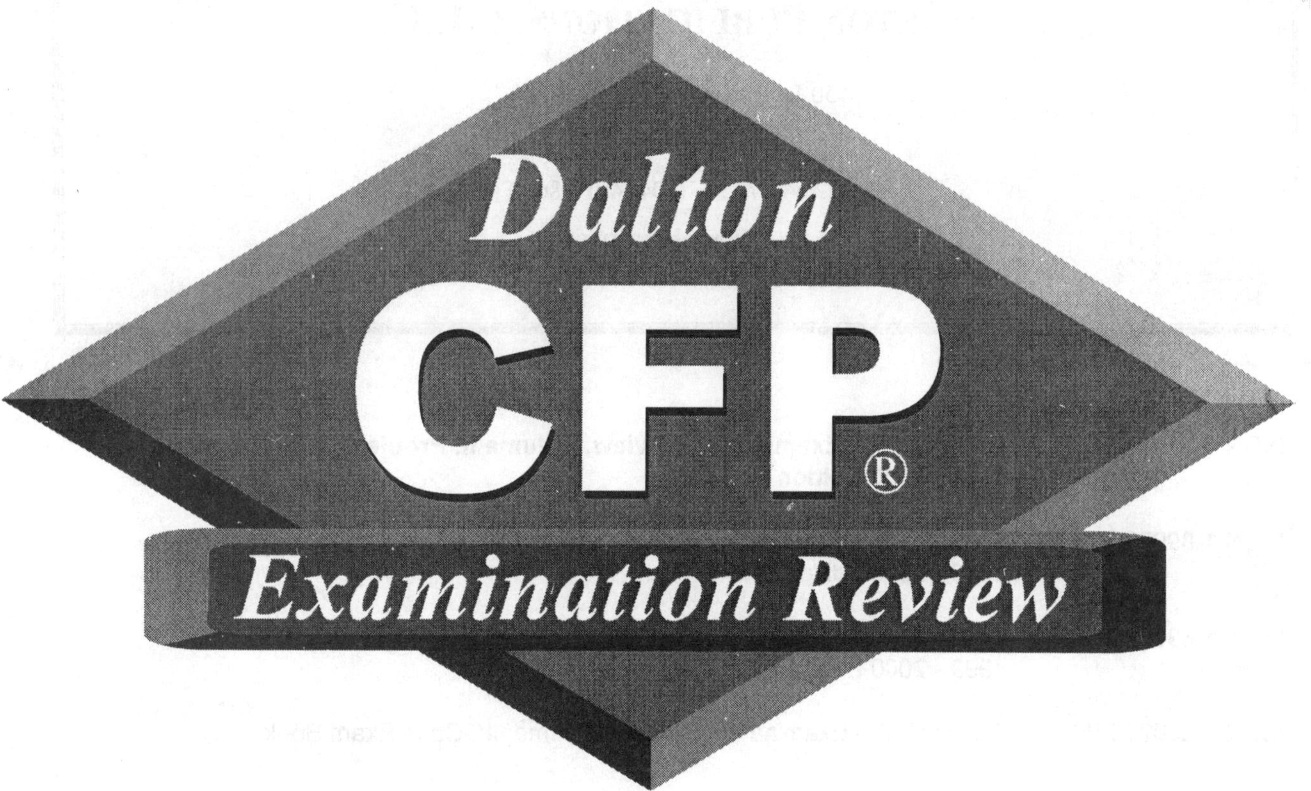

Volume II

Problems and Solutions

Michael A. Dalton, Ph.D., J.D., CPA, CFP, CLU, ChFC
James F. Dalton, MBA, MS, CPA/PFS, CFP

DALTON PUBLICATIONS, L.L.C.

150 James Drive East, Suite 100
St. Rose, Louisiana 70087
(504) 464-9772 • (504) 461-9860 Fax
www.daltonpublications.com

ISBN 1-890260-07-X	**Dalton CFP® Examination Review, Volume II: Problems and Solutions 1999 - 2000 Edition**
ISBN 1-890260-06-1	Dalton CFP® Examination Review, Volume I: Outlines and Study Guides 1999 - 2000 Edition
ISBN 1-890260-08-8	Dalton CFP® Examination Review, 3 Volume Set 1999 - 2000 Edition
ISBN 1-890260-09-6	Dalton CFP® Examination Review, Volume III: Case Exam Book

Cover designed by Donna D. Dalton

If found, please notify the following:

Name of CFP Candidate:______________________________

Address:______________________________

City, State, Zip: ______________________________

Phone: ______________________________

Additional Dalton CFP® Examination Review texts and information on the Dalton CFP® Live Instructional review course nearest you are available directly from:

Dalton Publications, L.L.C.
150 James Drive East, Suite 100
St. Rose, Louisiana 70087
(504) 464-9772
(504) 461-9860 FAX
http://www.daltonpublications.com

Dedicated to the users of the 1st and 2nd editions
who have made this product what it is today.
Thank you!

ADDITIONAL PRODUCTS AND SERVICES

LIVE INSTRUCTIONAL REVIEWS

Courses are offered in various cities around the country 4 - 8 weeks prior to each exam date. The program is designed to be both *effective and efficient*. The review is taught in two weekends (Friday, Saturday, and Sunday) for a total of 6 days. Two four hour sessions are taught each day in the classroom by exam specialists. Sessions cover Fundamentals of Financial Planning; Insurance Planning; Investment Planning; Income Tax Planning; Pensions, Fringe Benefits, & Retirement Planning; Estate Planning; and Case Analysis.

Our instructors lecture on each topic in a concise manner and provide selected readings and problems in the Dalton CFP Examination Review texts for each class. Instruction for the review course consists mainly of teaching substantive material and mastering both knowledge and application. The course also includes working problems, to assure that the substantive materials taught can be applied to the exam like questions, as well as actual exam management techniques.

The following are tentative locations for our live instructional reviews:

VOLUME I: OUTLINES AND STUDY GUIDES, 3rd Edition

Michael A. Dalton, James F. Dalton, and Cassie F. Bradley

This comprehensive text provides you with a complete reference outline in approximately 1,000 pages. Volume I includes detailed coverage of the six topics and is presented in an outline format. Each section contains examples, example questions, illustrations, and an index.

The introduction in Volume I presents helpful tips on what to expect when taking the exam, tips for studying, sample study plans, and a forecast of the number of questions expected in each area of the exam.

VOLUME III: CASE EXAM BOOK, 2nd Edition

Michael A. Dalton, James F. Dalton, and Patricia P. Houlihan

The third volume of the set contains 12 comprehensive case scenarios, with multiple choice questions and solutions and is updated for the recent tax law changes.

The case exam book provides the exam candidate with 12 comprehensive cases (each with 15 -19 multiple choice questions in each case) to simulate the comprehensive exam. Each case should be worked in 60 - 90 minutes. The answers and explanations for each multiple-choice question are provided. This text will prepare you for the three comprehensive cases given on the exam. Your preparation in this area is extremely important since these exam questions are weighted more heavily than the general multiple-choice questions.

The text also includes an excellent appendix for each section (43 total pages) containing tables, exhibits, charts, and other useful information for the candidate.

Our students who have used the *Case Exam Book* have said that this book is invaluable and a must if you want to be prepared for the cases on the exam!

MOCK EXAMS: SERIES A, EXAMS 1 AND 2

Michael A. Dalton and James F. Dalton

These supplements to the three-volume set simulate a session of the comprehensive exam. They take approximately 2 hours 45 minutes each. Each mock exam contains approximately 100 multiple choice and mini scenario problems and will assist you in evaluating your performance prior to the actual exam.

These supplements are diagnostic tools that can be used to assess your progress. They are useful in identifying your areas of strengths and weaknesses and are excellent tools for creating a study program to meet your individual study needs.

UNDERSTANDING YOUR FINANCIAL CALCULATOR

James F. Dalton

This text is designed to assist you in gaining proficiency in using and understanding your financial calculator. In addition to helping master the keystrokes for the financial calculator, it is also designed to assist students with the underlying financial theory type problems given on the CFP® Certification Exam. It is critical that you are familiar with the financial calculations, since mastering these problems is an important step to passing the exam.

All calculations are worked out ***step by step*** with keystrokes and displays on five of the most popular financial calculators. The calculators include HP 17B II, HP 12C, HP 10B, TI BAII Plus, and Sharp EL-733A.

This text covers the basic operations of the calculators, basic TVM calculations, fundamental problems (such as mortgages, education needs analysis, and retirement needs analysis), investment planning concepts and calculations (such as IRR, YTM, YTC, Sharpe, Treynor, Jensen, standard deviation), and more. This text also includes a student workbook with almost ***200*** practice (basic, intermediate, and advanced) problems and calculations. This is a great reference for the exam and for practitioners.

FINANCIAL PLANNING FLASHCARDS

Scott Wasserman and James F. Dalton

This product is created as a study supplement to the three-volume set and is a valuable tool for your review. This product includes 950 flashcards covering topics in each of the six areas on the exam and will help you learn basic concepts and definitions. Flashcards are an excellent way to learn the material since they prompt you to recall facts and information for the exam. It is a great addition to the texts for those studying on the go.

FUTURE PRODUCTS

Computerized Testbank (Available Soon)

This product is created in a similar format to Volume II. It will cover each of the six areas on the exam. The testbank includes over 1,000 questions with answers and explanations and will allow you to keep score, track your progress, and breakdown your scores by section. This software, developed by an employee of one of the leading software development companies, will focus your study on those areas that you need the most work.

Please contact Dalton Publications for additional information!

150 James Drive East, Suite 100

St. Rose, LA 70087

(504) 464-9772

(504) 461-9860 Fax

www.daltonpublications.com

PREFACE

This text is intended as a basis for the preparation of the Certified Financial Planner® Examination, either as self-study materials or as part of a review course. The materials in this volume are organized by the six different topic areas tested on the exam and presented in an outline format, with examples, example questions, and illustrations to help candidates quickly comprehend the material.

We have structured both volumes into six manageable study units

1. Fundamentals of Financial Planning
2. Insurance Planning
3. Investment Planning
4. Income Tax Planning
5. Retirement Planning
6. Estate Planning

The multiple choice problems and case problems in Volume II have been grouped into primary categories that correspond to the major topic headings in the outlines from Volume I. In addition, the answers also identify more specific topical categories within each study unit.

We are indebted to the CFP Board of Standards for permission to reproduce and adapt their publications and other materials.

We welcome any comments concerning materials contained in or omitted from this text. Please send your comments, in writing, to Dalton Publications, L.L.C., 150 James Drive East, St. Rose, Louisiana 70087 or fax to (504) 461-9860.

Wishing you success on the exam,

Michael A. Dalton
James F. Dalton

ABOUT THE AUTHORS

Michael A. Dalton, Ph.D., JD, CPA, CFP, CLU, ChFC

- Associate professor of Accounting and Taxation at Loyola University in New Orleans, Louisiana
- Ph.D. in Accounting from Georgia State University
- J.D. from Louisiana State University in Baton Rouge, Louisiana
- MBA and BBA in Management and Accounting from Georgia State University
- Former board member of the CFP® Board of Standards and Board of Governors
- Former chairman of the CFP® Board of Examiners
- Conducted in-house financial planning and training courses for Exxon corporation, ITT, Federal Express, the New Orleans Saints, and Chrysler Corporation
- Author of *Dalton CFP Examination Review - Volume I and II, Dalton CFP Examination Review Case Exam Book, Dalton CFP Examination Review Mock Exams, and CPA Review and Cost Accounting: Traditions and Innovations*
- Co-author of the *ABCs of Managing Your Money*

James F. Dalton, MBA, MS, CPA/PFS, CFP

- Manager with an international accounting firm, specializing in Personal Financial Planning, investment planning, and litigation support
- MBA from Loyola University in New Orleans, Louisiana
- Masters of Accounting in Taxation from the University of New Orleans
- BS in accounting from Florida State University in Tallahassee, Florida
- Completed two of three levels of CFA Examination
- Member of the CFP® Board of Standards July 1996, Comprehensive CFP® Exam Pass Score Committee
- Member of the AICPA and the Louisiana Society of CPAs
- Author of *Understanding Your Financial Calculator*
- Co-author of *Dalton CFP Examination Review - Volume I and II, Dalton CFP Examination Review Case Exam Book, and Dalton CFP Examination Review Mock Exam*

ABOUT THE CONTRIBUTING AUTHOR

Cassie F. Bradley, Ph.D.

- Assistant Professor of Accounting at Mercer College in Atlanta, Georgia
- Previously the Senior Tax Manager with Federal Express Corporation
- Ph.D. in Accounting from The University of Alabama
- BBA in Accounting from Georgia State University
- Past Southeast American Accounting Association Doctoral Consortium Representative
- Member of the American Accounting Association and the American Taxation Association
- Co-author to *Dalton CFP Examination Review - Volume I*
- Contributing author to *Dalton CFP Examination Review - Volume II*

ABOUT THE REVIEWERS

The following individuals assisted in the preparation of these texts by reviewing, rewriting, or editing sections of the outlines:

Arlene Nesser, CPA/PFS

Ms. Nesser is the Chief Financial Officer with the Commander's Palace family of restaurants in New Orleans, LA. Ms. Nesser has over 16 years experience with an international accounting firm where she specialized in financial planning. Ms. Nesser reviewed the Retirement Planning Problems and Solutions.

John B. Ohle, III, JD, MBA, CPA/PFS, CFP

Mr. Ohle is a Senior Manager with an international accounting firm where he specializes in personal financial planning and estate planning. Mr. Ohle reviewed the Estate Planning Planning Problems and Solutions.

Scott Wasserman, CPA, CFP

Mr. Wasserman is a Senior Manager with an international accounting firm where he specializes in financial planning practice and is currently developing software that is used by the financial planning professionals throughout the firm. Mr. Wasserman reviewed the Fundamentals of Financial Planning, Estate Planning, Insurance Planning, Tax Planning, Retirement Planning, and Investment Planning Problems and Solutions; Young, Martini, and Remolade Cases; and Mini Cases.

ACKNOWLEDGMENTS AND SPECIAL THANKS

We are most appreciative for the tremendous support and encouragement we have received from everyone throughout this project. We are extremely grateful to the users of our texts who were good enough to provide us with valuable comments concerning our first and second editions.

We have received so much help, from so many people; it is possible that we inadvertently overlooked thanking someone. If so, it is our shortcoming, and we apologize in advance. Please let us know if you are that someone, and we will correct it in our next printing.

We are grateful to the registered programs that provided us with confidence and support by using/adopting our latest edition. These schools include, but are not limited to: The American College, Boston University, Fairleigh Dickinson University, Florida Institute of Technology, Long Island University, Loyola University-Chicago, Merrimack College, New York University, NOVA Southeastern University, Oakland University, Oglethorpe University, University of California-Irvine, University of California-Los Angeles, University of Central Florida, University of Houston, University of North Texas/PDI, University of St. Thomas/PDI, University of South Florida, and University of Miami.

We especially want to thank DeDe Pahl, Vice President, Certification and Standards and Colleen McArdell, Manager, Initial Certification Services of the CFP® Board of Standards for their cooperation and assistance in providing disk copies of CFP® Board of Standards copyrighted materials and for their continued encouragement and enthusiasm about this project.

We deeply appreciate the cooperation of the CFP® Board of Standards for granting us permission to reproduce and adapt their publications and other materials.

This manual would not have been possible without the extraordinary efforts and dedication of Connie Powell, who managed the entire project; Michelle Bonnette and Donna Dalton, who incorporated most of the revisions into the 3rd Edition; Tina Collins, Kristi Mincher, and Robin Delle who helped with the revisions; Scott Wasserman who painstakingly reviewed all of the problems and solutions; and our families and friends for their support and assistance.

VOLUME II CONTENTS

THIS PAGE IS INTENTIONALLY LEFT BLANK.

INTRODUCTION

PURPOSE OF VOLUME II

This text is intended as a basis for the preparation of the Certified Financial Planner® Examination, either as self-study materials or as part of a review course. The materials in this Volume are organized by the six topic areas tested on the exam.

Volume II contains:

- Fundamentals of Financial Planning
- Insurance Planning
- Investment Planning
- Income Tax Planning
- Retirement Planning
- Estate Planning
- William and Marilyn Mathews Case
- Booth and Needa Martini Case A
- Booth and Needa Martini Case B
- David And Susan Young Case A
- David and Susan Young Case B

Before you begin your study, you might want to review the Table of Contents in both Volume I and II and familiarize yourself with the topics related to the exam.

ABOUT THE EXAM

Read the CFP® General Information Booklet.

Date Given

The exam is generally given on the third Friday and Saturday of March, July, and November each year.

Friday afternoon session	4 hours
Saturday 2 sessions	6 hours
Total	**10 hours**

For exact dates, contact the CFP® Board of Standards.

Question Type

The examination consists solely of objective questions, approximately 285. The majority of these are stand-alone multiple-choice questions that contain all relevant information within the body of the problem. A portion of the exam is in the form of a case analysis. These cases are on Friday and Saturday morning and will have numerous (10-20) questions per case. The information needed to answer these questions is generally found within the body of the case. These cases can be several pages long, making it difficult to organize the information in an efficient way to answer the questions.

Each question may test only one particular area of financial planning, such as investments. However, many of the questions are integrated questions, meaning that more than one topic is covered in the question. For example, a question might integrate investments and taxation. These integrated questions are designed to test your ability to analyze fact situations involving many planning considerations.

Distribution of Topics

The topics on the exam are distributed as follows:

Fundamentals	12%
Insurance	17%
Investments	20%
Income Tax	17%
Retirement	17%
Estates	17%
	100%

Cognitive Levels Tested (Target)	Percent of the Exam
Knowledge level	5%
Comprehension/application	35%
Analysis/Synthesis/Evaluation	60%
	100%

Scoring Method	Pt. Value Per Question	Approximate #	Points	Percent
Stand alone multiple choice	2 points	240	480	78%
Case multiple choice	3 points	45	135	22%
		285	615	100%

The examination division of the CFP® Board of Standards and the Board of Examiners assigns the value weights to questions according to type, cognitive level, and level of difficulty.

Time and Time Analysis

There are 10 hours of examination time.

1. Friday - (4 hours) 70 multiple choice questions & 1 case and mini cases
2. Saturday – Morning Session (3 hours) 2 cases and mini cases
3. Saturday – Afternoon Session (3 hours) Balance of multiple choice
4. Approximately 285 questions overall.
5. Case questions 10-20 per case.

	Time (minutes)	No. of Multiple Choice	Average Time
Average Indicated Time Per M/C Question	420	240	1.5 minutes each (Friday & Saturday)
Average Indicated Time Per Case M/C Question	180	40-50	4.0 minutes each (Friday & Saturday)
Average Indicated Time Per All M/C Question	600	285	2.1 minutes each (Overall)

The authors have concluded that you should strive to average 1.7 minutes per multiple choice question throughout your study in Volume II. The case and case analysis presented for the cases in Volume II and especially in the Case Exam Book should provide you with a realistic approximation of exam conditions regarding cases. The case multiple choice should take about 1 ¼ - 1 ½ hour per set, including reading the case.

Pass Rates

The pass rates have ranged from 42% to 66% on recent comprehensive exams. This exam is a pass/fail professional exam with no partial credit. Therefore, it is vitally important that you be thoroughly prepared for all the topics covered on this examination.

Examination Procedures

Read carefully the procedures outlined in Section B of the General Information Booklet. This section covers:

- Dates of Examinations
- Alternate Test Dates and Test Facilities
- Fees for the Examination
- Scheduling Confirmations
- Withdrawal from the Exam
- Medical Emergencies
- Items to Bring to the Examination
- Examination Misconduct
- Examination Scoring
- Score Reports
- Pass Score
- Re-Examination Procedures
- Answers to Frequently Asked Questions

A copy of the General Information Booklet may be obtained from the CFP® Board.

CFP Board of Standards
1700 Broadway, Suite 2100
Denver, CO 80290-2101
Telephone: (303) 830-7500
Fax: (303) 860-7388
Website: http://www.CFP-Board.org
E-mail: mail@CFP-Board.org

BEGINNING YOUR CFP® REVIEW

Be Prepared to Spend the Time

- The exam will demand a great deal of your time and effort. Make passing a priority in your life. If it is not in your top three or four priorities at this time, perhaps you should wait until it is.
- A comprehensive review will take you approximately 300 hours including any in class and out of class time. This time will vary from candidate to candidate depending on your level of knowledge in the base material and your experience in the practice or simulated practice of financial planning.
- Do not fool yourself! This exam is comparable to other professional exams and is extremely rigorous.

Know Your Financial Calculator

- You need to have very thorough knowledge of your financial calculator. It is imperative that you are familiar with the time value of money calculations, as well as the underlying financial theory. If you are deficient in this area, you should take the time (approximately 6-8 hours) to learn the calculator before beginning your study program.
- Work problems 71-118 in the Fundamentals section of Volume II as practice. Also, work thoroughly through the ***Understanding Your Financial Calculator*** book.
- It is especially helpful to learn the keystrokes. Pay close attention to where the cash flows occur in time. Mastering these problems is an important step in passing the exam.
- We recommend an HP12C, HP10B, or the equivalent.

Develop a Study Plan

- The exam is comprehensive and encompasses an enormous amount of material and information. Studying on a regular basis will be a great asset in accomplishing your goal of passing the CFP® exam. With work, family, eating, and sleeping, much of the day is already gone. For this reason, it is important to develop a study plan and keep study materials with you at all times.
- Get organized. Make a preliminary study plan keeping all specifics (such as date, number of problems attempted, number correct, total time (hours), etc.). Your study plan should be divided into the six subject areas for more manageable use of your study time. You may want to use the sample study plan at the end of this section to track your progress.
- You will need self-discipline to adhere to your plan.

Sample Your Knowledge

- It is crucial to begin your study program by first evaluating your current knowledge. Once you have an idea of what you currently know, you must then determine the areas in which you are deficient. Basically, you must determine where your strengths and weaknesses lie.
- We recommend that you sample your knowledge by taking a random sample of 20 multiple choice questions in each of the six major areas from Volume II. Be sure to mark the time that you start and the time that you finish. Put a (G) by any questions that you had to guess the answer.
- If you score above 70% in any area, go ahead and take another sample continuing with this method as long as your percentage correct stays above 70%. Continue until you have answered all the questions. Anytime you score less than 70%; you should carefully read the entire outline in Volume I that relates to the material you have been testing. Repeat the step above.
- Most candidates will have some topical areas in each of the above - don't be discouraged.
- We recommend that you write down your progress in your study plan. Try to get each topic to 65% - 70% correct with one or more above 80%. You are almost certain to pass.
- Evaluation:
  - 80% or more correct and 1.7 minutes or less per question = extremely well prepared.
  - 70% or more correct and 1.7 minutes or less per question = well prepared.
  - 50-60% or more correct and 2.0 minutes or less per question = marginally prepared (risk).
  - Less than 50% and/or over 2.0 minutes per question = need serious review (serious risk).

Time Management

After you determine your areas of strengths and weaknesses, you should be able to estimate the number of hours you will need to study in order to pass the exam. At this point, you should take out your calendar, and count the number of weeks you have remaining to study prior to the exam. Divide the number of hours you need to study by the number of weeks until the exam. This will allow you to determine the number of hours you must study per week. This figure can then be further refined into hours to study per weekday and per weekend, etc.

For example: Paul is taking the exam in November. It is now the beginning of August, and he has just received his Dalton Package. He purchased the full set, *Volume I and II*, *Volume III: Case Exam Book*, *Understanding Your Financial Calculator*, *Mock A-1,* and *Mock A-2*. He has 15 weeks until the exam and has decided that he needs to study a full 300 hours to pass. Based on this information, he will need to study 20 hours per week. To accomplish this goal, Paul decided to study 2 hours each weekday and 10 hours on the weekend. Using this information (along with Paul's knowledge of his own areas of strengths and weaknesses), Paul decided the following schedule would be appropriate:

Week	Topics to covers
1	Understanding your financial calculator
2	Fundamentals *Volume I* (all) and Fundamentals *Volume II* (half)
3	Fundamentals *Volume II* (half) and Insurance *Volume I* (all)
4	Insurance *Volume II* (all) and Investments *Volume I* (half)
5	Investments *Volume I* (half) and Investments (all)
6	Estates *Volume I* (all) and Estates *Volume II* (half)
7	Estates *Volume II* (half) and Retirement *Volume I* (all)
8	Retirement *Volume II* (all) and Tax *Volume I* (half)
9	Tax *Volume I* (half) and Tax *Volume II* (all)
10	Mini Cases and built in time for review and catch-up
11	*Volume II* Cases
12	*Case Exam Book* (half)
13	*Case Exam Book* (half)
14	*Mock A* and *Mock A-2*
15	Review

Monthly Calendar

- You might also find it beneficial to invest in a large monthly calendar and hang it where you will see it every day. Be sure to mark all of your upcoming commitments with regards to work, family, outside activities, etc. on your calendar. This will help you plan and anticipate any time constraints that may lead to obstacles in your study program. For example, during Week 3 of Paul's schedule, he knows that he must attend an out of town wedding and will only have time to study the two hours he is on the plane. Therefore, he must adjust his schedule to spend more time studying during Weekend 2 and on the weekdays during Weeks 2 and 3 in order to compensate for the fluctuation in his study program. You may find that you will need to cancel commitments or turn down new commitments you would otherwise accept in order to maintain your focus. Remember, your study time for the CFP Certification Exam is limited and must be one of your top priorities.
- You will also want to indicate on your calendar the subject area(s) on which you plan to focus your study time each week. This will help you plan which commitments you will and will not be able to accept as weeks go by. For example, in Week 8 Paul's brother calls and wants to schedule dinner for Week 9. Paul knows that he will be studying Tax (his hardest subject) and that this area might require more study time than other areas. Thus, Paul decides that he should not schedule any additional events for Week 9 and declines.

Weekly Calendar

- Before you begin your first week of study, list all of the activities in which you participate. Determine how long each activity takes to complete and whether or not this activity is performed at a specific time each day, week, month, etc.
- Make sure to include your work hours, drive time, family time, meals, sleep, and any other miscellaneous activities you might do that fill up your time. You may want to use the sample schedule at the end of this section to track your activities.

Once you have logged your activities in your weekly and monthly calendars, review your schedule, and decide which time slots are full and which are open. Using this information, you should be able to develop a realistic study plan for each day. If you find that your current activities do not leave you enough free time to study, you will need to eliminate enough activities so that you will have adequate study time to prepare for the exam. If you discover that you do not have the appropriate amount of time for exam preparation, it would be to your benefit to postpone taking the exam until it is a higher priority or until you have fewer commitments. Before each week begins, review your weekly schedule and update it for any new commitments. Although you will need to be flexible with your scheduled study time, it is important to stick with your scheduled study time as much as possible. Try to anticipate missed study time and be sure to reschedule the missed time for another day.

Make a Daily To-Do List

Before you begin each study session, make a tentative list of what you want to accomplish during your study time. You may also want to keep a spiral notebook or binder so you will be able to continuously evaluate and reevaluate your progress. Write down the number of pages that you plan to read and/or the number of problems that you plan to work during your study session. Be realistic when you write this list and work very hard to stick to your study plan.

PREPARE TO STUDY

There are many ways you can maximize the benefits of your study time. The following are some of our suggestions to most efficiently and effectively study.

Create a Suitable Study Environment

The most important thing you can do to help facilitate your studying is to create a suitable study environment. Your study area should be:

1. Quiet. You want to find a place that is free from all extraneous noise (including the television and disruptive people).
2. Away from distractions. Stay away from areas where there are a lot of distractions. For example, try not to study close to a telephone, since you might be tempted to answer it and talk. You might also want to try to avoid studying at work or at home if co-workers or family members will interrupt you.
3. Study in a well-lit location. You will want to study in an area where you will be able to see the information as well as stay awake and alert.
4. Be comfortable but not too comfortable. You want to be relaxed so that you see studying as a beneficial activity and not a punishment. However, you should not let yourself get so comfortable that you will be tempted to fall asleep.
5. Have all of your materials readily available. Gather everything you will need during your study session beforehand. This includes pencils, pens, books, highlighters, a calculator, and paper. Try to sit at a desk or table so that you have room for all of your materials, and a firm writing surface.

Use the Multiple Choice to Direct Your Study.

Keep in mind that you should **not** spend the majority of your study time on material you already know well. There is a natural tendency to do so, as it is a lot more fun and certainly more comforting but unfortunately counter productive. The subject that you scored the lowest in should be studied the most. The multiple choice can be used as a monitoring tool if you keep thorough records. We recommend that you study the multiple choice and the outlines as needed. You should use the three volumes to complement your comprehensive study plan.

Become Thoroughly Prepared with the Material

1. The exam is professionally rigorous and tests across Bloom's Taxonomy of Cognitive Learning. You can expect a small percentage of problems to test at the knowledge level and a much larger percentage to test at the application, synthesis, and evaluation levels.
2. The difference in passing and failing is the difference between being thoroughly prepared and pro-active, versus being casually acquainted and reactive. For example, if I mention IRAs, your mind should create a picture of the following topics that relate to IRAs:

➢ Eligibility	➢ Distribution prior to 70½
➢ Deductible/non-deductible	➢ Minimum distributions
➢ Allocation between spouses	➢ Roth and Education IRAs
➢ Transferability	➢ Death
➢ Rollover	➢ Inclusion in Gross Estate
➢ Assignment/pledging	➢ QDRO
➢ Investments	➢ Active participation in a pension plan
➢ Penalties	➢ Joint life distribution

3. You should be immediately prepared and ready to answer any question about any sub-topic in IRAs. If the mentioning of IRAs does not bring anything to mind, or if only few of the listed topics come to mind, you are not thoroughly knowledgeable.
4. The problem with being only casually acquainted with the material is twofold: (1) you take too much time and (2) you let the exam lead you to incorrect answers. You must discipline yourself to aggressively answer the questions and you must monitor the time it takes you to answer the average multiple choice question. Remember when you are thoroughly knowledgeable, the questions are pretty easy. When you are only casually acquainted, the questions are much harder and take longer to answer.

Textbook Previewing

1. As you are reviewing *Volume I*, there are two things you should do:
2. Be sure to study the title of each section. Not only will this preview what you are about to read, it will also help you to narrow your scope of study.
3. Look for relationships. By looking for relationships between current information and subjects you have read about previously, you can learn to group concepts together and increase memory retention.

Things to Mark

1. You should mark definitions. Often knowing a word's definition can help you to distinguish terms that might otherwise prove confusing. On the exam, knowing the definition of key words and concepts can often help you eliminate possible answers on multiple choice questions.
2. Signal words, such as "and", "or", "except", "not", and "also". These words indicate the relationships between concepts.
3. Key words and phrases. Key words are words or phrases that should instantly bring to mind a number of questions, issues, or ideas relating to the topics identified by the key words or phrases. For example, the phrase "substantial and reoccurring" is a key phrase that relates to the funding of profit sharing plans. Keywords and phrases are the foundation on which you should build your basis of knowledge.

Note Taking Methods

1. Flashcards or note cards. Notes taken on note cards can also be used as valuable tools for review. You can use them as flash cards, which are much more portable than textbooks or notebooks, and force memory recall, which is a requirement of the exam.
2. Study notes. Traditional study notes allow you to trigger key concepts that you have read about. This is crucial for review purposes. Study notes should be rewritten within 48 hours of taking them to clarify any areas that seem ambiguous.

Study Methods

SQ3R Study System

Survey. Glance through material and get a general idea about the key information within the text.

Question. Think about questions that could be asked about the material. If the section title is "Key Concept of Estate Planning," a possible question might be "What are key the concepts of estate planning?"

Read. Read through the material carefully, marking the text and taking notes as you go.

Recite. After each section, pretend that you are lecturing to a friend or colleague on the material. Are you able to retain the information?

Review. Be sure to go over each section and review information that you might be confused about.

SOAR Study formula

Survey the book. Skim over the outline topics. Review the table of contents to see the major categories of information. Review the index for important topics and keywords. Also look at each individual section and review the topics, major points, and information contained within each section.

Organize. Organize the information that you have read and taken notes on. Some ways to facilitate this are to:

- Underline books.
- Make notes for books (charts, notecards, etc.)

Anticipate. Anticipate the information that you think will be tested. Formulate possible test questions, and evaluate your ability to answer these questions correctly in a testing environment.

Recite and Review. Just as with the SQ3R method, the SOAR method places final emphasis on being able to recite information as if lecturing on its key points and reviewing any areas where you have deficiencies.

Mnemonics

Mnemonics literally translates to "to help the memory." These are techniques that can be incorporated into your study plan in order to increase your retention of information. The most common use of mnemonics is to create a sentence with the first letter of each keyword. For instance, "PRIME" is used to help students remember systematic risks. P-R-I-M-E stands for Purchasing Power Risk, Reinvestment Rate Risk, Interest Rate Risk, Market Risk, and Exchange Rate Risk.

Dalton's Final Tips

- **Avoid whining** - Avoid whining that you should not have to know or learn some area of financial planning that is technical and that most planners have to look up. One purpose of the exam is to be a gatekeeper to the profession; another is to help you develop a healthy sense of professional humility about what you know. Also, clients will expect you to know everything.
- **Study what you don't know** - The subject that you scored the lowest should be the subject you study the most.
- **Think positively** - It will help you pass.
- **Find a way to make it fun** - Don't fight the problem.

STUDY PLAN

Topic ______________________________

Date	# Attempted	# Correct	% Correct	Average Time per Question	Study Outline	Total Time	Notes

WEEKLY ACTIVITIES/COMMITMENTS

Time	Monday	Tuesday	Wednesday	Thursday	Friday	Saturday	Sunday
12am							
1							
2							
3							
4							
5							
6							
7							
8							
9							
10							
11							
12pm							
1							
2							
3							
4							
5							
6							
7							
8							
9							
10							
11							

EXPECTED QUESTION DISTRIBUTION

The authors have prepared an analysis of the likely topics and frequency of expected questions as indicated in this section.

FUNDAMENTALS OF FINANCIAL PLANNING EXAM ANALYSIS

	# of Expected Questions	% of Exam
Financial Planning Process	6-12 questions	
Economic Environment	4-8 questions	
Time value of Money	12-19 questions	
Legal Environment	3-7 questions	
Financial Analysis	3-5 questions	
Ethical and Professional	2-4 questions	
Total	**30-55 questions**	**9% - 17%**
Expected on Exam	**34 questions**	**12%**

INSURANCE PLANNING EXAM ANALYSIS

	# of Expected Questions	% of Exam
Principles of Insurance	1-2 questions	
Risk Exposure	2-7 questions	
Legal Aspects	2-6 questions	
Property and Liability	2-5 questions	
Life Insurance	9-14 questions	
Health Insurance	1-3 questions	
Disability Insurance	2-3 questions	
Employee Benefits	0-3 questions	
Social Insurance	0-3 questions	
Other-Including Tax	3-7 questions	
Total	**22-53 questions**	**7% - 17%**
Expected on Exam	**48 questions**	**17%**

INVESTMENT PLANNING EXAM ANALYSIS

	# of Expected Questions	**% of Exam**
Regulation	1-2 questions	
Investment Vehicles	17-31 questions	
Client Assessment	2-4 questions	
Theory and Markets	15-26 questions	
Strategies and Tactics	8-15 questions	
Modern Portfolio Theory	4-7 questions	
Integration	2-4 questions	
Total	**49-89 questions**	**15%-28%**
Expected on Exam	**57 questions**	**20%**

INCOME TAX PLANNING EXAM ANALYSIS

	# of Expected Questions	**% of Exam**
Fundamentals	3-8 questions	
Tax Computation & Concepts	7-13 questions	
Tax Planning Especially Property	22-38 questions	
Hazards & Penalties	4-9 questions	
Total	**36-68 questions**	**11% - 21%**
Expected on Exam	**48 questions**	**17%**

RETIREMENT PLANNING EXAM ANALYSIS

	# of Expected Questions	% of Exam
Ethics	1-2 questions	
Social Security plus Medicare	2-3 questions	
Retirement Plans/Types	12-21 questions	
Qualified Plan Characteristics	5-12 questions	
Distribution and Options	4-6 questions	
Group Insurance	3-6 questions	
Other Employee Benefits	2-4 questions	
Analysis of Factors	7-13 questions	
Total	**36-67 questions**	**11% - 21%**
Expected on Exam	**48 questions**	**17%**

ESTATE PLANNING EXAM ANALYSIS

	# of Expected Questions	% of Exam
Estate Planning Overview	4-8 questions	
Property Ownership Interest	4 questions	
Considerations and Constraints	14-27 questions	
Tools and Techniques (General)	11-17 questions	
Tools and Techniques (Special)	6-12 questions	
Total	**39-68 questions**	**12% - 21**
Expected on Exam	**48 questions**	**17%**

SOLVING MULTIPLE CHOICE QUESTIONS

1. **Read the last line (the requirement) first.**

   The last line will generally be the question part of the problem and will identify the types of important information that will be needed to answer the questions.

   From Example 1: "How many personal and dependency exemptions can Mike and Pam claim on their 1995 income tax return?"

   This last sentence of Example 1 identifies the type of information needed from the body of the problem. You can now look for key information while reading through the body of the problem.

2. **Read the question carefully.**

   Underline the concepts, words, and data and make important notes of data or relevant rules to help formulate your answer.

3. **Formulate your answer.**

   Do not look at the answer choices presented on the exam until you have formulated your answer. Looking at the answer choices may have a tendency to distract or change your thinking.

4. **Select your answer if it is presented.**

5. **Write it or circle it directly on the examination.**

   Watch the clock and enter answers on the answer sheet as you go, or all at once at the end. If at the end, be sure you have enough time. Be consistent.

6. **Review other answer choices for the following:**

   Was your answer sufficiently precise?

   Was your answer complete?

7. **If your answer is not presented.**

   You know you are incorrect. Alternatives:

   - Reread question and requirements.
   - Evaluate answers presented.
   - Guess.
   - Skip the question and come back to it later.
   - **Note:** You are not penalized for guessing, so, if time is running out, be sure to fill in all of the open questions.

SOLVING "A" TYPE QUESTIONS

Straight Multiple Choice Type Questions

1. Example.

Mike and Pam, ages 67 and 65, respectively, filed a joint tax return for 1998. They provided all of the support for their 19-year-old son, who had $2,200 of gross income. Their 23-year-old daughter, a full-time student until her graduation on June 25, 1998, earned $2,700, which was 40% of her total support during 1995. Her parents provided the remaining support. Mike and Pam also provided total support for Pam's father who is a citizen and life-long resident of Columbia. How many personal and dependency exemptions can Mike and Pam claim on their 1998 income tax return?

Question 1 Analysis

Step		
Step 1	Read last line and identify the topic: Personal and dependency exemptions.	
Step 2	Read question and make notes:	
	Mike and Pam	*2 personal exemptions*
	19 year old son	*1 dependency exemption (because gross income test is met).*
	23 year old daughter	*1 dependency exemption (because full time student for 5 months).*
	Pam's father	*None (because he is not a citizen).* ***Note:*** *He could qualify if a citizen of Mexico or Canada.*
Step 3	Count exemptions (4) and select answer C.	

a. 2.
b. 3.
c. 4.
d. 5.
e. None of the above.

Answer: C

Exemptions are allowed for Mike, Pam, their son, and their daughter. They are not entitled to an exemption for Pam's father because he was not a citizen or resident of the U.S. or other qualifying country. Their son qualifies as a dependent because his gross income was less than the exemption amount ($2,700 in 1998). The gross income test is waived for their daughter, who was a full-time student for at least 5 months during the year.

2. Example.

George, whose wife died in November 1998, filed a joint tax return for 1998. He did not remarry and has continued to maintain his home for his 2 dependent children. In the preparation of his tax return for 1999, what is George's filing status?

Question 2 Analysis

Step	
Step 1	Read last line and identify the topic: Filing status for George for 1999.
Step 2	Read question and make notes: *Wife died 11/98.* *Joint return filed for 1998.* *Unmarried with 2 dependents.*
Step 3	With these facts and notes, you should immediately recall that the surviving spouse's filing status can be used for the 2 years following the year of death of the first spouse if there is a dependent child.
Step 4	Delete the clearly wrong answer by striking through them (e.g., delete (d) he is not married). This will help you to focus on the viable alternatives.
Step 5	Select answer B.

a. Single.

b. Qualified widow/widower.

c. Head of household.

d. Married filing separately.

e. None of the above.

Answer: B

George, who filed a joint return in 1998, correctly filed a joint return in 1998. He will file qualified widower for 1999.

3. Example.

Brian, an employee of Duff Corporation, died December 25, 1998. During December, Duff Corp. made employee death payments of $10,000 to his widow, and $10,000 to his 17 year old son. What amounts can be excluded from gross income by the widow and son in their respective tax returns for 1998?

Question 3 Analysis

Step	
Step 1	Read last line and identify the topic: Amounts excluded from gross income for 1998.
Step 2	Read question and make notes: *Brian died during 1998.* *Employee death payments of $10,000 to widow and $10,000 to son.*
Step 3	With these facts and notes, you should recall that the law allowing an exclusion for death benefits was repealed.
Step 4	Analysis: *Total amount excludable = $0* *Total death benefits = 20,000*
Step 5	Select answer A.

	Widow	Son
a.	$0.	$0.
b.	$2,500.	$2,500.
c.	$5,000.	$5,000.
d.	$7,500.	$7,500.
e.	$10,000.	$10,000.

Answer: A

No death proceeds are excludable.

Note: After August 1996 there is no 5,000 death benefit exclusion effective with the Small Business Act of 1996. Therefore the answer would be 0 exclusion - Answer A, if this question were on the 1999 exam.

4. Example.

Clark Roberts wants to retire in 9 years. He needs an additional $300,000 (today's $) in 9 years to have sufficient funds to finance this objective. He assumes inflation will average 5.0% over the long run, and he can earn a 4.0% compound annual after-tax return on investments. What will be Clarks' payment at the end of the second year?

Question 4 Analysis

Step 1	Read last line and identify the topic: TVM Serial Payment 2nd year-end.			
Step 2	Read question and make notes: *Needs $300,000 in today's dollars in 9 years.* *Inflation rate = 5%, earnings rate = 4%.*			
Step 3	Analysis:			
	FV	=	*$300,000*	
	i	=	*-.9524*	*[((1.04/1.05) -1) x 100]*
	N	=	*9*	
	PV	=	0	
	PMT	=	*$34,623.42*	*Payment at the beginning of the year 1.*
			x 1.05 = $ 36,354.60	*Payment at the end of year 1.*
			x 1.05 = $ 38,172.33	*Payment at the end of year 2.*
Step 4	Select answer B.			

a. $38,244.62.
b. $38,172.33.
c. $36,354.60.
d. $34,623.42.
e. None of the above.

Answer: B

$36,354.60 x 1.05 = $38,172.33. This is an example of a serial payment. A serial payment is not an annuity due or ordinary annuity level payment. A serial payment increases annually at the rate of inflation

5. Example.

Taxpayer gives her son property with a basis to donor of $35,000 and a fair market value of $30,000. No gift tax is paid. Son subsequently sells the property for $33,000. What is his recognized gain (or loss)?

Question 5 Analysis

Step 1	Read last line and identify the topic: Gain or loss on sale of donated property. **Note:** This topic should bring to mind the important points for this area, such as basis and sales price.
Step 2	Read question and make notes: *FMV < Basis.* *FMV < Sales Price < Basis.* *If an asset is sold between the gain basis and the loss basis there will be no gain or loss.*
Step 4	Select answer A.

a. No gain or loss.

b. Loss.

c. Gain.

d. Gain.

e. None of the above.

Answer: A

The son's basis is $35,000 for gains. His loss basis is $30,000. Since his selling price of $33,000 is between the gain and the loss basis, there is no recognized gain or loss.

Calculation Type Questions

6. Example.

Helen (a single taxpayer) purchases an airplane for $130,000. In order to obtain financing for the purchase, Helen issues a lien on her personal residence in the amount of $130,000. At the time, the residence had a fair market value of $400,000 and a first mortgage of $320,000. For the plane loan, Helen may claim as qualified residence interest the interest on what amount?

Question 6 Analysis

Step	
Step 1	Read last line and identify the topic: Qualified residence interest/Home equity limit.
Step 2	Read question and make notes: *QRI limit to 1,000,000 debt or Fair Market Value, whichever is less.* *Home Equity line is limited to the lesser of equity or $100,000.*
Step 3	Analysis: *FMV* *$400,000* *1st Mortgage* *- 320,000* *= $80,000* *Equity Limit*
Step 4	Answer $80,000. Select answer B.

a. $30,000.

b. $80,000.

c. $100,000.

d. $130,000.

e. None of the above.

Answer: B

Home equity loans are limited to the lesser of:

(a) The fair market value of the residence, reduced by acquisition indebtedness, or

(b) $100,000.

Thus, $400,000 (fair market value) - $320,000 (first mortgage) provides a limit of $80,000. Interest on the remaining $50,000 of the loan will be treated under the consumer interest rules (i.e., not deductible).

7. Example.

Connie wants to withdraw $1,200 at the beginning of each month for the next 5 years. She expects to earn 10% compounded monthly on her investments. What lump sum should Connie deposit today?

Question 7 Analysis

Step 1	Read last line and identify the topic: TVM - PVAD.
Step 2	Read question and make notes: PV *problem.*
Step 3	Analysis: *PV* *N* *i* *PMT* *FV*
Step 4	Fill out information and identify objective. *Objective* *PV =* *N = 60* *i = 10 ÷ 12* *PMT= $1,200 (annuity due)* *FV = Not applicable (put 0 in cell to eliminate any numbers)*
Step 4	Calculate PV_{OA} = $56,478.44 (Incorrect). Note closeness of answers; check to make sure you used annuity due. Calculate PV_{AD} = $56,949.10 Answer B.

a. $56,478.44.

b. $56,949.10.

c. $58,630.51.

d. $59,119.10.

e. None of the above.

Answer: B

PMT_B	=	$1,200
i	=	.8333 (10 ÷ 12)
N	=	60 (5 x 12)
PV_{AD}	=	$56,949.10

8. Example.

Gary has received an inheritance of $200,000. He wants to withdraw equal periodic payments at the beginning of each month for the next 5 years. He expects to earn 12% compounded monthly on his investments. How much can he receive each month?

Question 8 Analysis

Step 1	Read last line and identify the topic: Analysis of PMT (AD)
Step 2	Analysis: *PV* *N* *i* *PMT* *N*
Step 3	Fill out information and identify objective. *PV* = *$200,000* *N* = *60* *i* = *12 ÷ 12* *Objective→* PMT_{AD} *= $4,404.84 therefore Answer A* *FV* = *Not applicable* **Note:** Closeness of answer B, make sure you have the annuity due, ordinary annuity issue correct. Does C or D make any sense - No, 60 payments at those levels would be 2-3 million.
Step 4	Select answer A.

a. $4,404.84.

b. $4,448.89.

c. $49,537.45.

d. $55,481.95.

e. None of the above.

Answer: A

PV	=	$200,000
i	=	1.00 (12 ÷ 12)
N	=	60 (5 x 12)
PMT_{AD}	=	$4,404.84

Evaluate Answers

9. Example.

On January 1, Father (Mike) loaned daughter (Allison) $90,000 to purchase a new personal residence. There were no other loans outstanding between Mike and Allison. Allison's only income was $30,000 salary and $4,000 interest income. Mike had investment income of $200,000. Mike did not charge Allison interest. The relevant Federal rate was 9%. Which of the following statements is correct regarding the transaction?

a. Allison must recognize $8,100 (.09 X $90,000) imputed interest income on the loan.
b. Mike must recognize imputed interest income of $4,000.
c. Mike must recognize imputed interest income of $8,100.
d. Allison is allowed a deduction for imputed interest of $8,100.
e. None of the above.

Question 9 Analysis

In order to answer this type of question, you must evaluate each presented option.

Step 1	Read last line and identify the topic: lenders imputed interest.
Step 2	Read question and make notes: *a) No interest on loans < 10,000.* *b) No interest on loans < 100,000 if no income.*
Step 3	Analysis of answer choices: *a. No - it is not Allison that would impute interest information.* *b. Looks correct, Mike's inputted interest is equal to lesser of Allison's interest income or Federal rate.* *c. Is Federal rate, therefore wrong.* *d. Allison is wrong person.* *e. B and C are both possible.*
Step 4	Select answer B.

Answer: B

The $100,000 exemption applies, and thus Mike's imputed interest income is limited to Allison's net investment income.

10. Example.

Judy Martin estimates her opportunity cost on investments at 12% compounded annually, which one of the following is the best investment alternative?

Question 10 Analysis

Step 1	Read last line and identify the topic: Present Value					
Step 2	Read question.					
Step 3	Analysis of answer choices:					
		A	***B***	***C***	***D***	***E***
	FV		*$250,000*	*$120,000*		*$60,000*
	N		*14*	*12*	*18*	*3*
	i		*12*	*12*	*6*	*12*
	PMT				*$5,000 AD*	
	Objective - PV	*$50,000*	*$51,154.95*	*$30,801.01*	*$57,386.30*	*$42,706.81*
	FV			*$40,000.00*		
	N			*4*		
	i			*12*		
	PV			*$25,420.72*		
	TOTAL			*$56,221.73*		
Step 4	Select answer D.					

a. To receive $50,000 today.
b. To receive $250,000 at the end of 14 years.
c. To receive $40,000 at the end of 4 years and $120,000 8 years later.
d. To receive $5,000 at the beginning of each 6-month period for 9 years compounded semiannually.
e. To receive $60,000 at the end of 3 years.

Answer: D

Option D:

PMT = $5,000

i = 6 (12 ÷ 2)

N = 18 (9 x 2)

PV_{AD} = $57,386.30

SOLVING "K" TYPE QUESTIONS

Evaluate each K Type Statement

11. Example.

Which, if any, of the following transactions are permissible regarding an IRA?

1. A non-spouse IRA beneficiary must distribute the balance of an IRA, where distribution had begun, over a period not exceeding 5 years.
2. A non-spouse IRA beneficiary may distribute the balance of an IRA, where distribution had not begun, over the life expectancy of the beneficiary.
3. A beneficiary spouse of a deceased owner of an IRA can delay any distribution of such IRA until April 1 following the year in which such heir or beneficiary is 70½.
4. A spouse beneficiary of a deceased owner IRA can roll such IRA balance into her own IRA, even if distributions had begun to the owner prior to death.

Question 11 Analysis

Step 1	Read last line and identify the topic: **Note:** positive/are or negative/are not. IRA/Distributions.
Step 2	Read question.
Step 3	Analysis of statements: 1. *False.* 2. *True.* 3. *True.* 4. *True.*
Step 3	Read answers.
Step 4	Select answer D.

a. 1 and 2.
b. 2 and 3.
c. 1, 2, and 3.
d. 2, 3, and 4.
e. 1, 2, 3, and 4.

Answer: D

Number 1 is incorrect. The option is to pay at least as fast as the original payment schedule. For K type questions anchor yourself in certainty. Include the answers that are certainly correct and exclude any answer with a statement that is certainly incorrect.

12. Example.

Which of the following is/are deductible for adjusted gross income?

1. Alimony paid to the taxpayer's ex-spouse.
2. Capital losses.
3. Ordinary and necessary expenses incurred in a business.
4. A deductible individual retirement account (IRA) contribution.

Question 12 Analysis

Step	
Step 1	Read last line and identify the topic: **Note:** Is/are verses are not/AGI.
Step 2	Read question.
Step 3	Analysis of statements: 1. *True.* 2. *Let's suppose I don't know.* 3. *Let's suppose I don't know.* 4. *True.*
Step 4	Evaluate answers. a. *1 only* — *definitely incorrect* b. *4 only* — *definitely incorrect* c. *1 and 4* — *possible answer* d. *1, 3 and 4* — *possible answer* e. *1, 2, 3, and 4* — *possible answer*
Step 5	Evaluate answers 2 and 3 above.
Step 4	Select answer E.

a. 1 only.
b. 4 only.
c. 1 and 4.
d. 1, 3, and 4.
e. 1, 2, 3, and 4.

Answer: E

All are deductible for adjusted gross income.

13. Example.

Jeffrey and Karen Jones have given cash gifts to their children.

Mark, age 13, earns $2,500 in salary.

Jennifer, age 14, earns $2,200 in dividends and capital gains.

Nancy, age 12, earns $1,900 in dividends and interest.

Steven, age 10, earns $900 in dividends and interest.

Whose income is subject to the tax at their parents' marginal rate?

Question 13 Analysis

Step	
Step 1	Read last line and identify the topic: **Note:** Not is/are verses are not/Kiddie Tax.
Step 2	Read question and make note: Topic : Kiddie tax relates to unearned income of children under 14 only for 1998. $1,300 of unearned income to child at child's rate, balance taxed at parents' rate, personal exemption for child, child's standard deduction of : a) 700 b) itemized deductions c) earned income + $250
Step 3	*Mark* - *No, earned income only.* *Jennifer* - *No, too old.* *Nancy* - *Yes.* *Steven* - *Yes, but income too low.*
Step 4	Evaluate answers.
Step 4	Select answer C.

a. Steven's.

b. Jennifer's and Nancy's.

c. Nancy's.

d. Steven's, Jennifer's and Nancy's.

e. Nancy's and Mark's.

Answer: C

The question related to the Kiddie tax, which applies only to unearned income in excess of $1,400 (1998), by a child under the age of 14. Mark, while under the age of 14, has only earned income excluding E. Jennifer is 14 excluding B and D, and Steven age 10 had unearned income less than $1,400. Therefore, the correct answer is C - Nancy, age 12, who had unearned income of $1,900.

14. Example.

Which of the following would best describe the action of a fiscal policy economist?

1. Increase in government spending.
2. Decrease in the money supply.
3. Decrease in income taxes.
4. Increase in the inflation rate.

Question 14 Analysis

Step 1	Read last line and identify the topic: Fiscal policy.
Step 2	Read question and make note: Fiscal is taxation and spending - monetary is interest rates.
Step 3	1. *Yes - fiscal.* 2. *Don't know.* 3. *Yes - fiscal.* 4. *Don't know.*
Step 4	Evaluate answers. a. *Possible answer.* b. *Possible answer.* c. *No.* d. *No.* e. *No.*
Step 5	Re-evaluate statements: #4 is incorrect, therefore A is incorrect.
Step 4	Select answer B.

a. 1, 2, 3, and 4.
b. 1 and 3.
c. 2 only.
d. 2 and 4.
e. 1 only.

Answer: B

Fiscal policy economists believe that the economy can be controlled through the use of government spending and income tax adjustments. Answer C is the answer to describe economists who believe that economic activity is controlled through the use of the money supply. A is incorrect since that answer describes all the choices that include both fiscal policy as well as monetary policy economists. Answer D is incorrect because inflation is determined by market factors. Answer E partially describes the actions of a fiscal policy economist.

HOW TO ANALYZE A CASE

- The sections on case analysis are given Friday and Saturday morning.
- Each case answer is worth 3 points.
- Generally each case contains 10-20 questions.
- There are 3 cases with 10-20 questions each; the questions will total about 130 points.
- You should practice the cases by working them under time pressure. Volume III: Case Exam Book is a great tool for practicing cases and for developing case analysis skills. If you have not practiced working cases, you may find yourself panicking on the exam.
- **Our advice is to complete the non-case multiple choice first, then go to the case.**

General Case Approach to the CFP Examination

Regardless of age or family; there are usually questions concerning insurance deficiencies, asset or property transactions, and the investment portfolio.

1. Every case should present some insurance deficiencies, coverages, exclusions, applications, or taxability of benefits issues.

   If you think about 4 distinct types of families (as provided below) based on:
   - Age.
   - Marital status (MS).
   - Children and grandchildren (C & GC).
   - Net worth (NW).
   - Income (INC).

2. There are always questions regarding asset or property transactions, such as:
   - Acquisition (basis) or disposition of asset (capital gain/loss). Examples:
   - Acquisition - Basis if received by gift- holding period.
   - Basis if received by inheritance.
   - Disposition - Sale/gift/installment sale/private annuity.
   - GRATs/SCINs/CRATs/CRUTs.

3. There are usually questions regarding investment portfolios. Examples:
   - Deficiencies in the current portfolio.
   - Risks associated with current portfolio. Ex. Purchasing power risk, systematic risk, unsystematic risk, lack of diversification, excess liquidity, insufficient growth.

4. Then there are questions regarding the family that are typically family specific.

	Family #1	Family #2	Family #3	Family #4
Age	25-35	35-45	45-60	60-70
M/S	M	M	M	M
C/GC #	2	3	2	4/2
NW	Low	moderate	high	High
Inc.	Moderate	moderate	high	High

QUESTIONS SUGGESTED BY EACH FAMILY			
Family #1	**Family #2**	**Family #3**	**Family #4**
Ed Funding Home refinancing or buying home Savings & investments Portfolio allocation	Educational Funding Retirement Tax savings Portfolio allocation Capital needs analysis	Retirement Planning Estate Planning Investments - Portfolio Analysis Qualified Plans Rollovers etc.	Estates & Probate Planning Gifts Qualified transfers Insurance ownership (life)

5. Obviously there can be strange situations [example: a 70 year old woman with a high net worth and 3 children age 50s, 4 grandchildren age 30s marries a 17 year old man]. Do not QTIP the 17-year-old if you expect to get the estate to the children and grandchildren – 17-year-old will out live children and grandchildren. You will just have to think through the objectives and apply your tools for accomplishing the objectives.

Applications of Case Analysis Strategies

- **Approach 1**

  Read the case carefully and slowly making sure you are involved in the case. Pay particular attention to age, marital status, the number of children and grandchildren, the net worth, and the income levels. These variables will give you a good idea what the case is about. Try to read so you do not have to flip back. Anticipate questions and make notes. When a topic comes up, make a mental or written note. When additional information is provided on that topic later in the case, it is a good bet that there will be a question unless the additional information negates the question. Read each question and answer. Skip the complex questions until last. Answer the easy ones first. An example of approach 1 and 2 using the Mathews case that was released by the CFP® Board is provided.

- **Approach 2**

Read questions quickly. Make notes. Answer any that do not require reading the case, then read the case only looking for answers to questions asked.

<u>Steps</u>:

1) Read questions - last line first.
2) Make notes.
3) Answer all questions that are possible without reading case - mark answer on test.
4) Read case to answer specific questions - record page number of information related to the question.
5) Make sure all questions are answered and then review the answers.

CASE ANALYSIS APPROACH 1

(Use Matthews Case in the back of this book)

Step 1 - Read case and make notes.

Step 2 - Analyze the case making notes in each of the six areas and other significant topic areas.

Step 3 - Anticipate questions.

Step 4 - Read question.

Notes by topical areas - questions anticipated.

Fundamentals

TVM - Installment Sale

Insurance	**Pg. 5**
Life	$200 K B insured Owner Bill/will be included in estate (weakness).
Health	No mention (medigap).
Disability	No mention - over 65.
HO	OK.
Auto	OK.
Umbrella/no umbrella	Inadequate.
HO	No mention of summerhouse insurance.

Tax

1.	Sale of business	Pg. 1				
2.	401K distribution	Pg. 2				
3.	Installment Sale	Pg. 3		N = 120	i = 10 ÷ 12	
4.	Sale of stocks on securities			1244 stock	PV = 1.5 - .3 = 1.2	PMT = ?
5.	SPDA $120,000	1981				
	Basis $40,000		FIFO	Basis $700,000		
	Withdrawal			CG $800,000		

Retirement

OI

PMT - 1993 = 5

PMT - 1994 = 12

Estates

Simple wills/over qualification/ failure to use credit equivalency

Improper ownership of insurance.

No gifts/no trusts/no qualified payments.

Investments

Little growth/Pg.1 low ST rates

Portfolio is 50% T Bills/small tax exempt/heavy liquidity

Other

Pg. 1 Ages 65/63 2 children 3 grandchildren

Sale of business

Objectives

Maintain lifestyle

Estate Planning	Transfers implies gifts/Crummey/GSTT/payment of qualified transfers
Review Investment Portfolio	Liquidity/diversification/risk/growth - some tax advantage; purchasing power/ income needs
Risk Management	
401(k) Distribution	IRA rollover 5/10 year averaging

Financial Statements

Large estate

No property titled

Business is worth 1.5 million $700,000 basis.

$800,000 Capital Gain + Ordinary Income on Installment sale at 10%.

Total Time = approximately 15 minutes.

Step 4:

Then answer questions - use same analysis as 1.

Question Number	Answer	Details
1.	E	No ordinary income from DP.
2.	A	n = 120 PV = 1.5 - .3 = 1.2 i=10/12 PMT = $15,858.09 x 5 = $79,290.44
3.	A	Deduction $1,200,000 x 10% x 5/12 of year = $50,000 because some principal was paid. Look for answer that is < $50,000, therefore A.
4.	C	Installment payment in 1993 = $79,290 from Quest ion 2, therefore some Social Security benefits will be taxed.
5.	A	Number 3 is incorrect. Numbers 1, 2, and 4 are possible.
6.	C	Number 1 is incorrect, number 2 is incorrect, number 4 is incorrect, therefore answer C is correct.
7.	D	Purchased before 1982, therefore FIFO.
8.	D	Section 1244 stock MFJ, therefore $100,000 limit/ordinary loss.
9.	B	Number 1 is correct , #2 is correct, #3 is correct, #4 is incorrect, therefore B.
10.	D	Number 1 is incorrect, #3 and #4 are correct, #2 is correct.
11.	E	All 4 are easy and correct.
12.	B	Calculation $345,800 - 192,800 = $153,000. No table.
13.	C	#2, #3, and #4 all work. #1 does not.
14.	A	See investment notes.
15.	C	Careful reading, installment notes are in gross income.
16.	E	#1, #2, #3, and #4 are all correct.
17.	D	#1 is incorrect, #2 is incorrect, #3 is incorrect, #4 is correct.
18.	E	None of the above are correct.
19.	A	Choice A is the only one that makes sense.

Total Time = approximately 29 minutes.

Comment:

This particular case, because of the shortness of information, was easier in terms of time to answer using the first approach. Dr. Dalton prefers approach 1 over approach 2 because it is more focused on understanding the overall financial picture and anticipating the questions.

Approach 2

Step 1 - Read questions (last line first for directions).

Step 2 - Make notes.

Question #	Need to Read Case	Answers	Page #	Topic	Quick Notes
1	No	E		Tax	Installment Sale; Down Payment; no ordinary income on down payment. Answer - E is correct. Stand alone *.
2	Yes		Pg. 3 and cal. A	TVM	Calculation of monthly payment; need PV = N, i calculate payment.
3	Yes		Pg. 3	TVM	Calculate interest income from installment sale.
4	Yes		Pg. 3 and cal.	Social Security Benefits	Installment payments not wages. Answer B/C – depending on amount of installment payments and basis.
5	No	A		401(k) Options	#3 is incorrect. Stand alone* Answer A is correct.
6	No	C		Life Insurance and Estates	#1 is incorrect; #2 is incorrect; #3 is possible; #4 is incorrect. Answer C is correct. Stand alone*.
7	Yes		Pg. 5	Tax and Annuities	Depends on date of annuity; D is possible; C is possible; A and B are obviously incorrect.
8	Yes		Pg. 5 and 6	Tax Impact	Sale of stock D & T; check basis and FMV and holding period. Read case.
9	No	B		Estate Planning	#1 is correct; #2 is usually correct; answer must be b; #4 is incorrect if he already has an installment sale. Stand alone*.
10	No	D		Taxation of Investments	#1 is incorrect; #2 is possible; #3 is correct; #4 is correct; answer must be D. Stand alone*.
11	Yes	E	Pg. 1	Estate - Grandchildren	Growth; 1 is correct; 2 is correct; 3 is correct - if there are grandchildren. Read case; 4 is correct; Answer E - there is not 1, 2, & 4 only; Answer E is correct - Stand alone*.
12	No	B		GSTT	Calculate GSTT tax - confirms grandchildren Answer B - Stand alone*. 345,800 - 192,800 = 153,000. Note wide differences in answers.
13	No	C	Pg. 1	Tax Shelter	Independent Contractor - Shelter current taxable income - #1 doesn't do that; #2 is OK; #3 is OK; #4 is OK. Answer C if Bill less than 70 ½. Stand alone*. Check age of Bill.
14	Yes		Pg. 3 and 6	Portfolio Analysis	Read Case!
15	No	C		Estate Duplication of Installment Notes	Answer A is incorrect; C is possible; D is incorrect; E is incorrect. Stand alone*.
16	Yes		Pg. 3 and 6	Estate Inadequacies	Read case; probably E - check case information.
17	Yes		Pg. 3 and 6	Asset Allocation to Meet Goals	Read Case.
18	Yes		Pg. 3 and 6	Asset Allocation to Meet Goals	Read Case.
19	Yes		Pg. 3 and 6	Asset Allocation to Meet Goals	Read Case.

* Stand Alone - Stand alone means you do not really need case information to answer the question.

Total time to make above chart = approximately 19 minutes.

Question No.	Initial Analysis of Questions before reading the case	After reading the case
1.	Answer E	
2.	Time Value of Money	Answer A
3.	Time Value of Money	Answer A
4.	Social Security Benefits	Answer C
5.	Answer A	
6.	Answer C	
7.	Tax - Annuities	Answer D
8.	Tax	Answer D
9.	Answer B	
10.	Answer D	
11.	Answer E	
12.	Answer B	
13.	Answer C	
14.	Asset Allocation	Answer A
15.	Answer C	
16.	Estates	Answer E
17.	Asset Allocation	Answer D
18.	Asset Allocation	Answer E
19.	Asset Allocation	Answer A

Numbers 2, 3, 4 - These are interrelated to the first questions regarding sale of business.

Numbers 1, 2, 3, 4.

Information Gathering

Bill	Age 65	Confirms #13	Pg. 1 in case
Grandchildren	Ages 3, 4, 5, and 7	Confirms #11	Pg. 1 in case
Children	Ages 32 and 30	Confirms #11	Pg. 1 in case

Installment Sale of Business **Answers questions 1, 2, 3 and 4**

Sales Price = \$1.5 million Basis = \$700,000 therefore Capital Gain = \$800,000

Down payment = \$300,000

PV = \$1.2 million

N = 120 months

i = 10% ÷ 12 = .83333

PMT_{OA} = \$15,858,09

Start August 1, 1993

Number of months in 1993 \$15,858.09 x (5) = \$79,290.44 Question 2 is answered A.

In 1994, 12 x 15,858.09 = \$190,297.06; therefore SS will be taxable Question 4 is answered C.

Interest income in 1993 = 10% x 120,000 x (5 ÷ 12) ≅ \$50,000. Total Payment = \$79,290.44

Therefore slightly less than \$50,000. Read answers then select A, the only one to qualify (Question 3).

Question 7

Case - Page 5 SPDA Purchase Date 1/1/81. Therefore FIFO the answer is D.

Question 8

D&T Stock Sale

Find Investments - See Balance Sheet p. 3 then p. 6

FMV \$ 25,000

Cost (76,000)

(\$51,000) loss/1244 stock ordinary loss

If married filing jointly 100,000 loss possible, therefore answer D.

Page 1 Section 1 MFJ.

Question 16

Note simple wills Pg. 1 Section 1.

Property not titled, Pg. 3 balance sheet.

See insurance owner Pg. 5.

No mention of durable powers or trusts, therefore answer E.

Questions 14, 17, 18, 19 (All are Investments.)

Question	14 A	17 D	18 E	19 A

Investments are $3.2 million in Invested Assets p. 3 very short-term risk less p. 6

Objectives are p. 2 maintain lifestyle.

Investment Risk Tolerance - Normal p. 2 some modest long-term growth.

After analysis, reread questions.

Question	14	Excessive liquidity, no growth, answer A.
Question	17	#3 is incorrect; #4 is correct; eliminate A and E.
		Reread economic environment p. 1.
		#2 is incorrect, therefore D is the correct answer.
Question	18	E None of the above.

Total Time = approximately 54 minutes. (**Note:** All correct answers.)

YOUR COMMENTS FOR VOLUME II – PROBLEMS AND SOLUTIONS

Our goal is to provide a high quality product to you and other CFP® candidates. With this goal in mind, we hope to significantly improve our texts with each new edition. We welcome your written suggestions, corrections, and other general comments. Please be as detailed as possible and send your ***written*** comments to:

Dalton Publications, L.L.C.
150 James Drive East, Suite 100
St. Rose, Louisiana 70087
(504) 461-9860 FAX

	Page	Ques.	Comments for Volume II (please be as specific as possible)
1.			
2.			
3.			
4.			
5.			
6.			
7.			
8.			
9.			
10.			
11.			
12.			
13.			
14.			
15.			

Name ______________________________

Address ______________________________

Phone ____________ (work) ____________ (home) ____________ (FAX)

E-mail ____________ **Do you require a response?** ______ **Yes** ______ **No**

THIS PAGE IS INTENTIONALLY LEFT BLANK.

FUNDAMENTALS OF FINANCIAL PLANNING PROBLEMS

FUNDAMENTALS OF FINANCIAL PLANNING

THE FINANCIAL PLANNING PROCESS

1. Which of the following publications would provide the best source of mutual fund rates of return, rankings, and expense ratios?

    a. A.M. Best.

    b. Standard and Poors.

    c. Dow Jones.

    d. Federal Reserve Publications.

    e. Time Series Data.

2. Processing and analyzing client information is one stage of the personal financial planning process. Which of the following tasks are completed in this stage?

    1. Identifying alternative investment vehicles.
    2. Identifying financial strengths and weaknesses.
    3. Recommending specific tax strategies.
    4. Preparing financial statements.

    a. 2 and 4.

    b. 1 and 3.

    c. 1, 2, and 3.

    d. 2, 3, and 4.

    e. 1, 2, 3, and 4.

3. Arrange the following financial planning functions into the logical order in which these functions are performed by a professional financial planner. **(CFP® Exam, released 3/95)**

    1. Interview clients, identify preliminary goals.
    2. Monitor financial plans.
    3. Prepare financial plan.
    4. Implement financial strategies, plans, and products.
    5. Collect, analyze, and evaluate client data.

    a. 1, 3, 5, 4, 2.

    b. 5, 1, 3, 2, 4.

    c. 1, 5, 4, 3, 2.

    d. 1, 5, 3, 4, 2.

    e. 1, 4, 5, 3, 2.

4. A client is concerned about the impact that inflation will have on her retirement income. The client currently earns $40,000 per year. Assuming that inflation averages 5.5% for the first five years, 4% for the next five years and 3½% for the remaining time until retirement, what amount must her first-year retirement income be when she retires thirteen years from now if she wants it to equal the purchasing power of her current earnings? **(CFP® Exam, released 3/95)**

   a. $62,550.
   b. $68,841.
   c. $70,520.
   d. $80,231.
   e. $83,157.

5. An inexperienced investment advisor recommends a RELP (Real Estate Limited Partnership) to a client and the client loses 80% of his investment. What do you advise client to do first?

   a. Contact manager at investment house.
   b. Sue or have attorney sue.
   c. Arbitration.
   d. Contact NASD.

6. You speak to a person for the first time. Which of the following would be appropriate if you are in the first 2 stages (goal setting and data gathering) of the financial planning process.

   1. Asking about the number of dependents.
   2. Asking about the age of the dependents or dates of birth.
   3. Determining which stocks to buy.
   4. Collecting personal financial statement information.

   a. 1 only.
   b. 1 and 2.
   c. 2 and 3.
   d. 1, 2, and 4.
   e. 1, 2, 3, and 4.

7. You are a CFP licensee. Your client tells you that his CPA advised him to purchase a tax shelter. He did so, and lost money. He mentions that he has no ill feelings toward the CPA. What should you advise your client as to his rights to recovery (assuming he wants to know his rights)?

   a. Inform him that this is beyond your scope.
   b. Inform him that he has no right to recovery.
   c. See his attorney.
   d. You should call the CPA and discuss issue.

PERSONAL FINANCIAL STATEMENTS

8. A client provides the following information regarding his assets and liabilities as of December 31, 1999. Determine which of the items listed below should be presented on the Statement of Financial Condition (Balance Sheet) as of December 31, 1999.

   1. Stock options granted September 30, 1999 exercisable one year from date of grant.
   2. A bonus receivable of $10,000. The client estimates the bonus based on the prior year bonus and cannot determine the amount precisely because the board of directors meets February 15, 2000 to determine if and when a bonus will be paid.
   3. Huge Oil, Inc. stock in the amount of $15,000. The client owns 1,000 shares priced at $10 per share at December 31, 1999. Huge Oil, Inc. declared a $5 per share dividend on December 10, 1999 payable January 15, 2000 to stockholders of record as of December 31, 1999. The client participates in the company's dividend reinvestment plan.
   4. The client is a cosigner on a loan. The proceeds were used to purchase an automobile by his son. The principal balance on the loan is $4,500 and his son has made all payments to date on a timely basis.
   5. Consulting fees receivable related to services performed by the client's spouse. The engagement was completed and an invoice was mailed December 10, 1999, the credit terms were net 30.

      a. 1, 3, and 4.
      b. 3 and 5.
      c. 4 and 5.
      d. 2, 3, and 5.
      e. 1, 2, and 4.

9. Determine the order of liquidity for the following assets for purposes of presentation on the Statement of Financial Condition (Balance Sheet).

   1. Cash surrender value of life insurance.
   2. Equity mutual fund.
   3. Jewelry.
   4. Personal residence.

      a. 1, 2, 3, 4.
      b. 2, 1, 4, 3.
      c. 2, 1, 3, 4.
      d. 1, 2, 4, 3.
      e. 3, 2, 1, 4.

10. What is the appropriate date to identify the Statement of Financial Condition (balance sheet) of a calendar year client for the year 1999?
    a. At December 31, 1999.
    b. For the period beginning January 1, 2000.
    c. For the period ending December 31, 1999.
    d. For the period January 1 to December 31, 1999.
    e. At January 1, 2000.

11. What is the appropriate date to identify the Statement of Cash Flows of a calendar year client for the year 1999?
    a. At December 31, 1999.
    b. For the period prior to January 1, 2000.
    c. For the period ending December 31, 1999.
    d. For the period beginning January 1, 1999.
    e. At January 1, 2000.

12. The estimated value of a real estate asset in a financial statement prepared by a Certified Financial Planner licensee should be based upon the: **(CFP® Exam, released 3/95)**
    a. Basis of the asset, after taking into account all straight line and accelerated depreciation.
    b. Client's estimate of current value.
    c. Current replacement value of the asset.
    d. Value that a well-informed buyer is willing to accept from a well-informed seller where neither is compelled to buy or sell.
    e. Current insured value.

13. Six months ago, a client purchased a new bedroom suite for $6,500. For purposes of preparing accurate financial statements, this purchase would appear as a(an): **(CFP® Exam, released 3/95)**

    1. Use asset on the client's net worth statement.
    2. Investment asset on the client's net worth statement.
    3. Variable outflow on the client's historic cash flow statement.
    4. Fixed outflow on the client's cash flow statement.

        a. 1, 2, and 3.

        b. 1 and 3.

        c. 2 and 4.

        d. 4 only.

        e. 1, 2, 3, and 4.

ANALYSIS OF FINANCIAL STATEMENTS AND IDENTIFICATION OF STRENGTHS AND WEAKNESSES

14. During a period of rising prices, ABC, Inc. switches from using FIFO to LIFO to determine its inventory valuation. Which of the following is correct, assuming inventory levels remain constant?

    1. The switch should have a dampening effect on net income.
    2. The switch should lower the value of inventory on the balance sheet.
    3. The balance sheet will be unaffected.
    4. The income will increase.

    a. 1 only.
    b. 1 and 2.
    c. 3 only.
    d. 3 and 4.
    e. 2 and 4.

15. Which of the following items would affect net worth?

    1. Repayment of a loan using funds from a savings account.
    2. Purchase of an automobile that is 75% financed with a 25% down payment.
    3. The S&P 500 increases, and the client has an S&P Indexed Mutual Fund.
    4. Interest rates increase, and the client has a substantial bond portfolio.

    a. 2 and 3.
    b. 3 and 4.
    c. 1, 3, and 4.
    d. 1, 2, and 4.

16. The Powells have a net worth of $200,000 before any of the following transactions:

    1. Paid off credit cards of $10,000 using a savings account.
    2. Transferred $4,000 from checking to their IRAs.
    3. Purchased $2,000 of furniture with credit.

    What is the net worth of the Powells after these transactions?

    a. $184,000.
    b. $186,000.
    c. $190,000.
    d. $200,000.

17. Mr. and Mrs. Claiborne, both age 30, have provided you the following information:

Abbreviated Balance Sheet Information			
Cash	$4,000	Credit Cards	$25,000
IRA	25,000	Student Loans	20,000
Investments	40,000	Residence Mortgage	200,000
Personal Residence	240,000		

Abbreviate Statement of Cash Flows	
Annual Income	$48,000
Annual Expenditures:	
Housing Payments (P&I)	$21,062
Housing Payments (T&I)	4,000
Credit Card Repayments	10,000
Student Loans	5,000
All Other Expenses	4,000

How much is Mr. and Mrs. Claiborne's net worth?

a. $64,000.

b. $103,938.

c. $107,938.

d. $148,000.

18. Mr. and Mrs. Claiborne, both age 30, have provided you the following information:

Abbreviated Balance Sheet Information			
Cash	$4,000	Credit Cards	$25,000
IRA	25,000	Student Loans	20,000
Investments	40,000	Residence Mortgage	200,000
Personal Residence	240,000		

Abbreviate Statement of Cash Flows	
Annual Income	$48,000
Annual Expenditures:	
Housing Payments (P&I)	$21,062
Housing Payments (T&I)	4,000
Credit Card Repayments	10,000
Student Loans	5,000
All Other Expenses	4,000

Which of the following is a correct statement regarding Mr. and Mrs. Claiborne?

a. Their net worth is inadequate for their age.

b. They have an insufficient emergency fund.

c. They could not qualify to refinance their home for her balance of the mortgage if interest rates fell from 10% to 8%.

d. Their debt to asset ratio is normal.

BUDGETING

19. Using the rule of 72, approximately how long would it take an investment earning 9% annually to double?

    a. 5 years.
    b. 6 years.
    c. 8 years.
    d. 9 years.
    e. 12 years.

PERSONAL USE-ASSETS AND LIABILITIES.

20. Frankie's house payments, including principal and interest, are $496.00 at the end of each month. She has a 15-year mortgage note with an 8.75% interest rate compounded monthly. What was the amount of Frankie's original mortgage note? (Round answer to the nearest hundred dollars).

    a. $55,600.
    b. $59,600.
    c. $49,600.
    d. $45,600.
    e. None of the above.

21. A young couple would like to purchase a new home using one of the following mortgages:

    #1: 10.5% interest with 5 discount points to be paid at time of closing.

    #2: 11.5% interest with 2 discount points to be paid at time of closing.

    Assuming the couple could qualify for both mortgages, which of the following aspects should be considered in deciding between these two mortgages? **(CFP® Exam, released 3/95)**

    1. Gross income.
    2. Estimated length of ownership.
    3. Real estate tax liability.
    4. Cash currently available.

    a. 1 and 2.
    b. 2 only.
    c. 2 and 4.
    d. 4 only.
    e. 1, 2, 3, and 4.

ECONOMIC ENVIRONMENT - BASIC CONCEPTS

22. Which of the following costs best describes the cost of foregone income which results from making an economic decision to use funds to purchase a piece of equipment?

    a. Marginal cost.

    b. Opportunity cost.

    c. Variable cost.

    d. Fixed cost.

    e. Cost of capital.

23. The inverse relationship between the price of a product and the number of units sold would describe which of the following?

    a. The Law of demand.

    b. Price controls.

    c. Supply side economics.

    d. The Law of supply.

    e. Market price.

24. If the demand for a product is inelastic, it means that:

    a. An increase in the price would lead to an increase in the total amount spent on purchases of the product.

    b. An increase in the price would lead to a decrease in the total amount spent on purchases of the product.

    c. An increase in the price would have no effect on the total amount spent on purchases of the product.

    d. The demand and supply are in equilibrium.

    e. The price of the product cannot be increased or decreased.

25. If the Federal Reserve wanted to lower interest rates, it would consider which of the following?

    1. Purchase government securities.
    2. Increase the reserve requirement of member banks.
    3. Increase the discount rate.
    4. Lower the margin requirement.

        a. 1 and 2.
        b. 2 and 3.
        c. 1 only.
        d. 1 and 4.
        e. 3 and 4.

26. The average number of times a dollar is used per year is also known as:

    a. Inflation.
    b. Price elasticity.
    c. Devaluation.
    d. Velocity of money.
    e. GDP.

27. A common measure of inflation is the Consumer Price Index (CPI). The index begins with a base of 100 at 1967. If the index as of December 1992 was 125.6 and the index as of December 1993 was 133.5, what was the CPI rate of inflation for 1993 rounded to the nearest one-tenth of a percent?

    a. 10.6%.
    b. 7.9%.
    c. 5.9%.
    d. 6.0%.
    e. 6.3%.

28. If the US dollar equivalent of a Mexican Peso is .30656 and the US dollar equivalent of a Peruvian Inti is .4717, what is the value of a Mexican Peso in Peruvian Inti?

    a. MN 00.6499.
    b. MN 01.5387.
    c. MN 64.9900.
    d. MN 00.0154.
    e. MN 00.1446.

29. In a random sample, the value that occurs most frequently is known as:

    a. Mean.
    b. Median.
    c. Mode.
    d. Standard deviation.
    e. Beta.

30. The demand for an economic product varies inversely with its price is the definition of which of the following:

    a. The Law of competition.
    b. The Law of supply and demand.
    c. The Law of demand.
    d. Laissez-faire.
    e. None of the above.

31. Supply for a product includes which of the following:

    1. Amount of a product available at any one time.
    2. Various amounts of a product that producers are willing to supply at all possible prices in the market.
    3. Total production in one year's time by a single firm.
    4. Amount that is supplied at equilibrium price.

    a. 1 only.
    b. 2 only.
    c. 3 and 4.
    d. 1, 2, 3 and 4.
    e. None of the above.

32. The adjustment process in a competitive market moves toward:

    a. Equilibrium.
    b. Shortage.
    c. Surplus.
    d. Capitalism.
    e. None of the above.

33. Which of the following describes pure competition?

    1. Buyers and sellers deal in a variety of products.
    2. Buyers and sellers act together.
    3. A large number of buyers and sellers exist.
    4. Buyers and sellers have little knowledge of the items for sale.

        a. 1 only.
        b. 3 only.
        c. 1 and 3.
        d. 1 and 4.
        e. 1, 2, 3, and 4.

34. A decrease, or shift to the left, in the supply curve occurs when:

    a. Some firms leave the industry.
    b. Government reduces regulations on production.
    c. The cost of inputs goes down.
    d. Taxes go down.
    e. Competition increases.

35. Which of the following occurs when the price of a product decreases and consumers buy more of the product?

    a. The product of a complementary product.
    b. There has been an increase in demand.
    c. A change in demand has taken place.
    d. A change in quantity demanded has taken place.
    e. None of the above.

36. Consumer demand for sugar at 80 cents per pound results in $1,000 in company revenue, and a drop in price to 50 cents per pound results in $1,250 in revenue. Which of the following may be concluded about demand?

    a. Is unit elastic.
    b. Is inelastic.
    c. Would overtake supply.
    d. Is elastic.
    e. None of the above.

37. What question can be asked to (in part) determine the elasticity of demand for an item?
    a. Should production be decreased?
    b. Can the purchase be made by cash only?
    c. Could something else be substituted and work just as well?
    d. Is there enough of the product available?
    e. All of the above.

38. Which of the following describes the law of downward sloping demand?
    a. Consumer demand has not changed significantly.
    b. Consumer demand had dropped drastically.
    c. Consumers demand more at lower prices.
    d. Consumer demand has increased significantly.
    e. None of the above.

39. An increase in the price of product A causes a decrease in the demand for product B. What are the two products?
    a. Complement products.
    b. Substitute products.
    c. Unrelated products.
    d. Demand elastic products.
    e. None of the above.

40. Which of the following explains the principle of diminishing marginal utility?
    a. The shape of the demand curve.
    b. A change in demand.
    c. The nature of inelastic demand.
    d. The substitution effect.
    e. None of the above.

41. The Law of Demand states that:
    a. Consumers select alternative ways of spending income.
    b. The relative change in price is caused by changes in demand.
    c. The relationship between changing prices and total receipts is a direct one.
    d. The demand for an economic product varies inversely with its price.
    e. None of the above.

42. Which of the following are reasons for a change in consumer demand?

    1. Changes in consumer tastes: advertising, news reports, trends, and seasons can all affect consumer tastes.
    2. Changes in consumer demand may result from changes in consumer income: as income rises, consumers tend to buy more, if income declines, consumers buy less.
    3. Prices of related products: sometimes substitutes can be used in place of other products.

       a. 1 only.
       b. 2 only.
       c. 3 only.
       d. 1 and 2.
       e. 1, 2, and 3.

43. The relationship between a demand schedule and a demand curve is best described as:

       a. The two present the same information in different ways.
       b. There is no relationship between the two.
       c. A demand curve is part of a demand schedule.
       d. A demand schedule is created from a demand curve.
       e. All of the above.

44. Which of the following are determinants of demand elasticity?

    1. Whether the purchase of the product can be delayed.
    2. Whether there are adequate substitutes for the product.
    3. Whether the purchase of the product requires a large portion of income.
    4. Whether the product has utility.

       a. 1 only.
       b. 2 only.
       c. 2 and 3.
       d. 1, 2, and 3.
       e. 1, 2, 3, and 4.

45. Which of the following might cause an increase in supply?

1. A decrease in productivity.
2. Fewer sellers in the marketplace.
3. More efficient technology.
4. A decrease in government subsidies.

a. 1 only.
b. 2 only.
c. 3 only.
d. 1 and 4.
e. 2 and 3.

46. Which of the following describes supply if the quantity supplied does not change significantly with a change in price?

a. Supply is unit elastic.
b. Supply is elastic.
c. Supply is inelastic.
d. Supply is fixed.
e. Supply is variable.

47. Which of the following describe why changes in supply occur?

1. Changes in the cost of inputs.
2. Changes in productivity.
3. Changes in technology.
4. Changes in taxes.

a. 1 only.
b. 3 only.
c. 1 and 2.
d. 2 and 3.
e. 1, 2, 3, and 4.

48. Inflation causes people living on a fixed income to have:

    1. No financial problems.
    2. No voice in the government.
    3. Declining purchasing power.
    4. Unlimited resources.

        a. 1 only.
        b. 2 only.
        c. 3 only.
        d. 1 and 4.
        e. 1, 2, 3, and 4.

49. Which of the following describes a rapid increase in the general level of prices?

    a. A market economy.
    b. A depression.
    c. Inflation.
    d. Deflation.
    e. None of the above.

50. Which economic goal does minimum wage support?

    a. Economic equity.
    b. Economic efficiency.
    c. Economic growth.
    d. Full employment.
    e. None of the above.

51. Movement through the phases of the business cycle is initiated by shifts in aggregate demand which create fluctuations in Gross Domestic Product (GDP). Which combination of the following statements would be the most significant contributor to the upward shift in aggregate demand shown in the graph? **(CFP® Exam, released 3/95)**

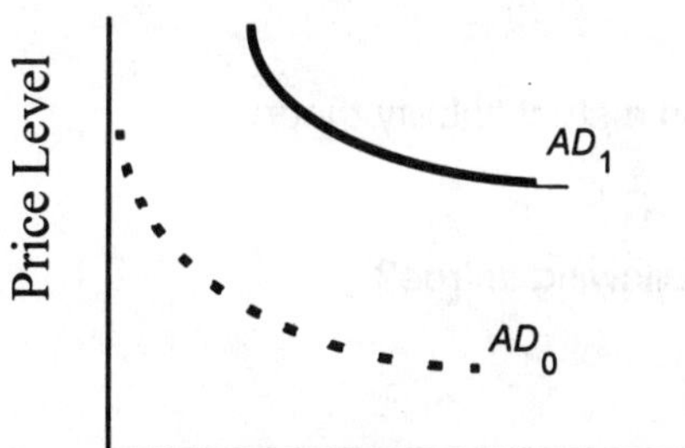

1. Increase in demand for capital goods.
2. Increase in interest rates.
3. Increase in disposable income.
4. Increase in savings.

   a. 1 and 3.
   b. 1, 2, and 3.
   c. 1, 3, and 4.
   d. 2 and 4.
   e. 3 and 4.

52. Under the Federal Fair Labor Standards Act, which of the following would be regulated?

1. Minimum wage.
2. Overtime.
3. Number of hours in the work week.

   a. 1 only.
   b. 2 only.
   c. 3 only.
   d. 1, 2, and 3.
   e. None of the above.

53. Which of the following provisions is basic to all workers' compensation systems?

    a. The injured employee must prove the employer's negligence.
    b. The employer may invoke the traditional defense of contributory negligence.
    c. The employer may invoke the defense of assumption of the risk.
    d. The employer's liability may be ameliorated by a co-employee's negligence under the fellow-servant rule.
    e. The injured employee is allowed to recover on a strict liability theory.

54. If you have product with inelastic demand, which of the following is true?

    a. As the price increases, revenue decreases.
    b. As the price increases, revenue increases.
    c. There is no relationship between price and revenues.
    d. None of the above.

55. Which best describes high unemployment, with low interest rates?

    a. Peak.
    b. Recession.
    c. Trough.
    d. Expansion.

56. When the economy is slowing and unemployment is increasing, what stage of the economic cycle are we in?

    a. Trough.
    b. Recession.
    c. Peak.
    d. Recovery.

57. Which of the following statements concerning supply and/or demand is/are true? **(CFP® Exam, released 12/95)**

1. If demand increases and supply simultaneously decreases, equilibrium price will rise.
2. There is an inverse relationship between price and quantity demanded.
3. If demand decreases and supply simultaneously increases, equilibrium price will fall.
4. If demand decreases and supply remains constant, equilibrium price will rise.

a. 1, 2 and 3.
b. 1 and 3.
c. 2 and 4.
d. 4 only.
e. 1, 2, 3 and 4.

58. If the demand for a product is inelastic, it means that:

a. An increase in the price would lead to an increase in the total amount spent on purchases of the product.
b. An increase in the price would lead to a decrease in the total amount spent on purchases of the product.
c. An increase in the price would have no effect on the total amount spent on purchases of the product.
d. The demand and supply are in equilibrium.
e. The price of the product cannot be increased or decreased.

59. If the Federal Reserve wanted to lower interest rates, it would consider which of the following?

1. Purchase government securities.
2. Increase the reserve requirement of member banks.
3. Increase the discount rate.
4. Lower the margin requirement.

a. 1 and 2.
b. 2 and 3.
c. 1 only.
d. 1 and 4.
e. 3 and 4.

MONETARY AND FISCAL POLICY

60. Which of the following actions would best describe a fiscal policy economist?

    1. Increase in government spending.
    2. Decrease in the money supply.
    3. Decrease in income taxes.
    4. Increase in the inflation rate.

       a. 1, 2, 3, and 4.
       b. 1 and 3.
       c. 2 only.
       d. 2 and 4.
       e. 1 only.

61. Which of the following economic activities represent(s) examples of monetary policy?

    1. The federal funds rate is increased.
    2. Congress passes a tax cut.
    3. Bank reserve requirements are lowered by the Federal Reserve.
    4. The Federal Open Market Committee sells securities.

       a. 1 only.
       b. 1 and 3.
       c. 1, 3, and 4.
       d. 1, 2, and 3.
       e. 2, 3, and 4.

62. The purposes of the Federal Reserve include?

    1. Establishing the Prime Lending Rate (PLR).
    2. Influencing and monitoring the flow of capital in the United States.
    3. Establishing wage and price controls as economic circumstances dictate.
    4. Functioning as the federal government's agency to influence or control inflation.

       a. 1 only.
       b. 2 only.
       c. 2 and 4.
       d. 2, 3, and 4.
       e. 1, 2, 3, and 4.

63. Which of the following monetary components would be included in the M-1 measure of the money supply?

1. NOW accounts.
2. Savings accounts.
3. Checking accounts.
4. Currency.
5. Certificates of Deposit (CD's).

a. 3 and 4.
b. 1, 2, and 5.
c. 1, 3, and 4.
d. 4 only.
e. All of the above.

64. Which of the following can the Fed do to reduce the money supply?

1. Purchase Treasury securities.
2. Decrease the reserve requirements for banks.
3. Increase the discount rate.

a. 1 only.
b. 2 only.
c. 3 only.
d. 1 and 2.
e. 2 and 3.

65. Which of the following can be done by the Fed to increase the money supply?

1. Decrease the margin requirements for banks from 8 percent to 6 percent.
2. Increasing expenditures of the Federal government, thereby circulating addition funds in the economy.
3. Open market transactions.

a. 1 only.
b. 2 only.
c. 1 and 2.
d. 1 and 3.
e. 1, 2 and 3.

66. What actions taken by the Fed will lead to increased money supply?

    a. Lowering the prime rate.
    b. Lowering the discount rate.
    c. Sell treasury securities.
    d. Increase reserve requirements.

67. Which of the following is/are methods that might be used to control the supply of money?

    1. Control of the Federal Reserve Discount Rate.
    2. Open market operations.
    3. Fiscal policy.

    a. 1 only.
    b. 2 only.
    c. 1 and 3.
    d. 2 and 3.
    e. 1, 2, and 3.

BUSINESS CYCLE THEORIES

68. The phases of a typical business cycle are as follows:

    a. Trough, Peak, Expansion, Recession.

    b. Peak, Recession, Expansion, and Trough.

    c. Trough, Expansion, Peak, Recession.

    d. Recession, Peak, Expansion, Trough.

    e. Recession, Expansion, Trough, Peak.

69. In a typical business cycle, which one of the following phases would exhibit periods of increasing employment and increasing output?

    a. Intensity.

    b. Trough.

    c. Peak.

    d. Expansion.

    e. Recession.

FINANCIAL INSTITUTIONS

70. An investor wishing to invest $150,000 is concerned about the safety of his investment if he invests the funds through a national bank. Which of the following statements is/are correct?

    1. If the investor deposits the funds in a savings account, the FDIC guarantees the full amount of his investment.
    2. If the FDIC guaranteed the funds in a savings account, none of the investment the investor deposits is guaranteed if the amount exceeds $100,000.
    3. If the funds were invested in a mutual fund sold by the national bank, the FDIC up to $100,000 affords the investor protection.
    4. If the investor deposits $75,000 into each of two savings accounts at the same bank in his name only, the full amount of his investment is afforded protection by the FDIC since neither account exceeds $100,000.

    a. 1 and 4.
    b. 4 only.
    c. 2 only.
    d. 3 only.
    e. None of the statements are correct.

TIME VALUE OF MONEY

71. Today Bob Jones purchased an investment grade gold coin for $50,000. He expects the coin to increase in value at a rate of 12% compounded annually for the next 5 years. How much will the coin be worth at the end of the fifth year if his expectations are correct?

    a. $89,792.82.
    b. $66,911.28.
    c. $88,117.08.
    d. $89,542.38.
    e. None of the above.

72. A client invested $10,000 in an interest bearing promissory note earning an 11% annual rate of interest compounded monthly. How much will the note be worth at the end of 7 years assuming all interest is reinvested at the 11% rate?

    a. $13,788.43.
    b. $20,762.60.
    c. $21,048.52.
    d. $21,522.04.
    e. None of the above.

73. Bill Barnett purchased $60,000 worth of silver coins 8 years ago. The coins have appreciated 7.5% compounded annually over the last 8 years. How much are the coins worth today?

    a. $107,008.67.
    b. $102,829.46.
    c. $99,719.03.
    d. $99,542.95.
    e. None of the above.

74. Sarah Attaya wants to give her daughter $25,000 in 8 years to start her own business. How much should she invest today at an annual interest rate of 8% compounded annually to have $25,000 in 8 years?

    a. $12,802.95.
    b. $13,506.72.
    c. $13,347.70.
    d. $13,210.34.
    e. None of the above.

75. Cassie expects to receive $75,000 from a trust fund in 6 years. What is the current value of this fund if it is discounted at 9% compounded semiannually?

    a. $57,592.18.
    b. $44,720.05.
    c. $44,224.79.
    d. $42,794.31.
    e. None of the above.

76. Bill McDowell expects to receive $75,000 in 5 years. His opportunity cost is 10% compounded monthly. What is this sum worth to Bill today?

    a. $45,584.14.
    b. $46,043.49.
    c. $46,569.10.
    d. $48,542.09.
    e. None of the above.

77. Mary Sue wants to accumulate $57,000 in 8.5 years to purchase a boat. She expects an annual rate of return of 10.5% compounded quarterly. How much does Mary Sue need to invest today to meet her goal?

    a. $23,529.87.
    b. $23,619.30.
    c. $23,883.56.
    d. $24,364.33.
    e. None of the above.

78. Joe purchased 10 shares of an aggressive growth mutual fund at $90 per share 7 years ago. Today he sold all 10 shares for $4,500. What was his average annual compound rate of return on this investment before tax?

    a. 17.46%.
    b. 19.58%.
    c. 21.73%.
    d. 25.85%.
    e. None of the above.

79. John borrowed $800 from his father to purchase a mountain bike. John paid back $1,200 to his father at the end of 5 years. What was the average annual compound rate of interest on John's loan from his father?

  a. 11.5646%.
  b. 8.4472%.
  c. 7.7892%.
  d. 5.1990%.
  e. None of the above.

80. Susan Jones purchased a zero coupon bond 6.5 years ago for $525. If the bond matures today and the face value is $1,000, what is the average annual compound rate of return (calculated semi-annually) that Susan realized on her investment?

  a. 11.3372%.
  b. 10.5713%.
  c. 10.400%.
  d. 10.163%.
  e. None of the above.

81. Mike Kibley purchased an Oriental rug for $8,000. Today, he sold the rug for $15,000. Mike determined the average annual compound rate of return on the rug was 12%. Approximately how may years did Mike own the rug? (rounded to the nearest .0000)

  a. 6.8452.
  b. 5.5468.
  c. 4.5337.
  d. 5.8451.
  e. 6.0000.

82. Today Raul put all of his cash into an account earning an annual interest rate of 9% compounded monthly. Assuming he makes no withdrawals or additions into this account, approximately how many years must Raul wait to double his money? (rounded to the nearest .00)

  a. 7.75.
  b. 8.25.
  c. 8.75.
  d. 7.25.
  e. 8.00.

83. Clarence Cushman has been investing $1,000 at the end of each year for the past 15 years. How much has accumulated assuming he has earned 10.5% compounded annually on his investment?

    a. $20,303.72.
    b. $23,349.28.
    c. $33,060.04.
    d. $36,531.34.
    e. None of the above.

84. Christine Valico has been dollar cost averaging into a mutual fund by investing $2,000 at the end of every quarter for the past 7 years. She has been earning an average annual compound return of 11% compounded quarterly on this investment. How much is the fund worth today?

    a. $78,266.19.
    b. $81,170.29.
    c. $82,721.95.
    d. $84,996.80.
    e. $86,875.47.

85. Bill Russell has been investing $3,000 at the beginning of each year for the past 15 years. How much has accumulated assuming he has earned 8% compounded annually on his investment?

    a. $91,896.04.
    b. $87,972.85.
    c. $84,696.81.
    d. $81,456.34.
    e. None of the above.

86. Chrissy Nables has been dollar cost averaging in a mutual fund by investing $2,000 at the beginning of every quarter for the past 7 years. She has been earning an average annual compound return of 11% compounded quarterly on this investment. How much is the fund worth today?

    a. $82,721.95.
    b. $93,902.42.
    c. $91,389.22.
    d. $84,996.80.
    e. None of the above.

87. Stuart Wood expects to receive $5,000 at the end of each of the next 4 years. His opportunity cost is 14% compounded annually. What is this sum worth to Stuart today?

    a. $14,568.56.
    b. $16,608.16.
    c. $19,568.56.
    d. $17,165.41.
    e. None of the above.

88. Tim, injured in an automobile accident, won a judgment that provides him $1,500 at the end of each 6-month period over the next 6 years. If the escrow account that holds Tim's settlement award earns an average annual rate of 11% compounded semiannually, how much was the defendant initially required to pay Tim to compensate him for his injuries?

    a. $6,345.81.
    b. $7,043.85.
    c. $12,927.78.
    d. $13,638.80.
    e. None of the above.

89. Jane wants to withdraw $4,000 at the beginning of each year for the next 7 years. She expects to earn 10.5% compounded annually on her investment. What lump sum should Jane deposit today?

    a. $19,157.21.
    b. $18,667.20.
    c. $20,627.25.
    d. $21,168.72.
    e. None of the above.

90. Connie wants to withdraw $1,200 at the beginning of each month for the next 5 years. She expects to earn 10% compounded monthly on her investments. What lump sum should Connie deposit today?

    a. $56,478.44.
    b. $56,949.10.
    c. $58,630.51.
    d. $59,119.10.
    e. None of the above.

91. Gary received an inheritance of $200,000. He wants to withdraw equal periodic payments at the beginning of each month for the next 5 years. He expects to earn 12% annual interest, compounded monthly on his investments. How much can he receive each month?

    a. $4,404.84.
    b. $4,448.89.
    c. $49,537.45.
    d. $55,481.95.
    e. None of the above.

92. Eugene wants to purchase a fishing camp in 5 years for $60,000. What periodic payment should he invest at the beginning of each quarter to attain the goal if he can earn 10.5% annual interest, compounded quarterly on investments?

    a. $2,319.42.
    b. $2,260.09.
    c. $8,805.91.
    d. $9,730.53.
    e. None of the above.

93. Tina wants to purchase a home 6 years from now. She anticipates spending $150,000. To attain this goal, how much should Tina invest at the end of each 6-month period if she expects to earn a 12% annual compound rate of return, compounded semiannually, on her investments?

    a. $18,483.86.
    b. $16,503.44.
    c. $8,891.55.
    d. $8,388.26.
    e. None of the above.

94. Janet purchased a car for $19,500. She is financing the auto at 11% annual interest rate, compounded monthly for 3 years. What payment is required at the end of each month to finance Janet's car?

    a. $606.71.
    b. $638.40.
    c. $632.61.
    d. $684.97.
    e. None of the above.

95. Shane estimates his opportunity cost on investments at 10.5% compounded annually. Which one of the following is the best investment opportunity for Shane?

    a. To receive $45,000 today.
    b. To receive $120,000 at the end of 10 years.
    c. To receive $5,500 at the beginning of each year for 15 years.
    d. To receive $5,500 at the end of each year for 19 years.
    e. To receive $5,750 at the end of each year for 17 years.

96. Richard estimates his opportunity cost on investments at 9% compounded annually, which one of the following is the best investment opportunity?

    a. To receive $100,000 today.
    b. To receive $310,000 at the end of 15 years.
    c. To receive $1,200 at the end of each month for 11 years compounded monthly.
    d. To receive $65,000 in 5 years and $125,000 5 years later.
    e. To receive $65,000 in 5 years and $200,000 10 years later.

97. Judy Martin estimates her opportunity cost on investments to be 12% compounded annually. Which one of the following is the best investment opportunity?

    a. To receive $50,000 today.
    b. To receive $250,000 at the end of 14 years.
    c. To receive $40,000 at the end of 4 years and $120,000 8 years later at the end of the 12th year.
    d. To receive $5,000 at the beginning of each 6-month period for 9 years compounded semiannually.
    e. To receive $60,000 at the end of 3 years.

98. Morris and JoAnn Simpson are ready to retire. They want to receive the equivalent of $25,000 in today's dollars at the beginning of each year for the next 20 years. They assume inflation will average 4% over the long run, and they can earn an 8% compound annual after-tax return on investments. What lump sum do Morris and JoAnn need to invest today to attain their goal?

    a. $265,089.98.
    b. $339,758.16.
    c. $353,348.49.
    d. $357,681.46.
    e. None of the above.

99. Stuart needs an income stream equivalent to $50,000 in today's dollars at the beginning of each year for the next 12 years to maintain his standard of living. He assumes inflation will average 4.5% over the long run, and he can earn a 9% compound annual after-tax return on investments. What lump sum does Stuart need to invest today to fund his needs?

   a. $480,878.04.
   b. $455,929.00.
   c. $476,445.85.
   d. $461,025.81.
   e. None of the above.

100. Clark Roberts wants to retire in 9 years. He needs an additional $300,000 (today's $) in 9 years to have sufficient funds to finance this objective. He assumes inflation will average 5.0% over the long run, and he can earn a 4.0% compound annual after-tax return on investments. What serial payment should Clark invest at the end of the first year to attain his objective?

   a. $34,623.42.
   b. $34,689.00.
   c. $36,354.60.
   d. $36,423.45.
   e. None of the above.

101. Judy Danos wants to retire in 9 years. She needs an additional $300,000 (today's $) in 9 years to have sufficient funds to finance this objective. She assumes inflation will average 5.0% over the long run, and she can earn a 4.0% compound annual after-tax return on investments. What will be Judy's payment at the end of the second year?

   a. $38,244.62.
   b. $38,172.33.
   c. $36,354.60.
   d. $34,623.42.
   e. None of the above.

102. John wants to start his own business in 6 years. He needs to accumulate $200,000(today's $) in 6 years to sufficiently finance his business. He assumes inflation will average 4%, and he can earn a 9% compound annual after-tax return on investments. What serial payment should John invest at the end of the first year to attain his goal?

a. $29,546.11.

b. $30,727.95.

c. $28,190.78.

d. $29,318.41.

e. None of the above.

103. Sarah wants to start her own business in 6 years. She needs to accumulate $200,000(today's $) in 6 years to sufficiently finance her business. She assumes inflation will average 4%, and she can earn a 9% compound annual after-tax return on investments. What will be Sarah's payment at the end of the second year?

a. $28,190.78.

b. $30,727.95.

c. $30,491.00.

d. $31,957.07.

e. None of the above.

104. Determine the future value of a periodic deposit of $6,100 made at the beginning of each year for 10 years to a mutual fund expected to earn 11.5% compounded annually during the projection period. Calculate the future value rounded to the nearest dollar.

a. $104,493.

b. $116,510.

c. $113,040.

d. $124,344.

e. $39,229.

105. Determine the future value of a periodic deposit of $6,100 made at the beginning of each year for 10 years to a mutual fund expected to earn 11.5% compounded quarterly during the projection period. Calculate the future value rounded to the nearest dollar.

a. $447,130.
b. $116,510.
c. $119,931.
d. $107,076.
e. $459,985.

106. A client is to receive $650 per month for 5 years beginning one year from today at the beginning of the month. What is the present value of all payments (rounded to the nearest dollar) assuming an annual discount rate of 9%?

a. $33,070.
b. $28,943.
c. $30,339.
d. $31,548.
e. $28,728.

107. The rate which produces a net present value of a series of discounted cash flows equal to zero is called the:

a. Return on investment (ROI).
b. Internal rate of return (IRR).
c. Average rate of return.
d. Cost of capital.
e. Inflation rate.

108. If the net present value of a series of discounted cash flows is greater than zero, one could interpret that:

1. The discounted cash flows exceed the investment outlay.
2. The rate of return is higher than the cost of capital.
3. The return on investment is lower than the internal rate of return.
4. The internal rate of return was the discount rate used.

a. 1 only.
b. 1 and 4.
c. 1, 2, 3, and 4.
d. 2 and 3.
e. 2 only.

109. If the net present value of a series of discounted cash flows is equal to zero, one could interpret that:

1. The discounted cash flows equal the investment outlay.
2. The rate of return is lower than the cost of capital.
3. The return on investment is lower than the internal rate of return.
4. The internal rate of return was the discount rate used.

a. 1 only.
b. 1 and 4.
c. 1, 2, 3, and 4.
d. 2 and 3.
e. 2 only.

110. If the net present value of a series of discounted cash flows is less than zero, one could interpret that:

1. The discounted cash flows are lower than the investment outlay.
2. The rate of return is lower than the cost of capital.
3. The return on investment is higher than the internal rate of return.
4. The internal rate of return was the discount rate used.

a. 1 only.
b. 1 and 4.
c. 1, 2, 3, and 4.
d. 2 and 3.
e. 2 only.

111. What is the monthly payment made at the end of each month required to accumulate a balance of $150,000 in 10 years at an assumed interest rate of 11% compounded monthly and a beginning savings balance of $2,500?

a. $684.97.
b. $691.25.
c. $656.81.
d. $650.85.
e. $712.14.

112. Joe wants to buy a business in 10 years. He estimates he will need $150,000 at that time. He currently has a Zero Coupon Bond with a market value of $1,157.98 that he will use as part of the required amount. The Zero Coupon Bond has a face value of $2,500 and will mature in 10 years. The bond has a semi-annual effective interest rate of 3.923%. In addition to the bond, he wants to save a monthly amount to reach his goal. What is Joe's required monthly payment made at the beginning of each month in order to accumulate the $150,000, including the Zero Coupon Bond, at an assumed interest rate of 11%?

a. $676.10.
b. $673.56.
c. $669.96.
d. $679.73.
e. $800.91.

113. A parent wishes to begin saving for a child's education. The child is born today, the first payment will be made today and the child will start college on his 18th birthday. The child will attend college for four years with the annual payment due at the beginning of the school year. The current cost of the college education is $25,000 per year. It is expected that the cost of a college education will increase at an average rate of 7% per year during the projection period and that the general rate of inflation will be 4%. The parent has the option of investing in the following: 1) A taxable mutual stock fund expected to earn 12.0% during the projection period and 2) A tax-free bond fund expected to earn 8.5% during the projection period. The parents marginal tax bracket is 31% and the average tax bracket is 21%. Exclusive of risk, what do you recommend?

a. The equity mutual fund because the after tax rate of return (assuming the average tax bracket) is greater than the tax-free bond fund.
b. The bond fund because the rate of return is greater than the after tax rate of return for the equity mutual fund (assuming marginal tax bracket).
c. Make the annual payment at the end of the year because the annual funding requirement is less than if made at the beginning of the year.
d. Either investment is appropriate as long as the after tax rate of return is greater than the underlying rate of inflation on an annual basis.
e. Invest in the equity mutual fund because the pre-tax rate of return is greater than the rate of return of the bond fund.

114. Philip purchased a house for $185,000 with a down payment of 20%. If he finances the balance at 10% over 15 years, how much will his monthly payment be?

a. $1,577.27.

b. $1,590.42.

c. $1,971.59.

d. $1,988.02.

115. David Gregory recently purchased a house for $120,000. He put 20% down and financed the remaining amount over 15 years at 7.5%. How much interest will be paid over the life of the loan assuming he pays the loan as agreed? (Round to the nearest dollar.)

a. $31,813.00.

b. $64,187.00.

c. $96,000.00.

d. $160,187.00.

116. Brian, age 48, plans to retire at 65 and wants to be debt free at retirement. The balance sheet mortgage is $114,042 at the end of the 10th year of a 30-year loan. The monthly payment from the income statement (P&I only) was $953.89. What was the original balance of the loan if the interest rate was 8%? (Select closest answer.)

a. $119,572.

b. $120,000.

c. $125,000.

d. $130,000.

e. $140,428.

117. Using the information from the previous question, assume Brian can refinance at a 15 year rate for 6.5% or a 30 year rate for 7% and will incur closing costs of 3% of the mortgage amount to be financed in the new mortgage balance. What will be his new mortgage payment under the circumstances to achieve his objectives?

a. $776.95.

b. $781.49.

c. $957.56.

d. $980.57.

e. $986.29.

118. Allen pays his mortgage as agreed. The mortgage is $120,000 for 15 years and has an interest rate of 7%. Allen makes payments monthly. What is the total amount of interest Allen will pay over the term of the mortgage? (Select closest answer.)

a. $75,000.

b. $80,000.

c. $85,000.

d. $90,000.

e. $100,000.

EDUCATIONAL FUNDING

119. Marleen and Billy Poor have two children ages 5 and 7. The Poors want to start saving for their children's education. Each child will spend 6 years at college and will begin at age 18. College currently costs $20,000 per year and is expected to increase at 6% per year. Assuming the Poors can earn an annual compound return of 12% and inflation is 4%, how much must the Poors deposit at the end of each year to pay for their children's educational requirements until the youngest is out of school? Assume that educational expenses are withdrawn at the beginning of each year and that the last deposit will be made at the beginning of the last year of the youngest child.

   a. $11,984.
   b. $12,386.
   c. $14,186.
   d. $14,989.
   e. $15,230.

120. Sandy was recently divorced and has two children. The divorce decree requires that she pay 1/3 of the college tuition cost for her children. Tuition cost is currently $15,000 per year and has been increasing at 7% per year. Her son and daughter are 12 and 16, respectively, and will attend college for four years beginning at age 18. Assume that her after-tax rate of return will be 9% and that general inflation has been 4%. How much should she save each month, beginning today for the next five years to finance both children's education?

   a. $745.01.
   b. $750.60.
   c. $2,235.04.
   d. $2,251.80.
   e. $2,500.00.

121. Sharon has a daughter, Debbie, who is 14 years old. College costs are currently $12,000 per year and are expected to increase 5% per year, including the 4 years Debbie is in college. Debbie will begin college at age 18. Pursuant to a divorce decree, Sharon is responsible for 1/3 of the total cost of Debbie's college tuition. Sharon wants to be able to have the total amount of tuition for which she is responsible by the time Debbie starts college but will pay the tuition at the beginning of each school year. She estimates she can put money in a fund that earns 9% after tax. What amount does Sharon have to deposit at the beginning of each month starting now to meet her goal?

  a. $317.56.
  b. $319.95.
  c. $341.80.
  d. $952.69.
  e. $959.84.

122. Scott and Arleen Smith have two children ages 4 and 6. The Smiths want to start saving for their children's education. Each child will spend 5 years at college and will begin at age 18. College currently costs $30,000 per year and is expected to increase at 7% per year. Assuming the Smiths can earn an annual compound return of 12% and inflation is 4%, how much must the Smiths deposit at the end of each year to pay for their children's educational requirements until the youngest goes to school? Assume that educational expenses are withdrawn at the beginning of each year and that the last deposit will be made at the beginning of the first year of the youngest child.

  a. $19,894.
  b. $20,674.
  c. $22,272.
  d. $22,886.
  e. $23,615.

BUSINESS ORGANIZATIONS

123. Which of the following describes a weakness of the proprietorship form of business?
   a. Owner has too many partners.
   b. Business is in constant danger of bankruptcy.
   c. Owner has no control.
   d. Business depends solely on the owner.
   e. None of the above.

124. A business fails and the owners lose their investment in the company, along with their personal residences, automobiles and other personal property. What type of business entity does this suggest?
   a. Common shareholders in a corporation.
   b. Preferred shareholders in a corporation.
   c. Limited partners in a limited partnership.
   d. General partners in a general partnership.
   e. None of the above.

125. Which of the following describes a main strength of the corporate form of business entity?
   a. Ease of establishment.
   b. Ease of management.
   c. Ease of raising capital.
   d. Freedom from business income taxes.
   e. None of the above.

126. Which of the following describe the corporate form of business entity?
   1. Limited liability.
   2. Limited life.
   3. Proxy.
   4. Board of directors.
   a. 1 only.
   b. 2 only.
   c. 3 only.
   d. 1 and 3.
   e. 1, 3, and 4.

127. Which of the following can be considered a strength of the partnership form of business entity?

1. Ease of management.
2. Ease of establishment.
3. Lack of special taxes.
4. Limited life.

a. 1 only.
b. 2 only.
c. 2 and 3.
d. 1, 2, 3, and 4.
e. None of the above.

128. A taxpayer is considering starting a new business. The taxpayer is concerned about liability issues affecting his business and expects to incur losses in the first year. Which of the following forms of organizations would be the most appropriate?

a. Sole proprietorship.
b. Partnership.
c. C corporation.
d. S corporation.
e. Personal holding company.

129. In order to elect S corporation status for the current year of a calendar year newly incorporated business, the following must be done:

1. Secure the consent of the board of directors of the corporation.
2. File the election (Form 2553) before March 15 of the year the election is to take place.
3. Issue two classes of stock.
4. File the election (Form 2553) at any time before the end of the corporation's tax year.
5. Elect S corporation status upon filing the corporation's initial tax return.

a. 1, 3, and 5.
b. 5 only.
c. 1 and 2.
d. 2 only.
e. 3 and 4.

130. Which of the following is/are disadvantages of electing S corporation status?

1. Fringe benefits are not tax deductible by the S corporation for shareholders owning 2% or more of the stock of the corporation unless included in W-2.
2. Individual income tax rates may be higher than corporate tax rates.
3. Section 179 election to expense certain capital expenditures are not allowed at the corporate or individual level.
4. The corporation cannot have more than 75 shareholders.

a. 3 and 4.
b. 1, 2, and 4.
c. 1, 2, 3, and 4.
d. 2 and 3.
e. 4 only.

131. Which of the following statements regarding partnerships, S corporations, and sole proprietorships is not true?

a. S corporation earnings are not eligible for Keogh retirement plans.
b. Sole proprietorships are subject to the self-employment tax at a rate of 15.3% of net earnings from self-employment.
c. Guaranteed payments made by a partnership are taxable to the individual partners.
d. Pass through earnings of an S corporation are subject to the self-employment tax.
e. Salary payments made to S corporation shareholders are subject to FICA taxes at the corporate level and not at the individual level.

132. Which of the following is correct with regard to the rights of a limited partner?

1. Has the right to take part in the management of the partnership.
2. May assign his or her interest in the partnership to anyone he/she wishes at any time.
3. Is subject to personal liability for partnership debts.

a. 1 only.
b. 2 only.
c. 3 only.
d. 1 and 3.
e. 1, 2, and 3.

133. Which of the following is correct regarding both a corporation and general partnership?

1. Can hold and convey property.
2. Are regarded as distinct entities for tax purposes.
3. Profits are divided equally.
4. Pay no federal tax on income.

   a. 1 only.
   b. 2 only.
   c. 1 and 2.
   d. 1 and 4.
   e. 1, 2, 3, and 4.

134. When is a corporation likely to elect S corporation status?

   a. A loss is anticipated especially at the start-up of a business.
   b. Desire to issue preferred stock.
   c. Place personal liability on the shareholders.
   d. Borrow money from shareholders.
   e. All of the above.

135. Your client, a wealthy physician in the top marginal tax bracket, is interested in purchasing a franchise in a fast-growing chain with five of his colleagues. After carefully reviewing the proposal, you have determined that apart from a large up-front investment, the business will <u>not</u> need to retain income and the income generated in subsequent years will be paid out to the investors.

Furthermore, your client wants to be assured that after investing so large an amount, the business would not be disrupted if one of his partners lost interest or encountered personal financial reversals.

What form of business makes the most sense given these circumstances? **(CFP® Exam, released 3/95)**

   a. Limited partnership.
   b. General partnership.
   c. C corporation.
   d. Professional corporation.
   e. S corporation.

136. A minority non-employee shareholder in an S corporation: **(CFP® Exam, released 3/95)**

1. Receives compensation when the corporation declares a dividend.
2. Votes for the Board of Directors at the annual shareholders' meeting.
3. Receives a K-1 annually in order to prepare a personal income tax return.
4. Reports on a personal income tax return a pro-rata share of corporate profit or loss.

a. 1, 2, and 3.
b. 1 and 3.
c. 2 and 4.
d. 4 only.
e. 1, 2, 3, and 4.

137. Bob and his brother, George, are interested in forming a business together. However, they are concerned about the following:

1. Whether the business will have losses for the next three years.
2. Whether or not the business would continue in the event that one brother would die.
3. Whether they will have some limited liability protection.

Based on the concerns of the brothers, which form of business is the most appropriate?

a. C corporation.
b. S corporation.
c. Partnership.
d. Limited partnership.
e. Trust.

CONTRACTS

138. Which of the following defenses could a surety assert successfully to limit the surety's liability to a creditor?

   a. A discharge in bankruptcy of the principal debtor.
   b. A personal defense the principal debtor has against the creditor.
   c. The incapacity of the surety.
   d. The incapacity of the principal debtor.
   e. The death of the principal debtor.

139. Bucky Corp. lent Forrest $50,000. At Bucky's request, Forrest entered into an agreement with Lanning and Snow for them to act as compensated cosureties on the loan in the amount of $100,000 each. Bucky Corp. released Snow without Lanning's or Forrest's consent, and Forrest later defaulted on the loan. Which of the following statements is correct?

   a. Lanning will be liable for 50% of the loan balance.
   b. Lanning will be liable for the entire loan balance.
   c. Bucky's release of Snow will have no effect on Forrest's and Lanning's liability to Bucky Corp.
   d. Forrest will be released to 50% of the loan balance.
   e. Snow will still be liable because Forrest and Lanning did not consent to the release.

140. Which of the following is/are required elements of a contract?

   1. A writing.
   2. Legality.
   3. Consideration.
   4. Legal capacity.

   a. 1 only.
   b. 2 only.
   c. 2 and 4.
   d. 1, 2, and 3.
   e. 2, 3, and 4.

141. Which of the following represent a distinction between a bilateral and a unilateral contract?

1. Two promises are invólved in a bilateral contract but only one promise is involved in a unilateral contract.
2. A formal written agreement is required for a bilateral contract but not a unilateral contract.
3. Rights are assignable in a bilateral contract but are not in a unilateral contract.
4. Specific performance is available for breach of a bilateral contract but is not available for a unilateral contract.

a. 1 only.

b. 3 only.

c. 1 and 2.

d. 3 and 4.

e. 1, 2, and 3.

142. Which of the following must exist for an offer to confer the power to form a contract by acceptance?

1. Be communicated in writing only.
2. Be sufficiently definite and certain.
3. Manifest an intent to enter into a contract.
4. Be communicated orally by the offeror to the offeree.

a. 1 only.

b. 2 only.

c. 1 and 2.

d. 2 and 3.

e. 1, 2, 3, and 4.

NEGOTIABLE INSTRUMENTS

143. Which of the following are correct regarding negotiable instruments?

    1. Must be written.
    2. Must be signed by the maker/drawer.
    3. Must contain an unconditional promise or order to pay.

        a. 1 only.
        b. 2 only.
        c. 3 only.
        d. 1 and 2.
        e. 1, 2, and 3.

144. Which of the following are correct regarding negotiable instruments?

    1. State a fixed amount in money.
    2. Payable to order/bearer.
    3. Payable on demand or at a definite time.

        a. 1 only.
        b. 2 only.
        c. 1 and 2.
        d. 2 and 3.
        e. 1, 2, and 3.

PROPERTY

145. Which of the following are characteristics of property ownership as community property?

   1. A joint interest held by husband and wife.
   2. Upon the death of a spouse both halves of community property are stepped to fair market value.
   3. Transfer of property requires consent of the other party.
   4. There is a right of survivorship for each spouse.

   a. 1 and 4.
   b. 3 and 4.
   c. 1, 2, and 3.
   d. 2, 3, and 4.
   e. 1, 2, 3, and 4.

146. What is one characteristic of tenancy by the entirety?

   a. Tenants have unequal rights in the property.
   b. Tenants have rights of survivorship in the property.
   c. Any tenant can exercise a general power of appointment over the property.
   d. Any tenant can bequeath interest in the property without consent of other tenants.
   e. None of the above.

147. Which of the following are characteristics of property ownership as tenants by the entirety?

   1. Joint interest held by husband and wife.
   2. If both spouses' names appear on the title, tenancy by the entirety is presumed.
   3. Transfer of property does not require consent of the other party.
   4. There is a right of survivorship for each spouse.
   5. Divorce does not affect tenancy by the entirety.

   a. 1, 3, and 5.
   b. 2, 3, and 4.
   c. 5 only.
   d. 1, 2, and 4.
   e. 3 and 5.

148. Of the following property ownership arrangements, which may be entered into by spouses only?

1. Tenancy in common.
2. Joint tenancy with right of survivorship.
3. Tenancy by the entirety.
4. Community property.

a. 3 only.

b. 2 and 4.

c. 3 and 4.

d. 2, 3, and 4.

e. 1, 2, 3, and 4.

CONSUMER PROTECTION

149. A client had five credit cards in his wallet when the wallet was stolen. He reported the cards as missing the next morning, but the following transactions had already occurred:

Discover Card	$350
MasterCard	$100
VISA	$425
Sears	$25
Marshall Fields	$685

How much is the client's expected liability for the fraudulent transactions on these cards? **(CFP® Exam, released 3/95)**

a. $50.
b. $225.
c. $250.
d. $1,235.
e. $1,585.

150. Under the Federal Age Discrimination in Employment Act, which of the following practices would be prohibited?

1. Compulsory retirement of employees below the age of 65.
2. Termination of employees between the ages of 65 and 70 for cause.
3. Termination of employees under the age of 65 for good cause.

a. 1 only.
b. 2 only.
c. 3 only.
d. 1 and 3.
e. 2 and 3.

BANKRUPTCY AND REORGANIZATION

151. Landry Plumbing, Inc. filed bankruptcy under the reorganization provisions of Chapter 11 of the Federal Bankruptcy Code. A plan of reorganization was confirmed, and a final decree closing the proceedings was entered. Which of the following events usually occurs next?

  a. Landry Plumbing, Inc. will be liquidated.
  b. Landry Plumbing, Inc. will have negotiated with all creditors except as otherwise provided in the plan and applicable law.
  c. Discharged creditors of Landry Plumbing, Inc. will file suit to recover amounts due.
  d. A trustee will continue to operate the debtor's business.
  e. Landry Plumbing, Inc. will not be allowed to continue in the same business.

152. Andrew Martin, CFP, is an unsecured creditor of Golf Expo Co. for $6,000. Golf Expo Co. has a total of 10 creditors, all of whom are unsecured. Golf Expo Co. has not paid any of the creditors for three months. Under Chapter 11 of the Federal Bankruptcy Code, which of the following statements is correct?

  a. Golf may not be petitioned involuntarily into bankruptcy because there are less than 12 unsecured creditors.
  b. Golf may not be petitioned involuntarily into bankruptcy under the provisions of Chapter 11.
  c. Three unsecured creditors must joint the involuntary petition in bankruptcy.
  d. Martin may file involuntary petition in bankruptcy against Golf.
  e. None of the above.

153. Which of the following claims will not be discharged in bankruptcy?

  a. A claim that arises from alimony or maintenance other than a lump sum property settlement.
  b. A claim that arises out of the debtor's breach of a contract.
  c. A claim brought by a secured creditor that remains unsatisfied after the sale of the collateral.
  d. A claim brought by a judgment creditor whose judgment resulted from the debtor's negligent operation of a motor vehicle.
  e. All of the above.

154. Under the liquidation provisions of Chapter 7 of the Federal Bankruptcy Code, which of the following statements applies to a person who has voluntarily filed for and received a discharge in bankruptcy?

1. The person will be discharged from all debts.
2. The person can obtain another voluntary discharge in bankruptcy under Chapter 7 after three years have elapsed from the date of the prior filing.
3. The person must surrender for distribution to the creditors amounts received as an inheritance, if the receipt occurs within 180 days after filing the bankruptcy petition.

a. 1 only.
b. 2 only.
c. 3 only.
d. 1 and 3.
e. 2 and 3.

155. Which of the following items can be discharged in a Chapter 7 bankruptcy?

1. Child support.
2. Student loans (10 years old).
3. Federal taxes (past two years).
4. Consumer debt.

a. 1 and 2.
b. 2 and 3.
c. 2 and 4.
d. 1, 2, and 4.
e. 2, 3, and 4.

156. Under the Bankruptcy laws, which of the following will not be discharged?

1. Credit card debt used to pay college tuition (within the last five years).
2. Taxes from four years ago in which the taxpayer purposely failed to report $10,000 of self-employment income.
3. Alimony.

a. 1 only.
b. 2 only.
c. 1 and 2.
d. 2 and 3.
e. 1, 2 and 3.

157. Under the Bankruptcy laws, which of the following will not be discharged?

1. Federal taxes from two years ago.
2. $4,000 debt from the embezzlement of funds from an insurance company.
3. Child support.

a. 1 only.
b. 2 only.
c. 1 and 2.
d. 2 and 3.
e. 1, 2 and 3.

TORTS

158. A tort is:

a. An offense against the state.

b. A breach of contract.

c. Based on socially unreasonable conduct.

d. Based on familiar obligations.

e. The civil equivalent of a crime.

159. Which of the following must the plaintiff establish with regard to intent necessary to establish a cause of action for fraud?

a. The defendant made a false representation of facts.

b. The plaintiff actually relied on the defendant's misrepresentation.

c. The defendant made a misrepresentation with a reckless disregard for the truth.

d. The plaintiff justifiably relied on the defendant's misrepresentation.

e. All of the above.

160. Which of the following is an essential element of the tort of battery?

a. The unauthorized use of a defendant's property.

b. A harmful or offensive bodily contact.

c. Actual physical danger.

d. The defendant need not have acted with intent.

e. The plaintiff must have been aware of the defendant's conduct.

161. Which of the following is a tort of negligence?

a. While playing golf, Jay swings a new golf club on the fairway and the head of the club flies off, and strikes another golfer standing 15 yards away.

b. Betty has a sudden chest pain while driving, which causes her to lose control of her car and hit an oncoming car.

c. Bubba throws a rock intending to hit a window and instead hits a pedestrian.

d. Stan takes medication that he knows makes him drowsy and then proceeds to drive. He later gets into an accident injuring the passenger in the other car.

e. Cherie locks Chris in a room to prevent him from leaving the building.

PROFESSIONAL LIABILITY - FINANCIAL PLANNERS

162. In which of the following common law actions, against a CFP, would lack of privity be a viable defense?

    a. The plaintiff is the client's creditor who sues the CFP for negligence.
    b. The plaintiff can prove the presence of gross negligence that amounts to a reckless disregard for the truth.
    c. The plaintiff is the CFP's client.
    d. The plaintiff bases the action upon fraud.
    e. The plaintiff is the CFP's employee.

REGULATORY REQUIREMENTS

163. Which of the following activities must be proven by a stock purchaser in order to prevail against a CFP in a suit brought under the provisions of Section 10(b) and Rule 10b-5 of the Securities Exchange Act of 1934?
   1. Intentional conduct by the CFP designed to deceive investors.
   2. Negligence by the CFP.
   3. Strict liability by the CFP.
      a. 1 only.
      b. 2 only.
      c. 3 only.
      d. 1 and 2.
      e. 1, 2, and 3.

164. Which of the following situations would require a company to be subject to the reporting provisions of the 1934 Act?
   1. Shares are listed on a national securities exchange.
   2. There are more than one class of stock.
   3. There are 100 shareholders.
      a. 1, 2, and 3.
      b. 1 only.
      c. 2 only.
      d. 3 only.
      e. None of the above.

165. Following registration, which of the following documents must a company subject to the reporting provisions of the 1934 act file with the SEC?
   1. Quarterly reports (Form 10-Q).
   2. Annual report (Form 10-K).
   3. Proxy statements.
      a. 1 only.
      b. 2 only.
      c. 3 only.
      d. 1, 2, and 3.
      e. None of the above.

166. When certain transactions or events occur affecting a company subject to the reporting requirements of the 1934 act, a report must be submitted to the SEC in conjunction with the transaction or event. Which of the following reports must also be submitted to the SEC?

1. A report of proxy solicitations by current stockholders.
2. A report by a party making a tender offer for a company's stock.
3. A report by the heirs of a deceased shareholder.

   a. 1 only.
   b. 2 only.
   c. 3 only.
   d. 1 and 3.
   e. 2 and 3.

167. Which of the following securities would be regulated by the provisions of the Securities Act of 1933?

   a. Securities issued by not-for-profit, charitable organizations.
   b. Securities guaranteed by domestic governmental organizations.
   c. Securities issued by savings and loan associations.
   d. Securities issued by insurance companies.
   e. Securities issued by a domestic government.

168. Under the Securities Act of 1933, which of the following statements most accurately reflects how securities registration affects an investor?

   a. The investor is provided with information on the stockholders of the offering corporation.
   b. The investor is provided with information on the principal purposes for which the offering's proceeds will be used.
   c. The investor is guaranteed by the SEC that the facts contained in the registration statement are accurate.
   d. The investor is assured by the SEC against loss resulting from purchasing the security.
   e. All of the above.

169. Which combination of the following statements concerning federal law is correct? **(CFP® Exam, released 3/95)**

1. The Securities Act of 1933 provides for protection from misrepresentation, deceit, and other fraud in the sale of new securities.
2. The Securities Investor Protection Act of 1970 is designed to protect individual investors from losses as a result of brokerage house failures.
3. The Investment Advisers Act of 1940 requires that persons or firms advising others about securities investment must register with the Securities and Exchange Commission.
4. The Investment Advisers Act of 1940 assures the investor safety of investment in companies engaged primarily in investing, reinvesting, and trading in securities.

   a. 1, 2, and 3.
   b. 1 and 3.
   c. 2 and 4.
   d. 2 and 3.
   e. 1, 2, 3, and 4.

170. Which of the following would require an individual to be registered as an investment adviser under the Investment Advisers Act of 1940?

1. The individual provides advice about a specific security.
2. The individual is in the business of providing advice about specific securities.
3. The individual receives compensation for providing advice.
4. The individual is a CFP licensee.
5. The individual has fewer than 15 clients.

   a. 1, 2, 3, and 4.
   b. 3, 4, and 5.
   c. 4 only.
   d. All would require the individual to register.
   e. 1, 2, and 3.

INVESTMENT ADVISERS REGULATION AND REGISTRATION

171. If an individual is required to be registered as an investment adviser, is NASD registration required?

  a. No, if he is licensed by the state to sell products.
  b. Yes, if the individual is a CFP licensee.
  c. Yes, if the individual sells products.
  d. No, if he agrees to be bound by the Code of Ethics.
  e. Further information is needed to answer the question.

CODE OF ETHICS AND PROFESSIONAL RESPONSIBILITY

172. Which of the following statements concerning a CFP's disclosure of confidential client data is generally correct?

   1. Disclosure may be made to any state agency without subpoena.
   2. Disclosure may be made to any party on consent of the client.
   3. Disclosure may be made to comply with an IRS audit request.

      a. 1 only.
      b. 2 only.
      c. 3 only.
      d. 1, 2, and 3.
      e. None of the above.

173. According to the Code of Ethics established by the Certified Financial Planner Board of Standards, which of the following are correct uses of the marks:

   1. Frank Smith, C.F.P.
   2. Frank Smith, CFP.
   3. Frank Smith, CERTIFIED FINANCIAL PLANNER.
   4. Frank Smith, Certified Financial Planner.
   5. Frank Smith & Co., PA, CFP's.

      a. 1, 2, 3, and 4.
      b. 1, 2, and 4.
      c. 2, 3, and 4.
      d. 2, 3, 4, and 5.
      e. All are correct uses.

174. A CFP licensee agrees to be bound by the Continuing Education (CE) Requirement established by the Certified Financial Planner Board of Standards. The Continuing Education (CE) Requirement for a regular continuing licensee (not a new licensee or a licensee who has been inactive) is as follows:

      a. 40 Hours of CE every year.
      b. The number of CE hours required by other designations the licensee may hold.
      c. 30 Hours of CE every year.
      d. 30 Hours of CE every two years.
      e. 40 Hours of CE every two years.

175. Which of the following is/are not a principle(s) of the Board of Standards Code of Ethics and Professional Responsibility?

   1. Integrity.
   2. Disclosure.
   3. Objectivity.
   4. Competence.
      a. 1 only.
      b. 2 only.
      c. 1 and 4.
      d. 1, 2, and 3.
      e. 1, 2, 3, and 4.

176. Which of the following is/are not a principle(s) of the Board of Standards Code of Ethics and Professional Responsibility?

   1. Proper Training.
   2. Fairness.
   3. Confidentiality.
   4. Professionalism.
      a. 1 only.
      b. 2 only.
      c. 1 and 4.
      d. 1, 2, and 3.
      e. 1, 2, 3, and 4.

177. Which of the following is/are not a principle of the Board of Standards Code of Ethics and Professional Responsibility?

   1. Independence.
   2. Objectivity.
   3. Competence.
   4. Disclosure.
      a. 1 only.
      b. 2 only.
      c. 1 and 4.
      d. 1, 2, and 3.
      e. 1, 2, 3, and 4.

178. Which of the following is/are not a principle of the Board of Standards Code of Ethics and Professional Responsibility?

1. Independence.
2. Diligence.
3. Confidentiality.
4. Fairness.

    a. 1 only.
    b. 2 only.
    c. 1 and 4.
    d. 1, 2, and 3.
    e. 1, 2, 3 and 4.

179. David Ramsey comes to you and wants you to invest $400,000 in such a way that will not attract the IRS. He refuses to allow you to do any financial planning and insists on paying you in cash. Which of the following would you do?

    a. Invest the money.
    b. Invest the money only after he signs a liability waiver.
    c. Refuse to help David.
    d. Inform the IRS.

180. Marion, a CFP licensee, has a habit of commingling his client's money with his own. However he keeps good records and knows how much belongs to whom. One day he needs to pay off a drug debt and he uses some of the client's money to pay the debt. He didn't have any other money in the account at the time except client money. Within 3 business days he promptly repays the money with winnings from gambling. His client is unaware of the above and is not affected. Which of the following is/are principles Marion has violated?

1. Integrity.
2. Objectivity.
3. Fairness.
4. Professionalism.

    a. 1 and 4.
    b. 1, 2, and 4.
    c. 1, 2, and 3.
    d. 1, 2, 3, and 4.
    e. None of the above.

MISCELLANEOUS

181. Which of the following statements correctly describes the funding of a noncontributory pension plan?

    a. The employees provide all of the funds.
    b. The employer provides all of the funds.
    c. The employer and employee each provide 50% of the funds.
    d. The employer provides 90% of the funds, and each employee contributes 10%.
    e. The employer provides 10% of the funds, and each employee contributes 10%.

182. For the entire year 1999, Fisher's Ace Hardware, Inc. conducted its business operations without any permanent or full-time employees. Fisher's employed temporary and part-time workers during each of the 52 weeks in the year. Under the provisions of the Federal Unemployment Tax Act (FUTA), which of the following statements is correct regarding Fisher's obligation to file a federal unemployment tax return for 1999?

    a. Fisher's is obligated to file a 1999 FUTA return only if at least one worker earned $50 or more in any calendar quarter of 1999.
    b. Fisher's must file a 1999 FUTA return only if aggregate wages exceeded $100,000 during 1999.
    c. Fisher's must file a 1999 FUTA return because it had temporary and part-time employees during at least 20 weeks of 1999.
    d. Fisher's does not have to file a 1999 FUTA return because it had no permanent or full-time employees in 1999.
    e. Fisher's must file a 1999 FUTA return because it had at least five workers during the last quarter of 1999.

183. Which of the following organizations provide bond-rating services?

1. NASDAQ.
2. Moody's.
3. Standard and Poors.
4. Duff & Phelps.

a. 2 only.
b. 3 only.
c. 1, 2, and 3.
d. 2, 3, and 4.
e. 1, 2, 3, and 4.

184. Betty purchased a zero coupon bond for $500. The bond matured last week, and Betty received the face amount of $1,000. If the bond had an average annual compound rate of 9% compounded semiannually, approximately how many years did Betty hold the bond? (Round to nearest year.)

a. 8 years.
b. 9 years.
c. 16 years.
d. 18 years.
e. 32 years.

185. What is one characteristic of a corporate zero-coupon bond?

a. It has little price volatility.
b. The investor receives semiannual interest payments.
c. It is subject to interest rate risk.
d. The investor pays taxes on interest only when the bond matures.
e. All of the above.

186. What is one description of the coinsurance provision in a major medical expense policy?

a. Charges are shared after the maximum policy limit has been reached.
b. Initial charges are borne entirely by the insured.
c. The insurer pays the insured directly for hospital charges.
d. A portion of charges is paid by the insured.
e. All of the above.

187. What is one similarity between HO4 and HO6 policies?

a. They include broad form coverage on personal property.

b. They cover all risks on dwelling and other structures.

c. They base contents coverage on dwelling coverage.

d. They cover all risks on personal property.

e. All of the above.

188. Which of the following are characteristic of splitting gifts?

1. A husband and wife together can give up to $20,000 per year per donee free of gift taxation.
2. Requires a filing of a gift tax return.
3. A person donating community property must split gift and file a gift tax return.

a. 1 only.

b. 2 only.

c. 1 and 2.

d. 2 and 3.

e. 1, 2, and 3.

189. Which is one description of a call option purchased by an investor?

1. An investment that allows the owner to sell shares of stock with no time restriction.
2. An investment that allows the owner to buy shares of stock with no time restriction.
3. An investment that allows the owner to sell shares of stock at a specified price.
4. An investment that allows the owner to buy shares of stock at a specified price.

a. 1 only.

b. 2 only.

c. 4 only.

d. 1 and 3.

e. 2 and 4.

190. Which statement best describes the replacement cost provision of a homeowners policy in the event of a covered loss?

   a. The insurer will pay the full cost of repair or replacement up to the policy limit.
   b. The insurer will pay the full cost of repair or replacement up to 80% of the coverage on the dwelling.
   c. If the insured carries coverage equal to the original dwelling cost minus depreciation, the full cost of repair or replacement will be paid.
   d. If the insured satisfies the 80% coverage requirement, the full cost of repair or replacement will be paid up to the policy limit.
   e. If the insured satisfies the 80% coverage requirement, the full cost of repair or replacement minus depreciation will be paid up to the policy limit.

191. What is one characteristic of a high-grade general obligation municipal bond?

   a. Its main source of investment risk is business risk.
   b. The taxing authority of the issuing government or municipality backs it.
   c. It retains a direct claim on specific property.
   d. Its periodic interest is paid to investors only when earned.
   e. Its main source of investment risk is financial risk.

192. What is one characteristic of a QTIP trust?

   a. The trust property does not qualify for the estate tax marital deduction.
   b. The trust property is automatically excluded from the gross estate of the surviving spouse.
   c. The recipient of the trust income has a general power of appointment over trust property.
   d. The grantor of the trust can determine the remainderman.
   e. All of the above.

THIS PAGE IS INTENTIONALLY LEFT BLANK.

FUNDAMENTALS OF FINANCIAL PLANNING SOLUTIONS

FUNDAMENTALS OF FINANCIAL PLANNING

1.	B	34.	A	67.	E	100.	C	133.	A	166.	E
2.	A	35.	D	68.	C	101.	B	134.	A	167.	D
3.	D	36.	D	69.	D	102.	B	135.	E	168.	B
4.	C	37.	C	70.	E	103.	D	136.	E	169.	A
5.	A	38.	C	71.	C	104.	B	137.	B	170.	E
6.	D	39.	A	72.	D	105.	C	138.	C	171.	C
7.	C	40.	A	73.	A	106.	B	139.	A	172.	B
8.	B	41.	D	74.	B	107.	B	140.	E	173.	C
9.	C	42.	E	75.	C	108.	A	141.	A	174.	D
10.	A	43.	A	76.	A	109.	B	142.	D	175.	B
11.	C	44.	D	77.	B	110.	A	143.	E	176.	A
12.	D	45.	C	78.	D	111.	C	144.	E	177.	C
13.	B	46.	C	79.	B	112.	B	145.	C	178.	A
14.	B	47.	E	80.	D	113.	B	146.	B	179.	C
15.	B	48.	C	81.	B	114.	B	147.	D	180.	D
16.	D	49.	C	82.	A	115.	B	148.	C	181.	B
17.	A	50.	A	83.	C	116.	D	149.	B	182.	C
18.	C	51.	A	84.	C	117.	E	150.	A	183.	D
19.	C	52.	D	85.	B	118.	A	151.	B	184.	A
20.	C	53.	E	86.	D	119.	D	152.	D	185.	C
21.	C	54.	B	87.	A	120.	A	153.	A	186.	D
22.	B	55.	B	88.	C	121.	A	154.	C	187.	A
23.	A	56.	B	89.	D	122.	D	155.	C	188.	C
24.	A	57.	A	90.	B	123.	D	156.	D	189.	C
25.	D	58.	A	91.	A	124.	D	157.	E	190.	D
26.	D	59.	D	92.	B	125.	C	158.	C	191.	B
27.	E	60.	B	93.	C	126.	E	159.	C	192.	D
28.	A	61.	C	94.	B	127.	D	160.	B		
29.	C	62.	C	95.	A	128.	D	161.	D		
30.	C	63.	C	96.	C	129.	D	162.	A		
31.	B	64.	C	97.	D	130.	B	163.	A		
32.	A	65.	D	98.	D	131.	D	164.	B		
33.	B	66.	B	99.	A	132.	B	165.	D		

THE FINANCIAL PLANNING PROCESS

Sources, Uses and Interpretation of Planning Information

1. **B**

A.M. Best is an insurance company ranking services. Federal Reserve Publications would not contain specific mutual fund information and Time Series Data is statistical analysis. In addition to Standard and Poors, Valueline and Morningstar rate and provide analysis for mutual funds. Dow Jones is a financial news service and does not provide detailed mutual fund information.

Financial Planning Process

2. **A**

Identifying financial strengths and weaknesses and preparing financial statements are completed in the third stage of the financial planning process. The other tasks would be done after the processing and analyzing stage.

Financial Planning Functions (CFP® Exam, released 3/95)

3. **D**

This is simply a matter of which function as a planner comes in what order. Interview, collect, prepare, implement, and monitor.

Financial Planning Functions (CFP® Exam, released 3/95)

4. **C**

Year 1 – 5	PV	=	($40,000)
	i	=	5.5%
	N	=	5
	PMT	=	$0
	FV	=	$52,278.40
Year 6 – 10	PV	=	($52,278.40)
	i	=	4.0%
	N	=	5
	PMT	=	$0
	FV	=	$63,604.67
Year 10 – r	PV	=	($63,604.67)
	i	=	3.5%
	N	=	3
	PMT	=	$0
	FV	=	$70,519.63

Fundamentals - Process

5. **A**

The most logical first step is to contact the manager at the brokerage house.

Fundamentals - Process

6. **D**

Everything (statements #1, #2, and #4) except pick stocks, which is the implementation stage.

Fundamentals - Process

7. **C**

See his attorney.

PERSONAL FINANCIAL STATEMENTS

Financial Statement Presentation – Accrual vs. Cash

8. B

In order to determine whether the items should be included in the Statement of Financial Condition, the asset or liability should have the following characteristics:

a. The asset or liability is a fixed and determinable amount.

b. The receipt or payment is not contingent on the occurrence of a particular event.

c. The receipt or payment does not require future performance of service.

Statement #1 is fixed and determinable but requires that one-year pass before the options become exercisable.

Statement #2 is not fixed and determinable and requires that the board of directors meets and authorizes the bonus.

Statement #3 addresses the issue of constructive receipt of the dividend. Since the date of record was December 31, 1999 and the client held the shares as of that date, the client will receive the payment regardless of whether the client owns the stock after December 31, 1999. The amount should be shown on the Statement of Financial Condition.

Statement #4 requires that the client's son defaults on the loan and therefore should not be included in the Statement of Financial Condition.

Finally, statement #5 should be included because the spouse is awaiting payment and no further service is required in order to receive the payment.

Since statements #3 and #5 are the only two items that should be included in the Statement of Financial Condition, B is correct.

Financial Statement Presentation

9. C

The Equity Mutual Fund is the most liquid asset presented. Following the mutual fund is the cash surrender value of the life insurance policy because redemption of those proceeds can be difficult and costly. Finally, the personal residence is not as liquid as the jewelry. Liquidity, in this sense, is the ability to convert to cash quickly, not the liquidity concept found in investments.

Financial Statement Presentation

10. A

The Statement of Financial Condition is presented as of a date in time (a snapshot as of a particular date). The responses B, C, and D identify a period of time and not a specific date. A period of time is appropriate for the Statement of Cash Flows. Answer E could be a correct answer because it is a specific date but the question specified that the date was for a calendar year client.

Financial Statement Presentation

11. C

Answers A and E specify a point in time, which is appropriate for the Statement of Financial Condition. Option B is not correct because it does not specify an ending date. Option D is not descriptive about the ending date.

Note: The question addresses the year 1999. It is possible to prepare quarterly statements of cash flow. In the case of any period less than a full year, the beginning and ending period must be specified (for example: For the Period Beginning April 1, 1999 and Ending June 31, 1999).

Client Data

12. D

The question is what value should be used in preparation of a personal financial statement. The answer is fair market value (FMV), and D is the definition of FMV.

Client Data (CFP® Exam, released 3/95)

13. B

This is a personal use asset and a variable outflow.

ANALYSIS OF FINANCIAL STATEMENTS AND IDENTIFICATION OF STRENGTHS AND WEAKNESSES

Analysis of Financial Statements

14. B

The ending inventory will be valued at old, lower prices using LIFO and, therefore, net income will decline and the inventory on the Balance Sheet will be less than under FIFO.

Analysis of Financial Statements

15. B

Statements #1 and #2 do not affect net worth. Statement #3 would increase net worth, and statement #4 would decrease net worth.

Analysis of Financial Statements

16. D

Net worth of $200,000 is not affected by any of the transactions.

Analysis of Financial Statements

17. A

Net worth is defined as assets minus liabilities.

Assets = $309,000 ($4,000 + $25,000 + $40,000 + $240,000)

Liabilities = $245,000 ($25,000 + $20,000 + $200,000)

Net Worth = $64,000 ($309,000 - $245,000)

Analysis of Financial Statements

18. C

They can not meet either the 28% or 36% hurdle to refinance the home at 8%. Their income is too low and indebtedness too high. It is unclear if they have an adequate emergency fund since they have the IRA and the investment account that they may choose to include or not in an emergency fund analysis. It is inconclusive whether they have an adequate net worth for their age; it depends on their goals.

BUDGETING

Budgeting

19. **C**

72 ÷ 9 = 8

The rule of 72 says to divide the rate of return into 72. The quotient is the approximate number of years to double the investment.

PERSONAL USE-ASSETS AND LIABILITIES

Home Mortgage

20. **C**

PMT_{OA}	=	\$496
N	=	180 (15 x 12)
i	=	.729 (8.75 ÷ 12)
FV	=	\$0
PV	=	(\$49,627) rounded to the nearest \$100 = \$49,600

Mortgages (CFP® Exam, released 3/95)

21. **C**

Cash to pay points and terms of ownership to reduce overall yield. Numbers 1 and 3 are irrelevant. The differential could be: (assume a \$100,000 mortgage and add discount).

PMT_{OA}	\$960.48/month	PMT_{OA}	\$1,010.10/month
i	10.5%	i	11.5%
N	360 months	N	360 months
PV	\$105,000	PV	\$102,000

The indifference term is where amortization crosses over at about 43 months assuming payments were equalized at \$1,010.10. If interest is to stay longer, use mortgage #1. If less, use mortgage #2.

ECONOMIC ENVIRONMENT – BASIC CONCEPTS

Economic Environment

22. B

Economists refer to foregone income as a cost. The decision to use resources means that other forms of income are not realized, for example, the funds expended for a piece of machinery are not available to derive interest income. The foregone income costs are known as opportunity costs. Marginal costs are the cost to produce one more unit of product. Variable costs are costs that fluctuate with some cost driver (e.g., units produced). Fixed costs are costs that do not change as a result of producing additional units (i.e., rent). Cost of Capital is an internal measure of a company's borrowing costs from stockholders or outside creditors.

Supply / Demand

23. A

The Law of Demand states that as the price of a product decreases the demand for the product increases and vice versa. Answer B, Price Controls, is an attempt to adjust the balance between supply and demand. Answer C, Supply Side Economics, is a belief that offering incentives to produce can accomplish stated objectives. Answer D, the Law of Supply, states that there is a positive relationship between the price of a product and the amount producers are willing to produce (i.e., The higher the price, the more producers will produce). Answer E, Market Price, is the price at which a willing buyer and a willing seller achieve their objectives.

Supply / Demand

24. A

Answer B is the description of a product whose demand is elastic. Answer C describes the demand of a product that is perfectly elastic. Answer D is a description of the equilibrium point in supply and demand. Answer E is incorrect because price can be changed in a market economy.

Changes in Economic Activity

25. D

The Federal Reserve has the power to affect all of the controls listed above. The manner in which it is done affects the objective of raising or lowering interest rates. If the Fed purchases securities on the open market, the money supply is increased and therefore interest rates are lowered. An increase in the reserve requirement causes the money supply to decrease because banks have to reduce their lendable reserves and this causes interest rates to rise. An increase in the discount rate causes banks to increase their interest rates to compensate for the spread between interest earned and interest paid. Finally, lowering the margin requirement means that the demand for funds is not as high in order to buy stocks and therefore, interest rates are lowered. Therefore, since #1 and #4 lower interest rates, the correct answer is D.

Economic Environment

26. D

The question is asking for the definition of the velocity of money and therefore all other answers are incorrect.

Inflation

27. E

This is determined by dividing the current years' index (133.5) by the prior years' index (125.6). The result is 1.063; that means the index of prices for 1993 is 1.063 times the index at the end of 1992, therefore, prices rose 6.3%. Answers A and D are distracters. Answer B is the difference between the two indexes and is incorrect. Answer C calculates the percentage using the December 1993 index as the denominator and the difference as the numerator.

International Economics

28. A

This is calculated by dividing the US dollar equivalent of a Mexican Peso by the US dollar equivalent of a Peruvian Inti. If a Mexican Peso buys less of a US dollar than a Peruvian Inti, then a Mexican Peso would buy less than one full Peruvian Inti (.30656 ÷ .4717). Answer B divides the US dollar equivalent of the Peruvian Inti by the US dollar equivalent of the Mexican Peso. Answer C is the same as A, except it is multiplied by 100. Answer D is the same as B, except the answer is divided by 100. Answer E multiplies the two US dollar equivalent amounts.

Statistical Series

29. C

Answer A, mean, is the mathematical average of all the values. Answer B, median, is the value where one half of the values are above the median and one half the values are below the median. The standard deviation, answer D, relates to the deviation from the mean. Answer E, Beta, is the correlation of a particular security to the market.

Supply / Demand

30. C

This is the classic definition of the Law of Demand.

Supply / Demand

31. B

This is the classic definition of supply.

Adjustment Process

32. A

The adjustment process is the price process and moves to equilibrium.

Pure Competition

33. B

Pure competition occurs with large numbers of buyers and sellers.

Supply / Demand

34. A

Less is produced at all price levels.

Supply / Demand

35. D

A change in quantity demanded.

Supply / Demand

36. **D**

Elasticity indicates a lower price will increase overall revenues.

Supply / Demand

37. **C**

If there is a substitute good, the product will be deemed elastic.

Supply / Demand

38. **C**

The option consumers demand more at lower prices is an example of elastic demand.

Supply / Demand

39. **A**

By definition, products are complements if an increase in the price of good A causes a decrease in the demand for its complementary good B. Therefore, the two products are examples of complements.

Supply / Demand

40. **A**

As the amount of goods consumed increases, the marginal utility of the good tends to decrease. From this concept, the law of downward sloping demand, the shape of the demand curve is formed. Therefore, answer A is correct.

Supply / Demand

41. **D**

The Law of Demand states that when the price of a good rises (at the same time all other things are constant) that less is demanded and vice versa. Therefore, answer D is correct.

Supply / Demand

42. **E**

All are reasons for changes in consumer demand.

Supply / Demand

43. A

The relationship between price and quantity purchased can be interpreted by a numerical table (demand schedule) or a graph where prices are measured on the vertical axis and quantity demanded on the horizontal axis (demand curve).

Supply / Demand

44. D

Elasticity of demand is an indicator of responsiveness of quantity demanded to changes in the market. Statements #1, #2, and #3, all of which may affect the demand for a product, are determinants of demand elasticity.

Supply / Demand

45. C

A key element that affects supply is the cost of production. More efficient technology will decrease the cost of production.

Supply / Demand

46. C

Elasticity of supply indicates the amount of quantity supplied in response to a given rise in competition. If the amount supplied is fixed, or does not change significantly, then supply is inelastic.

Supply / Demand

47. E

All affect supply – classic definition of supply.

Inflation

48. C

Inflation generally means rising prices for goods and services. Someone on a fixed income in a time of rising prices will be forced to purchase less and therefore, have declining purchasing power.

Economic Concepts

49. C

General definition of inflation.

Economic Concepts

50. A

Minimum wage is one example of government intervention to promote economic equity.

Economic Concepts (CFP® Exam, released 3/95)

51. A

Shifts in aggregate demand are stimulated by increase in demand for capital goods #1 and increases in personal disposable income #3. Increase in interest rates #2 and savings #4 dampen aggregate demand.

Economics

52. D

All are regulated by the FLSA.

Workers' Compensation

53. E

Strict liability is the basis for recovery according to most workers' compensation statutes. The worker need only prove that an injury was suffered arising out of and occurring during the course and scope of employment.

Economics

54. B

If the demand is inelastic, price increases raise revenues.

Economics

55. B

Recession is characterized by high unemployment and low interest rates.

Economics

56. **B**

Recession is characterized by a slowing economy and increasing unemployment.

Economics Supply and Demand (CFP® Exam, released 12/95)

57. **A**

Statements #1, #2, and #3 are true. Statement #4 is false (the price would decrease).

Supply / Demand

58. **A**

Answer B is the description of a product whose demand is elastic. Answer C describes the demand of a product that is perfectly elastic. Answer D is a description of the equilibrium point in supply and demand. Answer E is incorrect because price can be changed in a market economy.

Changes in Economic Activity

59. **D**

The Federal Reserve has the power to affect all of the controls listed. The manner in which it is done affects the objective of raising or lowering interest rates. If the Fed purchases securities on the open market, the money supply is increased and therefore interest rates are lowered. An increase in the reserve requirement causes the money supply to decrease because banks have to reduce their lendable reserves and this causes interest rates to rise. An increase in the discount rate causes banks to increase their interest rates to compensate for the spread between interest earned and interest paid. Finally, lowering the margin requirement means that the demand for funds is not as high in order to buy stocks and therefore, interest rates are lowered. Therefore, since statement #1 and #4 lower interest rates, the correct answer is D.

MONETARY AND FISCAL POLICY

Monetary and Fiscal Policy

60. B

Fiscal policy economists believe that the economy can be controlled through the use of government spending and income tax adjustments. Answer C is the answer to describe economists who believe that economic activity is controlled through the use of the money supply. A is incorrect since that answer describes all the choices that include both fiscal policy as well as monetary policy economists. Answer D is incorrect because inflation is determined by market factors. Answer E partially describes a fiscal policy economist.

Monetary and Fiscal Policy

61. C

Tax legislation is fiscal not monetary policy.

Monetary and Fiscal Policy

62. C

Commercial banks establish the prime rate. The executive branch or Congress initiates any price control legislation.

Monetary and Fiscal Policy

63. C

M-1 is the measure of the most liquid components of the money supply. M-1 specifically includes currency, checking accounts, NOW accounts, travelers checks and checking money market accounts. M-2 includes all items of M-1 plus savings accounts, certain money market mutual funds, Overnight Eurodollars and Overnight Repurchase Agreements. M-3 includes all of M-2 plus certificates of deposit. Answer A is incorrect because NOW accounts are included in M-1. Answer B is incorrect because savings accounts are M-2 and CD's are M-3. Answer D is incorrect because checking accounts and NOW accounts are included in M-1. Answer E is incorrect because only three of the five items are included in M-1.

Economics

64. C

Only increasing the discount rate will reduce the money supply.

Economics

65. D

All of the above have the potential to increase the money supply. However, the Fed does not control the expenditures of the Federal Government.

Economic Environment

66. B

Lowering discount rate stimulates the money supply.

Monetary Policy

67. E

Control of the Federal Reserve Discount Rate, open market operations, and fiscal policy are all methods of controlling the supply of money in the U.S. economy.

BUSINESS CYCLE THEORIES

Business Cycle

68. C

The terminology in each answer is the same, only the order is different. A typical business cycle can be measured from trough to trough or from peak to peak with expansion and recession in between. A recession follows a peak and expansion follows a trough which means the correct answer is C.

Business Cycle

69. D

An expansion is where employment and output are rising. When employment and output are no longer rising, the phase is the peak. If employment and output begins to decrease, this indicates a recession. Finally, when employment and output are no longer decreasing, the cycle has reached a trough. The intensity indicates the highest and lowest points of the peak or the trough.

FINANCIAL INSTITUTIONS

Safety of Financial Institutions

70. E

Statement #1 is incorrect because the FDIC guarantees amounts up to $100,000. The excess over $100,000 is at risk. Statement #2 is incorrect because deposits up to $100,000 are guaranteed. Statement #3 is incorrect because funds invested in a mutual fund are subject to market risk and are not guaranteed by the FDIC at all. Statement #4 is incorrect because the FDIC guarantees amounts by depositor and not by accounts.

TIME VALUE OF MONEY

TVM – Future Value/Annual Compounding

71. **C**

PV	=	($50,000)
i	=	12
N	=	5
PMT	=	$0
FV	=	$88,117.08

TVM – Future Value/Annual Compounding

72. **D**

PV	=	($10,000)
i	=	.91666 (11 ÷ 12)
N	=	84 (7 x 12)
PMT	=	$0
FV	=	$21,522.04

TVM – Present Value/Annual Compounding

73. **A**

PV	=	($60,000)
i	=	7.5
N	=	8
PMT	=	$0
FV	=	$107,008.67

TVM – Future Value/Annual Compounding

74. **B**

FV	=	$25,000
i	=	8
N	=	8
PMT	=	$0
PV	=	($13,506.72)

TVM – Present Value/Semi-Annual Compounding

75. C

FV	=	$75,000
i	=	4.5 (9 ÷ 2)
N	=	12 (6 x 2)
PMT	=	$0
PV	=	($44,224.79)

TVM - Present Value/Monthly Compounding

76. A

PV	=	$75,000
i	=	.8333 (10 ÷ 12)
N	=	60 (5 x 12)
PMT	=	$0
PV	=	($45,584.14)

TVM – Future Value/Quarterly Compounding

77. B

FV	=	$57,000
i	=	2.625 (10.5 ÷ 4)
N	=	34 (8.5 x 4)
PMT	=	$0
PV	=	($23,619.30)

TVM - Interest Rate

78. D

PV	=	($900)
FV	=	$4,500
N	=	7
PMT	=	$0
i	=	25.8499

TVM – Interest Rate

79. **B**

PV	=	($800)
FV	=	$1,200
N	=	5
PMT	=	$0
i	=	8.4472

TVM - Interest Rate

80. **D**

PV	=	($525)
FV	=	$1,000
N	=	13 (6.5 x 2)
PMT	=	$0
i	=	5.0815

Annual rate of return = 5.0815 x 2 = 10.163

TVM – Compounding Periods

81. **B**

PV	=	($8,000)
FV	=	$15,000
i	=	12
PMT	=	$0
N	=	5.5468

Note 1: Anytime you calculate for n (term) using a HP12C you may need to find the answer by trial and error. The HP12C calculator rounds to the nearest integer when calculating N and therefore your answer is not always precise when calculating the term. You must then take what you have and find the exact answer by trial and error methods. The HP will give you 5.533.

Note 2: If you are using an HP12C and use correct n of 5.5468 the FV will be $15,023.84 which, of course, looks incorrect. The error is in the way the HP works. If you are using a HP10B, HP17BII, Sharp EL-733A, or TIBAII Plus you will get 5.5468 (the correct N). You can mathematically prove this answer by taking 1.12 raised to the 5.5468 power and then multiply by $8,000 to get $15,000.04. (Oh well, it is not a perfect world!)

TVM – Compounding Periods

82. **A**

PV = ($1)

FV = $2

i = .75 (9 ÷ 12)

PMT = $0

N = 7.75 (93 ÷ 12) HP12C

7.73 (92.77 ÷ 12) other calculators

TVM – Future Value of an Ordinary Annuity

83. **C**

PV = $0

PMT_{OA} = ($1,000)

i = 10.5

N = 15

FV_{OA} = $33,060.04

TVM – Future Value of an Ordinary Annuity Compounded Quarterly

84. **C**

PV = $0

PMT_{OA} = ($2,000)

i = 2.75 (11 ÷ 4)

N = 28 (7 x 4)

FV_{OA} = $82,721.95

TVM – Future Value of an Ordinary Annuity Due Compounded Annually

85. **B**

PV = $0

PMT_{AD} = ($3,000)

i = 8

N = 15

FV_{AD} = $87,972.85

TVM – Future Value of an Annuity Due Compounded Quarterly

86. D

PV	=	\$0
PMT_{AD}	=	(\$2,000)
i	=	2.75 (11 ÷ 4)
N	=	28 (7 x 4)
FV_{AD}	=	\$84,996.80

TVM – Present Value of an Ordinary Annuity Compounded Annually

87. A

PMT_{OA}	=	\$5,000
i	=	14
N	=	4
FV	=	\$0
PV_{OA}	=	(\$14,568.56)

TVM – Present Value of an Ordinary Annuity Compounded Semi-Annually

88. C

PMT_{OA}	=	\$1,500
i	=	5.5 (11 ÷ 12)
N	=	12 (6 x 2)
FV	=	\$0
PV_{OA}	=	(\$12,927.78)

TVM – Present Value of an Annuity Due Compounded Annually

89. D

PMT_{AD}	=	(\$4,000)
i	=	10.5
N	=	7
FV	=	\$0
PV_{AD}	=	\$21,168.72

TVM – Present Value of an Annuity Due Compounded Monthly

90. B

PMT_{AD} = ($1,200)

i = .8333 (10 ÷ 12)

N = 60 (5 x 12)

FV = $0

PV_{AD} = $56,949.10

TVM – Present Value of an Annuity Due Compounded Monthly

91. A

PV = $200,000

i = 1.00 (12 ÷ 12)

N = 60 (5 x 12)

FV = $0

PMT_{AD} = ($4,404.84)

TVM – Payment Calculation for Annuity Due with Quarterly Compounding

92. B

FV = $60,000

i = 2.625 (10.5 ÷ 4)

N = 20 (5 x 4)

PV = $0

PMT_{AD} = ($2,260.09)

TVM – Payment Calculation for an Ordinary Annuity Using Semi-Annual Compounding

93. C

FV = $150,000

i = 6 (12 ÷ 2)

N = 12 (6 x 2)

PV = $0

PMT_{OA} = ($8,891.55)

TVM – Payment Calculation for an Ordinary Annuity Using Monthly Compounding

94. **B**

PV	=	\$19,500
i	=	.91666 (11 ÷ 12)
N	=	36 (3 x 12)
FV	=	\$0
PMT_{OA}	=	\$638.40

TVM – Present Value Analysis of Alternatives

95. **A**

Option A:	PV	=	\$45,000
Option B:	FV	=	\$120,000
	i	=	10.5
	N	=	10
	PMT	=	\$0
	PV	=	(\$44,213.86)
Option C:	PMT_{AD}	=	\$5,500
	i	=	10.5
	N	=	15
	FV	=	\$0
	PV_{AD}	=	(\$44,935.97)
Option D:	PMT_{OA}	=	\$5,500
	i	=	10.5
	N	=	19
	FV	=	\$0
	PV_{OA}	=	(\$44,523.35)
Option E:	PMT_{OA}	=	\$5,750
	i	=	10.5
	N	=	17
	FV	=	\$0
	PV_{OA}	=	(\$44,731.47)

TVM – Present Value Analysis of Alternatives

96. C

Option A:	PV	=	$100,000			
Option B:	FV	=	$310,000			
	i	=	9			
	N	=	15			
	PMT	=	$0			
	PV	=	($85,106.79)			
Option C:	PMT	=	$1,200			
	i	=	.75 (9 ÷ 12)			
	N	=	132 (11 x 12)			
	FV	=	$0			
	PV_{OA}	=	($100,327.70)			
Option D:	FV	=	$65,000	FV	=	$125,000
	i	=	9	i	=	9
	N	=	5	N	=	10
	PMT	=	$0	PMT	=	$0
	PV	=	($42,245.54)	PV	=	($52,801.35)

$42,245.54 + 52,801.35 = $95,046.89

Option E:	N	=	15
	i	=	9
	FV	=	$200,000
	PMT	=	$0
	PV	=	($54,907.61)

$54,907.61 + 42,245.54 = $97,153.15

TVM – Present Value Analysis of Alternatives

97. D

Option A:	PV	=	\$50,000

Option B:	FV	=	\$250,000
	i	=	12
	N	=	14
	PMT	=	\$0
	PV	=	(\$51,154.95)

Option C:	FV	=	\$40,000		FV	=	\$120,000
	i	=	12		i	=	12
	N	=	4		N	=	12
	PMT	=	\$0		PMT	=	\$0
	PV	=	(\$25,420.72)		PV	=	(\$30,801.01)

\$25,420.72 + 30,801.01 = \$56,221.73

Option D:	PMT	=	\$5,000
	i	=	6 (12 ÷ 2)
	N	=	18 (9 x 2)
	FV	=	\$0
	PV_{AD}	=	(\$57,386.30)

Option E:	FV	=	\$60,000
	i	=	12
	N	=	3
	PMT	=	\$0
	PV	=	(\$42,706.81)

TVM – Present Value on an Annuity Due Adjusted for Inflation Compounded Annually

98. D

PMT = $25,000

i = 3.84615 $\left(\frac{1.08}{1.04} - 1.00\right) \times 100$

N = 20

FV = $0

PV_{AD} = ($357,681.46)

TVM – Present Value on an Annuity Due Adjusted for Inflation Compounded Annually

99. A

PMT = $50,000

i = 4.3062 $\left(\frac{1.09}{1.045} - 1.00\right) \times 100$

N = 12

FV = $0

PV_{AD} = ($480,878.04)

TVM – Serial Payments Adjusted for Inflation

100. C

FV = $300,000

i = (.95238) $\left(\frac{1.04}{1.05} - 1.00\right)$ X 100 =

N = 9

PV = $0

PMT_{OA} = ($34,623.42) x 1.05 = $36,354.60 (change sign)

TVM – Serial Payments Adjusted for Inflation

101. B

$36,354.60* x 1.05 = $38,172.33

*See previous question.

TVM – Serial Payments Adjusted for Inflation

102. B

FV	=	$200,000	
i	=	4.8077	$\left(\frac{1.09}{1.04} - 1.00\right) \times 100 =$
N	=	6	
PV	=	$0	
PMT_{OA}	=	($29,546.11) x 1.04 = $30,727.95 (change sign)	

TVM – Serial Payments Adjusted for Inflation

103. D

$30,727.95* x 1.04 = $31,957.07

*See previous question.

TVM – Future Value of an Annuity Due with Annual Compounding

104. B

The question specifies that the deposits are made at the beginning of each year, therefore the student is required to calculate the future value of an annuity due. Answer A is the future value of deposits made at the end of the year. Answer C is incorrect because the calculation is based on the future value of the deposits made at the end of the year at 10% for 11.5 years, a reversal of the term and the interest rate. Answer D is similar to C except the calculation is based on an annuity due. Answer E is the present value of an annuity due instead of the future value of an annuity due. The keystrokes used with a financial calculator are:

PMT_{AD}	=	($6,100)
i	=	11.5
N	=	10
PV	=	$0
FV_{AD}	=	$116,510

TVM – Serial Payments Adjusted for Inflation

105. C

Step 1:

PV	=	($1)
N	=	4
i	=	2.875 (11.5 ÷ 4)
PMT	=	$0
FV	=	1.120055
Therefore i =		12.0055

Step 2:

PV	=	$0
PMT	=	($6,100)
i	=	12.0055
N	=	10
FV	=	$119,931

Answer A calculates the future value of a $6,100 deposit made at the end of each quarter for 40 quarters using i = 2.875 (11.5 ÷ 4). This is incorrect because the question specifies an annual deposit and not a quarterly deposit. Answer E calculates the future value of an annuity due of a $6,100 deposit made at the beginning of each quarter for 40 quarters using i = 2.875 (11.5 ÷ 4). Finally, answer B calculates the future value of an annuity due of a $6,100 deposit made annually for 10 years at i = 11.5.

TVM – Present Value of an Annuity Due with Lag Period

106. B

There are two steps in solving this question. The first step is to calculate the present value of an annuity of $650 per month for 60 months at a discount rate of 9%. Financial Calculations: PMT = $650, i = .75 (9 ÷ 12), n = 60 (5*12) and solve for PV_{AD} = $31,548. This provides the present value of an annuity one-year from now. Step 2: This amount is further discounted to the present, one year. Financial Calculations: FV = $31,548, i=9, n=1 and solve for PV = $28,943. Answer A is the present value of an annuity due of $7,800 (650 * 12) received for five years at a discount rate of 9%. Answer C is the present value of answer A discounted for one year at 9%. Answer D is the first part of the correct calculation. Finally, answer E is the present value of an ordinary annuity instead of an annuity due.

TVM – Capital Budgeting

107. B

The question presented is the definition of Internal Rate of Return.

TVM – Capital Budgeting

108. A

A positive net present value of a series of discounted cash flows means that the discounted cash flows exceed the investment outlay. Statements #2 and #3 cannot be correct because the question does not provide appropriate information. Statement #4 is not correct because if the internal rate of return were the rate used, the net present value amount would be equal to zero.

TVM – Capital Budgeting

109. B

Statements #1 and #4 are correct. A net present value of a series of discounted cash flows equal to zero means the discounted cash flows are equal to the investment outlay.

TVM – Capital Budgeting

110. A

A negative net present value of a series of discounted cash flows means the investment outlay exceeds the discounted cash flows.

TVM – Ordinary Annuity Payment Calculation Assuming Beginning Balance

111. C

There are two steps to solving this question. The first step is to compute the future value of the beginning savings balance. PV = $2,500, i = .92 (11 ÷ 12), N = 120 (10 * 12) and solve for FV = $7,472.87. This amount is subtracted from the required balance of $150,000 to arrive at the amount that needs to be funded of $142,527.13. Solving for this amount is as follows: FV = $142,527.13, i = .92 (11 ÷ 12), N = 120 (10 * 12) and solve for PMT_{OA} = $656.81. Answer D has the correct inputs except the answer is the calculation of an annuity due. Answer A calculates the annuity due assuming no beginning savings balance. Answer B calculates the payment required assuming no beginning savings balance. Answer E calculates the annual payment required assuming a beginning balance and divides that number by 12.

TVM – Capital Budgeting with Annuity Due and Beginning Balance

112. B

The amount to be funded is \$147,500, the required amount of \$150,000 less the face amount of the bond of \$2,500. FV = \$147,500, i =.92 (11 ÷ 12), N = 120 (10 * 12) and solve for PMT_{AD} = \$673.56. Answer A is incorrect because the payment is calculated as if the present value of the bond is projected at 11%, the assumed rate of return. It is unnecessary to project the present amount since the face value at the end is known. Answer C is the same as A except the payment is solved as an annuity due. Answer D calculates the future value correctly (\$147,500) except as a regular payment and not an annuity due. Answer E calculates the annuity due of \$147,500 except at an interest rate of 8%, which is the implicit rate of the bond.

TVM – Case Study

113. B

Answer A is an incorrect statement because the marginal tax rate is the appropriate tax rate to use and not the average tax rate. Answer C is incorrect because an annuity due payment will be less than a regular payment. Answer D is incorrect because the rates of return should be greater than the education rate of inflation and not the general rate of inflation. Finally, answer E does not compare the after tax rate of return and may not be appropriate advice.

Mortgage Payment Calculation

114. B

N	=	180
i	=	.8333 (10 ÷ 12)
PV	=	\$148,000 (\$185,000 x .80)
PMT_{OA}	=	\$1,590.42

Mortgage Interest

115. B

PV = \$96,000 (120,000 x 80%)

i = .625 (7.5 ÷ 12)

N = 180 (15 years x 12)

PMT_{OA} = \$889.93

Total Payments	\$160,187.40
Less Principal	(96,000.00)
Total Interest	\$64,187.40

TVM - PV

116. D

One Way

N = 120 (10 x 12)

i = .6667 (8 ÷ 12)

PMT_{OA} = \$953.89

FV = \$114,042

PV = \$130,000

Alternate Way

N = 360 (30 x 12)

i = .6667 (8 ÷ 12)

PMT_{OA} = \$953.89

FV = \$0

PV = \$130,000

TVM - PV

117. E

PV = \$117,463.26 = (\$114,042 x 1.03)

N = 204 (17 x 12)

i = .583333 (7 ÷ 12)

PMT_{OA} = \$986.29

TVM

118. A

PV = \$120,000

N = \$180

i = .583333 (7 ÷ 12)

PMT_{OA} = \$1,078.59 x 180 = \$194,146.90 – 120,000 = \$74,146.90

EDUCATIONAL FUNDING

Time Value of Money

119. **D**

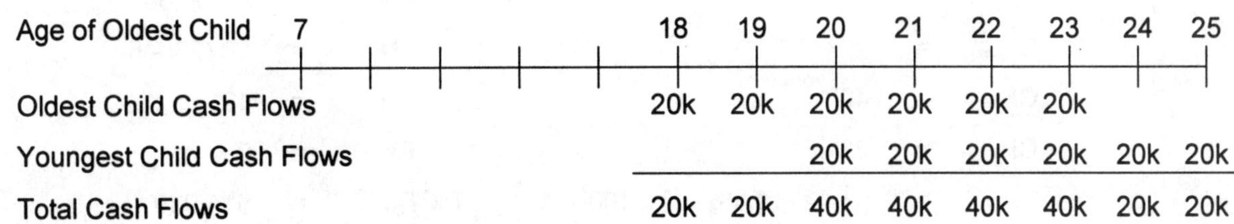

Method 1:

PV Youngest Child @ 20

FV	=	$0
N	=	6
i	=	5.66
PMT	=	$20,000
PV_{AD}	=	$105,032
FV	=	$105,032
N	=	13 (20 – 7)
i	=	5.66
PMT	=	$0
PV_{OA}	=	$51,343

$$\left[\left(\frac{1 + \text{Earnings Rate}}{1 + \text{Inflation Rate}}\right) - 1\right] \times 100$$

PV Oldest Child @ 18

FV	=	$0
N	=	6
i	=	5.66
PMT	=	$20,000
PV_{AD}	=	$105,032
FV	=	$105,032
N	=	11 (18 – 7)
i	=	5.66
PMT	=	$0
PV_{OA}	=	$57,320

Note: The inflation rate for this problem reflects the educational inflation rate of 6%.

Total cost in today's dollars

Youngest Child	=	$51,343
Oldest Child	=	57,320
		$108,663

Step 2:

Yearly Payment

PV	=	$108,663
N	=	18 (23 – 5)
i	=	12
FV	=	$0
PMT_{OA}	=	$14,989

Method 2: Uneven cash flows

Step 1:

		Cash flows
$CF_{7\text{-}17}$	=	(0)
$CF_{18\text{-}19}$	=	20k
$CF_{20\text{-}23}$	=	40k
$CF_{24\text{-}25}$	=	20k
i	=	[(1.12 ÷ 1.06) –1] x 100
NPV	=	$108,663

Step 2:

		Yearly Payment
PV	=	($108,663)
N	=	18 (23 – 5)
i	=	12
FV	=	0
PMT_{OA}	=	$14,989

TVM - Education

120. A

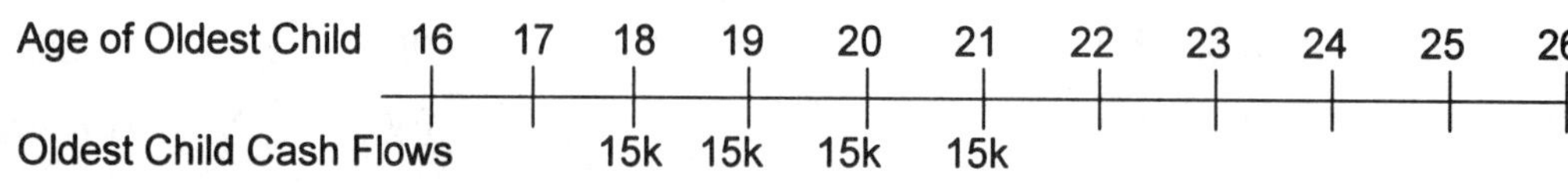

	16	17	18	19	20	21	22	23	24	25	26
Youngest Child Cash Flows							15k	15k	15k	15k	
Total Cash Flows			15k	15k	15k	15k	15k	15k	15k	15k	

CF_0	=	$0
N_j	=	2
CF_j	=	$15,000
N_j	=	8
i	=	1.86916 [[(1.09 ÷ 1.07) – 1] x 100]
f NPV	=	$108,476.87
Sandy's portion	=	$36,158.96 ($108,476.87 ÷ 3)

PV	=	($36,158.96)
i	=	.75 (9% ÷ 12)
N	=	60 (5 x 12)
PMT_{AD}	=	$745.01

TVM - Education

121. A.

Step 1: Calculate future value of first tuition payment

PV	=	$12,000
i	=	5
N	=	4
$FV_{@18}$	=	$14,586.08

Step 2: Calculate present value of 4 tuition payments

PMT_{AD}	=	$14,586.08
i	=	3.81 [[(1.09 ÷ 1.05) – 1] x 100]
N	=	4
PV_{AD}	=	$55,210.56

Step 3: Calculate monthly payment

$55,210.56 ÷ 3 = $18,403.51 (Sharon's share at age 18)

FV	=	$18,403.51
N	=	48 (4 x 12)
i	=	.75 (9 ÷ 12)
PMT_{AD}	=	$317.56 (Sharon's monthly payment made at the beginning of each month)

Note: There are numerous methods to calculate education need analysis. This question was solved using the method generally applied to capital needs analysis. If you used the traditional three-step approach illustrated in question 119 or the uneven cash flow method your answer should be $322 instead of $317.56 (which would change the answer to this question). The reason for this difference is that this problem has been calculated by switching from annual compounding to monthly compounding. Monthly compounding was necessary as indicated by the question. Generally, you should not encounter this problem, most questions will ask for annual payments instead of monthly payments.

Time Value of Money

122. **D**

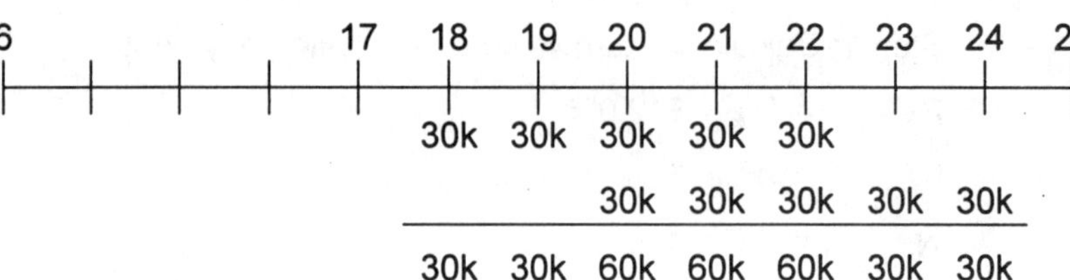

	6				17	18	19	20	21	22	23	24	25
Age of the oldest child	6				17	18	19	20	21	22	23	24	25
Oldest child cash flows						30k	30k	30k	30k	30k			
Youngest child cash flows								30k	30k	30k	30k	30k	
Total cash flows						30k	30k	60k	60k	60k	30k	30k	

Method 1:

PV Oldest Child @ 17

FV = \$0
N = 5
i = 4.6729
PMT = (\$30,000)
PV_{OA17} = \$131,067

$$\left[\left(\frac{1 + \text{Earnings Rate}}{1 + \text{Inflation Rate}}\right) - 1\right] \times 100$$

PV Youngest Child @ 19

FV = \$0
N = 5
i = 4.6729
PMT = (\$30,000)
PV_{OA17} = \$131,067

FV_{17} = \$131,067
N = 11 (17 – 6)
i = 4.6729
PMT = \$0
PV_{OA} = (\$79,308)

FV = \$131,067
N = 13 (19 – 6)
i = 4.6729
PMT = \$0
PV_{OA} = (\$72,385)

Total cost in today's dollars

Oldest Child = \$79,308
Youngest Child = 72,385
\$151,693

Step 2:

Yearly Payment

PV = (\$151,693)
N = 14 (20 – 6)
i = 12
FV = \$0
PMT_{OA} = \$22,886

Method 2: uneven cashflows

Step 1:			**Step 2:**		
Cash flows			Yearly Payment		
$CF_{6\text{-}17}$	=	0	PV	=	$151,693
$CF_{18\text{-}19}$	=	30,000	N	=	14 (20 – 6)
$CF_{20\text{-}22}$	=	60,000	i	=	12
$CF_{23\text{-}24}$	=	30,000	FV	=	0
i	=	[(1.12 ÷ 1.07) –1] x 100	PMT	=	($22,886)
NPV	=	($151,693)			

BUSINESS ORGANIZATIONS

Forms of Business Organizations

123. D

A sole proprietorship is owned by one individual who is personally liable for the business. Therefore, the business depends solely on the owner.

Forms of Business Organizations

124. D

Interest in the business being personal property is characteristic of a general partnership. More than one owner being personally liable indicates a general partnership business form.

Forms of Business Organizations

125. C

The ease of raising financial capital is a main strength of the corporate form of business entity.

Forms of Business Organizations

126. E

Limited liability, proxy, and a board of directors are all characteristics of the corporate form of entity. Therefore, Statements #1, #2, and #3 are correct. Limited life is incorrect because the death of a shareholder does not dissolve or otherwise automatically adversely affect the corporation (as with a partnership).

Forms of Business Organizations

127. D

All are strengths of the partnership form of business entity.

Forms of Business Organizations

128. D

The question specifies that the taxpayer is concerned about liability issues that would mean that forming a corporation is desirable in order to protect personal assets. A sole proprietorship and a partnership would expose the personal assets of the taxpayer to creditors. Since losses are expected in the first year, it would be desirable to take advantage of these losses on a personal level. An S corporation allows the benefit of pass through of corporate items to the individual, therefore, this is the more appropriate form to elect. A Personal Holding Company is a status, not a form of business organization, which is determined by an IRS test.

Forms of Business Organizations

129. D

Form 2553 – Election by a Small Business Corporation has to file by the 15th day of the third month of the tax year. Statement #1 is incorrect because the shareholders secure the consent to be taxed as an S corporation. Statement #3 is not correct because in general only one class of stock is allowed.

Forms of Business Organizations

130. B

All of the statements except #3 are disadvantages of electing S corporation status. Section 179 expenses are allowed at the individual level by virtue of the pass through of selected items to the individual shareholders. The answer would by B after January 1, 1997 due to law change regarding shareholder to 75 (Small Business Act of 1996).

Forms of Business Organizations

131. D

All other statements are true.

Forms of Business Organizations

132. B

A limited partner's interest in the partnership is personal property that may be freely assigned unless agreed to the contrary. Therefore, statement #2 is correct.

Forms of Business Organizations

133. A

One similarity of both a partnership and a corporation is that they may both hold and convey property.

Forms of Business Organizations

134. A

The taxable income/losses of an S corporation flow through to the shareholders. A is correct because losses can be utilized by the shareholders on their individual tax returns in order to reduce their own liability. D is incorrect because although a corporation may borrow money from shareholders, this is not exclusive to S corporations and is therefore not a valid reason to select such a corporate status. B and C are incorrect.

Financial Planning Functions (CFP® Exam, released 3/95)

135. E

The question asks about legal forms. Partnerships (A and B) are excluded due to disruption if a partner left. Corporation (C) is excluded due to implicit double taxation and no need for capital accumulation. Professional Corporation (D) is not available for a franchise operation. Therefore, the S corporation is the best choice – a flow through entity, offering limited liability and ease of continuation and exchange of ownership. A Limited Liability Corporation may well have accomplished the same goals had it been a choice.

Forms of Business Organizations (CFP® Exam, released 3/95)

136. E

Statements #1, #2, #3, and #4 describe an S corporation non-employee shareholder; therefore, E is the correct answer. Compensation is not as used in taxation. Compensation usually means earned income from employment when used in taxation. Dividends declared from an S corporation are non-taxable distributions to the extent of the accumulated adjustments account.

Fundamentals

137. B

An S corporation will allow losses to flow through to the brothers, continue in the event that one brother should die, and will have the protection of a C corporation.

CONTRACTS

Suretyship

138. C

The surety may assert a defense, personal to the surety, to limit his/her liability to a creditor. The surety may use the defense of incapacity of the surety to avoid liability to the principal debtor's creditor.

Suretyship

139. A

Release of a co-surety by a creditor without the consent or reservation of rights against the other co-surety releases the remaining surety to the extent that he/she can not obtain contribution from the released surety. Thus, Lanning remains liable for 50% of the loan balance.

Contracts

140. E

There are four essential elements of a contract:

- Agreement
- Consideration
- Legal Capacity
- Legal objective

A writing is not required. Therefore, Statements #2, #3, and #4 are correct.

Contracts

141. A

The promise of one party to perform is consideration for the promise of the other in a bilateral contract (two promises). On the other hand, in a unilateral contract, one party makes a promise in exchange for the other party's act (one promise).

Contracts

142. D

The manner of communications is irrelevant as long as it is communicated as intended by the offeror. Therefore, statements #2 and #3 are correct, and statements #1 and #4 are incorrect.

AGENCY RELATIONSHIPS

Note: For questions in this area refer to Insurance Planning

NEGOTIABLE INSTRUMENTS

Negotiable Instruments

143. E

All are correct. In order for an instrument to be negotiable, it must:

- Be written.
- Be signed by the maker/drawer.
- Contain an unconditional promise or order to pay.
- State a fixed amount in money.
- Be payable to order/bearer.
- Be payable on demand or at a definite time.

Negotiable Instruments

144. E

All are correct. In order for an instrument to be negotiable, it must:

- Be written.
- Be signed by the maker/drawer.
- Contain an unconditional promise or order to pay.
- State a fixed amount in money.
- Be payable to order/bearer.
- Be payable on demand or at a definite time.

PROPERTY

Legal Environment

145. **C**

The characteristics of community property include:

1. Joint interest held by husband and wife;
2. Community property gets a step up to FMV for taxable basis both halves at the death of the first spouses;
3. Transfer requires the consent of both parties;
4. There is no right of survivorship.

Property

146. **B**

The main characteristic of tenancy by the entirety (spouses) is that if one of the joint owners dies, interest in the property automatically passes to the other joint owner.

Legal Environment

147. **D**

The characteristics of tenancy by the entirety are:

1. Joint interest held by husband and wife;
2. Tenancy by the entirety is presumed when the names of both spouses are on the title;
3. Transfer requires the consent of both parties;
4. Each tenant has a right of survivorship;
5. Divorce creates a property ownership as tenants in common.

Property

148. **C**

Community property and tenancy by the entirety can only be entered into by spouses. Joint tenancy (JTWROS) is often used by spouses to avoid probate but is not limited to spouses.

CONSUMER PROTECTION

Consumer Legislation

149. B

Each credit card carries a $50 potential liability, which is mitigated with notice prior to any fraudulent use.

Discover Card	$50
Master Card	$50
VISA	$50
Sears	$25
Marshall Fields	$50
Total	$225

Age Discrimination

150. A

The ADEA is intended to prevent arbitrary discrimination based on age. Furthermore, compulsory retirement of most classes of employees before the age of 70 is prohibited.

BANKRUPTCY AND REORGANIZATION

Bankruptcy

151. B

At the end of Chapter 11 proceedings, a corporate creditor had negotiated with creditors for most of the debts of the business. Exceptions to negotiated debts include debts that are provided for in the plan of reorganization (approved by the creditors and the court) and certain non-dischargeable debts.

Bankruptcy

152. D

A single creditor may file an involuntary petition for relief under Chapter 11 if he/she has at least $5,000 of unsecured claims and if the debtor has fewer than 12 creditors.

Bankruptcy

153. A

Debts arising from alimony, maintenance, and child support may not be discharged in bankruptcy. This does not include lump sum property settlement awards.

Bankruptcy

154. C

The bankruptcy estate consists of all the debtor's legal and equitable interests in property, including gifts, insurance proceeds, property settlements, and inheritances received within 180 days of the commencement of bankruptcy proceedings.

Chapter 7 Bankruptcy

155. C

Child support is not dischargeable nor are Federal taxes within the last 3 years. Student debt older than 5 years and consumer debt may be discharged.

Bankruptcy

156. D

Credit card debt will be discharged but not alimony or self-employment tax.

Bankruptcy

157. E

None is dischargeable.

TORTS

Tort Law

158. C

Courts try to provide a remedy for injury when a freedom of action is outweighed by the harm caused by interference with the personal or property rights of another.

Tort Law

159. C

Intent (or scienter) exists when the defendant makes a false representation with knowledge of its falsity or with a reckless disregard for the truth.

Tort Law

160. B

A battery is an intentional unprivileged bodily contact that would be harmful or offensive to a reasonable person.

Tort Law

161. D

Negligence is "conduct that falls below the standards established by law for the protection of others against unreasonable risk of harm." Stan, who knowingly drove his car after taking medicine he knows makes him drowsy, behaved negligently.

PROFESSIONAL LIABILITY – FINANCIAL PLANNERS

Contract

162. A

Under common law, an accountant's liability for negligence is most often restricted to those parties in privity of contract or who are primary beneficiaries of the engagement. This liability may also extend to foreseen third parties.

Note: For additional questions in this area refer to the Ethics section of Fundamentals

REGULATORY REQUIREMENTS

Regulatory Requirements

163. A

Liability under Rule 10b-5 requires that the plaintiff (stock purchaser) prove that a CFP had the intent (scienter) to deceive investors, the existence of a misstatement or omission of a material fact, its connection with the securities transaction, and reliance on the misstatement (reliance is assumed in omission cases.)

Regulatory Requirements

164. B

In order to be subject to the reporting requirements, a company must have shares listed on a national security exchange or have at least 500 shareholders and total gross assets of at least $5,000,000.

Regulatory Requirements

165. D

The reports include the annual report (Form 10-K), the quarterly reports (10-Q), and a proxy statement. In addition, the current report (8-K) must be filed to disclose material events within 15 days of occurrence.

Regulatory Requirements

166. E

Statements #2 and #3 are correct.

Regulatory Requirements

167. D

The 1933 Act exempts certain types of securities from registration statements. These include securities issued by not-for-profit organizations, domestic governments, banks, savings and loan associations, companies in reorganization, parties regulated by the ICE, receivers or trustees in bankruptcy, and companies in exchange for existing securities if no commission is paid.

Regulatory Requirements

168. B

The 1933 Act states that prospective investors must be provided with a prospectus disclosing pertinent financial and other types of information. The principal purposes for which the offerings' proceeds will be used must also be disclosed. A, C, and D are not relevant to an informed decision regarding the purchase of a security.

Regulatory Requirements (CFP® Exam, released 3/95)

169. A

Nothing assures the investor safety while investing and trading in securities (Statement #4). Statements #1, #2, and #3 are correct.

Regulatory Requirements

170. E

If an individual has fewer than 15 clients, registration is not necessary. Therefore, answers B and D are incorrect. A CFP licensee does not necessarily have to register by virtue of the designation, therefore, answers A and C are incorrect.

INVESTMENT ADVISERS REGULATION AND REGISTRATION

Regulatory Environment

171. C

NASD registration is required when products are offered for sale.

CODE OF ETHICS AND PROFESSIONAL RESPONSIBILITY

Confidentiality – Ethics

172. B

Under Principle 5, a CFP may disclose any confidential client information with the specific consent of the client.

Code of Ethics

173. C

The Code of Ethics specifies that the CFP mark should never have periods between the letters CFP. Therefore, answers A, B, and E are incorrect. The Code of Ethics also specifies that the mark should not be used as part of or incorporated in the name of a firm. Therefore, answer D is incorrect. It is appropriate to capitalize all the letters as shown in answer 3 and also to capitalize only the first letter of each word as shown in answer 4.

Code of Ethics

174. D

30 hours of continuing education is required every 2 years. The 30 hours must be in at least three areas (e.g., tax, investments, and estates). Two hours of ethics must also be completed.

Code of Ethics

175. B

Integrity, objectivity, and competence are principles of the Board of Standards Code of Ethics and Professional Responsibility. Disclosure is not.

Code of Ethics

176. A

Fairness, confidentiality, and professionalism are principles of the Board of Standards Code of Ethics and Professional Responsibility. Proper training is not.

Code of Ethics

177. C

Objectivity and competence are principles of the Board of Standards Code of Ethics and Professional Responsibility. Independence and disclosure are not.

Code of Ethics

178. A

Diligence, confidentiality, and fairness are principles of the Board of Standards Code of Ethics and Professional Responsibility. Independence is not one of these principles.

Ethics

179. C

Never take a sleazy client. Integrity.

Fundamentals

180. D

Marion has violated all of the above principles.

MISCELLANEOUS

Retirement Plans

181. B

This is by definition a non-contributory pension plan. The employer makes all contributions.

Client Data

182. C

Although Fisher's did not have any full-time employees, it must file a FUTA return because it employed temporary and part-time employees for more than 20 weeks in 1999. An employer must file a return if it employs at least one person for some portion of the day during at least 20 weeks in the current or preceding calendar year.

Bonds

183. D

NASDAQ is an exchange. The other 3 provide bond-rating services.

Zero Coupon Bonds

184. A

PV = ($500)

FV = $1,000

i = 4.5 (9 ÷ 2)

calculate for N

N = 15.75 semi-annual period divided by 2 equals approximately 8 years. The HP17C will give you an answer of 16 semi-annual periods.

Zero Coupon Bonds

185. C

All bonds are subject to interest rate risk. However, a zero coupon bond would not be subject to reinvestment risk.

Coinsurance

186. D

A coinsurance policy provides that the insurance company and the insured will each pay a portion of any qualified claim.

Home Owners Insurance

187. A

HO-4 (renter's contents broad form) and HO-6 (for condominium owner's) both include broad form coverage on personal property.

Split Gift

188. C

Married persons can double their annual exclusion of up to $10,000 to each donee by making a split gift election. For tax purposes, the gift will be treated as if half were made by the spouse and the other half by the other spouse, however, a gift tax return must be filed for years where gift splitting is elected.

Call Option

189. C

A call option allows an investor to purchase securities at a specified price.

Homeowners Policy

190. D

The replacement cost provision of a homeowners policy provides that if the insured covers 80% of its replacement cost on the dwelling, the insurance will cover the full cost to repair or replace the damage without deducting depreciation.

Municipal Bonds

191. B

The taxing authority of the issuer backs a general obligation bond.

QTIPs

192. D

The grantor of the trust can name the remainderman. Choices A, B, and C are all false.

THIS PAGE IS INTENTIONALLY LEFT BLANK.

INSURANCE PLANNING PROBLEMS

INSURANCE PLANNING

INTRODUCTION TO INSURANCE

1. Conditions that increase either the frequency or severity of loss are called: **(CFP® Exam, released 3/95)**
   a. Subrogation.
   b. Risks.
   c. Hazards.
   d. Perils.
   e. Extenuating circumstances.

2. Which of the following statements is correct?
   a. Insurance is the dispersion of actual from expected results.
   b. A hazard is the cause of financial loss.
   c. Speculative risk involves the chance of loss or no loss.
   d. Insurance is a device for reducing risk by having a large pool of people share in the financial losses suffered by members of the pool.
   e. Peril is the indifference to the loss that creates carelessness and increases the chance of loss due to existence of insurance.

3. Which of the following statements is/are correct?
   1. Static risk includes losses caused by earthquake and flood.
   2. Particular risk is personal and individual risk.
   3. Fundamental risk involves the chance of loss or gain.
   4. Financial risk is the exposure to a risk that may cause financial loss.
   a. 1 only.
   b. 2 only.
   c. 2 and 3.
   d. 1 and 4.
   e. 1, 2, and 4.

4. Pure risk involves only the chance of loss or no loss. Which of the following is/are considered to be a pure risk?

    a. Property risk.
    b. Personal risk.
    c. Liability risk.
    d. Risk from failure of others.
    e. All of the above.

5. The nature of risk management includes:

    a. Choosing efficiently among methods to manage risk.
    b. A non-scientific process that focuses on ideals.
    c. Insurance management only.
    d. Catastrophic loss prevention only.
    e. None of the above.

6. Which of the following statements is/are true?

    1. Risk is the chance of loss.
    2. Risk is certainty.
    3. Risk is the expected variability of returns.

    a. 1 only.
    b. 2 only.
    c. 1 and 3.
    d. 2 and 3.
    e. 1, 2, and 3.

7. Risk may be:

    a. Avoided.
    b. Retained.
    c. Transferred.
    d. Shared.
    e. All of the above.

8. Which of the following characteristics must be present to be considered an insurable risk?

   1. The loss cannot be unintentional.
   2. The loss must be uncertain.
   3. The loss cannot be catastrophic to society.
   4. The loss must be measurable.

      a. 4 only.
      b. 1 and 3.
      c. 2 and 3.
      d. 3 and 4.
      e. 1, 2, and 3.

9. Ken owns a hardware store that fills customers' propane tanks. You are Ken's insurance agent and are attempting to explain insurance terms to Ken. Which of the following statements is/are correct in this situation?

   1. Fire is a peril.
   2. The handling of propane is a risk.
   3. The handling of propane is a hazard.
   4. A loss is the destruction or reduction in value.

      a. 1 only.
      b. 2 only.
      c. 1, 2, and 3.
      d. 1, 3, and 4.
      e. 1, 2, 3, and 4.

THE LEGAL NATURE OF INSURANCE

10. Which of the following statements is incorrect regarding Homeowners policies?
    a. The insured has the right to assign the policy without written consent of the insurance company.
    b. The policy covers the insured's interest in the property.
    c. The insurance company has the right to replace or repair the damage rather than settle in cash.
    d. The insurance company can cancel for nonpayment of premium but must give notice of 10 days to the insured.
    e. The insurance company must provide notice to the insured if the policy will not be renewed.

11. A tort predicated on negligence alone carries certain defenses that may negate legal liability in spite of the negligent behavior. Which defenses are generally available against negligence?
    1. Contributory negligence.
    2. Comparative negligence.
    3. Gross negligence.
    4. Assumption of the risk.
    a. 1 only.
    b. 2 only.
    c. 1 and 2.
    d. 1, 2, and 4.
    e. 1, 2, 3, and 4.

12. Which of the following statements is incorrect regarding liability insurance policies?
    a. Liability policies provide defense for the insured in any lawsuit involving the type of liability insured.
    b. Liability insurance is commonly referred to as third party coverage.
    c. The injured party's claim is against the insurance company and not the negligent insured.
    d. The contract provisions provide that the insurance company is only bound to pay when the insured is legally liable.
    e. Liability insurance provides protection against the consequences of negligent acts.

13. Which of the following statements about assignments is/are true? **(CFP® Exam, released 3/95)**

1. An absolute assignment is an irrevocable transfer of all ownership rights that can be accomplished through a sale or gift.
2. A collateral assignment is a temporary transfer of some or all of the ownership rights on the condition such rights revert to the assignee.
3. A collateral assignment is a temporary transfer of some or all of the ownership rights whereby such rights revert to the assignor upon satisfaction of agreed-upon conditions.
4. A collateral assignment is a temporary transfer of some or all of the ownership rights on condition such rights revert to the insurance company upon satisfaction of agreed-upon conditions.

   a. 1, 2, and 3.
   b. 1 and 3.
   c. 2 and 4.
   d. 4 only.
   e. 1, 2, 3, and 4.

14. A contract for variable life insurance may be characterized as a/an: **(CFP® Exam, released 3/95)**

1. Unilateral contract.
2. Aleatory contract.
3. Conditional contract.
4. Personal contract of adhesion.

   a. 1, 2, and 3.
   b. 1 and 3.
   c. 2 and 4.
   d. 3 and 4.
   e. 1, 2, 3, and 4.

15. Amy purchases health insurance from Joseph, who claims to be an agent for XYZ Insurance Company. XYZ insurance knows that Joseph uses XYZ's logo on his stationery, even though Joseph is not an agent for XYZ, but XYZ does nothing. XYZ will have to honor Amy's policy of health insurance based upon:

   a. Apparent authority.
   b. Implied authority.
   c. Relied authority.
   d. Detrimental authority.
   e. Expressed authority.

16. The contract of insurance has several unique characteristics. Which of the following is not a characteristic?

    a. A contract of adhesion.
    b. A personal contract.
    c. An aleatory contract.
    d. A bilateral contract.
    e. A contract of indemnity.

17. An insurance policy is a contract derived from the general law of contracts. What binds an insurance contract?

    a. Reduction of contract (policy) to writing.
    b. For life insurance, the payment of the 1st premium amount due if insurable.
    c. Assumption of the risk.
    d. All of the above.
    e. None of the above.

LIFE INSURANCE IN GENERAL

18. Mr. Smith bought a $250,000 whole life, double indemnity policy on his own life on ***August 1 of the current year*** (premiums were $200 per month). On ***September 30 of the next year***, Mr. Smith committed suicide. What is payable to Mr. Smith's beneficiary, assuming the premiums were paid as agreed up to September 1st of the next year?

    a. $0.

    b. $2,800.

    c. $2,800 plus interest.

    d. $250,000.

    e. $500,000.

19. Ms. Johnson is 40 years old, but her youthful looks allow her to claim her age as 35. She has applied for a life insurance policy that has a premium of $25 per $1,000 for age 40 and $15 per $1,000 for age 35. On the application, Ms. Johnson stated her age as 35 and purchased a $20,000 life insurance policy, paying the appropriate annual premium for someone at the of age 35. Ms. Johnson dies unexpectedly one year later at the age of 41. What is the amount of the benefits to be paid to Ms. Johnson's beneficiary assuming the insurance company discovers Ms. Johnson has misstated her age on the application?

    a. $0.

    b. $10,000.

    c. $12,000.

    d. $19,800.

    e. $20,000.

20. The grace period clause of a life insurance contract:

    a. Must be elected by the insured at the time the policy is taken out, or it is not effective.

    b. Allows for default premiums to be paid out of cash values.

    c. Is designed to prevent an unintentional lapse in the policy.

    d. Does not allow for payment of benefits if the insured dies within the grace period.

    e. None of the above.

21. Which of the following statements concerning beneficiary designations of a life insurance policy is incorrect?

    a. The beneficiary may be an individual or a group of individuals.
    b. A contingent beneficiary is only entitled to the proceeds if the primary beneficiary is deceased.
    c. At the death of the insured, the beneficiary acquires a legal interest in the insurance contract.
    d. Under an irrevocable beneficiary arrangement, the insured is the complete owner of the contract, and the beneficiary cannot interfere in any manner with the insured's right to change beneficiaries.
    e. A revocable beneficiary is nothing more than an expectancy subject to all the rights and privileges that the insured may exercise in the contract.

22. Which of the following is/are true regarding the ownership of life insurance? **(CFP® Exam, released 3/95)**

    1. A policy can only be issued to the insured.
    2. Generally, assigning a policy requires proof that the insured is still insurable (meaning still in good health).
    3. Only a person with an insurable interest, generally a relative, a business associate, or lender, can be named as a beneficiary.
    4. The owner can assign (transfer) the policy to whomever he or she chooses, even if the assignee has no insurable interest.

    a. 1, 2, and 3.
    b. 1 only.
    c. 2 and 4.
    d. 4 only.
    e. 1, 2, 3, and 4.

23. Which of the following statements are true regarding life insurance contracts and modified endowment contracts?
    1. Both types of contracts defer earnings throughout the life of the contract.
    2. The life insurance contract and the modified endowment contract are virtually indistinguishable prior to a withdrawal of cash value.
    3. Modified endowment contracts receive disfavorable tax treatment to the extent that there is a withdrawal of cash value.
        a. 1 only.
        b. 2 only.
        c. 3 only.
        d. 1 and 2.
        e. 1, 2, and 3.

24. Which of the following are settlement options from a lapsed cash value life insurance policy?
    1. Paid up whole life in a reduced amount.
    2. Term insurance for the face value of the whole life policy.
    3. A reduced term insurance policy for life.
    4. Cash equal to the surrender value.
        a. 4 only.
        b. 1 and 2.
        c. 1, 2, and 3.
        d. 1, 2, and 4.
        e. 1, 2, 3, and 4.

TYPES OF LIFE INSURANCE

25. Group life insurance is a less expensive form of insurance than individual life insurance polices because:
    - a. The medical examination for group participants is eliminated.
    - b. Commissions for the selling agent for a group policy are lower than for individual policies.
    - c. Group mortality experience has less risk than individual mortality experience.
    - d. The employer for a group policy performs some of the administrative functions.
    - e. All of the above.

26. Which of the following types of life insurance provide payment only if the insured dies during a specific time period?
    1. Pure Endowment life insurance.
    2. Ordinary life insurance.
    3. Term life insurance.
    4. Limited pay life insurance.
    - a. 1 only.
    - b. 1, 2, and 3.
    - c. 1 and 3.
    - d. 1, 2, and 4.
    - e. 1, 2, 3, and 4.

27. Whole life insurance contracts contain cash surrender values. These cash surrender values:
    - a. Are based on the past experience of the insurance company and cannot be guaranteed.
    - b. Represent an excess of the premiums collected over pure insurance costs.
    - c. Represent estimates based on projected mortality savings.
    - d. Are available only if the insured chooses to terminate the coverage under the policy.
    - e. None of the above.

28. Life insurance policies that are participating pay a dividend to the insured. These policy dividends are paid from:

 a. Contingency surplus reserves of the insurance company.
 b. Legal reserves of the insurance company.
 c. Surplus apportioned for distribution by the insurance company.
 d. Prepaid premium reserves of the insurance company.
 e. None of the above.

29. A life insurance contract with low fixed premiums during the first 3 to 5 years and then significantly higher fixed premiums for the remainder of the policy period is called:

 a. An increasing term policy.
 b. A modified whole life policy.
 c. A graded whole life policy.
 d. Family protection policy.
 e. A return of premium policy.

30. A recent college graduate who has 2 young dependents has decided to purchase a life insurance policy that will accumulate cash value. His best choice for this coverage would be:

 a. Term life insurance for $100,000.
 b. A single premium policy for $100,000.
 c. A modified whole life policy for $100,000.
 d. An ordinary whole life policy for $100,000.
 e. Any of the above.

31. In which of the following insurance policies are the excess premiums generally invested in equity securities?

 1. Equity life.
 2. Adjustable life.
 3. Universal life.
 4. Variable life.

 a. 1 only.
 b. 4 only.
 c. 2 and 4.
 d. 1, 2, and 4.
 e. 2, 3, and 4.

32. In the case where the insured has a need for permanent life insurance but cannot afford that form of insurance, which of the following would be a reasonable alternative?
    a. Purchase term to expectancy life insurance.
    b. Purchase a form of convertible term life insurance.
    c. Purchase the amount of permanent life insurance that he can afford.
    d. Purchase a term life policy.
    e. Purchase an annuity.

33. There are many types of life insurance available in the market. Of the following, which is not a type of life insurance?
    a. Decreasing term life insurance.
    b. Mortgage term life insurance.
    c. Single premium life insurance.
    d. Cash value term life insurance.
    e. Universal whole life.

34. When evaluating a universal life insurance policy, which factors should be considered in assessing the cost?
    a. The interest rates actually being credited to the policy.
    b. The guaranteed interest rate specified in the policy.
    c. The mortality charge specified in the policy.
    d. The mortality charge actually being assessed to the policy.
    e. All of the above.

35. Generally, the premiums of group life insurance paid by an employer:
    a. Are tax-deductible by the employee and the employer.
    b. Are tax-deductible by the employer and represent a tax liability for the employee.
    c. May be tax-deductible by the employer and not taxable to the employee.
    d. Are not tax-deductible by the employee or the employer.
    e. Are considered a part of compensation to the employee and included as gross income on their W-2.

36. Employer sponsored life insurance is usually referred to as group life insurance. Which type of life insurance (offered as group life) is beneficial to both the employer and the employee from a tax point of view?

    a. Term life insurance.
    b. Group ordinary life insurance.
    c. Group universal life.
    d. Group paid up life insurance.
    e. All of the above.

37. Which one of the following statements about life insurance products and their tax attributes is correct? **(CFP® Exam, released 3/95)**

    a. Modified endowment contracts do not provide a tax-free death benefit if the policyholder dies prior to age 59½.
    b. Tax-deferred annuities owned by a corporation are eligible for tax-deferred accumulation.
    c. Permanent life insurance owned by a pension plan is 100% income tax-free to the beneficiary of the plan.
    d. If a person purchased a life and 20-year term-certain immediate annuity at age 50, there would be no premature distribution penalty.
    e. Policyholders of single payment deferred annuity contracts purchased prior to 1987 may withdraw funds tax-free from their policy up to basis.

38. A modified endowment life insurance policy differs from a pure endowment policy because:

    1. A pure endowment policy does not pay the face of the policy if the insured survives beyond the endowment period.
    2. A pure endowment policy is usually not sold in the United States.
    3. A pure endowment policy uses an annuity to pay the face of the policy if the insured survives beyond the endowment period.

    a. 1 only.
    b. 2 only.
    c. 3 only.
    d. 2 and 3.
    e. 1, 2, and 3.

39. Rank from lowest to the highest the risk of annual premiums increasing on the following life insurance policies on a male age 35. Premiums are projected to vanish at 65. After a careful review of each company's Insurance Questionnaire, it is concluded that all companies use realistic expense, mortality and lapse assumptions. All companies have demonstrated good historical results for policyholders. Assume further that a 30-year Treasury bond yields 7% and that all companies will have similar future investment returns. **(CFP® Exam, released 12/95)**

    1. Variable universal life insurance (illustrated to endow at age 100, run at 8% gross and allocated 100% to common stock sub-account).
    2. Interest sensitive whole life insurance (illustrated at current rate of 8.5% and funded at full target premium).
    3. Universal life insurance (illustrated at current projected new money rate of 6.75%).
    4. Whole life insurance (25% base policy, with 5.5% guarantee; 75% term rider - ledger illustrated at company's portfolio rate of 9.5% - company's net investment yield is 9.66% for this current year).

    a. 3, 1, 2, 4.
    b. 2, 4, 1, 3.
    c. 2, 4, 3, 1.
    d. 2, 1, 3, 4.
    e. 3, 2, 4, 1.

BUSINESS USES OF LIFE INSURANCE

40. Life insurance purchased to fund a 2 person partnership buy/sell agreement on an entity plan basis:
    - a. Will be the same total amount as the amount under a cross-purchase plan.
    - b. Will be paid for with tax-deductible dollars.
    - c. Will be a greater amount than the total amount under a cross-purchase plan.
    - d. Will be taxable as income to beneficiaries when received.
    - e. Will benefit the partnership with a tax deduction for the premiums that are paid for by the partners.

41. Split-dollar life insurance is:
    - a. An insurance arrangement in which the employer pays the cost of the premium and the employee must name the employer as the beneficiary.
    - b. An insurance arrangement where the employer and the employee share the cost of the life insurance on the employee and the portion of the premium that is paid by the employer is the value of the term life portion of the policy.
    - c. An insurance arrangement in which the employee pays the majority of the premium while the employer names the beneficiary.
    - d. An insurance arrangement in which the employer is the owner of the policy and is also the beneficiary to the extent of the premiums paid by the employer.
    - e. An insurance arrangement in which the employee is the owner of the policy and is also the beneficiary to the extent of the cash value of the policy.

42. Under a key employee insurance policy, the beneficiary is usually:
    - a. The spouse of the employee.
    - b. The employee.
    - c. The employer.
    - d. The estate of the employee.
    - e. The stockholders of the company.

43. A business that has a value of $1,200,000 has 4 partners. If each of the 4 partners buys a $100,000 life insurance policy on each of the other partners, this is an example of:

    a. A business insurance equity plan.
    b. An insurable interest plan.
    c. A cross-purchase plan.
    d. A shared interest plan.
    e. A key person plan.

44. The MAD2 partnership has 4 partners. The partners have entered into a binding buy/sell agreement that binds the surviving partners to purchase the partnership interest of the first partner to die. The partnership has chosen to use an entity approach to establish this agreement. How many life insurance policies are necessary to accomplish this agreement?

    a. 1.
    b. 3.
    c. 4.
    d. 8.
    e. 12.

TAX TREATMENT OF LIFE INSURANCE AND ANNUITIES

45. The tax treatment of whole life insurance is favorable for several reasons. Which of the following is not a favorable tax treatment of whole life insurance?
    a. The investment gains are deferred until realized.
    b. When the taxable gain is computed, the insured can deduct all premiums that have been paid to arrive at the taxable portion of the gain.
    c. Surrender proceeds in excess of premiums are taxable.
    d. The proceeds to the beneficiary are usually not considered taxable income.
    e. None of the above.

46. John dies owning a $200,000 life insurance policy; he is the insured, his brother Tom is the beneficiary. Tom does not need all the benefits currently and elects to receive the benefits annually over a 10-year period. The benefit that Tom will receive is $23,500 per year. How much of this payment is includible in taxable income to Tom each year?
    a. $0.
    b. $1,750.
    c. $3,500.
    d. $20,000.
    e. $23,500.

47. Vicki purchased an annuity for $26,000 in 1999. Under the contract, Vicki will receive $300 each month for the rest of her life. According to actuarial estimates, Vicki will live to receive 100 payments and will receive a 3% return on her original investment.
    a. If Vicki collects $3,000 in 1999, the $3,000 is treated as a recovery of capital and thus is not taxable.
    b. If Vicki dies after collecting a total of 50 payments, she has an economic loss that is not deductible.
    c. If Vicki lives to collect more than 100 payments, she must amend her prior years returns to increase her taxable portion of each payment received in the past.
    d. If Vicki lives to collect more than 100 payments, all amounts received after the 100th payment must be included in her gross income.
    e. None of the above.

48. Robert retired on May 31, 1999 and receives a monthly pension benefit of $1,200 payable for life. His life expectancy at the date of retirement is 10 years. The first pension check was received on June 15, 1999. During his years of employment, Robert contributed $24,000 to the cost of his company's pension plan. How much of the pension amounts received may Robert exclude from taxable income for the years 1999, 2000, and 2001?

	1999	2000	2001
a.	$0	$0	$0
b.	$1,400	$2,400	$2,400
c.	$8,400	$8,400	$8,400
d.	$8,400	$14,400	$14,400
e.	$14,400	$14,400	$14,400

49. You have a client who has been diagnosed as being HIV positive and is expected to live less than 1 year. She has a life insurance policy of $300,000, and the insurance company is willing to buy it back for $150,000. What are the tax implications of this transaction?

a. No tax is due since the law has been changed regarding viatical settlements.
b. Fully taxable if she lives beyond the one year period.
c. Fully taxable to the named beneficiary upon client's death.
d. Fully taxable in the year of receipt.
e. Taxable to the extent the proceeds exceed the adjusted cost basis.

50. Thomas named his wife, Kim, the beneficiary of a $120,000 (face amount) insurance policy on his life. The policy provided that upon his death, the proceeds would be paid to Kim with interest over her remaining life expectancy (which was calculated at 20 years). Thomas died during the current year, and Kim received a regular annual payment of $15,000 from the insurance company. What amount must Kim include in her gross income for the current year?

a. $0.
b. $3,000.
c. $6,000.
d. $9,000.
e. $15,000.

CALCULATING LIFE INSURANCE AMOUNTS (NEEDS ANALYSIS)

51. An individual has decided to purchase life insurance and comes to you as his agent. In order to program a system of life insurance to meet his individual needs, your first step is:
    a. Review his will or have him write a will if he does not have one.
    b. Selection of an insurance company.
    c. Selection of policy type he wants to purchase.
    d. Analysis of his needs and determination of the amount of life insurance coverage needed.
    e. Determine the rate of return he would like to receive.

52. When utilizing the needs approach in the determination of life insurance, which of the following is/are factor(s) to be considered?
    1. The family expenses that will remain after the wage earner dies.
    2. The value of the wage earner's life in the event he or she dies.
    3. The income that can be generated by the surviving spouse.
    4. The number of dependents.
    a. 1 only.
    b. 3 only.
    c. 1, 2, and 3.
    d. 1, 3, and 4.
    e. 1, 2, 3, and 4.

53. The so-called blackout period is:
    a. The period of time immediately following the death of the wage earner.
    b. The period of time after the death of a wage earner when the family is adjusting to life without the individual.
    c. The period of time when the widow or widower and dependents receive Social Security benefits.
    d. The period of time when the dependents are in primary and secondary schools and colleges.
    e. The period of time when the dependents have reached age 16 and the spouse's Social Security retirement benefits have not started.

54. All of the following statements about a life insurance needs analysis program are true except:
    a. Once a program has been designed for an individual or family, there is relatively no need for changes.
    b. A life insurance program will allow the individual or family to purchase the most beneficial type and amounts of life insurance for their current needs.
    c. A life insurance program determines the amount of insurance for a specific point in time.
    d. A life insurance program for an individual is not as complicated as a life insurance program for a family.

55. When designing a life insurance needs analysis program, provisions should be made for funds to meet which of the following needs?
    1. Funds to cover the funeral expenses related to the death of the wage earner.
    2. Funds to cover the education of dependents.
    3. Funds to cover payment of debts and mortgages.
    4. Funds for the retirement of the surviving spouse.
    a. 1 and 2.
    b. 2 and 3.
    c. 1, 2, and 3.
    d. 2, 3, and 4.
    e. 1, 2, 3, and 4.

56. Life insurance programming provides protection for all but which of the following:
    a. Maintenance of family lifestyle.
    b. Total protection from loss of income.
    c. Immediate cash flow needs.
    d. Adequate levels of life insurance protection.
    e. Adequate income in the event of the wage earner's death.

57. Andrew is 25 years old and recently began a job with a salary of $35,000. He is single but has been dating Gina for 2 years. He expects to marry her within the next 5 years. Andrew lives with his parents. What is the amount of life insurance that Andrew currently needs?

    a. $0.
    b. $100,000.
    c. $35,000 x 6 = $210,000.
    d. $35,000 x 10 = $350,000.
    e. (65-25) $35,000 = $1,400,000.

58. Which of the following is not needed to calculate the client's human life value? **(CFP® Exam, released 3/95)**

    a. Average annual earnings to the age of retirement.
    b. Estimated annual Social Security benefits after retirement.
    c. Costs of self-maintenance.
    d. Number of years from the client's present age to the contemplated age of retirement.
    e. Selection of an appropriate capitalization rate.

LIFE INSURANCE AND ESTATE AND GIFT PLANNING (INCLUDING GSTT)

59. Connie dies insured by a life insurance policy that her husband Glennon owns. Their daughter Lexie is the named beneficiary. What are the tax consequences?
    - a. Lexie and Glennon would be subject to estate tax liability on the life insurance proceeds.
    - b. Connie's estate would be subject to federal income tax liability on the life insurance proceeds.
    - c. Glennon would be subject to gift tax liability on the life insurance proceeds.
    - d. Lexie would be subject to gift tax liability on the life insurance proceeds.
    - e. None of the above.

60. Jack and Jill Jones, age 65, have decided that, in order to best pay their $3,000,000 federal estate tax bill, they will purchase a second-to-die life insurance policy. In order to keep the proceeds out of their estate, they were advised to create an irrevocable life insurance trust. Jack and Jill applied for the insurance and the policy was issued to them. An irrevocable trust was drafted. The policy was transferred into the irrevocable trust, and 90 days later both Jack and Jill were killed in a plane crash. The Internal Revenue Service wants to include the insurance in the estate for tax purposes. Which statement(s) is/are correct? ? **(CFP® Exam, released 3/95)**
    1. The insurance will be included in the estate because the trust was drafted after the insurance was approved.
    2. The insurance will be included in the estate because the premiums were a gift from the insured.
    3. The insurance will be included in the estate because the insureds transferred the policy within three years of death.
    4. The Internal Revenue Service is wrong - the insurance will <u>not</u> be included in the estate.
    - a. 1, 2, and 3.
    - b. 1 only.
    - c. 2 and 3.
    - d. 3 only.
    - e. 4 only.

CHOOSING LIFE INSURANCE COMPANIES

61. When selecting a life insurance company, which of the following should be considered?

    1. The financial strength of the company.
    2. The integrity of the company.
    3. The types of policies the company has available.
    4. The claim turnaround time.

        a. 1 and 2.
        b. 3 and 4.
        c. 1, 2, and 3.
        d. 1, 3, and 4.
        e. 1, 2, 3, and 4.

DISABILITY INSURANCE

62. The chance of becoming disabled is:
    a. Less than the chance of premature death during middle age.
    b. Approximately equal to the chance of premature death.
    c. Greater than the chance of premature death during the working years.
    d. Less than the chance of death at any age.
    e. None of the above.

63. Which of the following statements is correct about disability insurance?
    a. It is only sold on a group basis.
    b. It is less important than life insurance because the probability of death at most ages is greater than the probability of disability.
    c. It should be purchased with an elimination period that is short enough to not place the insured in a financial bind.
    d. It should be purchased as an "any occupation" definition to provide the most protection to the specialized worker such as a surgeon.
    e. It is only available to insureds who are also covered by life insurance.

64. Joe has a disability income policy that pays a monthly benefit of $1,200. Joe has been disabled for 30 days, but he only received $600 from his disability insurance. Which of the following is the probable reason that he only received $600?
    a. The policy has a deductible of $600.
    b. The elimination period is 15 days.
    c. The policy has a 50% coinsurance clause.
    d. Joe is considered to be only 50% disabled.
    e. Joe has only owned the policy for half the year.

65. Disability income insurance programming is designed to protect loss of income from disability. Which of the following statements is/are true of disability programming?

    1. Disability programming should start with the concept that the individual will have Social Security disability benefits.
    2. The waiting period that is selected should be the shortest possible.
    3. The coverage should be obtained to provide lifetime benefits for accidents only.
    4. The cost of medical expenses incurred with disability should be considered and protection for these expenses should be included.

    a. 4 only.
    b. 1 and 4.
    c. 2 and 4.
    d. 1, 2, and 4.
    e. 1, 2, 3, and 4.

66. One need that is often overlooked in programming disability income insurance is:

    a. Provision for the education of the dependents.
    b. Provision for income for the disabled person.
    c. Provision for income for recreational needs.
    d. Provision for completion of a retirement program.
    e. Provision for medical expenses.

67. Which of the following is a characteristic of guaranteed renewability?

    1. Insurer guarantees to renew policy to stated age.
    2. The policy is non-cancelable.
    3. Renewal is solely at insured discretion.
    4. Insurer has right to increase premium rates for the underlying class in which the insured is placed. ***Note**: Not a single individual.

    a. 4 only.
    b. 1 only.
    c. 1 and 4.
    d. 1, 2, and 4.
    e. 1, 2, 3, and 4.

HEALTH INSURANCE FOR MEDICAL EXPENSES

68. Non-cancelable health insurance contracts are different from guaranteed renewable contracts because:
    a. Non-cancelable policies are not guaranteed renewable.
    b. Non-cancelable policies cannot be canceled in mid-term.
    c. Non-cancelable policies cannot have a premium change.
    d. Non-cancelable policies have more liberal disability benefits.
    e. All of the above.

69. Medical insurance is commonly known as health insurance and can be purchased from private insurance companies. Which of the following best describes the classes of medical insurance?
    a. Coverage for hospital expense, surgical expense, physician expense, and major medical expense.
    b. Coverage for hospital expense, non-major medical expenses, surgical expenses, and physician expense.
    c. Coverage for hospital expense, comprehensive major medical expenses, non-major medical expense, and physician expense.
    d. Coverage for comprehensive major medical expense, non-major medical expenses, surgical expense, and physician expense.
    e. Coverage for comprehensive major medical expense only.

70. Which of the following statements regarding hospitalization expense insurance is false?
    a. Hospitalization coverage is sold under 2 types of contracts: expense reimbursement contract and service contract.
    b. Hospitalization coverage pays for physician services in all contracts.
    c. Hospitalization coverage pays for the hospital room based on a flat rate per diem.
    d. Hospitalization coverage includes miscellaneous hospital charges such as X-rays, lab work, and medications.
    e. All of the above are true.

71. Ms. Hopkins has a major medical insurance policy with a $500 deductible and an 80% coinsurance clause. She becomes ill and is admitted to the hospital for several days. When she is discharged, her hospital bill is $7,500, and her doctor bills are $3,250. What is the amount that her insurance will pay?

    a. $7,000.
    b. $8,200.
    c. $9,250.
    d. $10,250.
    e. $10,750.

72. Which of the following best describes a major medical policy?

    a. A major medical policy is designed to protect the insured from both small and large medical bills.
    b. A major medical policy includes high limits on losses, higher deductibles and coinsurance clauses, and is designed to protect the insured against large medical expenses.
    c. A major medical policy is always a supplement to other health insurance coverage.
    d. A major medical policy covers the same items as a regular medical policy, only the insured must assume some of the risk of loss through deductibles and coinsurance.
    e. A major medical policy can only be written on a group basis.

73. The coordination of benefits provisions in insurance policies eliminates which of the following?

    1. Excess coverage.
    2. Duplication of coverage.
    3. Double payment of benefits.
    4. Deductibles.

    a. 1 only.
    b. 3 only.
    c. 1 and 2.
    d. 2 and 3.
    e. 1, 2, 3, and 4.

74. In which of the following events would COBRA rules apply for the benefit of the covered employee, employee's spouse, or dependent child?

    1. Death of the covered employee.
    2. Covered employee fired for incompetence.
    3. Employee changes status from full-time to part-time and as a result loses coverage.
    4. Divorce of covered employee.

        a. 1 only.
        b. 1 and 4.
        c. 1, 3, and 4.
        d. 2, 3, and 4.
        e. 1, 2, 3, and 4.

75. In which of the following events would COBRA rules apply for the benefit of employee, employee's spouse, or dependent child?

    1. Divorce of covered employee.
    2. Child reaches age 19 and ceases to be eligible dependent.
    3. Employee becomes eligible for Medicare at age 65, therefore, eliminating employer plan coverage.
    4. Employee is fired for gross misconduct.

        a. 1 only.
        b. 1 and 3.
        c. 1, 2, and 3.
        d. 1, 3, and 4.
        e. 2, 3, and 4.

76. Due to a slow down in business, Michelle Bonnette has voluntarily changed her status from full-time to part-time with her employer. Prior to the change, she and her husband were covered under the company health plan. Which statement regarding COBRA is correct?

    a. Because her change is voluntary, COBRA rules do not apply.
    b. COBRA rules allow continuation of coverage in this situation for up to 36 months.
    c. COBRA rules allow continuation of coverage in this situation for up to 18 months.
    d. COBRA rules allow continuation of coverage in this situation for 29 months.
    e. None of the above.

77. COBRA coverage is available for which of the following persons?
    1. Retiring employee.
    2. Employee terminated for incompetence.
    3. Spouses and dependents of a deceased employee.
    4. Employee no longer able to work due to disability.
        a. 3 only.
        b. 3 and 4.
        c. 1, 3, and 4.
        d. 1, 2, and 3.
        e. 1, 2, 3, and 4.

78. COBRA coverage is available for which of the following persons?
    1. A child who ceases to be an eligible dependent.
    2. A former spouse after divorce from covered employee.
    3. An employee who changes to part-time status.
    4. A dependent child of a deceased worker.
        a. 4 only.
        b. 2 only.
        c. 2 and 4.
        d. 2, 3, and 4.
        e. 1, 2, 3, and 4.

79. Which of the following statements regarding COBRA rules for group health plans is correct?
    a. COBRA rules apply to any employer with a health plan and 15 or more employees.
    b. COBRA rules allow an employer to charge up to 103% of the cost of an active employee to cover administrative costs.
    c. COBRA rules require the employee or dependent to notify the employer within 60 days of a qualifying event such as a divorce.
    d. COBRA rules allow an employer to collect premiums quarterly.
    e. None of the above.

80. John Black is an employee of XYZ Corporation. He has just divorced his former dependent spouse, Anne. Anne, who was on all of his group health plan coverage, wants to know to what COBRA coverage she is entitled. The following is a list of John's group health plan benefits, all are integral parts of the plan. Which of John's benefits is/are subject to COBRA rules?

    1. Medical expense plan.
    2. Dental plan.
    3. Vision care plan.
    4. Prescription care plan.

        a. 1 only.
        b. 1 and 4.
        c. 1, 3, and 4.
        d. 2, 3, and 4.
        e. 1, 2, 3, and 4 .

THE OLD-AGE, SURVIVORS, DISABILITY AND HEALTH INSURANCE PROGRAM (OASDHI)

81. Which of the following groups of employees are not covered under Social Security?

    a. Congress.

    b. Railroad workers with over 10 years of service.

    c. Agriculture employees.

    d. Members of the armed forces.

    e. Members of the clergy.

82. Social Security is funded through:

    1. Employee payroll tax.
    2. Employer payroll tax.
    3. Sales tax.
    4. Self-employment tax.

    a. 1 only.

    b. 1 and 2.

    c. 2 and 3.

    d. 1, 2, and 4.

    e. 1, 2, 3, and 4

83. Glen, now deceased, was divorced after 12 years of marriage. He had 2 dependent children, ages 4 and 6, who are cared for by their mother age 45. He also had a mother age 70. At the time of his death, he was currently but not fully insured under Social Security. His survivors are entitled to benefits that include, but are not limited to:

    1. A lump sum death benefit of $255.
    2. A children's benefit equal to 75% of Glen's PIA.
    3. A caretaker's benefit for the children's mother.
    4. A parent's benefit.

    a. 1 only.

    b. 1 and 2.

    c. 1, 2, and 3.

    d. 2, 3, and 4.

    e. 1, 2, 3, and 4.

84. Medicare Part A provides hospital coverage. Which of the following person(s) is/are covered under Part A?

1. A person 65 or older and receiving railroad retirement.
2. Disabled beneficiaries regardless of age that have received Social Security for 2 years.
3. Chronic kidney patients who require dialysis or a renal transplant.
4. A person 65 or older entitled to a monthly Social Security check.

   a. 4 only.
   b. 2 and 4.
   c. 2, 3, and 4.
   d. 1, 2, and 4.
   e. 1, 2, 3, and 4.

85. Part B of Medicare is considered to be supplemental insurance and provides additional coverage to participants. Which of the following is/are true regarding Part B coverage?

1. The election to participate must be made at the time the insured is eligible for Part A Medicare and at no time after.
2. The premiums for Part B are paid monthly through withholding from Social Security.
3. Once a participant elects Part B, they must maintain the coverage until death.
4. Coverage under Part B does not include deductibles or coinsurance.

   a. 1 only.
   b. 2 only.
   c. 1 and 2.
   d. 2 and 3.
   e. 2, 3, and 4.

86. A person receiving Social Security benefits under age 70 can receive income up to a maximum threshold without reducing Social Security benefits. However, there are certain types of income that do not count against the threshold. Which of the following do not count against the threshold?

1. Dividends from stocks.
2. Rental income.
3. Pensions and insurance annuities.
4. Gambling winnings.

   a. 1 only.
   b. 4 only.
   c. 1 and 2.
   d. 1, 2, and 3.
   e. 1, 2, 3, and 4.

87. It is possible for a person receiving Social Security benefits to lose eligibility (be disqualified) for those benefits. Which of the following is not considered grounds for disqualification?

1. Marriage.
2. Divorce.
3. Conviction of fraud.
4. Engaged in illegal employment.

   a. 3 only.
   b. 3 and 4.
   c. 1, 2, and 3.
   d. 2 and 4.
   e. 1, 2, 3, and 4.

88. A client, age 70, a widower with no close relatives, has crippling arthritis. The client is unable to walk and is confined to a custodial nursing home. Which of the following programs is/are likely to pay benefits towards the cost of the nursing home? **(CFP® Exam, released 3/95)**

1. Medicare may pay for up to 100 days of care after a 20-day deductible.
2. Long-term care insurance may pay part if coverage of the facility type is broad enough.
3. Private medical insurance may pay part if it is a comprehensive major medical policy.
4. Medicaid may pay if the client has income and assets below state mandated thresholds.

a. 1, 2, and 3.

b. 1 and 3.

c. 2 and 4.

d. 4 only.

e. 1, 2, 3, and 4.

OTHER COMPULSORY SOCIAL INSURANCE

89. Which of the following is/are principle(s) of the workers' compensation laws?
    1. The indemnity paid to the injured employee is partial but is to be considered final.
    2. The costs for workers compensation benefits are funded through payroll taxes, and the employee is expected to contribute.
    3. The injured employee is not required to prove negligence on the part of the employer.
    4. The benefits payable under workers compensation are to be periodic payments.
        a. 1 only.
        b. 2 only.
        c. 1 and 3.
        d. 1, 3, and 4.
        e. 1, 2, 3, and 4.

90. Which of the following statements about workers' compensation is/are correct?
    1. Workers' compensation applies to all occupations.
    2. Workers' compensation covers any injury of the employee while at work, even if the injury was deliberately self-inflicted.
    3. Workers' compensation coverage is mandated in all 50 states.
    4. Workers' compensation benefits are excluded from the employee's gross income for tax purposes.
        a. 1 only.
        b. 4 only.
        c. 1 and 2.
        d. 2 and 3.
        e. 1, 2, 3, and 4.

91. Joe was involved in an accident at the plant where he works and, as a result, lost his arm. This type of injury is considered to be an example of:
        a. Total permanent disability.
        b. Partial temporary disability.
        c. Total temporary disability.
        d. Partial permanent disability.
        e. Medical expense disability.

92. The benefits under workers' compensation include:

    1. Medical expenses.
    2. Disability benefits.
    3. Death benefits for survivors.
    4. Rehabilitation benefits.

        a. 1 only.
        b. 2 only.
        c. 1 and 2.
        d. 1, 2, and 4.
        e. 1, 2, 3, and 4.

93. Unemployment benefits are a form of insurance against loss of income due to loss of employment. Which of the following statements regarding unemployment compensation is/are false?

    1. The eligibility for unemployment compensation is uniform in all 50 states.
    2. A person who is unemployed is not required to be available for other employment as long as they are receiving benefits.
    3. Unemployment benefits are excluded from taxable income.
    4. The weekly compensation through unemployment is usually equal to approximately 90% of the workers normal weekly full-time compensation.

        a. 1 only.
        b. 3 only.
        c. 2 and 3.
        d. 1, 2, and 3.
        e. 1, 2, 3, and 4.

HOMEOWNERS INSURANCE - GENERAL PROVISIONS

94. Which of the following is included in the definition of a dwelling for homeowners insurance?

    a. Building materials that are to be used in the alteration of the dwelling.

    b. A garage that is detached from the house.

    c. A covered swimming pool that is attached to a detached garage.

    d. Air conditioning and refrigeration equipment.

95. Which of the following perils are ordinarily covered in an open perils HO3 policy?

    1. Ice damage.
    2. Lightning.
    3. Flood.
    4. Earthquake.

    a. 1 only.

    b. 1 and 2.

    c. 1, 2, and 4.

    d. 2, 3, and 4.

    e. 1, 2, 3, and 4.

96. An HO3 policy (Special form-"All risks of physical loss" except those specifically excluded) with no endorsements excludes which one of the following perils? **(CFP® Exam, released 3/95)**

    a. Flood.

    b. Fire.

    c. Collapse.

    d. Weight of ice.

    e. Volcanic eruption.

PERILS

97. The principal difference among the various homeowners forms of insurance is:
    a. The definition of extension of coverage in each form.
    b. The definition of the dwelling in each form.
    c. The liability coverage under Section II.
    d. The definition of personal property in each form.
    e. The property covered and the perils insured against in Section I.

98. The difference between named peril coverage and open peril coverage is:
    a. A named peril coverage is an all risk type of coverage.
    b. Named peril coverage is broad enough to encompass all perils other than those specifically excluded.
    c. Open peril coverage is only for Form 02 coverage.
    d. Open peril coverage is broad enough to encompass all perils other than those specifically excluded.
    e. Open peril coverage includes only 16 perils.

99. Homeowners dwelling coverage can be written on replacement value or actual cash value. A policy that is written as replacement value includes:
    a. A deduction for depreciation on the structure.
    b. Applies to personal property and buildings.
    c. An 80% coinsurance clause.
    d. Includes carpeting and appliances.
    e. None of the above.

100. Which of the following perils is not a named peril in an HO4, HO6 or HO2 policy?
    a. Volcanic eruption.
    b. Falling object.
    c. Theft.
    d. Flood.
    e. Loss caused by a non-owned vehicle.

101. Personal property is covered under Homeowners policies. Which of the following is considered personal property as defined by a Homeowners policy?

a. A pet.

b. A motorcycle.

c. A credit card.

d. A CD player that is installed in an automobile.

e. Borrowed property from a friend.

102. Which of the following is covered without a dollar limit under the personal property provision of a homeowners policy?

a. Money.

b. Jewelry.

c. Guns.

d. Water crafts.

e. None of the above.

103. Additional coverage can be purchased as an endorsement or supplemental extension of the Homeowners policy. Which of the following is not an example of additional coverage that can be purchased?

a. Damage to trees, shrubs, plants, and lawns.

b. Cost of removal of debris.

c. Damage from a mudslide.

d. Damage from a depositor's forgery.

e. Damage from loss on credit cards.

104. Edward built a house in Dallas in 1990, which now has a replacement value of $200,000 and an actual cash value of $150,000. Edward has purchased insurance on the house under a Homeowners Broad Form HO2 in the amount of $150,000. The roof of the house becomes damaged by fire. The determination has been that the roof was 25% depreciated and that the cost to replace the roof will be $20,000. How much will the insurer pay for the loss?

a. $20,000.

b. $20,000 less the deductible.

c. $18,750.

d. $18,750 less the deductible.

e. $15,000 less the deductible.

105. Bill Jones is covered by a homeowner's tenants Form HO4 policy. While he is at work, burglars steal his television, stereo, $150 cash and his $6,500 Ohle watch. Which of the following is true?

a. Of the loss, all will be covered subject to the deductible.
b. Only the television and stereo are covered.
c. None of the loss is covered.
d. All items are covered, but the watch is subject to a limitation on the value. All are subject to the deductible.
e. The cash is not covered.

106. Which of the following is excluded from all standard Homeowners forms under the General Exclusion Provisions?

a. Theft of money.
b. Wear and tear and gradual deterioration.
c. Loss resulting from friendly fire.
d. Earth movement.
e. Breakage of glass.

107. The major difference between the Homeowners special form and the broad form is:

a. The coverage on personal property.
b. The coverage of dwellings and other structures.
c. Broad form only includes the loss of use coverage.
d. All of the above.
e. None of the above.

108. Which of the following statements is true?

a. Condominium units are covered under Form 02 or 03, depending on the extent of coverage desired.
b. HO15 special personal property only applies to condominium units.
c. HO6 is a special exposure coverage for a condominium owner.
d. The insurance that is purchased by a condominium owner covers the common areas as well as the unit.
e. HO4 covers the personal property of condominium owners.

109. Which of the following types of property is/are not eligible for a homeowners policy?

1. Unoccupied property.
2. Rental property.
3. Three and four family homes.
4. Vacation homes.

a. 3 only.
b. 4 only.
c. 1 and 4.
d. 2 and 3.
e. 1, 2, and 3.

110. Different types of personal property can be covered by a separate form of insurance or floater. Which of the following cannot be covered separately by endorsement?

a. Golf equipment.
b. Wedding presents.
c. Stamps and coin collections.
d. Musical instruments.
e. Pets.

111. The personal property floater:

a. Provides a broad form open peril coverage for all personal property owned, used, or worn by the insured.
b. Rarely has a deductible.
c. Is not useful to people who do not own their homes.
d. Is not subject to the same exclusions as personal property under a homeowners policy.
e. Covers only personal property that is not scheduled.

112. When fine arts or antiques are insured under a homeowners policy by an endorsement: **(CFP® Exam, released 3/95)**

    a. Coverage is usually on a replacement cost basis.
    b. Coverage is usually on an actual cash value basis.
    c. Coverage is usually provided on a valued basis.
    d. The perils are the same as the homeowners policy to which the endorsement is attached.
    e. Coverage limits are the same as the homeowners policy to which the endorsement is attached.

113. Joe who owns a condo, unit 4F, and is covered by a HO6 Homeowners policy, also owns a detached shed located on the condominium property where he stores his bicycle. The shed was destroyed by fire and Joe has contacted you to determine which of the following are correct:

    a. The shed is covered under the HO6 Section A (dwelling).
    b. The shed is covered under the HO6 Section B (other dwelling).
    c. The shed is not within the confines of the condominium and, therefore, not covered.
    d. The shed is covered under the condominium association blanket coverage, not the HO6.
    e. None of the above is correct.

114. Mary has a homeowner's policy HO2 with no endorsements and a $250 deductible. Mary's house was burglarized and several items were stolen as follows:

	Loss
Cash	$400
Coin collection	$500
Jewelry	$1,200
Fur coat	$800
Silverware	$1,400

How much does Mary collect from the insurance company?

    a. $2,350.
    b. $3,150.
    c. $3,350.
    d. $3,550.
    e. $4,050.

115. Kelly Spyhawk purchased $150,000 of coverage on her dwelling Feb. 2, 1998 under an HO3 policy. On August 3, 1999, her house caught fire, and she suffered damages of $60,000. The current replacement value of her dwelling is $180,000 exclusive of land. Her deductible is $250. How much will the insurer pay for this loss?

a. $49,583.

b. $50,000.

c. $59,750.

d. $60,000.

116. John owns a house that is worth $120,000. John has insured his home for $96,000. Last week, John's house was hit by a tornado causing $97,250 worth of damage. If John has a $250 deductible, how much will he have to pay to fully repair his house?

a. $0.

b. $250.

c. $450.

d. $1,250.

e. $1,500.

OTHER PERSONAL FORMS OF PROPERTY INSURANCE

117. The primary difference in the coverage under the monoline fire dwelling policy without endorsements and Section I of the homeowners policy is:
    a. The extension of coverage under the homeowners form.
    b. The theft coverage that is included under the homeowners form.
    c. The absence of a building law exclusion in the dwelling form.
    d. The more liberal definition of contents in the dwelling form.
    e. The broader coverage on the dwelling under the homeowners form.

118. The National Flood Insurance Program provides subsidized flood insurance for property owners in qualified areas. This program:
    a. Is mandatory for all people in the qualified areas.
    b. Provides coverage including inundations from broken or stopped up sewers.
    c. Is considered to be in force immediately if elected during the first 30 days in which the insurance is available to a community.
    d. Provides coverage for the personal property that is not inside the structure.
    e. Does not have a deductible.

119. Boats and trailers that are specifically insured, but limited to $1,000, and not covered for theft away from premises, may receive broader coverage under:
    a. The homeowners policy.
    b. A special form endorsement.
    c. A special form rider.
    d. An inland marine form.
    e. A liability policy.

LIABILITY INSURANCE FOR THE INDIVIDUAL

120. Liability insurance is primarily concerned with the financial consequences of :

a. Unintentional torts.
b. Intentional torts.
c. All torts.
d. Crimes.
e. None of the above.

121. Insurable liability risk is best defined as:

a. The risk that confronts every person or business resulting from intentional or unintentional behavior that could result in the injury of another person or damage to property.
b. The risk that confronts every person or business resulting from intentional behavior that could result in the injury of another person or damage to property.
c. The risk that confronts every person or business resulting from a public wrong.
d. The risk that confronts every person or business resulting from negligence.
e. None of the above.

122. Vicarious liability involves a situation where one person becomes legally liable for the negligence of another. Which of the following is not an example of a situation where vicarious liability can be claimed?

a. An agent/principal relationship.
b. An owner of an automobile that is involved in a negligent act where the non-owner driver had the permission of the owner.
c. A husband is liable for the torts of his wife.
d. An employer has an employee who does not have liability insurance and uses his personal car for business, and the car is involved in an accident resulting in an injury.
e. All of the above are examples of vicarious liability.

123. A property owner owes a high degree of care to prevent injury to anyone on his property. To which of the following does the property owner owe the highest degree of care?

   a. A licensee.
   b. An invitee.
   c. A trespasser.
   d. A child.
   e. The same degree of care is afforded to each of the above.

124. Certain people can be held legally liable for negligence. Which of the following cannot be held liable?

   a. Minors.
   b. Persons that are incapable of determining what is reasonable and prudent.
   c. Charitable institutions.
   d. Government employees.
   e. All of the above can be held liable for negligence.

125. A drunk driver killed Mr. Jones and severely injured his mistress. The court awarded the mistress $50 million in damages. These damages most likely represent:

   a. Punitive damages.
   b. Special damages.
   c. General damages.
   d. Loss of consortium damages.
   e. Loss of property damages.

126. Ms. Smith has a homeowners policy. Her dog bites the mailman while it is three streets away from her house. What is the consequence of this event?

   a. Ms. Smith needed a personal liability umbrella policy for coverage of this type of risk.
   b. There is no coverage under this policy because pets are excluded.
   c. Only medical payments coverage applies not liability coverage.
   d. The medical payments coverage is applicable, and liability coverage is applicable if Ms. Smith is held liable.

127. A personal umbrella policy always covers:

1. General liability.
2. Automobile liability.
3. Water craft liability.
4. Aircraft liability.

a. 1 only.
b. 1 and 2.
c. 1 and 3.
d. 1, 2, and 3.
e. 2, 3, and 4.

128. Under a umbrella liability policy, the definition of persons insured does not include:

a. A grandmother living in your house.
b. The daughter, age 13, of a friend who is living in your house while the friend is in Europe for 2 years.
c. Your gardener using your riding lawnmower in your yard.
d. Your neighbor who is taking care of the family dog while the family is away on vacation.
e. A guest in the house.

AUTOMOBILE INSURANCE

129. Which of the following is/are a type(s) of automobile insurance coverage?

    1. Uninsured motorists.
    2. Liability insurance.
    3. Medical payments.
    4. Property damage.

        a. 1 and 2.
        b. 2 and 4.
        c. 1, 2, and 3.
        d. 2, 3, and 4.
        e. 1, 2, 3, and 4.

130. Most automobile insurance companies use a classification system to determine premiums. Which of the following is/are factor(s) traditionally used in such a classification system?

    1. The location of the auto.
    2. The age of the driver.
    3. The sex of the driver.
    4. The marital status of the driver.

        a. 1 only.
        b. 1 and 2.
        c. 1, 2, and 4.
        d. 1, 2, and 3.
        e. 1, 2, 3, and 4.

131. Under most of the modified no-fault laws that have been enacted by the states:

    a. Only the funeral and medical expenses of the injured party are covered.
    b. Suits for pain and suffering are not allowed.
    c. There is total exemption from tort liability.
    d. A dollar threshold determines if a suit for pain and suffering is permitted.
    e. None of the above.

132. In the rating system for automobile coverage, which of the following receives the most favorable rating?
   a. Farm use.
   b. Pleasure use.
   c. Business use.
   d. Drive to work less than 15 miles.
   e. Drive to work more than 15 miles.

133. Which of the following types of automobile insurance coverage would apply if a bird hits your windshield?
   a. Comprehensive.
   b. Collision.
   c. Neither.
   d. Both.

134. Which of the following types of automobile insurance coverage would apply if you back into a tree in your front lawn?
   a. Comprehensive.
   b. Collision.
   c. Neither.
   d. Both.

135. Which of the following types of automobile insurance coverage would apply if an uninsured motorist hits you, but does not hurt you, and you have liability insurance only?
   a. Comprehensive.
   b. Collision.
   c. Neither.
   d. Both.

THE PERSONAL AUTO POLICY

136. For which of the following situations would the personal auto policy not provide coverage under the liability section?
    a. The named insured borrows a truck for use in his business.
    b. The named insured borrows a van for vacation.
    c. A resident relative borrows a truck to haul some sod to the house.
    d. A nonresident borrows the insured auto for a business trip.
    e. All of the above are covered.

137. The personal auto policy (PAP) is a package policy that provides protection against certain types of losses. Which is the best description of the losses protected against?
    a. Gross negligence, injury to other parties, and damage to auto.
    b. Gross negligence, injury to the insured family members, and damage to auto.
    c. Legal liability, injury to the insured or members of his family, and damage to or loss of auto.
    d. Legal liability, injury to the insured or other parties, and damage to or loss of auto.
    e. Gross negligence, legal liability, and damage to or loss of auto.

138. Andy has a PAP on his car and decided to purchase a pickup truck. The new truck is:
    a. Not covered under the PAP.
    b. Covered automatically for 30 days.
    c. Covered automatically for 30 days if the truck is a replacement for the car.
    d. Covered automatically until the end of the policy period.
    e. Covered automatically for 30 days provided the pickup meets the eligibility requirements of the policy.

139. Which of the following is not considered to be an eligible type of vehicle for a PAP?
    a. Motorcycles.
    b. Golf cart.
    c. Snowmobile.
    d. A pickup that has a gross weight in excess of 10,500 pounds.
    e. A van that has a gross weight of 9,000 pounds.

140. The PAP provides liability coverage for:

   a. All the automobiles owned by the insured.
   b. Non-owned snowmobiles, motorcycles and recreational vehicles.
   c. Anyone operating the owned auto.
   d. The employer of the named insured if such employer is sued because of the incidental operation of the covered auto by an insured person.
   e. All of the above.

141. When purchasing a PAP, which of the following coverages should be considered essential coverage?

   1. Liability coverage.
   2. Comprehensive and collision.
   3. Uninsured motorists.
   4. Medical payments.

   a. 1 only.
   b. 1 and 3.
   c. 1 and 4.
   d. 1, 2, and 4.
   e. 2, 3 and 4.

142. Under a PAP policy, exclusions exist for liability coverage. Which of the following is/are considered an exclusion?

   1. Damage to personal property while being transported by an insured.
   2. Injuries to employees who are covered by workman's compensation.
   3. Liability where the auto is being used for public conveyance.
   4. Intentional acts injury or damage.

   a. 4 only.
   b. 3 and 4.
   c. 1, 3, and 4.
   d. 1, 2, and 3.
   e. 1, 2, 3, and 4.

143. Comprehensive coverage pays for damage to the insured auto from all of the following except:

a. Flood.

b. Hail.

c. Collision with an animal.

d. Earthquake.

e. Collision with a tree.

144. David Knight and his son Jeff each own a car. Each is insured under their own PAP with the owner of the car named as the insured. David is borrowing Jeff's car while his is in the shop and Jeff is away on a business trip. If David is in an accident:

a. Jeff's policy will be the primary policy, and David's policy will apply on an excess basis.

b. There is no coverage under either policy.

c. Both policies will apply on a pro-rata basis.

d. David's policy will be the primary policy, and Jeff's policy will apply on an excess basis.

e. Only David's policy will apply.

145. The term "uninsured motorist" under the uninsured motorist coverage of a PAP does not include:

a. A car insured by a company that becomes insolvent.

b. A hit and run driver.

c. A car that is operated without liability insurance.

d. A vehicle owned by or furnished on a regular basis to the named insured.

e. None of the above.

INSURANCE PLANNING SOLUTIONS

INSURANCE PLANNING

1.	C	26.	C	51.	D	76.	C	101.	E	126.	D
2.	D	27.	B	52.	D	77.	E	102.	E	127.	B
3.	E	28.	C	53.	E	78.	E	103.	C	128.	E
4.	E	29.	B	54.	A	79.	C	104.	D	129.	E
5.	A	30.	C	55.	E	80.	E	105.	D	130.	E
6.	C	31.	B	56.	B	81.	B	106.	D	131.	D
7.	E	32.	B	57.	A	82.	D	107.	B	132.	A
8.	D	33.	D	58.	B	83.	C	108.	C	133.	A
9.	D	34.	E	59.	C	84.	E	109.	E	134.	B
10.	A	35.	C	60.	D	85.	B	110.	E	135.	C
11.	D	36.	A	61.	C	86.	D	111.	A	136.	A
12.	C	37.	D	62.	C	87.	A	112.	C	137.	C
13.	B	38.	D	63.	C	88.	C	113.	A	138.	E
14.	E	39.	D	64.	B	89.	D	114.	A	139.	D
15.	A	40.	A	65.	A	90.	B	115.	C	140.	D
16.	D	41.	D	66.	D	91.	D	116.	D	141.	A
17.	B	42.	C	67.	C	92.	E	117.	B	142.	E
18.	B	43.	C	68.	C	93.	E	118.	C	143.	E
19.	C	44.	C	69.	A	94.	A	119.	D	144.	A
20.	C	45.	C	70.	B	95.	B	120.	A	145.	D
21.	D	46.	C	71.	B	96.	A	121.	D		
22.	D	47.	D	72.	B	97.	E	122.	C		
23.	E	48.	B	73.	B	98.	D	123.	D		
24.	D	49.	A	74.	E	99.	C	124.	E		
25.	E	50.	D	75.	C	100.	D	125.	A		

INTRODUCTION TO INSURANCE

Insurance (CFP® Exam, released 3/95)

1. **C**

This is the definition of a hazard (a condition which increases the likelihood (probability) or severity of a loss) usually distinguished from peril (cause of loss) and risk (expected variability of outcomes).

Insurance

2. **D**

This is the definition of insurance. The alternative definition of insurance is the transfer of risk. Pure risk involves the chance of loss or no loss.

Classifications of Risk

3. **E**

Statement #3 is incorrect. Speculative risk involves the chance of loss or gain.

Classification of Risk

4. **E**

All are pure risk.

Risk Management

5. **A**

Risk management includes a cost/benefit analysis. Cost/benefit analysis equals choosing efficiently.

Risk

6. **C**

Statement #2 is incorrect because risk is uncertainty.

Managing Risk

7. E

All are correct.

Insurable Risk

8. D

Losses need to be measurable and definite as to time, place, form and must be monetarily measurable. Losses also must be accidental in order to be considered insurable. The risk of loss must be uncertain, the loss certain.

Risk Distinguished from Peril, Hazard, Loss

9. D

Statement #2 is incorrect. Risk is the chance of loss. Peril is the cause of financial loss. Hazard is the condition that increases the probability that a peril will occur.

THE LEGAL NATURE OF INSURANCE

Homeowners Insurance

10. A

Homeowners insurance is a personal contract. The insured always has the right to assign property insurance to another without agreement by the insurance company. (**Note:** Pay close attention to the word "not" where it appears in a question.) A life insurance policy may be assigned without agreement. The benefits but not the coverage can be assigned for any insurance policy unless precluded under law or by contact.

Defenses

11. D

Gross negligence is not a defense to a negligence claim. All of the others are defenses although all may not be available in each jurisdiction.

Liability Insurance

12. C

An injured party's claim is against the negligent insured. The insured has a contract with the insurance company for the insurance company to pay the injured party for the insured, subject to the limits and conditions of the insurance contract.

Insurance (CFP® Exam, released 3/95)

13. B

Statements #2 and #3 cannot simultaneously exist. Therefore, only an answer without statements #2 and #3 in it can be correct. The issue is definitional. Statements #1 and #3 are correct, thus B is the answer.

Insurance (CFP® Exam, released 3/95)

14. E

Any contract for life insurance has each of the 4 characteristics.

Agency-Apparent Authority

15. A

The insurance company is bound by the acts of the agent because the insurance company had knowledge of the agent's actions and failed to act.

Insurance as a Contract

16. D

An insurance contract is unilateral because only the insurer promised to do anything. In a bilateral contract, both parties have made a promise to each other to do something. The insured has no duty to pay the premium.

Insurance as a Contract

17. B

Statement A is incorrect because an oral contract of insurance may be binding. However, most state insurance commissions require insurance contracts to be written. Statement C is a defense to negligence. Insurer is not bound without payment or consideration.

LIFE INSURANCE IN GENERAL

Life Insurance

18. B

The 2-year suicide clause will prevent the payment of the face amount of the policy. However, the premiums paid through the date of the suicide will usually be returned or repaid without interest. 14 months x $200 = $2,800.

Insurance Misrepresentation

19. C

The insurance company will adjust the face amount of the policy to reflect the amount of insurance that could have been purchased for the correct age with the premiums that were already paid.

Total premium paid annually (15 x 20)	$300	
Premium per $1,000 of insurance for insured (age 40)	$25	
Face Amount of Policy (adjusted for correct age)	$12,000	[($300 ÷ $25) x $1,000]

Or: 15/25 x $20,000 = $12,000

Life Insurance Grace Period

20. C

The purpose of the grace period is to allow the insurance policy to remain in effect even though the premium payments are in arrears by up to 30 days.

Life Insurance-Beneficiary Designations

21. D

Under an irrevocable beneficiary arrangement, the owner remains the owner. However, the beneficiary obtains a legal interest in the insurance contract, and the owner will be unable to change the owner or beneficiary without the express consent of the current beneficiary.

Insurance (CFP® Exam, released 3/95)

22. **D**

With reference to characteristics of life insurance, statement #1 is incorrect. Thus, A, B, & E are eliminated. Statement #4 is correct, so the issue is to read statement #2. Assignment of life insurance policy does not require insurability.

Insurance - Insurance v. Modified Endowment Contracts

23. **E**

All of the statements are correct.

Insurance

24. **D**

Statement #3 is not an option.

TYPES OF LIFE INSURANCE

Life Insurance and Employee Benefits

25. **E**

Group life is generally less expensive than individual life policies for all of the reasons cited.

Life Insurance

26. **C**

Both a pure endowment life insurance policy and a term life insurance policy provide for payment for death within a specified period. In the case of a pure endowment policy, the insured must outlive the endowment period for the beneficiary to collect. In the case of term insurance, the insured must die before the term expires for the beneficiary to collect. The other two options ordinary life and limited pay life stay in force as long as premiums are paid in a timely manner.

Life Insurance

27. **B**

Whole life policies have level premiums for life. The premiums will be greater than the true cost of term insurance during the early years of the policy and will be less than the term cost of insurance during the later years. The cash value represents the amount of the premiums in excess of the true cost of insurance. The cash value will grow over time by way of contributions and earnings.

Life Insurance

28. **C**

Dividends are paid to holders of participating policies that have a lower cost of insurance than the amount of the premiums paid. This surplus is effectively a partial return of the premiums paid.

Life Insurance

29. **B**

The modified whole life policy is designed for individuals, such as college students, who want permanent insurance currently, yet are unable to afford the high premiums. This type of policy has a period of 3 to 5 years in which the premiums are lower. After this period, the premiums increase significantly (which should match an increase in the insured's income).

Life Insurance

30. C

A recent college graduate with dependents will likely have high costs within the first 3 to 5 years. After this period, it is likely that income levels will have increased significantly, enabling him or her to afford more insurance than currently possible. Therefore, the best policy is the modified whole life policy because its premium payment schedule matches the graduate's ability to pay.

Life Insurance

31. B

Variable life insurance is the only type of policy that invests in equity securities. In fact, the SEC treats variable life as a security which must be registered under the Securities Act of 1933, and agents selling these policies must be registered as broker-dealers under the Securities and Exchange Act of 1934. Adjustable life and universal life do not invest in equities. Equity life is not a type of insurance.

Life Insurance

32. B

If there is a need for permanent insurance, then purchase convertible term. Convertible term allows for exchange of the policy for a permanent life policy without evidence of insurability.

Life Insurance Types

33. D

There is no such thing as cash value term insurance.

Universal Life

34. E

All of the items listed should be considered.

Employee Benefits

35. C

The payments are deductible to the employer and not includible to the employee up to the $50,000 death benefit of the group term life insurance.

Group Life Insurance

36. **A**

Group term life insurance premiums are deductible by the employer and excludable from income by the employee (up to $50,000) of death benefit. Group term provided by an employer in excess of $50,000 causes W-2 inclusion to the employee utilizing the Section 79 Schedule.

Insurance (CFP® Exam, released 3/95)

37. **D**

A is incorrect. Modified endowment policies have nothing to do with age. D is correct because an annuity creates a series of substantially equal payments.

Life Insurance

38. **D**

Pure endowment pays off only upon survival of the endowment period and then in the form of an annuity.

Insurance - Premium Ranking (CFP® Exam, released 12/95)

39. **D**

Analysis indicates that policy 4 will likely have the largest increase due to its projection being the greatest insurance over the T-bond yield. The interest sensitive policy is funded at full target premium, making it the least risky for premium increases. Universal life has a flexible premium, thus, if premiums are not paid there is great risk of premium increases.

BUSINESS USES OF LIFE INSURANCE

Life Insurance Uses

40. A

It will be the same total amount as a cross-purchase plan.

Types of Life Insurance

41. D

Split-dollar is generally a situation where the employer is the owner and will be repaid the premiums outlayed for the insurance.

Business Application of Life Insurance

42. C

Under key person insurance, the beneficiary is usually the employer because the employer has suffered the loss.

Business Application of Life Insurance

43. C

This is a classic cross-purchase life insurance plan $1,200,000 ÷ 4 = $300,000 per partner $100,000 x 3 = $300,000.

Buy/Sell Agreements

44. C

Four at the entity level, one for each partner.

TAX TREATMENT OF LIFE INSURANCE AND ANNUITIES

Insurance Taxation

45. C

Surrender proceeds in excess of premiums paid are taxable.

Insurance Taxation

46. C

Any amounts received above or equal to the face amount of $200,000 will be taxable to Tom.

$23,500
x 10 years
$235,000
(200,000)
$35,000 ÷ **10 = $3,500 per year**

Annuities

47. D

Options A, B, C, and E are incorrect and contrary to the scheme provided in the Code for the taxation of annuities. If Vicki dies after collecting only 50 payments (before she has recovered all of her capital), a loss can be claimed on her final return as a miscellaneous itemized deduction not subject to the 2% hurdle.

Annuities

48. B

$24,000 ÷ 144,000 = .1666 or 1/6 exclusion ratio or fraction x $1,200 = $200 (exclusion amount).
Therefore, 120 ÷ 144 = .8333 or 5/6 inclusion ratio x $1,200 = $1,000 (inclusion amount).
In 1999, June to December = 7 months x $200 (exclusion amount) = $1,400.
B is the only possible correct answer for 1999.
Year 2000 (12 parts x $1,200) x 1/6 = $2,400.
Year 2001 (12 parts x $1,200) x 1/6 = $2,400.

Insurance

49. A

If surrendered, a viatical policy does not cause taxable income.

Life Insurance

50. D

Expected proceeds over life = $15,000 x 20 years = $300,000.

Inclusion ratio = (Proceeds - Basis) ÷ Expected: ($300,000 - 120,000) ÷ $300,000 = 60%.

Exclusion ratio = Basis ÷ Expected Proceeds: $120,000 ÷ 300,000 = 40%.

Current year payment: $15,000 x 60% for inclusion = $9,000.

$15,000 x 40% for exclusion = $6,000.

CALCULATING LIFE INSURANCE AMOUNTS (NEEDS ANALYSIS)

Life Insurance Needs Analysis

51. D

First determine insurance needs.

Life Insurance Needs Analysis

52. D

The value of the life lost is not considered. Rather, the focus is on the needs of the surviving dependents.

Life Insurance Needs Analysis

53. E

The blackout period is after the children have reached age 16 and before the surviving spouse is eligible for social security retirement benefits.

Life Insurance Needs Analysis

54. A

Needs analysis does not assume that there will be no changes once a program has been designed. A child may have been forecasted to go to a state university and it is determined sometime later that the same child wants to go to a private university and then to medical school which would be more expensive.

Life Insurance Needs Analysis

55. E

Funds to cover all of the needs (statements #1-4) should be considered.

Life Insurance Needs Analysis

56. B

Needs analysis programming does not provide for total protection from loss of income.

Life Insurance Needs Analysis

57. A

Andrew's current needs for life insurance is $0 because he has no dependents.

Insurance (CFP® Exam, released 3/95)

58. B

This question asks what information is not needed to calculate the value of a life. Clearly you need A, C, D, and E. Social Security benefits are not earned; they are an entitlement.

LIFE INSURANCE AND ESTATE AND GIFT PLANNING (INCLUDING GSTT)

Life Insurance

59. C

The life insurance proceeds would be a gift to Lexie. The donor of a gift is liable for the gift tax. At the death of Connie, Glennon owned the policy and could have named himself the beneficiary. In effect, he gave the insurance proceeds to Lexie.

Life Insurance (CFP® Exam, released 3/95)

60. D

Insurance policies transferred within 3 years of death are included in the gross estate - referred to as the throwback rule.

CHOOSING LIFE INSURANCE COMPANIES

Life Insurance Selection

61. C

The first three statements are important (statements #1-3). The fourth probably will change before any claim is submitted. Claims also tend to bunch, making claim turnaround time dependent upon the number and nature of the claims submitted at any point in time.

DISABILITY INSURANCE

Disability

62. C

The chance of disability is significantly greater than the chance of premature death. For example, about 1 out of 3 people who reach age 35 will be disabled for a period of at least 3 months before reaching age 65. The probability of premature death is much lower.

Disability

63. C

Disability insurance is sold on a group or individual basis. It is at least as important as life insurance (probably more so because the likelihood of a disability event occurring is much greater than the likelihood of premature death for most groups). Disability insurance should be purchased with a waiting period that is short enough so as not to put a financial strain on the insured. Own Occupation Disability insurance will provide the most protection for a specialized worker. Life insurance coverage is not a requirement for disability insurance.

Disability

64. B

If the elimination period is 15 days, Joe will only have received half (15/30) of the monthly benefit. Disability policies do not have a deductible.

Disability

65. A

The first three statements (statements #1-3) are false. Shorter elimination periods raise premiums or lower benefits. Sickness causes many more disabilities than accidents. Social security disability benefits, in addition to being difficult to qualify for, are usually an offset to benefits from a group or private plan. Statement #4 is the only one that is correct because medical expenses during disability may be catastrophic.

Disability

66. D

The one need in disability programming most often overlooked is the need to complete a retirement program.

Insurance

67. C

Statements #1 and #4 are correct.

HEALTH INSURANCE FOR MEDICAL EXPENSES

Health Insurance

68. **C**

A non-cancelable health insurance policy is a continuous term contract guaranteeing the right to renew for a specified period of time with the premium at renewal guaranteed. If the premium was not guaranteed, then the insurance company would be able to raise the premium beyond affordability. Guaranteed renewable contracts allow for automatic renewal, but permit the insurance company to raise the premium for an entire class of insureds.

Health Insurance

69. **A**

The four major classes of medical insurance are hospital, surgical, physician, and major medical.

Health Insurance

70. **B**

Physician's services will often be written into hospitalization or surgical expense coverages, but is not always included into hospitalization coverage.

Health Co-Insurance

71. **B**

Loss	$10,750
Deductible	(500)
	$10,250
Less 20%	(2,050)
Insurance Benefit	$8,200

Health Insurance

72. **B**

Major medical policies are designed to cover very large medical expenses that would otherwise be financially devastating to an individual. Generally, these policies have very high coverage or loss limits.

Policy Limits

73. **B**

The coordination of benefits provision is specifically designed to eliminate double payment of benefits for the same incident.

COBRA

74. **E**

Statements #1, #2, #3, and #4 would apply.

COBRA

75. **C**

Statements #1, #2, and #3 would apply. Termination resulting from gross misconduct will not qualify for COBRA.

COBRA

76. **C**

B and D apply to other COBRA situations. A is incorrect because COBRA rules do apply.

COBRA

77. **E**

Statements #1, #2, #3, and #4 are correct. All of these persons qualify for COBRA coverage.

COBRA

78. **E**

Statements #1, #2, #3, and #4 are correct. All of these persons qualify for COBRA coverage.

COBRA

79. **C**

A is incorrect since it is 20 employees, not 15.

B is incorrect, it is 102%, not 103%.

C is correct.

D is incorrect, the beneficiary has an option to pay the premiums monthly.

COBRA

80. E

All are covered if included in the group health plan.

THE OLD-AGE, SURVIVORS, DISABILITY AND HEALTH INSURANCE PROGRAM (OASDHI)

Social Security

81. **B**

Railroad workers with 10 years of service are entitled to benefits from the Railroad Retirement Board. They are not covered by Social Security.

Social Security

82. **D**

Employee and employer payroll tax and self-employment tax are the sources of funding for social security. Sales tax does not fund Social Security.

Social Security

83. **C**

A lump sum death benefit of $255 is payable to the surviving spouse or children of the deceased worker if he was fully or currently insured. The children's benefit is payable because Glen was either currently or fully insured. It is 75% of his PIA. The children's mother would be entitled to a benefit for caring for the children. His mother is only entitled to a benefit if he was fully insured.

Medicare

84. **E**

Medicare Part A covers individuals meeting all of these characteristics.

Medicare

85. **B**

Only statement #2 is correct. Statement #1 is incorrect because participation can occur after the initial eligibility. Participation is not required to be maintained for life, and Part B does have deductibles and/or coinsurance.

Social Security Benefits

86. D

Gambling winnings are not an exempt type of income. All the others are not considered earned income for social security purposes.

Social Security Benefits

87. A

Conviction of fraud is the only one of the four that cannot be considered grounds for disqualification.

Insurance (CFP® Exam, released 3/95)

88. C

Medicare covers all costs for the first 20 days for nursing home; so, statement #1 is incorrect. This leaves C and D. Statement #4 is true as is statement #2; therefore, C is the correct answer.

OTHER COMPULSORY SOCIAL INSURANCE

Worker's Compensation

89. D

All except statement #2 are correct. Worker's compensation is paid through insurance premiums paid by the employer.

Worker's Compensation

90. B

Workers' compensation does not cover all occupations. Workers' compensation does not cover deliberately self-inflicted injuries and is not mandatory in all states.

Worker's Compensation

91. D

Losing an arm is an example of a permanent partial disability.

Worker's Compensation

92. E

All listed are benefits acceptable under worker's compensation. In addition, there are four categories of disability benefits: partial temporary, total temporary, partial permanent, and total permanent.

Unemployment Compensation

93. E

All four of the statements are false. Unemployment compensation is taxable in lieu of wages. A person receiving unemployment benefits must be available for work. The weekly compensation for unemployment ranges from 50% to about 80% of normal full-time compensation and is state dependent.

HOMEOWNERS INSURANCE -GENERAL PROVISIONS

Homeowners Insurance

94. A

The only one to be included is materials to be used to alter the dwelling (e.g., construction materials for renovation).

Homeowners Insurance

95. B

HO3 is an "All risks of physical loss" policy but the general exclusions in all HO policies include earth movement (earthquake) and flood.

Homeowners Insurance (CFP® Exam, released 3/95)

96. A

Options B through E are open perils covered by HO3. Flood is excluded as a general exclusion under Section 1 of all Homeowners forms.

PERILS

Homeowners Insurance

97. **E**

The principal differences between forms are the properties covered and the perils insured against in Section 1 of the form.

Homeowners Insurance

98. **D**

Open peril coverage covers all perils except those specifically excluded. The named perils coverage covers only those specific perils which were enumerated.

Homeowners Insurance

99. **C**

A coinsurance clause 80%/20%.

Homeowners Insurance

100. **D**

Flood is never a named peril except in a flood insurance policy.

Homeowners Insurance

101. **E**

Borrowed property from a friend is considered personal property. The other items are excluded without special endorsements.

Homeowners Insurance

102. **E**

All mentioned have dollar limits: watercraft $1,000, cash $200, jewelry $1,000, and guns $2,000.

Homeowners Insurance

103. C

Damage from a mudslide is not covered by endorsement.

Homeowners Insurance

104. D

$18,750 less the deductible. Edward does not meet the co-insurance requirements so the insurer will pay as follows:

$$\frac{\text{Did carry}}{\text{Should have carried}} \quad \frac{\$150,000}{\$200,000 \times .80} = \frac{\$150,000}{\$160,000} = 93.75\%$$

The loss is $20,000, the value is replacement value.

Insurer pays 93.75% of each loss.

Edward pays 6.25% of each loss.

$20,000 x .9375 = $18,750 (less the deductible)

Homeowners Insurance

105. D

The watch is considered jewelry and limited to $1,000. All are subject to the deductible. Cash is subject to a $200 limitation.

Homeowners Insurance

106. D

Earth movement is excluded from all standard homeowners forms as a general exclusion. Homeowners need to read exclusions with exceptions to exclusions. There are both general and other exclusions.

Homeowners Insurance

107. B

The principal difference between the special form open perils and the broad form listed perils is on the coverage of dwellings and other structures.

Homeowners Insurance

108. **C**

HO6 is coverage for condominium owners.

Homeowners Insurance

109. **E**

The first three (statements #1-3) are not eligible for a homeowners policy but may be covered under some other insurance policy. Vacation homes not used primarily for rental may be covered under a homeowners policy.

Floater Policies

110. **E**

Pets cannot be covered under a floater policy. All of the others can.

Personal Property Floater Policies

111. **A**

A personal property floater policy provides a broad form open peril coverage for all personal property used or worn by the insured. It has a deductible and is useful to renters. The exclusions are the same as the exclusions under HO15.

Insurance (CFP® Exam, released 3/95)

112. **C**

A predetermined value is placed on such objects. If loss is total, the insurance company pays the face value of the policy (predetermined). This is contrasted to usual cash value or replacement cost coverage. D and E are not correct with respect to endorsements.

Homeowners Policies Coverage

113. **A**

Because there is no dwelling coverage under an HO6, other structures (shed) are covered under Section A.

Homeowner's Coverage Special Limits

114. A

	Amount paid by Insurer
Cash	$200 (limit)
Coin collection	$0 (Money and coins limited to $200)
Jewelry	$1,000 (limit)
Fur coat	$0 (furs and jewelry same limit)
Silverware	$1,400 ($2,500 limit)

($200 + 1,000 + 1,400 - 250 = $2,350)

Co-Insurance

115. C

Kelly meets the 80/20 co-insurance clause.

$$\frac{\$150{,}000}{\$180{,}000} = 83.33\%$$

Therefore, the insurer will pay $60,000 less the $250 deductible.

Co-Insurance

116. D

80% x $120,000 = $96,000.

Insurer pays 100% of loss, less deductible [$97,250 - 250 = $97,000], up to the insured amount of policy [$96,000]. Therefore, John pays $97,250 - 96,000 = $1,250.

If the amount of damage had been less than $96,000 then the insurance company would have deducted the $250 and paid the rest. Since the damage is above the coverage amount, the insurance company pays the loss minus the deductible up to the insured amount.

OTHER PERSONAL FORMS OF PROPERTY INSURANCE

Homeowners Insurance

117. B

Theft coverage under a monoline dwelling policy is by endorsement only.

Flood Insurance

118. C

This program is immediately available if elected during the first 30 days available, otherwise there is a 5-day waiting period.

Other Insurance

119. D

An inland marine form.

LIABILITY INSURANCE FOR THE INDIVIDUAL

Liability Insurance

120. A

Liability insurance is primarily concerned with negligence and unintentional torts.

Liability Insurance

121. D

That risk resulting from negligence (carelessness).

Liability Insurance

122. C

A husband is not vicariously liable for the torts of his wife. The employer maybe held vicariously liable for the acts of an employee if the employee is in the course and scope of his employment.

Liability Insurance

123. D

It is well accepted that a child may not always act prudently. Therefore, a property owner must exercise a higher degree of care with regard to a child than he normally would (e.g., fence around swimming pool).

Liability Insurance

124. E

All of those listed can be held liable for negligence.

Liability Insurance

125. A

Because of the size of the award, these most likely represent punitive damages.

Liability Insurance

126. D

The location where the dog bites the mailman is probably irrelevant. Medical payments and liability are applicable if Ms. Smith is held to be liable for negligence. In some states there is strict liability for the damage caused by pet. In other states, the theory is that the first bite is free (sometimes called the "one bite" rule).

Personal Umbrella Policy

127. B

The question asks what is always covered - the answer is general liability and automobile. Such coverage may or may not be extended to watercraft.

Personal Umbrella Policy

128. E

A guest in the house. You are not liable for the acts of the guest.

AUTOMOBILE INSURANCE

Automobile Insurance

129. **E**

All are types of automobile coverage that can be purchased.

Automobile Insurance

130. **E**

All of the factors are used in such classification systems.

Automobile Insurance

131. **D**

Suits under a certain threshold are not permitted.

Automobile Insurance

132. **A**

Farm use received the most favorable rating because it is generally off road.

Comprehensive

133. **A**

Comprehensive (other than collision) covers live animals striking your vehicle.

Collision

134. **B**

Collision covers your car striking a fixed, inanimate object.

Liability

135. **C**

Neither comprehensive nor collision would cover this because you had liability coverage only.

THE PERSONAL AUTO POLICY

Automobile Insurance

136. A

There is an exclusion for vehicles operated by the insured while engaging in business.

Automobile Insurance

137. C

The most comprehensive is C, includes members of the insured's family, and includes largest liability.

Automobile Insurance

138. E

Must meet requirements; coverage is automatic for 30 days.

Automobile Insurance

139. D

A pickup in excess of 10,500 pounds is not an eligible vehicle for a PAP.

Automobile Insurance

140. D

Only the employer for vicarious liability.

Automobile Insurance

141. A

Liability only is essential.

Automobile Insurance

142. E

All are exclusions.

Automobile Insurance

143. E

Upset would be covered by collision.

Automobile Insurance

144. A

The policy on the auto involved in the accident is the primary coverage.

Automobile Insurance

145. D

Vehicle owned or furnished on a regular basis to the named insured is excluded.

INVESTMENT PLANNING PROBLEMS

INVESTMENT PLANNING

BASIC INVESTMENT CONCEPTS

1. Which of the following statements about risk are true?

    1. Systematic risk can be diversified away.
    2. Unsystematic risk plus systematic risk equals total risk.
    3. It is not possible for systematic risk to equal total risk.

    a. 1 only.
    b. 2 only.
    c. 1 and 2.
    d. 2 and 3.
    e. 1, 2, and 3.

2. Bobby has the following securities in his portfolio:

    ABC common stock
    XYZ common stock
    PQR mutual fund (Small cap)
    DEZ mutual fund (foreign small cap stocks)
    30-year treasury bond
    5-year treasury note

    With which of the following risks does Bobby <u>not</u> have to be concerned?

    a. Financial risk.
    b. Default risk.
    c. Reinvestment rate risk.
    d. Systematic risk.
    e. He must be concerned with all of the above risks.

3. Debt to Equity Ratios for companies are considered what type of risk?

    a. Systematic risk.
    b. Business.
    c. Market.
    d. Financial.
    e. B and D.

4. A mutual fund that invests in U.S. companies, foreign companies, U.S. corporate bonds, and U.S. Treasury bonds is not subject to which of the following risks?

   a. Business risk.
   b. Default risk.
   c. Systematic risk.
   d. Interest rate risk.
   e. All of the above are risks to which the Mutual Fund would be subject.

5. Which of the following statements about risk is true?

   1. Undiversifiable risk is termed unsystematic risk.
   2. Systematic risk includes business, financial, and purchasing power risk.
   3. Default risk affects both equity and fixed investments.

   a. 1 only.
   b. 2 only.
   c. 1 and 2.
   d. 1, 2, and 3.
   e. None of the above.

6. Business risk would include which of the following?

   1. Inflation.
   2. Fire.
   3. High debt to equity ratio.
   4. Recession.

   a. 1 only.
   b. 2 only.
   c. 1 and 3.
   d. 1 and 4.
   e. 1, 2, and 4.

7. Candi purchases a 30-year zero coupon bond. The bond was issued by Du Pont, one of the Fortune 500 companies. Which of the following risks might Candi be subject to?

   1. Default Risk.
   2. Reinvestment Rate Risk.
   3. Purchasing Power Risk.
   4. Liquidity Risk.

      a. 1 and 3.
      b. 2 and 3.
      c. 1, 2, and 3.
      d. 1, 3, and 4.
      e. 1, 2, 3 and 4.

8. To which of the following risks might a fixed income security be subject?

   1. Purchasing Power Risk.
   2. Liquidity Risk.
   3. Exchange Rate Risk.
   4. Reinvestment Rate Risk.
   5. Default Risk.
   6. Short Squeeze Risk.

      a. 1 through 6.
      b. 1 through 5.
      c. 2 through 5.
      d. 2 through 6.
      e. 1, 2, 4, and 5.

9. Should an investor who purchased a bond five years ago yielding 8%, with a coupon of 8%, sell or hold the bond if he is trying to maximize the yield to maturity for the 30 year period? Assume at the end of the first five years the prevailing interest rate drops from 8% to 7% and remains at 7% for the next 25 years. Also assume that the interest rate is 8% from purchase to the five-year period.
   a. He should sell the bond because the value of the bond with an 8% coupon will increase by over 10%.
   b. He should hold the bond because he will yield 8% over the life of the bond, whereas if he sells the bond he will have to invest the proceeds at 7%.
   c. He should sell the bond for $1,116.54 and invest the proceeds at 7% for the remaining 25 years because the weighted average yield will be equal to 7.77%
   d. Neither holding nor selling will yield a higher resulting yield to maturity.
   e. None of the above are true.

10. Which of the following are non-diversifiable risks? **(CFP® Exam, released 3/95)**
    1. Business risk.
    2. Management risk.
    3. Company or industry risk.
    4. Market risk.
    5. Interest rate risk.
    6. Purchasing power risk.
       a. 4, 5, and 6.
       b. 1, 2, and 3.
       c. 5, 6, and 2.
       d. 1, 3, and 4.
       e. 1, 4, and 6.

11. Investors seek out tax-advantaged investments to accomplish which of the following?
    1. Reduce risk.
    2. Avoid taxes.
    3. Build equity.
    4. Defer tax liability.
       a. 2 only.
       b. 1 and 3.
       c. 2 and 4.
       d. 2, 3, and 4.
       e. 1, 2, 3, and 4.

12. Which combination of the following statements about investment risk is correct? **(CFP® Exam, released 12/95)**

    1. Beta is a measure of systematic, non-diversifiable risk.
    2. Rational investors will form portfolios and eliminate systematic risk.
    3. Rational investors will form portfolios and eliminate unsystematic risk.
    4. Systematic risk is the relevant risk for a well-diversified portfolio.
    5. Beta captures all the risk inherent in an individual security.

        a. 1, 2, and 5.
        b. 1, 3, and 4.
        c. 2 and 5.
        d. 2, 3, and 4.
        e. 2 and 5.

Note: Choices C and E are the same. These were the choices printed by the CFP® Board in 12/95. No changes were made to any of the questions released by the CFP® Board.

SECURITIES (TYPES & CHARACTERISTICS)

13. Which of the following is the least risky investment transaction?
    a. Selling an uncovered call.
    b. Buying a call.
    c. Selling an uncovered put.
    d. Shorting a stock.
    e. Short against the box.

14. Which of the following is the most risky investment transaction?
    a. Selling a naked option.
    b. Short against the box.
    c. Sell a covered call.
    d. Buy a put option.
    e. Buy a call option.

15. John sells a call option for a $3 premium. The call has an exercise price of $20. Which of the following is true?
    a. John's loss is limited to $20.
    b. John hopes the price will go up.
    c. The call will most likely not be exercised while the stock is trading at $23.
    d. John's maximum gain is $3.
    e. The option will most likely not be exercised until the price is $17.

16. Dave sells a call for $3. The exercise price is $42. Which of the following is not true?
    a. The call will likely be exercised at a stock price of anything greater than $42.
    b. The buyer of the call option will not exercise at a price of $44 because he would lose $1 ($44 - $42 - $3 = -$1).
    c. Dave can theoretically lose an infinite amount.
    d. The net profit will be zero if the call is exercised when the stock price is $45.
    e. The most Dave can make is the premium of $3.

17. Assume a put and call each sell for a $4 premium and each is exercisable at $54. Which of the following is true if the stock price at expiration is $50?
    1. The call would be exercised but the net profit would equal zero.
    2. Purchasing both the put and call would result in a net loss of $8.
    3. The seller of the call should make a profit at $4.
    4. The seller of the put should make a profit of $4.
        a. 1 only.
        b. 3 only.
        c. 1 and 2.
        d. 2 and 3.
        e. 2, 3, and 4.

18. If Dave buys a put option for $3 with an exercise price of $32 and a call option for $6 and an exercise price of $42 for the same time and for the same stock, which of the following are true?
    1. The largest loss Dave can sustain is $9.
    2. At a market price of $31 Dave will lose $2.
    3. At a market price of $45 Dave will lose $6.
        a. 1 only.
        b. 2 only.
        c. 3 only.
        d. 1 and 3.
        e. 2 and 3.

19. Mary buys a put option for $3 with an exercise price of $32 and a call option for $6 with an exercise price of $42, for ABC stock. Both options expire in December. At what stock price(s) will Mary break even?
        a. $23.
        b. $32.
        c. $42.
        d. $51.
        e. A and D.

20. Robin wishes to short GM. She places a market order to short sell 100 shares of GM just after it has traded previously at 46 and then at 45. GM 's subsequently trades at 45, 44, 43½, 44½, 44, 45 and 43. If Robin later buys 100 shares of GM at $40, what will her profit be?

    a. $300.
    b. $350.
    c. $400.
    d. $450.
    e. $500.

21. Lisa short sells 100 shares of XYZ at $35. She then buys back the stock for $2,000. XYZ pays a dividend of $2.00 per share before she buys the stock back. What is her net profit or loss?

    a. $1,300 loss.
    b. $1,500 loss.
    c. $1,300 profit.
    d. $1,500 profit.
    e. $1,600 profit.

22. Angel short sells 100 shares of XYZ at $57 with a 50% initial margin. XYZ pays a dividend of $2.00 per share after she sells the stock. She then buys back the stock for $54. What is the percent profit or loss?

    a. 1.8%.
    b. 3.5%.
    c. 5.3%.
    d. 7.0%.
    e. 10.5%.

23. Amanda buys 75 shares of BR Enterprise stock for $67 per share on margin. The initial margin is 55% and there is a maintenance margin of 40%. If she sells the stock for $78 per share what is her return?

    a. 16%.
    b. 23%.
    c. 30%.
    d. 36%.
    e. 41%.

24. Amy buys 75 shares of BR Enterprise stock for $67 per share on margin. The initial margin is 55%, and there is a maintenance margin of 40%. At what market price will Amanda receive a margin call?

    a. $21.54.
    b. $26.80.
    c. $33.00.
    d. $50.25.
    e. $56.95.

25. Which of the following is/are not a variable in determining the price for a call option under the Black-Scholes Option Valuation Model?

    1. Price of the underlying security.
    2. Inflation rate.
    3. Standard deviation of returns (expected volatility).
    4. Option exercise price.

    a. 2 only.
    b. 3 only.
    c. 4 only.
    d. 1 and 2.
    e. 2, 3, and 4.

26. Which of the following is/are not a variable in determining the price for a call option under the Black-Scholes Option Valuation Model?

    1. Time to expiration.
    2. Risk free interest rate.
    3. Exercise price of the option.

    a. 1 only.
    b. 2 only.
    c. 3 only.
    d. 1 and 2.
    e. All of the above are elements of the Black-Scholes Option Valuation Model.

27. A bond with a coupon rate of 8% and a YTM of 10% is considered to be which of the following?

    a. At-the-money.
    b. In-the-money.
    c. By-the-money.
    d. Out-of-the-money.
    e. None of the above.

28. Black-Scholes valuation model is used to determine the price of which of the following.
    a. Call options.
    b. Put options.
    c. Forward contracts.
    d. Commodity prices.
    e. A and B.

29. Baylor stock is currently selling for $63/share. A call option for this security has an exercise price of $65/share and can be purchased for $4/share. The option expires in 3 months. Which of the following below best describes the option.
    a. In-the-money.
    b. At-the-money.
    c. Out-of-the-money.
    d. By-the-money.
    e. These phases do not apply to options.

30. Baylor stock is currently selling for $63/share. A put option for this security that has an exercise price of $65/share can be purchased for $4/share. The option expires in 3 months. Which of the following below best describes the option.
    a. In-the-money.
    b. At-the-money.
    c. Out-of-the-money.
    d. By-the-money.
    e. These phases do not apply to options.

31. Using the information in the table below, determine which call options (numbered 1 through 9) are In-the-money, At-the-Money, and Out-of-the-Money (assume it is January).

		Premium for each call option		
Market Price	Exercise Price	April	July	October
$53	$50	1. $4.50	4. $6.00	7. $7.00
$53	$55	2. $3.00	5. $5.00	8. $6.50
$53	$60	3. $2.00	6. $4.00	9. $5.25

	In-the-Money	At-the-Money	Out-of-the-Money
a.	1, 2, 3	4, 5, 6	7, 8, 9
b.	1, 4, 7	2, 5, 8	3, 6, 9
c.	3, 6, 9	2, 5, 8	1, 4, 7
d.	1, 4, 7	none	2, 3, 5, 6, 8, 9
e.	2, 3, 5, 6, 8, 9	none	1, 4, 7

32. Using the table below, determine which of the call options (numbered 1 through 9) is the most risky (assume it is January).

		Premium for each call option					
Market Price	Exercise Price		April		July		October
$53	$50	1.	$4.50	4.	$6.00	7.	$7.00
$53	$55	2.	$3.00	5.	$5.00	8.	$6.50
$53	$60	3.	$2.00	6.	$4.00	9.	$5.25

a. 1.
b. 3.
c. 5.
d. 7.
e. 9.

33. Using the table below, determine which of the following call options (numbered 1 through 9) is the least risky.

Market Price	Exercise Price		Premium for each call option April		July		October
$53	$50	1.	$4.50	4.	$6.00	7.	$7.00
$53	$55	2.	$3.00	5.	$5.00	8.	$6.50
$53	$60	3.	$2.00	6.	$4.00	9.	$5.25

a. 1.
b. 3.
c. 5.
d. 7.
e. 9.

34. What model was developed to determine the value of a put option?
a. Sharp Index.
b. Treynor Index.
c. Black Scholes Option Valuation Model.
d. Put-Call Parity Model.
e. None of the above.

35. Jim Bob Simple is a paper maker who purchases lumber from tree farmers around his state. If Jim Bob is concerned with rising lumber prices, what type of hedge position should he enter into?
a. A short hedge; Simple should buy lumber futures contracts to protect against rising lumber prices.
b. A short hedge; Simple should sell lumber futures contracts to protect against rising lumber prices.
c. A long hedge; Simple should buy lumber futures contracts to protect against rising lumber prices.
d. A long hedge; Simple should sell lumber futures contracts to protect against rising lumber prices.
e. A long hedge; Simple should buy lumber futures contracts to protect against increasing supplies of lumber.

36. Which of the following statements are true concerning the characteristics of bonds and preferred stock?

    1. Unlike common stock, the rights of preferred stock holders must be satisfied prior to debt creditors, such as bond holders.
    2. Like interest paid to bond holders, dividends paid to preferred stock holders are tax deductible.
    3. Like bonds paying a fixed amount of interest, preferred stock pays a fixed dividend only.
    4. Both bonds and preferred stock have definite maturities.

    a. 1 and 2.
    b. 2 and 3.
    c. 3 and 4.
    d. 2, 3, and 4.
    e. None of the above.

37. What is the duration of a bond purchased for $948.50 which matures in 5 years and has a coupon rate of 12.5%? (Assume annual coupon payments.)

    a. 3.919 years.
    b. 3.948 years.
    c. 3.977 years.
    d. 4.006 years.
    e. 5.000 years.

38. Consider the following 6 AAA rated bonds:

Bond 1: 5 year bond with 8% coupon.

Bond 2: 5 year bond with 12% coupon.

Bond 3: 7 year bond with 8% coupon.

Bond 4: 10 year bond with 12% coupon.

Bond 5: 10 year bond with a zero-coupon.

Bond 6: 30 year bond with a 12% coupon.

Which of the following statements about the above bonds are true?

1. The duration of Bond 1 is greater than Bond 2 because the cash flows for Bond 2 are higher.
2. Bond 2 has a greater potential for price fluctuation than Bond 1 because it has a larger coupon rate.
3. Bond 6 has the highest potential for price fluctuations among Bonds 2, 4, and 6 because it has the longest maturity.
4. Bond 5 has a higher potential for price fluctuations than Bond 4 because it has a lower coupon rate.
5. Bond 4 has a duration less than that of Bond 5.

a. 1 and 2.

b. 1, 3, and 4.

c. 2, 3, and 5.

d. 1, 3, 4, and 5.

e. 1, 2, 3, and 5.

39. What is the duration of the following portfolio of bonds?

Bond A: 5-year bond with a 12.5% coupon rate purchased for $1,055.44.

Bond B: 5-year bond with a 10.0% coupon rate purchased for $963.04.

Bond C: 7-year bond with a 8.5% coupon rate purchased for $882.20.

a. 3.78.

b. 4.35.

c. 4.50.

d. 4.73.

e. 7.84.

40. The dollar value of a T-bill quoted at 95.24 is:
    a. $9,575.00.
    b. $9,507.50.
    c. $9,524.00.
    d. $10,000.00.
    e. Cannot be determined.

41. Which of the following statements is true regarding Serial Bonds?
    a. They are secured by the taxing power of the issuer.
    b. They generally sell at a discount.
    c. They have multiple maturity dates.
    d. They are always long-term bonds.
    e. None of the above.

42. A bond that pays interest and principal from revenue generated by a particular project is called?
    a. Revenue Obligation Bond.
    b. Project Bond.
    c. General Obligation Bond.
    d. Municipal Bond.
    e. A and D.

43. David wishes to sell short 200 shares of ABC common stock. If the last two transactions were at 45 followed by a trade at 45 1/8, David can sell short on the next transaction at what price?
    a. 45 or above.
    b. 45 1/8 or above.
    c. 45 or lower.
    d. 45 1/8 or lower.
    e. Any price.

44. In the event of a declining market, what should an investor do?
    a. Buy index futures.
    b. Sell index futures.
    c. Buy a call option.
    d. Sell a put option.
    e. None of the above.

45. Which of the following strategies could be considered a protective strategy?

   a. Purchasing a call option on a stock you own.
   b. Selling a naked call.
   c. Buying a put on a stock already owned.
   d. Buying a put on a stock you sold short.
   e. Selling a call against a stock you sold short.

46. What is the duration of a zero coupon bond yielding 9% maturing in 10 years and selling for $422.41?

   a. 7 years.
   b. 8 years.
   c. 9 years.
   d. 10 years.
   e. 11 years.

47. Which of the following issues guaranteed investment contracts?

   a. Insurance companies.
   b. Stock brokers.
   c. Investment brokers.
   d. The Federal Reserve.
   e. None of the above.

48. Which of the following statements is true about open-end investment companies?

   1. They can sell at a premium or discount relative to NAV.
   2. The capitalization is not fixed.
   3. Shares will be redeemed based on supply and demand.
   4. Shares are traded on various exchanges.

   a. 1 only.
   b. 2 only.
   c. 2 and 3.
   d. 3 and 4.
   e. 1, 2, 3, and 4.

49. You buy 100 shares of XYZ stock for $60/share with an initial margin of 50% and a 30% maintenance margin. At what price will you receive a margin call?
    a. $44.00.
    b. $43.50.
    c. $42.85.
    d. $42.00.
    e. $40.00.

50. If stock drops to $40/share, how much cash will you be required to put up, assuming you bought 100 shares of XYZ stock for $60 per share with initial margin of 50% and a 30% maintenance margin?
    a. $0.
    b. $200.
    c. $285.
    d. $800.
    e. $2,000.

51. Which of the statements concerning stock options is correct?
    1. The writer of a put receives a premium.
    2. The writer of a call receives a premium.
    3. A writer of a call is bearish.
    4. A writer of a put is bullish.
    a. 1 only.
    b. 2 only.
    c. 1 and 3.
    d. 1, 2, and 4.
    e. 1, 2, 3 and 4.

52. Which of the statements below regarding the stock market is correct?
    1. When stock positions are held in a margin account, a margin call generally occurs when the value of the position falls to below 75% of its original value.
    2. OTC stocks are more likely to pay dividends than are listed stocks.
    3. Bull (stock) markets generally last longer than do bear markets.
        a. 1 only.
        b. 2 only.
        c. 1 and 3.
        d. 2 and 3.
        e. 1, 2, and 3.

53. A client with a large, well diversified common stock portfolio expresses concern about a possible market decline. However, he/she does not want to incur the cost of selling a portion of their holdings nor the risk of mistiming the market. A possible strategy for him/her would be: **(CFP® Exam, released 3/95)**
    a. Buy an index call option.
    b. Sell an index call option.
    c. Buy an index put option.
    d. Sell an index put option.
    e. None of the above.

54. According to fundamental analysis, which phrase best defines the intrinsic value of a share of common stock? **(CFP® Exam, released 3/95)**
    a. The par value of the common stock.
    b. The book value of the common stock.
    c. The liquidating value of the firm on a per share basis.
    d. The stock's current price in an inefficient market.
    e. The discounted value of all future dividends.

55. Which one of the following types of investor benefits most from the tax advantage of preferred stocks? **(CFP® Exam, released 3/95)**
    a. Government.
    b. Individual.
    c. Corporate.
    d. Mutual funds.
    e. Non-profit institutional.

56. Municipal bonds that are backed by the income from specific projects are known as: **(CFP® Exam, released 3/95)**

    a. Income bonds.
    b. Revenue bonds.
    c. General obligation bonds.
    d. Debenture bonds.
    e. Project bonds.

57. A call option with a strike price of $110 is selling for 3½ when the market price of the underlying stock is $108. The intrinsic value of the call is: **(CFP® Exam, released 3/95)**

    a. 0.
    b. 1½.
    c. 2.
    d. 3½.
    e. -2.

58. With the same dollar investment, which of the following strategies can cause the investor to experience the greatest loss? **(CFP® Exam, released 3/95)**

    a. Selling a naked put option.
    b. Selling a naked call option.
    c. Writing a covered call.
    d. Buying a call option.
    e. Buying the underlying security.

59. Which of the following is/are characteristics of a municipal bond unit investment trust? **(CFP® Exam, released 3/95)**

    1. Additional securities are not added to the trust.
    2. Shares may be sold at a premium or discount to net asset value.
    3. Shares are normally traded on the open market (exchanges).
    4. The portfolio is self-liquidating.

    a. 1 only.
    b. 1 and 4.
    c. 2 and 3.
    d. 2 and 4.
    e. 1, 2, 3, and 4.

60. American depository receipts (ADRs) are used to **(CFP® Exam, released 3/95)**
    1. Finance foreign exports.
    2. Eliminate currency risk.
    3. Sell U.S. securities in overseas markets.
    4. Trade foreign securities in U.S. markets.
        a. 1 and 3.
        b. 1 and 4.
        c. 2 and 4.
        d. 4 only.
        e. 1, 2, and 4.

61. Which of the following agencies issue bonds that are backed by the full faith & credit of the United States Government?
    a. FHLMC.
    b. FNMA.
    c. TVA.
    d. GNMA.
    e. None of the above.

62. Which of the following are characteristics of closed-end investment companies?
    1. Shares of closed-end investment companies are generally redeemable by the fund.
    2. Similar to stocks, shares of closed-end investment companies are generally traded on exchanges.
    3. Closed-end investment companies will often issue additional shares to raise more capital for the fund.
        a. 1 only.
        b. 2 only.
        c. 3 only.
        d. 1 and 2.
        e. 1, 2, and 3.

63. Which of the following statements regarding series EE bonds is/are correct?

  1. Investors may choose to defer taxation on the interest until the bonds mature.
  2. Interest is not actually paid on the bonds until maturity or redemption.
  3. The bonds are originally sold for two-thirds of maturity (face) value.
  4. Series EE bonds may be traded at maturity for series HH bonds to defer tax on accrued interest.

     a. 1 only.
     b. 2 only.
     c. 1 and 3.
     d. 1, 2, and 4.
     e. 1, 2, 3, and 4.

64. Mutual funds often have stated objectives indicating what type of fund the investor is choosing. Which of the following types of funds generally focuses their investment objective in narrow areas such as natural resources, technology, or health care?

     a. Sector funds.
     b. Growth and income funds.
     c. Balanced funds.
     d. Growth funds.
     e. Income funds.

65. Which of the following is not considered a short-term investment vehicle?

     a. Treasury bonds.
     b. NOW accounts.
     c. Repurchase agreements.
     d. Negotiable CDs.
     e. Commercial paper.

66. Which of the following are correct regarding the characteristic of warrants and call options?

		Warrants	Call Options
1.	Issued by the company	Yes	No
2.	Convertible into stock	No	Yes
3.	Often issued with bonds	Yes	Yes

a. 1 only.
b. 2 only.
c. 3 only.
d. 1 and 3.
e. 1, 2, and 3.

67. Alex has a put option with an exercise price of $50. The stock is currently selling for $46. If the option has a premium of $3, what is the intrinsic value?

a. 0.
b. 1.
c. (3).
d. (7).
e. 4.

68. With the same dollar investment, which of the following strategies can cause an investor to experience the greatest loss?

a. Selling a naked call option.
b. Selling a naked put option.
c. Selling a covered call option.
d. Selling a covered put option.
e. Selling a stock short.

69. Which of the following bonds is/are considered to be default risk free?

1. Federal National Mortgage Association bonds.
2. Collateral mortgage obligations.
3. Guaranteed National Mortgage Association bonds.

a. 1 only.
b. 2 only.
c. 3 only.
d. 1 and 2.
e. None are considered default risk free.

70. Kristen wants to invest in ABC stock, however, she must wait several months until her certificate of deposit matures. What type of option should she invest in to protect against the market value of the stock increasing before her money becomes available?

  a. Buy a put option.
  b. Write a put option.
  c. Buy a call option.
  d. Sell a call option.
  e. None of the above.

71. Which of the following is a benefit of a STRIP Treasury?

  a. There is no taxable income.
  b. Treasury strips avoids reinvestment risk.
  c. All income from strips will be treated as capital gains.
  d. Strips are much less volatile than other bonds.
  e. None of the above are true.

72. Which of the following factors directly affects the value of a call option and does the factor cause the value of the option to increase or decrease?

	Greater Standard Deviation	Greater time till maturity	Rise in inflation
a.	Increase	increase	increase
b.	Increase	decrease	decrease
c.	Increase	increase	not directly related
d.	Decrease	decrease	increase
e.	Decrease	increase	not directly related

73. Which one of the following products is designed to provide both growth and income? **(CFP® Exam, released 12/96)**

  a. Fixed premium annuity.
  b. Non-participating mortgage real estate investment trust (REIT).
  c. Aggressive growth mutual fund.
  d. Convertible bond.

74. Which of the following publications is likely to have the historical earnings of The Blue Sky mutual fund?

    a. Value Line investment survey.
    b. Wall Street Journal.
    c. Morningstar.
    d. Moody's.

75. Your client owns highly appreciated common stock but wants to defer any tax impact until the following tax year (12 months away). He is also concerned about the market dropping before year-end. Which of the following would best protect his current gain while deferring taxes to the next year?

    a. Buy a put.
    b. Sell a put.
    c. Sell short against the box.
    d. Buy a call.
    e. Sell a call.

76. Mike likes a stock and expects it to significantly increase in value fairly soon. He is expecting a bond to mature in 2 months and doesn't want to miss out on any appreciation on the stock while waiting for the funds to become available. Which of the following actions should he take?

    a. Buy a put.
    b. Sell a put.
    c. Buy on margin.
    d. Sell a call.
    e. Buy a call.

77. If you own a stock, what is the safest investment strategy in a market that is expected to be flat for several months?

    a. Buy a straddle.
    b. Buy a call.
    c. Sell a covered call.
    d. Buy a put.

78. Mutual funds will generally report earnings under which of the following methods?

    a. Time-weighted return.

    b. Dollar-weighted return.

    c. Average return.

    d. Absolute return.

    e. Annualized return.

SECURITY MARKETS

79. In which of the following markets are large blocks of stock traded between investors without the use of brokers?
    a. Primary.
    b. Secondary.
    c. Third.
    d. Fourth.
    e. Fifth.

80. Which markets are IPO's related to?
    a. Primary.
    b. Secondary.
    c. Third.
    d. Fourth.
    e. Fifth.

81. Which of the following statements about underwriting is <u>not</u> true?
    a. All risk is shifted to the underwriter in firm–commitment underwriting agreements.
    b. The investment banks will purchase the remaining securities after an initial offering in standard underwriting agreements.
    c. The investment bank incurs zero risk in "best efforts" underwriting.
    d. Private placement is done with no more than 20 buyers.
    e. Private placements do not need to be registered with the SEC.

82. Which of the following statements is not true about the secondary market?
    a. Floor traders are the liaison between the public and the specialist.
    b. Specialists maintain orderly markets and adjust market prices based on supply and demand.
    c. The majority of orders are market orders.
    d. A round lot includes 100 shares.
    e. Stop orders turn into market orders if the stock price reaches a certain point.

83. What type of order(s) will permit an investor to trade stock at a predetermined price?
    a. Market.
    b. Limit order.
    c. Stop order.
    d. Stop limit order.
    e. B and D.

84. Which type of underwriting would you prefer if you were concerned about minimizing cost and placing an offering quickly?
    a. Firm commitment.
    b. Stand-by underwriting.
    c. Public placement.
    d. Private placement.
    e. Best efforts.

85. Which of the following individuals exclusively execute stock orders for retail clients?
    a. Commission broker.
    b. Floor broker.
    c. Registered trader.
    d. Specialist.
    e. Market maker

86. What is the most common type of order?
    a. Market order.
    b. Limit order.
    c. Stop order.
    d. Stop-limit order.
    e. Good till cancel order.

87. Which of the following is not an example of a secondary market transaction?
    a. U.S. Treasury auctions $150,000,000 in T-bills.
    b. Arkansas State issues debt to finance a toll road.
    c. A mutual fund purchases 20% of an IPO.
    d. IBM issues new shares to its stockholders.
    e. All of the above.

SECURITIES LAW

88. If a company is interested in issuing securities in the primary market, which of the following securities laws should it be most concerned with?
    a. Glass-Steagall Act.
    b. Security Act of 1933.
    c. Securities Exchange Act of 1934.
    d. The Maloney Act of 1938.
    e. The Securities Investor Protection Corporation Act of 1970.

89. If a broker is concerned about the implication and requirements of The Securities Exchange Act of 1934, which market would he most likely be dealing in?
    a. Fifth.
    b. Fourth.
    c. Third.
    d. Secondary.
    e. Primary.

90. Which of the following statements about industry/regulatory relationships are true? **(CFP® Exam, released 3/95)**
    1. The insurance industry is primarily regulated by each of the 50 states.
    2. The majority of banks are subject to federal regulation by the Federal Reserve System and the Federal Deposit Insurance Corporation.
    3. Pension plan funds are primarily subject to federal regulation.
    4. The organized stock exchanges, such as the New York Stock Exchange, are primarily regulated by the individual states in which they are incorporated.
    a. 1, 2, and 3.
    b. 1 and 3.
    c. 2 and 4.
    d. 2 and 3.
    e. 1, 2, 3, and 4.

91. Under which of the following conditions will a private placement be exempt from SEC registration?

 1. The issue is sold to less than 35 unsophisticated investors.
 2. The issue is sold to no more than 50 sophisticated investors.
 3. The issue's registration statement is filed with the SEC.

 a. 1 only.
 b. 2 only.
 c. 1 and 2.
 d. 1 and 3.
 e. 1, 2, and 3.

92. Assuming you want to sell a tax shelter as a private placement, which of the following statements are true?

 1. You can sell to unlimited accredited investors.
 2. You must register with the SEC.
 3. The tax shelter can be sold to any number of unsophisticated investors represented by knowledgeable advisors.

 a. 1 only.
 b. 3 only.
 c. 1 and 2.
 d. 1 and 3.
 e. 1, 2, and 3.

93. Which of the following is the body that regulates investment advisors?

 a. SEC.
 b. NASD.
 c. FDIC.
 d. Congress.
 e. Individual states.

INVESTMENT CONCEPTS

94. Using Harry Markowitz's three rules for selecting efficient portfolios, determine which of the following portfolio sets are preferred.

P	E(r)	Beta
1	8%	1.1
2	9%	1.25
3	11%	1.25
4	12%	1.3
5	13%	1.1
6	14%	1.25

a. 1 and 2.
b. 2 and 3.
c. 3 and 4.
d. 4 and 5.
e. 5 and 6.

95. Which of the following is a consistent strategy with the belief in the Efficient Market Hypothesis?
a. Waiting to purchase a stock until it increases above the 40 day moving average.
b. Searching for undervalued securities.
c. Comparing the calculated value of a security, through fundamental analysis, to the market value of the stock.
d. Selecting a random set of stocks for a portfolio.
e. A and B.

96. Based on the following information about ABC Stock, which of the following is true?

Market price	$67
Current dividend	$2
Growth of dividend	8%
Required rate of return	12.5%
Risk free rate of return	5%
Market return	11%
Beta of ABC	1.15

1. The stock is overvalued by $19 according to the dividend growth model.
2. According to the CAPM the E(r) is 12.65%.
3. If the stock was purchased last year for $65, the holding period return would be 3%.

a. 1 only.
b. 2 only.
c. 3 only.
d. 1 and 2.
e. 2 and 3.

97. ABC Stock has a Beta of .85 and is currently selling for $8 per share. The dividend yield is expected to be 6.25% for the year. The value of the stock is forecasted at $10 per share at year-end. The risk free rate is 7% and the market premium is 8%. According to the capital asset pricing model, is this a good purchase?

a. No, because the required return exceeds the expected return.
b. No, because expected return exceeds the required return.
c. Yes, because the expected risk exceeds the required return.
d. Yes, because the forecasted rate of return exceeds the required rate of return.
e. Yes, because the Beta of the stock is below the market Beta.

98. Which of the following forms of the efficient market hypothesis supports technical analysis?

a. Weak.
b. Semi-strong.
c. Strong.
d. A & B.
e. None of the above.

99. Which of the following forms of the efficient market hypothesis does not support technical analysis?

    a. Weak.
    b. Semi-strong.
    c. Strong.
    d. B and C.
    e. All of the above do not support technical analysis.

100. Which of the following is/are not correct?

    a. The variability of individual stocks is not reduced as portfolio diversification increases.
    b. As the number of stocks within a portfolio increases, systematic risk will more closely represent total risk.
    c. Beta is not an appropriate measure of risk unless the portfolio is sufficiently diversified.
    d. Standard deviation is not an appropriate measure of risk unless substantially all unsystematic risk has been eliminated through diversification.

101. Given the following probability distribution, determine the standard deviation of returns for the stock of ABC Company.

Probability	Expected Return
.25	5%
.47	13%
.28	23%

    a. 0.43%.
    b. 0.81%.
    c. 6.58%.
    d. 9.92%.
    e. 13.67%.

102. Determine the expected return and standard deviation of the following distribution of returns:

Probability	Return
.2	45%
.3	25%
.4	13%
.1	3%

	Expected Return	Standard Deviation
a.	21.5%	18.07%
b.	22.0%	13.30%
c.	21.5%	13.30%
d.	20.5%	18.07%
e.	22.0%	18.07%

103. Gillice Corporation stock has a mean of 14% and a standard deviation of 10%. If the historical returns are normally distributed, what is the probability that the stock will have a return below 14%?

a. 20%.
b. 25%.
c. 33%.
d. 40%.
e. 50%.

104. Kate Corporation stock has a mean of 9% and a standard deviation of 0%. If the historical returns for Kate stock are normally distributed, what is the probability that this stock will yield a return greater than 9%.

a. 0%.
b. 25%.
c. 33%.
d. 50%.
e. 100%.

105. Robert Corporation stock has a mean of 9% and a standard deviation of 6%. If the historical returns for Robert stock are normally distributed, what is the probability that this stock will yield a return greater than 15%.

a. 0%.

b. 16%.

c. 32%.

d. 34%.

e. 50%.

106. Skate Corporation stock has an average return of 24% and a standard deviation of 10%. The risk free rate of return is currently 4%. If the historical returns for Skate stock are normally distributed, what is the probability that this stock will have a return in excess of the risk free rate of return?

a. 2.5%.

b. 34.0%.

c. 95.0%.

d. 97.5%.

e. 100.0%.

107. Security A has a standard deviation of 5.0 and the market has a standard deviation of 4.5. The correlation coefficient between Security A and the market is .80. What percent of the change in Security A can be explained by changes in the market?

a. 36%.

b. 50%.

c. 64%.

d. 80%.

e. 100%.

108. Portfolio A has a standard deviation of .55 and the market has a standard deviation of .40. The correlation coefficient between Portfolio A and the market is .50. What percent of the Total Risk is Unsystematic Risk?

a. 0%.

b. 25%.

c. 50%.

d. 75%.

e. 100%.

109. Of the five pairs of portfolios, which pair provides the highest level of diversification?

a. Portfolio 1 & 2: with a correlation coefficient of +0.92.

b. Portfolio 3 & 4: with a correlation coefficient of +0.37.

c. Portfolio 5 & 6: with a correlation coefficient of 0.

d. Portfolio 7 & 8: with a correlation coefficient of -0.42.

e. Portfolio 9 & 10: with a correlation coefficient of -0.78.

110. John Wiggens has a portfolio with 23 different equities. John's portfolio increased by 22% and has a beta of 1.50. By what percent did the market change (round to nearest .5%) (assume the risk free rate is 4%)?

a. 14.5%.

b. 15.5%.

c. 16.0%.

d. 16.5%.

e. 17.0%.

111. Beverly Drake has two stocks with a correlation coefficient of zero. Which of the following is true?

a. These stocks are well diversified because as one stock appreciates in value, the other decreases in value.

b. These stocks are well diversified because they will move in unison.

c. These stocks are not well diversified because they move in unison.

d. These stocks will move independently of each other.

e. These stocks are well diversified because they move in opposite directions.

112. Adding investments with a negative Beta to a portfolio that currently has a Beta of 1 will:

a. Cause the portfolio to be more risky in times of a bull market.

b. Cause the portfolio to be more risky in times of a bear market.

c. Cause the volatility of the portfolio to increase.

d. Cause the expected performance of the portfolio to increase in bear markets.

e. Cause the expected performance of the portfolio to decrease in bear markets.

113. Which of the following statements is/are true?

1. It is possible to eliminate almost all unsystematic risk by combining a larger number of stocks with correlation coefficients of 0.00.
2. The market portfolio is considered the most diversified of all portfolios.
3. If two securities have a correlation coefficient of 1.0, diversification by adding these securities together in a portfolio will not reduce unsystematic risk.

a. 1 only.
b. 2 only.
c. 1 and 3.
d. 2 and 3.
e. 1, 2, and 3.

114. Based on Markowitz's Theory of the efficient frontier, which one of the following portfolios could not lie on the efficient frontier?

Portfolio	Expected Return	Standard Deviation
1	8%	15%
2	10%	14%
3	12%	19%
4	14%	17%

a. Portfolio 1.
b. Portfolio 2.
c. Portfolio 3.
d. Portfolio 4.
e. Portfolios 1 and 3.

115. Which of the following statements are true about Beta and Standard Deviation?

1. Beta measures unsystematic risk.
2. Standard deviation measures systematic risk only.
3. Standard deviation measures both systematic and unsystematic risks.

a. 1 only.
b. 2 only.
c. 3 only.
d. 1 and 2.
e. 1 and 3.

116. According to the CAPM model, which of the following best explains portfolio returns?

  a. Economic factors.
  b. Systematic risk.
  c. Unsystematic risk.
  d. Interest rates.
  e. Diversification.

117. Which of the following statements is true regarding the Arbitrage Pricing Theory.

  a. Beta is not a pricing factor.
  b. Inflation is not a pricing factor.
  c. Multiple factors affect the return of a security.
  d. The risk free rate of return does not affect the return.
  e. None of the above.

118. Based on the efficient market hypothesis, which of the following statements is true concerning an efficient market?

  1. Security prices will adjust quickly to new information.
  2. Security prices are rarely far from their justified price.
  3. Security analysis will permit investors to consistently earn returns superior to the market.

  a. 1 only.
  b. 2 only.
  c. 1 and 2.
  d. 1 and 3.
  e. 1, 2, and 3.

119. Use the information below to calculate the standard deviation of a portfolio having an expected return of 11% instead of an average return of 11.67%.

Security	Actual Return
J	15%
K	12%
L	8%

  a. 3.0.
  b. 3.5.
  c. 3.6.
  d. 4.0.
  e. 4.2.

120. The capital asset pricing model (CAPM) supports which of the following statements below?

1. Returns can be expected to correspond directly with the Level of Risk undertaken.
2. Standard deviation is the measure of market risk.
3. Beta is the measure of market risk.
4. Risk is measured by the probability of losing a portion of the initial investment.

   a. 1 only.
   b. 1 and 2.
   c. 1 and 3.
   d. 3 and 4.
   e. 4 only.

121. Using the following information below, which of the portfolios would be a reasonable selection(s) assuming a rational investor believes in standard deviation as a viable measure of risk?

	Expected Portfolio Return	Standard Deviation
1.	15%	12%
2.	11%	12%
3.	11%	7%
4.	7%	4%

   a. 1 only.
   b. 3 only.
   c. 4 only.
   d. 2 and 4.
   e. 1, 3, and 4.

122. The standard deviation of the returns of a portfolio of securities will be ___________ the weighted average of the standard deviation of returns of the individual component securities. **(CFP® Exam, released 3/95)**

   a. Equal to.
   b. Less than.
   c. Greater than.
   d. Less than or equal to (depending upon the correlation between securities).
   e. Less than, equal to, or greater than (depending upon the correlation between securities).

123. In contrast to the Capital Asset Pricing Model, The Arbitrage Pricing Theory (APT) **(CFP® Exam, released 3/95)**

   a. Is usually a multi-factor model.
   b. Is primarily used by arbitrageurs to profit from imperfections in security markets.
   c. Assumes a market portfolio.
   d. Is a useful technical indicator.
   e. None of the above.

124. If the market risk premium were to increase, the value of common stock (everything else being equal) would **(CFP® Exam, released 3/95)**

   a. Not change because this does not affect stock values.
   b. Increase in order to compensate the investor for increased risk.
   c. Increase due to higher risk free rates.
   d. Decrease in order to compensate the investor for increased risk
   e. Decrease due to lower risk free rates.

125. Modern "asset allocation" is based upon the model developed by Harry Markowitz. Which of the following statements is/are correctly identified with this model? **(CFP® Exam, released 3/95)**

   1. The risk, return and covariance of assets are important input variables in creating portfolios.
   2. Negatively correlated assets are necessary to reduce the risk of portfolios.
   3. In creating a portfolio, diversifying across asset types (e.g., stocks and bonds) is less effective than diversifying within an asset type.
   4. The efficient frontier is relatively insensitive to the input variable.

   a. 1 and 2.
   b. 1, 2, and 3.
   c. 1 only.
   d. 2 and 4.
   e. 1, 2, and 4.

126. Under the efficient market hypothesis, which of the following terms best describes the movement of stock prices?

   a. Random walk.
   b. Statistical.
   c. Diverse.
   d. Predictable.
   e. None of the above.

127. If an investment has a correlation coefficient of .80 with the market, which of the following performance measures is the best measure of risk?

  a. Sharpe.
  b. Treynor.
  c. Jensen.
  d. Sharpe and Jensen.
  e. Sharpe, Treynor, and Jensen equally.

128. Under which of the following forms of the Efficient Market Hypothesis can an investor benefit from analyzing historical public information?

1. Weak.
2. Semi-strong.
3. Strong.

  a. 1 only.
  b. 2 only.
  c. 1 and 2.
  d. 2 and 3.
  e. 1, 2, and 3.

129. Given the following information about securities A and B:

Historical Returns for Securities

	A	B
Year 1	10%	18%
Year 2	6%	12%
Year 3	0%	2%

Which of the following are true about Securities A and B?

1. A is more risky because it has a higher standard deviation.
2. B is more risky because it has a higher standard deviation.
3. A has a higher risk - adjusted return.
4. B has a higher risk - adjusted return.
5. A and B have the same risk - adjusted return.

  a. 1 and 3.
  b. 1 and 4.
  c. 2 and 3.
  d. 2 and 4.
  e. 1 and 5.

130. Under the Efficient Market Hypothesis, when would fundamental analysis be useful?

1. Weak form.
2. Semi strong form.
3. Strong form.

a. 1 only.
b. 2 only.
c. 3 only.
d. 1 and 2.
e. 1, 2, and 3.

131. Assume that Clay invests $7,000 of his $10,000 available assets into Portfolio A with the remainder in the S&P 500. Changes in the S&P 500 account for or explain 25% of the returns for Portfolio A. If Portfolio A has a standard deviation of 20% and the S&P 500 has a standard deviation of 11.5%, what is the standard deviation of the combined $10,000 portfolio?

a. 15.0%.
b. 15.2%.
c. 16.0%.
d. 17.5%.
e. 18.3%.

132. In analyzing the position of a portfolio in terms of risk/return on the capital market line (CML), superior performance exists if the fund's positions is ____________ the CML, inferior performance exists if the fund's position is ____________ the CML, and equilibrium position exists if it is __________ the CML? **(CFP® Exam, released 12/96)**

a. Above; on; below.
b. Above; below; on.
c. Below; on; above.
d. Below; above; on.
e. On; above; below.

133. Which of the following statements are true regarding the standard deviation of a two asset portfolio?

1. Only if the correlation between the two assets is negative will the standard deviation for the portfolio be less than the weighted standard deviation of the two assets.
2. If the correlation between Assets A and B is .3 and 80% of the Portfolio is invested in A (which has a standard deviation of 12%) and 20% is invested in B (which has a standard deviation of 15%), then the standard deviation of the portfolio will be less than 11%.

a. 1 only.

b. 2 only.

c. Both 1 and 2.

d. Neither 1 or 2.

e. Not enough information to answer statement 1 and statement 2.

SECURITY ANALYSIS

134. If you believe in fundamental analysis, you would use or follow which one of the following approaches?
    a. Technical Analysis.
    b. Quantitative Analysis (searching for undervalued securities).
    c. Efficient Market Hypothesis-weak.
    d. Efficient Market Hypothesis-strong.
    e. Passive Diversified Portfolio Approach.

135. Amber purchased a bond for $1,038.90 exactly two years ago. The bond had a maturity of 5 years and a coupon rate of 10% (paid semi-annually) when Amber first purchased it. Assuming the rates below are the prevailing rates for this type of bond at different maturities, how much could Amber sell her bond for today?

Maturities	1 year	2 years	3 years	5 years	10 years	30 years
Interest Rates	6%	6.5%	7%	8.5%	10%	12%

    a. $1,038.31.
    b. $1,039.00.
    c. $1,060.08.
    d. $1,078.73.
    e. $1,079.93.

136. Melany inherited a bond from her grandmother 1.5 years ago. The bond had been purchased with a 10-year maturity 3.5 years before Melany received it. The interest rate at the time Melany's grandmother purchased this bond was about 8.5%. Melany has just determined that her bond is worth $836.00. If the interest rates below are indications of the current prevailing market interest rates for this type of bond, how much did Melany's grandmother purchase the bond for? (Assume coupon payments are made annually.)

Maturities	1 year	2 years	3 years	5 years	10 years	30 years
Interest Rates	5%	5.5%	6%	7%	8%	10%

    a. $580.51.
    b. $639.13.
    c. $697.69.
    d. $814.56.
    e. $1,000.00.

137. Which of the following statements is/are true:

1. Lower coupon bonds are more volatile than higher coupon bonds when interest rates change.
2. There is an inverse relationship between bond prices and changes in interest rates.
3. A direct relationship exists between coupon rates and duration.

a. 1 only.
b. 3 only.
c. 1 and 2.
d. 2 and 3.
e. 1, 2, and 3.

138. Which of the following is/are assumptions of the Constant Dividend Growth Model?

1. Dividends will grow at a constant rate.
2. Earnings of the company will grow at a constant rate.
3. The investors required rate of return is fixed and determinable.

a. 1 only.
b. 2 only.
c. 1 and 2.
d. 2 and 3.
e. 1 and 3.

139. Blonde Company's earnings increased from $5 to $7 per share. Its dividend increased from $2 to $2.20 per share and the share price increased from $50 to $60. Based on this information, which of the following statements about Blonde Co. is/are true?

1. Blonde's P/E ratio declined.
2. The dividend payout ratio increased.
3. Earnings increased more than dividends.

a. 1 only.
b. 2 only.
c. 1 and 2.
d. 1 and 3.
e. 1, 2, and 3.

140. The current annual dividend of ABC Corporation is $2.00 per share. Five years ago the dividend was $1.36 per share. The firm expects dividends to grow in the future at the same compound annual rate as they grew during the past five years. The required rate of return on the firm's common stock is 12%. The expected return on the market portfolio is 14%. What is the value of a share of common stock of ABC Corporation using the constant dividend growth model? (Round to the nearest dollar.) **(CFP® Exam, released 3/95)**

a. $11.

b. $17.

c. $25.

d. $36.

e. $54.

141. Which combination of the following statements about bond swaps is true? **(CFP® Exam, released 3/95)**

1. A substitution swap is designed to take advantage of a perceived yield differential between bonds that are similar with respect to coupons, ratings, maturities, and industry.
2. Rate anticipation swaps are based on forecasts of general interest rate changes.
3. The yield pickup swap is designed to change the cash flow of the portfolio by exchanging similar bonds that have different coupon rates.
4. The tax swap is made in order to substitute capital gains for current yield.

a. 1, 2, and 3.

b. 1 and 3.

c. 2 and 4.

d. 4 only.

e. 1, 2, 3, and 4.

142. Which of the following technical indicators measures the strength of the market by comparing the number of advancing stocks to the number of declining stocks?

a. Market volume.

b. Support level.

c. A - D ratio.

d. Breadth of the market.

e. Short interest.

143. John Smith originally purchased Zerex stock for $45 per share. He purchased 3 shares, which are currently trading at $62 per share. The stock has paid dividends of $2.00/share in year 1 and $2.20/share in year 2 (all paid at year-end). If John has held the stock for 2 years, what is the holding period return?

a. 19%.

b. 22%.

c. 23.5%.

d. 38%.

e. 47%.

144. A bond, which was purchased for par, is now selling for $1,050. The bond made semiannual coupon payments of $60 during the year. What is the single period rate of return for the owner of this bond at the end of year 1?

a. 60%.

b. 8.4%.

c. 11%.

d. 11.4%.

e. 17%.

145. Michael purchased 800 shares of ABC Stock for $75 per share. The stock paid a $1.25 dividend per share at the end of the year and there was a 2 for 1 stock split during the year. If the value of his investment at the end of the year was worth $65,000, what is the single period rate of return for the investment?

a. 8.3%.

b. 10%.

c. 11.67%.

d. 12.5%.

e. 14.0%.

146. A portfolio had an IRR (compound return) for a 2 year period of 12.5%. During this 2 year period, $75,000 in dividends was paid each year (at year-end) and the current FMV of this portfolio is $1.5 million. What was the portfolio worth when it was purchased 2 years ago?

a. $750 k.
b. $1.00 M.
c. $1.25 M.
d. $1.31 M.
e. $1.50 M.

147. A portfolio had an IRR (compound return) for a 3 year period of 8.5%. During this 3 year period the following dividends were paid, and the current FMV of this portfolio is $58.

Dividend year 1 (end) $1.25.
Dividend year 2 (end) $1.41.
Dividend year 3 (end) $1.58.

What was the portfolio worth when it was purchased 3 years ago? (round to the nearest dollar)

a. $45.
b. $47.
c. $49.
d. $54.
e. $58.

148. A portfolio had an IRR (compound return) for a 3 year period of 2.43% (including dividends). During this 3 year period the following dividends were paid and disbursed from the portfolio. The current FMV of this portfolio is $58.

Dividend year 1 (end) $1.25.
Dividend year 2 (end) $1.41.
Dividend year 3 (end) $1.58.

What was the portfolio worth when it was purchased 3 years ago?

a. $45.
b. $47.
c. $49.
d. $54.
e. $58.

149. A portfolio had an IRR for a 3 year period of 5.57%. During this 3 year period the following dividends were paid and the current FMV of this portfolio is $40.

Dividend year 1 (end) $4.80.

Dividend year 2 (end) $5.90.

Dividend year 3 (end) $7.25.

What was the portfolio worth when it was purchased 3 years ago?

a. $30.

b. $34.

c. $37.

d. $40.

e. $50.

150. Based on the current price, ABC Stock has a holding period rate of return of 23.75% for a 5 year period ending today. The stock was purchased 5 years ago for $20 and the stock paid a dividend at the end of Year 1 (one) of $2.00. The dividend grew each year at 10% (for example: year 2 dividend = $2.20) and is expected to continue to grow at 10%. What could the holder sell the stock for today if his required rate of return was 12% per year?

a. A loss of $7.46 from the original purchase price if you use the holding period rate of return method.

b. $161.00 if the dividend growth model is used.

c. $24.75.

d. A and B.

e. B and C.

151. 500 shares of stock was purchased 3 years ago for $20 per share. The holding period return is 18% and the following dividends have been paid at the end of each year.

Year	Div./Share
1	$1.25
2	$1.50
3	$2.00

How much could this investment be sold for today?

a. $8,500.

b. $9,425.

c. $10,000.

d. $11,800.

e. $12,000.

152. The XYZ mutual fund has had the following performance over the last four years.

X1	X2	X3	X4
30%	3.85%	(20%)	(7.41%)

What is the arithmetic average and geometric annualized return for the four-year period?

	Arithmetic	Geometric
a.	1.61%	0
b.	15.32%	14.85%
c.	15.32%	0
d.	1.61%	14.85%
e.	None of the above.	

153. The XYZ mutual fund has had the following performance over the last four years:

X1	X2	X3	X4
20%	10%	2%	16%

What is the difference between the average and geometric annualized returns?

a. 0.

b. .21%.

c. .42%.

d. 1.00%.

e. 44%.

154. Determine the geometric average of the following returns:

1990	45%
1991	25%
1992	13%
1993	3%

a. 18%.

b. 20.5%.

c. 21%.

d. 21.5%.

e. 22%.

155. For investors to accept the possibility of outcomes that may deviate from the expected outcome, they must be provided with what type of return?

a. Real Premium.
b. Risk Premium.
c. Market Premium.
d. Expected Return.
e. Actual Return.

156. Given the following returns for Stocks A and B, which of the following is true?

Year	A	B
1	11%	10%
2	13%	13%
3	14%	16%
4	12%	11%

1. The geometric annualized rate of return for B is greater than for A.
2. Stock B is more volatile than Stock A.
3. The average return for Stock A is higher than for Stock B.

a. 1 only.
b. 2 only.
c. 3 only.
d. 1 and 2.
e. 1, 2, and 3.

157. Based on the following chart, which of the following statement(s) is/are true? (Assume all bonds make coupon payments semi-annually)

Bond	Maturity	Coupon Rate	Current FMV
A	4 years	0	$ 730.69
B	5 years	10%	$1,039.56
C	10 years	5%	$ 688.44
D	30 years	0	$ 40.26

1. The order of the bonds ranked from highest to lowest YTM is: D, C, B, A.
2. The bond most sensitive to interest rate changes is Bond D.
3. The actual yield to maturity or realized return may change for all the bonds A, B, C, D (even when held to maturity) if prevailing interest rates change.

a. 1 only.
b. 3 only.
c. 1 and 2.
d. 2 and 3.
e. 1, 2, and 3.

158. Bill Smith owns treasury bonds worth $34,000, OTC stocks worth $22,500, and calls worth $15,000. If the expected return is 8%, 12.5%, and 23%, respectively, what is the overall weighted average expected return on Bill Smith's investments?

a. 8.0%.
b. 12.5%.
c. 14.3%.
d. 14.5%.
e. 23.0%.

159. Donna Catherine lives in Louisiana (assume Louisiana taxes municipal income from other states) and owns Tennessee municipal bonds with a FMV of $12,500, U.S. Treasury Bills with a FMV of $16,000, and XYZ stock worth $18,750. The expected returns for these investments are 9%, 7%, and 11.5%, respectively. Assuming returns consist of ordinary income (no capital gains) and assuming Donna has a federal tax rate of 36% and a state tax rate of 4%, what is the overall after-tax weighted average expected return for this group of investments?

a. 5.6%.
b. 6.4%.
c. 6.5%.
d. 5.5%.
e. 9.2%.

160. Assuming the following bonds are equivalent credit quality, which of the following bonds, when added to the portfolio independently would cause an investment portfolio with an expected return of 12% to increase its expected return.

1. A zero coupon bond selling for $314.76 maturing in 10 years.
2. A bond with an 8% annual coupon (paying semiannually) selling for $739.76 and maturing in 12 years.
3. A bond with a 12.5% annual coupon (paying semiannually) selling for $1,014.99 and maturing in 22 years.

a. 1 only.
b. 2 only.
c. 1 and 2.
d. 2 and 3.
e. 1, 2, and 3.

161. Hurley Bishop wishes to purchase a boat in 20 years when he retires so that he may sail around the world. If the boat presently costs $450,000 and inflation is 4%, how much should he deposit at the beginning of each year to have enough to purchase the boat at the end of 20 years? Assume that Hurley will earn an average compounded return of 12.5% on his investments.

a. $5,238.
b. $8,573.
c. $9,645.
d. $11,478.
e. $12,912.

162. Tina Thompson purchased 100 shares of ABC preferred stock 6 years ago for $7,300. Tina received the following amounts as dividends for the last 6 years:

Year:	1	2	3	4	5	6
Dividend:	$250	$260	$285	$270	$285	$300

The dividends were all paid at the end of the year and at the end of the sixth year Tina sold the 100 shares for $12,250. What is the effective yield over the six year period for this investment (IRR)?

a. 10.40%.
b. 11.72%.
c. 12.07%.
d. 12.45%.
e. 13.02%.

163. Jeff Robinson purchased a 30-year bond for $977.36 with a stated coupon of 8.5%. What is the Yield to Maturity for this investment if Jeff receives semi-annual coupon payments and expects to hold the bond to maturity?

a. 4.36%.
b. 5.68%.
c. 8.50%.
d. 8.71%.
e. 8.93%.

164. Davis Company stock has an average return of 11% and has a standard deviation of 4%. What is the probability that the stock will earn a return over 15% (round to the nearest whole number and assume a normal distribution)?

a. 10%.
b. 13%.
c. 16%.
d. 19%.
e. 33%.

165. Kimberly Morris is in the business of buying homes, fixing them up, and reselling them for a profit. She is considering purchasing a home, but knows that she will have to invest $25,000 at the end of the first month and $5,000 at the end of 6 months to restore the house before selling it. She expects to be able to sell the house at the end of 18 months for $176,000. If Kimberly requires a 25% annual return on her investments and there is a 6% real estate commission for selling, then what is the most she should pay for this house.

a. $85,236.
b. $87,285.
c. $90,677.
d. $92,522.
e. $94,157.

166. Of the four securities, which will provide the highest risk adjusted return for an investor?

Stock 1: Annual return of 15%, beta of 1.2.

Stock 2: Annual return of 12%, beta of 1.0.

Stock 3: Annual return of 10%, beta of .85.

Stock 4: Annual return of 8.5%, beta of .75.

a. Stock 1.
b. Stock 2.
c. Stock 3.
d. Stock 4.
e. Stocks 3 and 4.

167. If an investor, who is age 55, saving for his retirement, and is in a marginal tax bracket of 30%, requires an after tax return of 8.5%, which of the following securities would you suggest?

Bond 1: A 30 year municipal bond with a coupon of 6% (payments made semi-annually) selling for $1,010.

Bond 2: A AA rated 10 year corporate bond selling for $847.16 with a coupon payment of $50 twice a year.

Bond 3: A BB 30 year zero coupon bond selling for $22.86.

a. Bond 1 because its yield is greater than the after tax yields of the other two bonds.
b. Bond 2 because its yield is greater than the after tax yields of the other two bonds.
c. Bond 3 because its yield is greater than the after tax yields of the other two bonds.
d. Bond 2 because it has a high yield and seems to meet his goals.
e. Bond 3 because it has the highest YTM and all tax will be deferred because it is a zero coupon bond.

168. Assume John invests in a stock for two years. The stock earns a return of 15% the first year and a negative 10% return the second year. What was the annual geometric return?

a. 1.5%.
b. 1.7%.
c. 2.5%.
d. 3.0%.
e. 5%.

169. Assume John invests $100 in a stock for two years. The stock earns 15% the first year and looses 10% the second year. How much is the stock worth at the end of the second year?

a. 90.

b. 100.

c. 103.5.

d. 105.

e. 115.

170. What are the mean, medium, and mode for the series: 12, 11, 10, 10, 9, 8, 3?

	Mean	Median	Mode
a.	9	8	10
b.	8	10	9
c.	8	9	10
d.	10	9	10
e.	9	10	10

171. Donna acquired a bond today with a coupon of 10% with 5 years remaining until maturity (interest is paid semiannually). She acquired the bond for $1,080. Interest rates dropped overnight to 7%. What is Donna's yield (actual or calculated) on this investment if interest rates remain at 7% and she holds to maturity?

a. 6.7%.

b. 7.0%.

c. 7.5%.

d. 8.0%.

e. 10.0%.

172. Alvin purchases 200 shares of Harbor Stock for $23 per share. Alvin makes subsequent purchases at the end of the following years:

Year 1: 50 shares at $26/share.

Year 2: 75 shares at $29/share.

Year 3: 25 shares at $36/share.

If it is now the end of the 4th year and no dividends have been paid and Harbor is trading for $41/share. What is the annualized time weighted return for Harbor stock over the four-year period?

a. 13.8%.

b. 14.2%.

c. 15.0%.

d. 15.5%.

e. 16.0%.

173. Alvin purchases 200 shares of Harbor Stock for $23 per share. Alvin makes subsequent purchases at the end of the following years:

Year 1: 50 shares at $26/share.

Year 2: 75 shares at $29/share.

Year 3: 25 shares at $36/share.

If it is now the end of the 4th year and no dividends have been paid and Harbor is trading for $41/share. What is Alvin's annualized return on his investment for this four-year period?

a. 16%.

b. 15.5%.

c. 15%.

d. 14.5%.

e. 14%.

174. Your client, Tiffany Woodson, owns a portfolio that earned 12% during 1999. It had a beta of 1.3 and a standard deviation of 14%. During 1999 the market (S&P 500) earned 9%. The risk free rate of return was 5%. Which of the following statements are true?

1. The Treynor Index for the market is .0400.
2. The Treynor Index for Tiffany's portfolio is .00923.
3. The Treynor Index for Tiffany's portfolio is .0538.
4. Tiffany's portfolio outperformed the market on a risk-adjusted basis.

a. 1 only.
b. 2 only.
c. 1 and 3.
d. 1, 2, and 4.
e. 1, 3, and 4.

175. Which of the following models of Portfolio Performance Measurement and Modern Portfolio Theories use beta as the risk-element?

1. The Jensen Index.
2. The Sharpe Index.
3. The Treynor Index.
4. Markowitz's Capital Asset Pricing Model.

a. 1 only.
b. 2 only.
c. 1, 3, and 4.
d. 2, 3, and 4.
e. 1, 2, 3, and 4.

176. The Performance Fund had returns of 19% over the evaluation period and the benchmark portfolio yielded a return of 17% over the same period. Over the evaluation period, the standard deviation of returns from the Fund was 23% and the standard deviation of returns from the benchmark portfolio was 21%. Assuming a risk free rate of return of 8%, which one of the following is the calculation of the Sharpe index of performance for the fund over the evaluation period? **(CFP® Exam, released 3/95)**

a. .3913.
b. .4286.
c. .4783.
d. .5238.
e. .5870.

177. In computing portfolio performance, the Sharpe index uses ________, while the Treynor index uses ________ for the risk measure. **(CFP® Exam, released 3/95)**

1. Standard deviation.
2. Variance.
3. Correlation coefficient.
4. Coefficient of variation.
5. Beta.

a. 5; 1.
b. 1; 3.
c. 1; 4.
d. 1; 5.
e. 2; 5.

178. A $1,000 bond originally issued at par maturing in exactly 10 years bears a coupon rate of 8% compounded annually and a market price of $1,147.20. The indenture agreement provides that the bond may be called after five years at $1,050. Which of the following statement(s) is/are true? **(CFP® Exam, released 3/95)**

1. The yield to maturity is 6%.
2. The yield to call is 5.45%.
3. The bond is currently selling at a premium, indicating that market interest rates have fallen since the issue date.
4. The yield to maturity is less than the yield to call.

a. 1, 2, and 3.
b. 1 and 3.
c. 2 and 3.
d. 4 only.
e. 1, 3, and 4.

179. David invested $50,000 in a non-publicly traded partnership. This partnership generates $12,000 of passive income and $4,000 of interest and dividend income each year. The partnership generates total cash flow (both passive and portfolio) of $15,000 each year. David expects to receive $75,000 (after tax) at the end of the fifth year by selling his interest in the partnership. David also has another entity, which generates $2,000 of passive loss each year that is not being offset by any other passive income. If David's after-tax rate of return is 6%, what is the net present value of the investment? (Marginal tax bracket 36%).

a. $48,000.
b. $54,065.
c. $58,021.
d. $98,000.
e. $104,065.

180. Which of the following Portfolio Performance Measurements is an absolute measure of performance?

1. Jensen Index.
2. Sharpe Index.
3. Treynor Index.

a. 1 only.
b. 2 only.
c. 3 only.
d. 1 and 3.
e. 2 and 3.

181. Barney Smith, resident of Louisiana, has the following two bonds:

Bond A: 10% coupon, paid annually, matures in 3 years.

Bond B: 8% coupon, paid annually, maturities in 2 years.

Barney will invest all cashflows from the bonds into a money market yielding 5% (after tax) per year. Barney's marginal tax bracket is 36%. If Barney could buy those bonds today for $2,000, what would be his after tax yield at the end of 3 years (round to nearest whole number)?

a. 5%.
b. 6%.
c. 8%.
d. 9%.
e. 10%.

182. Immunization protects bond holders from which of the following:

1. Interest rate risk.
2. Reinvestment rate risk.
3. Purchasing power risk.

   a. 1 only.
   b. 3 only.
   c. 1 and 2.
   d. 1 and 3.

183. Bond A, which is selling for $924.18, has a coupon rate of 8% and is yielding 10%. The bond, which is a 5-year Treasury bond, has a duration of 4.7 years. At what time horizon will an investor owning bond A not be subject to interest rate risk.

   a. 2.50 years.
   b. 4.70 years.
   c. 4.85 years.
   d. 5.00 years.
   e. The investor will always be subject to interest rate risk, regardless of his time horizon.

184. XYZ Stock has a current dividend of $1.75 that has been growing at 8%. If the stock is currently selling for $100 and your required rate of return is 10%, would you buy the stock at today's price?

   a. Yes, because the stock is a good buy based on a risk-return relationship.
   b. Yes, because the stock is undervalued based on the dividend growth model.
   c. Yes, because the stock is overvalued based on the dividend growth model.
   d. No, because the stock is not a good investment based on its risk-return relationship.
   e. No, because the stock is overvalued based on the divided growth model.

185. John Sanders owns an apartment complex with 120 units, each renting for $750 per month. The complex has an occupancy rate of 80%. The expenses are $300,000 to maintain and run the apartment complex. Based on the capitalized earnings approach and a capitalization rate of 12%, how much is the complex worth?

   a. $4,700,000.
   b. $5,600,000.
   c. $6,000,000.
   d. $6,500,000.
   e. $9,000,000.

186. Determine the yield to maturity of a 20-year bond selling for $1,197.93 that has a coupon of 10% (paid semi-annually).

a. 4%.
b. 5%.
c. 6%.
d. 7%.
e. 8%.

187. Determine the price of a bond with a 10% coupon paid semi-annually, 3-year maturity, yielding 12%.

a. $950.83.
b. $951.96.
c. $1,000.00.
d. $1,049.74.
e. $1,050.76.

188. John's portfolio has $15,000 invested in Security A, $30,000 invested in Security B, and $45,000 invested in Security C. If Securities A, B, and C have Betas of 1.5, 1.2, and .9, respectively, what is the weighted beta of John's portfolio?

a. 1.1.
b. 1.0.
c. 1.2.
d. 0.9.
e. 1.3.

189. Your client purchased 100 shares of FAQ stock at $60 with a 50% margin requirement and 35% maintenance margin requirement. If the stock drops to $40, how much money does he have to put up?

a. $0.
b. $400.
c. $600.
d. $615.
e. $800.

INVESTMENT STRATEGIES

190. Danny and Clyde Floyd are both young and are willing to take above average risk for higher returns with their retirement savings. Based on the following historical data, which stock should they add to their portfolio.

	Stock A	Stock B
1990	21%	30%
1991	8%	5%
1992	30%	40%
1993	15%	(10%)
1994	16%	25%

a. Either stock would be appropriate because the average return of the stocks are equal.
b. Stock A because its risk adjusted rate of return is higher than Stock B.
c. Stock A because it has a lower standard deviation.
d. Stock B because it has a high return and a larger standard deviation than Stock A.
e. Stock B because the geometric average annual return for Stock B is greater than Stock A.

191. Sam Squeaky has been investing $350 into a mutual fund at the end of each month for the last 10 years and has been earning a compound return of 12%, consisting entirely of appreciation. Does Sam have enough money, after selling this investment and paying taxes at 28% to purchase his dream boat for $70,000?

a. No, because he only has $69,729.75 after paying the tax on the capital gain.
b. No, because he only has $57,969.75 after paying the tax on the capital gain.
c. Yes, because he has $80,513.54 after the sale of the investment.
d. Yes, because he has $72,176.34 after paying the tax.
e. None of the above.

CLIENT ASSESSMENT

192. A person who is willing to accept a large increase in risk without a large increase in return would be classified as what?

   a. Risk average.
   b. Risk neutral.
   c. Risk adverse.
   d. Risk seeking.
   e. Risk tolerant.

193. Adrean comes to you for advice. She has a large capital gain in IBM (approximately 100%). She has heard rumors that may make the stock price tumble and is concerned about losing her gain. However, because of her tax situation, she does not currently want to recognize a taxable gain. Assuming no transaction costs, what would you advise her to do to maintain her gain without selling her stock?

   a. Sell short against the box.
   b. Purchase a call option.
   c. Sell a put option.
   d. Hedge in the futures market.
   e. Her best solution is to sell the stock and incur the tax.

194. Joseph Gillmore, age 35, is an investor with a moderate to high risk level who is in the top tax bracket of 40% (State and Federal) and has a long-term perspective and expects to be in a lower tax bracket in 30 years. Which of the following mutual funds would you recommend for Joseph if he is investing for his retirement:

Fund 1: A bond fund comprised of high quality municipal and corporate bonds, which has yielded 9.3% over the last 10 years.

Fund 2: An equity growth fund, which has yielded 14.75% of income and annual appreciation of approximately 2% over the last 10 years and has a beta of 1.1.

Fund 3: An equity growth fund, which has yielded 2.4% of income and annual appreciation of approximately 14% over the last 10 years with a beta of 1.12.

a. Fund 1 because bond funds are less risky and this fund invests in municipal bonds, which are not subject to federal income tax, thus reducing his tax burden.
b. Fund 2 because the total yield is higher than Fund 1 or Fund 3.
c. Fund 2 because the Beta level is lower than Fund 3.
d. Fund 3 because the capital appreciation will accumulate without tax until the shares are sold.
e. Fund 3 because with a higher beta, the returns over a long-term horizon will be higher than a fund with a lower beta.

195. Birtch and Mary Marlin are interested in adding an equity to their portfolio. The Marlins require a 10% rate of return and are considering the following stocks.

Stock A: Dividends are currently $4.50 annually and are expected to grow at 5% annually; the market price is currently $80.

Stock B: Dividends are currently $2.75 annually and are expected to grow at 9% annually; the market price is currently $250.

Stock C: Dividends are currently $1.25 annually and are expected to grow at 7% annually; the market price is currently $35.

Using the dividend growth model, which stock would be most appropriate for the Marlins and why?

a. Stock A: because it has the largest dividend.
b. Stock A: because the market price is undervalued by the largest amount.
c. Stock B: because it has the largest growth rate of the three investments.
d. Stock B: because it is undervalued by the largest dollar amount.
e. Stock C: because it is undervalued the greatest amount and is the best buy for the amount of initial investment.

196. Holly and Jeff Davis have recently retired and are no longer drawing an income. They would like to change their asset allocation to provide more income in their retirement years. Which of the following investments would help the couple in achieving their financial objectives?

    1. Aggressive growth mutual fund shares.
    2. AA corporate bonds.
    3. Zero-coupon bonds.
    4. Equity income mutual fund shares.

        a. 2 and 3.
        b. 2 and 4.
        c. 1 and 3.
        d. 1, 2, and 4.
        e. 2, 3, and 4.

197. Buddy and Patty White own a farm in Colorado with a FMV of $300,000 (with an outstanding loan of $125,000 and a basis of $50,000). This farm is rental property and generates $5,000 in after tax income each year. The farm has suspended passive activity losses of $50,000 and it is expected to appreciate at 6% per year. If the Whites can earn 10% after tax and plan to purchase a farm when they retire in 30 years, would they be better, from a purely monetary standpoint, to sell the farm (assuming a 28% capital gains rate) and invest the proceeds or keep the farm?

    a. The Whites should keep the farm because they would be better by $55,255 in today's dollars.
    b. The Whites should sell the farm because they would be better by $55,255 in today's dollars
    c. The Whites should keep the farm because they would be better by $26,880 in today's dollars.
    d. The whites should sell the farm because they would be better by $8,120 in today's dollars.
    e. There is no difference monetarily between keeping the farm and selling the farm.

198. Buddy and Patty White own a farm in Colorado with a FMV of $300,000 (with an outstanding loan of $125,000 and a basis of $50,000). This farm is rental property and generates $5,000 in after tax income each year. The farm has suspended passive activity losses of $50,000 and it is expected to appreciate at 6% per year. If the Whites can earn 10% after tax and plan to purchase a farm when they retire in 30 years, would they be better, from a purely monetary standpoint, to sell the farm (assuming a 28% capital gains rate) and invest the proceeds or keep the farm? How much after tax income must the property generate to be at break-even regarding the sale vs. keeping the farm?

a. $2,851.
b. ($2,851).
c. $2,149.
d. $5,861.
e. ($2,149).

199. Allison Michaels comes to you to and asks you which of the following payout methods she should accept from her qualified plan (assume all Michaels live at least until they are 90 and that they can earn 8% after tax):

Option 1: Lump-sum payment of $204,000.
Option 2: An annuity paid for a term certain of 15 years of $24,000 per year.
Option 3: An annuity, second to die payment, paid over the joint-life expectancy of Allison and her son: 27.5 years, in the amount of $18,450.

a. Option 1 because it has the highest future value.
b. Option 1 because it has the highest present value.
c. Option 2 because it has the highest guaranteed present value.
d. Option 3 because it has the highest present value.
e. Option 3 because it has the highest future value.

200. What is the present value of an annuity if it pays $2,500 per year at year-end for 20 years and the annuity does not begin for 3 years? (Assume a discount rate of 15%.)

a. $10,289.
b. $13,627.
c. $16,438.
d. $23,721.
e. $50,000.

INVESTMENT PLANNING SOLUTIONS

INVESTMENT PLANNING

1.	B	35.	C	69.	C	103.	E	137.	C	171.	D
2.	B	36.	E	70.	C	104.	A	138.	E	172.	D
3.	D	37.	C	71.	B	105.	B	139.	D	173.	A
4.	E	38.	D	72.	C	106.	D	140.	E	174.	E
5.	E	39.	C	73.	D	107.	C	141.	A	175.	C
6.	B	40.	C	74.	C	108.	D	142.	D	176.	C
7.	D	41.	C	75.	C	109.	E	143.	E	177.	D
8.	B	42.	E	76.	E	110.	C	144.	E	178.	A
9.	D	43.	B	77.	C	111.	D	145.	C	179.	A
10.	A	44.	B	78.	A	112.	D	146.	D	180.	A
11.	D	45.	C	79.	D	113.	E	147.	C	181.	B
12.	B	46.	D	80.	A	114.	E	148.	E	182.	C
13.	E	47.	A	81.	D	115.	C	149.	E	183.	B
14.	A	48.	B	82.	A	116.	B	150.	D	184.	E
15.	D	49.	C	83.	E	117.	C	151.	B	185.	A
16.	B	50.	B	84.	D	118.	C	152.	A	186.	E
17.	B	51.	E	85.	A	119.	C	153.	B	187.	A
18.	D	52.	C	86.	A	120.	C	154.	B	188.	A
19.	E	53.	C	87.	E	121.	E	155.	B	189.	B
20.	D	54.	E	88.	B	122.	D	156.	B	190.	B
21.	C	55.	C	89.	D	123.	A	157.	C	191.	A
22.	B	56.	B	90.	A	124.	D	158.	B	192.	D
23.	C	57.	A	91.	A	125.	C	159.	C	193.	A
24.	D	58.	B	92.	D	126.	A	160.	D	194.	D
25.	A	59.	B	93.	A	127.	A	161.	D	195.	E
26.	E	60.	D	94.	E	128.	A	162.	C	196.	B
27.	E	61.	D	95.	D	129.	D	163.	D	197.	C
28.	A	62.	B	96.	A	130.	A	164.	C	198.	C
29.	C	63.	D	97.	D	131.	C	165.	A	199.	C
30.	A	64.	A	98.	E	132.	B	166.	A	200.	A
31.	D	65.	A	99.	E	133.	B	167.	D		
32.	B	66.	A	100.	D	134.	B	168.	B		
33.	D	67.	E	101.	C	135.	E	169.	C		
34.	D	68.	A	102.	B	136.	B	170.	E		

BASIC INVESTMENT CONCEPTS

Types of Risk

1. B

Statement #1 is false. Systematic risk is market risk and cannot be diversified away.

Statement #2 is true.

Statement #3 is false. If unsystematic risk equals zero then total risk is systematic risk.

Systematic risk is the risk that all securities are subject to and can not be reduced or eliminated through diversification. Unsystematic risk is company or industry specific risk that can be reduced or eliminated though diversification.

Types of Risk

2. B

Because treasuries are considered default risk free. Financial risk is the uncertainty (risk) introduced from the method by which a firm finances its assets (i.e., debt vs. equity financing). Reinvestment rate risk is the risk that as cash flows are received they will have to be invested at lower rates of return than the investment that generated the cash flows. Systematic risk is the risk that all securities are subject to and can not be reduced or eliminated through diversification.

Types of Risk

3. D

Financial risk deals with the leveraging of a company's capital structure (i.e., debt vs. equity financing). Business risk is the uncertainty (risk) of income cash flows caused by the nature of a firm's business. The more uncertain the income cash flows to the company, the more uncertain the cash flows to the investor. Market risk is a type of systematic risk (see question 2).

Types of Risk

4. E

U.S. companies would subject the portfolio to business risk (A).

Corporate bonds would subject the portfolio to default risk (B) and interest rate risk (D).

All investments are subject to systematic risk (D).

Types of Risk

5. **E**

Statement #1 is false. Systematic risk is undiversifiable.
Statement #2 is false. Business risk and financial risk are examples of unsystematic risk. Purchasing power risk is a systematic risk.
Statement #3 is false. Default risk relates only to fixed investments.

Types of Risk

6. **B**

Fire is the only business risk above. Statement #1 and statement #4 are forms of market risk and statement #3 is financial risk.

Types of Investment Risk

7. **D**

1. Default Risk - Yes. Because the company may have financial difficulty in the future.
2. Reinvestment Rate Risk - No. Because the bond does not have any coupon payments to reinvest.
3. Purchasing Power Risk - Yes. Inflation may exceed the yield to maturity (YTM).
4. Liquidity Risk – Yes. Although there will always be a ready market; if she sells when interest rates have gone up, she may have a price concession.

Types of Risk

8. **B**

All are possible risks except short squeeze risk. Short squeeze relates to shorting stocks. The key word in the question is might.

Interest Rate Risk and Reinvestment Risk

9. **D**

Either choice will yield the same result.

Sell			Hold		
Step 1:		***Price of Bond***	***Step 1:***		***Inflate payments @ 7%***
FV	=	$1,000	PMT	=	($80)
PMT	=	80	N	=	25
i	=	7	i	=	7
N	=	25	FV	=	$5,059.92
PV	=	($1,116.54)			
Step 2:		***Inflate PV for 25 years @ 7%***	***Step 2:***		***Add maturity value of bond***
PV	=	($1,116.54)			$5,059.92
N	=	25			+ 1,000.00
i	=	7			$6,059.92
PMT	=	$0			
FV	=	$6,059.92			

Types of Risk (CFP® Exam, released 3/95)

10. **A**

Non-diversifiable risks or systematic risks are those that affect the entire market, including market risk, interest rate risk and purchasing power risk. Business risk, management risk, company risk and industry risk are unsystematic risks, which can be reduced or eliminated through diversification.

Objectives

11. **D**

Tax advantaged investments do not necessarily reduce risk. For example, municpal bonds, limited partnerships, non-dividend paying growth stocks all have a certain amount of risk inherent in them. All investments should be entered into with the idea of building equity.

Investment Risk Returns (CFP® Exam, released 12/95)

12. B

Systematic risk cannot be eliminated; thus, statement #2 is false. Beta only measures systematic risk, thus statement #5 is false. All other statements are true.

SECURITIES (TYPES & CHARACTERISTICS)

Investment Risk

13. E

The least risky transaction is shorting against the box.

Investment Risk

14. A

The most risky transaction is selling a naked option.

Options

15. D

Seller's maximum gain is $3, but his maximum loss is unlimited. Since the call option was written as a naked call, the seller (John) will have to buy the stock at the market price if the option is exercised by the buyer. The buyer would exercise the option when the stock price exceeds $20.00. Any price level over $20 begins to reduce the option buyer's potential loss, and at $23 the seller and buyer break even.

Options

16. B

The buyer of the call option would have a loss of $1.00 if he exercised the option whereas the loss would equal $3.00 if he did not exercise. Therefore, he would exercise. The buyer would exercise the option when the stock price exceeds $42.00. Any price level over $42.00 begins to reduce the option buyer's potential loss, and at $45.00 the option buyer breaks even.

Options

17. B

Statement #1 is false. This is true for a put but not for a call.

Statement #2 is false. Call: Net loss of $4. Put: Net loss of Zero (in-money by $4.00 + $4 Premium = "0" Net). Therefore, total loss of $4.00.

Statement #3 is true. The call option would not be exercised.

Statement #4 is false. Because the put would be exercised, both the buyer and the seller would break-even.

Options

18. **D**

1. The largest loss is cost of the two premiums because the call will be profitable with higher stock prices and the put will be profitable with lower stock prices. True. Maximum loss any option buyer can sustain is the original premium. Out-of-money options expire with "0" premium.

2. False

	Put					Call		Total
	32					*Not*		
	(31)					*Exercised*		
	1	- 3	=	(2)	+	(6)	=	(8)

3. True

	Call					Put		Total
	45					*Not*		
	(42)					*Exercised*		
	3	- 6	=	(3)	+	(3)	=	(6)

Options

19. **E**

To break even, the price must be $9 above or below the exercise price to cover the two premiums.

	Put	Call
Exercise Price	$32.00	$42.00
Premiums ($6.00 + $3.00)	- 9.00	+ 9.00
Break-even	$23.00	$51.00

Short Sales

20. **D**

$44.50
($40.00)
$ 4.50 x 100 = **$450**

The Uptick rules only permit an investor to short a stock when the price has moved up one Tick (not on down Ticks). Therefore, she will short the stock at $44.50 because that is the first increase in the stock price. Her gain will be the difference between $44.50 and $40.00 multiplied by the number of shares.

Short Sales

21. **C**

Proceeds	$3,500
Cost	(2,000)
Gain	$1,500
Less Dividend Payment	(200)
Net Profit	**$1,300**

The short seller must pay any dividends due to the investor who lent the stock. The purchaser of the short-sale stock receives the dividend from the corporation, so the short seller must pay a similar dividend to the lender.

Short Sales

22. **B**

Angel's investment: $100 x 57 x .5 = $2,850.

Proceeds	5,700
Cost	(5,400)
Gain	300
Less Dividend Payment	(200)
Net Profit	$100

[(Net Profit)/(Investment)] = % Gain/Loss

$100 ÷ $2,850 = 3.5%

Financial Leverage

23. **C**

Proceeds	$78.00				
Cost	(67.00)				
Gain	$11.00	x	75 shares	=	$825.00
Investment	=		75 x 67.00 x 55%	=	$2,763.75

Therefore, $\frac{\$825}{\$2,763.75}$ = 29.85% = 30%

Financial Leverage

24. **D**

$$\text{Margin Call} = \frac{\text{Loan}}{1 - \text{Maintenance Margin}}$$

$$\left[\frac{\$67 \times (1 - .55)}{1 - .40}\right] = \frac{\$30.15}{.60} = \$50.25$$

Options

25. **A**

All variables except the inflation rate are elements of the Black Scholes option valuation model.

The five variables in the model are as follows:

1. Stock price.
2. Exercise price.
3. Risk free rate.
4. Time.
5. Volatility (standard deviation).

Options

26. **E**

All three are variables in the Black Scholes Option model.

The five variables in the model are as follows:

1. Stock price.
2. Exercise price.
3. Risk free rate.
4. Time.
5. Volitility (standard deviation)

Options

27. **E**

Phrases A, B, and D are used to describe the state of an option. None are used to describe bonds.

Options

28. **A**

The Black Scholes model is used to value call options.

Options

29. **C**

Out-of-the-money for a call option means that the exercise price is greater than the current market price for the security. At-the-money means that the stock price is equal to the exercise price. In-the-money for a call option means that the price of the security is higher than the exercise price of the call option. By-the-money is a non-existent phrase.

Options

30. **A**

A put option is in-the-money when the exercise price is greater than the current market price of the security. A put option is out-of-the-money when the stock price is greater than the exercise price.

Options

31. **D**

In the money:	MP > EP
At the money:	MP = EP
Out of the money:	MP < EP

The premium for the option is not considered in determining if a call option is in-the-money, at-the-money, or out-of-the-money.

Options

32. **B**

Because option #3 is out-of-the-money by the greatest amount and because it has the earliest expiration date (less time for the stock price to move into the money), it is the most risky.

(**Note:** The most risky will usually have the lowest premium.)

Options

33. D

Option #7 is the least risky because it has the most time to expiration and it is in the money by the largest amount.

Options

34. D

The Put-Call Parity Model is used to determine the value of a put option based on the value of a similar call option. Sharpe and Treynor are stock performance models. Black Scholes is a call option valuation model.

Hedging

35. C

Jim Bob should buy lumber futures contracts to protect against rising prices. This is called a long hedge.

Bonds and Preferred Stock

36. E

Statement #1 is false. Creditors are satisfied before preferred stock holders

Statement #2 is false. Dividends are not deductible.

Statement #3 is false. Can be participating.

Statement #4 is false. Preferred stock has an indefinite life, whereas bonds have a definite maturity.

Duration

37. **C**

Method 1

Pd	CF	Product	PV @ 14%
1	125	125	$ 109.65
2	125	250	192.37
3	125	375	253.11
4	125	500	296.04
5	1,125	5,625	2,921.45
			$3,772.62

Yield to Maturity		
PV	=	$948.50
N	=	5
PMT	=	125
FV	=	$1,000
i	=	14%

Duration = [($3,772.62)/($948.50)] = 3.977 years

Method 2

$$\text{Duration} = \frac{1 + y}{y} - \frac{(1 + y) + T(c - y)}{c[(1 + y)^T - 1] + y}$$

$$= \frac{1.14}{.14} - \frac{1.14 + 5(.125 - .14)}{.125[(1.14)^5 - 1] + .14}$$

$$= 8.1429 - \frac{1.065}{.2557}$$

$$= 8.1429 - 4.1654$$

$$= 3.977 \text{ years}$$

Influence of Time on Investments

38. **D**

Statement #1 is true. Duration of Bond I is higher because cash flows are lower.

Statement #2 is false. The lower the coupon the higher potential for price fluctuation.

Statement #3 is true. The longer the maturity the higher potential for price fluctuation.

Statement #4 is true. The lower the coupon the higher potential for price fluctuation.

Statement #5 is true. Duration and coupon rate are inversely related.

Duration

39. C

(YTM)	i	=	A	B	C
			11%	11%	11%

Period	A CF	B CF	C CF	Total CF	PV @ 11%	PV x Period
1	$125	$100	$85	$310	$279.28	$279.28
2	125	100	85	310	251.60	503.20
3	125	100	85	310	226.67	680.00
4	125	100	85	310	204.22	816.83
5	1,125	1,100	85	2,310	1,370.87	6,854.36
6	0	0	85	85	45.44	272.67
7	0	0	1,085	1,085	522.60	3,658.20
	$1,625	$1,500	$1,595	$4,720	$2,900.68	$13,064.54

$1,055.44
963.04
882.20
$2,900.68

$13,064 ÷ $2,900.68 = **4.504 years**

Treasury Bills

40. C

T-bills are quoted as a percent of par value thus, 95.24 is 95.24% of 10,000 or $9,524.00.

Serial Bonds

41. C

The most common type of bond is a term bond that has a single maturity date. Serial Bonds have a series of maturity dates. A portion of the bond issue matures each year. Serial Bonds are typically issued by municipalities.

Municipal Bonds

42. E

Revenue obligation bonds are sold to finance specific projects, and the debt and interest are paid off with the revenue generated from the project. These bonds are a type of municipal bond.

Short Sales

43. **B**

The Uptick rule requires that short sales only occur after the stock price has increased on the previous trade.

Portfolio Insurance

44. **B**

Selling a stock index future will hedge against declining markets. The other options will only profit in increasing markets.

Options

45. **C**

Purchasing a put will be profitable if the market or stock declines. If the market increases or the stock price increases then the investment in the security will be profitable. The combination of a put option and a long position will limit down side risk but not limit upside potential.

Duration

46. **D**

Because the bond is a zero coupon bond, the duration must be 10 years. No calculation is necessary.

Insurance Based Investments

47. **A**

Insurance companies issue GICs.

Open-End Investment Companies

48. **B**

Statement #2 is true; open-end investment companies can sell unlimited shares and thereby increase their capitalization. All other statements are characteristics of closed-end investment companies.

Margin Calls

49. **C**

$$\text{Margin Call} = \frac{\text{Loan}}{1 - \text{Maintenance Margin}}$$

$$= \frac{\$60.00 \times 50\%}{(1 - .30)}$$

$$= \frac{\$30}{.70}$$

$$= \$42.85$$

Margin Calls

50. **B**

Value	=	$40 x 100	=	$4,000
Loan	=			(3,000)
Equity	=			$1,000
Equity needed	=	$4,000 x 30%	=	$1,200
Cash needed	=			$200

Options

51. **E**

Statements #1 and #2 are true because the writer of any option will receive a premium. Statement #3 is true because the purchaser of a call hopes the price will increase, whereas the seller of the option hopes it will decline (or at least not increase). Statement #4 is the opposite of statement #3.

Stock Market

52. C

Statements #1 and #3 are true. Statement #2 is false because most OTC stocks are more likely to reinvest earnings into the company, and therefore not pay dividends as high as well established companies.

Statement #1

Assumed stock price: $100

Assumed initial margin: 50%

Assumed maintenance margin: 35%

$$\text{Margin Call} = \frac{\text{Loan}}{1 - \text{Maintenance Margin}}$$

$$= \frac{\$50.00}{(1 - .35)}$$

$$= \frac{\$50}{.65}$$

$$= \$76.92$$

A margin call will occur at a price below $76.92. Since $75.00 (75% of the original value of $100) is less than $76.92, this statement must be true.

Hedging (CFP® Exam, released 3/95)

53. C

The client will benefit if the market increases. His/her portfolio, because it is diversified, should move with the market. An index option also moves with the market and would therefore be a good hedge vehicle. A put should be used because it will increase in value if the market should decline.

Intrinsic Value of Common Stock (CFP® Exam, released 3/95)

54. E

The intrinsic value of a share of common stock is equal to the discounted present value of its cash flows.

Preferred Stock (CFP® Exam, released 3/95)

55. C

Corporations receive a deduction of 70%, 80%, or 100%, depending on ownership percentage for dividends received (IRC Section 243).

Municipal Bonds (CFP® Exam, released 3/95)

56. B

General obligation bonds are backed by full taxing authority of the municipality, whereas revenue bonds are only repaid from revenues of a particular project.

Options (CFP® Exam, released 3/95)

57. A

The call option is out of the money, therefore the intrinsic value is zero. To have an intrinsic value, the current price of the stock must exceed the strike price. The formula is market price – strike price = intrinsic value.

Options (CFP® Exam, released 3/95)

58. B

A call option has unlimited upside price potential which means that writing a call without the stock as a hedge will provide the greatest loss potential. In selling a put option, the seller does have downside price risk, but the stock price can only drop to zero. Writing a covered call only exposes the writer to lost profits. In buying a call option, the purchaser's only risk is the premium or cost of the option. Buying the underlying security only exposes the purchaser to downside price risk; the price of the stock can only drop to zero.

Unit Trusts (CFP® Exam, released 3/95)

59. B

Once capitalized, unit trusts do not accept additional funds. Unit trusts are almost always self-liquidating. The other characteristics apply to closed-end mutual funds. Also, unit trusts do not have shares like a mutual fund, they are sold in units.

International Investments (CFP® Exam, released 3/95)

60. D

ADRs are used to trade foreign securities in the U.S. ADRs are trust receipts issued by a U.S. bank for shares of a foreign branch of the bank. ADRs are legal claims against the equity interest that the bank holds. ADRs do not eliminate currency risks.

Agency Bonds

61. D

GNMA stands for Government National Mortgage Association. The bonds issued by this organization are backed by the full faith and credit of the U.S. Government. Therefore, they are considered to be default risk free.

Closed-End Investment Companies

62. B

Statement #1 is false. Shares of closed-end funds are traded in the secondary markets, not redeemed by the company.

Statement #2 is true.

Statement #3 is false. Closed-end funds have a capitalization that is fixed, unlike open-end funds.

Series EE Bonds

63. D

Bonds are sold at 50% of face. All other statements are true.

Mutual Funds

64. A

Sector funds tend to limit their investments to one sector of the economy, such as natural resources, technology, or health care.

Short-Term Investment Vehicle

65. A

Treasury bonds are long-term investment vehicles.

Derivatives

66. A

Statement #1 is true. Warrants are issued by the company. Call options are written by other investors.

Statement #2 is false. Both types of derivatives can be converted to stock

Statement #3 is false. Warrants are often issued as a sweetener for bonds, however, call options are not issued with bonds.

Securities

67. E

The premium is ignored when determining the intrinsic value of an option. Therefore, the intrinsic value is $4.00 ($50 - $46).

Securities

68. A

Selling a naked call option has the greatest potential for loss, because the upside risk is unlimited.

Securities

69. C

As an agency of the U.S. Government, Guaranteed National Mortgage Association bonds are backed by the full faith and credit of the U.S. Government. The other two are considered to have default risk.

Options

70. C

Buying a call option will allow Kristen to purchase the stock in the future at a pre-determined price if the market value should go up.

Securities

71. B

Since strips do not have coupons, reinvestment risk is avoided.

Securities

72. **C**

Inflation will not directly affect the value of an option. Standard deviation and increased time are directly related.

Securities (CFP® Exam, released 12/96)

73. **D**

Convertible bonds generate current income from coupon payments and allow for growth through the stock conversion feature.

Reporting

74. **C**

Morningstar publishes information regarding mutual funds.

Securities

75. **C**

Shorting against the box will allow the client to freeze his gain until January 31st of the year following the year the short against the box transaction was entered into. A short against the box is a transaction in which the owner of a stock (long position) enters into an equal and offsetting short position. The net result is that regardless of the movement of the stock price, no additional gains or losses will occur.

Securities

76. **E**

Mike can lock in the price of the stock by purchasing a call option.

Securities

77. **C**

Selling a coverd call will generate income from the option premium. Since the market is expected to be flat, there is little risk that the market price of the stock will increase to the point where the option could be exercised.

Mutual Funds

78. **A**

The time-weighted return measures the actual rate of return of a portfolio manager.

SECURITY MARKETS

Security Markets

79. D

The question is the definition of the fourth market. The Primary Market is for initial sales of securities issued to the public. The Secondary Market consists of the large exchanges, such as the New York Stock Exchange, American Stock Exchange, NASDAQ (over the counter (OTC) stocks), and regional exchanges. The Third Market consists of stocks traded both on the organized exchanges and on the OTC market. The orders on the Third Market are usually block trades of 10,000 shares or more.

Security Markets

80. A

IPOs are initial public offerings, which is one of the functions of the Primary Market.

Underwriting

81. D

Private placement can be done with 35 or less investors (not 20).

Security Markets

82. A

False because floor traders do not trade with public. They trade for themselves.

Types of Orders

83. E

Both limit orders and stop limit orders are correct: (B and D); therefore, the correct answer is e. Market orders trade at the market price, not a price specified by the purchaser. A Stop order, commonly referred to as a Stop-loss Order, is triggered at a specific stock price after a decline in the price of a stock. When the Stop order is triggered it converts into a Market Order and executes at the market price.

Underwriting

84. D

Private placement does not require registration with the SEC. Therefore, it is much quicker and less costly.

Underwriting

85. A

Definition of commission broker.

Types of Orders

86. A

75% to 80% of orders are market orders.

Security Markets

87. E

All of the transaction are primary market transactions.

SECURITIES LAW

Securities Regulations

88. B

The Securities Act of 1933 deals with securities issued in the primary market.

Securities Regulations

89. D

The Securities Exchange Act of 1934 deals with regulating the secondary market.

Government Regulation (CFP® Exam, released 3/95)

90. A

Organized exchanges are regulated by the SEC, which is a Federal agency. All other statements are true.

Securities Law

91. A

Statement #1 is true.

Statement #2 is false. There is no limit for sophisticated investors investing in a private placement.

Statement #3 is false. A registration statement is not required (which is the point of a private placement).

Securities Law

92. D

Statements #1 and #3 are true.

Statement #2 is false. Registration with the SEC is not required with a private placement.

Securities Law

93. A

The SEC regulates investment advisor.

INVESTMENT CONCEPTS

Markowitz

94. E

Because Portfolio 5 has the same risk with a 5% higher return than Portfolio 1, and Portfolio 6 has the same risk and a higher return than the remaining portfolios.

Efficient Market Hypothesis

95. D

Because the efficient market hypothesis says that on average you cannot outperform the market. Statement A relates to technical analysis. Statements B and C relate to fundamental analysis.

Holding Risk and Return, Dividend Growth Model and CAPM

96. A

Statement I - True	Statement II - False	Statement III - False
$\frac{\$2(1.08)}{12.5\% - 8\%} = 48$	$E(r) = 5\% + 1.15(11\% - 5\%)$ $= 11.9\%$	$\frac{(\$67 - \$65 + \$2)}{\$65} = 6.15\%$

Market price	$67
Constant Growth Dividend Model Price	(48)
Overvalued	$19

Capital Asset Pricing Model

97. D

$$\text{Gain} = \frac{\$10 - \$8}{\$8} + 6.25\% \text{ Dividend Yield}$$

$$= 25\% + 6.25\%$$

$$= 31.25\%$$

$$E(r) = 7\% + .85(8\%) = 13.8 \text{ (CAPM)}$$

Efficient Market Hypothesis

98. E

The Efficient Market Hypothesis is in direct contradiction to technical analysis because the Efficient Market Hypothesis is founded on the notion that all historical data, which is what is used by technical analysts, is already accounted for in the current stock price.

Efficient Market Hypothesis

99. E

The Efficient Market Hypothesis is in direct contradiction to technical analysis because the Efficient Market Hypothesis is founded on the notion that all historical data, which is what is used by technical analysts, is already accounted for in the current stock price.

Types of Risk and Diversification

100. D

Standard Deviation measures total risk (systematic and unsystematic) and is therefore, always an appropriate measure of risk.

Standard Deviation

101. C

Mean = (.25)(.05) + (.47)(.13) + (.28)(.23) = 13.80%

Variance =$(.05 - .138)^2$ (.25) +$(.13 - .138)^2$ (.47) + $(.23 - .138)^2$ (.28)

=.001936 + .00003008 + .0023699

=.004336

Standard deviation =$(.004336)^{½}$ = 6.58%

Measurements of Risk

102. B

Expected Return		
(.2) x (.45)	=	.090
(.3) x (.25)	=	.075
(.4) x (.13)	=	.052
(.1) x (.03)	=	.003
		.220

Standard Deviation

σ = $[(.45-.22)^2(.2) + (.25-.22)^2(.3) + (.13-.22)^2(.4) + (.03-.22)^2(.1)]^{1/2}$

= $[.01058 + .00027 + .00324 + .00361]^{1/2}$

= $[.01770]^{1/2}$ = 13.3%

Incorrect Method – This method does not work!

Standard Deviation Calculation using HP12C

F	clx
.45	Σ+
.45	Σ+
.25	Σ+
.25	Σ+
.25	Σ+
.13	Σ+
.13	Σ+
.13	Σ+
.13	Σ+
.03	Σ+

Note: 10 in screen of calculator

To calculate mean: Blue g 0 Answer: 22%

To calculate standard deviation: Blue g . (which is the period with the blue s below)

Answer: 14.02%

$.14024^2$ = .01967 x 2

= .177 / 10

= .0177

= $\sqrt{.0177}$

= 13.3%

Note: The 14.02% differs from the formula calculation of 13.3. The HP12C calculates standard deviation of actual historical returns, while the formula in problem 46 determines the standard deviation of returns with assigned probabilities. The HP12C is for past returns and the formula is for future returns.

Measurement of Risk

103. E

The mean for a normal distribution splits the distribution in half. Because the probability of all occurrences is 100%, the probability that the stock will have a return below 14% (the mean) is one-half (50%) of all possible occurrences.

Measurement of Risk

104. A

All returns must have been 9% for the standard deviation to be zero. Therefore, the probability of a return of 9% is 100%. Thus, anything else has a probability of zero.

Measurement of Risk

105. B

The probability of having a return above 9% is 50%. The probability of having a return between 9% and 15% is 34% [1/2 of 68% (1 standard deviation)]. Therefore, the probability of a return above 15% is 16% (50% - 34%).

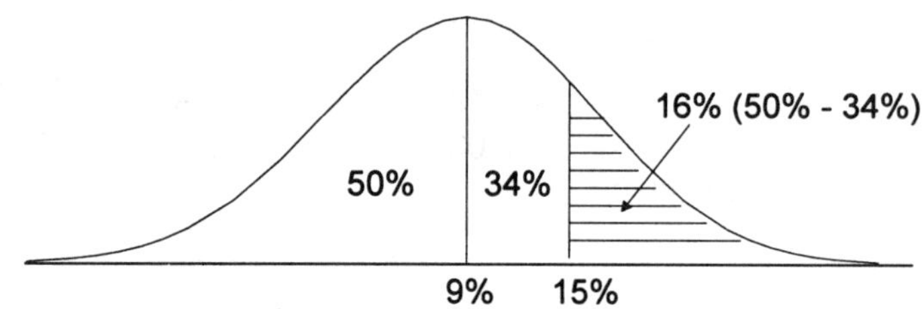

Measurement of Risk

106. D

The probability of a return above 24% is 50%. The probability of a return between 4% and 24% is 47.5% (95% divided by 2). Therefore, the probability of a return above 4% is 97.5% (50% + 47.5%).

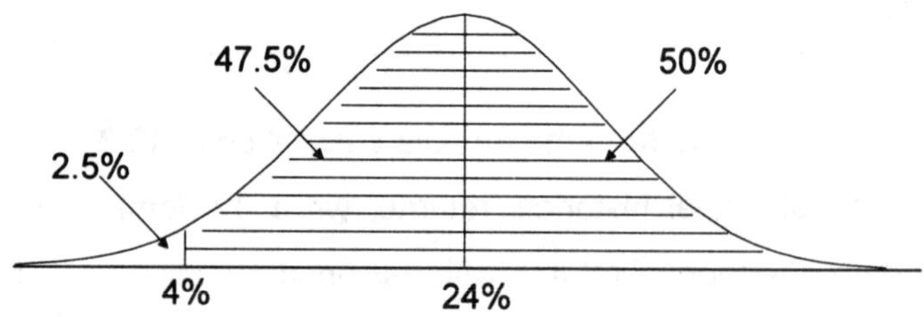

Measurement of Risk

107. C

$.8^2 = .64$. Since the correlation coefficient is .80, the coefficient of determination (R^2) is .64. Therefore, only 64% of investment returns can be explained by changes in the market (i.e., systematic risk represents 64%).

Measurement of Risk

108. **D**

$.5^2 = .25$

$(1 - .25) = .75$

The coefficient of determination (R^2), which is the correlation coefficient squared, explains the percent of change in the dependent variable that can be explained by changes in the independent variable. Therefore, 25% of returns are explained by changes in the market. To determine the percentage of returns that are explained by unsystematic risk, subtract the systematic risk from 1 (1 - .25).

Diversification

109. **E**

The highest level of diversification will occur when the correlation coefficient is closest to -1. Of the five pairs of portfolios, portfolios 9 and 10 offer the highest level of diversification because the correlation coefficient of -0.78 is closest to -1. Portfolios 9 and 10 should move in opposite directions because they are negatively correlated.

Beta

110. **C**

$E(r) = R_f + \beta(R_M - R_f)$ [Capital Asset Pricing Model]

$22\% = 4\% + 1.5(R_M - 4\%)$

$18\% = 1.5R_M - 6\%$

$1.5R_M = 24\%$

$R_M = 16\%$

Diversification

111. **D**

A correlation coefficient of zero means that the two stocks move independently. However, since most stocks are positively correlated, a correlation coefficient of zero should provide more diversification than most pairs of stocks.

Beta

112. D

A negative beta means that the investment will move in the opposite direction from the market (e.g., gold). Therefore, if the market is declining, then the security should increase in value, thereby increasing the value of the portfolio in a bear market.

Diversification

113. E

Statement #1 is true. Diversification is possible as long as the correlation coefficient is below one. Remember that most stocks are positively correlated which means that combining stocks with a correlation coefficient of zero will eliminate most, if not all, systematic risk.

Statement #2 is true. The market portfolio consists of all risky assets and is considered to be the most diversified portfolio.

Statement #3 is true. To reduce unsystematic risk, the correlation must be less than one.

Markowitz

114. E

The efficient frontier consists of portfolios with the highest expected return for a given level of risk. Because Portfolio 2 has a higher expected return and a lower standard deviation than Portfolio 1, Portfolio 1 cannot be on the efficient frontier. Since Portfolio 4 has a high expected return and lower risk than Portfolio 3, Portfolio 3 cannot be on the efficient frontier.

Measure of Risk

115. C

Beta only measures systematic risk. Standard deviation measures total risk. Therefore, only statement #3 is true.

Capital Asset Pricing Model

116. B

$CAPM = E(r) = R_f + \beta(R_M - R_f)$

Because Beta (β) measures systematic risk, the higher the Beta, the higher the expected return. Therefore, systematic risk best explains portfolio returns.

Arbitrage Pricing Theory

117. **C**

The APT determines returns based on multiple factors. These factors might include inflation, growth in GDP, major political upheavals, or changes in interest rates.

Efficient Market Hypothesis

118. **C**

Statements #1 and #2 are true. Statement #3 is false because efficient markets will not allow investors to consistently outperform the market.

Standard Deviation

119. **C**

Expected Return*	Actual Return	Difference	Squared Difference
11%	15%	4	16
11%	12%	1	1
11%	8%	(3)	+ 9
			26

Variance = 26/(3 - 1) = 26/2 = 13

Standard deviation = $(13)^{1/2}$ = 3.6055

* Normally, you would use the average return of 11.67% in this calculation. However, the question asked you to assume 11%.

Capital Asset Pricing Model

120. **C**

The CAPM model uses Beta as a risk measure. It also demonstrates that as the level of risk (measured by Beta) increases, so does the expected return.

Standard Deviation

121. **E**

Portfolio 2 should not be selected because portfolio 1 has the same standard deviation, but with an expected return that is 3% higher. Portfolios 1, 3 and 4 are all reasonable choices, each representing a different risk-return tradeoff.

Standard Deviation (CFP® Exam, released 3/95)

122. D

Unless the correlation coefficient between the stocks is equal to one, the standard deviation for the portfolio will always be lower than the weighted average standard deviation for the portfolio.

Arbitrage Pricing Theory (CFP® Exam, released 3/95)

123. A

Arbitrage Pricing Theory uses multiple regression (many factors) to determine the specific outcome.

Capital Asset Pricing Model (CFP® Exam, released 3/95)

124. D

Valuing a company is generally done by finding the present value of the cash flows generated from the company. With everything else being equal, to value the company when the market premium increased, you would be discounting the same stream of cash flows, but at a higher discount rate. The higher discount rate will cause the present value of the cash flows to be lower - a decrease in the stock price.

Markowitz (CFP® Exam, released 3/95)

125. C

Statement #1 is true.

Statement #2 is false. As long as the correlation coefficient between assets is less than 1, the risk of the portfolio will be reduced.

Statement #3 is false. Diversifying across asset types is more, not less, effective than within an asset type.

Statement #4 is false. All the input variables in statement #1 help to create the efficient frontier.

Efficient Marekt Hypothesis

126. A

Random walk is the term used to describe the pattern of movement of stock prices. Since only new information, which is unpredictable and random, will affect the price of a security, the pattern of price movement for a stock will be random.

Performance Measures and Correlation

127. A

Since the correlation coefficient is .80, the coefficient of determination (R^2) is .64. Therefore, only 64% of the returns from the investment can be explained by the market (i.e., systematic risk represents 64%). Beta only measures systematic risk which means that 36% of outcomes will not be captured with Beta. Thus, Treynor and Jensen are not appropriate because they use Beta. Since Sharpe uses standard deviation, it is always an appropriate measure.

Investment Concepts

128. A

Only the weak form.

Investment Concepts

129. D

	Security A	Security B
Standard Deviation (SD)	5.03%	8.08%
Average Return (AR)	5.33%	10.67%
AR ÷ SD	1.06	1.32

Therefore, statements #2 & #4 are true.

Investment Concepts

130. A

Only under the weak form would fundamental analysis be useful.

Investment Concepts

131. C

Since 25% of the change in Portfolio A can be explained by changes in the S&P 500, then the correlation between Portfolio A and the S&P 500 is the square root of 25% or .5. The coefficient of determination (R^2) is 25% and the correlation coefficient is 50%. The correlation coefficient is then used in the formula to calculate the standard deviation of a two-asset portfolio.

$\sigma^2 = W^2_A\sigma^2_A + W^2_B\sigma^2_B + 2W_A W_B\ [\sigma_A\sigma_B r_{AB}]$

$\sigma^2 = (.7)^2(.2)^2 + (.3)^2(.115)^2 + 2(.7)(.3)[(.2)(.115)(.5)]$

$\sigma^2 = .01960 + .00119 + .00483 = .02562$

$\sigma = .1600$

Investment Concepts (CFP® Exam, released 3/95)

132. B

Above the line would indicate higher return for the given risk level. On the line would indicate same return for the given risk level. Below the line would indicate lower return for the given risk level.

Investment Concepts

133. B

Statement #1 is false. The standard deviation of a two-asset portfolio will be less than the weighted average standard deviation of the two assets as long as the correlation between the assets is less than 1.0.

Statement #2 is true. The standard deviation of the two assets is equal to 10.89%.

$\sigma^2 = W^2_A\sigma^2_A + W^2_B\sigma^2_B + 2W_A W_B\ [\sigma_A\sigma_B r_{AB}]$

$\sigma^2 = (.8)^2(.12)^2 + (.2)^2(.15)^2 + 2(.8)(.2)[(.12)(.15)(.3)]$

$\sigma^2 = .00922 + .00090 + .00173$

$\sigma = .01185$

$\sigma = 10.89\%$

SECURITY ANALYSIS

Options

134. **B**

Fundamental analysis is based on comparing the intrinsic value of securities to the market value to determine which securities are undervalued.

Bond Valuation

135. **E**

FV = $1,000

i = 3.5 (7% ÷ 2)

PMT = $50 (100 ÷ 2)

N = 6 (3 x 2)

PV = ($1,079.93)

Bond Valuation

136. **B**

Melany			**Grandma**		
PV	=	($836)	FV	=	$1,000
N	=	5	N	=	10
i	=	7	i	=	8.5
FV	=	$1,000	PMT	=	$30 (calculated)
PMT	=	$30 (calculated) →	PV	=	($639.13)

Valuation of Bonds

137. **C**

Statement #3 is false. As the coupon rate increases, the duration of the bond will decline, because the investor is receiving cash flows sooner.

Dividend Growth Model

138. **E**

The model [$P_0 = D_1/(k-g)$] assumes dividends will grow at the same rate each year. It also assumes that the required rate of return for the investor (k) is fixed and determinable.

Equity Valuation

139. **D**

	Before	After	Result
P/E:	50 ÷ 5 = 10	60 ÷ 7 = 8.57	Decline
Div. Payout:	2 ÷ 5 = 40%	2.2 ÷ 7 = 31%	Decline

Earnings: $\frac{7 - 5}{5} = 40\%$

Dividends: $\frac{2.20 - 2.00}{2} = 10\%$

Thus, statements #1 and #3 are true.

Dividend Growth Model (CFP® Exam, released 3/95)

140. **E**

PV = ($1.36)

FV = $2.00

N = 5

i = 8.0185

Value of common stock = $\frac{d_1}{K - g} = \frac{1.080185 \times (2.00)}{.12 - .08} = \$54$

K = Required Rate of Return

g = growth rate of the dividend

Bond Swaps (CFP® Exam, released 3/95)

141. A

Statement #1 is true.

Statement #2 is true.

Statement #3 is true.

Statement #4 is false. Tax swaps generally take advantage of capital losses by selling bonds that have been devalued by increasing interest rates.

Technical Analysis

142. D

Breadth of the market is the technical indicator that attempts to measure the overall strength of the market by comparing the number of advancing stocks to the number of declining stocks.

PERFORMANCE MEASUREMENTS

Holding Period Return

143. E

$$\frac{(\$62 - \$45) + \$2 + \$2.20}{\$45} = 47\%$$

Holding Period Return is the same as Single Period Return.

Single Period Return

144. E

$$\frac{(\$1{,}050-1{,}000) + \$60 + \$60}{\$1{,}000} = 17\%$$

Single Period Return is the same as Holding Period Return.

Single Period Return

145. C

$$\frac{(\$65{,}000 - \$60{,}000) + (\$1\ 25)(800)(2)}{\$60{,}000} = 11.67\%$$

Do not forget about the stock split. The dividend is based on 1,600 shares. Single Period Return is the same as Holding Period Return.

Internal Rate of Return

146. D

To clear register hit f CLX

0	g	CF_0		FV	=	$1,500,000
$75,000	g	CF_j		PMT	=	$75,000
$1,575,000	g	CF_j	**OR**	N	=	2
12.5	i			i	=	12.5
f	NPV =>	$1,311,111		PV	=	$1,311,111

Internal Rate of Return

147. C

To clear register hit f CLX

0	g	CF_0
1.25	g	CF_j
1.41	g	CF_j
59.58	g	CF_j (58+1.58)
8.5	i	
f	NPV =>	$48.995

Internal Rate of Return

148. E

To clear register hit f CLX

0	g	CF_0
1.25	g	CF_j
1.41	g	CF_j
59.58	g	CF_j
2.43	i	
f	NPV =>	$58.004

Internal Rate of Return

149. E

To clear register hit f CLX

0	g	CF_0
4.8	g	CF_j
5.9	g	CF_j
47.25	g	CF_j (40 + 7.25)
5.57	i	
f	NPV =>	$49.99

Holding Period Return and Dividend Growth Model

150. D

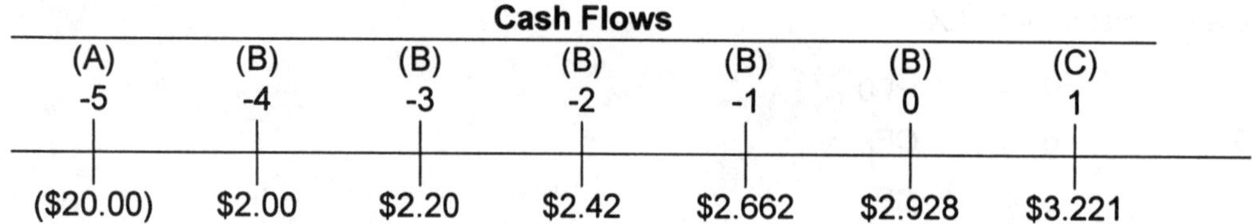

(A) Purchase price 5 years ago.

(B) Dividends paid to date.

(C) Dividend 1 period from today.

Holding Period Method:

$$\text{Holding period return} = \frac{\text{Sales price} - \text{Purchase price} +/- \text{cash flows}}{\text{Purchase Price}}$$

X = Sales price

1. [(x - 20) + 2 + 2.2 + 2.42 + 2.662 + 2.9282] ÷ 20 = 23.75%
2. [(x - 20) + 12.21] ÷ 20 = 23.75%
3. (x- 20) + 12.21 = 23.75 X 20
4. (x –20) = 4.75 – 12.21
5. x – 20 = -7.46
6. x = 20 – 7.46
7. x = 12.54

Sales price today	$12.54 (based on the holding period return)
Less the original price	(20.00)
Loss	($ 7.46)

Dividend Growth Model:

The dividend today (d_o) is $2.928 (from chart above).

The dividend growth model is: $v = \frac{d_1}{k - g}$ d_1 is $3.22 or ($2.928 x 1.1).

d_1 = $3.22 **OR** [$(1.1)^5$ x $2 = $3.22] **OR** $2.9282 x (1.1) = 3.22

$$\frac{\$3.22}{12\% - 10\%} = \$161.00$$

Note: The dividend is paid at the end of Year 1.

Note: $24.75 is a distracter [$20 x (1 + .2375)] = $24.75. This answer, however, is not correct.

Holding Period Return

151. **B**

$$\frac{(x - 20) + 1.25 + 1.5 + 2}{20} = 18\%$$

x = $18.85

Sales price = $18.85 x 500 = $9,425

Types of Returns

152. **A**

Average

30% + 3.85% + (20%) + (7.41%) = 6.44%

6.44% / 4 = 1.61%

Geometric

$[(1 + .30)(1 + .0385)(1 - .20)(1 - .0741)]^{1/4} - 1 = 0$

Types of Returns

153. **B**

Average

20% + 10% + 2% + 16% = 48%

48% ÷ 4 = 12%

Geometric

$[(1+.2)(1+.1)(1 + .02)(1 + .16)]^{1/4} - 1 = 11.79\%$

Diff: 12% - 11.79% = .21%

Types of Returns

154. **B**

$[(1+.45) \times (1 + .25) \times (1 + .13) \times (1 + .03)]^{1/4} - 1 = 20.5\%$

Types of Returns

155. **B**

Definition of Risk Premium.

Measurements of Risk and Types of Returns

156. B

Only statement #2 is true. The geometric return for A is 12.49% while it is 12.48% for B. The average return for both A and B is 12.5%.

Yield to Maturity and Interest Rate Sensitivity

157. C

Statement #1:

Bond	**A**	**B**	**C**	**D**
PV	($730.69)	($1,039.56)	($688.44)	($40.26)
N	8	10	20	60
PMT	$0	$50	$25	$0
FV	$1,000	$1,000	$1,000	$1,000
i(YTM)	4.0	4.5	5.0	5.5
i x 2	8	9	10	11

Bond	**YTM**
A	8
B	9
C	10
D	11

Statement #2 is true because of the term and fact that it is a zero coupon.

Statement #3 is false because zero coupon bonds held to maturity will always maintain the initial YTM and will be unaffected by changes in prevailing interest rates.

Weighted Average Return

158. B

Method 1:

FMV	(A) %	(B) Expected Return	(A) x (B) Weighted Return
$34,000	47.55%	8.0%	3.804%
22,500	31.47%	12.5%	3.934%
15,000	20.98%	23.0%	4.825%
$71,500	100.00%		12.563%

-OR-

Method 2:

(A) FMV	(B) Expecte d Return (%)	(A) x (B) Expected Return ($)
$34,000	8.0%	$ 2,720.00
22,500	12.5%	2,812.50
15,000	23.0%	3,450.00
$71,500		$ 8,982.50

$$\text{Weighted Average Return} = \frac{\$8{,}982.50}{\$71{,}500.00} = 12.56\%$$

Note: Method 2 eliminates the need to determine the percentages for each of the portfolio assets. You should also be aware that many of the financial calculators will calculate the weighted average ($\bar{x}$, w) by entering only a few keystrokes.

Weighted Average Return

159. **C**

FMV	(A) %	(B) Pre-Tax Return	(C) After Tax Yield	(A) x (B) x (C) Weighted Return
$12,500[1]	26.46%	9.00%	(1 - .04)	2.286%
16,000[2]	33.86%	7.00%	(1 - .36)	1.517%
18,750[3]	39.68%	11.50%	(1 - .40)	2.738%
$47,250				6.541%

[1]The municipal bonds will be taxed by Louisiana, but not by the Federal Government.

[2]The US Treasury Bills are not taxed at the state level, but are taxed at the Federal level.

[3]The gains on the stock will be taxed at both the Federal and state levels.

(A) FMV	(B) Pre -Tax Expected Return	(C) Tax Rate	(D) After - Tax Expected Return (%)	(A) x (D) After -Tax Expected Return ($)
$12,500	9.00%	4.00%	8.640%	$1,080.00
16,000	7.00%	36.00%	4.480%	716.80
18,750	11.50%	40.00%	6.900%	1,293.75
$47,250				$3,090.55

$$\text{Weighted Average Return} = \frac{\$3,090.55}{\$47,250.00} = 6.54\%$$

Yield to Maturity

160. **D**

	Bond 1	Bond 2	Bond 3
PV	($314.76)	($739.76)	($1,014.99)
N	20.00	24.00	44.00
PMT	0.00	40.00	62.50
FV	$1,000.00	$1,000.00	$1,000.00
YTM	11.90	12.18	12.30
	(5.95 x 2) = 11.90	(6.09 x 2) = 12.18	(6.15 x 2) = 12.30

Since bonds 2 and 3 both have a YTM greater than 12%, they will increase the investment portfolio expected return. The YTM for bond 1 should also be calculated semi-annually.

Types of Returns

161. D

Future Cost of Boat			**Yearly Deposit**		
PV	=	\$450,000	PV	=	0
N	=	20	N	=	20
i	=	4	i	=	12.5
PMT	=	0	FV	=	\$986,005
FV	=	(\$986,005)	PMT_{AD}	=	(\$11,477.75)

Remember it is an annuity due.

Internal Rate of Return

162. C

(7,300)	g	CF_0		
250	g	CF_j		
260	g	CF_j		
285	g	CF_j		
270	g	CF_j		
285	g	CF_j		
12,550	g	CF_j		
f	IRR		=	12.07%

Yield to Maturity

163. D

PV	=	(\$977.36)
N	=	60 (30 x 2)
PMT	=	42.5 (85/2)
FV	=	\$1,000
i	=	4.357
		4.357% x 2 = 8.71%

Types of Return

164. **C**

$$\text{Standard Deviation} = \frac{15\% - 11\%}{4\%} = 1.0$$

Approximately 68% of occurrences will fall within one standard deviation from the mean. Therefore, the probability of a return between 11% and 15% is 34%. Since there is a 50% chance of a return above 11%, the probability of a return in excess of 15% must be 16% (50% - 34%).

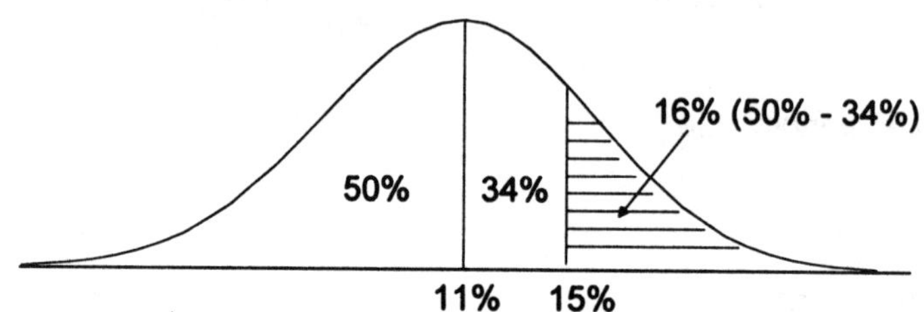

Internal Rate of Return

165. **A**

Sales Price	$176,000
(1 - Commission)	x .94
	$165,440

		A	B	C	
FV	=	($25,000)	($5,000)	$165,440	(from above)
N	=	1	6	18	
i	=	2.0833	2.0833	2.0833	(25% ÷ 12)
PMT	=	$0	$0	$0	
PV	=	$24,490	$4,418	($114,144)	

PV of Sales Price	(C)	$114,144
Less Costs:	1st month (A)	(24,490)
	6th month (B)	(4,418)
PV of Cash Flows		$85,236

Beta and Risk Adjusted Return

166. A

Stock	Return	Beta	Return / Beta
1	15	1.2	12.50%
2	12	1.0	12.00%
3	10	.85	11.76%
4	8.5	.75	11.33%

After Tax Yield

167. D

	YTM	After Tax YTM
Bond I	5.93%	5.93%
Bond II	**12.75%	8.922%
Bond III	13.00%	*

Bond I does not have a high enough YTM for the investor's objectives.

Bond II has a horizon of 10 years which will meet the investor's retirement needs better than the 30 year bonds. Also, it has a high rating and high yield.

Bond III will be subject to OID (original issue date) interest each year.

**YTM is calculated with 60 payments to reflect semi-annual compounding.

Internal Rate of Return

168. B

$R = [(1 + k_1)(1 + k_2) \ldots (1 + k_n)]^{1/n} - 1$

$R = [(1 + .15) * (1 - .10)]^{1/2} - 1$

$R = 1.017 - 1$

$R = .017$ or 1.7%

Annualized Return

169. C

$T_0 = 100$

$T_1 = 100 \times 1.15 = 115$

$T_2 = 115 \times .9 = 103.5$

Types of Return

170. E

Mean = Average: (12 + 11 + 10 + 10 + 9 + 8 + 3) / 7 = 63 ÷ 7 = 9

Median = The number in the middle = 10

Mode = Most frequently occurring = 10

Compound Yield

171. D

Step 1: Calculate future value of interest payments.

PMT = \$50

N = 10

i = 3.5 (reinvestment rate)

FV = \$586.57

Step 2: Calculate realized return

FV = \$1,586.57 (\$1,000 from maturity, 586.57 from step 1)

N = 10

PV = (\$1,080)

i = 3.921 x 2 = 7.84 ≈ 8.0%

Time Weighted Return

172. D

PV_0 = (\$23)

N = 4

PMT = \$0

FV = \$41

i = 15.5%

Time weighted returns do not consider cash flows of the investor, only appreciation and dividends for a portfolio or stock. The only cash flows that occurred over this time period from the investment are the initial purchase price and the sales price.

Internal Rate of Return

173. **A**

Step 1: List cash flows

Year	Cash Flow	
0	$4,600	(200 x 23)
1	1,300	(50 x 26)
2	2,175	(75 x 29)
3	900	(25 x 36)
4	(14,350)	(350 x 41)

Step 2: Calculate IRR

f	CLX		
4,600	g	CF_0	
1,300	g	CF_j	
2,175	g	CF_j	
900	g	CF_j	
(14,350)	g	CF_j	
f	IRR	=	16.05%

Treynor Index

174. **E**

Treynor = [Portfolio Return – Risk Free Return] divided by Beta

Market: Ti = (.09 - .05) ÷ 1.0 = .04000 (Statement#1 is true)

Tiffany: Ti = (.12 - .05) ÷ 1.3 = .05385 (Statement#2 is false; statement#3 is true)

The index number is higher for Tiffany's Portfolio than the market, which means that statement#4 is true.

Portfolio Performance Measurement

175. **C**

Sharpe uses standard deviation; all of the other models use beta as the measure of risk.

Sharpe Index (CFP® Exam, released 3/95)

176. C

$$\text{Sharp Index} = \frac{\text{Realized Return – Risk Free Return}}{\text{Standard Deviation of the Portfolio}}$$

$$= \frac{(.19 - .08)}{.23}$$

$$= .47826$$

Note:

1. All other information in the problem is for distraction purposes.
2. An easy way to remember the difference between the Sharpe Index and the Treynor Index is that Sharpe uses standard deviation (both begin with "S") and the other index, Treynor, uses Beta.

Portfolio Performance Measurement (CFP® Exam, released 3/95)

177. D

An easy way to remember the difference between the Sharpe Index and the Treynor Index is that Sharpe uses standard deviation (both begin with S) and the other index, Treynor, uses beta.

Bonds (CFP® Exam, released 3/95)

178. A

		YTM	YTC
PV	=	($1,147.20)	($1,147.20)
PMT	=	$80	$80
N	=	10	5
FV	=	$1,000	$1,050
i	=	6%	5.45%

The price of bonds is inversely related to changes in interest rates. Therefore, #1, #2, and #3 are all correct.

Passive Activity Losses and Tax Adjusted Returns

179. A

Period	**0**	**1**	**2**	**3**	**4**	**5**
Pre-tax cash flow	($50,000)	$15,000	$15,000	$15,000	$15,000	$15,000
Less income tax	--	(5,040)	(5,040)	(5,040)	(5,040)	(5,040)
After tax cash flow	($50,000)	$9,960	$9,960	$9,960	$9,960	$9,960
Plus sales proceeds	--	--	--	--	--	75,000
Total cash flow	($50,000)	$9,960	$9,960	$9,960	$9,960	$84,960

Calculation of tax

Passive Income	$12,000
Passive Loss	(2,000)
Net passive income	10,000
Dividend & Interest Income	+ 4,000
Total Taxable Income	$14,000
Tax rate	x 36%
Tax	$5,040

Present Value of cash flow

FV = $75,000

PMT = $9,960

i = 6

N = 5

PV = ($97,999.50) ≈ $98,000

NPV = $98,000 - $50,000 = $48,000

Note: NPV is the difference between the PV of the cash inflows and the initial outflow.

Performance Measures

180. A

Jensen's alpha is an absolute measure of performance. Sharpe and Treynor are both relative measures of performance.

Tax Adjusted Returns

181. B

Step 1: Find the future value of cash flows

	1	2	3	
Bond A coupon payments	$100.00	$100.00	$100.00	
Bond B coupon payments	80.00	80.00	0.00	
Total coupon payments	$180.00	$180.00	$100.00	
Times 1 - Tax Rate	.64	.64	.64	
After Tax Cash Flow	$115.20	$115.20	$64.00	
Plus Maturity Value		1,000.00	1,000.00	
	$115.20	$1,115.20	$1,064.00	
Cash Flow from Period 2		@ 5% →	$1,170.96	(1,115.20 x 1.05)
Cash Flow from Period 1	→	@ 5% →	+ 127.01	[115.20 x $(1.05)^2$]
			$2,361.97	

Step 2: Calculate the yield for the three year period

FV = $2,361.97

N = 3

PV = ($2,000)

i = 5.7% ≈ 6%

Security Analysis

182. C

Immunization protects bond holders from fluctuations in interest rates and from reinvestment rate risk. It will not protect against purchasing power risk.

Security Analysis

183. B

When the duration of the bond matches the time horizon of the investor, the bond is considered to be immunized.

Constant Growth Dividend Model

184. **E**

$$V = \frac{d_1}{k-g} = \frac{(1.75)(1.08)}{(.10 - .08)} = \$94.50$$

Since the value of $94.50 is less than the current market price, an investor should not purchase the stock if he believes in the dividend growth model.

Capitalized Earnings Approach to Valuation

185. **A**

Monthly Rent	$750	
Occupied Units	X 96	(120 x 80%)
Total monthly rent	$72,000	
Total yearly rent	$864,000	
Less yearly expense	(300,000)	
Yearly net income	$564,000	
Value of the company	$4,700,000	($564,000 ÷ .12)

Security Analysis

186. **E**

PV	=	($1,197.93)
N	=	40 (20 x 2)
PMT_{OA}	=	$50 ($100 ÷ 2)
FV	=	$1,000
i	=	3.9999 = 4% x 2 = 8%.

Security Analysis

187. **A**

FV	=	$1,000
PMT_{OA}	=	$50 ($100 ÷ 2)
i	=	6 (12% ÷ 2)
N	=	6 (3 x 2)
PV	=	($950.83)

Security Analysis

188. A

The weighted beta of a portfolio is determined by multiplying each security's percentage of the total portfolio times its relative beta. The weighted beta is then the sum of the three products.

Security	Amount Invested	Percentage of Portfolio	Beta	Weighted Beta
A	$15,000	.1667	1.5	0.2500
B	$30,000	.3333	1.2	0.4000
C	$45,000	.5000	0.9	0.4500
	$90,000	1.0000		1.1000

Or

(A) Security	(B) Amount invested	(C) Beta	(B) x (C)
A	$15,000	1.5	$22,500
B	$30,000	1.2	$36,000
C	$45,000	0.9	$40,500
	$90,000		$99,000

Weighted Beta = $99,000 ÷ $90,000 = 1.100

Security Analysis

189. B

Value	$40 x 100	$ 4,000
Loan	$6,000 x .50	(3,000)
Equity		$1,000
Equity needed	$4,000 x 35%	(1,400)
Cash needed		$400

INVESTMENT STRATEGIES

Integration

190. **B**

The average return for both Stock A and B is 18%. The standard deviation for Stock B is greater than Stock A. Therefore the risk adjusted return for Stock A is higher.

	A	B
Mean	18%	18%
Standard Deviation	8%	20%
Geometric	17.78%	16.54%

Note: Stock A should not be added simply because it has a lower standard deviation.

Dollar Cost Averaging

191. **A**

Note: If you chose answer b, then you forgot to subtract the basis from the proceeds when you were calculating the tax. It is a common mistake! Remember, the exam is integrated!

Step 1: Calculate value today →

PV	=	$0		
N	=	120	=	10 x 12 months
i	=	1%	=	(12% ÷ 12)
PMT	=	($350)		
FV	=	$80,513.54		

Step 2: Determine Sam's basis

Amount of payments	$350
Number of payments	x 120
Basis	$42,000

Step 3: Calculate tax →

Proceeds	$80,513.54
Less Basis	(42,000.00)
Gain	$38,513.54
Tax Rate	x 28%
Tax	$10,783.79

Step 4: Cash available

Proceeds	$80,513.54
Less Tax	(10,783.79)
After Tax Cash Flow	$69,729.75

Thus, he cannot purchase his dream boat.

CLIENT ASSESSMENT

Client Assessment

192. D

Definition of risk seeking.

Client Assessment

193. A

Selling short against the box will freeze her gain without the sale of the stock. None of the other choices will accomplish her goal. Buying a put option would also allow her to protect her gain.

Client Assessment

194. D

	Fund 2	**Fund 3**
Taxable Yield	14.75%	2.4%
1 - Tax Rate	x 60%	x 60%
After Tax Yield	8.85%	1.44%
Plus Appreciation	2.00%	14.00%
Total Return (after tax)	10.85%	15.44%
Beta	÷ 1.10	÷ 1.12
Risk Adjusted Return	9.86%	13.79%

Fund 1 is not an appropriate choice for Joseph's objectives.

Client Assessment

195. **E**

		A	B	C
Dividend growth model	$\frac{d_1}{k-g}$ =	$\frac{4.5\,(1.05)}{(.10 - .05)}$	$\frac{2.75(1.09)}{(.10 - .09)}$	$\frac{1.25(1.07)}{(.10 - .07)}$
Value of Stock		$94.50	$299.75	$44.58
Less Current Market Price		(80.00)	(250.00)	(35.00)
Amount Stock is Undervalued		$14.50	$49.75	$9.58
Undervalued as a % of Value		15.34%	16.59%	21.49%

Stock C is the most undervalued (as a percent), which makes it the best buy.

Client Assessment

196. **B**

Investments 2 and 4 are the only two that will provide current income for the Davis family.

Client Assessment

197. **C**

Alternative 1: Sell the Farm

Sale of the Farm	
Sales Price	$300,000
Less Outstanding Loan	(125,000)
Cash	$175,000
Less Tax	(56,000)
Net Cash	$119,000

Tax on the Sale of the Farm	
Sales Price	$300,000
Less Basis	(50,000)
Gain	$250,000
Less Passive Activity Loss	(50,000)
Realized Gain	$200,000
Tax Rate	x 28%
Tax	$ 56,000

Alternative 2: Keep the Home

Appreciation (FV) of the House			FV of the Rent	PV of Both		
PV	=	($300,000)	$0	FV	=	$2,545,517 (1,723,047 + 822,470)
N	=	30	30	N	=	30
i	=	6%	10%	i	=	10%
PMT	=	$0	($5,000)	PMT	=	$0
FV	=	$1,723,047	$822,470	PV	=	($145,880)

Keep Home (PV)	$145,880
Sell the Home (net cash)	(119,000)
Difference	$ 26,880

Another way to think of this comparison is to determine how much the Whites would have assuming they invested the $119,000 for 30 years at 10%. They would have $2,076,479, which is less than the value of the farm plus the value of the rental payments of $2,545,517.

Client Assessment

198. C

FV of Sale			FV of Keeping Farm	Difference
PV	=	($119,000)		
N	=	30		
i	=	10		
PMT	=	$0		
FV	=	$2,076,479	FV = $2,545,517	$469,038

Difference in Payments to Break Even

PV	=	$0	Current Rent	$5,000
FV	=	$469,038	Less	(2,851)
i	=	10	Rent to Break Even	**$2,149**
N	=	30		
PMT	=	($2,851)		

Time Value of Money

199. **C**

		Option 2	**Option 3**	
FV	=	$0	$0	
N	=	15	27.5	
i	=	8%	8%	
PMT	=	$24,000	$18,450	
PV	=	($205,427)	($202,844)	**Note:** HP12C shows ($193,994).

Security Valuation

200. **A**

Step 1:

N	=	20
i	=	15%
PMT	=	$2,500
FV	=	$0
PV_3	=	($15,648.33)

Step 2:

FV_3	=	$15,648.33
N	=	3
i	=	15%
PMT	=	$0
PV_0	=	($10,289)

THIS PAGE IS INTENTIONALLY LEFT BLANK.

INCOME TAX PLANNING PROBLEMS

INCOME TAX PLANNING

TAX LAW - TAX LEGISLATION, ADMINISTRATION AND JUDICIAL (CASE)

1. Ed lost his tax case in the U.S. District Court. He may appeal to the:
   a. U.S. Supreme Court.
   b. U.S. Tax Court.
   c. U.S. Court of Federal Claims.
   d. U.S. Court of Appeals.
   e. Any of the above.

2. From which court is there no appeal:
   a. U.S. Court of Appeals.
   b. U.S. District Court.
   c. U.S. Tax Court.
   d. Small Cases Division of the U.S. Tax Court.
   e. None of the above (All courts above can be appealed from.)

3. Which of the following are true regarding audits, procedures, and appeals for a taxpayer?
   1. The taxpayer must pay any tax deficiency assessed by the IRS and must sue for a refund to bring suit in the U.S. District Court.
   2. A taxpayer can obtain a jury trial in the U.S. Tax Court.
   3. The IRS must make letter rulings available for public inspection.
   4. The IRS or the taxpayer can appeal to the U.S. Tax Court for a decision rendered by the Small Cases Division of the Tax Court.

   a. 1 only.
   b. 1 and 2.
   c. 1 and 3.
   d. 2, 3, and 4.
   e. 1, 2, 3, and 4.

4. Which is the best source for obtaining information about the intent of a very recent change in the tax law? **(CFP® Exam, released 3/95)**
    a. RIA Federal Tax Coordinator.
    b. Congressional Committee Reports.
    c. Treasury Regulations.
    d. Tax Court Reports.
    e. U.S. Master Tax Guide.

5. Which entity is never subject to Federal income tax?
    a. Partnership.
    b. S corporation.
    c. C corporation.
    d. Individual.
    e. Trust.

6. Which types of entities are always pass through entities for Federal income tax purposes?
    1. Partnerships.
    2. S corporations.
    3. C corporations.
    4. Limited Liability Companies.
    5. Trusts.
        a. 1 and 2.
        b. 1, 2, and 3.
        c. 1, 2, and 4.
        d. 1, 2, 3, and 4.
        e. 2, 3, 4 and 5.

TAX RATES AND BRACKETS

7. Angie and Buddy, both age 55, filed a joint return for the current year. They provided all the support for their son who is 19 and had no income. Their daughter, age 23, and a full-time student at a university, had $5,000 of income and provided 70% of her own support during the current year. How many exemptions should Angie and Buddy claim on their current year joint income tax return?
   a. 5.
   b. 4.
   c. 3.
   d. 2.
   e. None of the above.

8. John, age 50, filed a joint return with his wife Joan, age 24. Their son Chip was born December 16 of the current year. John provided 60% of the support for his 73-year-old widowed mother until May 1, when she died. His mother's only income was from Social Security benefits totaling $3,000. How many exemptions should John and Joan claim on their joint tax return?
   a. 2.
   b. 3.
   c. 4.
   d. 5.
   e. None of the above.

9. Steve provided more than one-half of the support for the following relatives, none of them were members of Steve's household: cousin, nephew, and a foster parent. None of these relatives had any income, nor did any of them file an individual or joint return. All of the relatives are U.S. citizens. Which of these relatives could be claimed as a dependent on Steve's return?
   a. Cousin.
   b. Nephew.
   c. Foster parent.
   d. None of the above.
   e. b and c.

10. Mary Sue and Bob, who are married and file a joint return, provided over 50% of the support for Becky, Rachel, and Vicki during the year. Their daughter Becky, a college student, earned $3,300 during the year. Mary Sue and Bob's married daughter Rachel filed a joint return with her husband. Vicki, who is Mary Sue's mother, lives with Mary Sue and Bob. Vicki's only income during the year was $5,200 of Social Security benefits, and she used that entire amount for her own support. Which of the following statements is/are incorrect?

    1. Mary Sue and Bob can claim Becky as a dependent only if she is under 19 years of age or is a full-time college student under 24 years of age.
    2. Mary Sue and Bob may claim Rachel as a dependent if neither Rachel nor her husband was required to file a return.
    3. Mary Sue and Bob may not claim Vicki as a dependent because Vicki's gross income is too high.

    a. 1 only.
    b. 2 only.
    c. 3 only.
    d. 1 and 3.
    e. 1, 2, and 3.

11. Mike and Pam, ages 67 and 65, respectively, filed a joint tax return for the current year. They provided all of the support for their 19-year-old son, who had $2,200 of gross income. Their 23-year-old daughter, a full-time student until her graduation on June 25 of this year, earned $2,500, which was 40% of her total support during the year. Her parents provided the remaining support. Mike and Pam also provided total support for Pam's father, who is a Columbian citizen and life-long resident of Columbia. How many personal and dependency exemptions can Mike and Pam claim on their income tax return?

    a. 2.
    b. 3.
    c. 4.
    d. 5.
    e. None of the above.

12. Thomas and Cecilia Martinez are married and filed a joint income tax return for the current year. During this year they properly claimed a personal exemption for their dependent 17-year old daughter, Hazel. Since Hazel earned $5,400 in the current year from a part-time job at the college she attended full-time, Hazel was also required to file an income tax return. What amount was Hazel entitled to claim as a personal exemption on her individual income tax return for the current year?

    a. $0.
    b. $1,200.
    c. $2,450.
    d. $2,700.
    e. $5,400.

13. Arline provided 30% of her own support; the remaining 70% was provided by her three sons as follows:

James	12%
Brian	20%
Michael	38%
	70%

Assume that a multiple support agreement exists and that the brothers will sign multiple support declarations as required. Which of the brothers is eligible to claim the mother as a dependent for the current year?

    a. None of the brothers.
    b. Michael only.
    c. Brian or Michael.
    d. James, Brian, or Michael.
    e. Each brother gets to claim his percentage of contribution.

14. William, who is covered by a qualified retirement plan and is age 30 and single, provided the following information for his 1998 income tax return:

Salary	$30,000
Payment to a Roth Individual Retirement Account	$2,000
Total itemized deductions	$3,400
Number of exemptions claimed	1

William should report taxable income for 1998 of:

a. $21,050.
b. $22,050.
c. $23,050.
d. $24,600.
e. None of the above.

15. Calculate the taxable income for a single taxpayer, age 65 with no dependents, provided the following information for his 1998 income tax return:

Gross income	$46,000
Capital loss	$5,000
Total itemized deductions	$4,500

a. $34,050.
b. $35,000.
c. $36,050.
d. $35,050.
e. $36,750.

16. Peter, a single taxpayer, age 62, had adjusted gross income of $42,000 in 1998. He paid the cost of maintaining his dependent mother, age 90, in a home for the aged for the entire year. His itemized deductions totaled $5,400. What amount should Peter report as taxable income for 1998?

a. $30,350.
b. $32,350.
c. $33,050.
d. $35,050.

17. Which of the following is/are deductible for adjusted gross income?
    1. Alimony paid to the taxpayer's ex-spouse.
    2. Capital losses.
    3. Ordinary and necessary expenses incurred in a business.
    4. Contribution to a Roth IRA.
    5. Child support paid to ex-spouse.
        a. 3 and 5.
        b. 1, 3, and 5.
        c. 2, 3, and 5.
        d. 1, 2 and 3.
        e. 1, 2, 3, 4, and 5.

TAX DETERMINATION

18. Which of the following children have income subject to Federal income tax at his/her parents' highest marginal rate? **(CFP® Exam, released 3/95)**
    - Brittany, age 12, earns $3,000 in salary.
    - Kristen, age 5, earns $1,500 in interest on a savings account.
    - Trent, age 3, earns $500 in interest on a savings account.
    - Amanda, age 14, earns $1,800 in dividends and interest.

    a. Brittany.
    b. Kristen and Trent.
    c. Kristen.
    d. Kristen, Trent, and Amanda.
    e. All of the children will have income subject to FIT at parents' highest marginal rate.

19. Michael Christen, age 13 in 1998, has the following income: $3,000 investment income from mutual funds and $5,000 earned from a paper route. His parents claim him as a dependent. How much of Michael's income is taxed at the parents' highest marginal rate?

    a. $0.
    b. $1,600.
    c. $2,800.
    d. $3,000.
    e. $3,600.

20. Which of the following statements regarding the "kiddie tax" is/are correct?
    1. It only applies to unearned income from property transferred to a child from the child's parents.
    2. It applies to all children under the age of 15.
    3. A child's earned and unearned income may be subject to the tax.
    4. It is based on the additional tax the parents would have paid assuming the child's net unearned income had been included in the parents' taxable income.

    a. 4 only.
    b. 1 and 4.
    c. 1, 2, and 3.
    d. 1, 2, and 4.
    e. 1, 2, 3, and 4.

21. Allison Two, who is 12 years old, is claimed as a dependent on her parents' tax return. During 1998, she earned $2,200 from a summer job. She also earned $1,800 in interest and dividends from investments that were given to her by her maternal grandfather, Michael, five years ago. How much of Allison Two's income will be taxed at her parents' highest marginal rate in 1998?

    a. $0. The gift was from her grandparent.
    b. $400.
    c. $1,150.
    d. $3,300.
    e. $4,000.

FILING CONSIDERATIONS

22. George, whose wife died last November, filed a joint tax return for last year. He did not remarry and has continued to maintain his home for his two dependent children. In the preparation of his tax return for this year, what is George's filing status?

    a. Single.
    b. Surviving spouse.
    c. Head of household.
    d. Married filing separately.
    e. None of the above.

23. Beth Brown's husband died in 1996. Assume Beth does not marry, and continues to maintain a home for herself and her dependent infant child during 1997, 1998, and 1999, providing full support for herself and her child during these 3 years. For 1996, Beth properly filed a joint return. For 1999, Beth's filing status is:

    a. Single.
    b. Married filing joint return.
    c. Head of household.
    d. Qualifying widow with dependent child.
    e. None of the above.

GROSS INCOME - INCLUSIONS

24. Mary is single and has one dependent. Her financial records show the following items in the current year: $6,000 gift from uncle; $1,000 dividends received on domestic common stock; $12,000 prize won in state lottery; $50,000 salary from employer; $6,000 child support and $7,500 alimony received from ex-spouse; and, a $5,000 short-term capital loss. How much adjusted gross income must Mary report in the current year?

    a. $76,500.
    b. $70,500.
    c. $67,500.
    d. $65,500.
    e. None of the above.

25. Ken, age 23, a full-time student at State University, is claimed as a dependent by his parents. He earned $1,600 from a summer job in 1998. In addition, he earned $1,350 from a savings account established with funds inherited from his grandmother. He had total itemized deductions of $150 in the current year. What is Ken's taxable income for 1998?

    a. $0.
    b. $2,850.
    c. $1,100.
    d. $2,950.
    e. None of the above.

26. Arline, who is 75 years old and single, is claimed as a dependent on her son's tax return. During 1998, she received $1,700 interest on a savings account and $4,000 of Social Security benefits. She also earned $1,250 from a part-time job. What is her taxable income for 1998?

    a. $0.
    b. $400.
    c. $650.
    d. $1,650.
    e. None of the above.

27. In October 1998, Michele, a cash basis CPA, contracted to perform an audit during the month of December 1998. At the time the contract was being negotiated, the client offered to pay for the services in December 1998. However, Michele wanted to defer the income until 1999. Therefore, the final agreement called for a $2,000 payment in January 1999. Michele also prepared a corporate tax return in November 1998. When she completed the tax return on December 1, 1998, the client offered to pay the $450 charge, but Michele refused to accept payment until 1999. What amount must Michele report on her 1998 return?

    a. $0.
    b. $450.
    c. $2,000.
    d. $2,450.
    e. None of the above.

28. Steve, an accrual basis taxpayer, performed services for a customer and collected the amount due, $2,000 in 1998. Later that year the customer told Steve that he had not performed the services properly and the customer wanted a refund. The dispute was still in process at the end of 1998. Steve paid the customer $100 in 1999 to settle the suit.

    a. Steve is not required to recognize any income until 1999, when the suit is settled.
    b. Steve is required to recognize $1,900 income in 1998.
    c. Steve is required to recognize the $2,000 in 1998 as income received under a claim of right.
    d. Steve is required to recognize as income in 1998 his best estimate of the amount he will have left after satisfying the customer's claim.
    e. None of the above.

29. Cable TV Co., an accrual basis taxpayer, allows its customers to pay by the month ($30 each month), by the year ($300 per year), or two years in advance ($600). In December of 1998, the company collected the following amounts applicable to future services:

January 1999 services (monthly contracts)	$15,000
January 1999 - December 1999 services (annual contracts)	$38,000
January 1999 - December 2000 services (two year contracts)	$19,000

The income from the above that must be reported as gross income for 1998 is:

a. $15,000.
b. $19,000.
c. $34,000.
d. $38,000.
e. $72,000.

30. Ron and Marge, residents of a community property state, were married in 1997. Late that same year they separated (began living apart) and were divorced in 1999. Each earned a salary and together they received income from community owned investments in all relevant years. They filed separate returns in 1998 and 1999. Which of the following is correct?

a. In 1998 and 1999, Marge must report only her salary and one-half of the income from community property on her separate return.
b. In 1998, Marge must report on her separate return one-half of Ron and Marge's salaries and one-half of the community property income.
c. In 1999, Marge must report on her separate return one-half of Ron and Marge's salaries for the period they were married as well as one-half of the community property income and her income earned after the divorce.
d. In 1998, Marge must report only her salary on her separate return.
e. None of the above.

31. Vicki purchased an annuity for $26,000 in the current year. Under the contract, Vicki will receive $300 each month for the rest of her life. According to actuarial estimates, Vicki will live to receive 100 payments and will receive a 3% return on her original investment.
    a. If Vicki collects $3,000 in the current year, the $3,000 is treated as a recovery of capital and thus is not taxable.
    b. If Vicki dies after collecting a total of 50 payments, she has an economic loss that is not deductible.
    c. If Vicki lives to collect more than 100 payments, she must amend her prior years' returns to increase her taxable portion of each payment received in the past.
    d. If Vicki lives to collect more than 100 payments, all amounts received after the 100th payment must be included in her gross income.
    e. None of the above.

32. Kathy, age 70, is single and an employee of Expo Corporation. Her only sources of income this year are $80,000 of W-2 wages, $6,000 in Social Security benefits, and $1,000 interest on State of Alabama Bonds. Based on the above, Kathy's adjusted gross income for the current year is:
    a. $80,000.
    b. $81,000.
    c. $83,000.
    d. $85,100.
    e. $86,000.

33. Ruby, a widow, elected to receive the proceeds of a $100,000 face value insurance policy on the life of her deceased husband in ten annual installments of $11,900 each (beginning last year). In the current year, she received $11,900, which included $1,900 interest. Ruby dies in December of the current year after collecting the current year's payment. What is the amount subject to income tax on her final tax return?
    a. $0.
    b. $1,900.
    c. $5,000.
    d. $6,900.
    e. None of the above.

34. During the current year, a taxpayer collected $400 interest on U.S. Treasury bills, $750 on Baldwin County school bonds, and $100 interest on a state income tax refund (she itemized her deductions last year). She also received $200 in dividends from a U.S. common stock. Her gross income from the above is:

    a. $0.
    b. $300.
    c. $700.
    d. $1,350.
    e. $1,450.

35. Robert retired on May 31, 1999 and receives a monthly pension benefit of $1,200 payable for life. His life expectancy at the date of retirement was 10 years (120 months). The first pension check was received on June 15, 1999. During his years of employment, Robert contributed $24,000 to the cost of his company's pension plan. How much of the pension amounts received may Robert exclude from taxable income for the years 1999, 2000, and 2001?

	1999	2000	2001
a.	$0	$0	$0
b.	$1,400	$2,400	$2,400
c.	$8,400	$8,400	$8,400
d.	$8,400	$14,400	$14,400
e.	$14,400	$14,400	$14,400

36. Thomas named his wife, Kim, the beneficiary of a $120,000 (face amount) insurance policy on his life. The policy provided that upon his death, the proceeds would be paid to Kim with interest over her remaining life expectancy (which was calculated at 20 years). Thomas died during the current year, and Kim received a regular annual payment of $15,000 from the insurance company. What amount must Kim include in her gross income for the current year?

    a. $0.
    b. $3,000.
    c. $6,000.
    d. $9,000.
    e. $15,000.

37. David Jones is covered by a $180,000 group term life insurance policy and his daughter is the beneficiary. Jones' employer pays the entire cost of the policy for which the uniform annual premium is $8 per $1,000 of coverage. How much of this premium is taxable to Jones?

    a. $0.
    b. $640.
    c. $1,040.
    d. $1,440.
    e. $12,480.

38. Carol and Jack were divorced in January of the current year. In accordance with the divorce decree, Jack transferred the title of their home to Carol in the current year. The home, which had a fair market value of $150,000, was subject to a $70,000 mortgage that had 240 more monthly payments (20 more years). Monthly mortgage payments are $1,000. Under the terms of the settlement, Jack is obligated to make the mortgage payments on the home for the full remaining 20-year term of the indebtedness, regardless of how long Carol lives. Jack made 12 mortgage payments in the current year totaling $12,000. What amount is taxable as alimony to Carol for her current year tax return?

    a. $0.
    b. $12,000.
    c. $80,000.
    d. $92,000.
    e. $162,000.

39. With regard to the alimony deduction related to a post-1984 divorce, which one of the following statements is correct?

    a. Alimony is deductible by the payor spouse, and includible by the payee spouse, to the extent that payment is contingent on the status of the divorced couple's children.
    b. The divorced couple may be members of the same household at the time alimony is paid, provided that the persons do not live as husband and wife.
    c. Alimony payments must terminate on the death of the payee spouse.
    d. Alimony may be paid either in cash or in property.
    e. None of the above are correct.

40. Jon and Bonnie were divorced. Their only marital property was a personal residence with a value of $300,000 and cost of $125,000. Under the terms of the divorce agreement, which did not include the word "alimony," Bonnie would receive the house. She would pay Jon $20,000 each year for five years. If Jon died before the end of the five years, the payments were to be made to his estate. Bonnie and Jon lived apart when Jon received the payments.

   a. Jon does not recognize any income from the above transaction.
   b. Jon must recognize a $87,500 [1/2 x ($300,000 - $125,000)] gain on the sale of his interest in the house.
   c. Bonnie can deduct $20,000 a year for alimony paid.
   d. Bonnie can deduct $25,000 as alimony paid.
   e. None of the above.

41. Which of the following are requirements for alimony deductions under post-1984 decrees and agreements?

   1. The agreement specifies that the payments are alimony.
   2. The payor and payee are not members of the same household at the time the payments are made.
   3. There is no liability to make the payments after the payee's death.
   4. The payments are not for the support of the payor's children.

   a. 1 and 2.
   b. 1, 2, and 3.
   c. 2 and 3.
   d. 2, 3, and 4.
   e. 1, 2, 3, and 4.

42. John is single, with no dependents. During the current year, John received salary of $11,000 and state unemployment compensation benefits of $3,000. He had no other source of income. The amount of state unemployment compensation benefits that should be included in John's current year adjusted gross income is:

   a. $3,000.
   b. $2,000.
   c. $1,500.
   d. $1,000.
   e. $0.

43. Clark, age 25, bought a Series EE U.S. Savings Bonds after 1989. Redemption proceeds will be used for payment of college tuition for Clark's dependent child. One of the conditions that must be met for tax exemption of accumulated interest on these bonds is that the:

    a. Purchaser of the bonds must be the sole owner of the bonds (or joint owner with his or her spouse).
    b. Bonds must be bought by a parent (or both parents) and put in the name of the dependent child.
    c. Bonds must be bought before the owner of the bonds reaches the age of 24.
    d. Bonds must be transferred to the college for redemption by the college rather than by the owner of the bonds.
    e. None of the above.

44. Lois is single and has two dependents. Financial records show the following items in the current year:

Gift from a friend	$12,000
Dividends received on stock	$1,200
Prize won in state lottery	$1,000
Salary from employer	$35,000
Child support received from ex-spouse	$6,000
Alimony received from ex-spouse	$12,000
Long-term capital loss	$5,000

How much is Lois' adjusted gross income for the current year?

    a. $43,200.
    b. $44,200.
    c. $46,200.
    d. $48,200.
    e. $58,200.

45. Kent had the following items in the current year:

Salary	$60,000
Long-term capital loss	$500
Short-term capital loss	$4,500
Moving expenses	$4,000

What is Kent's adjusted gross income for the current year?

a. $51,500.
b. $52,000.
c. $53,000.
d. $56,000.
e. $57,000.

46. In 1998, Buddy is 65, single, and claimed as a dependent by his daughter on her tax return. During the current year, Buddy received Social Security payments of $6,000, interest on a bank account of $3,500, and $2,300 from a part-time job selling potato machines. What is Buddy's taxable income?

a. $0.
b. $550.
c. $1,450.
d. $2,200.
e. $2,250.

47. Nick and Nan were divorced in the current year (Year 1). Under the divorce agreement, Nan is to receive $100,000 in the current year, $60,000 next year (Year 2) and nothing thereafter. The payments were to cease upon Nan's death or remarriage. How much, if any, should Nick have to claim as alimony recapture in Year 3?

a. $0.
b. $15,000.
c. $30,000.
d. $90,000.
e. $122,500.

48. On January 1, Dennis loaned his daughter Betty $90,000 to purchase a new personal residence. There were no other loans outstanding between Dennis and Betty. Betty's only income was $30,000 salary and $4,000 interest income. Dennis had investment income of $200,000. Dennis did not charge Betty interest. The relevant Federal rate was 9 percent. For the current year:

    a. Betty must recognize $8,100 (.09 x $90,000) imputed interest income on the loan.
    b. Dennis must recognize imputed interest income of $4,000.
    c. Dennis must recognize imputed interest income of $8,100.
    d. Betty is allowed a deduction for imputed interest of $8,100.
    e. None of the above.

49. John, the majority shareholder in XYZ, Inc., received an interest-free loan from the corporation. Which of the following is/are correct?

    a. If the loan is classified as an employer-employee loan, the corporation's taxable income will not be affected by the imputation of interest.
    b. If the loan is classified as a corporation-shareholder loan, the corporation's taxable income will increase as a result of the imputation of interest.
    c. If John uses the funds to take a vacation, the imputation of interest will cause a net increase to his taxable income.
    d. All of the above.
    e. None of the above.

50. A client purchased a mutual fund with a $10,000 lump-sum amount four years ago. During the holding period, $4,000 of dividends was reinvested. Today the shares are valued at $20,000 (including any shares purchased with dividends). If the client sells shares equal to $13,000, which statement(s) is/are correct? **(CFP® Exam, released 3/95)**

    1. The taxable gain can be based on an average cost per share.
    2. The client can choose which shares to sell, thereby controlling the taxable gain.
    3. To minimize the taxable gain today, the client would sell shares with the higher cost basis.
    4. The client will <u>not</u> have a gain as long as he/she sells less than what he/she invested.

    a. 1, 2, and 3.
    b. 1 and 3.
    c. 2 and 4.
    d. 4 only.
    e. 2, 3, and 4.

GROSS INCOME - EXCLUSIONS

51. Scott, age 22, is a full-time student at Texas State University and a candidate for a bachelor's degree. During the current year, he received the following payments:

State scholarship for ten months (tuition and books)	$5,000
Loan from college financial aid office	2,000
Cash support from parents	5,000
Cash dividends	500
Cash prize awarded in contest	300
	$12,800

What is Scott's adjusted gross income?

a. $500.
b. $800.
c. $5,800.
d. $12,800.
e. None of the above.

52. Rick has been a night watchman at INVEST, Inc. for 10 years. During the current year, he received the following from his employer:

Salary	$20,000
Hospitalization premiums paid directly to provider	3,660
Lodging on company premises for employer's convenience as a condition to Rick's employment	3,000
Reward for discovering and preventing burglary	1,000

What amount is includible in Rick's adjusted gross income for the current year?

a. $20,000.
b. $21,000.
c. $23,000.
d. $23,660.
e. $27,660.

53. During this year, Matt was injured on his job. As a result of the injury, he received the following payments during this year:

Workman's compensation	$ 2,600
Reimbursement from his employer for medical expenses paid by Matt (medical plan)	1,200
Damages for personal injuries	10,000

What is the amount to be included in Matt's gross income for the current year?

a. $0.

b. $12,000.

c. $10,000.

d. $13,800.

e. None of the above.

54. Ron is the manager of a hotel. To be available in emergency situations, Ron's employer requires that he live in one of the hotel rooms (without charge). The value of the room is $1,500 per month if occupied each night. The hotel is ordinarily 70% occupied. If Ron did not live there, he would live in an apartment that would rent for $900 per month. Ron's inclusive monthly gross income from living in the hotel room is:

a. $0.

b. $900.

c. $1,350.

d. $1,500.

e. None of the above.

55. Tracy is employed by a large corporation with 500 employees. The corporation has an exercise facility within its office for the exclusive use of the employees. A health club membership at a similar public facility would cost Tracy $1,200 per year. How much must Tracy include in her adjusted gross income?

a. $0.

b. $500.

c. $600.

d. $1,200.

e. None of the above.

56. Under the Franklin Company, Inc. cafeteria plan, all full-time employees are allowed to select any combination of the benefits below. The total received by the employee cannot exceed $8,000 a year.

    1. Whole life insurance, $2,000.
    2. Group medical and hospitalization insurance for the employee only, $4,000 a year.
    3. Group medical and hospitalization insurance for employee's dependents, $2,000 a year.
    4. Child-care payments, actual cost but not more than $2,400 a year if one child or $4,800 if 2 or more children.
    5. Cash required to bring the total of benefits and cash to $8,000.

    Which of the following statements is true?

    a. Becky a full-time employee, selects choices 1 and 2 and $2,000 cash. Her gross income must include the $2,000 cash and the $2,000 from the life insurance.
    b. Bob, a full-time employee, elects to receive $8,000 cash because his wife's employer provided benefits for him. Bob is not required to include the $8,000 in gross income.
    c. Vicki, a full-time employee, elects to receive choices, 1, 2, and 3. She is not required to include any of the above in gross income.
    d. Don, a full-time employee, selects options 2 and 3 and $2,000 in child-care (4). Don must include $2,000 in gross income.
    e. None of the above.

57. Crescent Company allows a 10% discount to all non-officer employees. Officers, all highly compensated, are allowed a 30% discount on company products. Crescent's gross profit rate is 35%. Which of the following is true?

    a. An officer who takes a 30% discount must include the extra 20% (30% - 10%) in gross income.
    b. All discounts taken by employees are includible because the plan is discriminatory.
    c. All discounts taken by officers are includible because the plan is discriminatory.
    d. None of the discounts are includible in income because the discount in all cases is less than the company's gross profit percentage.
    e. None of the above.

58. Romig Company was experiencing financial difficulties, but was not bankrupt or insolvent. Shelby, the holder of a mortgage on Romig's building, agreed to accept $60,000 in full payment of the $90,000 due. Shelby had sold the property to Romig for $200,000 five years ago. Peoples Bank, which held a mortgage on other real estate owned by Romig reduced the principal from $75,000 to $35,000. The bank had made the loan to Romig when it purchased the real estate from Roper, Inc. As a result of the above, Romig must:

    a. Include $70,000 in gross income.
    b. Reduce the basis in its assets by $70,000.
    c. Include $130,000 in gross income and reduce its basis in its assets by $40,000.
    d. Include $40,000 in gross income and reduce its basis in the building by $30,000.
    e. None of the above.

59. Brian, an employee of Duff Corporation, died on July 25 of the current year. During July, Duff Corp. made employee death payments of $10,000 to his widow, and $10,000 to his 17 year old son. What amounts should be excluded from gross income by the widow and son in their respective tax returns for the current year?

	Widow	**Son**
a.	$0	$0
b.	$2,500	$2,500
c.	$5,000	$5,000
d.	$7,500	$7,500
e.	$10,000	$10,000

60. During the current year, Bill Hill sustained a serious injury in the course of his employment. As a result of this injury, Bill received the following payments:

Workman's Compensation	$3,000
Reimbursement from his employer's accident and health plan for medical expenses paid by Bill and not deducted by him.	$2,400
Compensatory damages for personal injuries	$6,000
Punitive damages for personal injuries	$5,000

The amount to be included in Hal's gross income should be:

a. $0.

b. $3,000.

c. $5,000.

d. $11,000.

e. $16,400.

61. On January 1 of the current year, David was awarded a post-graduate fellowship grant of $6,000 by a tax-exempt educational organization. David is not a candidate for a degree and was awarded the grant to continue his research. The grant was awarded for the period August 1 of the current year through July 31 of the following year. On August 1 of the current year, David elected to receive the full amount of the grant. What amount should be included in his gross income for the current year?

a. $0.

b. $2,500.

c. $3,000.

d. $4,500.

e. $6,000.

62. In July 1983, Bill leased a building to Bob for a period of fifteen years at a monthly rental rate of $2,000 with no option to renew. At that time, the building had a remaining estimated useful life of twenty years. Prior to taking possession of the building, Bob made improvements at a cost of $18,000. These improvements had an estimated useful life of twenty years at the commencement of the lease period. The lease expired on June 30 of the current year at which point the improvements had a fair market value of $2,000. The amount that Bill, the landlord, should include in his gross income for the current year is:

    a. $12,000.
    b. $14,000.
    c. $24,000.
    d. $26,000.
    e. $30,000.

DEDUCTIONS AND LOSSES: IN GENERAL

63. John is the sole shareholder of River Rafting, Inc., a C Corporation. In the current year, he receives a salary of $150,000 and dividends of $60,000 from River. River's taxable income for the current year is $400,000. On his audit, the IRS reduces John's salary by $60,000 to $90,000 because it was determined to be unreasonable. Which of the following statements is correct?

    a. John's gross income will increase by $60,000 as a result of the IRS adjustment.
    b. River's taxable income will not be affected by the IRS adjustment.
    c. John's gross income will decrease by $60,000 as a result of the IRS adjustment.
    d. River's taxable income will increase by $60,000 as a result of the IRS adjustment.
    e. None of the above.

64. Sylvia, a real estate broker, files a Schedule C and had the following income and expenses in her business:

Commissions income	$120,000
Expenses:	
Commissions paid to non-brokers for referrals (illegal under state law)	30,000
Commissions paid to other real estate brokers for referrals (not illegal under state law)	15,000
Travel and transportation	16,000
Auto expenses	4,200
Office, phone, and fax	3,500
Parking tickets for illegal parking	400

How much Schedule C net income must Sylvia report from this business?

    a. $50,900.
    b. $51,300.
    c. $81,300.
    d. $96,300.
    e. $96,700.

65. Randy, a calendar year cash basis taxpayer, owns and operates furniture rental outlets in Georgia. He wants to expand to other states. He spends $20,000 investigating furniture stores in Alabama and $12,000 investigating stores in Florida. He acquires the Alabama stores, but not the stores in Florida. As to the above expenses, Randy should:
    a. Capitalize $20,000 and not deduct $12,000.
    b. Expense $32,000.
    c. Expense $12,000 and capitalize $20,000.
    d. Capitalize $32,000.
    e. None of the above.

66. Sara pursued a hobby of selling antique furniture in her spare time. During the year she sold the furniture for $3,000. She incurred expenses as follows:

Cost of goods sold	$2,000
Supplies	1,200
Interest on loan to get business started	800
Advertising	750

Assuming that the activity is a hobby, and that she cannot itemize this year, how should she report these items on her tax return?
    a. Include $3,000 in income and deduct $4,750 for AGI.
    b. Ignore both income and expenses since hobby losses are disallowed.
    c. Include $3,000 in income and deduct nothing for AGI since hobby expenses must be itemized.
    d. Include $3,000 in income and deduct interest of $800 for AGI.
    e. None of the above.

67. Bob and Teddi own a house at the beach. The house was rented to unrelated parties for 8 full weeks during the current year. Bob and Teddi used the house 16 days for their vacation during the year. After properly dividing the expenses between rental and personal use, it was determined that a loss was incurred as follows:

Gross rental income			$6,400
Less:	Mortgage interest and property taxes	$7,000	
	Other allocated expenses	1,000	(8,000)
	Net rental loss		**($1,600)**

What is the correct treatment of the rental income and expenses on Bob and Teddi's joint income tax return for the current year?

a. A $1,600 loss should be reported.

b. The rental portion of interest and taxes can be deducted.

c. The rental expenses (other than interest and taxes) are limited to the gross rental income in excess of deductions for interest and taxes allocated to the rental use.

d. Since the house was used only 20% personally by Bob and Teddi, all expenses allocated to personal use may be deducted.

e. Include none of the income or expenses related to the beach house in their current year income tax return.

68. Frank paid the following expenses for his dependent son, Mitch, during the current year:

Principal payments on automobile loan	$15,000
Interest on the automobile loan	1,500
Payment of Mitch's medical expenses	4,000
Payment of Mitch's property taxes (ad valorem)	1,000

How much of the above may Frank deduct (ignoring any hurdles or thresholds) in computing his itemized deductions?

a. $4,000.

b. $5,000.

c. $5,500.

d. $6,500.

e. $21,500.

69. On January 10 of last year (Year 1), Todd sold stock with a cost of $6,000 to his son Trey for $4,000 (its fair market value). On July 31 of the current year (Year 2), Trey sold the same stock for $5,000 in a bona fide arms length transaction to Mary who is unrelated to Trey or Todd. What is the proper treatment for these transactions?

a. Neither Todd nor Trey has a recognized gain or loss in either Year 1 or Year 2.
b. Todd has a recognized loss of $2,000 in Year 1.
c. Trey has a recognized gain of $1,000 in Year 2.
d. Trey has a recognized gain of $2,000 in Year 2.
e. Todd has a recognized loss of $2,000 and Trey a recognized gain of $1,000 in Year 1 and Year 2 respectively.

70. Which of the following types of deductions can be claimed in arriving at an individual's adjusted gross income?

a. Unreimbursed business expenses of an outside employee-salesperson.
b. Personal casualty losses.
c. Charitable contributions.
d. Alimony payments.
e. Union dues.

DEDUCTIONS AND LOSSES: CERTAIN BUSINESS EXPENSES & LOSSES

71. Versa, Inc. is an accrual basis taxpayer. Versa uses the accounts receivable aging approach to calculate their accounting allowance for bad debts. The following information is available for the current year related to bad debts.

Credit sales	$450,000
Collections on credit sales	375,000
Amount added to the allowance account	60,000
Beginning balance in the allowance account	25,000
Bad debts written off in the current year	32,000

The tax deduction for bad debt expense for Versa for the current year is:

a. $32,000.
b. $35,000.
c. $53,000.
d. $92,000.
e. None of the above.

72. Three years ago, Eric loaned Robin $5,000 (Year 1) with the understanding that the loan would be repaid in two years. Last year, in Year 3, Robin filed for bankruptcy, and Eric learned that he would receive $0.10 on the dollar. In the current year, Year 4, the final settlement was made, and Eric received $300. Assuming the loan is a non-business bad debt, how should Eric account for the loan?

a. $4,700 ordinary loss in the current year.
b. $3,000 ordinary loss last year and $1,700 ordinary loss in the current year.
c. $4,700 short-term capital loss in the current year.
d. $3,000 short-term capital loss last year and $1,700 short-term capital loss in the current year.
e. $5,000 ordinary loss last year.

73. Two years ago, Kevin loaned his friend Randy $5,000. In the current year, Randy paid Kevin $1,500 in final settlement of the loan. Kevin has $100,000 of salary and $5,000 of capital gains for the current year. What amount of the loss may he use in the current year?

   a. $0.
   b. $1,500.
   c. $3,000.
   d. $3,500.
   e. $5,000.

74. On October 15, 1998, Erin purchased stock in Glennan Irish Ale Corporation (the stock is not small business stock) for $2,000. On June 15, 1999, the stock became worthless. How should Erin treat the loss in the current year?

   a. $1,000 long-term capital loss.
   b. $2,000 short-term capital loss.
   c. $2,000 long-term capital loss.
   d. $1,000 short-term capital loss.
   e. $2,000 ordinary loss.

75. On January 15 of last year, Pat, a single taxpayer, purchased stock in Fisher Corporation (the stock is small business stock) for $10,000. On January 10 of the current year, he sold the stock for $70,000. How should Pat treat the gain on his current year tax return?

   a. $60,000 ordinary income.
   b. $60,000 long-term capital gain.
   c. $50,000 ordinary income, $10,000 long-term capital gain.
   d. $50,000 ordinary income, $10,000 short-term capital gain.
   e. $60,000 short-term capital gain.

76. Which of the following is/are casualty losses?

   1. Erosion due to rain or wind.
   2. Termite infestation.
   3. Damages to personal automobile resulting from a taxpayer's negligent driving.
   4. Misplaced or lost items.

   a. 1 only.
   b. 3 only.
   c. 4 only.
   d. 1 and 3.
   e. 1, 2, 3, and 4.

77. Rick had art worth $10,000 (basis of $15,000) stolen from his apartment. During the year, he had a salary of $30,000 and no other deductions. Compute Rick's itemized deduction from the theft of the art.

    a. $6,900.
    b. $9,900.
    c. $10,000.
    d. $15,000.
    e. None of the above.

78. On September 19, 1998, an investor purchases 5,000 shares of Tenor Corporation for $6,000. On March 31, 1999, the stock became worthless. What is the recognized gain or loss and how is it classified?

    a. $3,000 STCL.
    b. $6,000 STCL.
    c. $3,000 LTCL.
    d. $6,000 LTCL.
    e. None of the above.

79. Buddy Short, CPA, is a cash basis taxpayer. In April of last year, Buddy billed a client $4,500 for the following professional services:

Estate planning	$3,000
Personal tax return preparation	$1,000
Compilation of business financial statements	$500

No part of the $4,500 was ever paid. In April of the current year, the client declared bankruptcy, and the $4,500 obligation became totally uncollectible. What loss can Buddy deduct on his current year tax return for this bad debt?

    a. $0.
    b. $500.
    c. $1,500.
    d. $3,000.
    e. $4,500.

80. Kurt, who worked as a manager for Review Corp., loaned Review Corp. $4,000 two years ago. Kurt did not own any of Review's stock, and the loan was not a condition of Kurt's employment by Review. This year, Review declared bankruptcy and Kurt's note receivable from Review became worthless. What loss can Kurt claim on his income tax return for this year assuming no other capital gains or losses?

    a. $2,000 ordinary loss.
    b. $2,000 long-term capital loss.
    c. $3,000 short-term capital loss.
    d. $4,000 business bad debt.
    e. $4,000 short-term capital loss.

DEPRECIATION, COST RECOVERY, AMORTIZATION DEPLETION

81. Last year, Black had a §179 deduction carryover of $8,000. In the current year, he elected §179 for an asset acquired at a cost of $10,000. Black's net income for the current year is $15,000. Determine Black's §179 deduction for the current year (assume no other income).

    a. $8,000.
    b. $10,000.
    c. $15,000.
    d. $17,500.
    e. $18,000.

82. In 1999, Adorn Corp. purchased and placed in service a machine to be used in its manufacturing operations. This machine cost $207,000. What portion of the cost may Adorn elect to treat as a current, deductible expense rather than as a capital expenditure assuming net taxable income of $400,000?

    a. $0.
    b. $11,500.
    c. $12,000.
    d. $13,000.
    e. $19,000.

83. A client purchased a piece of equipment in 1995 for the client's computer business. Which of the following depreciation methods should be used if the client wishes to maximize tax depreciation? **(CFP® Exam, released 3/95)**

    a. Modified accelerated cost recovery system (MACRS).
    b. Accelerated cost recovery system (ACRS).
    c. Units of production.
    d. Sum of the year's digits.
    e. Straight line.

PASSIVE ACTIVITY LOSSES

84. In the current year, Bob invested $50,000 for a 20% interest in a partnership in which he was a material participant during the year. The partnership incurred a loss, and Bob's share was $75,000. Which of the following statements is false?

    a. Since Bob has only $50,000 of capital at risk, he cannot deduct more than $50,000 against his other income.

    b. Bob's non-deductible loss of $25,000 can be carried over and used when the at-risk provisions allow.

    c. If Bob has taxable income of $45,000 from the partnership in the following year and no other transactions that affect his at-risk amount, he can use all of the $25,000 loss carried over from the current year.

    d. Bob's $75,000 loss is non-deductible in the current year and the following year under the passive loss provisions.

85. Joseph, who earned a salary of $180,000, invested $30,000 for a 15% interest in a passive activity in the current year. Operations of the activity resulted in a loss of $300,000, of which Joseph's share was $45,000. How is his loss for the current year characterized?

    a. $30,000 is suspended under the passive loss rules and $15,000 is suspended under the at-risk rules.

    b. $30,000 is suspended under the at-risk rules and $15,000 is suspended under the passive loss rules.

    c. $45,000 is suspended under the passive loss rules.

    d. $45,000 is suspended under the at-risk rules.

    e. None of the above.

86. In the current year, George invested $100,000 for a 20% partnership interest in an activity in which he is a material participant. The partnership reported a loss of $400,000 in the current year and $200,000 in the following year. George's share of the partnership's loss was $80,000 in the current year and $40,000 in the following year. How much of the loss from the partnership can George deduct?

	Current Year	Following Year
a.	$80,000	$40,000
b.	$80,000	$20,000
c.	$0	$0
d.	$80,000	$0
e.	None of the above.	

87. In the current year, Fred invested $25,000 for a 1/4 interest in a real estate partnership where he was a general partner and a material participant. Fred's AGI was $125,000 and his allocated loss from the real estate activity was $30,000. Fred has no passive income this year. What is Fred's deductible loss on his Federal tax return from the above transaction for the current year?

a. $0.
b. $12,500.
c. $15,000.
d. $25,000.
e. $30,000.

88. Philip, a professor, earned a salary of $140,000 from a university in the current year. He received $35,000 in dividends and interest during the year. In addition, he incurred a loss of $25,000 from an investment in a passive activity. His at-risk amount in the activity at the beginning of the current year was $15,000. What is Philip's adjusted gross income for the current year?

a. $115,000.
b. $150,000.
c. $160,000.
d. $175,000.
e. None of the above.

89. Arthur, an attorney, owns and participates in a separate business (not real estate) during the current year. He has one employee who works part-time in the business. Which of the following statements is correct?

    a. If Arthur participates for 500 hours and the employee participates for 520 hours during the year, Arthur qualifies as a material participant.
    b. If Arthur participates for 600 hours and the employee participates for 1,000 hours during the year, Arthur qualifies as a material participant.
    c. If Arthur participates for 120 hours and the employee participates for 120 hours during the year, Arthur does not qualify as a material participant.
    d. If Arthur participates for 95 hours and the employee participates for 5 hours during the year, Arthur probably does not qualify as a material participant.
    e. None of the above.

90. Ron has three separate passive activities and has an at-risk amount in excess of $100,000 for each. During the year, the activities produced the following income (losses):

First Activity (1)	($40,000)
Second Activity (2)	(20,000)
Third Activity (3)	15,000
Net passive loss	**($45,000)**

Ron's suspended losses are as follows:

    a. $40,000 to 1; $20,000 to 2.
    b. $30,000 to 1; $15,000 to 2.
    c. $0 to 1; $0 to 2.
    d. $22,500 to 1; $22,500 to 2.
    e. None of the above.

91. Carter, an unmarried individual, had an adjusted gross income of $180,000 in the current year before any IRA deduction, taxable social security benefits, or passive activity losses. Carter incurred a loss of $30,000 from rental real estate in which he actively participated. What amount of loss (attributable to this rental real estate) can be used in the current year as an offset against income from non-passive sources?

    a. $0.
    b. $12,500.
    c. $25,000.
    d. $30,000.
    e. None of the above.

92. Which of the following activities is/are treated as a "rental activity" under the passive activity rules?

    1. Property rental where average customer use is 7 days or less.
    2. Property rental where average customer use is 30 days or less and significant services are provided.
    3. Property rental where extraordinary services are provided on behalf of the owners.
    4. Property rental where the property is customarily made available during defined business hours for the non-exclusive use of customers.

    a. 1 only.
    b. 2 only.
    c. 2 and 3.
    d. 2, 3, and 4.
    e. 1, 2, 3, and 4.

93. Which of the following types of income is/are generally considered passive income?

    1. Interest income.
    2. Royalty income.
    3. Rental income.
    4. Dividend income.

    a. 3 only.
    b. 3 and 4.
    c. 2 and 3.
    d. 2, 3, and 4.
    e. 1, 2, and 4.

EMPLOYEE EXPENSES

94. Jenny holds two jobs: a full-time job with Continental Corporation and a part-time job with Delta Corporation. Jenny uses her car to get to work, and the mileage involved is as follows: from Jenny's home to Continental is 60 miles; from Continental to Delta is 10 miles; and from Delta to Jenny's home is 60 miles. Jenny's deductible mileage for each work day is:
    a. 0 miles.
    b. 10 miles.
    c. 60 miles.
    d. 70 miles.
    e. 120 miles.

95. When travel includes both business and pleasure:
    a. No transportation expenses can be deducted if foreign travel is included.
    b. Transportation expenses must be allocated if domestic travel is included.
    c. For foreign travel, no allocation of transportation expenses is required if the taxpayer was away from home for seven days or less.
    d. For foreign and domestic travel, no allocation of transportation expenses is required if the taxpayer spends at least 75 percent of the time on business.
    e. None of the above.

96. In the current year, Ashley took a trip from Montgomery, Alabama, to London, England. She was away from home for ten days. She spent two days vacationing and eight days on business (including the two travel days). Her expenses are as follows:

Air fare	$1,200
Lodging (10 days x $150)	1,500
Meals (10 days x $90)	900
	$ 3,600

Ashley's deduction is:
    a. $2,760.
    b. $3,120.
    c. $3,150.
    d. $3,600.
    e. None of the above.

97. In the current year, Kim is transferred by her employer from New Orleans to Houston. Her expenses are not reimbursed and are as follows:

Costs of moving household furnishings	$1,600
Transportation costs	300
Meals in route	400
Lodging in route	250
	$2,550

Her qualified moving expenses are:

a. $1,850.
b. $2,150.
c. $2,350.
d. $2,550.
e. None of the above.

98. Melinda, who holds a Bachelor of Arts degree in Art History, is a middle school teacher in New Orleans. The school board recently changed its minimum education requirement by prescribing five years of college training. Existing teachers, such as Melinda, were allowed 10 years in which to acquire the additional year of education. Pursuant to this requirement, Melinda spends her summer break attending the University of Hawaii taking art history courses. Her expenses are as follows:

Books and tuition	$2,000
Meals	1,000
Lodging	700
Laundry while in travel status	200
Transportation	700
Total	**$4,600**

Her education expense deduction before the 2% floor is:

a. $0.
b. $2,500.
c. $4,100.
d. $4,400.
e. $4,600.

99. Steve entertains one of his clients on January 1 of the current year. Expenses paid by Steve are:

Taxi	$30
Door fee cover	25
Dinner	128
Tips to waitress	25
	$208

Assuming proper substantiation, Steve's current year deduction is:

a. $119.

b. $162.

c. $183.

d. $208.

e. None of the above.

100. Robbins, the sales director for a software company, pays $2,000 to obtain a skybox for an evening production of "Cats." The skybox holds 15 seats and Robbins invites 14 clients. Non-luxury seats sell for $25 each. The refreshments served to Robbins and her clients cost $455. A substantial business discussion was held before and after the show and Robbins has all necessary substantiation. Robbins' deduction is:

a. $375.

b. $415.

c. $830.

d. $2,227.50.

e. $2,455.

101. Lance made the following gifts during the current year:

To Jack, a key client ($4 of the amount listed was for gift wrapping)	$104
To Vernon, Lance's secretary, on Vernon's birthday	24
To Steve, Lance's boss, at Christmas	28
	$156

Assuming proper substantiation, Lance's deduction is:

a. $49.

b. $53.

c. $75.

d. $79.

e. $156.

102. At Thanksgiving of the current year, Delle Corp. gave business gifts to 15 individual customers. These gifts, which were not of an advertising nature, had the following fair market values:

3 gifts at $12 each
4 gifts at $25 each
4 gifts at $60 each
4 gifts at $100 each

Of the total gifts given, how much was deductible as a business expense for the current year?

a. $0.
b. $336.
c. $375.
d. $575.
e. $776.

103. Foster, a corporate executive, incurred the following business-related, unreimbursed expenses in the current year:

Entertainment	$3,000
Travel	2,000
Education	1,000

Assuming that Foster does not itemize deductions, how much of these expenses can he deduct on his current year tax return?

a. $0.
b. $1,000.
c. $3,000.
d. $4,000.
e. $6,000.

ITEMIZED DEDUCTIONS: MEDICAL EXPENSES, TAXES PAID, INTEREST PAID, CHARITABLE CONTRIBUTIONS

104. Wing, a single, calendar year, cash basis taxpayer, has the following transactions for the current year:

Salary from job	$60,000
Alimony paid to ex-wife	5,000
Medical expenses	7,500

Based on this information, Wing has which of the following?

a. Adjusted Gross Income of $60,000.
b. Medical expense deduction of $3,000.
c. Medical expense deduction of $3,375.
d. Medical expense deduction of $4,125.
e. Medical expense deduction of $4,500.

105. Which, if any, of the following expenses qualify for deductibility under miscellaneous itemized deductions, subject to a 2% floor?

a. Cost of regular uniforms of U.S. Marine officer on active duty.
b. Job-hunting expenses of a recent college graduate looking for his first job.
c. Job-hunting expenses of an art history professor seeking employment as chef.
d. Cost of local service for a residential telephone which taxpayer uses for business.
e. None of the above.

106. Which of the following miscellaneous itemized deductions are not subject to the 2 percent floor?

a. Gambling losses to the extent of gambling gains.
b. Union dues.
c. Work uniforms (not suitable for street wear).
d. Home office expenses of an employee (the employer provides a regular office).
e. None of the above.

107. Which of the following, if any, qualify for the medical expense deduction?

a. Cremation expenses for dependent mother.
b. Non-prescribed cold remedy purchased at a drug store.
c. Non-prescribed vitamin supplements purchased from a mail-order catalogue.
d. Stop-smoking clinic.
e. None of the above.

108. During the current year, Abe incurred and paid the following expenses:

Psychiatrist bills for Alex (Abe's stepson)	$1,400
Tuition, room, and board and other expenses for Alex at the Dalton School	12,000
Doctor bills for Cynthia (Alex's mother, Abe's spouse)	2,000
Charges at Memorial Nursing Home for Cynthia	24,000

Alex qualifies as Abe's dependent. Alex's psychiatrist recommended the Dalton School because of its small class sizes and rigorous discipline control. The school provides no special medical facilities or care. Cynthia has been diagnosed as having deteriorating brain disease. Memorial offers the proper care Cynthia needs. For these expenses, the amount that qualifies for the medical deduction is:

a. $0.

b. $1,400.

c. $27,400.

d. $38,000.

e. $39,400.

109. Upon the recommendation of a physician, Sidney has an air filtration system installed in his personal residence since he suffers from severe allergy problems. Sidney incurs and pays the following amount during the current year:

Filtration system and cost of installation	$10,000
Increase in utility bills due to the system	1,000
Cost of certified appraisal of property	500

The system has an estimated useful life of 15 years. The appraisal was to determine the value of Sidney's residence with and without the system. The appraisal states that the system increased the value of Sidney's residence by $2,000. Expenses qualifying for the medical deduction in the current year total:

a. $1,500.

b. $8,000.

c. $9,000.

d. $11,000.

e. $11,500.

110. Upon the recommendation of a physician, David drives his dependent and disabled mother to the Mumford Clinic for treatment on an outpatient basis. Expenses for the four day trip were as follows:

Mileage (round-trip)	600 miles
Tolls and parking	$50
Meals	420
Lodging (2 rooms for 4 nights at $75 per room each night)	600

All expenses were incurred and paid for by David. He has qualifying medical expenses of:

a. $310.

b. $510.

c. $720.

d. $930.

e. $1,037.

111. Donna's employer withheld $4,200 in state income taxes from her salary in the current year. Donna also paid an additional $1,200 in estimated state income tax payments. She filed her previous year's state income tax return in April of the current year, and received a state tax refund of $700 in the current year. She claimed the standard deduction on her Federal return for the previous year. Which of the following statements is correct?

a. If she itemizes, she can deduct $4,700 in state income tax on her current year Federal income tax return.

b. If she itemizes, she can deduct $5,400 in state income tax on her current year Federal income tax return.

c. She is required to report the $700 state income tax refund as income in the current year.

d. Statements B and C are correct.

e. None of the above are correct.

112. During the current year, Ginny paid the following taxes:

Taxes on residence (for the period January 1 through August 31 of the current year)	$2,000
State motor vehicle tax (based on the value of the automobile)	$120

Ginny sold the residence on June 30 of the current year, and the real estate taxes were not prorated between the buyer and the seller. How much of these taxes qualify as a deduction from AGI for the current year for taxes (rounded to nearest dollar)?

a. $1,480.
b. $1,601.
c. $1,800.
d. $2,300.
e. None of the above.

113. Taxpayer is a resident of a state that imposes income tax. Information regarding Taxpayer's state income tax transactions is as follows:

Taxes withheld in the current year, 1999	$7,200
Refund received in 1999 from overpayment of 1997 tax liability	1,500
Deficiency assessed for 1997 (as a result of audit by the state)	3,000
Interest on the tax deficiency	500

The 1997 deficiency and interest thereon were paid by Taxpayer in 1999. If Taxpayer elects to itemize deductions for 1999, how much of the above transactions can be deducted?

a. $7,700.
b. $9,700.
c. $10,200.
d. $10,700.
e. None of the above.

114. During the current year, Horace paid the following interest charges:

Home mortgage	$9,000
On loan to purchase household furniture (personal)	800
On loan to purchase state of Louisiana general obligation bonds (tax-exempt)	750

If Horace itemizes his deductions from AGI for the current year, the amount deductible as interest expense is:

a. $800.
b. $1,550.
c. $9,000.
d. $9,800.
e. $10,550.

115. In the current year, Helen (a single taxpayer) purchases an airplane for $130,000. In order to obtain financing for the purchase, Helen issues a lien on her personal residence in the amount of $130,000. At the time, the residence had a fair market value of $400,000 and a first mortgage of $320,000. For the plane loan, Helen may claim as qualified residence interest the interest on what amount?

a. $30,000.
b. $80,000.
c. $100,000.
d. $130,000.
e. None of the above.

116. George graduated from Ball University. In the current year, he donated $2,000 to the athletic department of the university to guarantee priority to purchase two premium season tickets to home football games. In addition, George purchased two season tickets at the regular price of $500 ($250 each). George's charitable contribution for the current year is:

a. $1,000.
b. $1,600.
c. $2,000.
d. $2,500.
e. None of the above.

117. In the current year, Jeff makes the following charitable donations:

	Basis	Fair Market Value
Inventory held for resale in Jeff's business (a sole proprietorship)	$8,000	$6,000
Stock in Hetzer Co. held as an investment (acquired two years ago)	10,000	40,000
Coin collection held as an investment (acquired ten years ago)	1,000	7,000

The Hetzer Co. stock was given to Jeff's church, and the coin collection was given to the Boy Scouts. Both donees promptly sold the property for the stated fair market value. Ignoring percentage limitations, Jeff's charitable contribution for the current year is:

a. $19,000.

b. $47,000.

c. $53,000.

d. $55,000.

e. None of the above.

118. A calendar year taxpayer made the following charitable contributions in the current year:

	Basis	Fair Market Value
Cash to church	$5,000	$5,000
Unimproved land to the city of Kenner, Louisiana	40,000	70,000

The land had been held as an investment and was acquired 5 years ago. Shortly after receipt, the city of Kenner sold the land for $90,000. If the taxpayer's AGI is $120,000, the allowable charitable contribution deduction is:

a. $25,000 if the reduced deduction election is not made.

b. $75,000 if the reduced deduction election is made.

c. $37,000 if the reduced deduction election is not made.

d. $45,000 if the reduced deduction election is made.

e. None of the above.

119. During the current year Jack and Mary Dardis paid the following taxes:

Taxes on residence (for period January 1 to September 30 of the current year)	$3,600
Motor vehicle tax on value of the car	450

The Dardis' sold their home on May 31 of the current year under an agreement where the real estate taxes were not prorated between buyer and seller. What amount should the Dardis' deduct as taxes in calculating itemized deductions for the current year?

a. $2,000.
b. $2,428.
c. $2,450.
d. $3,600.
e. $4,050.

120. John, who resided in New Jersey, was unemployed for the last six months of last year. In January of the current year, he moved to Florida and obtained a full-time job in February. He kept this job for the balance of the year. John paid the following expenses in the current year in connection with his move:

Rental of truck to move his personal belongings to Florida	$1,200
Penalty for breaking the lease on his New Jersey apartment	500
Total	**$1,700**

How much can John deduct in the current year for moving expenses?

a. $0.
b. $500.
c. $1,200.
d. $1,450.
e. $1,700.

121. Vicki and Mike Kline are married and file a joint income tax return. Among their current year expenditures were the following discretionary costs that they incurred for the sole purpose of improving their physical appearance and self-esteem:

Face lift for Vicki, performed by a licensed surgeon	$3,800
Hair transplant for Mike, performed by a wallpaper hanger	4,000

Disregarding the adjusted gross income medical percentage threshold, what total amount of the bills may be claimed by the Klines in their current year tax return as qualifying medical expenses?

a. $0.

b. $3,800.

c. $4,000.

d. $7,800.

e. None of the above.

122. Last year, Marsha charged $3,000 on her credit card for her dependent son's medical expense. Payment to the credit card company had not been made by the time she filed last year's income tax return this year. Also, Marsha paid a physician $3,000 last year for the medical expenses of her mother, (qualified as a dependent) who died the previous year. Disregarding the adjusted gross income percentage for medical expenses, what amount could Marsha claim in last year's income tax return for medical expenses?

a. $0.

b. $3,000.

c. $4,500.

d. $6,000.

e. None of the above.

ALTERNATIVE MINIMUM TAX

123. Which of the following is included in computing the alternative minimum tax for an individual taxpayer?

 1. Interest from a savings account with $35,000.
 2. Net capital gain deduction on the sale of rental property.
 3. Excess accelerated depreciation over straight-line for real property placed in service before 1987.
 4. Capital gains on the sale of personal residence.

 a. 1 only.
 b. 3 only.
 c. 2 and 3.
 d. 2, 3, and 4.
 e. 1, 2, 3, and 4.

124. The alternative minimum tax applies to which of the following?

 1. Individuals.
 2. Trusts.
 3. Partnerships.
 4. Corporations.

 a. 1 only.
 b. 1 and 2.
 c. 1, 2, and 3.
 d. 1, 2, and 4.
 e. 2, 3, and 4.

125. Which of the following is a tax preference item for the purpose of calculating the alternative minimum tax?

 1. The accelerated portion of real property depreciation (purchased before 1/1/87).
 2. Cash contributions to charitable organizations.
 3. Cash flows from limited partnerships.
 4. Personal-service income in excess of tax losses.

 a. 1 only.
 b. 2 only.
 c. 1 and 2.
 d. 1, 3, and 4.
 e. 1, 2, 3, and 4.

TAX CREDITS

126. Which, if any, of the following properly describes the earned income credit (EIC) for the current year?
    a. Is available regardless of the amount of the taxpayer's adjusted gross income.
    b. Is not available to a surviving spouse.
    c. To take advantage of the credit, a taxpayer must have a qualifying child.
    d. If the taxpayer has a qualifying child, then the EIC is a refundable credit and may be received from an employer.
    e. None of the above.

127. To be eligible for the earned income credit, a taxpayer may be required to have a qualifying child. A qualifying child must meet which of the following test(s)?
    a. Relationship.
    b. Residency.
    c. Age.
    d. All of the above tests must be met.
    e. None of the above need be met (A - C).

128. Jack and Jill both age 69 are husband and wife and file a joint return. During the current year, they receive Social Security benefits of $4,000 and have adjusted gross income of $12,000. Their credit for the elderly is:
    a. $1,125.
    b. $750.
    c. $450.
    d. $375.
    e. None of the above.

129. Cynthia and Ted are married and file a joint return. They report $50,000 of adjusted gross income ($15,000 salary earned by Ted and $35,000 salary earned by Cynthia). They claim two exemptions for their dependent children. During the year, they paid the following amounts to care for their 5 year old son Alex, and 7 year old daughter Tedra, while they worked:

Day Care Center	$3,000
Housekeeping Services provided by Mrs. Skeckel while she is babysitting	1,000
Mrs. Skeckel (Ted's mother) for baby sitting	2,000

They may claim a credit for child and dependent care expenses of:

a. $960.
b. $1,000.
c. $1,440.
d. $1,500.
e. None of the above.

130. Guidry, unmarried, pays Hellen Smith (a housekeeper) $6,000 to care for his physically incapacitated mother so that he can be gainfully employed. He has adjusted gross income of $44,000 and claims his mother as a dependent. Guidry's credit for child and dependent care expenses is:

a. $0.
b. $480.
c. $960.
d. $980.
e. None of the above.

131. A widow maintains a home for herself and her two dependent preschool children. This year she had adjusted gross income of $31,000 (all earned income). She paid work-related expenses of $4,000 for a housekeeper to care for her children. How much can she claim as a child care credit in the current year?

a. $0.
b. $480.
c. $600.
d. $800.
e. $900.

PROPERTY TRANSACTIONS - CAPITAL GAINS AND LOSSES

132. John owned the following lots of FinPlan, Inc. stock.

Purchased date	No. of shares	Basis
April 24, 1998	100	$ 5,000
June 25, 1999	100	6,000
August 3, 1999	200	13,000

On December 15, 1999 John sold 100 shares for $5,500. John did not specifically identify the shares of stock sold. What is his recognized gain or loss?

a. No gain or loss.
b. $1,000 STCL.
c. $500 STCG.
d. $500 LTCG.
e. None of the above.

133. Jerry has the following capital gains and losses for the current year:

LTCG	$20,000	STCG	$20,000
LTCL	$15,000	STCL	$ 7,500

What are Jerry's net long-term and short-term gains?

a. NSTCG = $17,500 NLTCG = $0.
b. NLTCG = $15,000 NSTCG = $20,000.
c. NLTCG = $5,000 NSTCG = $20,000.
d. NLTCG = $5,000 NSTCG = $12,500.
e. None of the above.

134. This year, Mary has short-term capital losses of $6,000, short-term capital gains of $11,000, and long-term capital losses of $6,000. How much may Mary deduct against her ordinary income this year?

a. $0.
b. $1,000.
c. $3,000.
d. $6,000.
e. None of the above.

DETERMINATION OF GAIN OR LOSS

135. The following assets were used in John's business:

Asset	Holding Period	Gain/Loss
Equipment	4 years	$2,100
Truck	6 months	<$1,200>
Common Stock (capital asset)	3 years	$2,000

The equipment had a zero adjusted basis and was purchased for $8,000. The truck was purchased for $3,000 and sold for $1,800. The stock was purchased for $3,000 and sold for $5,000. In the current year (the year of the sale), John should report what amount of net capital gain and net ordinary income?

a. $2,100 LTCG.
b. $800 LTCG and $900 ordinary gain.
c. $2,000 LTCG and $900 ordinary gain.
d. $4,100 LTCG and $1,200 ordinary loss.
e. None of the above.

136. In the current year, Cecily had taxable income of $30,000 not considering capital gains and losses and her personal exemption. In the current year, she incurred a $5,000 net short-term capital loss and a $5,000 net long-term capital loss. What is her long-term capital loss carryover to the following year?

a. $0.
b. $2,000.
c. $4,000.
d. $5,000.
e. None of the above.

137. Gift property (no gift tax was paid by the donor):

a. Has a zero basis to the donee because the donee did not pay anything for the property.

b. Has the same basis to the donee as the donor's adjusted basis if the donee disposes of the property at a gain.

c. Has the same basis to the donee as the donor's adjusted basis if the donee disposes of the property at a loss, and the fair market value on the date of gift was less than the donor's adjusted basis.

d. Has a zero basis to the donee if the fair market value on the date of gift is less than the donors adjusted basis.

e. None of the above.

138. Craig gives Scott (his son) stock with a basis of $80,000 and a fair market value of $70,000. No gift tax is paid. Scott subsequently sells the stock for $78,000. What is his recognized gain or loss?

a. No gain or loss.

b. $2,000 loss.

c. $8,000 gain.

d. $78,000 gain.

e. None of the above.

139. Christine purchased 100 shares of Romig Corporation stock for $28,000 ten years ago. In the current tax year, she sells 30 shares of the 100 shares purchased for $8,000. Twenty-nine days earlier, she had purchased 30 shares for $7,500. What is Christine's recognized gain or loss on the sale of the stock, and what is her basis in the 30 shares purchased 29 days earlier?

a. $400 recognized loss, $7,500 basis in new stock.

b. $0 recognized loss, $7,500 basis in new stock.

c. $0 recognized loss, $7,900 basis in new stock.

d. $0 recognized loss, $8,250 basis in new stock.

e. None of the above.

140. William Barnhill gave his son, Simon, a house on August 1 of this year. No gift tax was paid. The fair market values of the house on January 1, August 1, and December 31 of the current year were as follows: $130,000, $140,000, and $150,000. Mr. Barnhill had purchased the property in 1990 for $60,000 and had used it as rental property the entire time he held it. He had taken cumulative straight-line depreciation through July 31 of the current year of $10,000. What is Simon Barnhill's initial tax basis?

a. Simon's initial tax basis is zero because he did not have to pay anything for the house.

b. Simon's initial tax basis is the same as William's cost.

c. Simon's initial tax basis is the same as William's cost, less depreciation regardless of what Simon does with the property.

d. Simon's initial tax basis is the fair market value on the date of the gift.

e. Simon's initial tax basis is the fair market value as determined on the last day of the year in which the gift was given.

PROPERTY TRANSACTIONS: NON-TAXABLE EXCHANGES

PART A: EXCHANGES

141. Taxpayer exchanges a machine (A) and building for another machine (B) in a like-kind exchange. The (A) machine had an adjusted basis of $40,000 and a fair market value of $30,000. The building had an adjusted basis of $20,000 and a fair market value of $35,000. The large machine (B) has a fair market value of $65,000. What is the taxpayer's recognized gain or loss? There was no cash exchanged and no mortgages.

    a. $0.
    b. $10,000 loss.
    c. $5,000 gain.
    d. $15,000 gain.
    e. None of the above.

142. On February 2 of the current year, taxpayer exchanged a bank building, having an adjusted basis of $600,000 and subject to a mortgage of $275,000 for another bank building with a fair market value of $800,000 and subject to a mortgage of $275,000. Transfers were made subject to outstanding mortgages. What amount of gain should taxpayer recognize in the current year?

    a. $0.
    b. $75,000.
    c. $200,000.
    d. $275,000.
    e. None of the above.

143. An office building with an adjusted basis of $120,000 was destroyed by fire on January 2 of last year. On January 15 of the current year, the insurance company paid the owner $200,000. The owner reinvested $190,000 in a new office building. What is the basis of the new building if §1033 (non-recognition of gain from an involuntary conversion) is elected?

    a. $110,000.
    b. $120,000.
    c. $180,000.
    d. $190,000.
    e. None of the above.

144. Which of the following is not a requirement for a non-taxable exchange?

   a. The form of the transaction is an exchange.
   b. Both the property transferred and the property received are held either for productive use in a trade or business or for investment.
   c. The property is like kind property.
   d. The exchange cannot involve related parties.
   e. All of the above are requirements for a non-taxable exchange.

145. Taxpayer's office building was condemned by a local government authority on May 10, 1998. The adjusted basis was $300,000. Condemnation proceeds of $500,000 were received on February 1, 1999. The taxable year is the calendar year. What is the latest date that the taxpayer can replace the office building to qualify for §1033 (non-recognition of gain from an involuntary conversion) treatment?

   a. May 10, 2000.
   b. February 1, 2001.
   c. December 31, 2001.
   d. December 31, 2002.
   e. None of the above.

146. Mike exchanged the following old machine in a like-kind exchange. What gain is recognized, and what is the basis in the new asset?

1.	Adjusted basis of old machine	$5,000
2.	Fair market value of new machine	$10,000
3.	Fair market value of boot received	$0
4.	Fair market value of boot given	$0

	Gain Recognized	Basis of New Asset
a.	$0	$5,000
b.	$0	$10,000
c.	$5,000	$5,000
d.	$5,000	$10,000
e.	$5,000	$0

147. Mike exchanged the following old machine in a like-kind exchange. What gain is recognized, and what is the basis in the new asset?

1.	Adjusted basis of old machine	$5,000
2.	Fair market value of new machine	$10,000
3.	Fair market value of boot received	$0
4.	Fair market value of boot given	$4,000

	Gain Recognized	Basis of New Asset
a.	$0	$5,000
b.	$0	$9,000
c.	$0	$10,000
d.	$4,000	$5,000
e.	$4,000	$10,000

148. Mike exchanged the following old machine in a like-kind exchange. What gain is recognized, and what is the basis in the new asset?

1.	Adjusted basis of old machine	$5,000
2.	Fair market value of new machine	$10,000
3.	Fair market value of boot received	$0
4.	Fair market value of boot given	$6,000

	Gain Recognized	Basis of New Asset
a.	$0	$5,000
b.	$0	$10,000
c.	$0	$11,000
d.	$5,000	$11,000
e.	$6,000	$11,000

149. Mike exchanged the following old machine in a like-kind exchange. What gain is recognized, and what is the basis in the new asset?

1.	Adjusted basis of old machine	$5,000
2.	Fair market value of new machine	$10,000
3.	Fair market value of boot received	$4,000
4.	Fair market value of boot given	$0

	Gain Recognized	Basis of New Asset
a.	$0	$5,000
b.	$4,000	$5,000
c.	$4,000	$10,000
d.	$5,000	$5,000
e.	$5,000	$10,000

150. Mike exchanged the following old machine in a like-kind exchange. What gain is recognized, and what is the basis in the new asset?

1.	Adjusted basis of old machine	$5,000
2.	Fair market value of new machine	$10,000
3.	Fair market value of boot received	$0
4.	Fair market value of boot given	$400

	Gain Recognized	Basis of New Asset
a.	$0	$5,000
b.	$0	$5,400
c.	$0	$10,000
d.	$4,600	$10,000
e.	$5,000	$5,000

151. Which of the following exchanges would qualify for tax deferral under a tax-free exchange?

a. Common stock for preferred stock.

b. Inventory for an apartment.

c. Vacant land for a bank building.

d. A building in Boston for a building in Paris.

e. None of the above.

PART B: SALE OF RESIDENCE

152. Karen bought a personal residence for $130,000 ten years ago. She builds an additional room on the house for $20,000. She sells the property for $200,000 in the current year and pays $12,000 in real estate commissions and $3,000 in legal fees in connection with the sale. What is her recognized gain or loss on the sale of the house?

    a. $0.
    b. $35,000.
    c. $38,000.
    d. $55,000.
    e. $58,000.

153. Neal and Amy sold their personal residence for a gain of $150,000. Which of the following conditions would prevent them from excluding the full gain from income under Section 121?

    a. Neal has owned the house for 3 years.
    b. Amy moved into the house when she and Neal got married one year ago.
    c. The principal residence was a houseboat.
    d. Neal and Amy are both 40 years old.
    e. None of the above will cause inclusion of the gain.

154. B.J. and Sarah own a house that they have resided in for the past 10 years. B.J. is 60 and Sarah is 58. They sell the house for $420,000 with realtor fees of $50,000. Their adjusted basis for the house is $70,000. What is their recognized gain on the sale of the residence if they make any possible election? Assume no reinvestment.

    a. $0.
    b. $125,000.
    c. $175,000.
    d. $250,000.
    e. $300,000.

155. As part of their divorce agreement, Ron transfers his ownership interest in their personal residence to Marge. The house had been jointly owned by Ron and Marge, and their adjusted basis was $160,000. At the time of the transfer to Marge, the fair market value is $210,000. What is the recognized gain to Ron, and what is Marge's new tax basis for the house?

a. $0 and $160,000.

b. $0 and $210,000.

c. $25,000 and $185,000.

d. $25,000 and $210,000.

e. None of the above.

156. Hugh, age 57, is a single taxpayer. In March of this year, Hugh sold his principal residence for $445,000 net of expenses and moved to a nursing home. Hugh paid $120,000 for the residence 18 years ago and has made no improvements to it. How much of the gain must Hugh include in his gross income this year as a result of the sale?

a. $0.

b. $55,000.

c. $75,000.

d. $120,000.

e. $180,000.

157. To take advantage of the $250,000 exemption for selling a principal residence (by a single taxpayer) which of the following requirements must be met?

1. The taxpayer or spouse must have attained age 55.
2. The taxpayer must have occupied the house as his or her primary residence for at least 2 of the last 5 years.
3. A new or replacement residence must be purchased no more than 2 years before or 2 years after the sale of the residence.
4. The exclusion must not have been previously claimed by the taxpayer or spouse.

a. 1 only.

b. 2 only.

c. 2 and 3.

d. 1, 2, and 4.

e. 1, 2, 3, and 4.

158. On July 1 of the current year, George, age 65, sold his principal residence (in which he lived for the last 20 years) for $300,000, which had an adjusted basis of $100,000. On December 1 of the same year, he purchased a new residence for $160,000. What should the taxpayer recognize as the gain on the sale of his residence in the current year?

a. $0.

b. $15,000.

c. $75,000.

d. $175,000.

e. None of the above.

SECTION 1231 AND RECAPTURE PROVISIONS

159. Bradley, Inc. sold some business equipment on June 30th of the current year for a $15,000 gain. The equipment was originally purchased 3 years ago and was classified as a Section 1231 asset. This was the only asset sale for this year. In the previous year, Bradley Inc. had an $8,000 net Section 1231 loss. For the current year, Bradley's net Section 1231 gain is treated as:

    a. A $15,000 ordinary loss.
    b. A $15,000 ordinary gain.
    c. A $7,000 long-term capital gain and a $8,000 ordinary gain.
    d. A $8,000 long-term capital gain and a $7,000 ordinary loss.
    e. None of the above.

AUDIT PROCESS

PART A: TYPES/STATUTES

160. Tom, a self-employed individual, had income transactions for last year (duly reported on his return filed in April of this year) as follows:

Gross receipts	$320,000
Less cost of goods sold and deductions	(256,000)
Net business income	$64,000
Capital gains	20,000
Net income	**$84,000**

Suppose that in February of next year, Tom discovers he had inadvertently omitted income on the return filed in April last year and retains a CPA to determine his position under the statute of limitations. The CPA should advise Tom that the six-year statute of limitations would apply to his return only if he omitted from gross income an amount in excess of:

a. $11,000.
b. $16,000.
c. $21,000.
d. $80,000.
e. $85,000.

161. Which of the following is/are correct regarding the chances of a taxpayer return being selected for audit?

1. Chances of selection increase with the size of refund claimed.
2. Chances increase for taxpayer who has been audited in the past regardless of the outcome.
3. Chances increase for people who deduct 10% of salary for charity simply because that is in excess of national norms.
4. Chances increase for self-employed individuals.

a. 2 and 4.
b. 1, 2, and 4.
c. 3 and 4.
d. 1, 3, and 4.
e. 1, 2, and 3.

PART B: INTEREST AND PENALTIES

162. Bill files his tax return 40 days after the due date. Along with the return, Bill remits a check for $5,000 (the balance of the tax owed). Disregarding the interest element, Bill's combined failure to file and failure to pay penalties are:

    a. $650.
    b. $600.
    c. $500.
    d. $550.
    e. None of the above.

163. Chip files a timely tax return but is later required to pay an additional $15,000 in tax. Of this amount, $6,000 is attributable to the taxpayer's negligence. The negligence penalty will be:

    a. $0, there is no penalty, the return filed timely.
    b. $500, there is a maximum of $500 penalty.
    c. $1,200, a 20% penalty is applied to the $6,000.
    d. $1,800, a 30% penalty is applied to the $6,000.
    e. $3,000, a 20% penalty is applied to all tax due.

164. Margo files her tax return 39 days after the due date. Along with the return, she remits a check for $6,000 (the balance of the tax owed). Disregarding any interest element, her combined failure to file and failure to pay penalties are:

    a. $660.
    b. $600.
    c. $400.
    d. $440.
    e. None of the above.

165. Sara filed an extension on April 15. On June 1, she filed her tax return and owed $400 on a tax liability of $4,100. Which one of the following will apply? **(CFP® Exam, released 3/95)**

    a. Failure to file on a timely basis.
    b. Failure to pay the total amount due.
    c. No penalty because of prepayment of over 90% of liability.
    d. Penalty on $400.
    e. Penalty and interest on $400.

MISCELLANEOUS

166. In the current year, deductible contributions to a defined contribution qualified pension plan on behalf of a self-employed individual, whose Schedule C income from self-employment is $20,000 and whose social security taxes are $3,060, are limited to:

   a. $3,000.
   b. $3,694.
   c. $4,000.
   d. $4,618.
   e. $5,000.

167. Which of the following is/are correct regarding SEP contributions made by an employer?

   1. Contributions are subject to FICA and FUTA.
   2. Contributions are currently excludable from employee's gross income.
   3. Distributions can be rolled into a qualified plan.
   4. Contributions are vested over five years.

   a. 1 only.
   b. 2 only.
   c. 1 and 2.
   d. 1, 2, and 4.
   e. 1, 2, 3, and 4.

168. Which of the following is/are correct regarding the 10% penalty tax for early withdrawal from a qualified plan (age 59½)?

   1. Termination of employment at age 55 or older will exempt distribution from penalty tax.
   2. Distributions used to pay medical expenses not to exceed deductible medical expenses of the taxpayer are exempt from the 10% tax.
   3. Distributions used for hardship situations are exempt from the 10% penalty.
   4. Distributions that are part of a series of equal periodic payments paid over the life (or life expectancy) of the participant are exempt from the 10% penalty.

   a. 1, 2, and 4.
   b. 1, 2, and 3.
   c. 1, 3, and 4.
   d. 2, 3, and 4.
   e. 1, 2, 3, and 4.

169. Brother A and Brother B each own 2,000 shares in corporation X. Each has a son with 200 shares. How many shares does A have through attribution?

a. 0.

b. 200.

c. 2,200.

d. 4,000.

e. 2,400.

170. Larry employs the following related persons as full time employees in his proprietorship:

1. Larry's spouse age 42.
2. Larry's son age 22.
3. Larry's son age 16.
4. Larry's daughter age 16.

Of the above, who is subject to FICA taxes?

a. 1 only.

b. 1 and 2.

c. 3 and 4.

d. 2, 3, and 4.

e. 1, 2, 3, and 4.

171. Joan has an error on a past tax return (not prepared by current tax preparer) which Joan refuses to correct. The current tax preparer:

1. Has a duty to notify the IRS or is subject to preparer penalties.
2. Should withdraw from engagement if error affects current return and is material in amount.
3. Must withdraw from engagement.
4. Should consider the materiality of the error even if it does not affect the current year.

a. 1 and 4.

b. 2 and 4.

c. 1 and 3.

d. 1, 3, and 4.

e. 1, 2, and 4.

172. Which of the following is considered a related party for the sale of stock where the basis is above the Fair Market Value?

    1. Mother.
    2. Aunt.
    3. Daughter.
    4. Niece.
    5. Sister.

        a. 1, 2, and 5.
        b. 1, 3, and 5.
        c. 3 and 4.
        d. 3 and 5.
        e. 5 only.

173. Which of the following incomes is/are not taxed under Social Security self-employment tax? **(CFP® Exam, released 3/95)**

    1. Rental real estate income.
    2. Small part-time repair shop income.
    3. Shareholder's share of S corporation's income in excess of salary.
    4. Income of an individual working as an independent contractor.

        a. 1, 2, and 3.
        b. 1 and 3.
        c. 2 and 4.
        d. 4 only.
        e. 1, 2, 3, and 4.

174. Which of the following are true concerning Non-Qualified Stock Options (NQSOs)?

    1. The gain upon exercise of NQSOs is determined on the date of issuance by multiplying the difference between the market price and the exercise price by the number of options.
    2. The gain upon exercise of NQSOs is subject to Federal tax.
    3. The gain upon exercise of NQSOs is subject to FICA.
    4. The gain upon exercise of NQSOs is reportable on Form 1099-Misc.

        a. 1 and 2.
        b. 2 and 3.
        c. 2 and 4.
        d. 2, 3, and 4.
        e. 1, 2, 3, and 4.

175. Which of the following statements regarding the tax treatment of employing a person's children in a family business is/are correct?

1. If the business is incorporated, services performed by a child under age 18 are excluded from social security coverage.
2. Dependent children are taxed on earned income from a family business at their own marginal rates.
3. The earned income of a minor child derived from a family business cannot be reduced by the standard deduction.
4. Parents who employ their minor children may still claim a dependency exemption if the parents meet the support rules.

a. 1 only.
b. 4 only.
c. 1, 2, and 4.
d. 1, 2, and 3.
e. 1, 2, 3, and 4.

176. Jimmy and Dee Dee are married and filed a joint return last year. Jimmy earned a salary of $60,000 and was covered by his employer's pension plan. Also, Jimmy and Dee Dee earned interest of $5,000 on their joint savings account. Dee Dee was not employed and the couple had no other income. On April 15 of this year, Jimmy contributed $2,000 to an IRA for himself and $2,000 to an IRA for Dee Dee for the previous tax year. The allowable IRA deduction in Jimmy and Dee Dee's last year's joint return is:

a. $0.
b. $250.
c. $2,000.
d. $2,250.
e. $4,000.

177. Thad and Debra Claiborne, both age 50, are married and filed a joint return for the current year. Their adjusted gross income was $100,000, including Thad's $95,000 salary. Debra had no income of her own. Neither spouse was covered by an employer-sponsored pension plan. What amount could the Claiborne's contribute to IRAs for the current year to take advantage of their maximum allowable IRA deduction in their return?

a. $0.

b. $250.

c. $2,000.

d. $2,250.

e. $4,000.

178. Judy Martin, who is divorced, received taxable alimony of $30,000 in the current year. In addition, she received $900 in earnings from a part-time job. Judy is not covered by a qualified pension plan. What was the maximum deductible regular IRA contribution that Judy could have made for the current year?

a. $0.

b. $250.

c. $900.

d. $1,125.

e. $2,000.

179. For the current year Mary Sue and Bob White reported the following items of income:

	Mary Sue	Bob	Total
Salary	$40,000	$30,000	$70,000
Interest income	1,000	200	1,200
Cash prize won on TV game show	--	10,000	10,000
	$41,000	**$40,200**	**$81,200**

Mary Sue is not covered by a qualified retirement plan, but Bob is covered. She and Bob established Individual Retirement Accounts (IRAs) during the year. Assuming a joint return was filed for the current year, what is the maximum amount that they can deduct for the contributions to their IRAs?

a. $0.
b. $250.
c. $2,000.
d. $2,250.
e. $4,000.

180. A single taxpayer, age 54, retired two years ago and is receiving a pension of $600 per month from her previous employer's qualified pension plan. She has recently taken a position in a small CPA firm that has no pension plan. She will receive $10,000 in compensation from the CPA firm as well as the $7,200 from her pension. What amount, if any, can she contribute to a deductible IRA?

a. $0.
b. $1,000.
c. $1,500.
d. $2,000.
e. $2,250.

181. Which of the following distributions from a Roth IRA are qualified distributions not subject to the additional 10% early withdrawal tax:

1. Distributions for taxpayers over the age of 59 ½, where the contributions were made at least 5 years ago.
2. Unlimited distributions for first time homebuyers.
3. Distributions prior to age 59 ½ that are a series of equal periodic payments paid over the life or life expectancy of the participant.
4. Distributions used for educational expenses.

   a. 2 only.
   b. 1 and 2.
   c. 1, 2, and 3.
   d. 1, 3, and 4.
   e. 2, 3 and 4.

182. Which of the following is/are correct regarding penalties associated with IRA accounts?

1. Generally, distributions made prior to 59½ are subject to the 10% premature distribution penalty.
2. There is a 50% excise tax on under-distributions not made by April 1 of the year following the year in which age 70½ is reached.
3. A 15% penalty will be imposed for distributions from an IRA that exceeds the greater of (1) $160,000 or (2) $112,000 indexed.
4. An excess accumulation tax of 15% will be applied at the estate level for accumulations in excess of the present value of an annuity of the greater of: (1) $160,000 or (2) $112,000 (indexed over the participants life expectancy at death).

   a. 1 and 2.
   b. 1, 2, and 3.
   c. 1, 3, and 4.
   d. 2 and 3.
   e. 1, 2, 3, and 4.

183. Which of the following individual(s) can contribute to a deductible IRA for the current year?

	Person	Marital Status	AGI	Covered by Pension Plan
1.	Jane	Single	$ 30,000	Yes
2.	Joe	Married	$100,000	No
3.	Barbie	Single	$ 20,000	Yes
4.	Maggie	Married	$ 40,000	Yes

a. 3 only.
b. 3 and 4.
c. 2, 3, and 4.
d. 1, 3, and 4.
e. 1, 2, 3, and 4.

184. Which of the following is/are investments which can be utilized in an IRA without penalty?

1. A mutual fund which invests exclusively in gold mining stock.
2. An international stock mutual fund.
3. Investment grade piece of art.
4. Gold coins minted by the United States Treasury.

a. 2 only.
b. 2 and 4.
c. 1, and 2.
d. 1, 2, and 4.
e. 1, 2, 3, and 4.

185. Which of the following is/are correct regarding distributions from a decedent's IRA?

1. Generally, if distributions have not commenced before death, the balance must be distributed within 5 years.
2. If the owner has a designated beneficiary, and distributions have not commenced, distributions can be made over a period not extending beyond the life expectancy of the beneficiary.
3. If distributions have not begun, and the beneficiary is the spouse of the decedent, distribution may be delayed until the beneficiary's spouse reaches 70½ without rolling to spouse's account.
4. If the owner dies after payments have begun, the payments must continue to the beneficiary or heir at least as soon as they would have under the method of distribution in effect during the owner's life (unless the heir or beneficiary is a spouse).

a. 1 only.
b. 2 only.
c. 1 and 3.
d. 1, 2, and 4.
e. 1, 2, 3, and 4.

186. Which, if any of the following transactions are permissible regarding a deceased person's IRA?

1. A non-spouse IRA beneficiary must distribute the balance of an IRA, where distribution had begun, over a period not exceeding 5 years.
2. A non-spouse IRA beneficiary may distribute the balance of an IRA, where distribution had not begun, over the life expectancy of the beneficiary.
3. A beneficiary spouse of a deceased owner of an IRA can delay any distribution of such IRA until April 1 following the year in which such beneficiary is 70½.
4. A spouse beneficiary of a deceased owner IRA can roll such IRA balance into his or her own IRA, even if distributions had begun to the owner prior to death.

a. 1 and 2.
b. 2 and 3.
c. 1, 2, and 3.
d. 2, 3, and 4.
e. 1, 2, 3, and 4.

187. Joe Schmurk took a lump sum distribution from his employer at age 52, when he terminated his service. He rolled over his distribution using a direct transfer to an IRA. Which of the following is/are correct regarding tax treatment of the transaction?

1. If at age 55 he distributes the IRA, he benefits from lump sum forward averaging.
2. If he rolls the entire IRA to his new employer, he will be eligible for forward averaging treatment in the future.
3. If he rolls over a portion of the IRA to his new employer's plan, he will preserve his eligibility for forward averaging.
4. If Joe immediately withdraws the entire amount from his IRA, he will benefit by virtue of forward averaging.

   a. 1 only.
   b. 2 only.
   c. 2 and 3.
   d. 2 and 4.
   e. 1, 2, 3, and 4.

188. Which of the following are characteristics of both a SEP and an IRA?

1. Investment options are limited.
2. Immediate vesting in entire balance.
3. Early withdrawal (pre-59½) penalties of 10% excepting death and disability.
4. Availability of forward averaging.

   a. 1 only.
   b. 2 only.
   c. 2 and 3.
   d. 2, 3, and 4.
   e. 1, 2, and 3.

189. A client, age 50 and single, chose early retirement and is receiving from his previous employer's qualified pension plan a monthly pension of $400. The client elects to work for a small company and will receive $30,000 in annual compensation. This company does not cover him under a qualified pension plan. The client wants to contribute the maximum deductible amount to an Individual Retirement Account (IRA). The amount of the IRA contribution that he can deduct from his gross income is: **(CFP® Exam, released 3/95)**

a. $0.
b. $200.
c. $400.
d. $1,000.
e. $2,000.

190. Which of the following is/are correct regarding tax sheltered annuities (TSAs)?

1. A catch up provision is available to all 501(c)(3) organization employers.
2. Active employees who make withdrawals from TSAs prior to 59½ are subject to a 10% penalty tax.
3. TSAs are available to all employees.
4. A catch up provision is allowed for employees with at least fifteen (15) years of service who have made no contributions, and who are employed by universities.

a. 2 only.
b. 1 and 2.
c. 2 and 4.
d. 2, 3, and 4.
e. 1, 2, 3, and 4.

NEW TAX LEGISLATION

191. Under the 1998 Act, the burden of proof rests on:

a. The taxpayer.
b. The IRS.
c. The IRS in cases of fraud with intent to evade.
d. The taxpayer but only in court proceedings.
e. None of the above.

192. In order to obtain innocent spouse relief, a taxpayer must meet the following conditions:

a. Have filed a separate return.
b. The understatement of tax must be attributable to a grossly erroneous item of the other spouse.
c. Spouse had no reason to know the extent of the understatement.
d. Be elected by taxpayer and taxpayer's spouse.
e. None of the above.

193. Which of the following statements is/are true?

1. The Hope Scholarship Credit is only available for the first two years of post-secondary education.
2. The Hope Scholarship has a $1,500 lifetime cap.
3. The credit is calculated as 100% of the first $1,000 and 50% of the next $1,000 of eligible expenses.
4. Eligible expenses include tuition and books.

a. 1, 3, and 4.
b. 2 and 3.
c. 1 and 3.
d. 1 only.
e. None of the statements are true.

194. The Lifetime Learning Credit:

a. Is available for a maximum of five years.
b. Will vary according to the number of students in the taxpayer's family.
c. Can be elected in conjunction with the Hope Credit.
d. Must be elected.
e. None of the above statements is correct.

195. George has returned to school to take a course that will help him pass a real estate broker's exam. The course fee was $1,300. His wife, Phyllis, a schoolteacher, has enrolled in a massage school with a goal of becoming a massage therapist. Tuition at the school totaled $4,000. George and Phyllis' AGI for the year is $90,000. What is the amount of Lifetime Learning Credit they can elect?

a. $0.

b. $500.

c. $1,000.

d. $1,300.

e. $2,650.

196. Lynn took out a total of $20,000 in student loans. She began her 10-year pay back in January 1996. Beginning in January 1998, how many monthly payments may she deduct interest on?

a. 0.

b. 36.

c. 60.

d. 96.

e. 120.

197. Which of the following statements regarding Education IRAs is/are true?

1. Contributions have a limit of $500/year.
2. Contributions must be made for a child under the age of 21.
3. When distributed for educational expenses, only the interest earned is taxable.
4. Room and board for a less than half time student is a qualified expense.

a. 1, 2, and 4.

b. 1, 3, and 4.

c. 2, 3, and 4.

d. 1 and 4.

e. 1 only.

198. Bob and Denise have two children, Caitlin, 18, and Matthew, 12. Both are claimed as dependents. Bob and Denise's AGI in 1999 is $110,400, and they file a joint return. What is the amount of Child Tax Credit they can claim?

a. $0.

b. $450.

c. $500.

d. $900.

e. $1,000.

INCOME TAX PLANNING SOLUTIONS

INCOME TAX PLANNING

1.	D	35.	B	69.	A	103.	A	137.	B	171.	B
2.	D	36.	D	70.	D	104.	C	138.	A	172.	B
3.	C	37.	C	71.	A	105.	E	139.	C	173.	B
4.	B	38.	A	72.	C	106.	A	140.	C	174.	B
5.	A	39.	C	73.	D	107.	E	141.	D	175.	C
6.	A	40.	A	74.	C	108.	C	142.	A	176.	C
7.	C	41.	D	75.	E	109.	C	143.	B	177.	E
8.	C	42.	A	76.	B	110.	B	144.	D	178.	E
9.	B	43.	A	77.	A	111.	B	145.	D	179.	C
10.	C	44.	C	78.	D	112.	B	146.	A	180.	D
11.	C	45.	C	79.	A	113.	C	147.	B	181.	D
12.	A	46.	D	80.	C	114.	C	148.	C	182.	A
13.	D	47.	E	81.	C	115.	B	149.	B	183.	E
14.	C	48.	B	82.	C	116.	B	150.	B	184.	D
15.	B	49.	D	83.	A	117.	B	151.	C	185.	D
16.	A	50.	A	84.	D	118.	D	152.	A	186.	D
17.	D	51.	B	85.	A	119.	B	153.	B	187.	B
18.	C	52.	B	86.	B	120.	C	154.	A	188.	E
19.	B	53.	A	87.	B	121.	A	155.	A	189.	E
20.	A	54.	A	88.	D	122.	D	156.	C	190.	C
21.	B	55.	A	89.	B	123.	C	157.	B	191.	C
22.	B	56.	A	90.	B	124.	D	158.	A	192.	C
23.	C	57.	C	91.	A	125.	A	159.	C	193.	A
24.	C	58.	D	92.	B	126.	D	160.	E	194.	D
25.	C	59.	A	93.	A	127.	D	161.	D	195.	B
26.	B	60.	C	94.	B	128.	D	162.	C	196.	B
27.	B	61.	E	95.	C	129.	A	163.	C	197.	E
28.	C	62.	A	96.	A	130.	B	164.	B	198.	B
29.	B	63.	D	97.	B	131.	D	165.	E		
30.	A	64.	C	98.	C	132.	D	166.	B		
31.	D	65.	B	99.	A	133.	D	167.	B		
32.	D	66.	C	100.	B	134.	B	168.	A		
33.	B	67.	C	101.	B	135.	C	169.	C		
34.	C	68.	A	102.	B	136.	D	170.	B		

TAX LAW - TAX LEGISLATION, ADMINISTRATION AND JUDICIAL (CASE)

Court System

1. **D**

Appeals from the U.S. District Court go to the taxpayer's home circuit of the U.S. Court of Appeals.

Court System

2. **D**

Small Cases Division of the U.S. Tax Court. In the Small Cases Division, the amount in controversy is limited to $10,000, and the proceedings are informal. Proceedings can be faster and less expensive in the Small Cases Division.

Appeals

3. **C**

Statement #2 is incorrect because the Tax Court is a judge trial (there is no jury). Statement #4 is incorrect because neither side may appeal from a decision in the Small Cases Division of the Tax Court.

Tax Research (CFP® Exam, released 3/95)

4. **B**

The question asks about very recent changes to tax law. The best source for recent bills passed and signed into law is Congressional Committee reports.

Taxable Entities

5. **A**

Partnerships are not subject to federal income tax.

Taxable Entities

6. **A**

A Limited Liability Company may be a pass through entity if it meets certain IRS tests.
C corporations and trusts (in which all income is not distributed) are not pass through entities.

TAX RATES AND BRACKETS

Exemptions

7. **C**

Three exemptions are allowed: one each for Angie, Buddy, and their son. No exemption is allowed for their daughter. Although the gross income test is waived, they did not meet the support test for her.

Exemptions

8. **C**

The couple is entitled to exemptions for John, Joan, their son Chip, and John's mother. An exemption is allowed for a dependent who was alive during any part of the taxable year. John's mother's Social Security income is earned income, thus it is not considered in applying the gross income test.

Dependents

9. **B**

Of the potential dependents listed, only the nephew is a qualifying relative.

Dependents

10. **C**

Vicki's Social Security benefits are not included in gross income. Therefore, she does not fail the gross income test and can be claimed by Mary Sue and Bob as a dependent.

Exemptions

11. **C**

Exemptions are allowed for Mike, Pam, their son, and their daughter. They are not entitled to an exemption for Pam's father, because he was not a citizen or resident of the U.S. or other qualifying country. Their son qualifies as a dependent, because his gross income was less than the exemption amount. The gross income test is waived for their daughter, who was a full-time student for at least five months during the year.

Exemptions

12. A

A person who <u>may</u> be claimed by another as a dependent can not claim a personal exemption.

Dependents

13. D

Multiple support agreement (MSA) between parties who provide > 50% support may claim dependency exemption. Any party to an MSA who has contributed more than 10% can claim the exemption; therefore, James, Brian, or Michael can claim Arline.

Taxable Income

14. C

($30,000 - 4,250 standard deduction - 2,700) = $23,050. The Roth IRA contribution is non-deductible. William should reduce income by the standard deduction since it is greater than his itemized deductions.

Taxable Income

15. B

	B Correct	**E Incorrect**	**A Incorrect**	**C Incorrect**	**D Incorrect**
	$46,000	$46,000	$46,000	$46,000	$46,000
CL	(3,000)	(5,000)	(5,000)	(3,000)	(3,000)
	$43,000	$41,000	$41,000	$43,000	$43,000
Standard Ded. or	(4,250)	(4,250)	(4,250)	(4,250)	(4,250)
Itemized Ded.	$38,750	**$36,750**	$36,750	$38,750	$38,750
Add'l Std. Ded.	1,050				1,000
	$37,700				$37,750
Personal exemp.	(2,700)		(2,700)	(2,700)	(2,700)
	$35,000		**$34,050**	**$36,050**	**$35,050**

Note: $4,250 standard deduction + $1,050 additional standard deduction exceed the itemized deduction of $4,500.

Adjusted Gross Income

16. **A**

Adjusted Gross Income	$42,000
Less: Standard deduction (head of household)	6,250
Less: Exemptions (self, mother) $2,700 x 2	5,400
Taxable income	**$30,350**

	A Correct	B Incorrect	C Incorrect	D Incorrect
	$42,000	$42,000	$42,000	$42,000
Std. Ded.	(6,250)	(4,250)	(6,250)	(4,250)
	$35,750	$37,750	$35,750	$37,750
P/E & D/E	(5,400)	(5,400)	(2,700)	(2,700)
Taxable Income	**$30,350**	**$32,350**	**$33,050**	**$35,050**

Adjusted Gross Income

17. **D**

Child support payments are excluded from income for the parent receiving the support, and the parent paying the support does not get a deduction. Contributions to Roth IRAs are not deductible for adjusted gross income.

TAX DETERMINATION

Kiddie Tax (CFP® Exam, released 3/95)

18. C

This question is related to the Kiddie tax, which applies to unearned income in excess of $1,400, by a child under the age of 14. Brittany, while under the age of 14, has only earned income. Amanda is 14, and Trent, age 3, had unearned income less than $1,400. Therefore, the correct answer is C. Kristen, age 5, had unearned income of $1,900.

Kiddie Tax

19. B

$3,000	Unearned income
5,000	Earned income
$8,000	Total
(4,250)	Standard deduction (note limit)
$3,750	
(1,400)	Unearned income at child's rate (700 x 2)
$2,350	
(750)	Earned income at child's rate (excess over standard deduction)
$1,600	Taxed at the parents rate

Optional method:

$3,000 Unearned income

(1,400) Unearned income taxed at child's rate

$1,600 Taxed at parent's rate.

Kiddie Tax

20. A

Statement #1 is incorrect; it applies to all unearned income of children under 14.

Statement #2 is incorrect; it should be under the age of 14.

Statement #3 is incorrect; it should be only unearned income.

Kiddie Tax

21. **B**

Unearned income	$1,800	
	(1,400)	
Net unearned income tax at parent's rate	$400	
Total income	$4,000	
Standard deduction	(2,450)	(earned income $2,200 + $250)
Taxable income	$1,550	
	(400)	Taxed at parent's rate ($1,800-$1,400)
	$1,150	Taxed at Allison's rate ($1,400-$250 from excess standard deduction)

FILING CONSIDERATIONS

Filing Status

22. B

George correctly filed a joint return in the year of his wife's death. He will file as a surviving spouse for the two years following his wife's death if he continues to maintain a home for his dependent children.

Filing Status

23. C

Beth's 1999 filing status is Head of Household. Surviving Spouse filing status is only for two years following death of spouse (1997 and 1998).

GROSS INCOME - INCLUSIONS

Gross Income

24. **C**

Mary must report adjusted gross income of $67,500. Gross Income = $70,500 ($1,000 dividends + $12,000 lottery prize + $50,000 salary + $7,500 alimony received). $70,500 gross income - $3,000 capital loss = $67,500. The gift and child support payments are excluded from gross income. The capital loss deduction is limited to $3,000.

Taxable Income

25. **C**

$1,600 earned income + $1,350 interest income = $2,950 - $1,850 (standard deduction limited to earned income + $250) = $1,350 taxable income. Because Ken is claimed as a dependent by his parents, he is not entitled to an exemption on his own return and his standard deduction is reduced.

Taxable Income

26. **B**

Because Arline is 65 or over, her standard deduction is equal to $2,550 ($1,250 earned income + $250 + $1,050 additional standard deduction). $2,950 gross income - $2,550 standard deduction = $400 taxable income. Social Security is not included in earned income. The additional $250 deduction was added by the 1997 Taxpayer Relief Act.

Constructive Receipt

27. **B**

$450. A taxpayer is not permitted to defer income for services in the current year by refusing to accept payment. The doctrine of constructive receipt does not reach income that the taxpayer is not yet entitled to receive by contract. Michele has not yet performed the audit

Tax Benefit Rule

28. **C**

The amount received by Steve, even though in dispute, is included in his 1998 gross income because he has received the $2,000. Steve will deduct $100 in 1999 to adjust his income for the refund.

Revenue Ruling 71-21

29. **B**

$19,000. Revenue Ruling 71-21 does not permit an accrual basis taxpayer to defer advance payments for services if any of the services will be performed after the tax year following the year of receipt of the advance payment. Therefore, the $19,000 amount from the two-year contracts must be included in 1998 gross income since part of that income will be unearned at the end of 1999.

Community Property

30. **A**

Because Ron and Marge lived apart for the entire year, she does not have to report one-half of Ron's salary on her separate return. She is required to report her share of the income from the community property.

Annuities

31. **D**

The options other than D are incorrect and contrary to the scheme provided in the Code for the taxation of annuities. If Vicki dies after collecting only 50 payments (before she has recovered all of her capital), a loss can be claimed on her final return as a miscellaneous itemized deduction not subject to the 2% hurdle. Therefore, B is incorrect.

Inclusion - Exclusion

32. **D**

Kathy's adjusted gross income is:

W-2 Income	$80,000
Interest on State of Alabama bonds (tax-exempt)	-0-
Social Security benefits (85% X $6,000)	5,100
	$85,100

Insurance Proceeds

33. **B**

($11,900 - 100,000) ÷ 10) = $1,900

Note: Because it is insurance proceeds there is no recapture of basis. The Inclusion/Exclusion Ratio applies.

Inclusions

34. C

Interest on Baldwin County school bonds is excluded under Section 103. Gross income is $700 (i.e., $400 + $100 + $200).

Annuities

35. B

$24,000 ÷ 144,000 = .1666 or 1/6 exclusion ratio or fraction x 1,200 = 200.

Therefore, 120 ÷ 144 = .8333 or 5/6 inclusion ratio x 1,200 = 1,000.

In 1999, June to December = 7 months x 200(exclusion) = 1,400.

Option B is only possible correct answer for 1999.

2000 (12 parts x 1,200) x 1/6 = 2,400.

2001 (12 parts x 1,200) x 1/6 = 2,400.

Life Insurance

36. D

Expected proceeds over life = $15,000 x 20 years = $300,000.

Inclusion ratio = (Proceeds - Basis)/Expected: ($300,000 - 120,000) ÷ $300,000 = 60%.

Exclusion ratio = Basis/Expected Proceeds: $120,000 ÷ 300,000 = 40%.

Current year payment $15,000 x 60% for inclusion = $9,000.

$15,000 x 40% for exclusion = $6,000.

Group Term Life Insurance

37. C

$50,000 of group term is non-taxable.

$180,000 - 50,000 = $130,000 x $8/thousand = $1,040 taxable.

Alimony

38. A

The monthly mortgage payments are not alimony because they are not support. They are not support because they do not terminate with Carol's death.

Alimony

39. C

For Post-1984 divorce agreements and decrees, payments to former spouses are alimony only if:

- The payments are in cash;
- The agreement or decree does not specify that the payments are not alimony;
- The payee and payor are not members of the same household at the time the payments are made; and
- There is no liability to make the payments for any period after the death of the payee.

Alimony

40. A

The payments are not alimony because the payments would continue after the death of the payee.

Alimony

41. D

It is not necessary to specify that payments are alimony. However, the agreement cannot specify that the payments are not alimony.

Unemployment Compensation

42. A

Unemployment is fully includible in gross income.

Series EE Bonds

43. A

In addition to option A, the other conditions are:

- The savings bonds are issued after December 31, 1989;
- The savings bonds are issued to an individual who is at least 24 years old at the time of issuance;
- The exclusion is limited by a MAGI threshold which begins to phaseout at $78,350 on a joint return ($52,250 for single);
- The exclusion is not available to married couples filing separate returns.

Adjusted Gross Income

44. **C**

$12,000 gift	Not includible by donee
$1,200 dividend	Includible in AGI
$1,000 won as prize	Includible in AGI
$35,000 salary	Includible in AGI.
$6,000 support	Not includible in AGI.
$12,000 alimony	Includible in AGI
$5,000 LTCG	Limited to $3,000 per year

$1,200	Dividend
1,000	Prize
35,000	Salary
12,000	Alimony
(3,000)	Long-term capital loss (carryover $2,000)
$46,200	

Adjusted Gross Income

45. **C**

$60,000 salary - $3,000 short-term capital loss - $4,000 moving expenses = $53,000.

The $1,500 balance of short-term capital loss is carried over.

The $500 balance of long-term capital loss is carried over.

Taxable Income

46. **D**

$3,500	Interest
2,300	Earned income
$5,800	Taxable income before standard deduction
(2,550)	Standard deduction (earned income + $250)
(1,050)	Additional standard deduction (over 65 and single)
$2,200	Taxable income (answer for 1998)

* Social Security benefits are not taxable at his income level.

* No personal exemptions can be claimed since he is classified as a dependent on another's return.

* The $250 additional standard deduction is indexed annually for inflation.

Alimony Recapture Front Loading

47. **E**

Calculation of Recapture:

$$R_3 = R_2 + R_1$$

$$R_2 = P_2 - (P_3 + \$15{,}000)$$

$$R_1 = P_1 - \left[\frac{(P_2 - R_2 + P_3)}{2} + \$15{,}000\right]$$

R_3 = amount recaptured in year 3

R_2 = amount recaptured in year 2

R_1 = amount recaptured in year 1

P_1, P_2, P_3 = payments 1, 2, and 3 respectively

Solve R_2 first:

$$R_2 = \$60{,}000 - (\$0 + 15{,}000) = \$45{,}000$$

$$R_1 = \$100{,}000 - \left[\frac{(\$60{,}000 - 45{,}000 + 0)}{2} + \$15{,}000\right] = \$77{,}500$$

$$R_3 = \$45{,}000 + \$77{,}500 = \$122{,}500$$

Low Interest Loans

48. **B**

The $100,000 exemption applies so Dennis' imputed interest income is limited to Betty's net investment income. Betty's imputed interest expense would also be $4,000.

Low Interest Loans

49. **D**

If the loan is classified as an employer-employee loan, the corporation must accrue interest income and compensation expense. Thus, the corporation's taxable income will not be affected. Thus, it follows that A is correct. Option B is also correct because the corporation will have interest income, and the offsetting adjustment is a dividend paid, which is not deductible by the corporation. If John uses the funds for a vacation, he must recognize either dividend income or compensation income. He will not have an offsetting deduction for the interest on funds used for personal expenditures. Therefore, C is also correct.

Mutual Funds (CFP® Exam, released 3/95)

50. A

The choice belongs to the client if he or she maintains adequate identification records. Statement #4 is clearly incorrect.

GROSS INCOME - EXCLUSIONS

Inclusion - Exclusion

51. B

$500 dividends + $300 prize. Scholarships for tuition, books, and fees (not room and board) are excluded from adjusted gross income. Loans are not income. The cash support from Scott's parents is a gift.

Gross Income Inclusion

52. B

$20,000 salary + $1,000 reward. The hospitalization premiums and lodging are non-taxable fringe benefits.

Gross Income Inclusion

53. A

None are includible. All payments are to make him whole.

Lodging

54. A

The room is furnished for the convenience of the employer and is required by the employer.

Employee Benefits

55. A

The value of a health facility or gymnasium provided by the employer, on the employer's premises solely for the use of employees is excluded from gross income by the employee.

Employee Benefits

56. A

Cash of $2,000 and whole life of $2,000 must be included. Option C is incorrect because the whole life insurance premiums of $2,000 cannot be excluded.

Employee Benefits

57. **C**

The plan is discriminatory to non-highly compensated employees; therefore, all discounts actually taken by officers are includible in income.

Discharge of Indebtedness

58. **D**

The $40,000 reduction by the People's Bank is includible in gross income (income from discharge of indebtedness). The $30,000 reduction by Shelby (seller and mortgage holder) is an exception to the general rule, and a $30,000 reduction in basis, in lieu of inclusion in income is taken.

Employee Health Benefits

59. **A**

The death benefits exclusion was repealed by the Small Business Act 1996. The entire payment is considered income.

Gross Income Inclusion

60. **C**

The question relates to inclusion in gross income.

Workman's compensation is to make a person whole and is excludable.

Compensatory damages for personal injuries are excludable.

Punitive damages are includable in income.

Reimbursements from an employer medical plan not previously deducted are not includable.

Scholarships

61. **E**

David is not a candidate for a degree and, therefore, must include all of the grant received. The issue of proration between years is not relevant in this case (Prop. Reg. 1.117 - 6(b)(2)).

Gross Income Exclusion

62. **A**

The lease payments in the current year equal 6 months x $2,000 = $12,000.

Improvements made by the lessee are not included until such time as property is disposed of and then only at the property's retained fair market value.

DEDUCTIONS AND LOSSES: IN GENERAL

Unreasonable Compensation

63. D

The $60,000 of salary is reclassified as a dividend. Thus, River's taxable income increases by $60,000 because dividends are not deductible. John's gross income remains the same. His salary income decreases by $60,000, but his dividend income increases by $60,000.

Proprietor's Income

64. C

The illegal commissions and parking tickets are in violation of public policy and are not deductible.

Income		$120,000
Expenses:		
Commissions to other brokers	$15,000	
Travel and transportation	16,000	
Supplies	4,200	
Office and phone	3,500	(38,700)
Net Income		**$81,300**

Investigation of Business

65. B

He is already in the business, therefore, expenses are deductible. Deductible expenses include travel, engineering and architectural surveys, marketing reports, and legal and accounting services.

Hobby Losses

66. C

Hobby expenses must be itemized - include $3,000 in income. Since this is a hobby, itemized deductions are limited to an amount equal to the income from the hobby. Hobby losses are itemized deductions to the extent the hobby expenses exceed 2% of AGI.

Vacation Home

67. **C**

Since the personal use (16 days) was more than the greater of 14 days or 10% of rental use (5.6 days), the property will not qualify as primarily rental. The property is classified as personal/rental property. Therefore, no loss is allowed.

Payment of Other's Obligations

68. **A**

Medical expenses for spouse and dependents are deductible. The other items are not incurred for the taxpayer's benefit or as a result of the taxpayer's obligation and are non-deductible.

Related Party Transactions

69. **A**

Todd's sale to Trey, his son, is a related party transaction and, therefore, Todd will not recognize a loss ($4,000-6,000). Trey's basis in the stock is $4,000. When he sells it for $5,000, he has a realized gain of $1,000. However, Trey will not recognize this gain since he can utilize $1,000 of his father's unrecognized loss.

Deductions for AGI

70. **D**

Alimony payments are deductible for AGI. The rest are itemized deductions or from AGI.

DEDUCTIONS AND LOSSES: CERTAIN BUSINESS EXPENSES & LOSSES

Bad Debts Expense

71. A

Only the specific charge-off method can be used. Allowances for estimated expenses are not allowed for tax purposes.

Personal Bad Debt

72. C

No deduction is allowed for partial worthlessness in the year of bankruptcy for a personal bad debt. Personal bad debts are classified as short-term capital losses.

Personal Bad Debt

73. D

Short-term capital loss of $3,500 is used entirely against $5,000 capital gains.

Worthless Securities

74. C

Worthless securities are treated as becoming worthless at year-end. Therefore, the loss is a long- term capital loss even though the actual holding period was only 8 months.

Capital Assets Gains & Losses

75. E

The gain of $60,000 is classified as a short-term capital gain. Small business stock rules are irrelevant to gains.

Casualty Losses

76. B

The key is sudden and non-recurring - negligence is not an issue unless it is willful negligence. To be a casualty loss the event causing the loss must be identifiable, damaging to property, sudden and unexpected, and unusual in nature.

Casualty Losses

77. **A**

Loss	$10,000
Less: $100 floor	(100)
10% AGI (10% x $30,000)	(3,000)
Itemized Deduction	$6,900

Worthless Securities

78. **D**

Section 165 (g)(1) provides that if a security becomes worthless during the tax year, the loss shall be treated as if it occurred on the last day of the tax year. The holding period will be long-term.

Note: The intent of the question is to determine the nature of the loss even though the holding period was less than a year and a day. The question does not ask what is the recognized loss for 1999, but what is the recognized loss from the transaction.

Bad Debt Losses

79. **A**

No loss is allowed because the indebtedness was never taken into income since the taxpayer was a cash basis taxpayer.

Personal Bad Debt

80. **C**

This is a non-business bad debt (personal bad debt). Regardless of the holding period it is treated as a short-term capital loss and the $3,000 limit applies. Kurt has a carryover short-term capital loss of $4,000 - 3,000 = $1,000.

Election to Expense

81. **C**

His Section 179 deduction is limited to $15,000 (due to net income limitation). A Section 179 deduction can not create a loss. He would still have $3,000 Section 179 carryover from the previous year.

Election to Expense

82. **C**

For 1999, the Section 179 election maximum is $19,000.
Reduce for purchases over $200,000, dollar for dollar. [$207,000 – 200,000 = $7,000]
$19,000 - 7,000 = $12,000
[For year 2000 the maximum is $20,000 and for 2001 and 2002 the maximum is $24,000]

Depreciation (CFP® Exam, released 3/95)

83. **A**

This is a depreciation question. MACRS is 200% declining balance depreciation and will accomplish the maximum allowable depreciation expense. Note Section 179 was not a choice but could have been coupled with any of the answers and probably would have accomplished the maximum write-off (election to expense up to the Section 179 limit plus the MACRS on the balance).

PASSIVE ACTIVITY LOSSES

At Risk/Passive Losses

84. **D**

Options A, B, and C are all true. The correct analysis of the tax treatment of Bob's income is Bob is limited to a $50,000 deduction against his other income. The remaining $25,000 would be a loss carryforward. Bob's at-risk investment would now be zero. He will have to increase his at-risk investment to use the $25,000 loss carry forward.

At Risk/Passive Losses

85. **A**

$15,000 of Joseph's loss is suspended under the at-risk rules, leaving a potential deduction of $30,000. The $30,000 loss is suspended under the passive loss rules.

At Risk/Passive Losses

86. **B**

George's losses are deductible in both years because he is a material participant in the activity. However, the at-risk rules limit his total losses to $100,000.

At Risk/Passive Losses

87. **B**

He has $5,000 suspended for at risk rules: $30,000 - 25,000 = $5,000. He has $12,500 phase out from his AGI: [(150,000 - 125,000) ÷ $50,000] x 25,000 = $12,500. It is irrelevant that he has no passive income.

At Risk/Passive Losses

88. **D**

Philip's AGI, after considering the passive investment, is $175,000 ($140,000 active income + $35,000 portfolio income). He would not have been allowed to offset the passive loss against active or portfolio income.

At Risk/Passive Losses

89. B

Option A is incorrect: Arthur would have to participate for more than 500 hours for option A to be correct. Option B is correct: an individual who participates for more than 500 hours is a material participant regardless of how much others participate. Option C is incorrect: Arthur participates for more than 100 hours and this is not more than the participation of any other individual. Option D is incorrect: Arthur's participation constitutes substantially all of the participation, even though Arthur's participation is less than 100 hours.

At Risk/Passive Losses

90. B

($40,000 ÷ $60,000) x $45,000 = $30,000 to Activity 1.
($20,000 ÷ $60,000) x $45,000 = $15,000 to Activity 2.

Passive Losses

91. A

An exception to passive loss limits regarding real estate allows individuals to deduct up to $25,000 of losses on real estate activities against active and portfolio income. The annual $25,000 deduction is reduced by 50% of the taxpayer's AGI in excess of $100,000. The deduction is entirely phased out at an AGI of $150,000.

Passive Activities

92. B

Only statement #2 is treated as a rental activity according to IRS regulations.

Passive Income

93. A

Rental income is passive; all of the others are portfolio income. Passive income is defined as income or loss from:

- Any trade, business, or income- producing activity in which the taxpayer does not materially participate, or;
- Any rental activity, whether the taxpayer materially participates or not.

Note: Remember there are exceptions to the rental activity classification.

EMPLOYEE EXPENSES

Employee Expense

94. B

The deduction is based on the distance between jobs. There is no deduction for commuting expenses (mileage) to or from a taxpayer's primary place of employment.

Travel

95. C

Less than 7 days of travel requires no allocation for foreign travel. Additional exceptions regarding allocation are:

(1) if less than 25% of the time is used for personal purposes

or

(2) if the taxpayer does not have substantial control over the trip arrangement.

Travel

96. A

($1,200 + (8 X 150) + 1/2 (8 x 90) = $2,760. Since Allison used less than 25% of the time (10 days x 25% > 2 days) on personal business her airfare does not have to be allocated. Lodging and meals are allocated based on the number of business days on the trip.

Moving Expense

97. B

($1,600 + $300 + $250) = $2,150. Meals while moving are not deductible. To deduct moving expenses, the new job must be at least 50 miles further from the taxpayer's old residence than the old residence was from the former place of employment. There are additional time requirements about length of employment on the new job.

Education Expense

98. C

($2,000 + .5(1,000) + 1,600) = $4,100. Taxpayers may deduct expenses of additional education if additional education is required by the employer or imposed by law. The education can not be for the purpose of meeting the minimum requirements for the job.

Employee Expenses

99. **A**

[$30 + .5 (25 + 128 + 25)] = $119. Transportation is not subject to a 50% reduction. The door cover fee, dinner, and tip are all considered part of the meal and are reduced by 50%.

Entertainment

100. **B**

50% [(15 x 25) + 455] = $415. The cost of the skybox is not deductible. The deduction is limited to the cost of the face value of non-luxury box seats. Meals (refreshments) and the seats are both subject to a 50% reduction.

Business Gifts

101. **B**

$29 + 24 = $53. The cost of gift-wrapping is allowed. No deduction is available for a gift to a superior. The limit on gifts is $25 per person.

Business Gifts

102. **B**

The limit is $25 per individual.

($3 x 12 = $36) + ($12 x 25 = $300) = $336.

Employee Expenses

103. **A**

All are itemized deductions. The listed deductions are all deduction from AGI.

ITEMIZED DEDUCTIONS: MEDICAL EXPENSES, TAXES PAID, INTEREST PAID, CHARITABLE CONTRIBUTIONS

Itemized Deductions

104. **C**

($60,000 - 5,000) x .075 = $4,125 is the floor for medical expenses.

$7,500 - 4,125 = $3,375 deduction.

Miscellaneous Itemized Deductions

105. **E**

Generally, full-time active duty military personnel cannot deduct the cost of uniforms (option A). Job-hunting expenses for the first job (option B) are not allowed. Nor are job-hunting expenses allowed when the taxpayer is changing a trade or business (option C). The basic cost of one telephone in home is not deductible, even if used for business (option D).

Itemized Deductions

106. **A**

Gambling is not subject to 2% miscellaneous itemized deduction hurdle.

Medical Expenses

107. **E**

All are excluded. Deductible medical expenses are defined as expenses incurred for the diagnosis, cure, mitigation, treatment, or prevention of disease, or for the purpose of affecting any structure or function of the body. Non-prescription drugs (except insulin) are not deductible.

Medical Expenses

108. **C**

The charge for tuition, room, and board to The Dalton School does not qualify, since the school does not provide qualified medical treatment.

Medical Expenses

109. **C**

Only $8,000 of the system qualifies since $2,000 of the $10,000 increased the value of Sidney's residence. The utilities count - $1,000. Total = $9,000. The appraisal fee is a 2% itemized deduction but not as a medical expense.

Medical Expenses

110. B

$60 ($.10 x 600 miles) + $50 (tolls and parking) + $400 [$50 x 8 (2 rooms for 4 nights)] = $510. Because the mother is disabled, David's accompaniment on the trip is necessary. Meals are not deductible.

Itemized Deductions - Taxes

111. B

Option A is incorrect because the $700 refund is not offset against the itemized deduction. Option C is incorrect since Donna claimed the standard deduction for the previous year.

Itemized Deductions - Taxes

112. B

[(180 days/243 days x $2,000) + $120] = $1,601. Real estate taxes for the entire year are apportioned between the buyer and seller on the basis of the number of days the property was held by each during the real estate tax year. The day of the sale goes to the buyer.

Itemized Deductions - Taxes

113. C

($7,200 + 3,000) = $10,200. The interest on the deficiency is personal interest and is not deductible. The refund is reported as income under the tax benefit rule. It does not affect the amount deductible.

Interest

114. C

The interest on the loan to purchase household furniture is nondeductible consumer interest. The interest on the loan to purchase Louisiana state bonds is not deductible under Section 265. The interest on the home mortgage is qualified residence interest and is deductible.

Qualified Residence Interest

115. B

Home equity loans are limited to the lesser of:

(1) The fair market value of the residence, reduced by acquisition indebtedness

or

(2) $100,000

Thus, $400,000 (fair market value) - $320,000 (first mortgage) provides a limit of $80,000. Interest on the remaining $50,000 of the loan will be treated under the consumer interest rules (i.e., not deductible).

Charitable Deductions

116. B

80% of the $2,000 is deductible. The $500 expenditure for the tickets cannot be claimed since it provided George with a benefit.

Charitable Contributions

117. B

Inventory is ordinary income property, but the fair market value ($6,000) must be used if lower than the basis ($8,000). Stock is intangible property and is not subject to the tangible personalty rules. Since a sale of the Hetzer Co. stock would have yielded a long-term capital gain, the full fair market value qualified for the deduction ($40,000). The coin collection comes under the tangible personality exemption, and the adjusted basis ($1,000) must be used. (6,000 + 40,000 + 1,000) = 47,000.

Charitable Contributions

118. D

$5,000 (cash) + $36,000 (30% x $120,000) = $41,000. The long-term capital gain property is limited to 30% of $120,000 AGI or $36,000. The carryover to the next five years is $34,000 [$70,000 (FMV of the land) - $36,000 (deduction allowed for current year)]. If the reduced deduction election is made, the deduction becomes $45,000 [$5,000 (cash) + $40,000 (basis of land) but does not carryover.

Itemized Deductions

119. B

Taxes accrue daily. Taxes are only deductible to the extent the taxpayer was both liable for and paid the taxes. Taxpayers cannot deduct taxes paid for someone else.

January 1st to May 31st = 150 days. (The date of sale belongs to the buyer.)
January 1st to September 30th = 273 days.
$3,600 x 150/273 = $1,978 + 450 = $2,428.

Part of the question is to realize that taxes are accrued on a daily basis (months do not have the same number of days). Do not count date of disposition.

Moving Expenses

120. C

Only the direct cost of the move is deductible. Lease penalty is no longer deductible. Additionally, the taxpayer must be employed on a full-time basis at the new location for 39 weeks in the 12-month period following the move.

Itemized Deductions - Medical

121. A

Qualifying medical expenses do not include cosmetic surgery.

Itemized Deductions - Medical

122. D

Taxpayer can pay medical expenses for those who could qualify as dependent without regard to joint return or gross income test. Both transactions are deemed to have taken place in the current year. The IRS considers the credit card charge as a payment to the service provider (e.g., the doctor) and a loan back to the credit card holder.

ALTERNATIVE MINIMUM TAX

Alternative Minimum Tax

123. C

Only statements #2 and #3 would be included in computing AMT. Other items included in computing the AMT for an individual taxpayer are: adding back personal exemptions and the standard deduction/itemized deductions; subtracting the refund of state and local taxes included in gross income; depreciation of leased personal property put in service before 1987; and, incentive stock options.

Alternative Minimum Tax

124. D

Alternative minimum tax does not apply to partnerships. AMT does apply to estates.

Alternative Minimum Tax

125. A

Statements #2, #3, and #4 are not preference items. Preference items also include: the part of the deduction for certain depletion that is more than the adjusted basis of the property, tax-exempt interest on certain private activity bonds, and a 42% exclusion for certain small business stock.

TAX CREDITS & PAYMENT PROCEDURES

Earned Income Credit

126. D

EIC may be received from an employer by filing Form W-5 with the employer. To qualify for the EIC, the taxpayer's AGI must be below a specific amount. A taxpayer does not have to have a child.

Earned Income Credit

127. D

All tests must be met. In addition to the tests, the taxpayer applying for the credit must provide the name, age, and taxpayer identification number of the qualifying child on the return.

Credit for Elderly

128. D

$7,500 (base amount) - $4,000 (Social Security benefits) - $1,000 (one-half of adjusted gross income in excess of $10,000) = $2,500 x 15% = $375.

Child Care Credit

129. A

Total qualifying childcare expenses are $6,000 ($3,000 + $1,000 + $2,000). A provider of childcare can also perform housekeeping chores. The amounts paid to Mrs. Speckle qualify since she was not a dependent. 20% x $4,800 (maximum allowed) = $960 child care credit.

Child Care Credit

130. B

$480 = 20% x $2,400. The maximum unreimbursed expense is $2,400 for one qualifying individual and $4,800 for two or more qualifying individuals.

Child Care Credit

131. D

$4,000 x 20% = $800. For AGI over $28,000, the applicable rate of credit is 20%.

PROPERTY TRANSACTIONS - CAPITAL GAINS AND LOSSES

Capital Gains

132. D

Amount realized		$5,500
Basis (FIFO)	(5,000)	
Realized gain	**$500**	
Recognized gain	**$500**	

Because John did not specifically identify the shares of stock sold, a FIFO presumption is made.

Capital Gains and Losses

133. D

The net long-term capital gain is $5,000 ($20,000 LTCG - $15,000 LTCL) and the net short-term capital gain is $12,500 ($20,000 STCG - $7,500 STCL).

Capital Gains and Losses

134. B

STCG	$11,000	LTCG	$0
STCL	(6,000)	LTCL	(6,000)
STCG	$5,000	LTCL	($6,000)

Net Long-Term Capital Loss = $1,000

(by netting $6,000 - 5,000)

DETERMINATION OF GAIN OR LOSS

Capital Gains

135. C

The sale of the equipment results in a $2,100 §1245 gain. The sale of the truck results in an ordinary loss of $1,200 because it was not held for the long-term holding period. The §1245 gain of $2,100 offsets the $1,200 ordinary loss for a net ordinary gain of $900. The sale of the stock results in a $2,000 LTCG.

Capital Loss Carryover

136. D

The capital loss deduction is limited to $3,000. In computing the $3,000 deduction, short-term capital losses must be used first. Therefore, $3,000 of the short-term capital loss is used, and none of the long-term loss is used. Therefore, $5,000 of the long-term loss is carried over. Her total capital losses carried forward are $7,000 ($5,000 long-term + $2,000 short-term).

Basis

137. B

Assuming no gift tax paid by the donor, the donee's gain basis for the property received is the same as that of the donor. The donee's loss basis is whichever is the lower of:

(1) the donor's adjusted basis

or

(2) the fair market value on the date of the gift.

Related Party Transactions

138. A

The son's gain basis is $80,000. His loss basis is $70,000. Since his selling price of $78,000 is between the gain basis and the loss basis, he has no recognized gain or loss.

Wash Sale Rule

139. C

Amount realized	$8,000
Adjusted basis (30 x $280)	(8,400)
Realized loss	**($400)**
Recognized loss	**$0**

Since the transaction qualifies as a wash sale, the realized loss of $400 is disallowed. This amount is added to the adjusted basis of the shares purchased 29 days earlier. Therefore, the adjusted basis for these shares is $7,900 ($7,500 + $400).

The Wash Sale rate applies to a loss sustained upon a sale or other disposition of a stock or security. The loss is not allowed if, within a period beginning 30 days before the date of the sale of disposition and ending 30 days after that date the taxpayer has acquired or has entered into a contract or option to acquire substantially identical stock or securities.

Basis

140. C

($60,000 - 10,000 = $50,000) carryover basis. Carryover basis on a gift for which no gift tax was paid is the basis of the donor unless the FMV on the date of the gift is lower than the donor's basis. If the FMV on the date of the gift is lower than the donor's basis, the donor will have a double basis. The FMV will be the basis for losses, and the donor's basis will be the basis for gains.

PROPERTY TRANSACTIONS: NON-TAXABLE EXCHANGES

PART A: EXCHANGES

Exchanges

141. D

	Machine (A)	Building
Amount realized	$30,000	$35,000
Adjusted basis	(40,000)	(20,000)
Realized gain (loss)	**($10,000)**	**$15,000**
Recognized gain (loss)	**$0**	**$15,000**

The realized loss on the like-kind exchange part of the transaction (i.e., the machines) is not recognized. The realized gain on the boot (i.e., building) is recognized. (Non like kind exchange on disposition).

Exchanges

142. A

Amount realized:			
Bank building (FMV)		$800,000	
Mortgage of transferor	275,000	$525,000	
Adjusted basis:			
Bank building		$600,000	
Mortgage of transferee	275,000	(325,000)	
Realized gain			**$200,000**
Recognized gain (net boot received equals net boot given)			**$ 0**

Involuntary Conversion

143. B

Gain realized equals $80,000; gain recognized equals $10,000 (i.e., $200,000 amount realized minus $190,000 amount reinvested); and basis equals $120,000 (i.e., $190,000 cost minus $70,000 postponed gain).

Exchanges

144. D

Related parties can enter into a non-taxable exchange although disposition before a two year holding period will trigger recognition.

Involuntary Conversion

145. D

The form of the involuntary conversion is the condemnation of real property used in a trade or business. Therefore, the taxpayer has three years, rather than the normal two years, from the close of the taxable year in which gain is first realized to replace the property.

Like Kind Exchanges (§1031)

146. A

	FMV New machine	$10,000
-	Boot Given	0
+	Boot Received	0
=	FMV Old machine	$10,000
-	Adjusted Basis (old)	(5,000)
=	Potential Gain (PG)	$5,000
-	Boot Received (recognized gain ≤ PG)	0
=	Remaining Gain	$5,000

	FMV New machine	$10,000
-	Unrecognized Gain	(5,000)
=	New Basis	$5,000

Like Kind Exchange

147. B

	FMV New machine	$10,000
-	Boot Given	(4,000)
+	Boot Received	0
=	FMV Old machine	$6,000
-	Adjusted Basis (old)	(5,000)
=	Potential Gain (PG)	$1,000
-	Boot Received (recognized gain ≤ PG)	0
=	Remaining Gain	$1,000

	FMV New machine	$10,000
-	Unrecognized Gain	1,000
=	New Basis	$9,000

Like Kind Exchange

148. C

	FMV New machine	$10,000
-	Boot Given	(6,000)
+	Boot Received	0
=	FMV Old machine	$4,000
-	Adjusted Basis (old)	(5,000)
=	Potential Gain (PG)	($1,000)
-	Boot Received (recognized gain ≤ PG)	0
=	Remaining Gain	($1,000)

	FMV New machine	$10,000
+	Unrecognized Loss	1,000
=	New Basis	$11,000

Like Kind Exchanges (§1031)

149. B

	FMV New machine	$10,000
-	Boot Given	0
+	Boot Received	4,000
=	FMV Old machine	$14,000
-	Adjusted Basis (old)	(5,000)
=	Potential Gain (PG)	$9,000
-	Boot Received (recognized gain ≤ PG)	(4,000)
=	Remaining Gain	$5,000

	FMV New machine	$10,000
-	Unrecognized Gain	(5,000)
=	New Basis	$5,000

Like Kind Exchanges (§1031)

150. B

	FMV New machine	$10,000
-	Boot Given	(400)
+	Boot Received	0
=	FMV Old machine	$9,600
-	Adjusted Basis (old)	(5,000)
=	Potential Gain (PG)	$4,600
-	Boot Received (recognized gain ≤ PG)	0
=	Remaining Gain	$4,600

	FMV New machine	$10,000
-	Unrecognized Gain	(4,600)
=	New Basis	$5,400

Like-Kind Exchange

151. **C**

The property must be of like-kind-realty for realty. Option A is incorrect since the stock is excluded. Option B is incorrect because inventory is excluded. Option D is incorrect because the property held must be in the U.S.

PART B: SALE OF RESIDENCE

Sale of Residence

152. **A**

Capital gains realized on the sale of a personal residence may not be recognized (if elected) for gains up to $250,000 for single taxpayers ($500,000 for married taxpayers filing jointly).

Sale of Personal Residence

153. **B**

Both spouses must use the home as a principal residence for at least 2 of the 5 years before the sale.

Sale of Personal Residence

154. **A**

Capital gains realized on the sale of a personal residence may not be recognized (if elected) for gains up to $250,000 for single taxpayers ($500,000 for married taxpayers filing jointly) if they have lived in their personal residence for 2 of the 5 preceding years.

Sale of Personal Residence

155. **A**

Section 1041 provides for non-taxable exchange treatment for the transfer of property between spouses or between former spouses as a result of divorce. The transferee's (Marge) basis is equal to transferor's (Ron) basis immediately before the transfer. Marge's carryover basis is $160,000.

Sale of Principal Residence

156. **C**

Single taxpayers can exclude up to $250,000 of gain on the sale of a personal residence.

Sale of Personal Residence

157. B

Age is no longer a factor. The exemption can be used every 2 years (more frequently if certain conditions are met).

Sale of Personal Residence

158. A

Capital gains realized on the sale of a personal residence may not be recognized (if elected) for gains up to $250,000 for single taxpayers ($500,000 for married taxpayers filing jointly).

SECTION 1231 AND RECAPTURE PROVISIONS

Section 1231 Gains and Losses

159. C

When the taxpayer has a net Section 1231 gain for the year, the lookback rules may recapture some or all of the net gain as ordinary income. To the extent the lookback rules do not apply, the net gain is treated as a long-term capital gain. The lookback goes back 5 taxable years, not including the current taxable year.

AUDIT PROCESS

PART A: TYPES/STATUTES

Statute of Limitations

160. E

25% ($320,000+$20,000) = $85,000. Section 6501(e) states that if the taxpayer omits from gross income (total receipts, without reduction for cost) an amount in excess of 25% of gross income as stated in the return, a six year limitation period on the assessment applies.

Tax Audits

161. D

Chances of an audit do not increase for those previously audited where the result was no change in tax liability.

PART B: INTEREST AND PENALTIES

Penalties

162. C

The penalty is determined as follows:

Failure to pay penalty		
[1/2% X $5,000 X 2 (2 months violation)]		$ 50
Plus: Failure to file penalty		
[5% X $5,000 X 2 (2 months violation)]	$500	
Less: Failure to pay penalty	(50)	450
Total penalties		**$500**

Negligence Penalty

163. C

A 20% penalty applies to the negligence component.

Failure to File and to Pay

164. B

The failure to file penalty is netted against the failure to pay penalty [$60 + (600 - 60)] = $600.

Penalties (CFP® Exam, released 3/95)

165. E

Sara owes a penalty and interest on the $400 that she owed on April 15th.

MISCELLANEOUS

Pension Plans for Self-Employed

166. B

Self-employed maximum = 25% of net income after pension contribution and 1/2 social security taxes:

$20,000	Schedule C Net Income
(1,530)	1/2 Social Security (3,060)
$18,470	
(3,694)	20% (pension maximum to 30,000)
$14,776	

$3,694 ÷ $14,776 = 25%

(Net Income - 1/2 S.S.) = 125% of net income after 1/2 S.S. and pension.

$18,470 ÷ 125% = $14,776 x 25% = $3,694 which happens in all cases to be 20% of pre-pension income.

This only applies to self-employed persons and not to their employees.

SEPs

167. B

Only statement #2 is correct. Employee salary reductions are subject to FICA and FUTA taxes. Distributions can not be rolled into a qualified plan. Employees are always immediately and fully vested in employer contributions, and these are not forfeitable.

Early Withdrawal Penalty

168. A

Statements #1, #2 and #4 are correct. Other distribution not subject to the 10% penalty tax include distributions upon death or disability of the participant; distributions to a non-participant under a divorce court order; and certain distributions by ESOPs of dividends in employer securities.

Attribution Rules

169. C

A is deemed to own his own stock and his son's stock. Siblings are not included in contribution rules. The only family members that qualify for attribution are spouse, children, grandchildren and parents.

Employing Related Parties

170. B

Larry's children under 18 are not subject to FICA (See Publication 334).

Preparer Ethics

171. B

Preparer must withdraw if error is material and affects current return (#2 and #4).

Related Parties

172. B

Spouses, lineal descendents and ancestors are considered related parties. The aunt and niece are not for the purposes of arms length transactions.

Social Security (CFP® Exam, released 3/95)

173. B

Income from rental property is not subject to social security tax nor are dividends to S Corporation shareholders/employees as long as employee's compensation is at or above FMV. Statements #2 and #4 are subject to FICA.

Nonqualified Stock Options

174. B

Statement #1 is false. Gain is determined on date of exercise not issuance.

Statement #2 is true.

Statement #3 is true.

Statement #4 is false. Reported on Form W-2.

Family Business

175. C

Earned income is offset by the standard deduction.

IRAs

176. C

Jimmy's IRA is not deductible (phaseout of deductibility of taxpayer covered by pension plan). Married filing joint phase out begins at $51,000 and ends at $61,000 for 1999. Dee Dee's IRA is fully deductible. Active participation in an employer's pension plan by one spouse (Jimmy) does not effect the full deductibility of the other spouse's (Dee Dee) IRA as long as:

- The other spouse (Dee Dee) is not an active participant in an employer sponsored pension plan, and
- The couple's joint adjusted gross income does not exceed $150,000. Phaseout of deductibility is between $150,000 - $160,000.

IRAs

177. E

Since the Clabornes are not covered by a pension plan, they are allowed a $2,000 IRA plus $2,000 spousal IRA. Total IRA contribution of $4,000.

IRAs

178. E

Alimony counts as earned income for IRA purposes. Judy is not covered by a pension plan. Therefore, her maximum IRA is $2,000.

IRAs

179. C

Since both spouses have earned income in excess of $2,000, each can make the maximum contribution to his or her IRA. Bob is covered by a qualified retirement plan, and therefore, his $2,000 deductible is phased-out. Married filing joint adjusted gross income phase out begins at $51,000 and ends at $61,000 for 1999. Mary Sue is not covered by a qualified plan, so she can deduct her $2,000 contribution (since the couple's AGI is less than $150,000.)

IRAs

180. D

She is not currently covered by a qualified pension plan and therefore, can contribute her earned income up to $2,000 to a deductible IRA.

IRAs

181. **D**

Statement #1 is specific to the Roth IRA; and Statement #3 covers both the Roth and traditional IRAs. All the previously established non-penalized distribution rules apply to both Roth and traditional IRAs. Statement #4 does qualify; however, the distribution may be subject to income tax. Statement #2 does not qualify. Distributions for first time homebuyers are limited to $10,000 (lifetime cap). Distributions are qualified for the taxpayer, spouse, child, grandchild, and/or ancestor who have not owned a house for 2 years.

IRAs

182. **A**

Excess distribution and excess accumulation taxes were repealed by the 1997 Taxpayer Relief Act.

IRAs

183. **E**

Jane can only make a partial contribution to a deductible IRA. The phaseout is $51,000-$61,000 for 1999 for active participants in an employer sponsored pension plan. For Married Filing Joint Taxpayers 1998 the phaseout was $50,000 - $60,000; and for 2000 the phaseout will be $52,000 - $62,000.

IRAs

184. **D**

Collectibles are not an appropriate investment for an IRA. Section 408(m) will penalize such investments by treating them as a distribution.

IRAs

185. **D**

Statement #3 is incorrect. For a spouse beneficiary, distribution may be delayed until the decedent would have reached 70½ unless rolled to spouse's account.

IRAs

186. D

Statement #1 is incorrect. The option is to pay at least as fast as the original payment was scheduled. The 5-year rule applies if distributions had not begun before the death of the IRA owner.

IRAs

187. B

Only statement #2 is correct. Once qualified funds and non-qualified funds are commingled, rollover to another qualified plan is not permitted.

SEP/IRAs

188. E

Forward averaging is not available for SEPs, SIMPLES, 403(b)'s or IRA's. Forward averaging is only available for Qualified Plans.

IRAs (CFP® Exam, released 3/95)

189. E

The question asks about deductible IRA contributions. He is single, not covered by a pension plan and therefore can contribute his earned income up to $2,000 to a deductible IRA without regard to his income. There is no phase out.

TSAs

190. C

Statements #1 and #3 are incorrect. The catch up provision requires a specified service and specific type of employer. TSA plans can be adopted only by certain tax-exempt private organizations, public schools, and colleges.

Burden of Proof

191. C

The 1998 Act shifted more of the burden of proof to the IRS (but not in all cases). The shift only applies to court proceedings where the taxpayer has maintained records, cooperated with the IRS, and met certain net worth limitations.

Innocent Spouse

192. C

Option A is wrong since liability arises from a joint return. Option B is incorrect since the 1998 Act relaxed the standard to simply "erroneous". Option D is incorrect because the election is made by the spouse seeking relief.

Hope Credit

193. A

The $1,500 limit is per student, per year, so statement #2 is incorrect.

Lifetime Learning Credit

194. D

Neither the Hope Credit nor the Lifetime Learning Credit is allowed unless elected by the taxpayers.

Lifetime Learning Credit

195. B

Qualifying expenses	$5,300
Limited to	$5,000
	x 20%
Maximum Credit	$1,000
AGI Phaseout (10,000/20,000)	x 50%
	$ 500

AGI phaseout begins at $80,000 AGI for married filing jointly and is completely phased out at $100,000.

Student Loan Interest

196. **B**

The deduction applies only to the first 60 months that interest payments are required. Lynn has already made 24 payments, so only 36 can be deducted beginning 1/1/98.

Education IRAs

197. **E**

Statement #2 is incorrect because the beneficiary must be under 18. Statement #3 is incorrect since the contribution is nondeductible (but the earnings are tax-free). Statement #4 is incorrect. A student must be enrolled at least half time in order to qualify room and board.

Child Tax Credit

198. **B**

A qualifying child must be under 17. The $500 credit is reduced by $50 for each $1,000 (or portion thereof) that AGI exceed $110,000 (married filing jointly).

THIS PAGE IS INTENTIONALLY LEFT BLANK.

RETIREMENT PLANS, SOCIAL SECURITY AND EMPLOYEE BENEFITS PROBLEMS

RETIREMENT PLANS, SOCIAL SECURITY, AND EMPLOYEE BENEFITS

QUALIFIED PLANS - REQUIREMENTS AND TAXATION

1. Sanders Wood, age 38, earning $250,000 a year, wants to establish a defined contribution plan. He has 3 employees, who each make $20,000, are between ages 22 and 26, and have been employed with the company for 4 years on the average. Which of the following would be the most appropriate vesting schedule for Sander's company plan?
   - a. 3 year cliff.
   - b. 3 - 7 year graded.
   - c. 5 year cliff.
   - d. Immediate vesting.
   - e. 2-6 year graded vesting.

2. The premature distribution penalty does not apply to qualified plan distributions:
   1. Made on or after the attainment of age 59½.
   2. Made to a qualified plan participant's beneficiary or estate on or after the participant's death.
   3. Made on or after the participant's disability.
   4. That are part of a series of substantially equal periodic payments made at least annually over the life or life expectancy of the participant.
   - a. 1 and 2.
   - b. 1 and 3.
   - c. 2 and 3.
   - d. 1, 2, and 4.
   - e. 1, 2, 3, and 4.

3. If a qualified plan has been designed using 3-7 year graded vesting, which of the following characteristics would cause an employee to be required to be included in the plan (select the characteristics which are minimally required)?
   1. 21 years of age or older.
   2. 25 years of age or older.
   3. Has completed 1 year of service.
   4. Has completed 3 years of service.
      a. 1 only.
      b. 2 only.
      c. 1 and 3.
      d. 1 and 4.
      e. 2 and 4.

4. Which of the following statements is/are correct regarding non-penalized loans from qualified plans?
   1. The limit on loans is generally ½ the participant's vested account balance not to exceed $50,000.
   2. The limit on the term of any loan is generally 5 years.
   3. After tax employee contributions are available for loans.
   4. Generally loans to a 100% owner employee are permissible as long as they are not discriminatory.
      a. 1 only.
      b. 2 only.
      c. 1 and 2.
      d. 1, 2, and 3.
      e. 1, 2, 3, and 4.

5. Which of the following statements is/are correct regarding non-penalized loans from qualified plans?
   1. Loans must bear reasonable rates of interest.
   2. Generally loans are repayable within 5 years.
   3. Loans used to acquire a personal residence may exceed 5 years.
   4. A loan of up to $10,000 may be made even if it is greater than one half (½) of the participants vested benefits.
      a. 1 and 2.
      b. 1, 2, and 3.
      c. 2, 3, and 4.
      d. 1, 3, and 4.
      e. 1, 2, 3, and 4.

6. Which of the following statements is/are correct regarding the 10% penalty tax for early withdrawal (age 59½) from an IRA?
   1. Termination of employment at age 55 or older will exempt distribution from penalty tax.
   2. Distributions used to pay medical expenses in excess of the 7.5% hurdle for a tax filer using the standard deduction are not exempt from the penalty.
   3. Distributions used for hardship situations are exempt from the penalty.
   4. Distributions that are part of a series of equal periodic payments paid over the life or life expectancy of the participant are exempt.

   a. 1 and 4.
   b. 1, 2, and 3.
   c. 1, 3, and 4.
   d. 2, 3, and 4.
   e. 1, 2, 3, and 4.

7. Laundry Helpers, Inc., a regular C Corporation, is considering the adoption of a qualified retirement plan. The company has had fluctuating cash flows in the recent past and such fluctuations are expected to continue. The average age of non-owner employees is 24 and the average number of years of service is 3 with the high being 4 and the low 1. Approximately 25% of the 12 person labor force turns over each year. The 2 owners receive about 2/3 of the total of covered compensation.

   Which is the most appropriate vesting schedule for Laundry Helpers, Inc.?

   a. Immediate vesting.
   b. 2-7 year graded vesting.
   c. 3 year cliff.
   d. 5 year cliff.
   e. 2-6 year graded vesting.

8. What is the minimum number of employees that a defined benefit plan must cover to be in conformity with IRS and ERISA regulations?

   a. 50 employees.
   b. 50 employees or 40% of all employees.
   c. 40 employees or 50% of all employees.
   d. 35 employees or 40% of all employees.
   e. 50 employees or 50% of all employees.

9. Which of the following statements are correct regarding permitted disparity rules as they relate to qualified pension plans?
   1. A defined benefit plan utilizing the permitted disparity rules may be an excess plan.
   2. A defined benefit plan utilizing the permitted disparity rules may be an offset plan.
   3. A defined contribution plan utilizing the permitted disparity rules may be an excess plan.
   4. A defined contribution plan utilizing the permitted disparity rules may be an offset plan.
      a. 1 only.
      b. 1 and 2.
      c. 1, 2, and 3.
      d. 2, 3, and 4.
      e. 1, 2, 3, and 4.

10. Which of the following individuals is/are highly compensated employees of XYZ Corporation for qualified plan purposes this year? Assume the election was made.
    1. Bill who owns 10% of XYZ and is an employee.
    2. Mary, the President, whose compensation was $81,000 last year and she was in the top 20% of paid employees.
    3. Ralph, an employee salesman, who made $125,000 last year and was the top paid employee in XYZ this year.
    4. Joe who made $82,000 last year as the XYZ Corporation legal counsel (not in top 20%).
       a. 1 and 2.
       b. 2 and 3.
       c. 1, 2, and 3.
       d. 2, 3, and 4.
       e. 1, 2, 3, and 4.

11. Which of the following qualified plans must offer benefits in the form of qualified joint and survivor spouse annuities for married persons who have been married 1 year or longer?
    1. Defined benefit plans.
    2. Money purchase plans.
    3. Cash balance plan.
    4. Target benefit plans (money purchase).
       a. 1 only.
       b. 1 and 3.
       c. 3 and 4.
       d. 1, 2, and 4.
       e. 1, 2, 3, and 4.

12. Which of the following distributions or rollovers from retirement plans is subject to the 20% withholding rule?
    1. A partial non-direct distribution from a qualified pension plan.
    2. A full rollover, trustee to trustee, of a defined contribution plan to an IRA.
    3. A distribution from an IRA when the individual intends to reinvest within 60 days.
    4. A distribution from an IRA when the individual has no intent to reinvest within 60 days.
        a. None of the above.
        b. 1 only.
        c. 1 and 4.
        d. 1, 3, and 4.
        e. 1, 2, 3, and 4.

13. Which of the following require immediate vesting?
    1. Employer contributions to a money purchase plan.
    2. Employer contributions to a SEP.
    3. Employer contributions to a 401(k) plan.
    4. Employer contributions to a profit sharing plan.
        a. 1 only.
        b. 2 only.
        c. 1 and 2.
        d. 1, 2, and 3.
        e. 1, 2, 3, and 4.

14. In which of the following retirement plans can forfeitures increase account balances of plan participants?
    1. Defined benefit plans.
    2. Profit sharing plans.
    3. Money purchase plans.
    4. SEPs.
        a. 2 only.
        b. 3 only.
        c. 2 and 3.
        d. 2, 3, and 4.
        e. 1, 2, 3, and 4.

15. Which of the following retirement plans generally have loan provisions?
    1. Defined benefit plans.
    2. 401(k) plans.
    3. Money purchase plans.
    4. SEPs.
        a. 2 only.
        b. 3 only.
        c. 2 and 3.
        d. 1, 2, and 3.
        e. 1, 2, 3, and 4.

16. Which retirement plans assets are protected from creditors under federal laws in the event of bankruptcy (ignoring any state laws)?
    1. IRAs.
    2. SEPs.
    3. Profit sharing plans.
    4. Money purchase plans.
        a. 1 only.
        b. 2 only.
        c. 1 and 2.
        d. 3 and 4.
        e. 1, 2, 3, and 4.

17. Which of the following types of qualified plans do not allow integration with social security?
    1. Defined benefit plan.
    2. Money purchase plan.
    3. Profit sharing plan.
    4. ESOP.
        a. 2 only.
        b. 4 only.
        c. 2 and 4.
        d. 2, 3, and 4.
        e. 1, 2, 3, and 4.

18. Which of the following types of qualified plans allow integration with social security?

    1. Defined benefit plan.
    2. Money purchase plan.
    3. Profit sharing plan.
    4. ESOP.

        a. 1 only.
        b. 1 and 2.
        c. 2 and 3.
        d. 1, 2, and 3.
        e. 1, 2, 3, and 4.

19. Which of the following types of plans must meet the qualified pre-retirement survivor annuity and the qualified joint and survivor annuity rules?

    1. Defined benefit plans.
    2. Money purchase plans.
    3. Target benefit plans.
    4. 403(b) TSA/TDA plans.

        a. 1 only.
        b. 1 and 2.
        c. 1, 2, and 3.
        d. 3 and 4.
        e. 1, 2, 3, and 4.

20. With regard to rollovers that are not direct (trustee to trustee), which of the following are not subject to the 20% mandatory withholding?

    1. IRA rollovers.
    2. 403(b) TSA/TDA rollovers.
    3. Money purchase rollovers.
    4. Profit sharing rollovers.

        a. 1 only.
        b. 1 and 2.
        c. 1, 2, and 3.
        d. 2, 3, and 4.
        e. 1, 2, 3, and 4.

21. Which of the following plans are eligible for 5 year or 10 year special forward averaging for tax purposes for lump sum distributions?
    1. Defined benefit plan (DB).
    2. Simplified employee pension plan (SEP).
    3. Individual retirement account (IRA).
    4. Tax deferred annuity (TDA/403(b)).
        a. 1 only.
        b. 1 and 2.
        c. 1 and 4.
        d. 2 and 3.
        e. 1, 2, 3, and 4.

22. Kim Ding wants his wife Ding to waive her rights to a pre-retirement survivor annuity. Which of the following statements is/are correct to accomplish the waiver?
    1. Ding Ding must sign a written waiver.
    2. The waiver must be witnessed by a notary or by an official of the plan.
    3. The waiver is irrevocable.
        a. 1 only.
        b. 1 and 3.
        c. 2 and 3.
        d. 1, 2, and 3.
        e. None of the above.

23. John is married to Billie. They have been married for the past 30 years and have 2 minor children. John has recently received an offer from his employer to receive an early retirement package. One of the plan payout options is a single life annuity. Which of the following statements is/are true regarding the above?

    1. John can elect a single life annuity without any spousal knowledge.
    2. A single life annuity would provide the largest monthly amount of payout.
    3. To accept a single life annuity, John must inform Billie but does not have to obtain her consent.
    4. To accept a single life annuity, John must get a written waiver from Billie.

        a. 1 only.
        b. 3 only.
        c. 4 only.
        d. 2 and 3.
        e. 2 and 4.

24. Which one(s) of the following types of qualified and pension plans generally requires the use of a pre-retirement survivor annuity option?

    1. Defined benefit plan.
    2. 401(k) plan/profit sharing plan.
    3. SEP plan.
    4. Target benefit plan (money purchase).

        a. 1 only.
        b. 1 and 4.
        c. 1, 2, and 4.
        d. 3 and 4.
        e. 1, 2, 3, and 4.

25. Which of the following types of qualified plans require the use of an actuary in establishing the plan?
    1. Money purchase plan.
    2. Profit sharing plan.
    3. Target benefit plan.
    4. Defined benefit plan.
        a. 1 only.
        b. 4 only.
        c. 1 and 4.
        d. 3 and 4.
        e. 1, 3, and 4.

26. Which of the following types of plan generally require the following (or more stringent) coverage and eligibility requirements: (1) Age 21 and (2) One year of service.
    1. Defined benefit plan.
    2. Money purchase plan.
    3. Profit sharing plan
    4. Target benefit plan.
        a. 1 only.
        b. 1 and 4.
        c. 2 and 4.
        d. 1, 2, and 4.
        e. 1, 2, 3, and 4.

27. ABC employs 200 non-excludable employees 20 of whom are highly compensated. 16 of the 20 highly compensated and 125 of the 180 non-highly compensated employees benefit from the ABC qualified pension plan. The average benefits accrued for the highly compensated is 8% and $9,000. For the non-highly compensated, the average accrued benefit is 3% and $3,000.

    Which of the following statements is/are true regarding coverage?
        a. The plan meets the ratio % test.
        b. While the plan does not meet the ratio % test, it meets the average benefits test.
        c. The plan does not meet the ratio % test.
        d. The plan does not meet the ratio % test or the average benefits test.
        e. None of the above are correct.

28. ABC employs 200 non-excludable employees 20 of whom are highly compensated. 16 of the 20 highly compensated and 125 of the 180 non-highly compensated employees benefit from the ABC qualified pension plan. The average benefits accrued for the highly compensated is 8% and $9,000. For the non-highly compensated, the average accrued benefit if 3% and $3,000. The ratio % test for the above plan is:

    a. .6944.
    b. .70.
    c. .80.
    d. .868.

29. ABC employs 200 non-excludable employees 20 of whom are highly compensated. 16 of the 20 highly compensated and 125 of the 180 non-highly compensated employees benefit from the ABC qualified pension plan. The average benefits accrued for the highly compensated is 8% and $9,000. For the non-highly compensated, the average accrued benefit is 3% and $3,000. Calculate the average benefits % test.

    a. 26.0%.
    b. 33.5%.
    c. 37.5%.
    d. 70.0%.

30. Which of the following is/are highly compensated for qualified plan purposes for this year? Assume the company had no relevant elections.

    1. Steve, a 6% owner of an incorporated law firm.
    2. Mike, whose salary was $122,000 last year and was the top paid employee.
    3. James, whose salary was the tenth highest of 40 people and who made $95,000 last year.
    4. Donna, the corporate vice president of marketing, and an officer, whose salary last year was $80,000.

    a. 1 only.
    b. 2 only.
    c. 1, 2, and 3.
    d. 1, 2, and 4.
    e. 1, 2, 3, and 4.

31. Which of the following are objectives of the Employee Retirement Income Securities Act (ERISA)?
    1. To establish criteria for investment selection for qualified retirement plan portfolios.
    2. To require plan sponsors (employers) to provide full and accurate information about qualified retirement plan activity and funding to plan participants and appropriate regulatory agencies (e.g., IRS).
    3. To establish minimum funding, eligibility, coverage, and vesting requirements.
    4. To guarantee future benefits at a minimal level from defined contribution plans under the Pension Benefit Guarantee Corporation (PBGC).
        a. 2 only.
        b. 3 only.
        c. 2 and 3.
        d. 1, 2, and 3.
        e. 1, 2, 3, and 4.

32. Under a divorce agreement, the assignment of the rights to receive benefits from a qualified retirement plan by a court to the former spouse of a participant is referred to as:
        a. Front-loaded alimony.
        b. A collateral assignment.
        c. A qualified domestic trust (QDOT).
        d. A qualified domestic relations order (QDRO).
        e. A judicial pension split.

33. Which of the following parties would be classified under ERISA as parties in interest?
    1. A 4% owner of the sponsor and participant in the plan.
    2. An employee participant in the plan.
    3. An individual providing services to the plan.
    4. A plan fiduciary.
        a. 1 only.
        b. 1 and 4.
        c. 1, 2, and 3.
        d. 3 and 4.
        e. 1, 2, 3, and 4.

34. Which of the following are requirements for a plan to be a qualified plan?
    1. The plan must operate under a binding legal written document.
    2. The plan must be communicated to employees.
    3. The plan must operate for the exclusive benefit of participants and their beneficiaries.
    4. Monies may not be diverted from the plan for any purpose other than to benefit participants.
        a. 2 only.
        b. 2 and 3.
        c. 2, 3, and 4.
        d. 1, 2, and 3.
        e. 1, 2, 3, and 4.

35. Which of the following statements is/are correct?
    1. Hardship withdrawals by participants who have not yet reached age 59½ are not subject to a 10% early-withdrawal penalty.
    2. Hardship withdrawals are generally available only with qualified retirement plans that are required to maintain minimum funding standards such as money purchase plans.
    3. For a withdrawal to qualify as a hardship withdrawal, other resources with which to meet the need must not be available.
    4. Plan earnings on investments may be distributed under a hardship withdrawal.
        a. 1 only.
        b. 3 only.
        c. 1, 2, and 3.
        d. 1, 2, and 4.
        e. 1, 2, 3, and 4.

36. Jack Jones, age 40, earning $100,000 a year, wants to establish a defined contribution plan. He employs 4 people whose combined salaries are $60,000 and who range in age from 23 to 30. The average employment period is 3½ years. Which vesting schedule is best suited for Jack's plan? **(CFP® Exam, released 3/95)**
    a. 3-year cliff vesting.
    b. 3- to 7-year graded vesting.
    c. 5-year cliff vesting.
    d. Immediate vesting.
    e. 2- to 6-year graded vesting.

37. In the current year, Jennifer who is 30 years old received a distribution from her pension plan of $200,000, which she spent on a vacation that year. How much penalty will she owe for the current year?

    a. $0.
    b. $6,000.
    c. $20,000.
    d. $26,000.
    e. $100,000.

38. The Actual Deferral Percentage (ADP) test is applicable to which of the following?

    1. All 401(k) Plans.
    2. All DC Plans.
    3. All Profit sharing plans.

    a. 1 only.
    b. 2 only.
    c. 3 only.
    d. 1 and 2.
    e. 1, 2, and 3.

39. Husband and wife will retire in 13 years. Their life expectancy in retirement will be 25 years. They will need $5,000 at the beginning of each month for retirement expenses. Social Security will provide $2,000 per month during retirement. They can expect to earn 8% before retirement (after-tax) and 7% (after-tax) during retirement. How much must they save for the next 13 years at the end of each month to fund their retirement? They are unconcerned about inflation.

    a. $1,553.97.
    b. $1,564.33.
    c. $2,589.95.
    d. $2,607.21

40. Donna, became age 70½ on February 12, 1998, and has an IRA account. She is unsure about how much she should withdraw to satisfy the minimum distribution requirements. Her IRA account had the following year-end balances:

    12/31/97 $250,000

    12/31/98 $300,000

    12/31/99 $350,000

    The life expectancy for a single life at ages 70, 71, and 72 are 20, 19.5, and 19 years, respectively. Based on the above information, which of the following statements is/are true (assume no-recalculation)?

    1. A distribution of $28,343.73 in 1999 might satisfy the minimum distribution rules for Donna for 1998 and 1999.
    2. A distribution of $12,500.00 in 1998 and a distribution of $15,789.47 in 1999 will satisfy the minimum distribution requirements for Donna for 1998 and 1999.
    3. If Donna receives a distribution of $10,820.51 in 1998, it will result in a penalty for 1998 of $1,000.

    a. 1 only.
    b. 2 only.
    c. 3 only.
    d. 1 and 3.
    e. 1, 2, and 3.

41. Butch, a 35-year-old investor wants to know which of the following penalties he might be subject to if he continues to invest in tax advantaged accounts:

    1. 10% early distribution penalty.
    2. 50% minimum distribution penalty.
    3. 15% excess distribution penalty.
    4. 15% excess accumulation excise tax.

    a. 1 only.
    b. 1 and 2.
    c. 2 and 3.
    d. 1 and 4.
    e. 1, 2, 3, and 4.

42. Which of the following is true regarding ERISA and qualified plans.
    1. Must meet ERISA requirements to be a qualified plan.
    2. PBGC is responsible for enforcing ERISA.
    3. Requires the fiduciary to invest for gain under the prudent man rule.
        a. 1 only.
        b. 2 only.
        c. 1 and 2.
        d. 2 and 3.
        e. 1, 2, and 3.

43. What is the minimum number of employees that must be covered in a defined benefit plan to conform to ERISA requirements for a company having 200 employees?
    a. 40.
    b. 50.
    c. 55.
    d. 80.
    e. 110.

44. The XYZ Company has 2 employees - John, who earns $300,000 annually and his assistant, Sally, age 26 who has worked for John for 4 years. Sally makes $20,000. XYZ has a contributing pension plan using graded vesting. Sally's account balance reflects the following:

Contributions		Earnings from Contributions		Total Balance
Employee	Employer	Employee	Employer	
$1,500	$2,000	$800	$1,200	$5,500

Reviewing the account and assuming that Sally terminated employment when the account balance was as above after 4 years of employment, how much could she take with her, plan permitting?
    a. $2,300.
    b. $2,940.
    c. $3,580.
    d. $4,220.
    e. $4,860.

45. In January of the current year, John Black (age 47) took a premature distribution from a rollover IRA in the amount of $500,000, leaving him a balance in his IRA of $5,000,000. On October 31 of the current year, John died with the IRA account balance of $5,000,000. Which of the following penalties will apply to John as a result of these facts?
    1. The 10% early withdrawal penalty.
    2. The 15% excess distribution excise tax.
    3. The 15% excess accumulation excise tax.
    4. The 20% withholding penalty.
        a. 1 only.
        b. 1 and 2.
        c. 1, 2, and 3.
        d. 1, 3, and 4.
        e. 2, 3, and 4.

46. Which of the following persons could be classified as highly compensated for the current year?
    1. John, a 1% owner who made $150,000 in the previous year.
    2. Bill a 6% owner who made $28,000 in the previous year.
    3. Mary an officer who made $84,000 in the previous year who is the 25th highest paid employee of 100 employees.
    4. Maria who made $70,000 in the previous year and is in the top 20% of paid employees.
    5. Anna who made $80,000 in the previous year and is in the top 20% of paid employees.
        a. 1, 2, and 3.
        b. 2, 3, 4, and 5.
        c. 1, 2, and 4.
        d. 1, 2, 3, and 5.
        e. None of these necessarily because we don't know what their situation is in the current year.

47. Which of the following qualified plans is/are subject to the 50/40 test?
    1. Defined benefit.
    2. Cash balance.
    3. Money purchase pension plan.
    4. Profit sharing plan.
        a. 1 only.
        b. 1 and 2.
        c. 1, 2, and 3.
        d. 1, 3, and 4.
        e. 2, 3, and 4.

FIDUCIARIES AND THEIR OBLIGATIONS

48. Which of the following person(s) is a fiduciary for the XYZ qualified pension plan?
    1. Joe is named as the administrator for XYZ's Pension Plan.
    2. Bill is named as the investment manager for XYZ's Pension Plan.
    3. Mary, a CFP, is the paid investment advisory of the XYZ Pension Plan.
    4. Ralph is the XYZ owner and selected Joe, Bill, and Mary.
       a. 1 and 2.
       b. 1, 2, and 3.
       c. 1, 2, and 4.
       d. 2 and 3.
       e. 1, 2, 3, and 4.

49. Which of the following statements is/are true regarding fiduciaries of a qualified plan?
    1. A fiduciary must manage plan assets solely in the interests of plan participants and beneficiaries.
    2. A fiduciary who is also a full time paid employee of the plan sponsor may receive additional payment for services rendered to the plan.
    3. A fiduciary cannot permit more than 10% of plan assets to be invested in employer securities or real property in a defined benefit plan.
       a. 1 only.
       b. 1 and 3.
       c. 2 and 3.
       d. 1, 2, and 3.
       e. None of the above statements are true.

50. Which of the following persons is a party in interest for a qualified plan?
    1. An officer of the pension plan.
    2. The sponsor company.
    3. Bill who owns exactly 50% of XYZ, the corporate sponsor.
    4. Merrily, CFP, the investment advisor to the plan.
       a. 1 only.
       b. 1 and 4.
       c. 2 and 4.
       d. 2, 3, and 4.
       e. 1, 2, 3, and 4.

51. Company A has a participant directed retirement plan that offers 6 investments options ranging from conservative to risky. Sam, an employee, had his account invested in the riskiest option. When he suffered severe losses in the account he sued the plan fiduciary. Which of the following is correct regarding the fiduciary's liability to Sam?

    a. The fiduciary is fully responsible for the loss to Sam because risky portfolios are not appropriate choices for participants to invest their accounts.
    b. The fiduciary is responsible for only 20% of the loss suffered by Sam.
    c. The fiduciary is not responsible for the loss suffered by Sam, but must replace the risky portfolio with a more conservative portfolio.
    d. The fiduciary is not responsible for the loss suffered by Sam because the investment options were sufficiently diverse and Sam chose the risky portfolio.

DEFINED BENEFIT PENSION PLANS

52. Which of the following statements is/are correct regarding defined benefit plans?

    1. Allows discretionary annual contributions.
    2. Favors older employee participants.
    3. Requires an actuary annually.
    4. Is insured by the Pension Benefit Guaranty Corporation (PBGC).

    a. 2 only.
    b. 1, 2, and 4.
    c. 2 and 3.
    d. 2, 3, and 4.
    e. 1, 3, and 4.

53. A businessman, Joe, age 46 with 18 years in the company and a retirement objective of age 70, has other employees, all of whom are older than Joe, and have average service of 4 years (1-8). Joe would like to install a qualified retirement plan that would favor him and reward employees who have rendered long service. Joe has selected a defined benefit plan with a unit benefit formula.

    Which of the following statement is/are correct regarding Joe's defined benefit plan?

    1. Increased profitability would increase both Joe's and his employees pension contributions.
    2. A unit benefit plan allows for higher levels of integration than other defined benefit plans.
    3. A unit benefit plan rewards older employees hired in their 50's or 60's.
    4. It could maximize Joe's benefits and reward long-term employees based on length of service.

    a. 4 only.
    b. 2 only.
    c. 2 and 4.
    d. 1, 2, and 4.
    e. 2, 3, and 4.

54. Which of the following would be expected to decrease the employer's annual contribution to a defined benefit plan using a percentage for each year of service formula?
    1. Forfeitures are higher than anticipated.
    2. Inflation is higher than expected.
    3. Plan investments returns are greater than expected.
    4. Benefits are cost of living adjusted.
        a. 1 only.
        b. 1 and 2.
        c. 1 and 3.
        d. 2 and 3.
        e. 1, 2, 3, and 4.

55. Which of the following would increase the employer's annual contribution to a defined benefit plan using a percentage for each year of service formula?
    1. Forfeitures are lower than expected.
    2. Salary increases are higher than expected.
    3. Investment returns are less than expected.
    4. Benefits are cost of living adjusted as expected.
        a. 1 only.
        b. 2 only.
        c. 1 and 2.
        d. 1, 2, and 3.
        e. 1, 2, 3, and 4.

56. Which of the following qualified plans must provide qualified joint and survivor annuities and pre-retirement survivor annuities?
    1. SEPs (profit sharing).
    2. Target benefit plan (money purchase).
    3. Profit sharing plan.
    4. Defined benefit plan.
        a. 4 only.
        b. 3 only.
        c. 2 and 4.
        d. 1, 2, and 4.
        e. 1, 2, 3, and 4.

57. Which of the following qualified retirement plans require Pension Benefit Guaranty Corporation insurance?
    1. Defined benefit plan.
    2. Target benefit plan.
    3. Money purchase plan.
    4. Profit sharing plan.
        a. 1 only.
        b. 2 only.
        c. 1 and 2.
        d. 1, 2, and 3.
        e. 1, 2, 3, and 4.

58. Which of the following facts and assumptions are used by an actuary to determine the employer contributions to a defined benefit plan?
    1. Each participant's age, sex, expected compensation, and length of service.
    2. Plan expected investment results.
    3. Plan expected administrative expenses.
    4. The benefit formula specified in the plan.
        a. 1 and 2.
        b. 1 and 3.
        c. 1, 2, and 3.
        d. 3 and 4.
        e. 1, 2, 3, and 4.

59. Which of the following statement(s) is/are correct regarding the favoring of older or younger employees by various types of qualified plans with regard to employees contributions?
    1. Defined benefit plans favor older employees.
    2. Target benefit plans favor younger employees.
    3. Money purchase plans favor younger employees.
    4. SEP plans favor older employees.
        a. 1 only.
        b. 2 only.
        c. 1 and 3.
        d. 1, 3, and 4.
        e. 1, 2, 3, and 4.

60. Of the statements below regarding actuarial cost methods for defined benefit plans which is/are correct?

    1. The accrued benefit cost method can be used with either a flat-benefit or a unit-benefit formulas.
    2. The projected benefit cost method seeks to level the employer's plan cost from year to year.
    3. Under the accrued benefit cost method, the normal cost reflects the benefit that is attributable to the current year.
    4. Under the projected benefit cost method, costs are projected up to the current date.

        a. 1 only.
        b. 2 only.
        c. 2 and 3.
        d. 1, 2, and 3.
        e. 1, 2, 3, and 4.

61. Which one of the following statements is <u>not</u> true for a defined benefit plan? **(CFP® Exam, released 3/95)**

    a. Favors older participants.
    b. Arbitrary annual contribution.
    c. Requires an actuary.
    d. Maximum retirement benefit of the lesser of $90,000 (indexed) or 100% of pay per year.
    e. Requires Pension Benefit Guaranty Corporation (PBGC) premiums.

62. Which of the following are common actuarial assumptions used in determining the plan contributions needed to fund the benefits of a defined benefit plan? **(CFP® Exam, released 3/95)**

    1. Investment performance.
    2. Employee turnover rate.
    3. Salary scale.
    4. Ratio of single to married participants.

        a. 1, 2, and 3.
        b. 1 and 3.
        c. 2 and 4.
        d. 4 only.
        e. 1, 2, 3, and 4.

63. For defined benefit plans, which of the following changes in actuarial assumptions would increase plan costs to an employer?

    1. Early retirement without a reduction in benefits.
    2. Longer life expectancy predicted.
    3. An increase in inflation expectations regarding labor costs.

        a. 1 only.
        b. 2 only.
        c. 3 only.
        d. 1 and 2.
        e. 1, 2, and 3.

64. XYZ Corp had a defined benefit plan with no lump sum distribution settlement option. Which of the following defined benefit assumptions will impact this plan's funding, assuming they are each different from what was expected?

    1. Mortality rate of plan participants.
    2. Employee turnover.
    3. Inflation.
    4. Expected rate of return on plan investments.
    5. Changes in salary levels.

        a. 1, 3, 4, and 5.
        b. 2, 3, 4, and 5.
        c. 1, 2, and 4.
        d. 1, 2, 4, and 5.
        e. 1, 2, 3, 4, and 5.

DEFINED CONTRIBUTION PLANS

65. Which of the following statements is/are correct regarding profit sharing plans?

    1. The maximum tax-deductible employer contribution to a profit sharing plan is 15% of total covered compensation or 15% of covered payroll, etc.
    2. Company profits and retained earnings are required to make contributions to a profit sharing plan.
    3. Companies adopting a profit sharing plan and having current profits are required to make a contribution to the plan.
    4. Profit sharing plans are best suited for companies with predictable cash flows.

        a. 1 only.
        b. 2 only.
        c. 1 and 2.
        d. 1, 2, and 3.
        e. 1, 2, 3, and 4.

66. Which of the following statements is/are correct regarding factors which can affect the retirement benefits from a defined contribution plan?

    1. The investment earnings assumption used by administration.
    2. The number of years of service multiplied by a formula.
    3. The selection of the investments by the participant.
    4. The value in dollars of the participant's account balance at retirement.

        a. 1 and 2.
        b. 3 and 4.
        c. 1, 2, and 3.
        d. 2, 3, and 4.
        e. 1, 2, 3, and 4.

67. Which of the following are subject to FICA and FUTA taxes?

    1. Thrift plan contributions.
    2. 401(k) deferral contributions by employees.
    3. Salary reduction SEP contributions by employees.
    4. Non-salary reduction arrangement SEP contributions by employers.

        a. 1 only.
        b. 1 and 4.
        c. 2 and 3.
        d. 1, 2, and 3.
        e. 1, 2, 3, and 4.

68. Which of the following retirement plans can be integrated with social security?

    1. Profit sharing plan.
    2. SEP.
    3. Money purchase plan.
    4. Defined benefit plan.

        a. 4 only.
        b. 1 and 4.
        c. 3 and 4.
        d. 1, 3, and 4.
        e. 1, 2, 3, and 4.

69. Which of the following qualified defined contribution plans permit in-service withdrawals?

    1. Money purchase plan.
    2. Profit sharing plan.
    3. 401(k) plan.
    4. SEP.

        a. 1, 2, and 4.
        b. 2 and 3.
        c. 1, 2, and 3.
        d. 2, 3, and 4.
        e. 1, 2, 3, and 4.

70. Which of the following qualified retirement plans allow unrestricted investment into sponsor company stock?

    1. Money purchase plans.
    2. Stock bonus plans.
    3. ESOPs.
    4. Profit sharing plans.

        a. 4 only.
        b. 2 and 3.
        c. 1, 2, and 3.
        d. 2, 3, and 4.
        e. 1, 2, 3, and 4.

71. Which of the following retirement plans allow unrestricted investment into sponsor company stock?

    1. Defined benefit plans.
    2. Money purchase plans.
    3. SEPs.
    4. Profit sharing plans.

        a. 2 only.
        b. 4 only.
        c. 3 and 4.
        d. 1, 2, and 3.
        e. 1, 2, 3, and 4.

72. ABC Corporation is trying to set up a qualified pension plan and has established the following criteria:

- Simplicity.
- Must be able to be integrated with social security.
- Funding flexibility.
- Ability to invest in company stock is unrestricted.
- Employees can make in-service withdrawals.
- Employees cannot vote their stock if any in the plan.
- Distribution of benefits can be in the form of cash.
- ABC can deduct value of any stock contributed to plan.

Which of the following types of qualified plans would meet their criteria?

1. ESOP.
2. Stock bonus plan.
3. Profit sharing plan.
4. Money purchase plan.

a. 1 only.
b. 3 only.
c. 1 and 2.
d. 1, 2, and 3.
e. 1, 2, 3, and 4.

73. Which of the following types of retirement plans allow in-service withdrawals?

1. SEPs.
2. Money purchase plans.
3. Profit sharing plans.
4. 403(b) plans.

a. 1 only.
b. 3 only.
c. 1 and 3.
d. 1, 3, and 4.
e. 1, 2, 3, and 4.

74. Which of the following statements correctly applies to employer contributions to money purchase plans?
    1. Employer contributions may not exceed 25% of covered compensation.
    2. Money purchase plans are not subject to a minimum funding standard.
    3. Investment earnings and losses do not effect employer contributions.
    4. Forfeitures may be allocated to remaining participants.
        a. 2 and 4.
        b. 1, 2, and 3.
        c. 2, 3, and 4.
        d. 1, 3, and 4.
        e. 1, 2, 3, and 4.

75. Which one of the following statements is not correct? **(CFP® Exam, released 3/95)**
    a. Profit-sharing plans fall under the broad category of defined contribution plans.
    b. Profit-sharing plans are best suited for companies that have unstable earnings.
    c. A company that adopts a profit-sharing plan is required to make contributions each year.
    d. The maximum tax-deductible employer contribution to a profit-sharing plan is 15% of covered compensation. Neither company profits nor retained earnings are required in order to make contributions.
    e. All of the above.

76. In a money purchase pension plan that utilizes plan forfeitures to reduce future employer plan contributions, which of the following components must be factored into the calculation of the maximum annual addition limit? **(CFP® Exam, released 3/95)**
    1. Forfeitures that otherwise would have been reallocated.
    2. Annual earnings on all employer and employee contributions.
    3. Rollover contributions for the year.
    4. Employer and employee contributions to all defined contribution plans.
        a. 1, 2, and 3.
        b. 1 and 3.
        c. 2 and 4.
        d. 4 only.
        e. 1, 2, 3, and 4.

77. A client's employer has recently implemented a Cash or Deferred Arrangement (CODA) as part of his profit-sharing plan to provide incentive to his employees. The client is advised not to elect to receive the bonuses in cash but to defer receipt of them until retirement for which of the following reasons? **(CFP® Exam, released 3/95)**

    1. The client will not pay current federal income taxes on amounts paid into the CODA.
    2. The client will not pay Social Security (FICA) taxes on amounts paid into the CODA.
    3. The accrued benefits derived from elective contributions are non-forfeitable.
    4. The accrued benefits from non-elective contributions are non-forfeitable.

    a. 1, 2, and 3.
    b. 1 and 3.
    c. 2 and 4.
    d. 3 only.
    e. 1, 2, 3, and 4.

78. Which statements is/are true regarding qualified profit sharing plans? **(CFP® Exam, released 3/95)**

    1. A company must show a profit in order to make a contribution for a given year.
    2. A profit-sharing plan is a type of retirement plan and thus is subject to minimum funding standards.
    3. Forfeitures in profit-sharing plans must be credited against future years' contributions.
    4. Profit-sharing plans should make contributions that are "substantial and recurring" according to the IRS.

    a. 1, 2, and 3.
    b. 1 and 3.
    c. 1, 2, and 4.
    d. 1, 2, 3, and 4.
    e. 4 only.

79. Which of the following statements is/are correct regarding factors which can affect the retirement benefits from a defined contribution plan?
    1. The investment earnings assumption used by administration.
    2. The number of years of service multiplied by a formula.
    3. The selection of the investment alternatives by the participant.
    4. The value in dollars of the participant's account balance at retirement.
        a. 1 and 2.
        b. 3 and 4.
        c. 1, 2, and 3.
        d. 2, 3, and 4.
        e. 1, 2, 3, and 4.

HYBRID PLANS

80. Which of the following statements is/are correct with regard to a target benefit (not profit sharing) plan for Bill, a 59-year-old making $80,000, when the plan was designed to provide maximum benefits to a 38-year-old key employee/officer, and there is substantial employee turnover?

    1. Bill knows exactly what retirement benefit to expect.
    2. Bill's contributions to the plan are available for in-service withdrawals.
    3. Forfeitures are likely to be allocated equally to Bill and the 38-year-old.
    4. Contributions to the plan are certain.

    a. 1 only.
    b. 4 only.
    c. 2 and 4.
    d. 2, 3, and 4.
    e. 1, 2, 3, and 4.

81. Which of the following is/are disadvantage(s) of a target benefit (not profit sharing) plan for Lamonte, a 59-year-old making $80,000? The plan was designed to provide maximum benefits to a 38-year-old key employee/officer (Mike) and there is substantial employee turnover.

    1. Lamonte does not know exactly what retirement benefit to expect.
    2. The employer bears the investment risk.
    3. Forfeitures are likely to be allocated to Mike in a discriminatory manner.
    4. Contributions to the plan are flexible.

    a. 1 only.
    b. 1 and 2.
    c. 1, 2, and 3.
    d. 2, 3, and 4.
    e. 1, 2, 3, and 4.

82. Garces Product Wholesalers Inc., a regular C Corporation, is considering the adoption of a qualified retirement plan. The company has had fluctuating cash flows in the recent past and such fluctuations are expected to continue. The average age of non-owner employees is 24 and the average number of years of service is 3 with the high being 4 and the low 1. Approximately 25% of the 12 person labor force turns over each year. The two owners gross about 2/3 of covered compensation.

    Which is the most appropriate plan for Garces Product Wholesalers?

    a. Tandem plan (10% money purchase/15% profit sharing).
    b. Target benefit plan.
    c. Defined benefit plan.
    d. Money purchase plan.
    e. Profit sharing plan.

83. Which statement(s) is/are true for a target benefit plan? **(CFP® Exam, released 3/95)**

    1. It favors older participants.
    2. It requires actuarial assumptions.
    3. The maximum contribution is 25% of payroll.
    4. The maximum individual allocation is the lesser of 25% of pay or $30,000 as indexed.

    a. 1 and 4.
    b. 2 and 3.
    c. 1, 2, and 4.
    d. 4 only.
    e. 1 and 3.

HR 10 (KEOGH) PLAN

84. The deductible contribution to a defined contribution qualified pension plan on behalf of a self-employed individual whose income from self-employment is $20,000 and whose social security taxes are $3,060 is limited to:

    a. $3,000.
    b. $3,694.
    c. $4,000.
    d. $4,618.
    e. $5,000.

SIMPLIFIED EMPLOYEE PENSION (SEP)

85. Which of the following are characteristics of both a SEP and an IRA?
    1. Investment options are limited.
    2. Immediate vesting in entire balance.
    3. Early withdrawal (pre-59½) penalties of 10% apply excepting death and disability.
    4. Availability of forward averaging.
        a. 1 only.
        b. 2 only.
        c. 2 and 3.
        d. 2, 3, and 4.
        e. 1, 2, and 3.

86. Which of the following statements is/are correct regarding SEP contributions made by an employer?
    1. Contributions are subject to FICA and FUTA.
    2. Currently excludable from employee's gross income.
    3. Subject to withholding for income tax.
    4. Capped at $10,000.
        a. 1 only.
        b. 2 only.
        c. 1 and 2.
        d. 2 and 4.
        e. 2, 3, and 4.

87. Which of the following statements is/are correct regarding SEPs?
    1. Employees can rollover money from a SEP into an IRA within 60 days without withholding or penalty.
    2. Employees can make direct trustee to trustee transfers as often as desired.
    3. Non-direct rollovers can occur only once every 12 months.
    4. A regular SEP can be integrated with social security.
        a. 2 and 4.
        b. 2, 3, and 4.
        c. 1, 2, and 3.
        d. 1, 3, and 4.
        e. 1, 2, 3, and 4.

88. Which of the following retirement plans require immediate vesting?

    1. SEPs.
    2. SIMPLEs.
    3. 403(b) plans.
    4. 401(k) plans – employer contributions.

    a. 1 only.
    b. 2 only.
    c. 1 and 2.
    d. 1, 2, and 3.
    e. 1, 2, 3, and 4.

INDIVIDUAL RETIREMENT ACCOUNT (IRA)

89. A single taxpayer, age 54, has retired (2 years ago) and is receiving a pension of $600 per month from her previous employer's qualified pension plan. She has recently taken an employment position in a small CPA firm that has no pension plan. She will receive $10,000 in compensation from the CPA firm as well as the $7,200 from her pension. How much can she contribute and deduct to an IRA this year?

    a. $0.
    b. $1,000.
    c. $1,500.
    d. $2,000.
    e. $2,250.

90. Which of the following statement is/are correct regarding penalties associated with IRA accounts for the years after 1997?

    1. Generally, distributions made prior to 59½ are subject to the 10% premature distribution penalty.
    2. There is a 50% excise tax on under-distributions not made by April 1 of the year following the year in which age 70½ is reached.
    3. A 15% penalty will be imposed for distributions from an IRA that exceeds the greater of (1) $160,000 or (2) $112,000 indexed.
    4. An excess accumulation tax of 15% will be applied at the estate level for accumulations in excess of the present value of an annuity of the greater of (1) $160,000 or (2) $112,000 indexed over the participant's life expectancy at death.

    a. 1 and 2.
    b. 1, 2, and 3.
    c. 1, 3, and 4.
    d. 2 and 3.
    e. 1, 2, 3, and 4.

91. Which of the following individuals can contribute to a deductible IRA in the current year?

	Person	Marital Status	AGI	Covered by Pension Plan
1.	Jane	Single	$ 35,000	Yes
2.	Joe	Married	$100,000	No
3.	Betty	Single	$ 20,000	Yes
4.	Mary Sue	Married	$ 40,000	Yes

a. 2 only.
b. 3 and 4.
c. 2, 3, and 4.
d. 1, 3, and 4.
e. 1, 2, 3, and 4.

92. Which of the following is/are investments which can be purchased in an IRA without penalty?

1. A mutual fund which invests exclusively in gold mining stock.
2. An international stock mutual fund.
3. Investment grade piece of art.
4. Gold coins minted in the United States by the treasury.

a. 2 only.
b. 2 and 4.
c. 1 and 2.
d. 1, 2, and 4.
e. 1, 2, 3, and 4.

93. Which of the following statements is/are correct regarding distributions from a decedent's IRA or qualified plan?
    1. Generally, if distributions have not commenced before death, the balance must be distributed within 5 years.
    2. If the owner has a designated beneficiary, and distributions have not commenced, distributions can be made over a period not extending beyond the life expectancy of the beneficiary.
    3. If distributions have not begun, and the beneficiary is the spouse of the decedent, distribution may be delayed until the decedent would have reached 70½.
    4. If the owner dies after payments have begun, the payments must continue to the beneficiary or heir at least as fast as under the method of distribution in effect during the owner's life, unless the heir or beneficiary is a spouse.
        a. 1 only.
        b. 2 only.
        c. 1 and 2.
        d. 1, 2, and 3.
        e. 1, 2, 3, and 4.

94. Which, if any, of the following transactions is permissible regarding an IRA or qualified plan (QP) distribution?
    1. A non-spouse IRA/QP beneficiary must distribute the balance of an IRA/QP, where distribution had begun over a period not exceeding 5 years.
    2. A non-spouse IRA/QP beneficiary may distribute the balance of an IRA/QP, where distribution had not begun over the life expectancy of the beneficiary.
    3. A spousal beneficiary of a deceased owner of an IRA/QP can delay any distribution of such IRA/QP until April 1 following the year in which such beneficiary is 70½.
    4. A spouse beneficiary of a deceased owner IRA/QP can roll such IRA/QP balance into his/her own IRA/QP, even if distributions had begun to the owner prior to death.
        a. 1 and 2.
        b. 2 and 3.
        c. 1, 2, and 3.
        d. 2, 3, and 4.
        e. 1, 2, 3, and 4.

95. Tom Schmurk took a lump sum distribution from his employer at age 52, when he terminated his service. He rolled over his distribution using a direct transfer to an IRA.
Which of the following is/are correct regarding tax treatment of the transaction?
    1. If at age 55 he distributes the IRA, he benefits from lump sum forward averaging.
    2. If he rolls the entire IRA to his new employer's qualified plan; he will be eligible for forward averaging treatment in the future.
    3. If he rolls over a portion of the IRA to his new employer's qualified plan, he will preserve any eligibility for forward averaging on that portion.
    4. If Tom immediately withdraws the entire amount from his IRA, he will benefit by virtue of forward averaging.
        a. 1 only.
        b. 2 only.
        c. 2 and 3.
        d. 2 and 4.
        e. 1, 2, 3, and 4.

96. James and Donna Delle are married and filed a joint return for 1999. James earned a salary of $70,000 in 1999 and is covered by his employer's pension plan. James and Donna earned interest of $5,000 in 1999 on their joint savings account. Donna is not employed, and the couple had no other income. On April 15, 2000, James contributed $250 to an IRA for himself and $2,000 to an IRA for his spouse. The maximum allowable IRA deduction on the Delle's 1999 joint return is:
    a. $0.
    b. $250.
    c. $2,000.
    d. $2,250.
    e. $4,000.

97. Thad and Debra Claiborne, both age 50, are married and filed a joint return for 1999. Their 1999 adjusted gross income was $100,000, (including Thad's $95,000 salary). Debra had no income of her own. Neither spouse was covered by an employer-sponsored pension plan. What amount could the Claiborne's contribute to IRAs for 1999 to take advantage of their maximum allowable IRA deduction on their 1999 return?
    a. $0.
    b. $250.
    c. $2,000.
    d. $2,250.
    e. $4,000.

98. Judy Martin, who is divorced, received taxable alimony of $30,000 in 1999. In addition, she received $900 in earnings from a part-time job in 1999. Judy is not covered by a qualified pension plan. What was the maximum deductible IRA contribution that Judy could have made for 1999?

    a. $0.
    b. $250.
    c. $900.
    d. $1,125.
    e. $2,000.

99. For the year 1999, Mary Sue and Bob Oehlke reported the following items of income:

	Mary Sue	Bob	Total
Salary	$40,000	--	$40,000
Interest income	1,000	$200	1,200
Cash prize won from lottery		10,000	10,000
	$41,000	$10,200	$51,200

Neither Mary Sue nor Bob is covered by a qualified retirement plan and she and Bob established individual retirement accounts during the year. Assuming a joint return was filed for 1999, what is the maximum amount that they can be allowed for the contributions to their individual retirement accounts?

    a. $0.
    b. $250.
    c. $2,000.
    d. $2,250.
    e. $4,000.

100. A client, age 50 and single, chose early retirement and is receiving from his previous employer's qualified pension plan a monthly pension of $400. The client elects to work for a small company and will receive $30,000 in annual compensation. This company does not cover him under a qualified pension plan. The client wants to contribute the maximum deductible amount to an Individual Retirement Account (IRA). The amount of the IRA contribution that he can deduct from his gross income is: **(CFP® Exam, released 3/95)**

    a. $0.
    b. $200.
    c. $400.
    d. $1,000.
    e. $2,000.

101. Which of the following investments can be held in an IRA account?

   a. A U.S. gold coin.
   b. A Canadian gold coin.
   c. An African gold coin.
   d. A German gold coin.
   e. None of the above.

102. Which of the following investments can be held in an IRA?

   a. Krugerrands.
   b. Sovereigns.
   c. Eagles.
   d. Pandas.
   e. Maple Leafs.

103. Beverly's husband, age 67, dies with $1.2 million in his IRA. Beverly, who is the designated beneficiary, would like to know what her options are regarding the inherited IRA account. Which of the following are true?

   1. Beverly has five years to withdraw the funds from the IRA account.
   2. Beverly can roll over the IRA to her IRA.

   a. 1 only.
   b. 2 only.
   c. 1 and 2.
   d. None of the above.

104. John and Mary Lutz are married and file a joint income tax return for the current year. John is self-employed as an engineering consultant and makes $120,000 of Schedule C income and pays $14,000 in Social Security taxes. Mary is a full time homemaker and is not employed outside the home. What is the maximum deductible IRA John and Mary can claim on their current year federal income tax return?

   a. $0.
   b. $250.
   c. $1,250.
   d. $2,250.
   e. $4,000.

105. Amounts within a Roth IRA may have come from contributions, conversions from a traditional IRA, or earnings. Roth IRA distributions are required to be treated as occurring in a specific order. What is the order in which distributions are made from a Roth IRA?

   a. Contributions, conversions, earnings.
   b. Conversions, earnings, contributions.
   c. Earnings, conversions, contributions.
   d. Earnings, contributions, conversions.
   e. Contributions, earnings, conversions.

106. Judd, who is currently age 50, made his only contribution to his Roth IRA in 1998 in the amount of $2,000. If he were to receive a total distribution of $5,000 from his Roth IRA in the year 2004, how would he be taxed?

   a. Since Judd waited five years, the distribution will be classified as a "qualified distribution" and will, therefore, not be taxable or subject to the 10% early distribution penalty.
   b. Since Judd waited five years, the distribution will be classified as a "qualified distribution" and will, therefore, not be taxable, but will be subject to the 10% early distribution penalty.
   c. Although Judd waited five years, the distribution will not be classified as a "qualified distribution" and will, therefore, be taxable and will be subject to the 10% early distribution penalty.
   d. Although Judd waited five years, the distribution will not be classified as a "qualified distribution" and will, therefore, be taxable to the extent of earnings and will be subject to the 10% early distribution penalty on the amount that is taxable.
   e. Although Judd waited five years, the distribution will not be classified as a "qualified distribution" and will therefore be taxable to the extent of earnings and will be subject to the 10% early distribution penalty on the entire distribution.

107. Which of the following is not permitted as a method of converting a traditional IRA to a Roth IRA?

    a. An amount distributed from a traditional IRA can be rolled over to a Roth IRA within 60 days after the distribution.
    b. An amount in a traditional IRA can be transferred in a trustee-to-trustee transfer from the trustee of the traditional IRA to the trustee of the Roth IRA.
    c. An amount in a traditional IRA can be transferred to a Roth IRA maintained by the same trustee.
    d. An amount from a qualified plan can be transferred via a trustee-to-trustee transfer to a Roth IRA.

108. Alley, who is age 35, converts an $80,000 traditional IRA to a Roth IRA in 1998. Alley's basis in the traditional IRA is $20,000. She decides to spread the income from the conversion over the four-year period, 1998 to 2001. She also makes a contribution of $2,000 to a Roth IRA in 1998. If Alley makes a $2,000 distribution from her Roth IRA during 1998, how much total federal tax, including penalties, is due as a result of the distribution, assuming a Federal tax rate of 31 percent?

    a. $0.
    b. $200.
    c. $620.
    d. $820.

109. Jim and Jan are married and file a joint tax return. Jan has made a $2,000 contribution to her traditional IRA account and has made a contribution of $500 to their son's education IRA for the same year. What is the most that can be contributed to a Roth IRA for Jim or Jan this year?

    a. $0.
    b. $1,500.
    c. $2,000.
    d. $3,500.
    e. $4,000.

110. Bailey and Jen are married and file a joint tax return. They have AGI of $155,000 and have each contributed $1,000 to a Roth IRA during 1998. Bailey's mother contributed $500 to an Education IRA for each of their two children. What is the most that Bailey and Jen can contribute in total together to a traditional IRA for 1998?

    a. $0.
    b. $1,000.
    c. $2,000.
    d. $3,500.
    e. $4,000.

111. What is the first year in which a taxpayer, age 53 in 1998, could receive a qualified distribution from a Roth IRA, if he made a $2,000 contribution to a Roth IRA on April 1, 1999 for the tax year 1998?

    a. 1999.
    b. 2001.
    c. 2003.
    d. 2005.
    e. 2007.

112. Sally is single, recently divorced and has received the following items of income this year:

- Pension income from QDRO $25,000
- Interest & dividends $5,000
- Alimony $1,000

What is the most that Sally can contribute to a Roth IRA this year?

    a. $0.
    b. $500.
    c. $1,000.
    d. $1,500.
    e. $2,000

TAX DEFERRED ANNUITY - 403(b) PLANS

113. Which of the following statements is/are correct regarding tax sheltered annuities (TSAs)?

1. A catch up provision is available to all 501(c)(3) organization employers.
2. Active employees who make withdrawals from TSAs prior to 59½ are subject to a 10% penalty tax.
3. TSAs are available to all employees of 501(c)(3) organizations who adopt such a plan.
4. A catch up provision is allowed for employees with at least fifteen (15) years of service who have made no contributions and are employed by universities.

a. 2 only.
b. 1 and 2.
c. 1, 2, and 3.
d. 2, 3, and 4.
e. 1, 2, 3, and 4.

114. Which of the following statements is/are correct regarding TSAs and 457 plans?

1. Both plans require contracts between employer and employee.
2. Both plans have the same limits on salary deferral.
3. Both plans are able to use forward averaging tax treatment.
4. Both plans must meet minimum distribution requirements that apply to qualified plans.

a. 1 only.
b. 1 and 4.
c. 2, 3, and 4.
d. 1, 3, and 4.
e. 1, 2, 3, and 4

115. What is the maximum contribution (salary reduction) for a TSA in 1999, assuming no catch up provision?

a. $7,000.
b. $9,500.
c. $10,000.
d. $10,500.
e. $11,000.

116. Which of the following are permitted investments in a 403(b) TSA (TDA) plan?

1. Annuity contract from insurance company.
2. Growth stock fund (mutual fund).
3. A self-directed brokerage account using U.S. Stocks and Bonds.
4. Gold coins minted in the U.S.

a. 1 only.
b. 2 only.
c. 1 and 2.
d. 1, 2, and 3.
e. 1, 2, 3, and 4.

117. Which of the following are common features of a TSA (TDA) plan?

1. Salary reduction plan.
2. The benefit is dependent on the investment results.
3. The investment risk is borne by the employee.
4. Permits in-service withdrawals.

a. 1 and 3.
b. 2 and 3.
c. 1 and 3.
d. 1, 2, and 3.
e. 1, 2, 3, and 4.

118. Which of the following are correct regarding TSAs (TDAs)?

1. The sponsor must be organized under 501(c)(3).
2. Distributions are eligible for 5 or 10 year averaging.
3. In-service withdrawals are permitted.
4. The plan can invest in individual stocks and bonds but not options or futures.

a. 1 and 2.
b. 1 and 3.
c. 1, 3, and 4.
d. 1, 2, and 3.
e. 2, 3, and 4.

119. Which of the following statements concerning provisions of tax-sheltered annuities (TSAs) is not true? **(CFP® Exam, released 3/95)**

a. A catch up provision is allowed for all employees with at least 15 years of service and who made no prior contributions (and who belong to the correct type of organization*).

b. TSAs are available to all employees of a 501(c)(3) organization under provisions of the Internal Revenue Code.

c. Contributions to TSAs are made through the use of an exclusion allowance, salary reduction agreement under section 403(b) of the Internal Revenue Code.

d. If withdrawals are made from a TSA prior to age 59½, an active employee is subject to a 10% penalty tax.

e. A catch-up provision is available to all employees of a 501(c)(3) organization under the provisions of the Internal Revenue Code.

* ( ) added by author.

120. Which of the following statements are true regarding 403(b) plans?

1. 403(b) plans are eligible for rollover treatment to IRA accounts.
2. 403(b) plans permit 5 and 10 year averaging.
3. 403(b) plans are never permitted to have graded vesting, only cliff vesting.

a. 1 only.

b. 2 only.

c. 3 only.

d. 1 and 2.

e. 1 and 3.

NON-QUALIFIED DEFERRED COMPENSATION

121. Nick Twist has a 15% non-qualified deferred compensation plan that is funded annually by his employer. Payments are made to a separate trustee (not a Rabbi trust) who was mutually agreed upon by Nick and his employer. The employer contributions are discontinued at Nick's death, disability or employment termination. At Nick's retirement or termination of employment he will receive the proceeds from the trust.

Which of the following is/are correct regarding the deferred compensation plan?

1. The employer contributions are currently taxable to Nick because they are not subject to a substantial risk of forfeiture.
2. The employer contributions to the plan are tax deferred to Nick because they are less than 25% of his compensation.
3. The contributions to the plan are currently subject to payroll taxes.
4. The employer cannot deduct the contributions to the plan until they are actually paid to Nick.

a. 1 only.
b. 3 only.
c. 1 and 3.
d. 2 and 4.
e. 2, 3, and 4.

SOCIAL SECURITY BENEFITS (OASDHI)

122. In order to qualify for OASDHI disability benefits, which of the following definitions of disability must be met?
   a. The inability to perform the complete duties of the occupation engaged in prior to the disability.
   b. The inability to engage in any occupation for which one is reasonably suited by training, education, or experience.
   c. The inability to engage in any substantial gainful activity by reason of disability expected to last at least 12 months or result in death.
   d. The inability to perform substantially all duties required of your prior occupation and inability is caused by disability expected to last 12 months or result in death.
   e. The inability to perform substantially all duties of any occupation for which you are reasonably suited by training, education, or experience and the disability is expected to last 12 months or result in death.

123. Philip began his professional corporation single practitioner CPA Firm 38 years ago at age 27. He worked profitably as a sole practitioner for the full 38 years and is now age 65. He retired December 31. On January 1st of this year he sold his practice for $400,000 to be received in 4 equal annual annuity due payments to be made on January 1st of each of the next four years beginning January 1st, this year.

   Is Philip eligible for social security retirement benefits during this year? Why or why not?
   a. Yes, he is eligible because he is 65, retired, and fully insured.
   b. No, he is retired and 65 but the proceeds from the sale of his practice will delay his receiving social security retirement benefits.
   c. No, he is not considered retired for social security purposes.
   d. Yes, he is entitled to benefits, but they will be reduced because of the payments from the sale of his practice.
   e. No, single practitioners of professional corporations are not covered by social security retirement benefits.

124. Under OASDHI (Social Security), immediate survivor income benefits based on a deceased worker's Primary Insurance Amount (PIA) and coverage are available to which of the following persons?

1. A surviving spouse age 55 or older caring for an under 16-year-old child.
2. Unmarried children under age 18 who are dependents.
3. Unmarried disabled children who became disabled before age 22.
4. Any surviving divorced spouse over 50, with no children who was married to decedent for over 10 years and who is disabled.

a. 1 only.
b. 2 only.
c. 1 and 2.
d. 1, 2, and 3.
e. 1, 2, 3, and 4.

125. Which of the following statements regarding a worker's insured status under Social Security is/are correct?

1. To achieve currently insured status under social security, a worker must have at least 6 quarters of coverage out of 13 calendar quarters prior to retirement, disability, or death.
2. To achieve fully insured status, a worker must have at least one quarter of coverage for each year after the attainment of age 22 until, but not including, age 62, disability or death.
3. Any worker with 40 covered quarters is fully insured forever.
4. To achieve a disability insured status, a worker must be fully insured.

a. 1 only.
b. 3 only.
c. 1 and 3.
d. 1, 3, and 4.
e. 1, 2, 3, and 4.

126. Under Social Security (OASDHI), which of the following benefits would be available to the survivors of a deceased but currently insured worker?

1. A $255 lump-sum death benefit which his generally payable to the insured's spouse.
2. A widow's or widower's income payable to a deceased worker's spouse at age 65 or at age 50 if the widowed spouse is disabled.
3. Mother's or father's income to a surviving spouse with a dependent child under the age of 16.
4. Monthly retirement income of 100% of the worker's primary insurance amount at the insured's normal retirement age.

a. 1 only.
b. 2 only.
c. 3 only.
d. 1 and 3.
e. 1, 2, 3, and 4.

127. Larry was married at the following ages and to the following wives. Larry is now 62 and married to Dawn.

	Wife	Current Age	Larry's Age at Marriage	Current Marital Status	Length of Marriage
1.	Alice	62	20	Single	10 years, 1 month
2.	Betty	63	31	Single	10 years, 1 month
3.	Claire	64	42	Single	9 years
4.	Dawn	65	53	Married	9 years

Who, among the wives, may be eligible to receive Social Security retirement benefits based upon Larry's earnings if Larry is retired or not retired?

	Retired	Not Retired
a.	1 and 2.	1, 2, and 4
b.	1, 2, and 4	1 and 2
c.	1, 2, and 3	1, 2, and 3
d.	1, 2, 3, and 4	1, 2, 3, and 4
e.	4 only.	No one.

128. Michael was divorced after 12 years of marriage. He had 2 dependent children ages 4 and 6 who are cared for by their mother. He was currently, but not fully, insured under Social Security at the time of his death. The benefits that his survivors are entitled to include:

1. A lump sum death benefit of $255.
2. A children's benefit equal to 75% of Michael's PIA.
3. A widow's benefit at age 60.
4. A parent's benefit for deceased workers parents who are over the age of 62.

a. 1 only.
b. 1 and 2.
c. 1, 2, and 3.
d. 2, 3, and 4.
e. 1, 2, 3 and 4.

129. In 1999, James earned $4,000 from employment subject to Social Security between January 1 and March 31. He was then unemployed for the remainder of the year. How many quarters of coverage does he earn for Social Security for 1998?

a. 0.
b. 1.
c. 2.
d. 3.
e. 4.

130. Charles, age 38, has just died. He has been credited with the last 30 consecutive quarters of social security coverage since he left school. He had never worked before leaving school. Which of the following persons are eligible to receive Social Security survivor benefits as a result of Charles' death?

1. Charles' child Bill, age 16.
2. Charles' child Dawn, age 18.
3. Charles' widow Margaret, age 38.
4. Charles' dependent mother Betty, age 60.

a. 1 only.
b. 1 and 2.
c. 1, 2, and 3.
d. 1, 3, and 4.
e. 2, 3, and 4.

GROUP INSURANCE

131. Vicki purchased an annuity for $26,000 in 1998. Under the contract, Vicki will receive $300 each month for the rest of her life. According to actuarial estimates, Vicki will live to receive 100 payments and will receive a 3% return on her original investment. Which of the following is correct?

a. If Vicki collects $3,000 in 1998, the $3,000 is treated as a recovery of capital basis and thus is not taxable.

b. If Vicki dies after collecting a total of 50 payments, she has an economic loss that is not deductible.

c. If Vicki lives to collect more than 100 payments, she must amend her prior years' returns to increase her taxable portion of each payment received in the past.

d. If Vicki lives to collect more than 100 payments, all amounts received after the 100th payment must be included in her gross income.

e. None of the above.

132. Robert retired on May 31, 1998 and receives a monthly pension benefit of $1,200 payable for life. His life expectancy at the date of retirement is 10 years. The first pension check was received on June 15, 1998. During his years of employment, Robert contributed $24,000 to the cost of his company's pension plan. How much of the pension amounts received may Robert exclude from taxable income for the years 1998, 1999, and 2000?

	1998	1999	2000
a.	$0	$0	$0
b.	$1,400	$2,400	$2,400
c.	$8,400	$8,400	$8,400
d.	$8,400	$14,400	$14,400
e.	$14,400	$14,400	$14,400

133. W is a 55-year-old woman who has begun receiving a retirement annuity over her life expectancy of 25.5 years. She is to receive $1,500 per month. Her contributions to the plan were post-tax and amounted to $91,800. Payments begin April 1, this year. How much of the pension income can she exclude from income tax this year?

a. $0.

b. $1,800.

c. $2,700.

d. $3,000.

e. $3,600.

134. W is a 55-year-old woman who has begun receiving a retirement annuity over her life expectancy of 25.5 years. She is to receive $1,500 per month. Her contributions to the plan were post-tax and amounted to $91,800. How much must W include in taxable income this year assuming payments began last year?

   a. $0.
   b. $3,600.
   c. $9,000.
   d. $12,000.
   e. $14,400.

135. W is a 55-year-old woman who has begun receiving a retirement annuity over her life expectancy of 25.5 years. She is to receive $1,500 per month. Her contributions to the plan were post-tax and amounted to $91,800. Assume the distribution began January 1, last year, and W dies October 15, this year, after receiving her October payment. Which of the following is/are correct?

   1. W can exclude $3,000 from this year's income.
   2. W must include $12,000 in this year's income.
   3. W's final income tax return receives a deduction for $85,200 as recovery of basis.

   a. 1 only.
   b. 2 only.
   c. 1 and 2.
   d. 1, 2, and 3.
   e. None of the above.

CAFETERIA PLAN

136. Under the Cheers, Inc. cafeteria plan, all full-time employees are allowed to select any combination of the benefits below, but the total received by the employee cannot exceed $8,000 a year.

1. Whole life insurance, $2,000.
2. Group medical and hospitalization insurance for the employee only, $4,000 a year.
3. Group medical and hospitalization insurance for employee's dependents, $2,000 a year.
4. Child-care payments, actual cost but not more than $2,400 a year if 1 child, or $4,800 if 2 or more children.
5. Cash required to bring the total of benefits and cash to $8,000.

Which of the following statements is true?

a. Becky a full-time employee, selects choices 2 and 3 and $2,000 cash. Her gross income must include the $2,000 cash.

b. Bob, a full-time employee, elects to receive $8,000 cash because his wife's employer provides benefits for him. Bob is not required to include the $8,000 in gross income.

c. Vicki, a full-time employee, elects to receive choices 1, 2, and 3. She is not required to include any of the above in gross income.

d. Don, a full-time employee, selects options 2 and 3 and $2,000 in child-care (IV). Don must include $2,000 in gross income.

e. None of the above.

OTHER EMPLOYEE FRINGE BENEFITS

137. Ruby, a widow, elected to receive the proceeds of a $100,000 face value insurance policy on the life of her deceased husband in ten annual installments of $11,900 each beginning last year. This year, she received $11,900, which included $1,900 interest. Ruby dies in December this year after collecting the annual income tax payment. What amount of the annuity received is subject to income tax on her final return?

    a. $0.
    b. $1,900.
    c. $5,000.
    d. $6,900.
    e. None of the above.

138. Thomas named his wife, Kim, the beneficiary of a $120,000 (face amount) insurance policy on his life. The policy provided that upon his death, the proceeds would be paid to Kim with interest over her remaining life expectancy, which was calculated at his death to be 20 years. Thomas died this year and Kim received a regular annual payment of $15,000 from the insurance company. What amount must Kim include in her gross income for this year?

    a. $0.
    b. $3,000.
    c. $6,000.
    d. $9,000.
    e. $15,000.

139. David Jones is covered by a $180,000 group-term life insurance policy of which his daughter is the beneficiary. Jones' employer pays the entire cost of the policy, for which the uniform annual premium is $8 per $1,000 of coverage. How much of this premium is taxable income to Jones?

    a. $0.
    b. $640.
    c. $1,040.
    d. $1,440.
    e. $12,480.

140. Roberto, an employee of Dusk Corporation, died December 25, this year. During December, Dusk Corp. made employee death payments of $10,000 to his widow, and $10,000 to his 16-year-old daughter. What amounts should be excluded from gross income by the widow and daughter in their respective tax returns for this year?

	Widow	**Daughter**
a.	$0	$0
b.	$2,500	$2,500
c.	$5,000	$5,000
d.	$7,500	$7,500
e.	$10,000	$10,000

141. James lives and is employed as a consultant in Boston. He frequently works late and his employer gives him $15.00 for his evening meal. Occasionally, he works so late that he believes it is not practical to return home after work. On those nights his employer pays for James' hotel room. Which of the following is correct?

a. Neither the value of the meals nor the hotel rooms affect James' gross income.
b. The value of the meals are taxable, but the rooms are not.
c. The value of the rooms are taxable, but the meals are not.
d. The value of the meals and rooms must both be included in James' gross income.
e. None of the above is correct.

142. Cresent Company allows a 10% discount to all non-officer employees. Officers are allowed a 30% discount on company products. Cresent's gross profit rate is 35%.

a. An officer who takes a 30% discount must include the extra 20% (30% - 10%) discount in gross income.
b. All discounts taken by employees are includible because the plan is discriminatory.
c. All discounts taken by officers are includible because the plan is discriminatory.
d. None of the discounts are includible in income because the discount in all cases is less than the company's gross profit percentage.
e. None of the above.

143. What is the number of employees covered by a health plan that a business can have and not be subject to the COBRA rules?

a. 19.
b. 24.
c. 49.
d. 74.
e. 99.

144. For a highly compensated employee, which of the following fringe benefits would be included in gross income if discriminatory?

1. No additional cost services.
2. Free parking.
3. Working condition fringes.
4. De minimus fringes.

a. 1 only.
b. 1 and 3.
c. 1, 2, and 3.
d. 1, 3, and 4.
e. 2, 3, and 4.

145. The rule excluding premiums from income to an employee, for health insurance premiums provided by an employer is applicable to:

1. The employee, if currently employed.
2. The employee's spouse.
3. The employee's dependents other than a spouse.
4. The employee, if retired.

a. 1 only.
b. 1 and 4.
c. 1 and 2.
d. 1, 2, and 3.
e. 1, 2, 3, and 4.

146. Meals are excludable from income if:

1. Provided by the employer.
2. On the employer's premises.
3. For the convenience of the employer.

a. 3 only.
b. 1 and 2.
c. 1 and 3.
d. 1, 2, and 3 must all be met.
e. Meals are not excludable from income except for 50%.

147. Jack, a busy CFP and author, has an assistant Pam. When Pam is not doing anything else (not regularly), Jack sends her to pick up his laundry, go to the bank, etc. This is an example of:

a. A non-cash benefit.
b. A de minimus fringe.
c. A no additional cost service.
d. An employee discount.
e. None of the above.

148. JoJo, a publisher, lets Penelope, his employee, use his business computer after business hours for her own personal use. Which of the following is correct?

a. The value of the computer and office can be excluded from income under a no additional cost benefit.
b. The value can be excluded as a working condition fringe.
c. As long as other employees have the same usage it is excludable.
d. The value of the computer is not excludable.
e. None of the above.

MISCELLANEOUS

149. In which one(s) of the following types of qualified plans is the investment risk generally borne by the employer?

   1. Target benefit plans.
   2. Money purchase plans.
   3. Defined benefit plans.
   4. Hybrid plans.

      a. 1 only.
      b. 2 only.
      c. 3 only.
      d. 1 and 3.
      e. 1, 2, 3, and 4.

150. Your client, ABC Corporation, is considering implementing some form of retirement plan. The client states its objectives for a plan to be, in the order of importance: **(CFP® Exam, released 3/95)**

   1. Rewarding long-term employees.
   2. Retention of employees.
   3. Providing a level of income at retirement equal to 50% of an employee's earnings.
   4. Tax-deductible funding.
   5. No risk to employees of benefits available.

   The company indicates it is willing to contribute an amount equal to 30% of payroll to such a plan. The company has been in business for 22 years, and during the past decade has consistently been profitable. They furnish you with an employee census. Based upon the stated objectives, you advise ABC Corporation that the most suitable retirement plan for the corporation would be a:

      a. Money purchase pension plan.
      b. Non-qualified deferred compensation plan for long-term employees.
      c. Combination of defined benefit and 401(k) plan.
      d. Defined benefit plan.
      e. Profit sharing plan.

STOCK OPTIONS

151. Bob is granted 10,000 stock options four years ago with an exercise price of $15.00 (the market price is $15.00). Two years ago he exercises the options when the market price is $22.00. In the current year, he sells the stock, which he received from exercising his options. Which of the following statements are true?

    1. If the options were ISOs, then Bob would have both ordinary income and capital gain in the year of the sale of the stock, however FICA and FUTA would not apply.
    2. Only a portion of original grant would qualify as ISOs.
    3. If the options were ISOs, Bob would have an AMT adjustment when he exercised the options and in the current year.

        a. 1 only.
        b. 2 only.
        c. 2 and 3.
        d. 1 and 2.
        e. 1, 2, and 3.

152. Which of the following can create a current tax liability upon exercise?

    1. Incentive Stock Options.
    2. Non-Qualified Stock Options.

        a. 1 only.
        b. 2 only.
        c. 1 and 2.
        d. None of the above.

PLAN TO MEET OBJECTIVES (PTMO)

153. The goal of the Company is to maximize retirement benefits to the highly compensated employees, who happen to be the oldest. Which of the following best accomplishes this goal assuming a new plan?

   a. Aged based profit sharing plan.
   b. A Tandem plan.
   c. A MPP Plan.
   d. A Target Benefit Plan.
   e. A Defined Benefit Plan.

154. Your client says she has a retirement plan with the following characteristics:

   1. Separate accounts.
   2. 40% of salary as projected benefit.

   What type of plan does she probably have?

   a. MPPP.
   b. DB.
   c. Target Benefit.
   d. Cash Balance.

155. Which of the following retirement plans can provide for deferral of taxable income for retirement?

   1. Non-deductible IRA account.
   2. Incentive Stock Options.
   3. SIMPLE plans.
   4. Deferred compensation plans.

   a. 1 only.
   b. 1 and 3.
   c. 2 and 3.
   d. 1, 3, and 4.
   e. 1, 2, 3, and 4.

156. Which of the following plans allows the Excess Method of Permitted Disparity?

1. Money purchase pension plans.
2. Defined benefit plans.
3. Employee stock ownership plan.
4. Simplified employee pension plan.

a. 1, 2, and 3.
b. 2, 3, and 4.
c. 1, 2, and 4.
d. 1, 3, and 4.
e. 1, 2, 3, and 4.

157. XYZ Inc. has 80 employees in the current year and is expected to employ the same number in next year. They are considering the adoption of a retirement plan next year. The objectives are to use salary reduction of employees, with an appropriate match and immediate vesting. Which of the following plans would be appropriate?

1. SARSEP.
2. 403(b).
3. SIMPLE Plan - 401(k).
4. SIMPLE Plan - IRA.

a. 1 only.
b. 1 and 3.
c. 2 and 3.
d. 3 and 4.
e. 1, 2, 3, and 4.

158. Qualified Plans that require the use of the three highest consecutive years for earning purposes of determining the maximum benefit that can be planned for include which of the following?

1. Money purchase pension plan.
2. Stock bonus plan.
3. Profit sharing plan.
4. Defined benefit plan.

a. 4 only.
b. 1 and 2.
c. 1, 2, and 4.
d. 1, 3, and 4.
e. All plans listed have the requirement.

CAPITAL NEEDS ANALYSIS

159. Harry and Wendy have $130,000 in a retirement account. They are 20 years away from retirement and they expect to be in retirement for 25 years. They estimate they can earn 9% on the retirement account before retirement and 7% after retirement. If they made no additional contributions to the account and they receive a fixed monthly benefit for life, what is the amount they will receive at the beginning of the first month of retirement?

    a. $4,869.10.
    b. $5,119.54.
    c. $5,149.40.
    d. $6,068.65.
    e. $6,114.16.

SIMPLE PLANS

160. Which of the following is/are not characteristics of a SIMPLE Plan?

1. Can be organized as an IRA or 401(k).
2. Must match 3% of employees deferrals.
3. Allows 5-year cliff vesting.
4. Allows employee deferrals up to $9,500.

   a. 4 only.
   b. 3 and 4.
   c. 2, 3, and 4.
   d. 1, 3, and 4.
   e. 1, 2, 3, and 4.

THIS PAGE IS INTENTIONALLY LEFT BLANK.

RETIREMENT PLANS, SOCIAL SECURITY AND EMPLOYEE BENEFITS SOLUTIONS

RETIREMENT PLANS, SOCIAL SECURITY, AND EMPLOYEE BENEFITS

1.	E	28.	D	55.	D	82.	E	109.	C	136.	A
2.	E	29.	C	56.	C	83.	C	110.	C	137.	B
3.	C	30.	C	57.	A	84.	B	111.	C	138.	D
4.	C	31.	C	58.	E	85.	E	112.	C	139.	C
5.	E	32.	D	59.	C	86.	B	113.	D	140.	A
6.	A	33.	D	60.	C	87.	E	114.	B	141.	C
7.	E	34.	E	61.	B	88.	D	115.	C	142.	C
8.	B	35.	B	62.	A	89.	D	116.	C	143.	A
9.	C	36.	E	63.	E	90.	A	117.	E	144.	A
10.	C	37.	C	64.	E	91.	E	118.	B	145.	E
11.	E	38.	A	65.	A	92.	D	119.	E	146.	D
12.	B	39.	B	66.	B	93.	E	120.	A	147.	B
13.	B	40.	A	67.	D	94.	D	121.	C	148.	B
14.	C	41.	B	68.	E	95.	B	122.	C	149.	C
15.	A	42.	A	69.	D	96.	C	123.	A	150.	D
16.	D	43.	B	70.	D	97.	E	124.	E	151.	C
17.	B	44.	D	71.	B	98.	E	125.	C	152.	C
18.	D	45.	A	72.	B	99.	E	126.	D	153.	E
19.	E	46.	A	73.	D	100.	E	127.	B	154.	C
20.	A	47.	B	74.	D	101.	A	128.	B	155.	E
21.	A	48.	E	75.	C	102.	C	129.	E	156.	C
22.	D	49.	B	76.	D	103.	B	130.	A	157.	D
23.	E	50.	E	77.	B	104.	E	131.	D	158.	A
24.	B	51.	D	78.	E	105.	A	132.	B	159.	B
25.	D	52.	D	79.	B	106.	D	133.	C	160.	C
26.	E	53.	A	80.	B	107.	D	134.	E		
27.	A	54.	C	81.	A	108.	A	135.	D		

QUALIFIED PLANS - REQUIREMENTS AND TAXATION

Vesting

1. E

The plan is top heavy due to the salary of Sanders. He has to choose between immediate vesting, 3-year cliff, and 2 - 6 year graded vesting. The 2 - 6 year graded would be better from the employer's perspective because of the possibility of termination and forfeitures.

Distribution Penalties

2. E

All of these exceptions are taken from the IRS regulations.

Participation Qualification

3. C

Participation requirements are (statement #1) age 21, and (statement #3) completion of 1 year of service. Statements #2 and #4 are incorrect. This is clearly not a top-heavy plan or the plan could not use 3 – 7 graded vesting.

Loans from Qualified Plans

4. C

After-tax employee contributions are not available for loans. Loans to 100% shareholders are non-permissible and are prohibited transactions. Statements #1 and #2 are correct.

Loans from Qualified Plans

5. E

All of the statements regarding loans are correct. If a participant has an account balance of between $10,000 and $20,000, he may borrow up to $10,000 even if the $10,000 exceeds 50% of the account balance.

Penalties

6. A

Statement #2 is incorrect because this is an exempt transaction. Statement #3 is also incorrect. There are no hardship rules related to IRA distributions. Statement #1 and #4 are correct.

Appropriate Plans

7. E

The plan will definitely be top heavy. Only immediate vesting, 3-year cliff, and 2 - 6 year graded vesting are appropriate. 2 - 6 year vesting is the best form of vesting from the perspective of the employer.

Coverage Requirements for Qualified Plans

8. B

Code Section 401 (9) (26) specifically states that a plan must cover 50 employees or 40% of all employees. (This requirement no longer applies to defined contribution plans after 1996.)

Permitted Disparity Rules

9. C

A defined contribution plan can satisfy the permitted disparity rules only if it uses an excess plan. Therefore, statement #4 is incorrect. Statements #1, #2, and #3 are correct. Defined contribution plans cannot use an offset plan because they have no benefit formula. Defined benefit plans can use either an offset or an excess plan for integration.

Highly Compensated

10. C

Statement #4 is not correct if the election maintained below was made.

Highly Compensated Rules After 1996:

- A 5% or greater than 5% owner (this year or the preceding year).
- Compensation > $80,000 last year.
- Compensation > $80,000 and in the top 20% if elected (preceding year).
- The $80,000 is indexed for inflation IRC Sections 414 (q) and 415 (d).

Qualified Join and Survivor Spouse Annuities

11. E

All qualified pension plans require joint and survivor annuities except some profit sharing plans.

Distributions

12. B

IRAs and SEPs are not subject to the 20% withholding rule. Statement #1 is correct because it is non-direct. Statement #2 is not subject to the withholding rules because the rollover is direct trustee to trustee.

Qualified Plans

13. B

Of those listed, only SEPs require immediate and full vesting. All of the other plans can use regular vesting schedules (5 year cliff, 3 – 7 graded).

Forfeitures

14. C

SEPs are 100% vested; therefore, there are no forfeitures. Defined benefit plan forfeitures must be used to reduce plan costs. Therefore, only the profit sharing and money purchase plans can use forfeitures to increase the account balances of remaining participants. Deferred compensation plans can choose either to allocate or to reduce plan costs.

Qualified Plan - Loans

15. A

Defined benefit plans, SEPs, and money purchase pension plans do not generally have loan provisions. Loan provisions are established in the plan document and are usually limited to plans like 401(k) and 403(b), which have employee pre-tax contributions. Some profit sharing plans also have loan provisions.

Creditor Protection

16. D

Only the profit sharing and money purchase plan assets are protected from creditors because they are qualified plans. IRAs and SEPs are not qualified plans and are not protected from creditors under federal law. There could be state law protection for IRAs and SEPs.

Social Security Integration

17. **B**

The only one that cannot use integration is ESOP.

Social Security Integration

18. **D**

ESOPs cannot be integrated with social security.

Qualified Plans - Joint and Survivor Annuity

19. **E**

All of the listed plans are required to meet pre-retirement and joint and survivor annuity rules.

Rollovers

20. **A**

Of those listed, only IRAs are not subject to 20% withholding. All qualified plans and 403(b)s require withholding. SEPs, while not listed, are not qualified plans and therefore do not require withholding.

Distributions - Favorable Tax Treatment

21. **A**

SEPs, IRAs, and TDAs 403(b)s are not eligible for special 5-year averaging.

Note: 5-year averaging is repealed for distributions after 1999.

Pre and Joint Survivor Annuities

22. **D**

All of the statements are correct. An effective waiver requires writing, witness by a notary or plan official, and is generally irrevocable.

Distributions

23. **E**

John must get a written spousal waiver to accept or elect a single life annuity. Statement #2 is correct. John cannot elect a single life annuity without a written spousal waiver. Therefore, Statements #1 and #3 are incorrect.

Pre-Retirement Joint Annuities

24. B

A SEP plan does not require a joint and survivor annuity option at pre-retirement because it is not a qualified plan. The 401(k) will usually not provide joint and survivor options because it is usually a profit sharing plan.

Use of Actuaries

25. D

Both target benefit and defined benefit plans use actuarial calculations. The difference is that defined benefit plans require annual actuarial calculations whereas the target benefit plan only requires the use of an actuary at the inception of the plan.

Qualified Plan Coverage and Eligibility

26. E

All require the same eligibility and have the same coverage requirements because they are all qualified plans. These plans can allow coverage after 2 years of service if 100% vested.

Qualified Plan Coverage

27. A

Ratio % test is 70%. It is calculated as follows:

Non-highly compensated	125 ÷ 180 = .6944
Highly compensated	16 ÷ 20 = .80
	.6944 ÷ .80 = 86.80%

Therefore, the plan meets the ratio % test of 70%.

Qualified Plan Coverage Ratio % Test

28. D

The ratio % test is 86.8%. (.6944 ÷ .80 = .868).

Qualified Plan Coverage Average Benefit % Test

29. **C**

The average benefits % test is in percentage terms, not dollars, and must be greater than or equal to 70%. This plan would fail this particular test.

A is incorrect. \$9,000 x 16 = \$144,000
\$3,000 x 125 = \$375,000
\$375,000 ÷ \$144,000 = 26%

B is incorrect. \$3,000 ÷ 9,000 = 33.3%

C is correct. 3% ÷ 8% = 37.5%

D is incorrect.

Highly Compensated Employees

30. **C**

James is not in the top 20% but does make > \$80,000. For 1997, the answer would be Statements #1, #2 and #3 because the company did not make the election to limit to top 20%. Donna is not highly compensated because her salary did not exceed \$80,000 last year. All of the others are highly compensated because (statement #1) Steve is a 6% owner (greater than 5% rule); (statement #2) Mike's salary is greater than \$80,000; and (statement #3) James' salary was greater than \$80,000 last year.

ERISA

31. **C**

Statements #2 and #3 are correct. Statement #1 is incorrect because ERISA does not set any investment criteria. Statement #4 is incorrect because the PBGC provides insurance for defined benefit plans not defined contribution plans.

Plan Distribution

32. **D**

A qualified domestic relations order (QDRO).

ERISA

33. **D**

Statement #1 is incorrect. The threshold is 50% ownership. Statement #2 is incorrect. An employee participant is not a party in interest without additional criteria. Statements #3 and #4 refer to parties in interest.

Qualified Plan Requirements

34. **E**

All are requirements of a qualified plan.

Hardship Distributions

35. **B**

Only statement #3 is correct; all of the other statements are incorrect.

Vesting (CFP® Exam, released 3/95)

36. **E**

This is a top-heavy plan as evidenced by the salary of Jack in comparison to other employees. The choices for vesting in a top-heavy plan are (a) immediate, (b) 3-year cliff, or (c) 2 - 6 graded. Due to the average length of employment, the most suitable vesting schedule from Jack's point of view (cash flow if termination occurs and forfeiture) is graded vesting. B and C would be unavailable to Jack due to top heaviness.

Retirement

37. **C**

Distribution before age 59½

$200,000	
x 10%	penalty
$ 20,000	

The 15% excess distributions tax was repealed for all distributions received after December 31, 1996.

Total Penalty = $20,000

Retirement - ADP Test

38. **A**

The ADP Test only applies to the 401(k) plan because the 401(k) plan is the only one to have employee deferrals.

Retirement - Needs Analysis

39. B

PMT_{AD}	=	\$3,000 (5,000 - 2,000)
i	=	.5833 (7 ÷ 12)
N	=	300 (25 x 12)
PV_{AD}	=	\$ 426,936.73
FV	=	\$426,936.73
i	=	.666 (8 ÷ 12)
N	=	156 (13 x 12)
PV	=	\$0
PMT_{OA}	=	\$1,564.33

Retirement

40. A

1998 Minimum Distribution	
Balance at 12/31/97	\$250,000
Life expectancy at 12/31/98	19.5 (age 71)
1998 Minimum distribution	\$12,820.51

Note: Distribution can be deferred up until 4/1/99.

1999 Minimum Distribution	1999 Distribution after 12/31/98 on or before 4/1/99	
Balance at 12/31/98	\$287,179.49*	
Life expectancy (no recalculation)	18.5 (19.5 - 1)	
1999 minimum distribution	\$15,523.22 (12/31/99)	
* (300,000 - 12,820.51)	Total for 1999=\$28,343.73	(\$12,820.51 + \$15,523.22)

Statement 1: True. See above.

Statement 2: False. See above. (These are calculated using life expectancy at 20, not 19.5.)

Statement 3: False. No penalty will be levied for 1998 because the 1998 minimum distribution is not required to be taken until April 1, 1999.

Tax

41. **B**

He could possibly be subjected to each of the first two penalties. The last two penalties (statements #3 and #4) have been repealed.

Retirement

42. **A**

Statements #2 and #3 are incorrect.

Retirement

43. **B**

50/40 Rule-50 employees or 40% of the workforce.

Retirement

44. **D**

The plan is top heavy therefore must use 2-6 graduated vesting. She has vested interest in 60% of employer's contribution and earnings and 100% of her own.

Retirement

45. **A**

Both the excess distributions excise tax and the excess accumulation excise taxes are repealed for distribution made after decedents dying after December 31, 1996. Statement #1 is correct. Statement #4 only applies to distributions from qualified plans.

Retirement

46. **A**

Going back to the previous year, then any greater than 5% owner or a person who makes more than $80,000, therefore #1,#2, and #3.

Retirement

47. B

Only defined benefit plans are subject to the 50/40 test after December 31, 1996. A cash balance plan is a defined benefit plan.

FIDUCIARIES AND THEIR OBLIGATIONS

Fiduciaries

48. E

All of those listed are fiduciaries.

Fiduciaries

49. B

Statements #1 and #3 are correct. Statement #2 is incorrect. Statement #1 is an obligation, and statement #2 is a prohibited transaction.

Fiduciaries

50. E

All of those listed are parties in interest. The rule for statement #3 is 50% or more.

Retirement

51. D

Investment options that cover the entire investment spectrum are appropriate. The participant chose the option and will benefit or suffer accordingly.

DEFINED BENEFIT PENSION PLANS

Defined Benefit Plans

52. **D**

The only incorrect answer is statement #1. Defined benefit plans have mandatory contribution formulas, require an actuary, and require PBGC insurance. Additionally, these plans tend to favor older participants.

Defined Benefit Plans

53. **A**

Statement #1 is incorrect; defined benefit plans have nothing to do with profitability. Statement #2 is incorrect, because all integration levels are the same. Statement #3 is incorrect, because a unit credit method favors workers with longevity.

Defined Benefit Plans

54. **C**

Defined benefit plan contributions decrease due to statements #1 and #3 only. Statements #2 and #4 are incorrect. Inflation would likely cause salaries to increase thereby causing contributions to increase. Likewise, statement #4 would cause increases.

Defined Benefit Plans

55. **D**

Defined benefit plan contributions would increase due to statements #1, #2, and #3. Statements #4 is as expected. The issue is expectations in the assumptions.

Joint and Survivor Annuities

56. **C**

SEPs and profit sharing plans do not have to provide for pre- or retirement joint and survivor annuities. Profit sharing plans pay non-forfeitable balances to surviving spouses as an alternative provision to pre and post joint and survivor annuities.

PBGC Insurance

57. A

Money purchase, profit sharing plans, and target benefit plans do not require PBGC insurance. Defined benefit plans require PBGC insurance.

Plan Distribution

58. E

All of the items listed are utilized in the calculation of the contributions by the actuary for an employer with a defined benefit plan.

Appropriate Plan

59. C

Statements #2 and #4 are incorrect. Target benefit plans favor older employees. SEPs favor younger employees as do all non-age weighted defined contribution plans.

Actuarial Method

60. C

Statement #1 is incorrect because a unit benefit formula must be used with the accrued benefit cost method. You cannot use the accrued benefit cost method with a flat benefit formula. Statement #4 is incorrect, because costs are determined by projecting benefits to retirement.

Defined Benefit Plans (CFP® Exam, released 3/95)

61. B

Defined benefit plans require mandatory contributions. A, C, D, and E are correct statement regarding DB plans.

Actuarial Assumptions (CFP® Exam, released 3/95)

62. A

Actuarial assumptions used in a defined benefit plan do not include the ratio of single to married participants because it is irrelevant in the determination of contributions. The ratio is relevant to distribution options and survivor options. Statements #1, #2, and #3 are correct; therefore, A is the correct answer.

Retirement

63. E

Each assumption (statements 1#, #2, and #3) would increase the plan costs to an employer with a defined benefit plan.

Retirement - Defined Benefit Funding Assumptions

64. E

All of these will impact funding one direction or the other depending on whether they are positive or negative to expectations. Inflation ultimately affects labor, administrative, and actuarial costs. The others should be obvious.

DEFINED CONTRIBUTION PLANS

Profit Sharing Plans

65. A

Statements #2, #3, and #4 are incorrect. Neither profits nor retained earnings are required to make a contribution to a profit sharing plan. Profit sharing plans are most suitable for companies with unstable earnings due to the discretion over contributions. An age-weighted profit-sharing plan allows up to 25% of compensation for any one participant but is limited to 15% of overall covered compensation

Defined Contribution Plans

66. B

Factors affecting retirement benefits from a defined contribution plan are the investments selected by the participant (statement #3) and the account balance (statement #4). Statements #1 and #2 are related to defined benefit plans, not defined contribution plans.

Qualified Plans

67. D

Statement #4 is not subject to FICA and FUTA taxes. All others are subject to FICA and FUTA taxes. No new SARSEPS after 1996. All employee contributions to all plans are subject to FICA and FUTA except a flexible spending account. Alternatively, no employer contributions are subject to FICA or FUTA.

Social Security Integration

68. E

All of the plans listed may be integrated with social security.

In Service Withdrawals

69. D

Money purchase plans do not allow in-service withdrawals. All of the others listed allow for in-service withdrawals if the plan document permits. No pension plans (DB/Cash Balance/Target Benefit MP or Money Purchase) allow in-service withdrawals.

Qualified Plans - Investments

70. **D**

Money purchase plans allow only 10% contributions in stock (restricted). All of the other plans may invest 100% in company stock.

Qualified Plans - Investments

71. **B**

Only profit sharing plans allow unrestricted investments in company sponsored securities.

Appropriate Plan

72. **B**

Profit sharing plan is correct.

ESOP - cannot be integrated with social security.

Money purchase plans - cannot invest unrestricted in company stock.

Profit sharing plans - employees cannot vote stock.

In-Service Withdrawals

73. **D**

Money purchase plans do not allow in service withdrawals. All of the others allow them if the plan document permits, but may subject the participant to penalties (early withdrawal).

Money Purchase Plans

74. **D**

Money purchase plans require mandatory funding from the % selected 1 - 25%. Investment earnings and losses do not affect employer contributions. Most pension plans are subject to minimum funding standards.

Profit Sharing (CFP® Exam, released 3/95)

75. **C**

Profit sharing plans do not require that to make a contribution in a given year the company need to have made a profit that year. A, B, D, and E are all characteristics of profit sharing plan. Most pension plans are subject to minimum funding standards.

Money Purchase Plans (CFP® Exam, released 3/95)

76. **D**

This is a multi-plan question of a relatively high level of sophistication. Statement #1 is obviously incorrect; statement #2 is incorrect because defined contribution plans do not consider earnings on investments when calculating contributions.

CODA (CFP® Exam, released 3/95)

77. **B**

Statement #3 is correct. Statement #1 is also correct. Election deferral is both subject to FICA and non-forfeitable.

Profit Sharing Plans (CFP® Exam, released 3/95)

78. **E**

Statements #1, #2, and #3 are all incorrect regarding profit-sharing plans. Statement #4 is correct. This is a very easy question once you establish that #1 is incorrect.

Defined Contribution Plans

79. **B**

Factors affecting retirement benefits from a defined contribution plan are statements #3 and #4. Statements #1 and #2 are related to defined benefit plans not defined contribution plans.

HYBRID PLANS

Target Benefit Plans

80. B

Only statement #4 is correct in a target benefit plan. Benefits (statement #1) depend on the account balances. Forfeitures are likely to be unequal due to unequal compensation and contributions are not available for in-service withdrawals.

Target Benefit Plans

81. A

Lamonte will not know what benefit to expect (statement #1). Benefits depend on investment returns. Statements #2, #3, and #4 are incorrect statements not disadvantages.

Appropriate Plans

82. E

Irregular cash flow suggests a profit sharing plan. All of the other plans listed have some mandatory contribution component.

Target Benefit Plans (CFP® Exam, released 3/95)

83. C

Characteristics of a target benefit plan do not include a maximum contribution of 25% of payroll but rather 25% of a participant's compensation up to $30,000 indexed.

HR 10 (KEOGH) PLAN

Pension Plans for Self-Employed

84. B

Self-employed maximum = 25% of net pension income.

After pension contribution and 1/2 social security taxes:

$20,000	Sch. C Net Income
(1,530)	1/2 S.S. ($3,060)
$18,470	
(3,694)	20% (pension maximum to $30,000)
$14,776	

$3,694 ÷ 14,776 = 25%

(Net Income - 1/2 S.S.) = 125% of net income after 1/2 S.S. and pension.

$18,470 ÷ 125% = 14,776 x 25% = $3,694 which happens in all cases to be 20% of pre-pension income.

This only applies to self-employed persons and not to their employees.

SIMPLIFIED EMPLOYEE PENSION (SEP)

SEPs - IRAs

85. **E**

SEPs and IRA do not qualify for forward averaging. Statements #1, #2, and #3 are correct.

SEPs

86. **B**

Statement #2 is the only correct response. Statements #1, #3, and #4 are incorrect. Employer contributions to a SEP are not subject to FICA and FUTA. $10,000 is the 403(b) limit. The SEP limit is 15% of covered compensation up to $30,000.

SEPs

87. **E**

All are true.

Note: SEPs use excess (not offset) integration.

Vesting

88. **D**

Statements #1, #2, and #3 require immediate vesting. A 401(k) plan does not require immediate vesting for employer contributions.

INDIVIDUAL RETIREMENT ACCOUNT (IRA)

IRAs

89. **D**

She is not currently covered by a qualified pension plan, and therefore, can contribute her earned income up to $2,000 to a deductible IRA.

IRAs Penalties

90. **A**

Only statements #1 and #2 are correct. The penalties associated with statements #3 and #4 have been repealed.

IRAs Eligibility

91. **E**

All of these persons can take a deductible IRA, although Jane can only make a partial contribution to a deductible IRA until the year 2003 when the phaseout starts at $40,000 for single people.

IRAs

92. **D**

Collectibles (art) are prohibited as an investment for an IRA under Section 408(m). Such investments will result in penalties by treating them as a distribution. Statements #4 is the exception to collectibles and is permitted as an investment, as are statement #1 and #2, which are stock funds.

IRAs - Qualified Plans Distributions

93. **E**

All of the choices are correct (statements #1-4).

IRAs - Qualified Plans

94. **D**

Statements #1 is incorrect. The option is to pay within 5 years or the life expectancy of the heir. All other options statement #2-4 are correct.

IRA Distributions

95. **B**

Only statement #2 is correct. His new employer's qualified plan may or may not allow him to roll previous distributions into it. His IRA rollover should only have had qualified plan distribution and earnings in it.

IRAs

96. **C**

One spouse is an active participant and the joint AGI is less than the limit for deductibility by the spouse who is not an active participant (phase-out of AGI from $150,000 to $160,000); up to $4,000 could be contributed. Donna's deduction is $2,000. She can use James' earned income as her own. The $250 for James is not deductible.

IRAs

97. **E**

$2,000 IRA plus $2,000 spousal IRA. Not covered by a pension plan. The rules on spousal IRAs changed to $4,000 for 1997 and after.

IRAs

98. **E**

Maximum IRA is $2,000. Alimony counts as earned income for IRA purposes. Not covered by pension plan.

IRAs

99. **E**

They can contribute $4,000 ($2,000 + $2,000).

IRAs (CFP® Exam, released 3/95)

100. **E**

The question asks about deductible IRA contributions. He is single, not covered by a pension plan and therefore can contribute his earned income up to $2,000 to a deductible IRA without regard to his income. There is no phase-out.

Retirement- IRA Accounts

101. A

Only gold and silver coins minted by the U.S. can be held as an investment in an IRA.

Retirement

102. C

Only Eagles are coined by the U.S. Treasury.

Retirement

103. B

Statement #1 is not true, she can take the distribution over her husbands table life expectancy.

Retirement

104. E

Apparently neither John nor Mary is an active participant in an employer retirement plan, qualified retirement plan, SEP, governmental plan, or Section 403(b) plan; therefore, they can take $4,000 in a deductible IRA for the current year.

Roth IRA Distributions

105. A

According to Prop. Reg. 1.408A-6, any amount distributed from an individual's Roth IRA is treated as made in the following order (determined as of the end of a taxable year and exhausting each category before moving to the following category):

1. From regular contributions;
2. From conversion contributions, on a first-in-first-out basis; and
3. From earnings.

All distributions from all an individual's Roth IRAs made during one taxable year are aggregated.

Roth IRA Distributions

106. D

According to Prop. Reg. 1.408A-6, a distribution from a Roth IRA is not includible in the owner's gross income if it is a qualified distribution or to the extent that it is a return of the owner's contributions to the Roth IRA. A qualified distribution is one that is:

1. Made after a 5 taxable year period; and
2. Made on or after the date on which the owner attains age 59 ½, made to a beneficiary or the estate of the owner on or after the date of the owner's death, and attributable to the owner's being disabled or for a first-time home purchase.

According to Prop. Reg. 1.408A-6, the 10 percent additional tax under IRC Section 72(t) applies to any distribution from a Roth IRA includible in gross income. The 10 percent additional tax under IRC Section 72(t) also applies to a nonqualified distribution, even if it is not then includible in gross income, to the extent it is allocable to a conversion contribution, if the distribution is made within the 5 taxable year period beginning with the first day of the individual's taxable year in which the conversion contribution was made.

Roth IRA Conversions

107. D

According to Prop. Reg. 1.408A-4, an amount can be converted by any of three methods:

1. An amount distributed from a traditional IRA can be rolled over to a Roth IRA within 60 days after the distribution.
2. An amount in a traditional IRA can be transferred in a trustee-to-trustee transfer from the trustee of the traditional IRA to the trustee of the Roth IRA.
3. An amount in a traditional IRA can be transferred to a Roth IRA maintained by the same trustee.

Amounts in a qualified plan or annuity plan described in IRC Section 401(a) or 403(a) cannot be converted directly to a Roth IRA. Rather, they must first be transferred to a traditional IRA and then converted to a Roth IRA.

Roth IRA Distributions

108. A

According to Prop. Reg. 1.408A-6, any amount distributed from an individual's Roth IRA is treated as made in the following order (determined as of the end of a taxable year and exhausting each category before moving to the following category):

1. From regular contributions;
2. From conversion contributions, on a first-in-first-out basis; and
3. From earnings.

All distributions from all an individual's Roth IRAs made during a taxable year are aggregated.

According to Prop. Reg. 1.408A-6, the 10 percent additional tax under IRC Section 72(t) applies to any distribution from a Roth IRA includible in gross income. The 10 percent additional tax under IRC Section 72(t) also applies to a nonqualified distribution, even if it is not then includible in gross income, to the extent it is allocable to a conversion contribution, if the distribution is made within the 5 taxable year period beginning with the first day of the individual's taxable year in which the conversion contribution was made.

Although the distribution is not a qualified distribution, it will not be taxable because it will be deemed to come from regular contributions first. Thus, the basis in the distribution will equal the amount of the distribution. Since the $2,000 is not includible in gross income, nor does it relate to a conversion within the last five years, it will not be subject to the 10% penalty.

Roth IRA Contributions

109. C

The maximum contribution to traditional and Roth IRAs is $2,000 per year per person. Therefore, Jim and Jan would have a total of $4,000 to allocate between traditional and Roth IRAs. The Education IRA is not included in the $2,000 limit.

Roth IRA Contributions

110. C

The maximum contribution to traditional and Roth IRAs is a total of $2,000 per year per person. They have contributed the maximum amount to their Roth IRAs for the year since their income is between the phase-out limits of $150,000 and $160,000. However, they can still contribute $2,000 ($1,000 each) to a traditional IRA for 1998.

Roth IRA Distributions

111. C

A qualified distribution can only occur after a five-year period has occurred and is made on or after the date on which the owner attains age 59 ½, made to a beneficiary or the estate of the owner on or after the date of the owner's death, and attributable to the owner's being disabled or for a first-time home purchase. The five-year period begins at the beginning of the taxable year of the initial contribution to a Roth IRA. The five-year period ends on the last day of the individual's fifth consecutive taxable year beginning with the taxable year described in the preceding sentence. Therefore, the first year in which a qualified distribution **could** occur is 2003.

Roth IRA Contributions

112. C

Contributions to Roth IRAs, as well as traditional IRAs, are limited to the lesser of earned income or $2,000. Sally has earned income of $1,000 from the alimony she received. Thus, she is limited to a contribution of $1,000. The other $30,000 of income is not earned income and, therefore, is unavailable for contributions to any IRA.

TAX DEFERRED ANNUITY - 403(b) PLANS

TSAs

113. D

Statement #1 is incorrect. The catch up provision requires specified service and the correct kind of employer. Statements #2, #3, and #4 are correct.

TSAs

114. B

Statements #1 and #4 are correct. 403(b) plans (TSA) limit is $10,000. 457 plan limit is $8,000; therefore, statement #2 is incorrect. There is no forward averaging (statement #3 is incorrect).

TSA (TDA)

115. C

1998	$10,000
1999	$10,000
2000	$10,500 estimated

TSA (TDA)

116. C

TSA (TDA) funds are limited to annuity contracts (statement #1) and mutual funds (statement #2). Statements #3 and #4 are not permitted.

TSA (TDA)

117. E

All of the features described are common to TDA (403b) plans.

TSA (TDA)

118. B

Statements #1 and #3 are correct.

Statement #2 is incorrect as is statement #4 (only annuities and mutual funds are permitted investments). Special 5 and 10 year averaging is not available to TSAs.

TSA (CFP® Exam, released 3/95)

119. E

The question is which statement is incorrect. E is incorrect because it says all employees of 501(c)(3) organizations. Make up provisions are limited to educational institutions, hospitals, home health services, health and welfare service agencies, and churches, not all 501(c)(3) organizations (e.g., Boy Scouts).

Retirement

120. A

Of the answers only A is correct.

NON-QUALIFIED DEFERRED COMPENSATION

Deferred Compensation

121. C

This fails as a deferred compensation plan; therefore, statements #1 and #3 are correct. Because the trust is not subject to the general creditors of the employer, this is straight compensation. Nick must treat the payments as constructively received and the employer may deduct the payments as compensation.

SOCIAL SECURITY BENEFITS (OASDHI)

OASDHI Disability

122. C

Disability is defined for social security as the inability to perform any gainful activity and the disability is expected to last at least 12 months or result in death.

Social Security

123. A

Proceeds of sale are not considered earned income for social security retirement benefits. He is 65 and retired and therefore eligible for social security. Some of his benefits may be included in taxable income as a result of the ordinary income and capital gains associated with the installment sale (i.e., MAGI will go up).

Social Security

124. E

All are eligible including statement #4 who is disabled.

Social Security

125. C

Currently insured is 6 of the most recent 13 quarters prior to death, disability, or retirement. Fully insured is 40 quarters or ten years. To be eligible for disability benefits, a worker needs to be disability insured but not fully insured. Statement #2 is incorrect as is statement #4.

Social Security

126. D

Only statements #1 and #3 are correct for a person who is currently insured.
Statements #2 and #4 require fully insured status.

Retirement

127. B

Any divorced spouse age 62, and married to Larry for 10 years, and his current wife if he is retired. His current spouse cannot collect if he is not retired.

Death Benefits

128. B

A lump sum death benefit of $255 is payable to the surviving spouse or children of the deceased worker if he was fully or currently insured. The children's benefit of 75% of PIA is payable because Michael was either currently or fully insured. The mother of the children would be entitled to a benefit if Michael was fully insured. The parents are not entitled because Michael is not fully insured.

Coverage

129. E

For 1999, a worker receives 1-quarter credit for each $740 in annual earnings on which Social Security taxes are withheld up to a maximum of 4 quarters. It is irrelevant that he earned the $4,000 all in the first quarter.

Benefits Eligibility

130. A

Dawn (statement #2) is too old; Margaret (statement #3) does not have a child under 16; and Betty (statement #4) is not eligible due to Charles being currently but not fully insured. Thus, only Bill (statement #1) is eligible.

GROUP INSURANCE

Annuities

131. **D**

The options other than D are contrary to the scheme provided in the Code for the taxation of annuities. If Vicki lives after collecting only 50 payments, before she has recovered all of her capital, a loss can be claimed on her final return. Therefore, A, B, C, and E are incorrect.

Annuities

132. **B**

$24,000 ÷ 144,000 = .1666 or 1/6 exclusion ratio or fraction x 1,200 = $200.

Therefore, 120 ÷ 144 = .8333 or 5/6 inclusion ratio x 1,200 = $1,000.

In 1998, June to December = 7 months x 200(exclusion) = $1,400.

Note: B is the only possible correct answer for 1998.

1999 (12 parts x 1,200) x 1/6 = $2,400.

2000 (12 parts x 1,200) x 1/6 = $2,400.

Annuity Distributions

133. **C**

Exclusion ratio is $91,800 ÷ (1,500 x 12 x 25.5) = 20%.

20% x 1,500 x 9 months = $2,700.

Annuity Distributions

134. **E**

Inclusion ratio is 80%.

$367,200 ÷ 459,000 = 80% x 18,000 = $14,400.

Annuity Distributions

135. **D**

All of the statements are correct.

$1,500 x 10 months x .20 exclusion ratio = $3,000 exclusion.

$1,000 x 10 months x .80 inclusion ratio = $12,000 inclusion.

W's estate is entitled to deduct her remaining basis on the estate income tax return.

$91,800 - (22 mo. X $300) = $85,200.

CAFETERIA PLANS

Employee Benefits

136. A

C is incorrect because the whole life insurance premiums of $2,000 cannot be excluded. A is correct, cash must be included in income. D is incorrect, as childcare payments are excludible benefits.

OTHER EMPLOYEE FRINGE BENEFITS

Insurance Proceeds

137. B

($11,900 - 100,000) ÷ 10 = $1,900.

Note: Because it is life insurance proceeds there is no recapture of basis. Inclusion/Exclusion Ratio applies.

Life Insurance

138. D

Expected proceeds over life = $15,000 x 20 years = $300,000.

Inclusion ratio = (Proceeds - Basis)/Expected: ($300,000 - 120,000) ÷ 300,000 = 60%.

Exclusion ratio = Basis/Expected Proceeds: $120,000 ÷ 300,000 = 40%.

Payment $15,000 x 60% for inclusion = $9,000. (Inclusion)

$15,000 x 40% for exclusion = $6,000. (Exclusion)

Group Term Life Insurance

139. C

$50,000 of group term is non-taxable.

$180,000 - 50,000 = 130,000 x $8/thousand = $1,040 taxable.

Employee Benefits

140. A

After 1996, the answer is A. $5,000 of death proceeds are no longer excludable due to the Small Business Act of 1996 (after the date of enactment - August 8, 1996).

Employee Benefits

141. C

The cost of the meals is de minimus. The room is income. His belief is not relevant. He is not required to stay in the hotel and he is not out of town overnight. The employer's payment for the hotel is disguised compensation.

Employee Benefits

142. **C**

The plan is discriminatory; therefore, all discounts actually taken by officers must be included in income.

Employee Benefits - COBRA Coverage

143. **A**

A company having less than 20 (e.g., 19) employees is not subject to COBRA.

Fringe Benefits

144. **A**

Statements #2, #3, and #4 may be provided on a discriminatory basis.

Fringe Benefits

145. **E**

All premiums (statements #1-4) are excludable.

Fringe Benefits

146. **D**

Must be provided on the premises of and for the convenience of the employer.

Fringe Benefits

147. **B**

A de minimus fringe and it can be discriminatory.

Fringe Benefits

148. **B**

A is incorrect; Jack is not selling computer services. Working condition fringes can be discriminatory.

MISCELLANEOUS

Investment Risk

149. C

Only in defined benefit plans is the investment risk borne by the employer.

Appropriate Plans (CFP® Exam, released 3/95)

150. D

Statement #5 alone answers the question. "No risk to employees of benefits available" is the definition of a defined benefit plan. Rewarding long time employees explains why it is not answer C - Defined benefit plan plus 401(k).

STOCK OPTIONS

Tax

151. C

Statement #1 is false because in the year of sale, Bob would only have capital gain income. Statements #2 and #3 are true.

Tax

152. C

Both ISOs and NQSOs may create a current tax liability. The exercise of NQSOs creates additional W-2 income. Although the exercise of ISOs does not create a regular tax liability, it does create an AMT adjustment. This adjustment, if large enough, may create AMT.

PLAN TO MEET OBJECTIVE (PTMO)

Retirement

153. E

The DB plan is the best for old employees in a new plan.

Retirement

154. C

Probably a target benefit plan due to the individual account (DC) and projected benefit.

Retirement

155. E

Each of the items will provide deferral but in different ways.

Retirement

156. C

All plans are allowed to integrate with social security except ESOPs and SARSEPs. The excess method is allowed for all plans allowing integration, while the offset method is only allowed for defined benefit plans.

Retirement

157. D

There can be no new SARSEPs after 1/1/97. 403(b)s are for 501 (c)(3) organizations and there is no indication that this is a 501(c)(3). Statement #3 and #4 are ok.

Retirement

158. A

Only the Defined Benefit plan requires the use of the 3 highest consecutive years of earning to drive the maximum benefit.

CAPITAL NEEDS ANALYSIS

Retirement

159. **B**

PV	=	\$130,000
i	=	9
N	=	20
FV	=	\$728,573.40
PV	=	\$728,573.40
i	=	.58333 (7 ÷ 12)
N	=	30 (25 x 12)
PMT_{AD}	=	\$5,119.54

SIMPLE PLANS

Retirement

160. C

The only correct answer is statement #1. Statement #2 is wrong because it says "must".

THIS PAGE IS INTENTIONALLY LEFT BLANK.

ESTATE PLANNING PROBLEMS

ESTATE PLANNING

BASIC CONCEPTS

1. Which of the following would be included in a broad definition of estate planning?
   1. Wealth accumulation.
   2. Management of assets.
   3. Conservation of assets.
   4. Transfer of assets.
      a. 2 only.
      b. 3 only.
      c. 2 and 4.
      d. 2, 3, and 4.
      e. 1, 2, 3, and 4.

2. Which of the following persons need estate planning?
   1. John, who has a wife and one small child, and a net worth of $250,000.
   2. Dean, married with ten children, five grandchildren, and a net worth of $5,000,000.
   3. Marge, divorced, whose only son is severely challenged intellectually.
   4. Cynthia, who is single, has a net worth of $100,000, and has two dogs that are like her children.
      a. 2 only.
      b. 3 only.
      c. 2 and 3.
      d. 1, 2, and 3.
      e. 1, 2, 3, and 4.

3. What is the proper order for the process of estate planning?
   1. Establish priorities for estate objectives.
   2. Prepare a written plan.
   3. Define problem areas including liquidity, taxes, etc.
   4. Gather client information and establish objectives.
      a. 1, 2, 3, 4.
      b. 2, 1, 3, 4.
      c. 4, 3, 1, 2.
      d. 3, 2, 1, 4.
      e. 4, 1, 3, 2.

BASIC DOCUMENTS INCLUDED IN AN ESTATE PLAN

4. Making arrangements to deal with possible physical or mental incapacity is a rapidly developing area of estate planning. Which of the following arrangements is/are plausible when dealing with unanticipated incapacity?
   1. Springing durable powers of attorney.
   2. Revocable living trusts.
   3. Joint tenancies.
   4. Living wills.
      a. 1 only.
      b. 2 and 4.
      c. 2, 3, and 4.
      d. 1, 2, 3, and 4.
      e. None of the above.

5. Which of the following is/are considered potential problems of an estate plan?
   1. Ancillary probate.
   2. The rule against perpetuities.
   3. A will which includes funeral instructions.
   4. A will which attempts to disinherit a spouse and/or a minor child.
      a. 1 only.
      b. 3 only.
      c. 1 and 3.
      d. 1, 3, and 4.
      e. 1, 2, 3, and 4.

6. Which of the following is/are common provisions in a well drafted will?
   1. Establishment of the domicile of testator.
   2. An appointment and powers clause.
   3. A survivorship clause.
   4. A residuary clause.
      a. 1 only.
      b. 3 only.
      c. 1 and 3.
      d. 1, 2, and 3.
      e. 1, 2, 3, and 4.

7. Which of the following statements is/are correct?
   1. A durable power of attorney for health care is always a direct substitute for a living will.
   2. A living will only covers a narrow range of situations.
   3. A living will must generally meet the requirements of a formally drafted state statute.
   4. Many well-intentioned living wills have failed due to vagueness and/or ambiguities.
      a. 3 only.
      b. 2 and 3.
      c. 1, 2, and 3.
      d. 2, 3, and 4.
      e. 1, 2, 3, and 4.

8. Which of the following statements is/are correct regarding durable powers of attorney?
   1. The power survives disability.
   2. The power survives the death of the principal.
   3. The power may be springing.
   4. A principal must be 18 and competent.
      a. 4 only.
      b. 1 only.
      c. 1 and 4.
      d. 1, 3, and 4.
      e. 1, 2, 3, and 4.

9. Patty, who is single, is diagnosed with a serious disease from teaching with Mike. Patty expects to be completely incapacitated in two years. Patty has one son, one daughter, and two grandchildren. She has $500,000 in net worth including her principal residence. Which of the following should Patty do?
   1. Set up a durable power of attorney.
   2. Immediate gift annual exclusion amounts to children and grandchildren.
   3. Set up a revocable living trust.
   4. Set up an ABC trust arrangement for her estate.
      a. 1 only.
      b. 1 and 3.
      c. 1, 2, and 3.
      d. 2, 3, and 4.
      e. 1, 2, 3, and 4.

10. Mary has a general power of appointment over her mother's assets. Which of the following is/are true regarding the power?
    1. Mary can appoint her mother's money to pay for the needs of her mother.
    2. Mary can appoint money to Mary's creditors.
    3. Mary must only appoint money using an ascertainable standard (health, education, maintenance, and support).
    4. If Mary were to die before her mother, Mary's gross estate would include her mother's assets although they were not previously appointed to Mary.
        a. 1 only.
        b. 1, 3, and 4.
        c. 2, 3, and 4.
        d. 1, 2, and 4.
        e. 1, 2, 3, and 4.

11. Doris Jenkins is a 71 year-old widow with a son and daughter ages 43 and 45 and six grandchildren. Doris has an estate currently worth $572,000, which includes her home worth $250,000 and a life insurance policy on her life with a face value of $160,000. Her children are named as primary beneficiaries. Doris recently suffered a severe stroke that left her paralyzed on her right side. She is home from the hospital but her health will continue to decline and she will need to go into a nursing home within one year. The only estate planning she has done to date is to write a will in 1989 which left all her assets to her children equally. Of the following estate planning considerations, which is/are appropriate for Doris at this time? **(CFP® Exam, released 12/95)**
    1. Transfer ownership of her home to her children so it will not be counted as a resource should she have to go into a nursing home and apply for Medicaid.
    2. Execute a durable general power of attorney and a durable power of attorney for health care.
    3. Place all of her assets in an irrevocable family trust with her children as beneficiaries.
    4. Start a gifting program transferring assets up to the annual exclusion amount to each of her children and grandchildren.
        a. 1, 2, 3, and 4.
        b. 2 and 3.
        c. 1 and 4.
        d. 4 only.
        e. 2 only.

OWNERSHIP OF PROPERTY AND HOW IT IS TRANSFERRED

12. Which of the following estate transfer methods is the least appropriate for a relationship of same sex individuals who both have donative intent exclusively to each other?
    - a. Qualified Pension Plan assets with a named beneficiary.
    - b. Intestate probate
    - c. Testate probate.
    - d. Named beneficiary of contract for life insurance.
    - e. Property held joint tenancy (WROS).

13. Which of the following is/are (an) appropriate method(s) of property transfer at death between persons of the same sex who are committed to a long-term relationship?
    1. Tenancy in common with each other, no will.
    2. Fee simple ownership with no will.
    3. Tenancy by the entirety.
    4. Community property.
    - a. 1 only.
    - b. 1 and 3.
    - c. 2 and 3.
    - d. 1, 2, and 4.
    - e. None of the above.

14. Of the following property ownership arrangements, which may be entered into by spouses only?
    1. Tenancy in common.
    2. Joint tenancy with right of survivorship.
    3. Tenancy by the entirety.
    4. Community property.
    - a. 3 only.
    - b. 2 and 4.
    - c. 3 and 4.
    - d. 2, 3, and 4.
    - e. 1, 2, 3, and 4.

15. Which of the following statements regarding joint tenancy is/are correct?
    1. Under a joint tenancy, each tenant has an undivided interest in the property.
    2. Joint tenancies may only be established between spouses.
    3. Community property is the same as joint tenancy and has been adopted in many states.
    4. Assuming a spousal joint tenancy, the full value of the property will be included in the probate estate of the first spouse to die without regard to the contribution of each spouse.
       a. 1 only.
       b. 1 and 2.
       c. 1 and 3.
       d. 2 and 3.
       e. 1, 2, 3, and 4.

THE PROBATE PROCESS

16. Generally speaking, which of the following property is included in the probate estate?
    1. Property owned outright in one's own name at the time of death (Fee Simple).
    2. An interest in property held as a tenant in common with others.
    3. Life insurance, and other death proceeds, payable to one's estate at death.
    4. The decedent's half of any community property.
        a. 1, 2, and 4.
        b. 1 and 2.
        c. 2, 3, and 4.
        d. 1, 2, and 3.
        e. 1, 2, 3, and 4.

17. It is sometimes argued that having property included in a probate estate is unwise. Which of the following statements regarding disposition of property through a probate estate is/are true?
    1. Creditors can never "get at" the probate estate.
    2. Disgruntled heirs have a better chance of "getting at" non-probate property rather than probate property.
    3. Overall, state and federal taxes are less in reference to a probate estate than to non-probate assets.
    4. The contents of a probate estate can become public knowledge.
        a. 2 only.
        b. 4 only.
        c. 1 and 2.
        d. 2, 3, and 4.
        e. 1, 2, 3, and 4.

18. Although the probate system is a common method for disposing of property after death, it is by no means the only way to transfer property. Which of the following methods is/are an excellent non-probate transfer device?
    1. Life insurance with a named beneficiary.
    2. Payable-on-death bank accounts (Totten Trust).
    3. A living trust.
    4. Joint tenancy with survivorship rights
        a. 1 and 3.
        b. 3 and 4.
        c. 1, 3, and 4.
        d. 1, 2, and 4.
        e. 1, 2, 3, and 4.

19. Which of the following statements is/are correct regarding the probate process?
    1. The probate process may be costly and create delays in the distribution of assets.
    2. The probate process is open to public scrutiny.
    3. The probate process protects creditors.
    4. The probate process provides heirs and/or legatees with clear title to property.
        a. 1 only.
        b. 2 only.
        c. 1 and 2.
        d. 1, 2, and 3.
        e. 1, 2, 3, and 4.

20. Which of the following property interests of a decedent will pass through probate?
    1. Property held in fee simple.
    2. Life insurance proceeds with decedent's spouse as beneficiary.
    3. Property owned with brother of decedent as tenants in common.
    4. Pension plan assets with a named beneficiary.
        a. 1 only.
        b. 2 and 4.
        c. 1 and 3.
        d. 1, 2, and 4.
        e. 1, 2, 3, and 4.

21. Which of the following is/are advantages of the probate process?

    1. Protects creditors.
    2. Provides clear title to heir or legatee.
    3. Improves the likelihood that parties in interest will receive notice and the opportunity to be heard.
    4. Provides for an orderly administration of decedent's assets.

        a. 1 only.
        b. 2 only.
        c. 1, 2, and 4.
        d. 2, 3, and 4.
        e. 1, 2, 3, and 4.

22. Which of the following is/are considered to be a disadvantage(s) of probate?

    1. The process may be costly.
    2. The process can result in delays.
    3. The process is open to public scrutiny.
    4. The process provides clear title to heirs and legatees.

        a. 1 only.
        b. 1 and 2.
        c. 2 and 4.
        d. 1, 2, and 3.
        e. 1, 2, 3, and 4.

23. Which of the following would be an alternative to probate regarding disposition of property?

    1. Property held tenants by the entirety.
    2. Property held within a revocable living trust.
    3. Property held within an irrevocable trust.
    4. Proceeds of an insurance policy (second-to-die) with named beneficiary.

        a. 1 only.
        b. 1 and 2.
        c. 1 and 3.
        d. 1, 2, and 3.
        e. 1, 2, 3, and 4.

24. Of the following items of property, which would be included in a decedent's probate estate?
    1. Solely owned securities held in a brokerage account.
    2. An interest in a business held as tenants in common with a brother of the decedent.
    3. Life insurance policy death proceeds made payable to the decedent's estate.
    4. A stamp collection owned jointly (JTWROS) with the decedent's spouse.
        a. 1 only.
        b. 2 only.
        c. 1 and 2.
        d. 1, 2, and 3.
        e. 1, 2, 3, and 4.

FEDERAL UNIFIED GIFT AND ESTATE TAXATION

25. The unified credit can offset the tax liability for which of the following transfers?

    1. A gift to a citizen spouse.
    2. Lifetime gifts to children.
    3. Testamentary transfers to friends.
    4. A gift to a public charity.

    a. 1 and 2.
    b. 1 and 3.
    c. 2 and 3.
    d. 1, 2, and 3.
    e. 1, 2, 3, and 4.

THE FEDERAL GIFT TAX

26. A transferred $100,000 to his son and $100,000 to his daughter. A's wife also transferred $5,000 to their son. No other gifts were made during the year. A and his wife elected to split the gifts on their gift tax returns. What is the amount of taxable gifts made by A and A's wife?

	A	A's Wife
a.	$82,500	$82,500
b.	$92,500	$92,500
c.	$160,000	$5,000
d.	$180,000	$0
e.	$200,000	$5,000

27. Which of the following situations would not constitute a taxable transfer under the gift tax statutes?
    1. Father creates an irrevocable trust under the terms of which his son is to receive income for life and his grandson the remainder at his son's death.
    2. Father, with personal funds, purchases real property and has title conveyed to himself and his brother as joint tenants with right of survivorship.
    3. Father creates a trust giving income for life to wife and providing that, at her death, the corpus is to be distributed to their daughter. Father reserves the right to revoke the transfer at any time.
    4. Father, with personal funds, purchases an U.S. Savings Bond made payable to himself and his wife. His wife surrenders the bond for cash to be used for her personal benefit.

    a. 1 only.
    b. 2 only.
    c. 3 only.
    d. 3 and 4.
    e. 1, 2, 3, and 4.

28. Jeff created a joint bank account for himself and his friend, Kim. There is a gift to Kim when:
    a. The account is created.
    b. Jeff dies.
    c. Kim draws on the account for her own benefit.
    d. Kim is notified by Jeff that the account has been created.
    e. None of the above.

29. Which of the following represents a taxable gift(s)?
    1. Transfer of assets to a dependent family member that represents legal support ($9,000).
    2. Payment of $12,000 to the law school for child's tuition.
    3. Payment of $16,000 of medical bills to the hospital for a friend.
        a. None of the above is a taxable gift.
        b. 2 only.
        c. 1 and 2.
        d. 2 and 3.
        e. 1, 2, and 3.

30. Which of the following statements relating to qualified transfers for gift tax purposes is not correct?
    a. The exclusion for a qualified transfer is in addition to the annual exclusion.
    b. A qualified transfer is allowed without regard to the relationship between the donor and the donee.
    c. Only that part of a payment to a qualified educational institution that applies directly to tuition costs is a qualified transfer.
    d. A payment made directly to an individual to reimburse him for his medical expenses is a qualified transfer.
    e. None of the above.

31. During this year, Mr. and Mrs. B made joint gifts of the following items to their son:
    1. A bond with an adjusted basis of $12,000 and a fair market value of $40,000.
    2. Stock with an adjusted basis of $22,000 and a fair market value of $33,000.
    3. An auto with an adjusted basis of $12,000 and a fair market value of $14,000.
    4. An interest free loan of $6,000 for a computer (for the son's personal use) on January 1st, which was paid by their son on December 31st. Assume the applicable federal rate was 8% per annum.

    What is the gross amount of gifts includible in Mr. and Mrs. B's gift tax returns for this year?
    a. $87,480.
    b. $87,000.
    c. $46,480.
    d. $46,000.
    e. $52,000.

32. December 1st, Rosario gave her son, Alex, stock with a fair market value of $20,000. Rosario paid gift tax of $5,000. Rosario had purchased the stock two years ago, and her adjusted basis on the date of the gift was $12,000. On January 10th, of the following year, Alex sold the stock for $24,000. What was Alex's basis on January 10th?

    a. $12,000.
    b. $14,000.
    c. $17,000.
    d. $20,000.
    e. $24,000.

33. Janet made the following gifts:

Gift	Donee	Value
Cash	Jack, Nephew	$12,000
6-month CD	Jill, Niece	$8,000
Antique rifle	George, Friend	$20,000
Bonds gifted to irrevocable trust		
Life estate	Joel, Father	$60,000
Remainder	Jill, Niece	$18,000

Janet's taxable gifts total:

    a. $68,000.
    b. $70,000.
    c. $78,000.
    d. $80,000.
    e. $118,000.

34. During the year, Mary Sue, who is single, made the following gifts:

1. Paid $16,000 in medical bills for her friend, Vicki. The payments were paid directly to her friend's hospital.
2. $18,000 to her mother to pay for her apartment rent, utilities, and food.
3. $14,000 to her nephew, Mike, to get him started in business.
4. Mary Sue also had made a $30,000 interest-free demand loan to her nephew, Mike, the previous year. The loan is still outstanding at the end of this year. The applicable federal interest rate during the year remained constant at 8%.

What is the amount of Mary Sue's taxable gifts?

a. $12,000.
b. $14,400.
c. $18,000.
d. $20,400.
e. $50,400.

35. Mr. B, a U.S. citizen, made the following gifts:

1. $20,000 cash to his son; $60,000 to his wife (also an U.S. citizen).
2. Auto to his brother (fair market value $15,000, adjusted basis $9,000).
3. $100,000 in land to the City for new library.

Without considering gift splitting, what is the total of Mr. B's exclusions and deductions for his gift tax return?

a. $160,000.
b. $169,000.
c. $170,000.
d. $177,000.
e. $180,000.

36. Allison, who is single, gave an outright gift of $60,000 to a friend, Stacy, who needed the money to pay her medical expenses. In filing the gift tax return, Allison was entitled to a maximum exclusion of:

a. $0.
b. $10,000.
c. $20,000.
d. $60,000.
e. None of the above.

37. When Ron and Bonnie became engaged in August, Ron gave Bonnie a ring that has a fair market value of $68,000. After their wedding in October, Ron gave Bonnie $45,000 in cash so that Bonnie could have her own bank account. Ron and Bonnie are U.S. citizens. What is the amount of Ron's gift tax marital deduction?

   a. $0.
   b. $35,000.
   c. $45,000.
   d. $103,000.
   e. $113,000.

38. Clint R. made the following gifts:

   1. $2,000 each month to a university to pay tuition costs for his friend, Ernesto.
   2. Tract of land to his mother that had an adjusted basis to Clint of $7,000 and a fair market value of $30,000.
   3. Stock to his wife that had an adjusted basis to Clint of $30,000 and a fair market value of $50,000.

   Clint's spouse did not consent to gift splitting. What is his total amount of taxable gifts?

   a. $20,000.
   b. $30,000.
   c. $39,000.
   d. $59,000.
   e. $109,000.

39. Which of the following statements regarding gift-splitting is/are true?

1. The annual gift tax exclusion allows spouses who consent to split their gifts to transfer up to $20,000 to any one person during any calendar year without gift tax liability, if the gifts are of a present interest.
2. To qualify for gift-splitting, a couple must be married at the time the gift is made.
3. For gift tax purposes, a husband and wife must file a joint income tax return to qualify for the gift-splitting benefits.
4. Both spouses must consent to the use of gift-splitting and at least one gift tax return must be filed.

a. 1 only.
b. 1 and 2.
c. 1, 2, and 4.
d. 2, 3, and 4.
e. 1, 2, 3, and 4.

40. Ron made the following gifts:

• Cash to son, Ron Jr.	$ 60,000
• Stock to wife Bonnie	120,000
• Cash to Church	40,000
• Auto to nephew	30,000

Ron and Bonnie elect gift-splitting. Bonnie's only gift during the year is a $30,000 cash gift to her mother. What is the amount of the taxable gifts to be reported by Ron?

a. $0.
b. $30,000.
c. $60,000.
d. $110,000.
e. $140,000.

41. For transfers by gift, one must file a gift tax return for which of the following?

a. A transfer of a present interest in property that is less than the annual exclusion.
b. A qualified transfer for educational or medical expenses.
c. A transfer to one's spouse that qualified for the unlimited marital deduction.
d. A transfer of $18,000 to a son for which one's spouse has agreed to gift-splitting.
e. A transfer of $10,000 by a father to his son.

42. George and his spouse Mary made joint gifts to their daughter as follows:

- Stock with an adjusted basis of $20,000 and a fair market value of $50,000.
- Bonds with an adjusted basis of $27,000 and a fair market value of $35,000.
- A truck with an adjusted basis of $16,000. FMV of truck is $8,000.
- An interest free loan of $10,000 to purchase a sailboat. The applicable federal rate was 9%. Loan was outstanding for the entire year.

What is the total gross amount of gifts includible in George's and Mary's gift tax returns?

a. $63,900.
b. $73,900.
c. $93,000.
d. $103,900.
e. $113,000.

43. William and his spouse Betty made joint gifts to their daughter as follows:

- Stock with an adjusted basis of $20,000 and a fair market value of $50,000.
- Bonds with an adjusted basis of $27,000 and a fair market value of $35,000.
- A truck with an adjusted basis of $16,000. FMV of the truck is $8,000.
- An interest free loan of $10,000 to purchase a sailboat. The applicable federal rate was 9%. The loan was outstanding for the entire year.

What is the amount of total taxable gifts made by William and Betty to their daughter?

a. $63,000.
b. $73,000.
c. $93,000.
d. $103,900.
e. $113,000.

44. Which, if any, of the following transfers is subject to the Federal gift tax?

a. Donations to political organizations.
b. Payments of a nephew's tuition to the University.
c. A taxpayer pays hospital for medical care provided to her aunt.
d. In advance of their marriage, H pays $50,000 to W as a prenuptial settlement.
e. None of the above.

45. Which, if any, of the following transfers would be subject to the Federal gift tax?

1. H designates W as beneficiary of his life insurance policy.
2. H dies and the insurance company pays the $300,000 life insurance proceeds to W (the designated beneficiary of H's policy).
3. H makes a donated capital contribution to Z Corporation. The stock of Z Corporation is held equally by H and D (H's daughter).
4. H creates a revocable trust for the benefit of his son and funds it with $25,000.

a. 2 only.
b. 3 only.
c. 1 and 2.
d. 2 and 3.
e. 1, 2, 3, and 4.

46. Mother (M) loans Daughter (D) $200,000. D signs a note promising to repay the loan in 5 years. No interest is provided for. Which, if any, of the following is not a tax consequence of this arrangement?

a. M has made a gift to D of the imputed interest.
b. M has an interest expense deduction as to the imputed interest.
c. M has interest income as to the imputed interest.
d. D may be allowed an income tax deduction as to the imputed interest.
e. None of the above.

47. Which of the following situations constitutes a transfer that comes within the gift tax statutes?

1. Kurt creates a trust under the terms of which his son is to get income for life and his grandson the remainder at his son's death.
2. Kurt purchases real property and has the title conveyed to himself and to his brother as joint tenants.
3. Kurt creates an irrevocable trust giving income for life to his wife and providing that upon her death the corpus is to be distributed to his daughter.
4. Kurt purchases an U.S. Savings Bond made payable to himself and his wife. The wife surrenders the bond for cash to be used for her benefit.

a. 1 only.
b. 1 and 2.
c. 2, and 3.
d. 1, 2, and 4.
e. 1, 2, 3, and 4.

48. Which of the following situations would not constitute a transfer that comes within the gift tax statutes?
    a. A mother creates a trust under the terms of which the daughter is to get income for life and her granddaughter the remainder at the daughter's death.
    b. Bill purchases real property and has title conveyed to himself and to his brother Joe as joint tenants.
    c. A father creates an irrevocable trust giving income for life to his wife and providing that at her death the corpus is to be distributed to his son.
    d. Joe purchases an U.S. Savings Bond made payable to himself and his wife, Mary. Mary cashes the bond to be used for her own benefit.
    e. Mary Sue creates a joint bank account for herself and her daughter, Rachel. There have been no withdrawals from the account.

49. Mary Sue creates a joint bank account for herself and her daughter, Rachel. There is a gift to Rachel when:
    1. Mary Sue creates the account.
    2. Mary Sue dies.
    3. Rachel withdraws part of the cash from the account for her own benefit.
    4. Rachel is notified by Mary Sue that the account has been created.
        a. 1 only.
        b. 3 only.
        c. 2 and 3.
        d. 1, 2, and 3.
        e. 1, 2, 3, and 4.

50. Which of the following regarding the opening of a joint bank account between a father and daughter would constitute a completed gift?
    1. The father creates the account.
    2. The father dies.
    3. The daughter draws on the account for her own benefit.
    4. The father notifies the daughter that the account has been created and that she may draw on the account.
        a. 3 only.
        b. 4 only.
        c. 3 and 4.
        d. 2, 3, and 4.
        e. 1, 2, 3, and 4.

51. Which of the following represent taxable gifts?
    1. The transfer of wealth by a parent to a dependent child that represents legal support.
    2. Payment to Loyola of a child's tuition to Loyola's Law School by a parent.
    3. The payment of $11,000 of medical bills for a friend paid directly to the medical institution.
    a. 1 only.
    b. 2 only.
    c. 2 and 3.
    d. 1, 2, and 3.
    e. None of the above.

52. Which statements regarding qualified transfers for gift tax purposes is/are true?
    1. The exclusion for a qualified transfer is in addition to the annual exclusion.
    2. A qualified transfer is allowed without regard to the relationship between donor and donee.
    3. Only that part of a payment to a qualified educational institution that applies to direct tuition costs is qualified.
    4. A payment made directly to an individual for reimbursement of medical expenses is a qualified transfer.
    a. 1 only.
    b. 3 only.
    c. 1 and 3.
    d. 1, 2, and 3.
    e. 1, 2, 3, and 4.

53. George decided to begin a program of lifetime giving to his 5 grandchildren and 3 great-grandchildren. He wants to control the amount of annual gifts to avoid the imposition of federal gift tax, and he does not desire to use any of his or his wife's (Sue) unified tax credit. Sue is willing to split each gift over a period of 10 years. George can give a total amount of gifts (exclusive of indexing), including the gift splitting, over the 10 year period of:
    a. $1,376,000.
    b. $1,600,000.
    c. $800,000.
    d. $600,000.
    e. $900,000.

54. Which, if any, of the following statements correctly reflects the rules regarding the Federal gift tax return (Form 709)?

    1. A donor who uses a fiscal year for income tax purposes uses the same filing date for Form 709.
    2. For a calendar year taxpayer, an extension of time for filing Form 1040 also extends the time for filing Form 709.
    3. A father gives $20,000 of separate property to his son. If the Father's wife elects to split gifts with the Father, they must file a gift tax return.
    4. A father and mother give $20,000 of community property to their son. No gift tax return need be filed.

        a. 1 only.
        b. 2 only.
        c. 1, 2, and 3.
        d. 2, 3, and 4.
        e. 1, 2, 3, and 4.

55. Which of the following statements correctly reflects the rules regarding the federal gift tax return Form 709?

    1. For a calendar year taxpayer, an extension of time for filing Form 1040 also extends the time for filing Form 709.
    2. George gives $10,000 of separate property to his son. If Mary, George's wife, elects to split the gift with George, they must file a gift tax return.
    3. George and Mary give $20,000 of community property to their son. No gift tax return need be filed.
    4. An extension of time for filing the gift tax return does not extend the time for payment of the gift tax.

        a. 1 and 2.
        b. 2 and 3.
        c. 1, 2, and 3.
        d. 2, 3, and 4.
        e. 1, 2, 3, and 4.

56. Lifetime gifts can be an attractive estate planning and tax-saving technique. Which of the following statements is/are true regarding lifetime gifts?

    1. Amounts qualifying for the annual exclusion will escape gift taxation and will not be included in the donor's estate.
    2. Future appreciation in the value of gifted property will escape gift taxation and estate taxation.
    3. Income from gift property generally will be taxed to the donee for income tax purposes.
    4. Generation skipping transfer taxes do not apply to "lifetime" gifts.

    a. 1 only.
    b. 1, 2, and 3.
    c. 2, 3, and 4.
    d. 3 and 4.
    e. None of the above.

57. Roy and his wife have 2 children, each over the age of majority, 1 grandchild age 21, and 3 minor grandchildren. Roy and his wife want to make gifts to their children and grandchildren sufficient to make maximum use of the tax provisions providing for annual exclusions from federal gift tax. Considering that desire only, Roy and his wife can make gifts during the year totaling:

    a. $30,000.
    b. $60,000.
    c. $120,000.
    d. $192,800.
    e. $600,000.

58. Which of the following independent situations would constitute a transfer that comes within the gift tax statutes?

    1. A father purchases real estate and makes his son joint tenant.
    2. A father opens a joint bank account and funds it with his own $1,000 and makes his non-contributory son joint owner.
    3. A father gives his son $9,999 in cash.
    4. A father creates a charitable remainder annuity trust with his son as the income beneficiary and State University as remainderman. The father funds the trust with personal money.

    a. 4 only.
    b. 1 and 3.
    c. 1 and 4.
    d. 1, 3, and 4.
    e. 1, 2, 3, and 4.

59. Generally, gift property:
    a. Has a zero basis to the donee because the donee did not pay anything for the property.
    b. Has the same basis to the donee as the donor's adjusted basis if the donee disposes of the property at a gain.
    c. Has the same basis to the donee as the donor's adjusted basis if the donee disposes of the property at a loss, and the fair market value on the date of gift was less than the donor's adjusted basis.
    d. Has a zero basis to the donee if the fair market value on the date of gift is less than the donor's adjusted basis.
    e. None of the above.

60. Taxpayer gives her son property with a basis to her of $35,000 and a fair market value of $30,000. No gift tax is paid. Son subsequently sells the property for $33,000. What is his recognized gain (or loss)?
    a. No gain or loss.
    b. $2,000 loss.
    c. $3,000 gain.
    d. $33,000 gain.
    e. None of the above.

61. Bill gifts his daughter bonds with a basis to Bill of $1,800 and a fair market value of $1,000. Daughter subsequently sells the bonds for $2,000. What is her recognized gain or loss?
    a. No gain or loss.
    b. $200 gain.
    c. $1,000 gain.
    d. $2,000 gain.
    e. None of the above.

62. Donna received a gift of rental real estate with an adjusted basis of $75,000 to the donor and fair market value of $50,000 on the date of gift. The donor paid gift tax of $3,000. Donna subsequently sold the property for $60,000. What is her recognized gain or loss?
    a. $10,000 gain.
    b. $7,000 gain.
    c. $15,000 loss
    d. $12,000 loss.
    e. None of the above.

63. James was given a house during the current year. At the date of the gift, the house had a fair market value of $175,000, and its adjusted basis to the donor (his father, Michael) was $105,000. The donor paid a gift tax of $12,000 on the gift. What is James' basis for gains?

a. $105,000.
b. $109,800.
c. $117,000.
d. $175,000.
e. $187,000.

64. Tom received a gift of bonds from his cousin. The basis of the bonds to the cousin was $42,000 and the fair market value on the date of the gift was $60,000. The cousin paid gift tax of $4,500. What is Tom's basis for the bonds?

a. $0 for gains and $0 for losses.
b. $43,350 for gains and $43,350 for losses.
c. $48,000 for gains and $40,000 for losses.
d. $50,000 for gains and $42,000 for losses.
e. None of the above.

65. Matt gives Jim securities. Matt's adjusted basis for the securities is $48,000, and the fair market value is $40,000. Matt pays gift tax of $2,000. What is Jim's basis for the stock for gain and for loss?

a. $0 for gain and $0 for loss.
b. $40,000 for gain and $40,000 for loss.
c. $48,000 for gain and $40,000 for loss.
d. $50,000 for gain and $42,000 for loss.
e. None of the above.

66. The holding period of property acquired by gift begins on:

a. The date the property was acquired by the donor only.
b. The date of gift only.
c. The date the property was acquired by the donor or the date of gift, depending on whether the property was sold at a gain or a loss.
d. a, b, or c as elected by donee.
e. None of the above.

67. Jack gives John a machine to use in his business with a fair market value of $4,500 and a basis to Jack of $4,800. What is John's basis for depreciation?

    a. $0.
    b. $4,500.
    c. $4,650.
    d. $4,800.
    e. None of the above.

68. Which of the following transactions requires the donor to file a gift tax return?

    1. Donor lends $125,000 to son interest free. The federal rate is 10%.
    2. Donor and wife using split gift technique give son $12,500 for son's birthday.
    3. Donor transfers $11,000 to revocable inter vivos trust for son who is both income and remainder beneficiary.
    4. Donor gifts jointly with spouse community property worth $14,500 to daughter for daughter's birthday.

    a. 4 only.
    b. 1 and 2.
    c. 1, 2, and 3.
    d. 1, 2, and 4.
    e. 1, 2, 3, and 4.

69. Which of the following is correct regarding a net gift?

    a. In a net gift, the donor pays the gift tax prior to the gift.
    b. A net gift is by definition a gift of a future interest.
    c. A net gift will cause the donor taxable income to the extent the gift tax paid exceeds the donor's adjusted basis in the gift.
    d. Net gifts do not qualify for the annual exclusion.
    e. None of the above.

70. Which of the following gifts would constitute a taxable gift? **(CFP® Exam, released 3/95)**
    1. $25,000 to the donor's adult child.
    2. $10,000 to a friend.
    3. $35,000 paid to a friend for medical expenses.
    4. $15,000 to a college to cover a friend's tuition.
        a. 1, 2, and 3.
        b. 1 and 3.
        c. 2 and 4.
        d. 4 only.
        e. 1, 2, 3, and 4.

71. Which of the following circumstances would definitely cause the date-of-death value of the gifted property to be included in the donor's gross estate? **(CFP® Exam, released 3/95)**
    1. Donor retains a life estate in the gift property.
    2. Donor retains the power to revoke or amend the gift.
    3. Donor gives more than $10,000 to one donee in one year.
    4. Donor dies within three years of the date of the gift.
        a. 1, 2, and 3.
        b. 1 and 2.
        c. 2 and 4.
        d. 3 and 4.
        e. 1, 2, 3, and 4.

72. William Barnhill gave his son, James, a house on August 1st. The fair market value of the house on January 1st, August 1st, and December 31st of the same year were as follows: $130,000, $140,000, and $150,000. Mr. Barnhill had purchased the property in 1992 for $60,000 and had used it as rental property the entire time he held it. He had taken cumulative straight-line depreciation through July 31st of the current year of $10,000. What is James Barnhill's adjusted taxable basis?
    a. $0.
    b. $50,000.
    c. $60,000.
    d. $130,000.
    e. $150,000.

73. William Barnhill gave his son, James, a house on August 1st. The fair market value of the house on January 1st, August 1st, and December 31st of the same year were as follows: $130,000, $140,000, and $150,000. Mr. Barnhill had purchased the property in 1992 for $60,000 and had used it as rental property the entire time he held it. He had taken cumulative straight-line depreciation through July 31st of the current year of $10,000. What is James Barnhill's adjusted taxable basis if William had paid $30,000 in gift tax?

    a. $0.
    b. $50,000.
    c. $69,286.
    d. $65,000.
    e. $130,000.

74. John and Mary are married and have two children, Patrick and Kurt. They would like to gift the maximum amount of cash possible without paying gift tax to their children. They have made no previous gifts during their lifetime and are willing to make maximum usage of whatever techniques are available to make these gifts as long as they don't have to pay any gift tax. How much total can they gift to Patrick and Kurt?

    a. $10,000.
    b. $20,000.
    c. $40,000.
    d. $665,000.
    e. $1,290,000.

75. Jeannine transferred, by gift, $100,000 to her son and $100,000 to her daughter. Jeannine's husband, Scott, also transferred, by gift, $50,000 to their son. No other gifts were made. Jeannine and Scott elected to split the gifts on their gift tax returns. What is the total amount of taxable gifts made by Jeannine and Scott?

	Jeannine	Scott
a.	$105,000	$105,000
b.	$115,000	$115,000
c.	$160,000	$50,000
d.	$180,000	$40,000
e.	$200,000	$50,000

76. Robin inherited 10 acres of land on the death of her father during the current year. A Federal estate tax return was filed, and the land was valued at $25,000, its fair market value at the date of the father's death. The father had originally acquired the land in 1962 for $5,000. What is Robin's basis in the land she inherited?

    a. $5,000.
    b. $10,000.
    c. $15,000.
    d. $25,000.
    e. None of the above.

77. Which of the following is/are true regarding split gifts? Gift splitting:

    1. Can utilize another persons unified credit.
    2. Applies to all gifts in a given year.
    3. Doubles the annual exclusion for gifts of a present interest.
    4. Requires the filing of a gift tax return.

    a. 3 only.
    b. 3 and 4.
    c. 2, 3, and 4.
    d. 1, 2, 3, and 4.

78. Husband and wife own property JTWROS and they contemplate a transfer from wife to husband. Assuming the transfer occurs, which of the following is/are correct?

    1. A taxable gift occurs.
    2. The transfer avoids capital gain tax.
    3. If the wife dies within 3 years of the transfer, the value of the gift she transferred is included in her gross estate.

    a. 1 only.
    b. 2 only.
    c. 1 and 2.
    d. 2 and 3.
    e. 1, 2, and 3.

79. What is the maximum gift that Bob and Sue Thompson can give to a third party in 1999 without paying any gift tax, assuming they have not made any previous taxable gifts?

    a. $10,000.
    b. $20,000.
    c. $1,270,000.
    d. $1,320,000.
    e. $1,370,000.

80. Which of the following represents a taxable gift(s)?

    1. Transfer of assets to a dependent family member that represents legal support ($9,000).
    2. Payment of $12,000 to the law school for child's tuition.
    3. Payment of $16,000 of medical bills to the hospital for a friend.

    a. None of the above is a taxable gift.
    b. 2 only.
    c. 1 and 2.
    d. 2 and 3.
    e. 1, 2, and 3.

81. Lifetime gifts can be an attractive estate planning and tax-saving technique. Which of the following statements is/are true regarding lifetime gifts?

    1. Annual exclusion gifts will escape gift taxation and will not be included in the donor's estate.
    2. Future appreciation in the value of gifted property will escape gift taxation and estate taxation.
    3. Income from gift property will generally be taxed to the donee for income tax purposes.
    4. Generation skipping transfer taxes do not apply to "lifetime" gifts.

    a. 1 only.
    b. 1, 2, and 3.
    c. 2, 3, and 4.
    d. 3 and 4.
    e. None of the above.

82. Donna received a gift of rental real estate with an adjusted basis of $75,000 to the donor and fair market value of $50,000 on the date of gift. Gift tax of $3,000 was paid by the donor. Donna subsequently sold the property for $60,000. What is her recognized gain or loss?

    a. $10,000 gain.
    b. $7,000 gain.
    c. $15,000 loss.
    d. $12,000 loss.
    e. None of the above.

THE FEDERAL ESTATE TAX

83. A decedent's gross estate includes the value of all property to the extent of the decedent's interest in the property at the time of death. Which of the following items is/are included in the gross estate?
    1. Medical insurance reimbursements that were due the individual at death.
    2. The value of the part of a deceased husband's real property allowed to his widow for her lifetime (dower interest).
    3. Proceeds of life insurance on the decedent's life if the decedent possessed incidents of ownership in the policy.
    4. Outstanding dividends declared to decedent after the date of death.
        a. 1 only.
        b. 2 only.
        c. 1 and 3.
        d. 1, 2, and 3.
        e. 1, 2, 3, and 4.

84. Which of the following items of property would be included in the gross estate of a decedent who died during the current year?
    1. Jewelry of the decedent.
    2. Cash of $200,000 given to decedent's friend in 1998. No gift tax was paid on the transfer.
    3. Stock purchased by decedent and held as joint tenants with rights of survivorship with decedent's brother.
        a. 1 only.
        b. 1 and 3.
        c. 2 only.
        d. 2 and 3.
        e. 1, 2, and 3.

85. Taxpayer died on September 8th. His will called for the transfer of all of his possessions to his mother. At the date of death, the assets transferred were:

	Adj. Basis	FMV
House	$140,000	$180,000
Common Stock	$20,000	$50,000
Dividends on above stock(declared 9/30)	$2,000	$2,000
Medical insurance reimbursement (check received 8/31 but not cashed)	$2,500	$2,500
Cash	$42,000	$42,000

The executrix did not elect the alternate valuation date. What is taxpayer's gross estate for purposes of an estate tax return, Form 706?

a. $125,000.
b. $272,000.
c. $274,500.
d. $276,500.
e. None of the above.

86. The fair market values of Art's assets at the date of death were:

- Personal effects $125,000
- Real estate bought by Art 5 years prior to death and held with Art's brother as joint tenants with right of survivorship (brother made no contribution) $700,000

The executor of Art's estate did not elect the alternate valuation date. The amount includible in Art's gross estate on the federal estate tax return is:

a. $125,000.
b. $525,000.
c. $700,000.
d. $825,000.
e. None of the above.

87. Dr. Goodbar died on July 31st. His assets and their fair market value at the time of his death were:

- Cash $20,000
- Personal Residence $200,000
- Life insurance payable to Dr. Goodbar's estate $100,000
- Series EE bonds $50,000
- State of Louisiana bonds $250,000

Dr. Goodbar had a balance on his residence mortgage of $15,000. What is Dr. Goodbar's gross estate?

a. $305,000.
b. $555,000.
c. $605,000.
d. $620,000.
e. None of the above.

88. Mrs. B died on August 1st this year. What is Mrs. B's gross estate?

- In 1998, B gave cash of $30,000 to her friend. No gift tax was paid on the gift.
- B held property jointly with her brother. Each paid $45,000 of the total purchase price of $90,000. Fair market value of the property at date of death was $200,000.
- In 1998, B purchased a life insurance policy on her own life and gave it as a gift to her sister. B retained the right to change the beneficiary. Upon B's death, her sister received $200,000 under the policy.
- In 1983, B gave her son a summer home (fair market value in 1982, $100,000). B continued to use it until her death pursuant to an understanding with her son. The fair market value at date of death was $190,000.

a. $200,000.
b. $250,000.
c. $375,000.
d. $425,000.
e. $490,000.

89. Which of the following is not an allowable deduction against a decedent's gross estate?

   a. Administration and funeral expenses.
   b. Claims against the estate.
   c. Penalty incurred as the result of a late payment of the federal estate tax.
   d. Casualty and theft losses.
   e. None of the above (all are deductions).

90. Decedent died during the current year. The state of residence and domicile was not a community property state. From the items listed below, what are the allowable deductions from the gross estate?

Funeral expenses	$4,500
Executor and administrative fees	$6,000
Total mortgage on jointly held property, one-half purchase price paid by decedent	$90,000
Bequest of cash to spouse	$75,000
Expense of filing estate's fiduciary income tax return	$1,000

   a. $56,500.
   b. $130,500.
   c. $131,500.
   d. $175,500.
   e. $176,500.

91. An U.S. citizen died on July 4, during the current year, leaving an adjusted gross estate with a fair market value of $1,400,000 at the date of death. Under the terms of the will, $375,000 was bequeathed outright to his widow. The remainder of the estate was left to his mother. No taxable gifts were made during his lifetime. In computing the taxable estate, the executor should claim a marital deduction of:

   a. $250,000.
   b. $375,000.
   c. $700,000.
   d. $975,000.
   e. $1,025,000.

92. What amount of a decedent's taxable estate is effectively tax-free in 1999 if the maximum unified estate credit and gift credit is taken?

    a. $0.
    b. $10,000.
    c. $202,050.
    d. $650,000.
    e. $1,000,000.

93. Form 706, United States Estate Tax Return, was filed for an estate in the current year. The gross estate tax was $350,000. All of the following items are credited against the gross estate tax to determine the net estate tax payable, except:

    a. Unified credit.
    b. Credit for gift taxes paid.
    c. Marital deduction.
    d. Credit for state and foreign death taxes.
    e. Credit for estate tax on prior transfers.

94. Roger died in 1998 with a taxable estate of $2,000,000. He had made no taxable gifts during his lifetime. His estate will receive a credit for state death tax of $100,000. His federal estate tax due is:

    a. $478,750.
    b. $578,750.
    c. $680,800.
    d. $681,200.
    e. $780,800.

95. Jack died in 1999 with a taxable estate of $1,600,000 and adjusted taxable gifts of $700,000. During his life he used unified credits of $64,800. The unified credit that his estate will subtract from tentative estate tax due is:

    a. $15,200.
    b. $64,800.
    c. $137,250.
    d. $202,050.
    e. $211,300.

96. Which of the following rules does not apply to the filing of an estate tax return of an U.S. citizen?

    a. Form 706 is the form that is used to file an estate tax return.
    b. The return is due 9 months after the date of death unless an extension of time for filing has been granted.
    c. The return is filed with the Internal Revenue Service Center for the state in which the decedent was domiciled.
    d. For 1998, the value of the gross estate must be over $600,000.
    e. All of the above apply.

97. If a citizen or resident of the United States dies during 1999, an estate tax return must be filed if the gross estate at the date of death was valued at more than:

    a. $600,000.
    b. $625,000.
    c. $650,000.
    d. $750,000.
    e. $1,000,000.

98. Unless an extension of time to file is granted, an estate tax return, Form 706 (United States Estate and Generation Skipping Transfer Tax Return) is due:

    a. 3 months after the date of the decedent's death.
    b. 6 months after the date of the decedent's death.
    c. 9 months after the date of the decedent's death.
    d. 12 months after the date of the decedent's death.
    e. None of the above.

99. The executor of an estate may request an extension of time to pay the estate tax. Which of the following statements are true?

    1. The general extension of time to pay is up to 12 months for reasonable cause.
    2. The IRS may extend the time for payment for up to 12 years.
    3. A request for an extension of time to pay estate tax is filed on Form 4768.

    a. 1 only.
    b. 2 only.
    c. 3 only.
    d. 1 and 3.
    e. 1, 2, and 3.

100. An extension of time to pay estate tax may be granted if the executor can show reasonable cause for requesting the extension. Which of the following would be an illustration of reasonable cause?
   1. Litigation is required to collect assets of the decedent.
   2. Liquid assets of the estate are located in several jurisdictions and are not, nor will be, within the immediate control of the executor due to ancillary probate.
   3. The estate would have to borrow funds at an interest rate higher than generally available to satisfy claims against the estate that are currently due and payable.
   4. Payment of estate taxes would require the liquidation of > 50% of the assets of the estate.
      a. 1 only.
      b. 1 and 3.
      c. 1 and 2.
      d. 1, 2, and 3.
      e. 1, 2, 3, and 4.

101. The unified credit against federal gift and estate tax for 1999 is:
      a. $10,000 per donee per year.
      b. $211,300.
      c. $650,000.
      d. $1,000,000.
      e. None of the above.

102. Which of the following alternatives is an effective method of limiting, reducing, or avoiding federal estate taxes:
   1. Use of the $10,000 annual gift tax exclusion.
   2. Creation of an irrevocable life insurance trust.
   3. Use of gift tax exclusions for tuition and medical expenses payments made directly to the provider.
   4. Use of the unlimited marital deduction.
      a. 2 and 4.
      b. 1, 2, and 4.
      c. 1 and 3.
      d. 1, 3, and 4.
      e. 1, 2, 3, and 4.

103. Husband and wife reside in Louisiana, a community property state. Their community property consists of real property with an adjusted basis of $90,000 and a fair market value of $300,000 and other property with an adjusted basis of $50,000 and a fair market value of $20,000. Husband dies and leaves his estate to his wife. What is wife's adjusted basis in the real property and other property after husband's death? (Assume no children).

	Real	Other
a.	$90,000	$50,000
b.	$195,000	$50,000
c.	$195,000	$35,000
d.	$300,000	$20,000
e.	None of the above.	

104. Which of the items below is/are deductions from the gross estate to arrive at the taxable estate on Form 706?

1. Medical (last illness) and funeral expenses.
2. Debts of the decedent.
3. Bequests to a spouse.
4. Charitable bequests.

a. 1 only.
b. 2 only.
c. 1 and 2.
d. 1, 2, and 3.
e. 1, 2, 3, and 4.

105. Decedent had made substantial lifetime gifts such that her estate is in the 50% marginal bracket. In the will, she made a bequest of $100,000 to her adult son with no special arrangements, or allocations, for the payment of the estate taxes. The balance of her estate goes to her husband. How much of this bequest will the son actually receive, assuming no other bequests to him from her estate? **(CFP® Exam, released 3/95)**

a. $50,000 because estate taxes of $50,000 would be charged against the bequest.
b. $55,000 because the $10,000 per beneficiary exclusion reduces the taxable amount.
c. $90,000 because the $10,000 per beneficiary exclusion applies even for adult children.
d. $100,000 because the estate tax will be paid from the residual estate.
e. The amount cannot be determined unless one knows whether a QTIP election was made.

106. On which IRS form do you file funeral expenses?
    1. Form 706 Estate tax return.
    2. Personal income tax return Form 1040.
    3. Form 1041 fiduciary return.
        a. 1 only.
        b. 2 only.
        c. 3 only.
        d. 1 and 2.
        e. All of the above.

107. Which of the following sections might apply to an estate with a closely held corporation as an asset of the estate?
    1. IRC Section 303.
    2. IRC Section 6166.
    3. IRC Section 2032.
    4. IRC Section 2032A.
        a. 1 only.
        b. 2 only.
        c. 1 and 2.
        d. 1, 2, and 3.
        e. 1, 2, 3, and 4.

VALUATION OF ASSETS

108. On July 13, Michael gave his brother, James, one share of XYZ stock, which was traded on an exchange. July 13 was a Thursday, and these were the quoted prices on Wednesday the 12th and Friday the 14th. The market was closed on Thursday:

Sales Price

Date	High	Low	Closing
7/12/98	60	56	58.5
7/14/98	62	58.5	59

What is the fair market value of Michael's gift?

a. $58.00.
b. $58.75.
c. $59.50.
d. $59.125.
e. $60.25.

109. Bill Cole died on August 29th. At that time, he owned stock in XYZ Corporation. The stock traded on both August 28th and August 29th. Given the following excerpt from the Wall Street Journal for both days, what is the reported value of XYZ stock on Form 706?

August 28th			August 29th		
High	Low	Close	High	Low	Close
63	52	57	60	58	59.5

a. 57.
b. 58.
c. 59.
d. 59.5.
e. 60.

110. ABC stock does not trade on a regular basis. If John Smith dies on Thursday, June 5th, and the most recent trades for ABC stock are as follows:

Mon., 6/2	27
Wed., 6/4	25
Mon., 6/9	28
Tues., 6/10	29

What is the date of death value that should be used for the Federal Estate Return?

a. 25.

b. 26.

c. 26.5.

d. 27.

e. 28.

THE MARITAL DEDUCTION

111. Which of the following qualify for the unlimited marital deduction?

1. Outright bequest to resident alien spouse.
2. Property passing to citizen spouse in QTIP.
3. Income beneficiary of CRUT is a non-resident alien spouse (Trust is not a QDOT).
4. Outright bequest to resident spouse who, prior to the decedent's death was a non-citizen, but who after the decedent's death and before the estate return was filed became an U.S. citizen.

a. 2 only.
b. 2 and 4.
c. 2, 3, and 4.
d. 3 and 4.
e. 1, 2, 3, and 4.

112. Which of the following is/are exception(s) to the terminable interest rule regarding property which qualified for the marital deduction?

1. An outright bequest of $100,000 to spouse with a condition that the spouse must survive decedent husband by 6 months and she does <u>not</u> survive by 6 months.
2. An outright bequest of $100,000 to a spouse with a condition that the spouse must survive the decedent husband by 6 months and she does survive.
3. Spouse is the sole income beneficiary of a CRAT; charity is the remainderman.
4. Spouse is the sole income beneficiary of a CRUT; charity is the remainderman.

a. 2 only.
b. 1 and 3.
c. 1, 2, and 4.
d. 2, 3, and 4.
e. 1, 2, 3, and 4.

TRUSTS

113. The advantage(s) of a revocable trust, compared to a will is/are:

1. Saves taxes.
2. Keeps one's affairs private.
3. Provides for joint tenancy.

a. 1 only.
b. 2 only.
c. 3 only.
d. 1 and 2.
e. 1, 2, and 3.

114. A Marital Power of Appointment Trust:

a. Cannot be elected for the federal estate tax marital deduction.
b. Can be elected for the federal estate tax marital deduction.
c. Qualifies automatically for the federal estate tax marital deduction.
d. Can qualify for the federal estate tax marital deduction only if the trust produces reasonable income that the trustee, at the trustee's discretion, decides to distribute.
e. None of the above.

115. A springing power is:

a. One which springs from a 1st agent to a 2nd agent after the 1st agent resigns.
b. Springs back to the principal upon revocation.
c. Springs into existence upon the incompetency of the principal.
d. Authorizes only 1 of 2 named agents to act, depending upon the power to be exercised.
e. None of the above.

116. Which of the following charitable trusts allow for additional inter vivos contributions to be made after the inception of the trust?

1. CRATs.
2. CRUTs.
3. Pooled Income Fund.

   a. 1 only.
   b. 2 only.
   c. 3 only.
   d. 2 and 3.
   e. 1, 2, and 3.

117. Which of the following charitable trusts allow investments in securities that are exempt from taxes?

1. CRATs.
2. CRUTs.
3. Pooled Income Fund.

   a. 1 only.
   b. 2 only.
   c. 1 and 2.
   d. 1 and 3.
   e. None allow such investments.

118. Which of the following charitable trusts allow sprinkling provisions?

1. CRATs.
2. CRUTs.
3. Pooled Income Fund.

a. 1 only.
b. 2 only.
c. 1 and 2.
d. 2 and 3.
e. 1, 2, and 3.

119. Which of the following charitable trusts allow both term certain ≤ 20 years and life annuities?

1. CRATs.
2. CRUTs.
3. Pooled Income Funds.

a. 1 only.
b. 2 only.
c. 1 and 2.
d. 1, 2, and 3.
e. None of the above.

120. On January 15th, Glennon transfers property to a trust over which he retains a right to revoke one-forth of the trust. The trust is to pay Connie 5% of the trust assets valued annually for her life with the remainder to be paid to a qualified charity. On September 1st, Glennon dies and the trust becomes irrevocable. Which of the following trusts does this qualify as?

a. A CRAT.
b. A CRUT.
c. A pooled income fund.
d. All of the above.
e. None of the above.

121. On January 15th, Linval transfers property to a trust over which he retains a right to revoke one-fourth of the trust. The trust is to pay Desiree 5% of the trust assets valued annually for her life with the remainder to be paid to a qualified charity. On September 1st, Linval dies and the trust becomes irrevocable. Which of the following statements is/are correct?

1. The trust is created January 15th.
2. The trust is created when it becomes irrevocable at September 1st.
3. Linval receives a charitable deduction equal to the present value of 75% of the remainder interest.
4. Linval receives a charitable deduction equal to the present value of 75% of the remainder interest.

a. 1 only.
b. 1 and 2.
c. 3 only.
d. 3 and 4.
e. None of the above.

122. Of the statements below regarding trusts, which is/are incorrect?

1. A trust has only two parties: the grantor and the trustee.
2. A revocable trust's assets pass through probate.
3. A testamentary trust is created at the grantor's death.
4. A trust is a legal arrangement rather than an entity.

a. 1 only.
b. 2 only.
c. 1 and 2.
d. 1, 2, and 3.
e. 1, 2, 3, and 4.

123. What are the parties to a guardianship?

1. The ward.
2. The guardian.
3. The state government.
4. The federal government.

a. 1 only.
b. 1 and 2.
c. 1, 2, and 3.
d. 2 and 3.
e. 1, 2, 3, and 4.

124. Which of the following charitable trusts allow for additional inter vivos contributions to be made after the inception of the trust?

    1. CRATs.
    2. CRUTs.
    3. Pooled Income.

        a. 1 only.
        b. 2 only.
        c. 3 only.
        d. 2 and 3.
        e. 1, 2, and 3.

125. Which type of charitable remainder trusts permit additional contributions to the trust after its' inception?

    1. CRATs.
    2. CRUTs.

        a. 1 only.
        b. 2 only.
        c. 1 and 2.
        d. None of the above.

126. Troy and Anne have the following in their combined estate. Assume that Troy wants to set up the optional standard A B trust arrangement for himself, which of the following would be correct?

Troy separate property	$500,000
Anne separate property	$700,000
Community property	$1,600,000

	A Trust	B Trust
a.	$800,000	$500,000
b.	$675,000	$625,000
c.	$625,000	$675,000
d.	$1,400,000	$1,400,000

127. Which of the following statements regarding self-canceling installment notes (SCINS) is/are correct?

1. To be effective, a self-canceling installment note must reflect a risk premium to compensate the seller for the possibility of cancellation.
2. A seller who accepts a self-canceling installment note may accept security without jeopardizing the installment sale treatment.
3. At the seller's death, the present value of any remaining self-canceling installment note balance is excluded from the seller's gross estate.
4. A self-canceling installment note is a debt that ordinarily is extinguished at the seller's death.

a. 1 only.
b. 3 only.
c. 1 and 3.
d. 1, 2, and 3.
e. 1, 2, 3, and 4.

128. A correct statement regarding the use of a Grantor Retained Annuity Trust (GRAT) as an estate-planning technique is that such a strategy: **(CFP® Exam, released 12/95)**

a. Is appropriate only if the remainder beneficiary is the grantor's spouse.
b. Saves estate taxes only if the grantor lives beyond the trust term.
c. Guarantees that the trust property will receive a stepped-up basis at the grantor's death.
d. Is generally inappropriate if the trust corpus consists of income-producing assets.

LIFE INSURANCE IN ESTATE PLANNING

129. Proceeds of a life insurance policy on the decedent's life payable to the decedent's estate are:

   a. Includible in the decedent's gross estate only if the premiums had been paid by the insured.
   b. Includible in the decedent's gross estate only if the policy was taken out within 3 years of the insured's death under the "contemplation of death" rule.
   c. Always includible in the decedent's gross estate.
   d. Never includible in the decedent's gross estate.
   e. None of the above.

130. A buy/sell agreement was funded by a cross-purchase insurance arrangement. John bought a policy on Jack's life to finance the purchase of Jack's interest in the event of Jack's death. John, the beneficiary, paid the premiums and retained all incidents of ownership. On the death of Jack the insurance proceeds will be:

   a. Includible in Jack's gross estate if Jack owns 50% or more of the stock of the corporation.
   b. Includible in Jack's gross estate only if Jack had purchased a similar policy on John's life at the same time and for the same purpose.
   c. Includible in Jack's gross estate if John has the right to veto Jack's power to borrow on the policy that Jack owns on John's life.
   d. Excludable from Jack's gross estate.
   e. None of the above.

131. Jack and Jill Jones, age 65, have decided that, in order to best pay their $3,000,000 federal estate tax bill, they will purchase a second-to-die life insurance policy. In order to keep the proceeds out of their estate, they were advised to create an irrevocable life insurance trust. Jack and Jill applied for the insurance and the policy was issued to them. An irrevocable trust was drafted. The policy was transferred into the irrevocable trust, and 90 days later both Jack and Jill were killed in a plane crash. The Internal Revenue Service wants to include the insurance in the estate for tax purposes. Which statement(s) is/are correct? **(CFP® Exam, released 3/95)**

1. The insurance will be included in the estate because the trust was drafted after the insurance was approved.
2. The insurance will be included in the estate because the premiums were a gift from the insured.
3. The insurance will be included in the estate because the insureds transferred the policy within three years of death.
4. The Internal Revenue Service is wrong - the insurance will <u>not</u> be included in the estate.

   a. 1, 2, and 3.
   b. 1 only.
   c. 2 and 3.
   d. 3 only.
   e. 4 only.

THE GENERATION SKIPPING TRANSFER TAX (GSTT)

132. The generation skipping transfer tax is imposed:
   a. Instead of the gift tax.
   b. Instead of the estate tax.
   c. As a separate tax in addition to the gift and estate taxes.
   d. On transfers of future interest to beneficiaries who are more than one generation above the donor's generation.
   e. All of the above.

133. Which of the following is subject to the generation skipping transfer tax?
   a. Vicki wrote her will in 1985 establishing a generation skipping trust. Her will was unchanged when she died on December 31, 1986.
   b. Orion wrote his will in 1970 but amended it in 1984 to add a generation skipping trust. Orion was permanently mentally incompetent from December 1986 until his death in July 1996.
   c. Bill wrote a will in July 1986, which established a generation skipping trust. He made no changes in his will before his July 1996 death.
   d. In 1984, Thad established a generation skipping trust as a gift for the benefit of his grandchildren. The irrevocable trust was unchanged and no corpus was added prior to his death in 1996.
   e. None of the above are subject to GSTT.

134. Which of the following is a correct statement about what a generation skipping transfer tax applies to?
   a. A taxable termination only.
   b. A taxable distribution only.
   c. A taxable termination or a taxable distribution but not a direct skip.
   d. A taxable termination, a taxable distribution, or a direct skip.
   e. None of the above.

135. James (age 63) established a trust and named his wife, Carol, (age 40) as income beneficiary for 20 years. After 20 years, James' son, Bill, (age 30) and nephew, Bob, (age 22) are to receive lifetime income interests. After the death of both Bill and Bob, the remainder passes equally to James' granddaughter, Allison, (age 20) and great-grandson, Michael, (age 1). How many younger generations are there in this trust arrangement?

   a. 4.
   b. 3.
   c. 2.
   d. 1.
   e. 0.

136. James (age 63) established a trust and named his wife Carol (age 40) as income beneficiary for 20 years. After 20 years, James' son Bill (age 30) and nephew Bob (age 22) are to receive lifetime income interests. After the death of both Bill and Bob, the remainder passes equally to James' granddaughter Allison (age 20) and great-grandson Michael (age 1). Assume Bill died 22 years after the trust was established and Bob died 34 years after the trust was established. Assuming both Allison and Michael were alive when Bob died, how many times is the generation skipping transfer tax levied?

   a. Never.
   b. Once.
   c. Twice.
   d. Three times.
   e. Four times.

137. Julie, age 53 years exactly, wants to provide for the financial security of her secretary, Carolyn, and other unrelated friends. She establishes a trust. Carolyn, age 66, will receive income from the trust for her life. On Carolyn's death, Abe, another friend who is currently 58, will receive income for his lifetime. Upon his death, the remainder interest will be divided equally between Peter (age 36) and Jimmy (age 40). How many times will this trust be subject to a GSTT?

   a. None. No GSTT will be assessed.
   b. One.
   c. Two.
   d. Three.
   e. Four.

138. $1,000,000 is the:

a. Aggregate lifetime exemption from gift tax, for annual exclusion of gifts.
b. Unified credit shelter exemption equivalent.
c. GSTT aggregate, lifetime exemption.
d. Maximum marital deduction for non-QTIP transfers.
e. None of the above.

139. Which of the following types of transfers are subject to the GSTT?

1. Direct skips.
2. Taxable terminations.
3. Taxable distributions.

a. 1 only.
b. 1 and 2.
c. 1 and 3.
d. 2 and 3.
e. 1, 2, and 3.

140. Who among the following would be skip persons for purposes of the GSTT? Bill is the transferor and is 82 years old.

1. John, the grandson of Bill whose mother, Donna, is living but whose father, Frank, is deceased.
2. Mary is the great-grandchild of Bill. Both Mary's parents and grandparents are living.
3. Hazel is the 21-year-old wife of Bill's second son, Mike, age 65.

a. John only (1 only).
b. Mary only (2 only).
c. John and Mary (1 and 2).
d. Mary and Hazel (2 and 3).
e. John, Mary, and Hazel (1, 2, and 3).

141. Which of the following statements is/are correct regarding the GSTT?

1. There is a $10,000 per donor/per donee annual exclusion.
2. The annual exclusion permits gift splitting.
3. Qualified transfers are excluded from GSTT.
4. Each person is allowed a $1 million (indexed after 1998) lifetime exemption against all skips.

a. 1 and 4.
b. 1, 2, and 4.
c. 1, 2, and 3.
d. 1, 3, and 4.
e. 1, 2, 3, and 4.

142. John owns a small business, which is worth $1.2 million. How should life insurance be held if John is trying to benefit his minor grandson with the insurance policy?

a. John should be the owner.
b. John's spouse should be the owner.
c. The grandson should be the owner.
d. An Irrevocable trust should be set up with the grandchild as beneficiary.
e. A Revocable life insurance trust should be established for the grandchild.

POST- MORTEM PLANNING

143. With regard to the federal estate tax, the alternate valuation date:

a. Is required to be used if the fair market value of the estate's assets has increased since the decedent's date of death.

b. If elected on the first return filed for the estate, may be revoked in an amended return provided that the first return was filed on time.

c. Must be used for valuation of the estate's liabilities if such date is used for valuation of the estate's assets.

d. Can be elected only if it decreases the value of the gross estate as well as the estate tax liability.

e. None of the above.

144. Mr. Blue died on July 10th. The assets in his estate were valued on his date of death and an alternate valuation date respectively as follows:

Asset	Date of Death Valuation	Alternate Valuation
Residence	$300,000	$350,000
Common Stock	$400,000	$450,000
Municipal Bonds	$180,000	$90,000
Patent	$80,000	$65,000

The patent had 8 years of life remaining at the time of Mr. Blue's death. The executor sold the residence on August 1st for $325,000. If Mr. Blue's executor properly elects the alternate valuation date method, what is the value of Mr. Blue's gross estate?

a. $940,000.

b. $945,000.

c. $955,000.

d. $960,000.

e. $970,000.

145. Ordinary and necessary administration expenses paid by the fiduciary of an estate are deductible:

a. Only on the fiduciary income tax return (Form 1041) and never on the Federal estate tax return (Form 706).
b. Only on the Federal estate tax return and never on the fiduciary income tax return.
c. On the fiduciary income tax return only if the estate tax deduction is waived for these expenses.
d. On both the fiduciary income tax return and on the estate tax return by adding a tax computed on the proportionate rates attributable to both returns.
e. None of the above.

146. Upon the death of the grantor of a revocable or living trust, the trust assets receive:

a. A carry over basis, with capital gains tax consequences but no estate tax consequences.
b. A carry over basis, with no capital gains tax consequences but with estate tax consequence.
c. A stepped-up basis, with no capital gains tax consequences but with estate tax consequences.
d. A stepped-up basis, with capital gains tax consequences but with no estate tax consequences.
e. A stepped-up basis with capital gains tax consequences and estate tax consequences.

147. If the executor of a decedent's estate elects the alternate valuation date and none of the property included in the gross estate has been sold or distributed, the estate assets must be valued as of how many months after the decedent's death?

a. 3.
b. 6.
c. 9.
d. 12.
e. None of the above.

148. Section 6166 contains provisions for extending the time for paying estate taxes when the estate consists largely of an interest in a closely held business. An interest in a closely held business could include:

1. An interest as a proprietorship in a business carried on as a proprietorship.
2. An interest in a partnership carrying on a trade or business if 20% or more of the capital interest in such partnership is included in the gross estate or there are ≤15 partners.
3. Stock in a corporation carrying on a trade or business if 20% or more in value of the voting stock of such corporation is included in the gross estate or there are ≤15 shareholders.
4. Stock in an S corporation carrying on a trade or business if 15% or more of the value of the voting stock of such corporation is included in the gross estate or there are ≤ 75 shareholders.

   a. 1 only.
   b. 1 and 2.
   c. 2, 3, and 4.
   d. 1, 2, and 3.
   e. 1, 2, 3, and 4.

149. Which of the following statements correctly reflects the rules applicable to the alternate valuation date?

1. The general rule is the election covers all assets included in the gross estate and cannot be applied to only a portion of the property.
2. Assets disposed of within six months of decedent's death must be valued on the date of disposition.
3. The election can be made even though an estate tax return does not have to be filed.
4. The election must decrease the value of the gross estate and decrease the estate tax liability.

   a. 1 only.
   b. 2 and 4.
   c. 1 and 2.
   d. 1, 2, and 4.
   e. 1, 2, 3, and 4.

150. Which of the following is/are correct regarding disclaimers?

1. Must be in writing.
2. Disclaiming party could not have previously benefited from interest.
3. Must be issued within 9 months of interest creation.
4. Disclaiming party cannot direct the interest to other parties.

a. 1 only.
b. 2 only.
c. 1 and 2.
d. 1, 2, and 4.
e. 1, 2, 3, and 4.

151. A Section 6166 election to pay federal estate taxes on an installment basis includes or permits:

1. An executor to pay the federal estate tax, but not the generation skipping transfer tax which corresponds to a decedent's interest in a closely held business in installments over a period not extending beyond 12 years.
2. Payments during the first four years may be for interest only on unpaid federal estate tax including GSTT tax.
3. The value of a decedent's closely held business must exceed 35% of the value of a decedent's adjusted gross estate both inclusive and exclusive of transfers made within three years of the decedent's death.
4. Multiple businesses may not be aggregated for determining the minimum percentage that qualifies as a closely held business.

a. 1 only.
b. 2 only.
c. 2 and 3.
d. 1, 2, and 3.
e. 1, 2, 3, and 4.

152. Assuming the following facts about Davidson Corporation's annual dividend:

Date declared	June 5th
Ex-dividend	August 7th
Dates of record	August 15th
Date of payment	September 1st

Which of the following statements is/are true about the treatment of the Davidson dividend with respect to the Federal Form 706?

1. If the decedent dies on June 15th, the dividend should be ignored for purposes of the 706.
2. If the decedent dies on August 12th, the dividend should be simply added to the date of death stock price.
3. If the decedent dies on August 28th, the dividend should be accrued and listed separately on the 706.
4. If the decedent dies after September 1st, the dividend should be ignored for purposes of the stocks and bonds section of the 706.

a. 1 and 4.

b. 2 and 3.

c. 1, 2, and 3.

d. 1, 3, and 4.

e. All of the above are true.

ESTATE PLANNING SOLUTIONS

ESTATE PLANNING

1.	E	27.	C	53.	B	79.	D	105.	A	131.	D
2.	E	28.	C	54.	D	80.	A	106.	A	132.	C
3.	C	29.	A	55.	E	81.	B	107.	E	133.	C
4.	D	30.	D	56.	B	82.	E	108.	D	134.	D
5.	E	31.	B	57.	C	83.	D	109.	C	135.	B
6.	E	32.	B	58.	D	84.	B	110.	B	136.	B
7.	D	33.	D	59.	B	85.	C	111.	B	137.	A
8.	D	34.	A	60.	A	86.	D	112.	D	138.	C
9.	B	35.	E	61.	B	87.	D	113.	B	139.	E
10.	D	36.	B	62.	E	88.	E	114.	C	140.	B
11.	E	37.	C	63.	B	89.	C	115.	C	141.	E
12.	B	38.	A	64.	B	90.	B	116.	D	142.	D
13.	E	39.	C	65.	C	91.	B	117.	C	143.	D
14.	C	40.	B	66.	C	92.	D	118.	C	144.	B
15.	A	41.	D	67.	D	93.	C	119.	C	145.	C
16.	E	42.	C	68.	B	94.	A	120.	E	146.	C
17.	B	43.	B	69.	C	95.	E	121.	A	147.	B
18.	E	44.	D	70.	B	96.	D	122.	C	148.	D
19.	E	45.	B	71.	B	97.	C	123.	C	149.	D
20.	C	46.	B	72.	B	98.	C	124.	D	150.	E
21.	E	47.	E	73.	C	99.	D	125.	B	151.	C
22.	D	48.	E	74.	E	100.	D	126.	B	152.	E
23.	E	49.	B	75.	A	101.	B	127.	E		
24.	D	50.	A	76.	D	102.	E	128.	B		
25.	C	51.	E	77.	D	103.	D	129.	C		
26.	A	52.	D	78.	B	104.	E	130.	D		

BASIC CONCEPTS

Estate Planning

1. **E**

All are incorporated in the definition of estate planning.

Estates

2. **E**

All of those persons have need for a will, a plan for incapacity, and a need to care for persons or dogs.

Estates

3. **C**

The establishment of priorities occurs after the definition of problem areas.

BASIC DOCUMENTS INCLUDED IN AN ESTATE PLAN

Incapacity

4. **D**

All of the arrangements are methods of providing for incapacity.

Estate Pitfalls

5. **E**

All of the items are potential problems:

1. Ancillary probate indicates the estate owns property outside the decedent's state of domicile and may cause excessive costs and delays - could have used JTWROS.
2. The rule against perpetuities may make trust arrangements void.
3. A will that includes funeral instructions - will may be lost or delays in proving could cause funeral instruction not to be carried out.
4. Attempts to disinherit spouses and/or minor children should be approached with great care - see an attorney.

Estate Planning Documents

6. **E**

All are important and common provisions in a well drafted will.

Estate Documents

7. **D**

Statement #1 is incorrect. A durable power of attorney does not always substitute for a living will because in many states a specific statute governs living wills, and unless the durable power meets that specific language, it will not be a valid living will. The other statements (#2 - #4) are correct.

Estate Documents

8. **D**

A durable power of attorney does not survive the death of the principal. The rest of the statements (#1, #3, and #4) are correct.

Basic Documents

9. **B**

She should not gift; she may need the money. She is single and under the exemption equivalent therefore has no need for ABC.

General Power of Attorney

10. **D**

This is a general power, statements #1, #2, and #4 are correct. Statement #3 is incorrect; she can appoint for any reason and to any person.

Durable Powers (CFP® Exam, released 12/95)

11. **E**

Statement #1 is inappropriate, may create serious problems, and will not accomplish what is intended. Statement #2 is appropriate due to her declining health. Statement #3 is inappropriate due to the irrevocability. Statement #4 is inappropriate because it is unnecessary. She is below the $625,000 (650,000 for 1999).

OWNERSHIP OF PROPERTY AND HOW IT IS TRANSFERRED

Estate Planning for Nontraditional Relationships

12. B

The question asks which is least appropriate. Intestate probate is probate without a will. Assuming that the individuals are not blood related, they would be unlikely to receive anything in an intestate probate.

Estate Planning for Nontraditional Relationships

13. E

None of the above will accomplish transfers between these parties. Statements #1 and #2 go through probate. Statements #3 and #4 are between husband and wife.

Property

14. C

Community property and tenancy by the entirety can only be entered into by spouses. Joint tenancy (JTWROS) is often used by spouses to avoid probate but is not limited to spouses.

Property

15. A

Only statement #1 is correct, anyone may establish a joint tenancy. Only half the value in a spousal joint tenancy is deemed included in the estate of the first spouse to die. Community property is not joint property. The first spouse to die can transfer his share of community to anyone he selects. Unlike a joint tenancy, in community property there is no survivorship transfer to the surviving spouse.

THE PROBATE PROCESS

Probate

16. **E**

All are examples of property that passes through probate.

Probate

17. **B**

Only statement #4 is true.

Probate

18. **E**

All are excellent methods of non-probate disposition devices.

Probate

19. **E**

All of the statements are correct.

Probate

20. **C**

Both properties held fee simple and as tenants in common will pass through probate.

Probate

21. **E**

All are advantages of probate.

Probate

22. **D**

Clear title to heirs and legatees is not a disadvantage.

Probate

23. E

All are substitutes for the probate process. Revocable living trusts become irrevocable at death of trustor.

Probate

24. D

The JTWROS property will avoid probate (statement #4).

FEDERAL UNIFIED GIFT AND ESTATE TAXATION

Unified Credit

25. C

There is no estate or gift tax liability for transfers to a spouse or to a public charity. Therefore, statements #1 and #4 are incorrect.

THE FEDERAL GIFT TAX

Gifts

26. A

($205,000 - 40,000) ÷ 2 = $82,500 each. When gifts are split, all gifts for that year must be split. "Taxable gifts" is a term of art meaning net of the annual exclusion. The two donees allow for $40,000 in annual exclusion.

Gifts

27. C

By reserving the right to revoke, the individual has not completed the gift in statement #3.

Gifts

28. C

No gift until the account is drawn on by the donee for donee's own benefit.

Gifts

29. A

Statements #2 and #3 are qualified transfers. Statement #1 is not a gift because it is legal support. Therefore, answer A is correct.

Gifts

30. D

Payments for medical expenses must be to the institution, not the person.

Gifts

31. B

The interest in statement #4 is not a gift because it is less than $10,000.

Gifts

32. B

Rosario's basis	$12,000
FMV at date of gift	$20,000
Donee's basis before gift tax	$12,000 (donor's basis)
Gift tax paid	$5,000
$8,000/20,000 X 5,000 =	$2,000 Gift tax paid adjustment

Donee's basis: $12,000 + 2,000 = $14,000.

Gifts

33. D

Donee	FMV	Annual Exclusion	Taxable Gifts
Nephew	$12,000	$10,000	$2,000
Niece	$8,000	$8,000	0
Friend	$20,000	$10,000	$10,000
Father	$60,000	$10,000	$50,000
Niece	$18,000	0	$18,000
	$118,000	**$38,000**	**$80,000**

Possible mistakes:

1. Not knowing the difference between gross gifts and taxable gifts - incorrect answer: $118,000.
2. Not knowing remainder interest does not qualify for gift of present interest: $18,000 - 2,000 = $16,000. Therefore, $78,000.
3. Taking the annual exclusion of $10,000 from remainder interest = $70,000.
4. Five donees x $10,000 = $50,000 ($118,000 - 50,000 = $68,000).

Gifts

34. **A**

1. Payment directly to hospital is a qualified transfer, not a gift.
2. Generally, support payments to a parent are not a legal obligation and, therefore, will be treated as a gift. $18,000 to her mother is reduced by $10,000, therefore, taxable gift, is: $8,000
3. $14,000 to Mike is reduced by $10,000, therefore, taxable gift, is : $4,000
4. Loan is less than $100,000; therefore, imputed interest is not a gift. $ 0

$12,000

Gifts

35. **E**

Question asks for exclusion and deductions:

	Total		Exclusions/ Deductions		Taxable Gift	Reason
1a.	$20,000	-	10,000	=	$10,000	Annual exclusion
1b.	$60,000	-	60,000	=	$0	Unlimited gifts to spouse
2.	$15,000	-	10,000	=	$5,000	Annual exclusion
3.	$100,000	-	100,000	=	$0	Charitable gift
			$180,000			

Gifts

36. **B**

The gift is outright to Stacy and, therefore, qualifies for the $10,000 exclusion. This is not a qualified transfer for educational or medical purposes, because the payee is not an institution.

Gifts

37. **C**

The engagement ring does not qualify for the deduction, because they were not married at the time of the gift.

Gifts

38. **A**

Statement #1 is a qualified transfer; statement #3 is to the spouse; and statement #2 ($30,000 - $10,000 = $20,000) is a gift of a present interest and exceeds the $10,000 annual exclusion.

Gi'. ,

39. **C**

Husband and wife do not have to file a joint income tax return to gift split.

Gifts

40. **B**

	TOTAL GIFTS	EXCLUSIONS	NET GIFTS
Son	$60,000	$20,000	$40,000
Wife	$120,000	$120,000	- 0 -
Church	$40,000	$40,000	- 0 -
Nephew	$30,000	$20,000	$10,000
Mother	$30,000	$20,000	$10,000
	$280,000	$220,000	$60,000 ÷ 2=$30,000

Gifts

41. **D**

Split gift election requires the filing of a gift tax return, even when there is no tax due.

Gifts

42. **C**

The interest free loan is a gift loan of $10,000 or less, therefore, there is no imputed income, and thus, no gift. Gift = ($50,000 + 35,000 + 8,000) = $93,000.

Gifts

43. **B**

Taxable gifts are the net of $93,000 - 20,000 annual exclusion = $73,000.

Gifts

44. **D**

Answer A is a nondeductible donation.

Answers B and C are qualified transfers not subject to gift tax.

Answer D occurs before the marriage; therefore, it is a gift.

Gifts

45. **B**

H has made a gift to D equal to the increase in the value of D's stock.

Gifts

46. **B**

Mother (M) must impute the interest but receives no deduction. Answers A, C, and D are correct.

Gifts

47. **E**

All are gifts subject to gift tax.

Gifts

48. **E**

A gift does not occur until the withdrawal by Rachel for her own benefit.

Gifts

49. **B**

Gift occurs when Rachel withdraws money from the account for her own benefit. The mere fact of creating the bank account does not constitute a gift nor does Rachel's notification that an account has been created. If Mary Sue were to die, this would not be a gift but rather a device.

Gifts

50. **A**

Only by drawing on the account for her own benefit is a gift made complete under the circumstances.

Gifts

51. **E**

None of the above is a taxable gift. Support is not a gift. Neither is the direct payment of tuition or medical bills paid to an institution a gift, since the transfer qualifies as a qualified transfer under 2503(e).

Gifts

52. **D**

Statement #4, a payment made directly to an individual to reimburse for medical expenses, is not a qualified transfer. All the other statements are true.

Gifts

53. **B**

Calculated as follows:

$10,000 per donee there are eight donees which is $800,000 for 10 years x 2 = $1,600,000. Split gift.

Gifts

54. **D**

The gift tax return is always due April 15th; therefore, statement #1 is incorrect. All of the others (statements #2, #3 and #4) are correct descriptions of rules regarding the Federal gift tax return.

Gifts

55. **E**

Statements #1, #2, #3, and #4 are all correct descriptions regarding the federal gift tax return.

Gifts

56. **B**

Only statement #4 is false. Statements #1, #2, and #3 are true.

Gifts

57. **C**

($10,000 x 6) x 2 = $120,000.

Gifts

58. **D**

The opening of a joint bank account does not constitute a gift. A gift arises when son withdraws funds for his own benefit. The $9,999 gift in statement #3 is within the statute even though it will not be a taxable gift due to the annual exclusion of $10,000.

Basis of Gift

59. **B**

The donee's gain basis for the property received is the same as that of the donor. The donee's loss basis is the lower of either the donor's adjusted basis or the fair market value as of the date of the gift.

Basis of Gift

60. **A**

The son's gain basis is $35,000. His loss basis is $30,000. Since his selling price of $33,000 is between the gain and the loss basis, there is no recognized gain or loss.

Basis of Gift

61. B

The daughter's gain basis is $1,800. She has a recognized gain of $200, which is calculated as follows:

Amount realized	$2,000
Basis for stock	(1,800)
Realized gain	$200
Recognized gain	$200

If the daughter had sold the bonds for less than $1,000, she would use her loss basis of $1,000.

Basis of Gift

62. E

The gain basis for Donna is $75,000, and the loss basis is $50,000. Because the sales price is within this range, no gain or loss is recognized. The gift tax paid is irrelevant, because there was no unrealized appreciation as of the date of the gift. If FMV < adjusted basis at the date of the gift, no basis adjustment is made for gift tax paid.

Basis of Gift

63. B

James' basis is calculated as follows:

Donor's Adjusted Basis + [(Unrealized appreciation ÷ FMV at date of gift) x Gift tax paid]
$105,000 + [($70,000 ÷ 175,000) x $12,000] = $109,800

Basis of Gift

64. B

Tom's basis is $42,000 + [(18,000 ÷ 60,000) x 4,500] = $43,350. Gain and loss basis are equal when FMV exceeds the donor's adjusted basis at the time of the gift.

Basis of Gift

65. C

The donee's gain basis for the property received is the same as the donor's basis. The donee's loss basis is the lower of the donor's adjusted basis or the fair market value on the date of the gift. If FMV < adjusted basis at date of gift, no basis adjustment is made for gift tax paid.

Basis and Holding Periods

66. **C**

The holding period associated with the gain basis rule includes the holding period of the donor. The holding period associated with the loss basis rule begins on the date of the gift.

Basis of Gift

67. **D**

The basis for depreciation is John's gain basis of $4,800. However, Jack cannot depreciate the asset more than $4,500, (the fair market value).

Gift Tax Filing

68. **B**

Statements #1 and #2 require filing; statement #3 is not a completed gift; and statement #4 is a gift of community property and is less than the annual exclusion.

Net Gift

69. **C**

Net gifts are considered part sale and part gift. Therefore, the donor will have taxable income to the extent gift tax paid actually exceeds donor's adjusted basis.

Gifts (CFP® Exam, released 3/95)

70. **B**

Taxable gifts include statement #1 to the adult child in excess of $10,000. Statement #2 is not correct due to the annual exclusions. Statement #3 is not a qualified transfer because it is paid to the individual, thereby subjecting it to the gift tax statutes. Statement #4 is a qualified transfer and therefore is not a taxable gift.

Gifts (CFP® Exam, released 3/95)

71. **B**

Donor retains power in statement #2 and life estate in statement #1. Both situations will cause inclusion. Gifts are not included in the gross estate; therefore, statements #3 and #4 do not cause inclusion.

Gifts

72. **B**

$60,000 (cost) - 10,000 (depreciation) = $50,000.

Gifts

73. **C**

$50,000 + [(90,000 ÷ 140,000) x 30,000] = $69,286.

Gifts

74. **E**

$20,000 per child for annual exclusion	=	$40,000
$625,000 per parent unified credit equivalency	=	$1,250,000
Total		$1,290,000

Gifts

75. **A**

($250,000 - 40,000) ÷ 2 = $105,000 each.

Basis of Inherited Property

76. **D**

The basis for inherited property is the fair market value at the date of death (primary valuation date) or the alternative valuation date. The alternative valuation date was not elected so Robin's basis for the land is $25,000.

Gift Splitting

77. **D**

All are correct.

Transfers

78. **B**

Only statement #2 is correct.

Annual Exclusion

79. **D**

Annual exclusion plus credit equivalency for each total $1,270,000 (1998 answer). For 1999, the answer would be (650,000 x 2) + 20,000 = $1,320,000. For 2000 and 2001, the answer would be (675,000 x 2) + 20,000 = $1,370,000.

Gifts

80. **A**

Statements #2 and #3 are qualified transfers. Statement #1 is not a gift, because it is legal support.

Gifts

81. **B**

Only statement #4 is false. Statements #1, #2, and #3 are true.

Basis of Gift

82. **E**

The gain basis for Donna is $75,000, and the loss basis is $50,000. Because the sales price is within this range, no gain or loss is recognized. The gift tax paid is irrelevant, because there was no unrealized appreciation as of the date of the gift. If FMV < adjusted basis at date of gift, no basis adjustment is made for gift tax paid.

THE FEDERAL ESTATE TAX

Gross Estate - Inclusion

83. D

The dividends declared to the decedent after death are excluded from the gross estate.

Gross Estate - Inclusion

84. B

Statement #2 is not included in the gross estate, because gifts made within 3 years of death are not included in the gross estate. However, such gifts are added back to the taxable estate.

Gross Estate - Inclusion

85. C

The dividend is not included in the gross estate, because it was declared after the death of taxpayer. $180,00 + $50,000 + $2,500 +$42,00 = $274,500.

Gross Income - Inclusions

86. D

Both assets are includible in the gross estate ($825,000).

Gross Estate - Inclusions

87. D

All assets are includible in the gross estate. Liabilities are irrelevant to the determination of the gross estate ($620,000).

Gross Estate - Inclusions

88. E

The gift is not included in the gross estate. Post-1976 gifts are added to the taxable estate. The jointly held property is 50% included. The last two items are included fully due to incidence of ownership and retained interest, respectively.

Estate Tax Deductions

89. C

Penalties are never deductible under administrative expenses.

Gross Estate and Deductions

90. B

($4,500 + 6,000 + 45,000 + 75,000) = $130,500.

The $1,000 is not deductible on the estate return. However, it is deductible on the fiduciary tax return (Form 1041).

Gross Estate and Deductions

91. B

The marital deduction is $375,000 (the amount bequeathed to the widow).

Taxable Estate - General

92. D

$650,000 for 1999.

Estates - General

93. C

The marital deduction is not a credit. It is a deduction from the gross estate.

Estates - General

94. A

The calculation is ($780,800 - 202,050 - 100,000) = $478,750.

Estates - General

95. E

The credit is $211,300. Gifts are added back to the taxable estate, and then the entire credit is taken.

Estates - General

96. D

The value of the gross estate must be over $625,000, not $600,000.

Estates - General

97. C

$650,000 is the exemption equivalency for 1999.

Estates - Filing

98. C

9 months is correct.

Estate Tax - Extensions

99. D

The IRS may grant extensions up to a maximum of 10 years, not 12 years.

Estate Tax - Extensions

100. D

Statement #4 is incorrect. Any 55% tax might cause liquidation. Statements #1, #2, and #3 are correct. See Regulation 20.6161.

Estates

101. B

$211,300 is the credit for $650,000, the lifetime exemption for 1999.

Gross Estate

102. E

All of the items listed will reduce the gross estate or the taxable estate.

Community Property Basis

103. D

Both decedent's and survivor's shares of the community property receive a basis adjustment to the fair market value on the date of decedent's death (or alternative valuation date, if properly elected).

Estate Deductions

104. **E**

All are deductions from the gross estate to arrive at the taxable estate.

Estate Tax Liability (CFP® Exam, released 3/95)

105. **A**

If the decedent is in the 50% marginal tax bracket, then she must have utilized her lifetime exemption. Therefore, tax is due on the $100,000 bequest. Since she has made no provisions to the contrary, the 50% tax will come out of the bequest to the son. The bequest to the husband qualifies for the unlimited marital deduction. B and C are wrong because this is not a gift subject to the annual exclusion. D is incorrect because there is no stipulation for the residual estate to pay the estate tax. E is incorrect.

Federal Estate Tax

106. **A**

Funeral expenses are deducted on the estate tax return (Form 706).

Federal Estate Tax

107. **E**

IRC Section 303 - Complete stock redemption.

IRC Section 6166 - Election to pay estate tax in installments.

IRC Section 2032 - Alternate valuation date.

IRC Section 2032A - Special use valuation of real estate.

VALUATION OF ASSETS

Valuation

108. D

The value is the mean [(High + Low) ÷ 2] on the date of sale. Since Thursday the market was closed, it is the mean average (high and low) selling price for the 2 days. It is not the closing price. (60 + 56 + 62 + 58.5) ÷ 4 = 59.125. We can average the values since the sale date is equidistant from the valuation date. See Volume I for the treatment of valuation where sale dates are not equal.

Valuation of Securities for an Estate

109. C

The value of the stock reported on the Form 706 will be the mean of the high and the low stock price on the date of death. It is not the stock's closing price for stock on the trading day.
(60 + 58) ÷ 2 = 59.

Valuation of Stock

110. B

$$\frac{(1 \times 28) + (2 \times 25)}{3} = \frac{78}{3} = 26$$

According to the IRS Regulations, the next trading price following the death should be multiplied by the number of trading days between the first trade before the date of death and the date of death (in this case, 1 day). Added to this number is the first trading price before the death multiplied by the number of trading days between the date of death and the first trade following the date of death (in this case, 2 days). This sum should be divided by the sum of trading days between trades.

THE MARITAL DEDUCTION

Marital Deduction

111. B

If the spouse is a non-resident, non-citizen, a QDOT must be used to qualify for the marital deduction.

Marital Deduction

112. D

Spouse must actually survive the condition. If the spouse does not survive, the property is not qualified.

TRUSTS

Trusts

113. **B**

Revocable trusts do not save taxes, nor create joint tenancy.

Trusts

114. **C**

A marital power of appointment trust is a general power and, therefore, automatically qualifies for the marital deduction as an exception to the terminable interest rule.

Powers of Appointment

115. **C**

Answer C is the only correct answer. A springing power may also spring on incapacity.

Charitable Remainder Interest

116. **D**

CRATs specifically preclude additions to trust property post-inception.

Charitable Remainder Interest

117. **C**

Pooled income funds are prohibited from investing in tax exempt securities.

Charitable Remainder Interest

118. **C**

Pooled income funds do not allow sprinkling provisions.

Charitable Remainder Interest

119. **C**

Statements #1 and #2 are correct. Pooled income funds do not allow a term other than the actual life of the beneficiary.

Charitable Remainder Interest

120. E

At the creation, the trust is revocable, therefore, it does not qualify as A, B, or C.

Charitable Remainder Interest

121. A

The trust is created when funded, but because of the right to revoke, it does not qualify for any charitable deduction.

Trusts

122. C

A revocable trust becomes irrevocable at death and assets pass according to the trust instrument. A trust has at least 3 parties: the grantor, the trustee, and the beneficiaries. All three parties may be the same person, however, if a grantor creates an inter vivos revocable trust and names himself both initial trustee and income beneficiary.

Guardianship

123. C

Appointments relative to the "person" are usually called guardianships. A ward is deemed by a court to be incapable of managing his/her personal and/or financial affairs in response to a hearing sought by an interested party. A guardian is appointed by the court to protect the ward according to the state's rules for guardianships. The state government must provide ongoing supervision of a guardianship. The federal government is not a party to guardianships that fall exclusively under state laws.

Charitable Remainder Interest

124. D

CRATs specifically preclude additions to trust property post-inception.

CRATs v. CRUTs

125. B

Only CRUTs permit additional contributions after inception.

Trusts

126. B

Troy puts $625,000 in the B trust (credit equivalency) and the balance in the A trust.

Installment Notes (SCINS)

127. E

All are correct. The present value of a self-canceling installment note balance is not included in the gross estate of the seller (decedent).

GRATs (CFP® Exam, released 12/95)

128. B

A GRAT is only effective if the grantor survives the GRAT term. GRATs are usually created with a related party remainderman. If the grantor does not outlive the GRAT, then the value of the GRAT is brought back into the estate.

LIFE INSURANCE IN ESTATE PLANNING

Life Insurance

129. C

Always includible in the gross estate.

Life Insurance

130. D

The policy is owned by John and not included in Jack's estate.

Life Insurance (CFP® Exam, released 3/95)

131. D

Insurance policies transferred within 3 years of death are included in the gross estate (referred to as the throw back rule).

THE GENERATION SKIPPING TRANSFER TAX (GSTT)

GSTT

132. C

As a separate tax in addition to the gift and estate tax.

GSTT

133. C

No exception for C because he died after January 1, 1987.

GSTT

134. D

All are subject to GSTT rules.

GSTT

135. B

Son, granddaughter, and great-grandson.

GSTT

136. B

The GSTT is only levied once at Bob's death (taxable termination).

GSTT

137. A

There are no skip persons in this example. In this case, the unrelated person must be 37½ years younger than the transferor to be a skip person.

GSTT

138. C

GSTT aggregate, lifetime exemption.

GSTT

139. **E**

All are subject to GSTT.

GSTT

140. **B**

John is not a skip person because of the predeceased parent rule. Hazel is not because she is not in a skipped generation.

GSTT

141. **E**

All statements are correct. In addition, there is the predeceased parent rule.

GSTT

142. **D**

The grandchild is a minor. Set up an irrevocable trust and use the GSTT lifetime exemption against premiums.

POST-MORTEM PLANNING

Post-Mortem Planning

143. D

To utilize the alternate valuation date there are two requirements:

1. Must reduce the estate tax liability.
2. Must reduce the gross estate.

Post-Mortem Planning

144. B

($325,000 + 450,000 + 90,000 + 80,000) = $945,000.

There are three rules applicable to the valuation of assets assuming that the alternate valuation date is properly elected. Rule 1 - generally all assets are valued on the alternate valuation date. Rule 2 – (1st exception) any asset disposed of between the date of death and the alternate valuation date is valued on the date of disposition. Rule 3 – (2nd exception) all wasting assets (leases, installment notes, annuities, and patents) which decline in value due to time as opposed to market conditions are always valued on the date of death.

Post-Mortem Planning

145. C

Only if waived on the estate return.

Post-Mortem Planning

146. C

Stepped-up basis means basis to FMV, no capital gains tax but inclusion in gross estate.

Alternative Valuation Date

147. B

The alternate valuation date is 6 months from the date of death.

Estates - Liquidity

148. **D**

Statement #4 is wrong because of the ≤ 75 shareholders. The rule is properly expressed in statement #3. S Corp can qualify if ≤ 15 shareholders or if value in gross estates is 20% or more of the total value of the voting stock.

Estate Taxation

149. **D**

The election must be made on Form 706 to be valid. Therefore, statement #3 is incorrect. Statements #1, #2, and #4 are correct.

Disclaimers

150. **E**

All are correct.

Installments

151. **C**

Statements #2 and #3 are correct. Statement #1 is incorrect. (1) The 6166 election permits installment payments of both FET (Federal Estate Tax) and GSTT (Generation Skipping Transfer Tax) and (2) the installment payment period can be up to 14 years--not 12. Statement #4 is incorrect, because interests in corporations, partnerships, and sole proprietorships may be aggregated in order to arrive at the 35% requirement if the decedent's interest has over 20% of each business.

Income in Respect of a Decedent

152. **E**

All are correct.

THIS PAGE IS INTENTIONALLY LEFT BLANK.

MINI CASE SCENARIOS

MINI CASE SCENARIO 1

Bob and Ann Crow wish to begin saving for their child's education. The child, Lee Schan, is born today. The first payment will be made today, and she will start college on her 18th birthday. Lee Schan will attend college for four years with the annual payment due at the beginning of the school year. The current cost of the college education is $25,000 per year. It is expected that the cost of a college education will increase at an average rate of 7% per year during the projection period and that the general rate of inflation will be 4%. The Crows have the option of investing in the following funds: 1) A taxable mutual stock fund expected to earn 12.0% during the projection period and 2) A tax-free bond fund expected to earn 8.5% during the projection period. The Crows' marginal tax bracket is 31% and the average tax bracket is 21%.

1. Which fund should the Crows invest in for the purpose of funding their child's education?
   a. The stock fund because it has a higher return.
   b. The bond fund because it is a safer investment.
   c. The stock fund initially, but they should allocate more of the funds to the bond fund as Lee Schan gets closer to attending college.
   d. The choice can not be made without determining the required rate of return necessary to fund the college education.
   e. The bond fund because it has a higher after-tax rate of return.

2. Calculate the sum total of the projected withdrawals (rounded to the nearest dollar).
   a. $350,623.
   b. $375,168.
   c. $401,429.
   d. $206,792.
   e. $215,063.

3. Calculate the annual payment required to fund the cost of college education assuming the Crows invest in the tax-free fund and make deposits on every birthday, exclusive of Lee Schan's 18th birthday. (Round to the nearest dollar.)
   a. $9,373.
   b. $7,759.
   c. $8,419.
   d. $8,793.
   e. $8,638.

MINI CASE SCENARIO 2

Al and Irma Dell have resided in New Orleans for several years. During 1999, a fire struck them, and they sustained damage to their home, automobiles, and personal property as follows:

Description	FMV Prior to Fire	FMV After Fire
Dwelling	$100,000	$60,000
Personal Property	$50,000	$25,000
Honda Accord	$18,000	$14,500
Toyota Camry	$20,000	$18,000

Fortunately, the Dells had insurance on the house, automobiles, and personal property*.

Homeowners Insurance	
Policy Type	HO3
Coverage	$75,000
Deductible	$500
Premiums (amount)	$1,025
Liability	$100,000
Medical Payments	$1,000

Automobile Insurance	Honda Accord (USAA)	Toyota Camry (State Farm)
Premium	$1,200	$950
Coverage	$50,000/100,000	$50,000/100,000
Comprehensive	$250	$500
Collision	$300	$550

* They also have an endorsement for personal property to be valued at replacement value.

1. How much will the insurance company pay to have the dwelling repaired?

    a. $40,000.

    b. $37,500.

    c. $37,000.

    d. $32,000.

    e. $30,000.

2. How much will the Dells have to pay personally to have the automobiles fixed?

   a. $5,500.

   b. $4,750.

   c. $4,650.

   d. $850.

   e. $750.

3. Assume the Dell's adjusted gross income for 1999 is $60,000, and assume that they receive the following amounts of insurance proceeds:

Dwelling	$30,000
Personal Property	$20,000
Honda Accord	$1,000
Toyota Camry	$1,000

   How much of a casualty loss can the Dells deduct on their 1999 Federal income tax return?

   a. $12,400.

   b. $12,500.

   c. $18,400.

   d. $18,500.

   e. $64,400.

MINI CASE SCENARIO 3

John, a happily single man, had the following stock transactions during 1999:

1. Sold 1,000 shares of Bachelor, Inc. for $15,000 on 6/1/99. The stock was originally purchased on 1/1/99 for $12,000.
2. Purchased 500 shares of Bachelor, Inc. on 6/15/99 for $16/share.
3. Sold 200 shares of Freedom Corp. stock (Sec. 1244 stock) for $35,000 on 9/1/99. The stock was originally purchased for $125,000 on 12/15/97.
4. Sold 500 shares of Footloose, Inc. on 6/1/99 for $12,000. Stock was inherited from his uncle on 3/1/99. Uncle's basis was $2,000 and the fair market value on 3/1/99 was $11,000.
5. Shares of Clueless, Inc. became worthless on 9/1/99. John originally purchased the stock on 10/1/98 for $5,000.
6. On 7/15/99, John sold 200 shares of Wild'n'Crazy for $3,000. John had received the stock on 1/15/99 in exchange for 300 shares of Diddly stock (Diddly FMV at date of exchange was $3,700). John originally purchased Diddly on 6/15/97 for $3,000.

1. What is the capital gain/loss on the sale of Bachelor, Inc. 6/1/99?

   a. $3,000 LTCG.

   b. $3,000 STCG.

   c. $4,500 LTCG.

   d. $2,500 STCG.

   e. No gain or loss currently recognized.

2. What is the nature of the gain/loss on the sale of Freedom Corp. 9/1/99?

   a. $90,000 STCL.

   b. $90,000 LTCL.

   c. $90,000 ordinary loss.

   d. $50,000 ordinary loss and $40,000 STCL.

   e. $50,000 ordinary loss and $40,000 LTCL.

3. Regarding all of these stock sales, which of the following statements is/are incorrect?

   1. John's maximum deductible capital loss for 1999 is $3,000.
   2. It is irrelevant how the uncle acquired the Footloose stock in Transaction #4.
   3. The sale of Bachelor, Inc. (Transaction #1) falls under the wash sale rules.
   4. John's basis in Diddly stock is $3,000 (Transaction #6).

   a. 2 only.
   b. 2 and 3.
   c. 2, 3, and 4.
   d. 1 and 4.
   e. 3 and 4.

4. What is John's long-term capital gain/loss for 1999 (without netting with short-term gains/losses)?

   a. $35,000 LTCL.
   b. $38,000 LTCL.
   c. $39,000 LTCL.
   d. $44,000 LTCL.
   e. $94,000 LTCL.

5. What is John's short-term capital gain/loss for 1999 (without netting with long-term gains/losses)?

   a. No short-term gains or losses.
   b. $2,800 STCL.
   c. $2,300 STCG.
   d. $3,000 STCG.
   e. $3,800 STCG.

MINI CASE SCENARIO 4

Harold is a 55-year-old corporate executive employed with one of the Fortune 500 companies. He is planning to retire at age 65 and has accumulated the assets listed below for his retirement. Harold is willing to accept enough risk to meet his goals, but he does not want to accept additional risk, nor does he ever want to die with less than $1,000,000 (in today's dollars) in his account (i.e., he hopes to have at least this much in his estate at the end of the 25 year retirement period).

	Stock Portfolio Various stocks	**Bond Portfolio Various Bonds**
Market Value	$572,160	$143,040
Average Historic Return	12%	7%
Standard Deviation	15%	9%
Current YTM	N/A	7%
Duration	N/A	5 yrs.
Correlation to the Stock Market	77.5%	N/A

Note: The correlation coefficient between stocks and bonds is +40%.

1. If Harold needs $100,000 each year (in today's dollars) during retirement and his retirement period is estimated to be 25 years, what allocation between his stock and bond portfolio is appropriate to meet his financial goals? Assume inflation is expected to be 3.2%.

	Stock %	Bond %
a.	40%	60%
b.	50%	50%
c.	60%	40%
d.	70%	30%
e.	100%	0%

2. Harold is concerned about the volatility of his portfolio and would like some help in assessing the risk. Based on his current allocation between his bond portfolio and his stock portfolio, what is the standard deviation of his entire portfolio (stock and bond portfolio together)?

   a. 12.0%.
   b. 12.4%.
   c. 12.8%.
   d. 13.4%.
   e. 13.8%.

3. Harold has taken an active role in developing his financial goals by reading Money Magazine. After reading about diversification, he has become concerned about the diversity of his stock portfolio. What portion of the risk in his stock portfolio is inherent to a specific business or industry?

   a. 20%.
   b. 40%.
   c. 60%.
   d. 80%.
   e. 100%.

4. With recent changes in the economy, there has been significant talk about the Federal Reserve raising interest rates. What would be the approximate decline in the value of Harold's bond portfolio if interest rates increase to 7.43%?

   a. 1.0%.
   b. 2.0%.
   c. 3.0%.
   d. 5.8%.
   e. 6.1%.

5. Harold knows that the bond market has been performing well and would like to know what the probability is of having a return of at least 16% from his bond portfolio.

   a. 9%.
   b. 16%.
   c. 22%.
   d. 28%.
   e. 34%.

6. Harold's previous financial planner told him that he should have about 45% of his portfolio in stocks and 55% in bonds. How much would his portfolio be worth when he retired, if he followed this advice? Assume the portfolio retains this 45%/55% asset allocation.

   a. $1,732,375.
   b. $1,772,428.
   c. $1,773,385.
   d. $1,813,313.
   e. $1,872,385.

MINI CASE SCENARIO 5

During the year 2000, Smallco, Inc. has 3 employees as indicated below:

Employee	Age	Status	401(k) Deferral	Compensation	Coverage in Health Plan
Aaron	30	Single	$3,000	$34,000	Single coverage
Barbara	65	Married	$6,000	$60,000	Family coverage
Charlie	50	Married	$4,000	$47,500	Family coverage

Smallco has a health plan that has the following annual deductibles:

For single coverage $2,000

For family coverage $4,000

Smallco pays the health insurance premiums.

Barbara is also employed by ABC Corporation, where she is covered under a health plan as an employee with single coverage. The employer pays the premiums.

1. How much, if any, can Aaron contribute to a Medical Savings Account (MSA) for the year 2000?
   a. $0.
   b. $1,000.
   c. $1,300.
   d. $1,500.
   e. $2,000.

2. Assume that in 2000 and 2001, Aaron made a contribution to a MSA. In 2001, he married Doris who is employed with XYZ Corporation and covered under the XYZ health care plan. In late 2001, Doris became sick and Aaron made a distribution from his MSA to cover her deductible and her coinsurance from major medical. What are the tax consequences to Aaron of such a transaction?
   a. The withdrawal was medically related; therefore, there are no tax consequences.
   b. The withdrawal was medically related; therefore, it is included as ordinary income for the withdrawal amount, but there is no penalty.
   c. The withdrawal is treated as ordinary income and is subject to a 15% penalty tax.
   d. None of the above.

3. Barbara would like to open her own MSA. How much may she deduct from her taxes and contribute to the MSA for 2000?
   a. $0.
   b. $1,000.
   c. $2,000.
   d. $2,600.
   e. $3,000.

4. Assume that in 2000, Barbara establishes a MSA, contributes $500, and makes no withdrawals during 2000. What are the tax consequences to Barbara related to the establishment of the MSA account during 2000?
   a. There are no tax consequences.
   b. She can deduct $500 from income.
   c. She cannot deduct the $500 from income.
   d. She has no deduction and a $30 penalty.
   e. None of the above.

5. Barbara has a working spouse who is not an active participant in a qualified plan. What is the maximum deductible IRA that Barbara's husband can make for 2000?
   a. $0.
   b. $1,000.
   c. $2,000.
   d. $2,250.
   e. $4,000.

6. Charlie has a non-working spouse and wishes to establish an IRA for his wife. What is the maximum deductible IRA that Charlie can establish for himself and his wife for year 2000?
   a. $0.
   b. $500.
   c. $1,000.
   d. $2,000.
   e. $4,000.

MINI CASE SCENARIO 6

Margaret believed that she and her husband, Steve, were America's most happily married couple. Margaret was a full-time housewife and mother while Steve owned a retail paper goods store. Quite by accident, Margaret discovered that one week while Steve was supposed to be attending a paper goods convention he was actually spending the week in the unoccupied half of their rental duplex with his youthful and shapely secretary. Margaret has no intention of getting a divorce and plans to file a joint tax return with her husband for 1999. She does, however, feel that Steve needs to suffer as a result of his thoughtless behavior. Therefore, the next Monday (October 8, 1999) she embarks on a program of charitable giving as follows:

1. She donates all of his custom tailored leisure suits to the Salvation Army.

   Cost basis = $4,000.

   Fair market value = $50.

2. She donates paper plates, cups, and napkins from Steve's store to a Democratic Fundraiser. Steve is a staunch Republican.

   Cost basis = $300.

   Fair market value = $600.

3. She donates the rental duplex to their church to be used as a home for wayward girls.

   Cost basis = $55,000 on September 1, 1993.

   Fair market value = $155,000.

4. She donates Steve's favorite picture, a Leroy Neiman lithograph of "Harry's Bar" to the Boys Scouts of America who hang it in the lobby of their headquarters.

   Cost basis = $2,500 on January 1, 1983.

   Fair market value = $17,500.

5. The youthful and shapely secretary is a faux blonde. Consequently, Margaret donates all of their Clairol stock to Troy State University's Department of Accounting.

   Cost basis = $900 on June 2, 1999 (date of purchase).

   Fair market value = $1,100 (date of contribution).

6. Margaret donates Steve's new white Toyota Supra with leather interior to a private non-operating foundation that is not a 50% organization.

   Cost basis = $40,000 on January 1, 1999.

   Fair market value = $34,000.

1. Which of the following statements is/are correct?

   1. The paper plates, cups, and napkins are ordinary income property; therefore, the charitable contribution deduction is limited to $300 (cost).
   2. The Clairol stock is capital gain property; therefore the charitable contribution deduction is the FMV at the date of the contribution.
   3. The donation of the duplex to the church will be an adjustment for AMT.
   4. Since Steve had only held his car for nine months, he can only deduct the basis of $40,000 as a charitable contribution.

      a. 1 and 2.
      b. 1, 2, and 3.
      c. 2 and 3.
      d. 3 and 4.
      e. None of the statements are correct.

2. Steve and Margaret's charitable deduction for the rental duplex is:

      a. $55,000 with a 50% of AGI ceiling.
      b. $55,000 with a 30% of AGI ceiling.
      c. $155,000 with a 50% of AGI ceiling.
      d. $155,000 with a 30% of AGI ceiling.
      e. Either A or D (their choice).

3. Which of the following statements is/are correct?

   1. The car has a charitable deduction of 20% of FMV.
   2. The duplex can either be subject to the 50% or the 30% of AGI ceiling.
   3. The suits are subject to a 50% of AGI ceiling.

      a. 1 only.
      b. 2 only.
      c. 2 and 3 only.
      d. 1, 2, and 3.
      e. None of the above.

4. The deduction for the Leroy Neiman lithograph contribution to the Boy Scouts would be equal to the fair market value if:

   a. The organization had used it as part of an art appreciation program for the Boys Scouts.

   b. Margaret believed they were going to use it as part of an education program for the Boys Scouts, but they did not.

   c. The organization had sold the painting and used the proceeds for scouting programs.

   d. A and B.

   e. A, B, and C.

MINI CASE SCENARIO 7

Mrs. Anna Bartoromo, age 64, died September 8, 1999. At the time of her death, she had a table life expectancy of 17 years and the applicable Federal rate of interest was 7% (Section 7520). She had been employed with the XYZ Corporation, where she had a vested retirement account and a completely vested 401(k) account. In addition, she had an IRA and other property listed below. She had not started any distributions.

Asset	Valuation of Her Interest 9/08/99	Date of Disposition 1/1/00	3/08/00	Adjusted Cost Basis	Titling or Beneficiary *
Qualified retirement account	$1,000,000		$800,000	$0	Beneficiary H
401(k)	750,000		600,000	0	Beneficiary S
IRA	2,000,000		1,700,000	0	Beneficiary D
½ personal residence	400,000		450,000	280,000	JTWROS with H
Annuity (10 year certain)(8%)	300,000		290,000	200,000	Beneficiary H
Installment notes (5 year/9%)	200,000		183,789	160,000	Willed to H
Other property	250,000	$300,000	250,000	80,000	Willed to H

* H = Husband
S = Son
D = Daughter

1. How much is Mrs. Bartoromo's gross estate for the purpose of the U.S. Federal estate tax return (Form 706)? Assume any appropriate election is made.

   a. $4,273,789.
   b. $4,323,789.
   c. $4,350,000.
   d. $4,900,000.

2. How much does Mrs. Bartoromo have to pay in excess accumulations excise tax?

   a. $0.
   b. $238,005.
   c. $335,505.
   d. $562,500.

3. How much is Mrs. Bartoromo's approximate probate estate?

   a. $450,000.
   b. $750,000.
   c. $1,150,000.
   d. $2,150,000.

4. Which of the following are Mr. Bartoromo's options regarding Mrs. Bartoromo's qualified retirement account?

   1. He can roll over her balances into his IRA account and must begin distributions by his age 70½.
   2. He can maintain the same account and begin distribution when Mrs. Bartoromo would have attained 70 ½.
   3. He can roll over the account to his own name and name another beneficiary and at 70 ½ take a joint life distribution.

   a. 1 only.
   b. 2 only
   c. 1 and 2.
   d. 1 and 3.
   e. 1, 2, and 3.

5. Which of the following are the son's options regarding the 401(k) balance?

    1. Son could leave the balance in Mrs. Bartoromo's name and begin distributions over 5 years.
    2. Son could leave the balance in Mrs. Bartoromo's name and begin distribution over the son's life expectancy.
    3. Son could roll over the 401(k) to his own IRA and delay distributions until son is 70 ½.

        a. 1 only.
        b. 2 only
        c. 1 and 2.
        d. 1 and 3.
        e. 1, 2, and 3.

MINI CASE SCENARIO 8

Mrs. Keri Mayer, age 64, died September 8, 1999. At the time of her death, she had a table life expectancy of 17 years and the applicable Federal rate of interest was 7% (Section 7520). She had been employed with the Reed Corporation, where she had a vested retirement account and a completely vested 401(k) account. In addition, she had an IRA and other property listed below. She had not started any distributions. Assume her executor makes any appropriate elections.

	Valuation of Her Interest				
Asset	**9/08/99**	**Date of Disposition 1/1/00**	**3/08/00**	**Adjusted Cost Basis**	**Titling or Beneficiary ***
Qualified retirement account	$1,000,000		$800,000	$0	Beneficiary H
401(k)	750,000		600,000	0	Beneficiary S
IRA	2,000,000		1,700,000	0	Beneficiary D
½ personal residence	400,000		450,000**	280,000***	JTWROS with H
Annuity (10year certain)(8%)	300,000		290,000	200,000	Beneficiary H
Installment notes (5yr/9%)	200,000		183,789	160,000	Willed to H
Other property	250,000	$300,000	250,000	80,000	Willed to H

* H = Husband
S = Son
D = Daughter

** Represents ½ of value of personal residence
*** Represents 50% of total basis

1. What is her husband's adjustable taxable basis in the installment notes?
   a. $0.
   b. $160,000.
   c. $183,789.
   d. $200,000.
   e. None of the above.

2. What is her husband's adjusted taxable basis in the "other property"?
   a. $0.
   b. $80,000.
   c. $250,000.
   d. $300,000.
   e. None of the above.

3. What is her husband's basis in the annuity?

   a. $0.
   b. $200,000.
   c. $290,000.
   d. $300,000.
   e. None of the above.

4. What is her husband's basis in the personal residence?

   a. $450,000.
   b. $560,000
   c. $705,000.
   d. $730,000.
   e. $900,000.

5. What is her son's basis in 401(k)?

   a. $0.
   b. $300,000.
   c. $600,000.
   d. $350,000.
   e. $700,000.

MINI CASE SCENARIO 9

On August 23, 1999, Fred, a single taxpayer, gave his son, Sammy, a gift of ABC stock with a fair market value of $100,000, as of the date of the gift. This was the only gift made this year. Fred had an adjusted taxable basis (cost) in the ABC stock of $160,000 and had acquired the stock on July 31, 1993. Fred had made only one previous taxable gift in his lifetime, and that gift was to Sammy in the amount of $600,000, made August 23, 1998. Fred has a remaining net worth of $1,000,000.

1. What was Fred's gift tax on the gift of the ABC stock?
   a. $14,800.
   b. $24,050.
   c. $33,300.
   d. $37,000.
   e. $59,400.

2. Assume that on December 31, 1999, Sammy sold the ABC stock for $140,000. What are the income tax consequences to Sammy for this sale?
   a. No gain or loss.
   b. Short-term capital gain of $40,000.
   c. Long-term capital gain of $40,000.
   d. Short-term capital loss of $20,000.
   e. Long-term capital loss of $20,000.

3. Assume that Sammy sold the ABC stock on December 31, 1999 for $90,000. What are the income tax consequences to Sammy for this sale?
   a. No gain or loss.
   b. Short-term capital loss of $10,000.
   c. Long-term capital loss of $10,000.
   d. Short-term capital loss of $70,000.
   e. Long-term capital loss of $70,000.

4. Regardless of what Sammy does with the stock, what happened to Fred in 1999 with regard to income tax for the ABC stock transaction?

   a. No gain or loss.
   b. Short-term capital loss of $60,000 fully deductible.
   c. Long-term capital loss of $60,000 fully deductible.
   d. Short-term capital loss of $60,000 limited to $3,000 deductible.
   e. Long-term capital loss of $60,000 limited to $3,000 deductible.

5. Assume that Fred died December 31, 2000. How much, if any, of the ABC stock transaction and other gifts would be included in Fred's gross estate?

   a. $14,800.
   b. $24,050.
   c. $33,300.
   d. $100,000.
   e. $700,000.

6. Assume Fred died December 31, 2001 with $1,000,000 in cash, no debts and no life insurance. Utilizing all of the information in the original statement and the following information:

Funeral and administrative expenses	$50,000
Charitable contributions	$150,000

   What is Fred's tentative tax base?

   a. $800,000.
   b. $814,800.
   c. $837,000.
   d. $1,490,000.
   e. $1,504,800.

MINI CASE SCENARIO 10

Grandfather, single, age 99, gave his granddaughter a gift of $1,510,000 on her 18th birthday that was October 27, 1999. Grandfather has previously made the following taxable gifts to the following individuals:

Previous taxable gifts made by grandfather				Gift Tax Paid
Gift 1	Daughter	$400,000	Jan. 1, 1995	$0
Gift 2	Son	$400,000	Jan. 1, 1995	$75,000
Gift 3	Grandson	$1,500,000	Aug. 23, 1997	$797,750

On July 1, 2000, Grandfather died with no assets to his name. Those who saw him at the wake said he had a smile on his face because he thought he had beat the estate tax man.

1. Regarding the gift the grandfather made to his granddaughter, how much, if any, was the generation skipping transfer tax (GSTT)?
   - a. $275,000.
   - b. $280,800.
   - c. $825,000.
   - d. $830,500.
   - e. None of the above.

2. What was the grandfather's gift tax liability for the gift made to his granddaughter on October 27, 1999?
   - a. $555,800.
   - b. $816,500.
   - c. $940,050.
   - d. $1,251,750.
   - e. $2,335,800.

3. What was Grandfather's gross estate when he died?

   a. $0.
   b. $1,251,750.
   c. $1,614,000.
   d. $2,049,250.
   e. $3,000,000.

4. What was Grandfather's tentative tax base assuming there were no funeral, administrative debts, or other deductions?

   a. $0.
   b. $5,422,500.
   c. $5,867,750.
   d. $6,949,250.
   e. $7,500,000.

MINI CASE SCENARIO 11

Bill, a single taxpayer, is contemplating selling his business to Mike on September 1st of the current year for a sale price of $400,000. Bill had purchased the business on January 1st, 10 years ago for $160,000 and the stock is Section 1244 Small Business stock. Mike has proposed that he pay 30% down on September 1st of the current year, and the balance in equal payment over 60 months beginning October 1st of the current year at 10% annual interest. Bill has come to you with the following questions:

1. What is Bill's tax treatment of the down payment made on September 1st of the current year, for Bill's current year income tax return?
   a. The $240,000 gain is a long-term capital gain.
   b. The down payment is entirely a return of capital.
   c. The long-term capital gain from the down payment is $72,000.
   d. The down payment will result in return of basis, capital gain, and ordinary income.
   e. Because it is Section 1244 stock, the entire gain of $240,000 is ordinary income for the current year.

2. Excluding the down payment, what will be the total installment payments made by Mike to Bill in the current year? (Round to nearest dollar.)
   a. $23,600.
   b. $23,797.
   c. $17,000.
   d. $17,750.
   e. $17,848.

3. The amount of ordinary income that Bill will have to claim in his current year tax return as a result of the installment payment is? (Round to nearest dollar.)
   a. $3,500.
   b. $6,909.
   c. $7,000.
   d. $8,150.
   e. $9,333.

4. How will the installment payments affect the benefits that Bill expects to receive under Social Security retirement next year? Bill is 65, and fully insured and will not have any other income except interest from tax-free municipal bonds of $66,000 per year. He will be filing a joint tax return.

   a. His Social Security benefits will be reduced $1 for every $2 of the installment payments.

   b. Because he is 65, his Social Security benefits will only be reduced $1 for every $3 of the installment payments.

   c. His Social Security benefits will not be reduced by the installment payments, but 85% of his Social Security benefits will be taxable.

   d. His Social Security benefits will not be reduced by the installment payments, but 50% of his Social Security benefits will be taxable.

   e. His Social Security benefits will not be reduced and his Social Security benefits will not be taxable because he only has tax-free income.

5. If Bill were to die prior to the completion of the installment term, which of the following is correct?

   a. The installment notes are includible in his gross estate at the total of all remaining principal and interest.

   b. The installment notes are includible in his gross estate at the discounted present value of the remaining payments at his death.

   c. The installment payments would stop because they are an annuity and therefore would not be included in his gross estate.

   d. Since Bill is married, only one half of the installment notes are included in his gross estate regardless of who owns them.

MINI CASE SCENARIO 12

Robert DuCharm is 65 and planning to retire and wants to transfer his 100% ownership interest in the XYZ Corporation to his daughter Veronica. The current fair market value of XYZ is $1,000,000. Robert's adjusted basis in the property is $300,000. Robert is married to Kelly Spyhawk, a citizen of Peru, who is also 65 and does the morning local radio show on traffic from her helicopter. Veronica is 32 and works full-time as the vice president of XYZ. Robert is in excellent health and has a family history of long life. His table life expectancy is 17 years and his joint life expectancy with Kelly is 25 years. Any installment sale would be made over the life expectancy of Robert. An appropriate market rate of interest is 9%. Assume interest rates remain stable.

1. Assuming that it is Robert's intention that neither the property nor the balance of indebtedness be included in his gross estate if he were to die prior to his life expectancy, which of the following devices would be appropriate in this situation?

   1. Private annuity.
   2. Installment sale.
   3. Grantor Retained Annuity Trust (GRAT) for 17 years.
   4. Self-canceling installment notes (SCIN).

      a. 1 only.
      b. 2 and 3.
      c. 2 and 4.
      d. 1 and 4.
      e. 1, 2, 3, and 4.

2. Robert has decided to use a traditional installment sale to transfer the property to Veronica. The terms of the sale are 20% down on July 31, 1999 and the balance paid in equal monthly installments beginning August 31, 1999 over a period of twelve years at 9% interest. How much cash does Robert expect to receive in 1999?

      a. $45,521.
      b. $236,417.
      c. $245,521.
      d. $254,625.
      e. $309,251.

3. Of the amount received from the down payment and the periodic payments how much ordinary income does Robert have in 1999?

    a. $14,195.
    b. $17,743.
    c. $21,292.
    d. $29,760.
    e. $30,000.

4. Unfortunately, Robert died on July 31, 2003, the same day he received his regular installment payment. What amount, if any, should be included in his gross estate as a result of the installment sale?

    a. $0.
    b. $565,865.
    c. $621,442.
    d. $800,000.
    e. $874,008.

5. Robert has a simple will leaving all of his assets to his wife, Kelly Spyhawk. Which of the following statement is correct regarding the installment notes?

    a. The present value of the notes will qualify for the unlimited marital deduction.
    b. The full amount of the remaining payments will qualify for the unlimited marital deduction.
    c. The income tax basis to Kelly on the inherited installment notes is the fair market value at the date of death.
    d. Kelly will continue to receive a partial return of basis, part capital gain, and part ordinary income from the continuing installment payments.
    e. None of the above.

MINI CASE SCENARIO 13

You invest $5,000,000 in investment A and it is worth $6,500,000 at the end of year one. You invest $8,000,000 in investment B and it is worth $10,000,000 at the end of year one.

1. Your after tax hurdle rate is 10%. Which of the following investments has a net present value of $909,090.90 and an IRR of 30%
   a. Investment A.
   b. Investment B.
   c. Both investment A and investment B.
   d. Neither.

2. Your after tax hurdle rate is 10%. Which of the following investments has a net present value of $1,090,909.09 and an IRR of 25%.
   a. Investment A.
   b. Investment B.
   c. Both investment A and investment B.
   d. Neither.

3. Your after tax hurdle rate is 10%. Which of the following investments has a net present value of $909,090.90 and an IRR of 100%.
   a. Investment A.
   b. Investment B.
   c. Both investment A and investment B.
   d. Neither.

4. Your after tax hurdle rate is 10%. Which of the following investments has a net present value of $1,090,909.09 and an IRR of 100%.
   a. Investment A.
   b. Investment B.
   c. Both investment A and investment B.
   d. Neither.

5. Your after tax hurdle rate is 10%. Which of the following investments has an IRR of 25%?

    a. Investment A.

    b. Investment B.

    c. Both investment A and investment B.

    d. Neither.

MINI CASE SCENARIO 14

Doris buys 1,000 shares of ABC stock for $100 per share with an initial margin of 55% and a maintenance margin of 30%.

1. At what price will Doris receive a margin call?
   a. $45.00.
   b. $55.00.
   c. $64.29.
   d. $69.23.
   e. $78.57.

2. If the stock drops to $70 per share, how much cash per share will Doris be required to deliver?
   a. $5.00.
   b. $6.00.
   c. $6.54.
   d. $8.57.
   e. No cash will be required.

3. If the stock drops to $50 per share, how much cash per share will Doris be required to deliver per share?
   a. $2.00.
   b. $5.00.
   c. $10.00.
   d. $19.22.
   e. $78.57.

MINI CASE SCENARIO 15

You have a two-asset portfolio with equal weighting with the following characteristics:

	Return	Risk (Standard Deviation)
A	5%	20%
B	15%	40%

1. If the correlation coefficient between asset A and B is 0.6, where does the standard deviation of the two-asset portfolio fall?
   a. Below 15%.
   b. 15 - 30%.
   c. 30 - 50%.
   d. Over 50%.
   e. Cannot calculate.

2. If the correlation coefficient between asset A and B is equal to 1, where does the standard deviation of the two-asset portfolio fall?
   a. 15 - 29%.
   b. 30%.
   c. 31 - 50 %.
   d. Cannot determine.

MINI CASE SCENARIO 16

Jennifer is in the process of purchasing a house for $175,000 with a down payment of 20%. She will finance the balance over 30 years at 8%.

1. Assuming she purchases the above house, what will be Jennifer's monthly payment?

   a. $1,020.47.

   b. $1,027.27.

   c. $1,275.58.

   d. $1,284.09.

2. Assume Jennifer buys the house on January 1st, of the current year. If payments are due the first of each month, how much qualified residence interest can she deduct for the current year on her tax Form 1040?

   a. $10,266.67.

   b. $10,231.53.

   c. $11,157.74.

   d. $11,299.97.

3. If Jennifer financed the house over 15 years instead of 30, how much interest would she save over the life of the loan (assuming the same interest rate)?

   a. $0.

   b. $55,915.20.

   c. $89,175.60.

   d. $128,993.40.

MINI CASE SCENARIO 17

Diana, a U.S. citizen, has a portfolio of $1,000,000 and has AGI of $200,000 per year. She is 40 years old and is very concerned about her disabled child, Kevin, who is 8 years old. Diana is well off and wants to provide an inflation protected life income for Kevin beginning when he reaches the age of 21. In addition, Diana wants to leave the principal of her portfolio to the New Orleans Museum of Art. She has a cost basis in the portfolio of $800,000. Her AGI is expected to remain constant for the next 10 years. If sold, the portfolio would result in long-term capital gains.

1. Which of the following devices should she use if she wants to make certain the charity gets at least the original principal?
    a. CRAT.
    b. CRUT.
    c. NIMCRUT.
    d. Charitable Lead Trust.
    e. Pooled Income Trust.

2. Which of the following parties could Diana name as a replacement remainder beneficiary for the New Orleans Museum of Art (NOMA), assuming that she no longer wanted to benefit the NOMA, and she had a properly drafted trust?
    1. Loyola University.
    2. Kevin himself.
    3. Diana herself.
    4. Buffy, the friend of Diana's husband.
        a. The trust is irrevocable and she cannot change the remainderman.
        b. 1 only.
        c. 2 only, because he is already the beneficiary.
        d. 3 only, because she is the grantor.
        e. 1, 2, 3, and 4.

3. Ignoring the first question, and assuming that the income is to start now and is in a 5% CRAT, what is the amount of the charitable deduction to Diana if Kevin's life expectancy is 60 years and the federal rate is 8% (closest number)?

   a. $9,876.
   b. $53,536.
   c. $381,172.
   d. $427,172.

4. Suppose that Diana changes her mind and considers donating the entire portfolio directly to the charity with no income to Kevin. How much is the maximum charitable deduction that she can take in the current year?

   a. $60,000.
   b. $100,000.
   c. $800,000.
   d. $1,000,000.

5. What is the maximum total amount of charitable contributions she can deduct over the next 10 years from this contribution, if Kevin is not a beneficiary, and this is a straight charitable contribution of the $1,000,000 portfolio?

   a. $300,000.
   b. $360,000.
   c. $500,000
   d. $600,000.
   e. $1,000,000.

MINI CASE SCENARIO 18

1. The Guffins refinanced their home exactly two years ago on January 1st, at a 30-year rate of 7.5%. If the remaining mortgage balance at the time of refinancing was $104,000 and the closing costs of 3% of the amount being financed was added to the mortgage balance, how much do they owe today? (Assume they made all payments as agreed, including today's.)

    a. $103,922.
    b. $105,068.
    c. $105,160.
    d. $106,133.
    e. $107,120.

2. The Guffins refinanced their home two years ago on January 1st, at a 30-year rate of 7.5%. The initial loan was for $112,820 and was paid as agreed. The balance at refinancing was $104,200 with a remaining term of 22 years. Closing costs of 3% were financed. Assuming the old loan was at a rate of 9%, how much interest will they save over the remaining life of the old loan?

    a. $20,204.
    b. $26,748.
    c. $32,109.
    d. $36,400.
    e. $41,538.

MINI CASE SCENARIO 19

Matching: You may use an answer more than once or not at all.

Auto Coverage

A. UM (bodily injury).

B. Collision.

C. Comprehension (other than collision).

D. None of the above.

Event

1. ______ Bird collides with your windshield.

2. ______ You back your car into a tree on your property.

3. ______ An uninsured motorist damages your automobile but does not hurt you.

4. ______ An uninsured motorist strikes you while you are walking.

MINI CASE SCENARIO 20

Matching: You may use an answer more than once or not at all.

A. CRAT.

B. CRUT.

C. Both CRAT and CRUT.

D. Neither CRAT nor CRUT.

1. _______ Charitable deduction, fixed amount of annuity payment regardless of income.

2. _______ Charitable deduction, revocable.

3. _______ Estate tax advantage, variable amount of annuity depending on annual revaluation of trust assets.

4. _______ Charitable deduction, remainder interest paid to charity.

MINI CASE SCENARIO 21

Matching: You may use an answer more than once or not at all.

A. General Power of Appointment over property.

B. Special Power of Appointment over property.

C. Both General Power and Special Power.

D. Neither General Power nor Special Power.

1. _______ Permits holder to dispose of property.
2. _______ Terminates at death of grantor.
3. _______ Holder of power includes property subject to power in holder's gross estate.
4. _______ Creates an income tax event to holder of power.

MINI CASE SCENARIO 22

Brett has invested 40% in Portfolio A and 60% in Portfolio B. The correlation between Portfolio A and Portfolio B is .4, and the respective standard deviations are 15.5% and 13.5%.

1. What is the standard deviation of Portfolio A and B together?

   a. 11.0%.
   b. 12.0%.
   c. 14.3%.
   d. 14.5%.
   e. 16.0%.

2. How would the answer to the above question change if there was no relationship between Portfolios A and B?

   a. 10.2%.
   b. 11.0%.
   c. 12.0%.
   d. 14.3%.
   e. 14.5%.

MINI CASE SCENARIO 23

Marleen, who turned age 70 ½ on June 30th of the current year, owns 12% of ABC Company. She has amassed $5,000,000 in her qualified plan account as of December 31st of the previous year and $5,500,000 as of December 31st of the current year. Life expectancies are as follows:

Age	Life Expectancy
70	20.0
71	19.2
72	18.4

1. What is the minimum distribution that Marleen must receive for the current tax year?
   a. $0.
   b. $250,000.
   c. $260,417.
   d. $275,000.
   e. $286,458.

2. If she receives a distribution of $190,000 during the current year, then how much in penalties will she be required to pay for the current tax year?
   a. $0.
   b. $4,500.
   c. $30,000.
   d. $34,500.
   e. $60,000.

3. Which of the following statements is/are true regarding Marleen?

   1. If Marleen continues to work for ABC company, she is permitted to defer her minimum distribution until after she retires.
   2. Marleen can roll over her account balance into an IRA rollover account if she no longer is employed by ABC Company.
   3. If she rolls over her account balance into an IRA rollover account and she does not commingle the funds with other IRA funds, then she will be permitted to use 5 year averaging on the entire balance.
   4. Marleen's election to recalculate or not recalculate will impact any distribution she could receive after December 31st of the current year.

      a. 2 only
      b. 1 and 2.
      c. 2 and 4.
      d. 3 and 4.
      e. 1, 2, and 4.

MINI CASE SCENARIO 24

Bob Pruit, the CEO of Tango, Inc. was awarded the following stock options from his company:

Stock Option	Grant date	Type	Exercise Price	# Shares
A	1995 Feb. 1	ISO	$20	100
B	1996 July 1	NQSO	$25	100
C	1997 Aug.1	ISO	$30	100
D	1998 May 1	NQSO	$30	100

During 1998, Bob had the following transactions regarding the above stock options:

Stock Option	Date	Action	# Shares	Market Price on Action Date
A	2/1/98	Exercised	100	$42
A	2/1/98	Sold	100	$42
B	2/14/98	Exercised	100	$45
C	2/14/98	Exercised	100	$45
D	5/1/98	Exercised	100	$50
D	6/1/98	Sold	100	$60

1. Which of the following is correct regarding the A options for 1998?
   a. Bob has a long-term capital gain of $2,200.
   b. Bob has a short-term capital gain of $2,200.
   c. Bob has ordinary income of $4,200.
   d. Bob has W-2 income of $2,200.
   e. None of the above is correct.

2. Which of the following is correct regarding the B options for 1998?
   a. There are no tax consequences to exercising the option B in 1998 because it was not sold.
   b. $2,000 of LTCG.
   c. $2,000 of STCG.
   d. $2,000 of W-2 income subject to payroll taxes.
   e. AMT income of $2,000 but no ordinary income.

3. Which of the following is correct regarding the C options for 1998?

   a. Bob has LTCG of $1,500.

   b. Bob has AMT income of $1,500 but not regular taxable income.

   c. Bob has STCG of $1,500.

   d. Bob has W-2 income of $1,500.

   e. Bob has ordinary income of $1,500 but not W-2 income.

4. Which of the following is correct regarding the D options for 1998?

   a. Bob must recognize $3,000 of STCG and $2,000 LTCG.

   b. Bob must recognize $3,000 of LTCG and no STCG.

   c. Bob must recognize $3,000 of ordinary income (not W-2).

   d. Bob must recognize $1,000 of STCG and $2,000 of W-2 income.

   e. Bob must recognize $1000 of LTCG and $2,000 ordinary income (not W-2).

MINI CASE SCENARIO 25

Jack, who had never married, died last year. Two years before his death he paid gift tax of $15,000 as a result of making the following gifts (these were the only gifts he made that year):

A. Stock worth $40,000 to Mickey;

B. A $300,000 (proceeds value) life insurance policy on his life to Molly. (The policy was worth $5,000 at the time of transfer.)

At Jack's death, the stock had increased in value to $70,000 and the life insurance company paid the $300,000 to Molly. Consider the two transfers and the gift taxes paid when answering the following questions.

1. By how much will Jack's gross estate be increased?

   a. $15,000.

   b. $60,000.

   c. $315,000.

   d. $355,000.

2. The adjusted taxable gifts will be:

   a. $0.

   b. $30,000.

   c. $40,000.

   d. $370,000.

3. If the two gifts had been made four years before Jack's death, how much would his gross estate have been increased by?

   a. $0.

   b. $15,000.

   c. $30,000.

   d. $300,000.

MINI CASE SCENARIO 26

Smith invests in a limited partnership that requires an outlay of $9,200 today. At the end of years 1 through 5, he will receive the after-tax cash flows shown below. The partnership will be liquidated at the end of the fifth year. Smith is in the 28% tax bracket.

YEARS	CASH FLOWS	
0	($9,200)	CF0
1	$600	CF1
2	$2,300	CF2
3	$2,200	CF3
4	$6,800	CF4
5	$9,500	CF5

1. The after-tax IRR of this investment is:
   a. 17.41%.
   b. 19.20%.
   c. 24.18%.
   d. 28.00%.
   e. 33.58%.

2. Which of the following statements is/are correct?
   1. The IRR is the discount rate that equates the present value of an investment's expected costs to the present value of the expected cash inflows.
   2. The IRR is 24.18% and the present value of the investment's expected cash flows is $9,200.
   3. The IRR is 24.18%. For Smith to actually realize this rate of return, the investment's cash flows will have to be reinvested at the IRR.
   4. If the cost of capital for this investment is 9%, the investment should be rejected because its net present value will be negative.

   a. 2 and 4.
   b. 2 and 3.
   c. 1 only.
   d. 1, 2, and 3.
   e. 1 and 4.

MINI CASE
SCENARIO SOLUTIONS

MINI CASE SCENARIOS

Case 1
1. E
2. B
3. B

Case 2
1. C
2. E
3. A

Case 3
1. B
2. E
3. B
4. D
5. C

Case 4
1. D
2. C
3. B
4. B
5. B
6. A

Case 5
1. C
2. C
3. A
4. D
5. C
6. E

Case 6
1. E
2. E
3. D
4. D

Case 7
1. C
2. A
3. A
4. E
5. C

Case 8
1. B
2. D
3. B
4. D
5. A

Case 9
1. A
2. A
3. B
4. A
5. A
6. E

Case 10
1. C
2. D
3. D
4. D

Case 11
1. C
2. E
3. B
4. C
5. B

Case 12
1. D
2. C
3. D
4. C
5. D

Case 13
1. A
2. B
3. D
4. D
5. B

Case 14
1. C
2. E
3. C

Case 15
1. B
2. B

Case 16
1. B
2. B
3. D

Case 17
1. C
2. B
3. C
4. B
5. D

Case 18
1. B
2. A

Case 19
1. C
2. B
3. B
4. A

Case 20
1. A
2. D
3. B
4. C

Case 21
1. C
2. C
3. A
4. D

Case 22
1. B
2. A

Case 23
1. C
2. A
3. A

Case 24
1. D
2. D
3. B
4. D

Case 25
1. C
2. B
3. A

Case 26
1. C
2. D

MINI CASE SCENARIO 1

Fundamentals - After-Tax Rate of Return

1. E

	Return	Tax Rate	After-Tax Return
Stock Fund	12%	31%	8.28%
Bond Fund	8.5%	0	8.50%

Thus, the bond fund has a higher after-tax rate of return.

Fundamentals - Calculating Future Value

2. B

		Tuition Yr.1	Tuition Yr. 2	Tuition Yr. 3	Tuition Yr. 4
PV	=	$25,000	$25,000	$25,000	$25,000
N	=	18	19	20	21
i	=	7	7	7	7
PMT	=	$0	$0	$0	$0
FV	=	$84,498.31 ❖	$90,413.19 ❖	$96,742.11 ❖	$103,514.06 ❖

Σ ❖ = $375,167.67

Fundamentals - Education Funding

3. B

Step 1:

FV = \$0

PMT_{AD} = \$25,000

i = 1.402 [((1.085 ÷ 1.07) - 1) X 100]

N = 4

$PV_{AD@18}$ = \$97,945.13

Step 2:

$FV_{@18}$ = \$97,945.13

N = 18

i = 1.402

PMT = \$0

PV_0 = \$76,233.43

Step 3:

PV_0 = \$76,233.43

N = 18

i = 8.5

FV = \$0

PMT_{AD} = \$7,758.98

MINI CASE SCENARIO 2

Insurance - Homeowners Loss Calculation

1. **C**

80% of \$100,000 = \$80,000. Since they only have \$75,000, they are in a co-insurance position.

$\frac{\$75,000}{\$80,000}$ = 93.75% (insurer's portion)

Loss	\$40,000	
Insurer %	.9375	
	\$37,500	Rounded
Deductible	(500)	
	\$37,000	will be paid by the insurance company

Insurance - Automobile Insurance

2. **E**

	Honda	**Toyota**	**Total**
Total Loss	\$3,500	\$2,000	\$5,500
Less Deductible	(250)	(500)	**(750)**
Loss Payable by Insurance Company	\$3,250	\$1,500	\$4,750

Amount payable by the Dells is \$750 for the two deductibles.

Tax - Casualty Loss

3. **A**

Total Loss	\$ 70,500	(40,000 + 25,000 + 3,500 + 2,000)
Less Insurance Proceeds	(52,000)	(30,000 + 20,000 + 1,000 + 1,000)
	\$18,500	
Less 10% AGI	(6,000)	(60,000 x 10%)
Less \$100	(100)	(casualty and loss reduction - \$100 per occurrence)
Deductible Loss	\$ 12,400	

MINI CASE SCENARIO 3

Tax - Capital Gains and Losses

1. **B**

The gain on the stock is $3,000. The gain is short-term (held for 5 months).

Tax - Section 1244 Stock

2. **E**

John incurred a $90,000 loss ($125,000 - 35,000). The stock had been held long-term and so the loss would normally be all long-term capital loss. The stock, however, is Section 1244 stock and so John will have a $50,000 ordinary loss and a $40,000 long-term capital loss.

Tax – Stock Sales

3. **B**

Statement #2 is incorrect because the possibility exists that the uncle received it as a gift from John within a year of his death; therefore, John would not get a stepped up basis. Thus, it is relevant how the uncle acquired the stock. Statement #3 is incorrect because the wash sale rules apply only to losses, not gains, so repurchase in Transaction #2 within 30 days has no effect on Transaction #1. John's basis in Diddly is $3,000. Transaction #6 cannot be a non-taxable exchange.

Tax - Capital Gains and Losses

4. **D**

$40,000 LTCL (Transaction #3).
$1,000 LTCG (Transaction #4).
$5,000 LTCL (Transaction #5).
Net $44,000 LTCL.

Regarding Transaction #4: John's basis in the inherited stock is the FMV at the date of death, $11,000. John has a gain of $1,000 on the transaction ($12,000 - $11,000). Inherited property automatically gets a long-term holding period.

Regarding Transaction #5: Worthless securities are deemed to have become worthless on the last day of the year, in this case, 12/31/99. Therefore, John will have a long-term capital loss of $5,000.

Tax - Capital Gains and Losses

5. **C**

$3,000 STCG (Transaction #1).
$700 STCL (Transaction #6).
Net $2,300 STCG.

Regarding Transaction #6: Securities do not qualify for nontaxable exchanges. Therefore, John's basis in the Wild'n'Crazy stock is $3,700. John has a short-term capital loss of $700.

MINI CASE SCENARIO 4

Investments – Portfolio Allocation

1. D

TIME LINE

Age	55	56	57	58	59	60	61	62	63	64	65	75	85	89	90
Cashflow	(715,200)	0	0	0	0	0	0	0	0	0	100k →				$1MM
Cashflow #	0	1	2	3	4	5	6	7	8	9	10	20	30	34	35

Note:
1. Retirement is from age 65 to 90 = 25 years.
2. $100,000 must occur at beginning of the year.
3. $100,000 is withdrawn each year for years 65 through 89, inclusive.

Step 1: Find IRR

Period		Cashflow	
0	=	($715,200)	= ($572,160 + 143,040)
1 - 9	=	$0	
10 - 34	=	$100,000	
35	=	$1,000,000	

Keystrokes (HP 12C)

(715,200)	[g] [CF_0]
0	[g] [CF_j]
9	[g] [N_j]
100,000	[g] [CF_j]
25	[g] [N_j]
1,000,000	[g] [CF_j]
	[f] [IRR]

Solution: IRR = 7.088

Step 2: Find Realized Return

IAR = [(1 + RR) ÷ (1 + IR) - 1] x 100 (IAR = Inflation Adjusted Return)

7.088 = [(1 + RR) ÷ (1.032) - 1] x 100

.07088 = (1 + RR) ÷ (1.032) - 1

1.07088 = 1 + RR ÷ 1.032

1.105 = 1 + RR

Therefore: RR = 10.5%

Thus, a realized return of 10.5% with 3.2% inflation is equivalent to an inflation-adjusted return of 7.088%.

Step 3: Find % of stocks and bonds

x = % of stock

.105 = .12(x) + .07(1 - x)

.105 = .12x + .07 - .07x

.035 = .05x

x = 70% Therefore, 30% must be invested in bonds.

Investments – Standard Deviation

2. C

Percent of stock = 80%

Percent of bonds = 20%

$$\sigma^2 = x_s^2\sigma_s^2 + y_b^2\sigma_b^2 + 2x_s y_b[(\sigma_s)(\sigma_b)(r_{sb})]$$

$$\sigma^2 = (.8)^2(.15)^2 + (.2)^2(.09)^2 + 2(.8)(.2)[(.15)(.09)(.40)]$$

$$\sigma^2 = .0144 + .00032 + .001728$$

$$\sigma^2 = .016448$$

$$\sigma = (.016448)^{1/2} = 12.825\%$$

Investments – Risk & Diversity

3. B

Correlation coefficient = .775

Coefficient of determination = $(.775)^2$ = .60

Thus, 60% of the performance of Harold's stock portfolio is directly attributable to the performance of the market. Therefore, 40% of the returns of his portfolio are related to risk of a particular stock or industry.

Investments – Economic Changes

4. B

$$\frac{\Delta P}{P} = \left(\frac{-D}{(1 + YTM)}\right)(\Delta\ YTM)$$

$$\frac{\Delta P}{P} = \left(\frac{-5}{1.07}\right)(0.0743 - 0.07)$$

ΔP = (.02) or (2%) Therefore, there is a decline of two (2) percent.

Investments – Probability of a Return

5. B

$$\frac{16\% - 7\%}{9\%} = 1 \text{ standard deviation}$$

The probability of a return falling within one standard deviation is 68%. Thus, the probability of a return between 7% and 16% must be 34% (one half of 68%). Since 50% of returns will fall below and above the mean of 7%, it follows that the probability of a return above 16% is 16% (50% - 34%).

Investments – Portfolio Valuation

6. A

Weighted return = (.45)(.12) + (.55)(.07) = .0925 or 9.25%

PV	=	$715,200
N	=	10 years
i	=	9.25%
PMT	=	$0
FV	=	$1,732,375

Incorrect method:

The following method is incorrect, because it assumes that the portfolio will begin with a 45% - 55% split and will continue to grow without rebalancing the portfolio.

	Stock	Bond	Total
PV	$321,840	$393,360	$715,200
N	10	10	
i	12%	7%	
FV	$999,586	$773,799	$1,773,388

MINI CASE SCENARIO 5

Retirement – MSA Contributions

1. **C**

65% of the high deductible may be placed pre-tax into a MSA (65% of $2,000).

Tax – MSA Distributions

2. **C**

Unfortunately, because Doris is covered under another plan, Aaron's distribution is subject to inclusion in income and because he is under 65. He is also penalized 15%.

Tax – MSA Deductions & Contributions

3. **A**

Barbara cannot have a MSA, because she is covered under another health plan at ABC.

Tax – MSA Contributions

4. **D**

There is a 6% excise tax penalty for over-funding an MSA. Barbara is covered by a health plan so she cannot establish a MSA. The entire contribution has a penalty of 6% x $500 = $30.

Tax – IRA Maximum Deduction

5. **C**

Barbara is an active participant in Qualified Pension Plan (401(k)). While her income exceeds $52,000, she is under the threshold of $150,000. Therefore, her active participant status will have no effect, and she can have a deductible IRA of $2,000.

Tax – IRA Maximum Deduction

6. **E**

The maximum deductible contribution is $4,000 for both spouses. Charlie is an active participant in Qualified Pension Plan (401(k)), but he is under the threshold of $52,000 for year 2000.

MINI CASE SCENARIO 6

Tax – Charitable Contribution

1. **E**

None of the statements are correct. The Democratic Party contribution is not deductible at all. The stock is not held long-term: thus, the adjusted basis is the deduction. No adjustment for AMT is necessary. Steve's holding period for the car is irrelevant.

Tax – Charitable Deduction

2. **E**

Either A or D. When donating long-term capital gain property to a 50% organization, the taxpayer has the choice of taking a deduction of adjusted basis and 50% of AGI or FMV and 30% of AGI.

Tax – Charitable Contribution

3. **D**

All three statements are correct. The car is given to a 20% charity (private non-operating). The duplex can either be subject to the 50% or 30% of AGI ceiling, depending on the election. All other donations have 50% of AGI ceilings.

Tax - Charitable Deduction

4. **D**

If appreciated capital gain personal property is put to a related use, the deduction is the FMV. If the property is put to an unrelated use, the deduction is the adjusted basis. Answer A is correct because the use would be related to the charitable purpose of the organization. Answer B is correct. If the taxpayer has reason to believe that the property will be put to a related use, even though the property was not put to that use, the FMV will be used. Answer C is incorrect, since this use would be considered an unrelated use.

MINI CASE SCENARIO 7

Estates – Gross Estate

1. **C**

The annuity and installment note are valued on the date of death because they are so-called "wasting assets". The other property is valued on the date of disposition. All remaining property is valued on the alternate valuation date.

QRA	$800,000	Alternate valuation date
401(k)	600,000	Alternate valuation date
IRA	1,700,000	Alternate valuation date
Personal Residence	450,000	Alternate valuation date
Annuity	300,000	Date of death
Note	200,000	Date of death
Other Property	300,000	Date of disposition
	$4,350,000	

Retirement – Excess Accumulations Excise Tax

2. **A**

The excess accumulations excise tax was repealed for the tax year beginning in 1997.

Estates – Probate Estate

3. **A**

Probate is determined at the date of death (includes the "note" and the "other property"). All other assets are non-probate assets. ($200,000 + 250,000) = $450,000.

Retirement – Qualified Retirement Account

4. **E**

All of the options are available for a spouse beneficiary of a qualified retirement account.

Retirement – 401(k)

5. **C**

The son cannot rollover the account into his own account. Statements #1 and #2 are correct alternatives.

MINI CASE SCENARIO 8

Tax – Adjustable Taxable Basis

1. **B**

$160,000 - There is no step to fair market value at death for installment notes (Code Sections 1014(c) and 691(a)(4)).

Tax – Adjustable Taxable Basis

2. **D**

$300,000 - The fair market value on the date of disposition. The executor should have elected the alternate valuation date.

Tax - Basis

3. **B**

$200,000 – The carryover basis. There is no step to FMV for annuities (Code Section 1014(a)(9)(A)).

Tax - Basis

4. **D**

He owed ½ already ($280,000 + 450,000 = $730,000). Step to FMV at death for decedent's ½.

Tax - Basis

5. **A**

The son has a zero basis in the 401(k) due to it being a qualified plan. There is no step to FMV at death for qualified retirement plans.

MINI CASE SCENARIO 9

Tax – Gift Tax

1. **A**

$90,000	Taxable gift ($100,000 - 10,000) annual exclusion
+600,000	Previous taxable gifts
$690,000	Total taxable gifts
226,100	Total tax ($155,800 + (.37 x $190,000))
(211,300)	Unified credit (1999)
$14,800	Gift tax liability

Tax - Sale

2. **A**

The son's adjusted taxable basis for gain is $160,000. His basis for losses is $100,000. The sale was in-between the gain basis and the loss basis, therefore, there is no recognized gain or loss.

Tax - Sale

3. **B**

The basis for losses is $100,000. Because this sale results in a loss (i.e., the loss basis of $100,000 is used), the holding period starts on the date of the gift. Therefore, this a short-term capital loss of $10,000. The holding period of the son would tack to the Father's holding period if the gain basis was used.

Tax – Stock Transaction

4. **A**

This is a gift. There is no gain or loss recognition.

Estates – Gross Estate

5. **A**

Gift tax paid on gifts made within 3 years of death is included in the gross estate. See question 1 for calculation of the gift tax.

Estates – Tentative Tax Basis

6. **E**

	$1,014,800	Gross estate ($1,000,000 + $14,800)
-	200,000	Deductions (funeral and administrative)
=	$814,800	Taxable estate
+	690,000	Post-'76 taxable gifts
=	$1,504,800	Tentative tax base

MINI CASE SCENARIO 10

Estates - GSTT

1. **C**

$1,510,000 - 10,000 (annual exclusion) = $1,500,000 x .55 = $825,000.

Note: Grandfather had already used his $1,000,000 exemption for GSTT on the previous gift to his grandson.

Estates – Gift Tax Liability

2. **D**

Gift tax calculation:

	Taxable Gifts		Gift Tax Paid
Gift 1	$400,000		
Gift 2	$400,000	$267,800 - 192,800	$75,000
Gift 3	$1,775,000*	$1,065,550 - 192,800 - 75,000	$797,750
	$2,575,000		$872,750

*The 1.5 million gift was taxed as follows: GSTTx = $500,000 @ 55% = $275,000

The $275,000 is added to the gift for purposes of determining gift tax.

Gift 4

$1,510,000 - 10,000 annual exclusion + 825,000 (GSTT) = $2,325,000 (taxable gift).

Total of all previous taxable gifts (1 - 3).

$2,575,000	(from above)
2,325,000	Total gift to granddaughter for gift tax (1,500,000 + 825,000)
$4,900,000	Total taxable gifts
$2,335,800	Gift tax amount (from unified gift and estate table)
(211,300)	Credit equivalency (1999)
(872,750)	Gift tax previously paid (from above)
$1,251,750	Gift tax liability for this gift to granddaughter (gift 4)

Estates – Gross Estate

3. **D**

Gift tax paid (does not include GSTT) on gifts made within 3 years of death is included in the gross estate.

($1,251,750 + 797,500) = $2,049,250.

Estates – Tentative Tax Base

4. **D**

Add back all taxable gifts (post-1976) plus taxable estate from question 3.

$4,900,000	Post-'76 gifts
+2,049,250	Gross estate (from problem 3)
$6,949,250	

Post-'76 Gifts

$400,000	
400,000	
1,500,000	
1,500,000	
$3,800,000	Total gifts
275,000	GSTT
825,000	GSTT
$4,900,000	Total post-'76 gifts

MINI CASE SCENARIO 11

Tax - Installment Sales & Capital Gains

1. **C**

SP	$400,000	100%	**Note:** Section 1244 only relates to losses.
Basis	(160,000)	40%	
	$240,000	60%	

Down Payment 30% x $400,000 =	$120,000	(100%) down payment
	(48,000)	(40%) return of basis
	$72,000	(60%) long-term capital gain

Fundamentals – Present Value

2. **E**

$400,000	N	=	60
(120,000)	i	=	.8333 (10 ÷ 12)
$280,000	PV	=	$280,000
	PMT	=	$17,847.52 ($5,949.1725 x 3)

Tax – Ordinary Income from Installment Sale

3. **B**

	PMT	Principal Reduction	Interest Income	Principal Debt
Oct.	$5,949.17	$3,615.83	$2,333.34	$280,000.00
Nov.	5,949.17	3,645.97	2,303.20	276,384.16
Dec.	5,949.17	3,676.35	2,272.82	272,738.19
			$6,909.36	

Note: Only answer possible < $7,000

$280,000 x .10 x (3 ÷ 12) = $7,000

The interest must be slightly < $7,000 due to the reduction of principal.

Retirement – Earnings Test for Social Security

4. **C**

Installment payments are not earned income. However, due to the MAGI of $66,000 plus the ordinary income of the installment notes, 85% of his Social Security benefits will be taxable.

Estates – Installment Notes

5. **B**

Installment notes are includible in the gross estate at the discounted present value of the remaining payments.

MINI CASE SCENARIO 12

Estates – Gross Estate

1. **D**

If Robert dies early, the installment notes (at remaining present value) would be included in his gross estate. The SCIN would not be included in his gross estate. The GRAT would cause inclusion in the gross estate. The private annuity would not cause inclusion.

Fundamentals – Installment Sale

2. **C**

$1,000,000	Sale Price	PV	=	$800,000
(200,000)	Down Payment	FV	=	$0
$800,000	Present Value	N	=	144 months
		i	=	.75 (9 ÷ 12)
		PMT_{OA}	=	$9,104.25

$245,521 = $200,000 + 45,521 [$9,104.25 (pmt) x 5]

Tax – Ordinary Income from Installment Sale

3. **D**

N	=	5 months
PV	=	$800,000
PMT	=	$9104.25
i	=	.75 (9 ÷ 12)
FV	=	$784,239.10

Total Payments $45,521 = [$9,104.25x5] less principal reduction.

Original debt	$800,000	Total Payment	$45,521
Remaining debt at 12/31	(784,239)	Principal reduction	(15,761)
Principal reduction	$15,761	Ordinary income from interest	$29,760

Estates – Inclusion in Gross Estate

4. **C**

N	=	96 (144 months - 48 months)
FV	=	$0
PMT_{OA}	=	$9,104.25
i	=	.75 (9 ÷ 12)
PV	=	$621,442

Estates - Marital Deduction

5. **D**

Installment notes do not receive a step to FMV at death. Because Kelly is a non-citizen, the property does not qualify for the unlimited marital deduction.

MINI CASE SCENARIO 13

Solutions to Questions 1 – 5.

		Investment A		Investment B	
IRR:	PV	($5,000,000)		($8,000,000)	
	N	1		1	
	PMT	$0		$0	
	FV	$6,500,000		$10,000,000	
	IRR(i)	30%		25%	**#5**
NPV:	FV	$6,500,000		$10,000,000	
	N	1		1	
	i	10		10	
	PMT	$0		$0	
	PV	$5,909,090.90		$9,090,909.09	
Less initial investment		(5,000,000.00)		(8,000,000.00)	
NPV		$909,090.90	**#1**	$1,090,909.09	**#2**

Fundamentals - TVM

1. **A**

Fundamentals - TVM

2. **B**

Fundamentals - TVM

3. **D**

Fundamentals - TVM

4. **D**

Fundamentals - TVM

5. **B**

MINI CASE SCENARIO 14

Investments – Margin Call

1. **C**

$$\frac{\text{Loan}}{(1 - \text{maintenance margin})} = \text{Margin Call}$$

Loan = (.45) x \$100 = \$45 per share

Therefore, a margin call will occur at \$64.29 (\$45 ÷ .7).

Investments – Cash Price Per Share

2. **E**

	Current Equity	Required Equity
Stock Price	\$70	\$70
Loan	(45)	X 30%
Equity	\$25	\$21

Equity is required to be \$21 = (30% of \$70). Since equity is \$25 = (\$70 - 45), no margin call will occur.

Investments – Cash Price Per Share

3. **C**

	Current Equity	Required Equity
Stock Price	\$50	\$50
Loan	(45)	X 30%
Equity	\$5	\$15
	Difference = \$10	

Required equity = \$15 = (30% of \$50)

Equity = \$5 = (\$50 - 45)

Difference = \$10

MINI CASE 15

Investments – Standard Deviation

1. **B**

σ^2 = $W_A^2\,\sigma_A^2 + W_B^2\,\sigma_B^2 + 2W_AW_B\,[\sigma_A\sigma_B r_{AB}]$

σ^2 = $(.5^2)(.2^2) + (.5^2)(.4^2) + 2(.5)(.5)[(.2)(.4)(.6)]$

σ^2 = $.01 + .04 + .024$

σ^2 = $.074$

σ = 27.2%

Note: The weighting is 50% for A and B.

Investments – Standard Deviation

2. **B**

σ^2 = $W_A^2\,\sigma_A^2 + W_B^2\,\sigma_B^2 + 2W_AW_B\,[\sigma_A\sigma_B r_{AB}]$

σ^2 = $(.5^2)(.2^2) + (.5^2)(.4^2) + 2(.5)(.5)[(.2)(.4)(1.0)]$

σ^2 = $.01 + .04 + .04$

σ^2 = $.09$

σ = 30%

Note: The weighting is 50% for A and B.

MINI CASE SCENARIO 16

Fundamentals - TVM

1. **B**

FV = $0

N = 360

i = .6667 (8 ÷ 12)

PV = $140,000 (175,000 x 80%)

PMT_{OA} = ($1,027.27)

Fundamentals - TVM

2. **B**

Beginning amount $140,000

N = 11

i = .6667 (8 ÷ 12)

PMT_{OA} = $1,027.27

FV = $138,931.55

Principal reduction $140,000 - 138,931.55 = $1,068.45.

Total Payments ($1,027.27 x 11) - 1,068.45 = $10,231.53 interest expense.

Note: If you get a figure that is slightly off, it may be due to a failure to round to a monthly payment of $1,027.27.

Fundamentals - Savings

3. **D**

$1,027.27 x 360 =	$369,817.20	
$1,337.91 x 180 =	240,823.80	
	$128,993.40	savings

MINI CASE SCENARIO 17

Estates – Trusts

1. **C**

NIMCRUT = No income must be paid unless earned – buy non-dividend stocks until the child is age 21. Notice that the portfolio will be revalued annually providing the possibility of an increase in the annuity payment once the portfolio begins to make income.

Estates – Charitable Remainderman

2. **B**

She can reserve the right to change the name of the charitable remainderman to some other "charitable remainderman". She cannot name 2, 3, or 4 nor can she reserve that right and still qualify as an irrevocable charitable remainder trust.

Estates - CRAT

3. **C**

PMT_{OA} = $50,000 ($1,000,000 x .05)
i = 8%
N = 60
PV = $618,828 the present value of the annuity

Value of the charitable deduction ($1,000,000 – 618,828 = $381,172).

Tax – Charitable Deduction

4. **B**

She can elect to deduct the basis and is then limited to 50% of AGI. If she elects to deduct the FMV she is limited to 30% of AGI or $60,000.

Tax – Charitable Deduction

5. **D**

She gets the deduction this year and a carryover for 5 years (total 6 x $100,000 or $600,000 if she elects to deduct the basis, as opposed to the FMV). If the FMV were chosen, she would get to deduct a total of $360,000.

MINI CASE SCENARIO 18

Fundamentals - TVM

1. **B**

PV	=	$107,120 ($104,000 x 1.03)	PV	=	$107,120
N	=	360	N	=	24 months
i	=	.625 (7.5 ÷ 12)	PMT_{OA}	=	$749
PMT_{OA}	=	$749.00 (rounded)	i	=	.625 (7.5 ÷ 12)
			FV	=	$105,068

Fundamentals - TVM

2. **A**

Old Payment	$907.78 x 22 x 12 =	$239,654
New Payment	$831.25 x 22 x 12 =	$219,450
		$20,204

Old Payment			New Payment		
N	=	360	N	=	22 x 12
PV	=	$112,820	PV	=	$104,200 x 1.03
i	=	.75 (9 ÷ 12)	i	=	.625 (7.5 ÷ 12)
PMT	=	$907.78	PMT	=	$831.25

MINI CASE SCENARIO 19

Insurance – Automobile Coverage

1. C

Contact with a bird or animal is specifically excluded from the category of collision and will, therefore, be covered as comprehensive.

Insurance - Automobile Coverage

2. B

Backing your car into a tree would fall within the definition of collision.

Insurance - Automobile Coverage

3. B

Damage to your automobile would fall under the definition of collision.

Insurance - Automobile Coverage

4. A

This is an example of uninsured motorist coverage.

MINI CASE SCENARIO 20

Estates – Charitable Remainder Trusts

1. **A**

CRATs pay a fixed annuity; whereas, CRUTs will pay an amount that varies based on the valuation of the assets in the trust.

Estates - Charitable Remainder Trusts

2. **D**

Both CRUTs and CRATs are irrevocable trusts.

Estates - Charitable Remainder Trusts

3. **B**

Only CRUTs will have a variable annuity.

Estates - Charitable Remainder Trusts

4. **C**

Both CRATs and CRUTs provide for the remaining property to be left to charity.

MINI CASE SCENARIO 21

Estates – Powers of Appointment

1. **C**

Both general power of appointment and special power of appointment may permit holder to dispose of property.

Estates - Powers of Appointment

2. **C**

All powers of appointment terminate at the death of the grantor.

Estates - Powers of Appointment

3. **A**

General power only, regardless of whether property was appointed.

Estates - Powers of Appointment

4. **D**

Neither granting of general power of appointment or special power of appointment has any income tax consequences.

MINI CASE SCENARIO 22

Investments – Standard Deviation

1. **B**

Based on a correlation of .4, the standard deviation of the two portfolios is approximately 12% .

$\sigma^2 = W^2_A\sigma^2_A + W^2_B\sigma^2_B + 2W_A W_B\ [\sigma_A\sigma_B r_{AB}]$

$\sigma^2 = (.4)^2(.155)^2 + (.6)^2(.135)^2 + 2(.4)(.6)[(.155)(.135)(.4)]$

$\sigma^2 = .00384 + .00656 + .00402 = .01442$

$\sigma = 12.009\%$

Investments – Standard Deviation

2. **A**

The key to this question is to understand that the correlation between two assets that have no relationship is zero. The correlation of zero is then used in the formula for the standard deviation of a two-asset portfolio.

$\sigma^2 = W^2_A\sigma^2_A + W^2_B\sigma^2_B + 2W_A W_B\ [\sigma_A\sigma_B r_{AB}]$

$\sigma^2 = (.4)^2(.155)^2 + (.6)^2(.135)^2 + 2(.4)(.6)[(.155)(.135)(0)]$

$\sigma^2 = .00384 + .00656 + 0 = .01040$

$\sigma = 10.2\%$

MINI CASE SCENARIO 23

Retirement – Minimum Distribution

1. **C**

The minimum distribution for the current tax year is found by dividing the balance at December 31 of the previous year by the factor for age 71 (since she will be age 71 on December 31). The result is $260,417 ($5,000,000 divided by 19.2). The minimum distribution does not have to be received until April 1st of the year after Marleen turns 70 ½. The distribution is received "for" the year in which she is 70 ½ but not "in" the year in which she is 70 ½.

Retirement - Penalties

2. **A**

No penalties will be assessed for current year, because Marleen will have until April 1 of next year to receive her minimum distribution. The penalty for excess distributions has been eliminated in the 1997 Taxpayer Relief Act.

Retirement – Minimum Distribution

3. **A**

Because Marleen is a 5% or greater owner, she is not allowed to defer her minimum distribution until April 1 of the year following the year she retires. Marleen is permitted to roll her account balance into an IRA rollover account. She will not be permitted to use 5 year averaging if the balance has been transferred to an IRA rollover account. Her choice of whether or not to recalculate will not impact her current year distribution that could be received up until April 1 of next year.

MINI CASE SCENARIO 24

Retirement – ISOs

1. **D**

Bob has W-2 income of $2,200, the difference between the exercise price and the sale price. Because this option is an ISO, and he has not held it for longer than 2 years from the date of the grant and one year from the exercise date, the result is ordinary income. Because he has sold it within the same year as he exercised it, the ordinary income is W-2 income and subject to payroll taxes.

Retirement - NQSOs

2. **D**

Bob must recognize $2,000 of W-2 income upon exercising the NQSO.

Retirement - ISOs

3. **B**

Bob recognizes AMT income at the exercise date of $1,500 but does not recognize any regular taxable income until he sells the stock.

Retirement - NQSOs

4. **D**

Recognize $2,000 as W-2 income on exercise date then $1,000 STCG on sale date.

MINI CASE SCENARIO 25

Estates - Gross Estate Inclusions

1. C

$300,000	Life insurance
15,000	Gift tax paid on gifts made within 3 years of death
$315,000	Increase in the gross estate

Estate - Taxable Gift

2. B

$40,000	Stock to Mickey
(10,000)	Annual exclusion
$30,000	Taxable gift

Note: The value of the life insurance given to Molly was less than $10,000 and therefore qualified for the annual exclusion. Adjusted taxable gift is a term of art, meaning net of any annual exclusion.

Estates - Gross Estate Inclusion

3. A

The correct answer is zero because neither the life insurance proceeds nor the gift tax would be included in the gross estate.

MINI CASE SCENARIO 26

Fundamentals - Uneven Cash Flows

1. **C**

	(Key strokes for HP12C)
	CLX
(9,200)	[g] CF_o
600	[g] CF_j
2,300	[g] CF_j
2,200	[g] CF_j
6,800	[g] CF_j
9,500	[g] CF_j
	[f] IRR = 24.18%

Fundamentals - Uneven Cash Flows

2. **D**

Statement #4 is false, because, if the cost of capital is less than the IRR, then the project should be accepted (NPV > $0). Thus, A and E are incorrect. Statements #1, #2, and #3 are correct.

WILLIAM AND MARILYN MATHEWS CASE SCENERIO

Instructions: Read the information provided about William and Marilyn Mathews and choose the best answer to the multiple-choice questions that follow.

WILLIAM AND MARILYN MATHEWS

Case Scenario and Multiple Choice

The following case scenario with multiple-choice questions appeared on CFP Board Comprehensive CFP Certification Examinations. The case has been approved for publication by the CFP Board of Examiners. If you have a question about the technical content of the case, please address your question to the Board of Examiners by writing to them at the CFP Board address: 1700 Broadway, Suite 2100, Denver, CO 80290-2101.

Your clients, Bill and Marilyn Mathews, have asked you to help them with a number of issues facing them as Bill prepares to sell his business and formally retire. Marilyn will also retire, having worked as the company bookkeeper for twenty years. Negotiations for the sale of Bill's business, Calculator City, are almost concluded, pending resolution of a number of questions Bill raised regarding installment payments for the business as well as a request from the proposed owner that Bill continue to provide consulting services.

I. PERSONAL INFORMATION

	Age	Health	Occupation
William Mathews	65	Excellent	Business Owner
Marilyn Mathews	63	"	Bookkeeper
John Mathews (son)	32	"	Engineer
James Mathews (son)	30	"	CPA
Grandchildren	3, 4, 5, and 7	"	

Neither son has any intention of becoming involved in the business. The Mathews file a joint tax return. Client and spouse have simple wills leaving all to each other.

II. Economic Environment

The current economic environment exhibits low real short-term rates, high real long-term rates, little economic growth, and high unemployment.

III. Client Objectives

1. Maintain current lifestyle, including frequent travel.
2. Revise estate plan to minimize taxes, take advantage of opportunities in various elections available in the Internal Revenue Code, and maximize amounts passing to children and grandchildren.
3. Review investment portfolio and make changes as necessary to reflect different priorities and risk tolerance levels during retirement. Initial indications are that the clients are willing to take normal investment risks, desirous of adequate current income, reasonable safety of principal, inflation protection, tax advantage, and some modest long term appreciation, in that order of priority.
4. Review and revise total risk management and insurance situation as necessary to provide adequate protection, and eliminate gaps and overlaps.
5. Determine the most advantageous method of taking distributions from the 401(k) accounts.

IV. FINANCIAL STATEMENTS

William And Marilyn Mathews
Statement of Financial Position
12/31/92

ASSETS		LIABILITIES AND NET WORTH	
Invested Assets			
Cash/Cash Equivalents	$8,000	Auto Loan	$6,000
Marketable Securities[1]	1,580,000	Mortgage [2]	12,000
Business Interest [3]	1,500,000	Mortgage[4]	74,000
Life Ins. Cash Value[5]	60,000		$92,000
Annuity	120,000		
	$3,268,000		
Use Assets			
Primary Residence	$188,000		
Summer Home	126,000		
Personal Property	60,000		
Automobiles	26,000	Net Worth	$3,951,000
	$400,000		
Retirement Plan Assets[6]			
IRA (H)	$27,000		
IRA (W)	28,000		
401(k) (H)	280,000		
401(k) (W)	40,000		
	$375,000		
Total Assets	**$4,043,000**	**Total Liabilities and Net Worth**	**$4,043,000**

[1]See separate Investment Portfolio Supplement.

[2]Principal residence; originally, 30 years @ 7%.

[3]Business is to be sold for $1.5 million. Purchase price was $700,000 in 1982. Terms of sale include $300,000 down payment on July 1, 1993, with the balance to be paid over 120 months starting August 1, 1993, at 10% interest.

[4]Summer home; originally, 15 years @ 9%.

[5]Face Amount: $200,000; Bill is insured, Marilyn is beneficiary.

[6]Spouse is beneficiary for IRA and 401(k). The IRAs are invested in a common stock growth mutual fund. The 401(k) plans are invested in 3-year Treasury notes.

WILLIAM AND MARILYN MATHEWS

Projected Monthly Cash Flow Statement

1/1/93 through 12/31/93

(Incomplete)

Cash Inflows	
Social Security (H)	$820
Social Security (W)	$410
Installment Payments (120 pmts @ 10%)	?
Interest Income (tax-exempt)	$600
Dividend Income	$540
Interest Income (taxable)	?
Other Investment Income	?

Outflows	
Savings and Investment	?
Mortgage (residence: PITI)	$600
Mortgage (summer home: PITI)	$1,100
Food	$300
Utilities	$400
Transportation (gas, oil, maintenance)	$200
Car Payment	$600
Clothing	$250
Entertainment	$450
Travel	$1,680
Family Gifts	$1,666
Charitable Gifts	$500
Life Insurance	$300
Hospitalization (Medigap/Medicare)	$100
Automobile Insurance	$150
Miscellaneous	?
Federal Income Tax	$5,800
State Income Tax	$900
Other	?

V. INSURANCE AND ANNUITY INFORMATION

Person Insured/Owner	Bill
Type of Policy	Whole Life
Face Amount	$200,000
Dividend Option	Paid Up Additions
Issue Date	2/13/77
Beneficiary	Marilyn
Current Cash Value	$60,000
Premium	$300 per month

Person Insured/Owner	Bill
Type of Policy	Single Premium Deferred Annuity
Fixed or Variable	Fixed
Current Value	$120,000
Current Interest Rate	6.5%
Issue Date	1/1/81
Purchase Price	$40,000

Homeowners Policy	
Type	HO-3
Amount on Dwelling	$175,000
Personal Property Coverage	$ 87,500
Personal Liability	$100,000

Automobile Policy	
Type	Personal Auto Policy
Bodily Injury/Property Damage	$300,000 Combined Single Limit
Collision	$250 Deductible
Comprehensive	Full, with $100 Deductible
Uninsured Motorist	$300,000 Single Limit

VI. INVESTMENT PORTFOLIO SUPPLEMENT

These securities were accumulated over a period of years and are essentially unmanaged.

Common Stocks	Fair Market Value
AT & T	$30,000
Bell South	10,000
Bell Atlantic	9,000
Ameritech	8,500
NYNEX	7,000
Pacific Telesis	8,000
Southwestern Bell	8,000
U.S. West	7,000
Canon	22,000
Comerica Bank	29,000
Danko	7,000
de Beers	8,000
du Pont	29,000
Disney	12,000
Dow Chemical	9,000
Detroit Edison	24,000
General Motors	8,000
GM E	10,500
D&T, Inc.*	25,000
Common stock mutual fund (IRAs)	55,000
Municipal Bonds	
Franklin Intermediate Tax Exempt Fund	$100,000
Annuities & Insurance	
Cash value life insurance	$ 60,000
Single Premium Deferred Annuity	120,000
Bonds	
Treasury notes (401(k))	$320,000
U.S. EE Savings Bonds	75,000
Cash and Equivalents	
Cash	$8,000
Cash equivalents, incl. Money Markets	134,000
Treasury Securities (T-Bills)	1,000,000
TOTAL	**$2,143,000**

*Small Business Corporation (1244 stock) solely owned by Bill and originally purchased for $76,000 on 1/1/87.

1. The tax treatment of the down payment made to Bill for the sale of his business is:
   a. Not taxable as a return of basis.
   b. Fully taxable as a capital gain.
   c. Partially a return of basis and partially taxable as ordinary income.
   d. Partially a return of basis, partially a capital gain, and partially ordinary income.
   e. Partially a return of capital and partially a capital gain.

2. How much will Bill receive from the monthly installment payments during 1993 (rounded to the nearest dollar)?
   a. $79,290.
   b. $95,149.
   c. $190,297.
   d. $379,290.
   e. $395,149.

3. The amount of interest income from the installment sale for the year ending 12/31/93 is approximately:
   a. $49,000.
   b. $59,000.
   c. $60,000.
   d. $72,000.
   e. $120,000.

4. How will Bill's receipt of installment payments for the sale of his business affect his Social Security benefits?

   a. His Social Security benefits will be reduced because of his installment payments.
   b. His Social Security benefits will not be taxable because installment payments are not wages.
   c. Receipt of installment payments will increase the amount of Modified Adjusted Gross Income, causing some of the Social Security benefits to be taxable.
   d. Because Bill is 65, his Social Security benefits will be subject to the excess earnings test applied to the installment payments. Benefits will be reduced $1 for every $2 earned over the base amount.
   e. Because Bill is 65, his Social Security benefits will be subject to the excess earnings test applied to the installment payments. Benefits will be reduced $1 for every $3 earned over the base amount.

5. Bill and Marilyn both have account balances in the 401(k) Plan, and they want to determine what options they can pursue.

   Which of the following statements describe options available for Bill and Marilyn?

   1. Bill can make an IRA Rollover with his account; Marilyn can elect 10-Year Special Averaging for hers.
   2. Both Bill and Marilyn can make IRA Rollovers.
   3. Bill can elect a partial rollover and use 5-Year Special Averaging on the balance; Marilyn can roll over her entire amount.
   4. Both Bill and Marilyn can elect either 5-Year or 10-Year Special Averaging for their respective distributions.

   a. 1, 2, and 4.
   b. 1 and 3.
   c. 2 only.
   d. 2 and 3.
   e. 1, 2, 3, and 4.

6. The Mathews family is considering the purchase of a survivorship life insurance policy, payable on the second death of either Bill or Marilyn, for the primary purpose of providing liquidity for the payment of the federal estate tax. The ownership and beneficiary arrangements are being studied for the best overall result.

   Which of the following options for ownership and beneficiary arrangements are viable?

   1. Bill and Marilyn can purchase the policy and retain ownership; the proceeds will <u>not</u> be includible in either estate because of the unlimited marital deduction.
   2. Bill and Marilyn can purchase the policy, and then transfer ownership to one or both of their sons, so that the proceeds avoid inclusion in either Bill's or Marilyn's estate <u>no</u> matter when death occurs because they do <u>not</u> have any incidents of ownership.
   3. Ownership can be vested immediately in an irrevocable life insurance trust, with appropriate "Crummey" provisions, to avoid inclusion of the proceeds in either estate.
   4. The Mathews family Revocable Living Trust can be the initial owner and beneficiary, in order to avoid estate taxes in either estate, because life insurance death proceeds retain their tax-free character in the trust.

   a. 1, 3, and 4.
   b. 2 and 4.
   c. 3 only.
   d. 2 only.
   e. 1 and 4.

7. If Bill decides to make a partial withdrawal from his Single Premium Deferred Annuity, what income tax result will ensue?

   a. The withdrawal will be taxed as long-term capital gain, subject to a maximum rate of 28%.
   b. The withdrawal will be subject to ordinary income tax, since there is <u>no</u> preference for long-term capital gain.
   c. The withdrawal will be taxed according to the annuity rules, so that a portion will be taxable as ordinary income and the balance will be a tax-free recovery of capital.
   d. The withdrawal will be tax-free up to Bill's cost basis, since FIFO treatment applies to this annuity.
   e. The withdrawal will be taxable on a LIFO basis to the extent of earnings in the contract.

8. Bill is contemplating selling his D&T, Inc. stock for the fair market value. Assuming he sold D&T on 12/31/92, the tax impact would be:
   - a. A fully deductible capital loss of $51,000.
   - b. A capital loss limited to $3,000 assuming no other investment transactions; carryover $48,000 long-term capital loss.
   - c. An ordinary loss of $50,000 with a $1,000 loss carryover.
   - d. An ordinary loss of $51,000.
   - e. A short-term capital loss of $51,000 because of Sec. 1244 status.

9. In view of the combined estate values for Bill and Marilyn, which of the following estate planning techniques may be appropriate?
   1. Placing life insurance in an irrevocable trust.
   2. Making use of annual gift tax exclusion.
   3. Establishing a revocable living trust, using the unlimited marital deduction and the full unified credit.
   4. Arranging for a preferred stock recapitalization for Bill's business interest.
      - a. 2 and 3.
      - b. 1, 2, and 3,
      - c. 1, 3, and 4.
      - d. 1, 2, and 4.
      - e. 1, 2, 3, and 4.

10. The Mathews currently own a number of tax-advantaged financial instruments. Which of the following statements is/are true with respect to these various instruments?
    1. Interest income and capital appreciation from the municipal bond fund is federally tax exempt.
    2. An initial partial withdrawal from the single premium deferred annuity is fully taxable.
    3. When redeemed, the return on the savings bonds is <u>not</u> subject to state income taxes.
    4. The Treasury bills are federally taxed only upon maturity.
       - a. 1, 2, and 3.
       - b. 2 and 4.
       - c. 3 only.
       - d. 3 and 4.
       - e. 1, 2, 3, and 4.

11. If Bill and Marilyn wish to limit the growth of their combined estate, which techniques may be advisable?

    1. Use of the annual gift tax exclusion and split gift election.
    2. Current use of both unified credits.
    3. Payment of tuition for grandchildren.
    4. Payment of direct medical expenses for children and grandchildren.

    a. 1 and 2.
    b. 2, 3, and 4.
    c. 1 only.
    d. 1, 2, and 3.
    e. 1, 2, 3, and 4.

12. Assume that Bill wants to take advantage of the $1,000,000 Generation Skipping Transfer Tax exemption, by giving his grandson this amount now. What is the amount of the gift tax, given that there have been <u>no</u> prior taxable gifts?

    a. $121,800.
    b. $153,000.
    c. $390,000.
    d. $345,800.
    e. $410,000.

13. Assume Bill provides consulting services for the new owner and is properly classified as an independent contractor. Which statements properly describe Bill's ability to shelter current taxable income?

    1. Bill may take a non-deductible IRA for $2,000.
    2. Bill may set up a profit-sharing Keogh.
    3. Bill can set up a money purchase plan.
    4. Bill can set up a combined money purchase and profit-sharing plan, but his contributions will be limited to 20% of Schedule C income.

    a. 2 and 3.
    b. 1, 2, and 3.
    c. 2, 3, and 4.
    d. 1, 2, 3, and 4.
    e. 1 and 3.

14. In reviewing Bill and Marilyn's cash-flow projections as well as the investment portfolio supplement, you question the appropriateness of some of the holdings. Which combination of portfolio weaknesses best summarizes a valid critique of their investments?
    a. Excessive liquidity, inadequate tax advantage, marginal equity diversification.
    b. Inadequate tax advantage, excessive growth orientation, marginal equity diversification.
    c. Excessive liquidity, excessive growth orientation, inadequate tax advantage.
    d. Excessive reliance on Treasury Bills, insufficient growth opportunities, inadequate current income.
    e. Insufficient growth opportunities, inadequate liquidity, excessive tax advantage.

15. Assuming that Bill reaches agreement with the new owner as to the installment payments for the business interest, what are the estate tax ramifications if Bill dies at the end of the third year of the ten-year payout schedule?
    a. The remaining value of the installments is not includible in Bill's estate, because the payments continuing to Marilyn qualify for the marital deduction.
    b. Seventy percent of the original cash purchase price upon which the installments were based is includible in Bill's estate but qualifies for the marital deduction because payments will continue to Marilyn.
    c. The present value of the future income stream to Marilyn is included in Bill's estate, but the continuing payments qualify for the marital deduction.
    d. The present value of the future income stream to Marilyn is included in Bill's estate, but the continuing income payments do not qualify for the marital deduction because it is a terminable interest.
    e. Nothing is included in the estate because the installment payments are not guaranteed.

16. The inadequacies in their estate planning can be summarized as follows:

    1. Failure to take full advantage of each unified credit.
    2. Failure to avoid probate.
    3. Lack of proper documents to address the potential problem of incapacity.
    4. Failure to coordinate titling of assets with documentation.

    a. 1 and 2.
    b. 1, 2, and 3.
    c. 2, 3, and 4.
    d. 2 and 4.
    e. 1, 2, 3, and 4.

Regarding questions 17 and 18 and given the current economic conditions, you recommend allocating the Mathews' investment funds into three asset categories: equity, debt, and cash.

17. Which of the following statements describe(s) action(s) that you would recommend in order to meet the Mathews' goals?
    1. Because of the economic environment, the Mathews should immediately increase the proportion of equity investments to provide for growth for the estate.
    2. This is the opportune time to lengthen the maturity of the fixed income proportion of the portfolio.
    3. Because of the current economic scenario and their retired status, the Mathews should liquidate the equity portion of the portfolio.
    4. The Mathews should gradually increase the equity proportion of the portfolio over the next 3 years to provide for growth in their estate.
        a. 3 and 4.
        b. 1 and 2.
        c. 2 and 4.
        d. 4 only.
        e. 2, 3, and 4.

18. In order to meet their goals, the Mathews should:
    1. Reduce cash level, expand fixed income securities.
    2. Expand fixed income securities.
    3. Increase cash level, decrease equities.
    4. Expand fixed income securities, decrease equities.
        a. 1 only.
        b. 1 and 4.
        c. 2 and 3.
        d. 2, 3, and 4.
        e. None of the above.

19. You are considering liquidating the individual equity holdings and moving this amount into equity mutual funds. The following alternative allocations have been proposed

Choice A		**Choice B**	
Market index fund	40%	Growth fund	33%
Growth fund	20%	International equity fund	33%
Value-oriented fund	20%	Value-oriented fund	34%
International equity fund	20%		
Choice C		**Choice D**	
Market index fund	30%	Small company fund	25%
Gold stock fund	50%	Aggressive growth fund	45%
Equity-income fund	20%	Growth fund	30%

a. Choice A is preferred because it includes multiple management styles and market diversification.
b. Choice B is preferred because it employs both active and passive funds.
c. Choice C is preferred because it best meets the Mathews' goals.
d. Choice D is preferred because it maximizes growth while meeting the Mathews' goals.
e. Do <u>not</u> liquidate the current portfolio.

THIS PAGE IS INTENTIONALLY LEFT BLANK.

WILLIAM AND MARILYN MATHEWS

MULTIPLE CHOICE SOLUTIONS

WILLIAM AND MARILYN MATHEWS

The alphabetical answer was provided by the CFP® Board of Standards and is used with permission.
Explanations have been added to the answers, all prepared by or
under the direction of Michael A. Dalton and James F. Dalton, the authors,
and are not part of the CFP® Board of Standards' materials.

1.	E	5.	A	9.	B	13.	C	17.	D
2.	A	6.	C	10.	D	14.	A	18.	E
3.	A	7.	D	11.	E	15.	C	19.	A
4.	C	8.	D	12.	B	16.	E		

Installment Sale

1. E

The return of capital portion is determined by the gross profit % of this installment sale. Since it is the down payment there is no income component. There is however a portion of capital gain.

Selling Price	$1.5
Basis	$7
Capital Gain	$8

$7 ÷ 15 = 46.67% return of capital

$8 ÷ 15 = 53.33% capital gain

Time Value Calculations

2. A

N = 120

i = 10 ÷ 12

PV = $120,000

PMT = $15,858 X 5 = $79,290 ordinary annuity as of July 1, 1993 for 5 months.

It should either because an ordinary annuity or an annuity due of $120,000 and 1 month's interest $121,000 in which case PV = $121,000 and PMT = $79,951.

Below is the CFP Board of Examiner's response to a candidate's question regarding this exam item.

#2 is based on a sale price of $1.5 million with a down payment of $300,000, leaving a balance of $1.2 million. Payments are for 120 months at an interest rate of 0.83% per month (10% divided by 12). By the end of 1993, Bill will have received five payments. The answer to the question can be arrived through normal annuity calculation. I would agree that it probably should be calculated as an annuity due, in which case, the answer would have been slightly different, the amount of $78,635. Even if calculated this way, clearly the closest and best answer would be A.

Installment Sale

3. **A**

Total 1993 payments $15,858.09 x 5 = $79,290.45

Balance of Liability as of 12/31/93

Interest is $49,507.74 (See Amortization table)

Principal reduction was $29,782.71

Balance	Principal	Interest	Payment
$1,200,000.00	$5,858.09	$10,000.00	$15,858.09
$1,194,141.91	$5,906.91	$9,951.18	$15,858.09
$1,184,235.00	$5,956.13	$9,901.96	
$1,182,278.87	$6005.77	$9,852.32	
$1,176,273.10	$6055.81	$9,802.28	
		$49,507.74	

To approximate:

$1,200,000
x .10
$120,000
x .41667 (5 ÷ 12)
$50,000

The answer has to be less due to payments! 50 payments at $15,858.09. First payment = $10,000 interest. 5 payments must be less than $50,000.

Below is the CFP Board of Examiner's response to a candidate's question regarding this exam item.

Explanation:

Installment Note - $1,200,000

Monthly payment - $15,858.09

# of payments in 1993 - 5

Installment note balance as of 12-31-93 - $1,170,217.29

Total 1993 Principal payments - $29,782.71

Total 1993 interest payments - $49,507.74

Social Security

4. C

The interest income from the installment sale will increase modified AGI. The sale of an asset or an installment basis is not earned income and therefore will not affect the collection of social security retirement benefits. The test is earned income. A, D, and E are incorrect. B is incorrect; his social security benefits will be taxed. C is correct.

401(k) Distributions

5. A

Bill and Marilyn can make rollovers so #2 is correct. They can also elect 10 year averaging making #1 correct. They also could elect 5 year averaging making #4 correct. Bill cannot use 5-year averaging and have a partial rollover.

Life Insurance in Estates

6. C

The objective is to provide estate liquidity at the death of the second spouse. Obviously inclusion in the estate of the second to die is undesirable. #1 is absolutely incorrect making A and E incorrect. #2 is incorrect because of the 3-year throwback rule making B and D incorrect. You need go no further. However, #4 is a revocable trust and therefore would cause inclusion due to incidents of ownership issues.

Annuities

7. D

1. The annuity starting date is unknown.
2. This withdrawal would appear to be a non-periodic type payment as described in IRS 590 (1994 p. 11).
3. The answer D is correct if this contract was entered into before August 14, 1982. It is clear as to when the annuity was purchased 1/1/81. See Insurance and annuity information.

Below is the CFP Board of Examiner's response to a candidate's question regarding this exam item.

See IRS publication 575 which is on point.

Stock

8. **D**

Sale of Section 1244 stock will result in an ordinary loss of $51,000 assuming married filing jointly.

Estate Planning

9. **B**

#1, #2, and #3. Bill has already agreed to sell business on installment basis. Any of #1, #2 or #3 could be effective for estate planning. Preferred stock recapitalization is a technique that is no longer available under the current Internal Revenue Code.

Tax Inclusion

10. **D**

T-Bills only pay income at maturity because they are bought at a discount. Therefore, #4 is correct only if the bills are held to maturity. If sold prior to maturity, they would be subject to a tax on any gain. #1 is incorrect because appreciation of a municipal bond is taxable. Those 2 eliminate A and E. Savings bonds are not subject to state income tax; therefore, B is eliminated and D must be chosen. #2 is false because the SPDA is a pre '82 SPDA.

Gross Estate

11. **E**

This does not even require a reading of the case except to verify that children and grandchildren exist. Each item #1-4 will reduce their gross estate.

Generation Skipping Transfer Tax

12. B

Calculation of Gift Tax:

	Assuming no split gift	Assuming split gift	Assuming no annual exclusion
Gift	$1,000,000	$1,000,000	$1,000,000
Annual Exclusion	10,000	20,000	- 0 -
	$990,000	$980,000	$1,000,000
Tax	341,600	337,700	345,800
Less Unified Credit	192,800	192,800	192,800
Gift Tax Due	$148,800	$144,900	$153,000 *

* The question assumes that the gift is a taxable gift of $1,000,000.

Below is the CFP Board of Examiner's response to a candidate's question regarding this exam item.

The purpose of question #12 was to determine if the candidate can perform a gift tax calculation. We wanted the candidate to be able to use a table to determine the tentative tax on a taxable gift of $1,000,000 and then apply the unified credit available. You will note that this question was not an attempt to be "tricky" and indeed, your computer gave the answer closest to the "keyed" answer. The question should have specified taxable gift to indicate the amount of the annual exclusion. The incorrect answers were chosen so there would be no doubt what the correct answer would be. Our goal in writing test questions for the Comprehensive CFP Certification Examination is not to trick anyone. We have tried to make the questions straightforward to test each of the 175 areas of emphasis but occasionally some are unintentionally complicated.

Retirement Plans

13. C

#1 is wrong because it does not shelter current taxable income except to the extent of earnings on such an IRA. #2, #3, and #4 are correct except #4 should be modified to read Schedule C income less 1/2 Social Security.

Investment Integration

14. A

A review of the balance sheet and investment portfolio supplement reveals excessive liquidity (T-Bills), a lack of growth orientation (common stocks), a lack of marginal diversification and low tax advantaged investments. E, C, and B can be quickly eliminated. D fails due to large income. Answer A is by deduction.

Installment Sales

15. **C**

The question could have stated gross estate instead of just estate but the value of the installment notes is the present value and would be included in the gross estate and would qualify for the marital deduction based on the simple wills.

Estate Weaknesses

16. **E**

#1 is correct because they have simple wills. #2 is correct due to titling of assets. #3 is correct due to lack of durable powers, trusts, living wills. #4 is correct because financials do not indicate clear ownership interest.

Below is the CFP Board of Examiner's response to a candidate's question regarding this exam item.
(4) would be correct since there is no indication on the statement of financial position as to who holds title to many of the assets. This is what is meant by "failure to coordinate titling of assets with documentation."

Asset Allocation

17. **D**

The current economic environment is not conducive to substantive growth in equities. However, the Mathews should begin to increase their equity positions to provide additional growth. Review the economic environment. Nominal interest rates are low while real long-term rates are high. Therefore, this would not be a good time to invest in long term bonds.

Asset Allocation

18. **E**

The Mathews need to increase their equity holdings. None of the answers are consistent with this strategy. Long term fixed income securities should not be bought at this time.

Asset Allocation

19. **A**

Choice A is the only one that meets the needs of the Mathews. Choice B is a possible choice except that none of the funds are passive. Choice C has too much risk with 50% in gold. Choice D contains 70% in very aggressive funds - too risky for the Mathews.

BOOTH AND NEEDA MARTINI

CASE SCENERIO

TABLE OF CONTENTS

BOOTH AND NEEDA MARTINI

CASE A & CASE B INFORMATION

In our opinion, this case is more analytically rigorous and longer than cases we would expect to be on the CFP Exam. However, it is an excellent study case to build student's analytical skills.

Time to read case = 30 minutes for each case (A and B).
Time to answer questions = 60 minutes for each case (A and B).
Total time for both Case A and Case B together = 180 minutes.

BOOTH AND NEEDA MARTINI
Case Scenario for
Case A and Case B

Booth and Needa Martini have come to you, a financial planner, for help in developing a plan to accomplish their financial goals. From your initial meeting together, you have gathered the following information:

I. PERSONAL BACKGROUND AND INFORMATION

(As of January 1, 1999)

Booth Martini

Age 60, employed 25 years as a Vice-President for an oil field service. He participates in a defined benefit plan. Booth's first wife died in 1996.

Needa Martini

Age 28, owns Publications, Inc. and Needa's Advertising, Inc.

Booth and Needa Martini

They met July 4, 1996 on a cruise, fell in love, and married November 23, 1996. They have no children together.

Booth's Children

Michael	Age 34
James	Age 33
Brian	Age 32
Lucy	Age 31

All are healthy, employed, married, and none are living with Booth and Needa.

II. PERSONAL AND FINANCIAL GOALS

1. Needa plans to sell her businesses.
2. Booth plans to retire in 1999 (January 1, 1999). Booth's life expectancy is 25.833 years.
3. They plan to sell their primary residence.
4. They plan to refinance their vacation home.
5. They plan to travel extensively before deciding where to permanently relocate.

III. ECONOMIC INFORMATION

- They expect inflation to average 3.0% (CPI) annually over both the short-term and the long-term.
- Expected stock market return of 11% on S & P 500 Index.
- T-Bills are currently yielding 5%.
- Current mortgage rates are:

Fixed 15 year	6.75%
Fixed 30 year	7.25%

- Closing costs are expected to be 3% of any mortgage.
- They will finance closing costs in any refinance.

IV. INSURANCE INFORMATION

Life Insurance

	Policy 1	Policy 2
Insured	Booth	Needa
Owner	Booth	Needa
Beneficiary	Children	Booth
Face Amount	$150,000	$150,000
Cash Value	0	0
Type of Policy	Term	Term
Settlement Options	Lump Sum	Lump Sum
Premium (annual)	$450	$150

Health Insurance

Employer provided both during employment and while retired (Booth's employer). Coverage for both Booth and Needa.

Disability Insurance

Neither has disability insurance.

Homeowner's Insurance

HO3 on both primary residence and vacation home.

	Residence	Vacation Home
Dwelling	$200,000	$150,000
Co-Insurance	80/20	80/20
Deductible	$250	$250

Umbrella Policy

$3 Million.

Automobile Insurance

Maximum liability, no comprehensive or collision.

V. INVESTMENT DATA

- Emergency fund is adequate at $20,000.
- They can accept moderate risk.
- Booth's IRA investment portfolio is $200,000 with all but $100,000 invested in low to medium risk equity mutual funds. Needa is the beneficiary.
- The $100,000 is invested in staggered maturity short-term treasury notes.
- Booth expects to use the income and some of the principal from the $100,000 to make up any shortfall between his retirement needs and his defined benefit plan annuity for the period of time until Social Security benefits are received (2 years at age 62).
- Booth is currently earning 6.5% on the $100,000 and expects the earnings rate to continue until the notes mature.

VI. INCOME TAX INFORMATION

(See also Assets)

- Booth and Needa file a joint tax return and are both average and marginal 28% taxpayers with no state income tax.

VII. RETIREMENT INFORMATION

Booth

- Has an employer provided defined benefit plan that will pay him a joint and survivor annuity equal to 80% of single life annuity at any retirement age 60 and over. No reduction for retirement at 60 and over.
- The defined benefit formula is 1.25% per year multiplied by the number of years multiplied by the last salary with no offset for Social Security (Booth's final salary for 1998 was $100,000).
- The present value of his projected annual Social Security benefits at 65 is $13,500 per year or 80% of that amount at age 62. Social Security benefits are expected to increase directly with the inflation rate.
- Booth is expected to retire January 1, 1999. He has three options he can elect regarding his Defined Benefit plan:
  1. Take a lump sum of $400,000.
  2. Take a single life annuity beginning January 1, 1999.
  3. Take a joint and survivor annuity beginning January 1, 1999.

VIII. GIFTS, ESTATES, TRUSTS, AND WILL INFORMATION

Gifts

Lifetime taxable gifts made are as follows:

- In 1989, Booth gifted $200,000 to each of his four children. The $800,000 was put in an irrevocable trust. During the same year he gave $10,000 to each child (total $40,000) to use the 1989 annual exclusion. He paid gift tax of $78,000 at the time. He inherited the $918,000 ($800,000 + $40,000 + $78,000) as the primary legatee from his mother in 1989. The successor legatees were the four grandchildren (children of Booth).
- In December 1996, Booth gave each of his four children $60,000 ($50,000 taxable and $10,000 annual exclusion) and paid gift tax of $75,000 April 15, 1997.
- Needa has made no taxable gifts during her lifetime.

Estates

For purposes of estimating estate tax liability (of either spouse):

- Last illness and funeral estimated at $20,000.
- Estate administration expense estimated at $30,000.

Wills

Booth and Needa have simple wills leaving all probate assets to the other. Debts and taxes are to be paid from the probate residue of the decedent.

IX. STATEMENT OF FINANCIAL POSITION

Booth and Needa Martini
Statement of Financial Position
As of January 1, 1999

ASSETS[1]

Cash/Cash Equivalents		
JT H W	Cash (Money Market)	$40,000
	Total Cash/Cash Equivalents	$40,000
Invested Assets		
WS	Publications, Inc.	$300,000
WS	Needa' Advertising, Inc.	100,000
WS	Needa's Investment Portfolio (see detail)	90,000
HS	SPDA	110,801
HS	Booth's Investment Portfolio (IRA) (see detail)	200,000
HS	Defined Benefit Plan (Vested)	400,000
	Total Investments	$1,200,801
Personal Use Assets		
JT H W	Primary Residence (Dwelling)	$300,000
JT H W	Primary Residence (Land)	20,000
JT H W	Vacation Home	160,000
JT H W	Personal Property & Furniture	100,000
HS	Auto1	20,000
WS	Auto2	22,000
	Total Personal Use	$622,000
Total Assets		**$1,862,801**

LIABILITIES AND NET WORTH[2]

Liabilities		
Current:		
HS	Bank Credit Card 1	$5,000
WS	Bank Credit Card 2	7,000
WS	Bank Credit Card 3	8,000
HS	$Auto_1$ Note Balance	10,000
WS	$Auto_2$ Note Balance	10,000
	Current Liabilities	$40,000
Long-Term:		
	Mortgage - Primary Residence	$150,000
	Mortgage - Vacation Home	120,000
	Long-Term Liabilities	$270,000
	Total Liabilities	$310,000
Net Worth		$1,552,801
Total Liabilities & Net Worth		**$1,862,801**

Notes to financial statements:

1 All assets are stated at fair market value.
2 Liabilities are stated at principal only.

Titles and Ownership Information

HS = Husband separate property.
WS = Wife separate property.
JTHW = Joint husband and wife (with survivorship rights).

X. INFORMATION REGARDING ASSETS AND LIABILITIES

Assets

Publications, Inc. (Needa 100% shareholder of C Corporation).

- Fair Market Value $300,000.
- Original and present tax basis $75,000 (acquired by purchase January 1, 1995).
- Needa has agreed to sell the company for $300,000 on April 1, 1999. Terms are 20% down on April 1 and the balance paid in equal monthly installments over 10 years at 11% interest beginning on May 1, 1999.

Needa's Advertising, Inc. (Needa 100% shareholder of C Corporation - Section 1244 stock).

- She started the business January 1, 1993, and her tax basis is $250,000.

SPDA (Single Premium Deferred Annuity) (Booth's)

- Acquired January 1, 1981 for $25,000. The current fair market value is $110,801.
- Contract has back and surrender charges of 5% for first 7 years.
- The current earnings rate is 6% compounded quarterly.
- Annuity start date is October 1, 1999 and will consist of quarterly payments over Booth's life (Booth's life expectancy is exactly 25 years as of 10/1/99).
- Needa is the named beneficiary, if Booth dies before the annuity start date.

Defined Benefit Plan

- Vested benefits $400,000 FMV.
- In the event of Booth dies before his retirement benefits begin, the entire balance is paid directly to Needa as his named beneficiary.

Primary Residence

- Was owned by Booth, gifted half to Needa as a wedding present.
- Fair market value $320,000, cost basis $140,000.
- Expect to pay 6% real estate commission on sale.

Vacation Home

- Fair market value $160,000.
- Original mortgage at 9%, 15 years.
- Current payment $1,522 per month (Principal and Interest).
- Current mortgage balance $120,000, remaining term is 120 months.

IRA Investments (Booth)

- Beneficiary is Needa.

XI. NEEDA'S DETAILED INVESTMENT PORTFOLIO

Description	Quantity	FMV	Beta	Maturity	Coupon	Yearly Returns 98	97	96	95	94
Best Buy	200	$6,000.00	1.15			10%	15%	12%	6%	-5%
Texaco	500	$10,000.00	0.90			5%	6%	3%	7%	-6%
Kroger	1,250	$10,000.00	0.85			5%	9%	8%	8%	-1%
Intel	400	$20,000.00	1.20			11%	15%	12%	10%	3%
Growth Fund	1,400	$21,000.00	1.15			5%	11%	14%	9%	2%
Treasury A (1 Bond)	1	$929.64		2	$50					
Treasury B (2 Bonds)	2	$2,050.62		3	$100					
Treasury C (2 Bonds)	2	$2,272.28		5	$125					
Cash		$17,747.46								
Total		**$90,000.00**								

Note: The correlation coefficient between Needa's portfolio and the market is 0.9.

All bonds have a par value of $1,000. The coupon amount represents the amount per bond.

THIS PAGE IS INTENTIONALLY LEFT BLANK.

BOOTH AND NEEDA MARTINI CASE A MULTIPLE CHOICE

BOOTH AND NEEDA MARTINI
CASE A

Assumption Regarding Dates

In answering this case (unless directed otherwise), assume that today is January 1, 1999.

1. Excluding the down payment, what is the total of the expected installment payments to be received by Needa in 1999, from the sale of Publications, Inc. (round to nearest dollar)?

   a. $26,208.
   b. $26,448.
   c. $29,484.
   d. $29,754.
   e. $39,672.

2. Calculate the first annuity payment from the SPDA for Booth, assuming he starts the annuity as scheduled (October 1, 1999).

   a. $2,114.56.
   b. $2,146.28.
   c. $2,211.15.
   d. $2,244.32.
   e. None of the above.

3. Booth and Needa have decided to refinance their vacation home over the remaining life of their existing current mortgage. What will be the monthly P & I payment as a result of refinancing?

   a. $1,061.89.
   b. $1,093.75.
   c. $1,370.18.
   d. $1,377.89.
   e. $1,419.23.

4. Assuming Booth and Needa sell their primary residence for the fair market value today, what are their 1999 tax consequences, assuming they do not plan to reinvest for three or four years and that they take advantage of any available elections?

   a. $37,000 LTCG.
   b. $55,000 LTCG.
   c. $162,000 LTCG.
   d. $180,000 LTCG.
   e. No gain or loss.

5. Booth is contemplating gifting his life insurance policy to his children who are the current beneficiaries. What is the correct valuation for gift tax purposes of such a gift?

   a. The interpolated terminal reserve.
   b. The replacement cost.
   c. The interpolated terminal reserve plus unearned premiums.
   d. The unearned premiums at the date of the gift.
   e. None of the above.

6. In the event of a $25,000 loss on the personal residence, how much will the homeowners insurance company pay for such a loss?

   a. $16,667.
   b. $20,000.
   c. $20,583.
   d. $25,000.
   e. None of the above.

7. You review the insurance coverage on Needa and Booth for catastrophic coverage and estate planning. Which of the following is/are deficiencies in the insurance arrangement considering catastrophic coverage and estate planning?

   1. Disability insurance for Needa.
   2. Lack of comprehensive and collision auto insurance.
   3. Insufficient umbrella coverage.
   4. Life insurance for estate liquidity at Booth's death.

      a. 1 and 4.
      b. 1, 2, and 3.
      c. 1, 2, and 4.
      d. 1, 2, 3, and 4.
      e. None of the above.

8. What are the weighted beta and the weighted geometric average return of Needa's investment portfolio over the last five years based on current market values (excluding bonds and cash)?

	Beta	**Return**
a.	1.05	6.96%
b.	1.05	7.20%
c.	1.08	6.96%
d.	1.08	7.51%
e.	1.08	7.61%

9. Which of the following risks should Needa be concerned about with regard to her investment portfolio?

   1. Systematic risk.
   2. Unsystematic risk.
   3. Market risk.
   4. Reinvestment rate risk.
   5. Interest rate risk.
   6. Default risk.

      a. 1, 2, and 6.
      b. 1, 3, 4, 5, and 6.
      c. 2, 3, 4, 5, and 6.
      d. 1, 3, 4, 5, and 6.
      e. 1, 2, 3, 4, and 5.

10. Considering Needa's current Bond Portfolio, which of the following risks is she not subject to, if she holds the bonds to maturity?

    1. Purchasing power risk.
    2. Reinvestment rate risk.
    3. Exchange rate risk.
    4. Default risk.
    5. Financial risk.

        a. 1 and 2.
        b. 1, 3, and 4.
        c. 2, 4, and 5.
        d. 3, 4, and 5.
        e. 1, 3, 4, and 5.

11. Determine which of the following bonds Needa should purchase if she wants to increase the duration of her bond portfolio.

    1. Bond 1: Three year zero coupon bond selling for $772.18 (Duration = 3 years).
    2. Bond 2: Four year bond selling for $1,923.32 with an annual coupon of $375 (Duration = 2.985 years).
    3. Bond 3: Four year bond selling for $983.80 with an annual coupon of $85 (Duration = 3.55 years).

    Note: All bonds have a maturity of $1,000.

        a. 1 only.
        b. 2 only.
        c. 3 only.
        d. 2 and 3.
        e. 1, 2, and 3.

12. Is Needa's portfolio of common stocks (including the mutual fund) subject to unsystematic risk?
    a. Yes, because unsystematic risk includes business risk and common stocks naturally contain this risk.
    b. Yes, because the coefficient of determination of the portfolio is not at its maximum level.
    c. Yes, because unsystematic risk includes market risk and all common stock and common stock portfolios are subject tc market risk.
    d. No, because the portfolio contains enough stocks to be completely diversified.
    e. No, because the market and the portfolio will not move precisely together as the market changes.

13. Using the Capital Asset Pricing Model and assuming that the market had yielded an annual compound return of 7.4% over the past five years, has Needa's portfolio outperformed the expected return?
    a. Yes, because the expected return is 7.59%, which is less than the return for the portfolio of 7.61%.
    b. Yes, because the return of 7.4% is lower than the actual return.
    c. No, because the expected return, which is 7.99%, is greater than the actual return.
    d. No, because the expected return, which is 7.59%, is greater than the actual return.
    e. The case does not provide sufficient information to answer this question.

14. Using the Treynor performance measure, which of the common stocks (including the mutual fund) falls in the middle as the five securities are ranked highest to lowest (use the geometric average return over the five year period).
    a. Best Buy.
    b. Texaco.
    c. Kroger.
    d. Intel.
    e. Growth Fund.

THIS PAGE IS INTENTIONALLY LEFT BLANK.

BOOTH AND NEEDA MARTINI CASE A SOLUTIONS

BOOTH AND NEEDA MARTINI CASE
CASE A

(Case A covers the following topics: Fundamentals, Insurance, and Investments)

1.	B	4.	E	7.	E	10.	D	13.	D
2.	C	5.	D	8.	D	11.	C	14.	A
3.	E	6.	C	9.	E	12.	B		

Summary of Question Types

1. Fundamentals-Installment Sale
2. Fundamentals-Time Value of Money
3. Fundamentals-Time Value of Money
4. Tax-Sale of Personal Residence
5. Estates-Gifts
6. Insurance-Homeowners
7. Insurance-Deficiencies
8. Investments-Beta & Geometric Return
9. Investments-Risk
10. Investments-Bond Portfolio
11. Investments-Bonds
12. Investments-Risk
13. Investments-CAPM
14. Investments-Treynor

Fundamentals-Installment Sale

1. **B**

N	=	120	Sale Price	$300,000
i	=	.9166 (11 ÷ 12)	Down Payment	(60,000)
PV	=	$240,000	Balance of Installment Note	$240,000
PMT_{OA}	=	$3,306.00		
x 8	=	$26,448		

*only 8 payments are made in 1999.

Fundamentals-Time Value of Money

2. **C**

You must first calculate the value of the annuity as of October 1, 1999, and then calculate the annuity due for 100 quarters.

Correct	Incorrect Answers		
	A	**B**	**D**
N = 3			
i = 1.5 (6 ÷ 4)			
PV = $110,801			
FV/PV = $115,862.20	PV = $110,801	PV = 110,801	PV = $115,862.20
N = 100 (quarterly pmts)	N = 100	N = 100	N = 100
i = 1.5	i = 1.5	i = 1.5	i = 1.5
PMT_{AD} = $2,211.15	PMT_{AD} = $2,114.56	PMT_{OA} = $2,146.28	PMT_{OA} = $2,244.32

Fundamentals-Time Value of Money

3. E

They would finance the 3% closing costs and pay over a period of 120 months at a 15 year fixed rate of 6.75%.

N	=	120
i	=	.5625 (6.75 ÷ 12)
PV	=	$123,600 ($120,000 x 1.03)
PMT	=	$1,419.23

Incorrect Answers				
	A	B	C	D
N	180	180	120	120
i	6.75 ÷ 12	6.75 ÷ 12	6.75 ÷ 12	6.75 ÷ 12
PV	$120,000	$123,600	$120,000	$120,000
PMT	$1,061.89	$1,093.75	$1,370.18 (Beg)	$1,377.89

Tax-Sale of Personal Residence

4. E

They can exclude up to $500,000 gain from the sale of a personal residence that was owned and used for a period of two years.

Estates-Gifts

5. D

This is a term policy. The value of the policy as a gift is equal to the unearned premium at the date of the gift.

Insurance-Homeowners

6. **C**

$$\$300,000 \times .80 = \frac{\$200,000 \text{ Insurance}}{\$240,000 \text{ Required insurance}} = .833 \times \$25,000 = \$20,833 - 250 = \$20,583$$

Insurance-Deficiencies

7. **E**

None are deficiencies. Net worth is strong, umbrella coverage is good, and there are no estimated estate taxes due. They have simple wills, and no liquidity problem at Booth's death. They chose not to insure for comprehensive and collision on auto. They are retired and, therefore, do not need disability insurance.

Investments-Beta & Geometric Return

8. **D**

Comments:

6.96% is the simple average of all returns.

7.20% is the simple average of the 94 returns.

1.05 is the simple average beta (not weighted).

7.61 uses simple average and not geometric average.

Answer D Solution (correct)

FMV	%	Geometric Return	Weighted Return
$6,000.00	9%	7.37%	0.66%
10,000.00	15%	2.89%	0.43%
10,000.00	15%	5.74%	0.86%
20,000.00	30%	10.13%	3.02%
21,000.00	31%	8.12%	2.54%
$67,000.00	**100%**		**7.51%**

FMV	%	Beta	Weighted Beta
$6,000.00	9%	1.15	0.10
10,000.00	15%	0.90	0.13
10,000.00	15%	0.85	0.13
20,000.00	30%	1.20	0.36
21,000.00	31%	1.15	0.36
$67,000.00	**100%**		**1.08**

Answer E Solution (incorrect)

FMV	%	Average	Weighted Simple Average
$6,000.00	9%	7.60%	0.68%
10,000.00	15%	3.00%	0.45%
10,000.00	15%	5.80%	0.87%
20,000.00	30%	10.20%	3.04%
21,000.00	31%	8.20%	2.57%
$67,000.00	**100%**		**7.61%**

FMV	%	Beta	Weighted Beta
$6,000.00	9%	1.15	0.10
10,000.00	15%	0.90	0.13
10,000.00	15%	0.85	0.13
20,000.00	30%	1.20	0.36
21,000.00	31%	1.15	0.36
$67,000.00	**100%**		**1.08**

Geometric return = -1 + the nth root of $[(1+R_1)*(1+R_2)*...*(1+R_n)]$

Investments-Risk

9. **E**

All risks apply, except default risk, because treasury bonds are considered default risk free.

Investments-Bond Portfolio

10. **D**

The Bond Portfolio is all Treasuries; therefore, it will not have any default risk. Exchange rate risk involves foreign bonds, and financial risk relates to common stock, not bonds.

Investments-Bonds

11. **C**

	Treasury A	Treasury B	Treasury C	Bond 1	Bond 2	Bond 3
PV	$929.64	$1,025.31	$1,136.14	$772.18	$1,923.32	$983.80
FV	$1,000.00	$1,000.00	$1,000.00	$1,000.00	$1,000.00	$1,000.00
N	2	3	5	3	4	4
PMT	$50	$100	$125	$0	$375	$85
i	9.00%	9.00%	9.00%	9.00%	9.00%	9.00%

Note: i above represents the YTM.
All bonds have a YTM of 9%.
PV of Current Bond Portfolio = $5,252.54.

	Cash Flow					
Period	Treasury A	Treasury B	Treasury C	Total	PV	PV * Period
1	$50	$200	$250	$500	$458.72	$458.72
2	$1,050	$200	$250	$1,500	$1,262.52	$2,525.04
3	-	$2,200	$250	$2,450	$1,891.85	$5,675.55
4	-	-	$250	$250	$177.11	$708.44
5	-	-	$2,250	$2,250	$1,462.35	$7,311.75
	$1,100	$2,600	$3,250	$6,950	$5,252.55	$16,679.50

Note: There are two bonds for Treasuries B & C.
Duration for this portfolio equals 3.176 years. ($16,679.50 ÷ $5,252.55)
Therefore, Needa should purchase a bond with a duration greater than 3.176 years.

Bond 1:

Period	Cash Flow	PV	PV x Period
1	-	-	-
2	-	-	-
3	$1,000	$772.18	$2,316.54
4	-	-	-
5	-	-	-
	$1,000	$772.18	$2,316.54

Duration for this portfolio equals 3 years. ($2,316.54 ÷ $772.18)
A zero coupon bond always has a duration equal to its maturity.

Bond 2:

Period	Cash Flow	PV	PV x Period
1	$375	$344.04	$344.04
2	$375	$315.63	$631.26
3	$375	$289.57	$868.71
4	$1,375	$974.08	$3,896.32
5	-	-	-
	$2,500	$1,923.32	$5,740.33

Duration for this portfolio equals 2.985 years. ($5,740.33 ÷ $1,923.32)

Bond 3:

Period	Cash Flow	PV	PV x Period
1	$85	$77.98	$77.98
2	$85	$71.54	$143.08
3	$85	$65.64	$196.92
4	$1,085	$768.64	$3,074.56
5	-	-	-
	$1,340	$983.80	$3,492.54

Duration for this portfolio equals 3.55 years. ($3,492.54 ÷ $983.80)

Answer: The portfolio has a duration of 3.176 years. Therefore, to increase the duration of the bond portfolio, bonds with durations greater than the current portfolio would have to be added. Only Bond 3 has a duration greater than the current portfolio. Thus, the answer is c.

Investments-Risk

12. **B**

The coefficient of determination is the square of the correlation coefficient. Therefore, because the correlation coefficient is .9, the coefficient of determination is .81. Thus, 81% of the changes in Needa's investment portfolio can be explained by changes in the market. However, 19% is explained by some other source. Because this other source is not systematic risk (which would have been explained by the changes in the market), it must be unsystematic risk. Therefore, B is the correct answer.

Investments-CAPM

13. **D**

Solution:

FMV	%	Geometric Return	Weighted Geometric Return
$6,000.00	9%	7.37%	0.66%
$10,000.00	15%	2.89%	0.43%
$10,000.00	15%	5.74%	0.86%
$20,000.00	30%	10.13%	3.02%
$21,000.00	31%	8.12%	2.54%
$67,000.00	**100%**		**7.51%**

FMV	%	Beta	Weighted Beta
$6,000.00	9%	1.15	0.10
$10,000.00	15%	0.90	0.13
$10,000.00	15%	0.85	0.13
$20,000.00	30%	1.20	0.36
$21,000.00	31%	1.15	0.36
$67,000.00	**100%**		**1.08**

Capital Asset Pricing Model

E(R) = Rf + B(Mr-Rf)

E(R) = 5% + 1.08(7.4%-5%) = 7.59%

Because the actual return of Needa's portfolio (7.51%) is less than the expected return of 7.59%, the portfolio has not outperformed the expected return.

Note: Geometric return = -1 + the nth root of $[(1+R_1)*(1+R_2)*...*(1+R_n)]$

Investments-Treynor

14. A

Treynor index = (R-Rf)/beta

	R	Rf	Beta	Treynor Index
Best Buy	7.37%	5.00%	1.15	2.06%
Texaco	2.89%	5.00%	0.90	-2.34%
Kroger	5.74%	5.00%	0.85	0.87%
Intel	10.13%	5.00%	1.20	4.27%
Growth Fund	8.12%	5.00%	1.15	2.71%

Note: R = geometric return

Geometric return = -1+ the nth root of $[(1+R_1)*(1+R_2)*...*(1+R_n)]$

	R	Rf	Beta	Treynor Index
Intel	10.13%	5.00%	1.20	4.27%
Growth Fund	8.12%	5.00%	1.15	2.71%
Best Buy	**7.37%**	**5.00%**	**1.15**	**2.06%**
Kroger	5.74%	5.00%	0.85	0.87%
Texaco	2.89%	5.00%	0.90	-2.34%

THIS PAGE IS INTENTIONALLY LEFT BLANK.

BOOTH AND NEEDA
MARTINI
CASE B
MULTIPLE CHOICE

BOOTH AND NEEDA MARTINI
CASE B

1. What is the tax treatment for 1999, of the down payment made on April 1, 1999 when Needa sells Publications, Inc., assuming that she treats the sale as an installment sale?
    a. Long-term capital gain $225,000.
    b. $60,000 return of capital.
    c. Long-term capital gain of $45,000.
    d. Ordinary income of $6,600.
    e. Long-term capital gain, return of basis, and ordinary income.

2. Calculate the amount of ordinary income and capital gain that Needa will have in 1999 from the sale of Publications, Inc. (round to the nearest dollar).

	Ordinary Income	Capital Gain
a.	$17,311	$51,853
b.	$17,311	$53,608
c.	$17,311	$53,848
d.	$17,600	$53,608
e.	$17,600	$53,848

3. Assume that Needa immediately sells Needa's Advertising, Inc. for the current fair market value. What is the impact of such a transaction on the Martinis' joint tax return for 1999?
    a. A $50,000 ordinary loss.
    b. A $100,000 ordinary loss.
    c. A $150,000 ordinary loss.
    d. A $150,000 long-term capital loss.
    e. A $100,000 ordinary loss and a $50,000 long-term capital loss.

4. Assume Booth decides to withdraw $15,000 from his SPDA today, January 1, 1999. The insurance company has informed him that his quarterly annuity (ordinary) payment will be reduced to $1,911.81 per quarter. What is the income tax effect of Booth's proposed withdrawal?

   a. $15,000 is ordinary income.
   b. $3,384 is ordinary income.
   c. $11,615.55 is ordinary income.
   d. $11,615.55 is ordinary income, and there is a 10% penalty.
   e. $15,000 is a return of basis, not taxable.

5. Assume that Booth begins his SPDA annuity as scheduled. What is the portion of that monthly annuity that is includible in taxable income in 1999?

   a. $477.11.
   b. $498.90.
   c. $1,712.25.
   d. $1,734.04.
   e. $1,961.15.

6. Calculate Booth's expected Defined Benefit monthly annuity payment assuming he elects the single life annuity (round to the nearest dollar).

   a. $2,049.
   b. $2,083.
   c. $2,209.
   d. $2,604.
   e. $2,763.

7. Assume Booth elects to take the lump sum benefit from his defined benefit plan. He believes that his after tax earnings rate on such a portfolio would be 10% and that inflation would be equal to the projected CPI. What real amount of a single life monthly annuity could he create assuming the payments were made at the beginning of each month and began October 1, 1999?

   a. $2,083.33.
   b. $2,604.17.
   c. $2,759.68.
   d. $2,775.31.
   e. $3,604.76.

8. Assuming Booth decides to take Social Security retirement benefits beginning January 1, 2001, calculate his expected annual Social Security benefits for 2001 (round to the nearest dollar).

   a. $10,800.
   b. $11,458.
   c. $12,500.
   d. $13,500.
   e. $14,322.

9. Assume that Booth was to die today, what is the total of his probate estate?

   a. $0.
   b. $20,000.
   c. $190,000.
   d. $440,000.
   e. $590,000.

10. Assuming that Booth was to die today, what is the total of his gross estate?

   a. $440,801.
   b. $640,801.
   c. $1,040,801.
   d. $1,190,801.
   e. $1,265,801.

11. What would be Booth's tentative tax base?

   a. $0.
   b. $150,000.
   c. $1,150,000.
   d. $1,225,000.
   e. None of the above.

12. What could Booth have done in 1989 to avoid his current estate situation and still have achieved the same result as his initial gifting?

    a. He could have orally disclaimed the inheritance from his mother.

    b. He could have given a written disclaimer to the executor directing that the monies should be paid to the successor legatees in trust.

    c. He could have accepted the money and used it until the filing date on the 706. Then he could have given the remainder to the successor legatees, and it would not have been a taxable gift.

    d. To disclaim, he would have had to do so within (6) six months. This would have to be done in writing.

    e. None of the above.

BOOTH AND NEEDA MARTINI CASE B SOLUTIONS

BOOTH AND NEEDA MARTINI CASE
CASE B

(Case B covers the following topics: Income Tax, Retirement, And Estates)

1.	C	3.	E	5.	E	7.	C	9.	B	11.	D
2.	A	4.	E	6.	D	8.	B	10.	E	12.	E

Summary of Question Types

1. Tax-Installment Sale
2. Tax-Installment Sale
3. Tax-Property Disposition
4. Tax-Annuities
5. Tax-Annuities
6. Retirement-Defined Benefit Plan
7. Fundamentals-Time Value of Money\Annuities
8. Retirement-Social Security
9. Estates-Probate Estate
10. Estates-Gross Estate
11. Estates-Estate Tax Base
12. Estates-Planning

Tax-Installment Sale

1. **C**

The down payment does not include any ordinary income.

Sales Price	$300,000	100%	Down Payment	$60,000	100%
Basis	(75,000)	25%	Return of Basis	(15,000)	25% Ratio
Capital Gain	$225,000	75%	LTCG	$45,000	75% Ratio

Tax-Installment Sale

2. **A**

1996				
	TP **Total Payments**	**CG** **Capital Gains**	**CR** **Basis Recovery**	**OI** **Ordinary Income**
Down Payment	$60,000	$45,000	$15,000	$0
Installment Payment	26,448	6,853	2,284	17,311
Total	$86,448	$51,853	$17,284	$17,311

It is not necessary to calculate the interest exactly. If no installment payments were made during the year, it is sufficient to know that it is less than $17,600, since ($240,000 x 11% x 8/12) = $17,600. Therefore, the interest must be $17,311.

PV	=	$240,000
PMT	=	$3,306
i	=	11 ÷ 12
(8 f N)Keystroke	=	$17,310.86 for interest on loan in year 1.

Balance of Installment Notes

PV = $240,000

i = 11 ÷ 12

PMT_{OA} = $3,306

FV = $230,862.86

Beginning Balance	$240,000
Ending Balance	$230,862.86
Principal Balance	$9,137.14
x 75% CG	$6,852.85
x 25% CR	$2,284.29

An alternative way to determine the interest is:

Total Payments	$3,306 x 8 =	$26,448.00	CG = $6,852.85
Principal Reduction		(9,137.14)	
Ordinary Income (interest)		$17,310.86	CR = $2,284.29

Tax-Property Disposition

3. **E**

Sales Price	$100,000	
Tax Basis	(250,000)	
	($150,000)	Loss
	(100,000)	Ordinary Loss (1244 stock)
	($50,000)	LTCL used against other capital gains

Note: Section 1244 stock entitles the owner to receive up to $100,000 (for married filing jointly) in ordinary losses instead of capital losses (per year); the remaining $50,000 is a long-term capital loss.

Tax-Annuities

4. **E**

Pre-1982 annuities use the FIFO rule. He may withdraw up to his basis tax-free.

<u>Calculation Check:</u>

					$110,801	
					(15,000)	Return of Basis
1/1/99	PV	$110,801		PV	$95,801	
	N	3		N	3	
	i	1.5		i	1.5	
10/1/99	FV/PV	$115,862.21		FV/PV	$100,177.03	
	N	100	Quarters	N	100	
	i	1.5		i	1.5	
	PMT_{AD}	$2,211.15		PMT_{AD}	$1,911.81	

Tax-Annuities

5. **E**

PV @ 10/1/99	$115,862						
Basis	$25,000						
Exclusion Ratio	$25,000 ÷ $221,115	=	11.3063 %	x	$2,211.15	=	$250.00
Inclusion Ratio		=	88.6937%	x	$2,211.15	=	$1,961.15
			100.0000 %				

Incorrect Answer

Exclusion Ratio	$25,000 ÷ $110,801	=	22.5629 %				
Inclusion Ratio		=	77.4371 %	x	$2,211.15	=	$1,712.25
			100.0000 %				

Annuity Payment

10/1/99	PV	=	$115,862
	N	=	100
	i	=	1.5
	PMT_{AD}	=	$2,211.15

Total of annuity payments is $221,115 = ($2,211.15 x 100).

Retirement-Defined Benefit Plan

6. **D**

$100,000 x 25 years x 1.25% = $31,250 ÷ 12 = $2,604.17. (This is the single life annuity.)

Joint life annuity would be $2,604.17 x .80 = $2,083.33.

Fundamentals-Time Value of Money\Annuities

7. **C**

Correct	Incorrect	
PV = $400,000	PV = $400,000	PV = $400,000
i = [((1.10 ÷1.03) - 1.00)x100]/12	i = [((1.10 ÷ 1.03) - 1.00)x100]/12	i = 10% ÷ 12
n = 300	n = 300	n = 300
PMT_{AD} = $2,759.68	PMT_{OA} = $2,775.31	PMT_{AD} = $3,604.76

Retirement-Social Security

8. **B**

Booth receives 80% of $14,322, because he will be 62 in 2001.

PV	=	$13,500
i	=	3
N	=	2
FV	=	$11,457.72 ($14,322.15 x .80)

The analysis to problems 9, 10, and 11 directly follows the answers.

Estates-Probate Estate

9. **B**

$20,000 (see chart on next page).

Estates-Gross Estate

10. **E**

$1,265,801 (see chart on next page). Gift tax paid on gifts within 3 years of death is included in the gross estate (gross up rule).

Estates-Estate Tax Base

11. **D**

$1,225,000 (see chart on next page).

CHART

(Answers problems 9, 10, and 11)

Assets	%	Probate Estate	Gross Estate	Marital Deduction	Children	His Debts
Cash	50%	0	20,000	20,000		5,000 (Credit Card)
SPDA	100%	0	110,801	110,801		
IRA Investments	100%	0	200,000	200,000		
Defined Benefit	100%	0	400,000	400,000		
Residence	50%	0	160,000	160,000		75,000
Vacation Home	50%	0	80,000	80,000		60,000
Personal Prop.	50%	0	50,000	50,000		
Auto1	100%	20,000	20,000	20,000		10,000
		$20,000	$1,040,801	$1,040,801		
Life Insurance Proceeds		0	150,000	0	150,000	
Gift tax paid 1997		0	75,000	0		
TOTALS		**$20,000#9**	**$1,265,801*#10***	$1,040,801	$150,000	$150,000
			Debts	(150,000)		
			F/Adm.	(50,000)		
Wife Marital Deduction				$840,801		

Gross Estate		$1,265,801
Deductions		
Funeral	$20,000	
Administrative	30,000	
Debts	150,000	
Marital	840,801	(1,040,801)
Taxable Estate		$225,000
Add: Post-76 Gifts (taxable)		1,000,000
Tentative Tax Base		**$ 1,225,000*#11***

Estates-Planning

12. **E**

An effective disclaimer has four elements:

1) It must be in writing.
2) It must be made within 9 months of the interest arising.
3) The disclaimant cannot have benefited from the interest he is now disclaiming.
4) He cannot direct the interest that is disclaimed.

THIS PAGE IS INTENTIONALLY LEFT BLANK.

DAVID AND SUSAN YOUNG CASE SCENARIO

TABLE OF CONTENTS
DAVID AND SUSAN YOUNG
CASE A & CASE B INFORMATION

Time to read case scenario = 20 minutes for each case (A and B).

Time to answer questions = 40 minutes for each case (A and B).

Total time for both Case A and Case B together = 120 minutes.

DAVID AND SUSAN YOUNG

Case Scenario for Case A and Case B

David and Susan Young have come to you, a financial planner, for help in developing a plan to accomplish their financial goals. From your initial meeting together, you have gathered the following information:

I. PERSONAL BACKGROUND AND INFORMATION

(As of January 1, 1999)

David Young

Age 26, employed as a salesperson for a rapidly growing air conditioning and heating service company. He has been employed with this company since July 1, 1995. David has tremendous potential and has positioned himself for advancement.

Susan Young

Age 26, a Canadian citizen, employed as an interior design consultant for a home-decorating center. Susan is studying for her interior design license and plans to become an independent design consultant in 3 years.

David and Susan Young

They met May 3, 1995, while attending a mutual friend's birthday party and were married May 3, 1997. They have 1 child, Kim, and Susan is pregnant. The latest ultrasound has determined that she will give birth to twins.

Miscellaneous

They like to take vacations (twice a year), with an average cost of $2,250 per vacation. David and Susan love to go out and entertain weekly with friends.

David and Susan's Children

Kim - Born January 1, 1998.

Twins - Expected late January, 1999.

Kim is perfectly healthy. There is no history of pregnancy complications in either Susan's or David's family.

Parents

David's parents, Kelly and Mike, are fairly well-off and live in California. They own all of their property as community property. They have known Susan for a long time and any gift that they make will be to both David and Susan. Kelly and Mike have made no previous taxable gifts.

The Young's expect David's parents either to lend them interest free or to give them a $30,000 down payment (27%) to buy a house.

II. PERSONAL AND FINANCIAL GOALS

- David wants to start his own business in 10 years. In the meantime, he plans to advance up the corporate ladder in his current job. He wants to open a business similar to his current employer's. He expects he will need $100,000 in today's dollars to start the company.
- The Youngs want to buy a house. They are looking for an $110,000 house, in a neighborhood with a low to moderate crime rate. They expect taxes and homeowner's insurance to average $200 per month.
- Susan would like to pursue a license in interior design license. David wants to sharpen his business skills by attending a local MBA program, which he expects to begin in September 2000. He expects to pay for the program himself. Expected cost is $18,000 ($600 per credit hour in today's dollars).
- They want to create a fund for their children's private education. Current cost of desired school is $2,500 per child per year for elementary, and $5,000 per year for middle and high school. College tuition is expected to be $8,000 per year per child (See **Economic Information).**
- They want to buy a new car within six months ($20,000 - $25,000 desired).
- They would like to buy new furniture for the new house ($8,000 - $10,000).
- They plan to create an Emergency Fund of at least six months salary ($24,000). Currently, they only have a small savings balance; therefore, this amount needs to be saved in installments over the next 4 years.
- They plan to retire in 30 years and travel extensively.
- They expect their raises to average 3.5% over their remaining work life expectancy.
- They both expect to live until age 90.

III. ECONOMIC INFORMATION

- Expected inflation will average 3.5% (CPI) annually.
- Expected return of 11% for the S&P 500 Index.
- T-Bills are currently yielding 5%. The long-term riskless rate is 7% (Treasury Bonds).
- Current mortgage rates are:

  Fixed 15 year: 7.5%

  Fixed 30 year: 8.0%
- Home closing costs are expected to be 3% of any mortgage.
- Savings accounts currently yield 1.5% annually compounded monthly.
- Certificates of Deposit are currently yielding 5% for 1 year.
- Unemployment is currently 6%.
- College: $8,000 / year (expected to increase 5% per year).

IV. INSURANCE INFORMATION

Life Insurance

Insured	David
Owner	David
Beneficiary	Susan
Face Amount	$50,000
Cash Value	0
Type of Policy	Term
Settlement Options	Lump-Sum
Premium	Employer provided

Assumptions For the Purpose of Life Insurance Needs Calculations:

- The surviving spouse will continue working.
- Education fund needed is $50,000 in today's dollars.
- Establish an emergency fund of $24,000 for the survivor.
- Funeral and debt expenses will be $50,000 (including any probate costs).
- Survivor income needs are $3,200 per month in today's dollars for a period of 22 years at which time either spouse would be age 48 (this is $1,200 more than is currently earned).
- From age 48 - 67 survivor needs will be $3,000 ($1,000 above earnings in today's dollar). At age 67 Social Security will provide $750 per month in today's dollars.
- Retirement needs from age 67 - 90 for the survivor are $2,400 per month in today's dollars.
- Life insurance proceeds can be invested at the long-term riskless rate.
- If either David or Susan dies before retirement, the other will continue working until age 67.

Health Insurance

Premium	Employer provided for David
	Susan and the children are dependents under David's policy
Coverage	Major medical with a $500,000 limit on a 80/20 basis
	Maternity coverage also has 80/20 basis
	Dental coverage is not provided
Deductible	$250 per person (3 person maximum)
Family out of pocket limit	$2,500

Disability Insurance -Neither David nor Susan has disability insurance.

Renter's Insurance

Type	HO 4
Contents Coverage	$35,000
Premium	$600 annually
Deductible	$250
Liability	$100,000
Medical Payments	$1,000 per person

Automobile Insurance

Premium	$1,000 total annual premium for both vehicles
Coverage	$10,000/$25,000 liability on each vehicle
Comprehensive	$250 deductible
Collision	$500 deductible

V. INVESTMENT DATA

- Both David and Susan have a high tolerance for risk.
- They currently have $3,840 in David's 401(k) provided by his employer. He is currently deferring 4% of his salary, and the plan will allow up to 10%. The 401(k) offers a variety of mutual funds from aggressive growth stock funds to Treasury money market funds. David currently has 100% invested in the Growth Fund.
- In 1997, David's grandfather gave him ABC stock. The fair market value at the date of the gift was $6,000. David's grandfather originally paid $2,000 for the stock and paid gift tax of $600 on the gift.
- The Young's required rate of return for investments is 1% below the S&P 500 Index return.

VI. INCOME TAX INFORMATION

- David and Susan file a joint tax return. Their total tax rate is 24% (Federal income tax average rate is 15%; State income tax amounts to 2% each year; FICA taxes amount to 7%).

VII. RETIREMENT INFORMATION

- David is a participant in his employer's 401(k) plan.
- Susan is planning a $2,000 IRA contribution for 1999.

VIII. WILL INFORMATION

- David and Susan have simple wills leaving all probate assets to each other.

IX. STATEMENT OF FINANCIAL POSITION

David and Susan Young

Statement of Financial Position

As of January 1, 1999

ASSETS[1]		LIABILITIES[7] AND NET WORTH	
Cash/Cash Equivalents		**Current Liabilities[8]**	
Checking[2]	$750	Credit Card 1 (David)	$1,500
Savings[3]	1,000	Credit Card 2 (Susan)	1,200
Certificate of Deposit[4]	3,000	Credit Card 3 (Susan)	4,800
EE Savings Bonds[5]	500	Credit Card 4 (Susan)	950
Total Cash/ Cash Equivalents	$5,250	Gas Card 1 (David)	200
		Total Current Liabilities	$8,650
Invested Assets			
ABC Stock	$10,000	**Long-Term Liabilities[8]**	
Stock Portfolio[6]	22,000	Student Loans	
David's 401(k)	3,840	David 1	$20,000
Total Invested Assets	$35,840	David 2	15,000
		Susan 1	6,000
Personal Use Assets		***Total Long-Term Liabilities***	$41,000
Auto 1	$7,500		
Auto 2	4,500	**Total Liabilities**	**$49,650**
Furniture	6,000		
Personal Property	7,000	**Net Worth**	**$16,440**
Total Personal Use Assets	$25,000		
Total Assets	**$66,090**	**Total Liabilities and Net Worth**	**$66,090**

Notes to financial statements:

Assets

1 All assets are stated at fair market value.
2 Checking is a non-interest bearing account.
3 Savings Interest of 1.5% annually, compounded monthly.
4 Certificate of Deposit mature December 1, 1999; Interest of 4.5% annually, compounded monthly.
5 EE Savings Bonds, 5 bonds with present value of $100 each; interest of 6% annually; Maturity date of 2027.
6 Stock Portfolio in stock account managed by David.

Liabilities

7 Liabilities are stated at principal only.
8 All liability payments are as indicated on monthly cash flow statement.

X. CASH FLOW STATEMENT (MONTHLY)

David and Susan Young

1999 Monthly Statement of Cash Flow

Projected

CASH INFLOWS/ INCOME			
David-Salary[1]		$2,000	
Susan-Salary[2]		2,000	
Interest Income		15	
Total Inflows		**$4,015**	
CASH OUTFLOWS/ EXPENSES			
401(k) Deferral Savings			$80
Rent			650
Groceries			370
Utilities			70
Water			25
Telephone			40
Auto Fuel			100
Auto Repair			50
Cable TV			35
Child Care			200
Entertainment			300
Vacations[3]			375
Insurance			
Auto	84		
Life	0		
Medical	0		
Renters (HO4)	50		134
Tax			
State Income	80		
Federal Income	600		
FICA	306		986
Student Loan David 1			144
Student Loan David 2			111
Student Loans Susan			45
Credit Card 1 David			51
Gas Card David			9
Credit Card 2 Susan			42
Credit Card 3 Susan			165
Credit Card 4 Susan			33
Total Outflows			**$4,015**
FUNDS TO INVEST			**$0**

Notes to financial statements:

[1] $2,000/month salary = $24,000 per year.

[2] $2,000/month salary = $24,000 per year.

[3] Vacation = Two vacations costing $4,500 per year. $4,500 ÷ 12 months = $375.

XI. DETAILED INVESTMENT PORTFOLIO

David's 401(k) plan

Description	Shares	Price/Share	Total Value	1996 Return	1997 Return
Growth Fund	93.00	$41.29	$3,840.00	13%	7%

Stock Portfolio

Stock	Date Acquired	Cost Basis	Fair Market Value As of 1/1/99	Beta	Current Dividend	Growth of Dividend
A	1/95	$300	$2,800	1.3	200	3.50%
B	3/97	3,000	700	1.6	33	5.00%
C	5/98	5,000	7,000	1.0	400	4.00%
D	6/98	12,000	2,500	1.1	197	2.00%
E	7/98	9,000	9,000	1.2	500	4.25%
TOTAL		$29,300	$22,000	N/A	$1,330	N/A

THIS PAGE IS INTENTIONALLY LEFT BLANK.

DAVID AND SUSAN YOUNG
CASE A
MULTIPLE CHOICE

DAVID AND SUSAN YOUNG CASE

CASE A

1. Assuming they have no savings set aside, how much should be saved at the end of each month, beginning this month, to be able to acquire David's business? Assume they will invest in a no load S&P 500-index fund and will pay all current taxes out of their regular budget. They will reinvest all earnings in this account.
   a. $456.65.
   b. $460.83.
   c. $566.53.
   d. $569.96.
   e. $650.05.

2. Will the Youngs currently qualify for a home mortgage loan, assuming that they make a down payment of $30,000 and finance the closing costs in the mortgage? Which of the following statements is correct?
   a. They can qualify for both the 15-year and the 30-year loan.
   b. They can qualify for the 30-year loan but not the 15-year loan.
   c. They can qualify for the 15-year loan but not the 30-year loan.
   d. They cannot currently qualify for either the 15 or 30-year loan.

3. How much additional life insurance should be purchased on David's life using the needs approach method? (Approximate to the nearest $100,000)
   a. $100,000.
   b. $200,000.
   c. $300,000.
   d. $400,000.
   e. $500,000.

4. How much additional life insurance should be purchased on Susan's life using the needs approach method? (Approximate to the nearest $25,000.)

   a. $125,000.
   b. $225,000.
   c. $325,000.
   d. $375,000.
   e. $425,000.

5. How much additional life insurance is needed on David's life using a human value approach net of state and federal income taxes? (Round to nearest $50,000.) For purposes of this question only, assume David's pay increases are 5%.

   a. $300,000.
   b. $400,000.
   c. $450,000.
   d. $500,000.
   e. $550,000.

6. Regarding the contribution to Susan's IRA for 1999, which of the following statements is/are correct?

   1. David is an active participant in a qualified plan.
   2. Susan's contribution is fully deductible.
   3. Susan's contribution is non-deductible.
   4. Susan's contribution is partially deductible.

   a. 1 and 2.
   b. 2 only.
   c. 1 and 3.
   d. 1 and 4.
   e. 4 only.

7. If David were to sell the ABC stock today, what would be the 1999 tax consequences to the Youngs?

   a. Long-Term Capital Gain of $3,600.
   b. Long-Term Capital Gain of $4,000.
   c. Short-Term Capital Gain of $8,000.
   d. Long-Term Capital Gain of $8,000.
   e. Long-Term Capital Gain of $7,600.

8. Assume David has only the following sale transactions in his stock trading account for 1999:

Sold stock	Date	Sales Price/ Net of Commissions
A	August 15, 1999	$2,750
B	August 15, 1999	$600
C	April 1, 1999	$8,000
D	April 1, 1999	$3,000
		$14,350 total proceeds

What are the net tax consequences of David's stock transactions during 1999?

a. Long-Term Capital Loss $2,400.

b. Short-Term Capital Gain $3,000.

c. Long-Term Capital Gain $2,450.

d. Short-Term Capital Loss $5,950.

e. Short-Term Capital Loss $9,000.

9. If the stock market yields 17%, what is the expected return for the Young's stock portfolio under the CAPM, based on the value as of January 1, 1999?

a. 19.4%.

b. 19.0%.

c. 18.8%.

d. 18.5%.

e. 18.2%.

10. Based on the constant growth dividend model, which of the stocks in the Young's stock portfolio are over-valued as of January 1, 1999?

1. A.
2. B.
3. C.
4. D.
5. E.

a. 1 and 5.

b. 2 and 3.

c. 1, 4, and 5.

d. 2, 3, 4, and 5.

e. 1, 2, 3, 4, and 5.

THIS PAGE IS INTENTIONALLY LEFT BLANK.

DAVID AND SUSAN YOUNG
CASE A
SOLUTIONS

DAVID AND SUSAN YOUNG CASE
CASE A

Case A covers the following topics: Fundamentals, Insurance, Investments, Tax, and Retirement)

1.	E	3.	C	5.	B	7.	E	9.	C
2.	B	4.	C	6.	A	8.	D	10.	B

Summary of Question Types

1. Fundamentals-Time Value of Money
2. Fundamentals-Mortgage Qualification
3. Insurance-Life Insurance Need Calculation (Needs Approach)
4. Insurance-Life Insurance Need Calculation (Needs Approach)
5. Insurance-Life Insurance Need Calculation (Human Value Approach)
6. Retirement-IRA
7. Tax-Sale of Stock
8. Tax-Capital Transactions
9. Investments-Capital Asset Pricing Model
10. Investments-Constant Growth Dividend Model

Fundamentals-Time Value of Money

1. **E**

Step 1	Step 2
PV = \$100,000	FV = \$141,060
N = 10	N = 120
i = 3.5	i = .9166 (11 ÷ 12)
FV = \$141,060	PMT_{OA} = \$650.05

Incorrect answers:

A	B	C	D
N = 120	N = 120	N = 120	N = 120
i = 11 ÷ 12	i = 11 ÷ 12	i = 7.246 ÷ 12	i = 7.246 ÷ 12
FV = \$100,000	FV = \$100,000	FV = \$100,000	FV = \$100,000
PMT_{AD} = \$456.65	PMT_{OA} = \$460.83	PMT_{AD} = \$566.53	PMT_{OA} = \$569.96

Fundamentals-Mortgage Qualification

2. **B**

House	\$110,000	
Down Payment	(30,000)	
	\$80,000	
Closing	2,400	(\$80,000 x .03)
Total mortgage	\$82,400	

Credit card and debt payments are \$600 per month.

	Loan 1	Loan 2
Term	15 years	30 years
N	180	360
i	7.5 ÷ 12	8 ÷ 12
PV	\$82,400	\$82,400
PMT_{OA}	\$763.86	\$604.62
Taxes and insurance	\$200.00	\$200.00
Housing costs	\$963.86	\$804.62
Total housing and debt payments	\$1,563.86	\$1,404.62
Gross income (per month)	\$4,015.00	\$4,015.00

		Loan 1		Loan 2	
	Principal and interest	$763.86		$604.62	
+	Taxes and insurance	200.00		200.00	
=	Housing costs	$963.86		$804.62	
÷	Gross income	$4,015.00		$4,015.00	
=	**Ratio 1**	**24.01%**	✓	**20.04%**	✓
	Housing costs	$963.86		$804.62	
+	Other debt payments	600.00		600.00	
=	Total monthly payments	$1,563.86		$1,404.62	
÷	Gross income	$4,015.00		$4,015.00	
=	**Ratio 2**	**38.95%**	✖	**34.98%**	✓

✓ = Yes **✖ = No**

Note: Principal and interest (P & I) and taxes and insurance (T & I), plus any association fees must be less than or equal to 28% of gross income (for most lenders). In addition, P & I and T & I plus association fees and other monthly indebtedness payments must be less than or equal to 36% of gross income. Both the 28% hurdle and the 36% hurdle must be met to qualify for a mortgage loan. The Youngs do not qualify for the 15-year loan because of the second ratio. They do, however, qualify for the 30-year loan, though they are close to the second ratio hurdle.

Insurance-Life Insurance Need Calculation (Needs Approach)

3. **C**

See explanation on next page.

Insurance-Life Insurance Need Calculation (Needs Approach)

4. **C**

See explanation on next page.

Explanation to problems 3 and 4:

Cash Needs

$50,000	Funeral and Debt
24,000	Emergency Fund
50,000	Education Fund
$124,000	(5)

	Dependency Period		First 4 years of Black Out	Remaining Black Out	Retirement
Period	18 years		4 years	19 years	23 years
Needs	$3,200		$3,200	$3,000	$2,400
Salary	(2,000)		(2,000)	(2,000)	(0)
Social Security	(1,125)	*	(0)	(0)	(750)
PMT$_{AD}$	**$75**		**$1,200**	**$1,000**	**$1,650**
N	18 x 12		4 x 12	19 x 12	23 x 12

i = 1 + 7/1 + 3.5 - 1 = 3.3816425 ÷ 12 = .2818 (same for all)

PV at Date	**12,156**	**53,955**	**168,518**	**317,111**
FV	$12,156	$53,955	$168,518	$317,111
N	0	18	22	41
i	3.3816425	3.3816425	3.3816425	3.3816425
PV now	**$12,156 (1)**	**$29,652 (2)**	**$81,076 (3)**	**$81,102 (4)**

Income needs	$203,986	Σ of present value (1 - 4)
Cash needs	124,000	from above (5)
Life insurance needs	**$327,986**	**for her (4)**
His current insurance	(50,000)	
Additional life insurance needed	**$277,986**	**for him (3)**

* This number reflects 150% of the Social Security payment. When a parent has died, the child is entitled to 150% of PIA, but there is a maximum family limit.

Insurance-Life Insurance Need Calculation (Human Value Approach)

5. **B**

Age 26	$24,000
Work life expectancy	30 years
Pay raises expected	5%
Investment Rate of return	7%
PV_{AD} of life income	$554,994
1 - tax rate	.83

Note: FICA taxes would be inapplicable.

N	=	30	=	
PMT	=	$24,000	=	
i	=	1.9047619	=	[(1.07 ÷ 1.05) – 1] x 100
PV_{AD}	=	$460,645	=	$554,994 x .83

$460,645 - 50,000 = $410,645

Retirement-IRA

6. **A**

Statement #1 is correct. Statement #2 is correct. Since David is an active participant in a qualified plan and Susan is not, the phaseout begins at $150,000.

Tax-Sale of Stock

7. **E**

<u>Step 1: Establish David's basis.</u>

Carryover basis of donor	=	$2,000
PLUS Pro rata share of gift tax paid on appreciation by Donor*	=	400
David's basis	=	$2,400

<u>Step 2: Determine Gain.</u>

Proceeds	$10,000
Basis	(2,400)
Long-Term Gain	**$7,600**

$$* \ \frac{\text{Appreciation}}{\text{FMV}} \times \text{gift tax paid} = \frac{\$4,000}{\$6,000} \times \$600 = \$400$$

Tax-Capital Transactions

8. **D**

STCG	=	$3,000	C	LTCG	=	$2,450	A
STCL	=	(9,000)	D	LTCL	=	(2,400)	B
Net STGL	=	$6,000		Net LTCG	=	$50	

Net STGL	=	$6,000
Net LTCG	=	(50)
Net STCL	=	$5,950

Investments-Capital Asset Pricing Model

9. **C**

Step 1: Find the beta for the portfolio

$2,800	x	1.3	=	$3,640
700	x	1.6	=	1,120
7,000	x	1.0	=	7,000
2,500	x	1.1	=	2,750
9,000	x	1.2	=	10,800
$22,000				$25,310

$25,310 ÷ $22,000 = 1.15045

Step 2: Determine expected return

$E(R) = Rf + B(R_M - Rf)$

$E(R) = .05 + 1.15(.17 - .05)$

$E(R) = 18.8\%$

Use 5%, because it is the T-bill rate.

Investments-Constant Growth Dividend Model

10. **B**

Stock	Current dividend	d_1	Required return	Growth rate	Diff.	d_1/diff.	FMV
A	$200	$207.00	10%	3.5%	6.5%	$3,185	$2,800
B	33	34.65	10%	5%	5.0%	693	700
C	400	416.00	10%	4.0%	6.0%	6,933	7,000
D	197	200.94	10%	2.0%	8.0%	2,512	2,500
E	500	521.25	10%	4.25%	5.75%	9,065	9,000

Stocks B and C are over-valued.

DAVID AND SUSAN YOUNG
CASE B
MULTIPLE CHOICE

DAVID AND SUSAN YOUNG CASE

CASE B PROBLEMS

USE THE FOLLOWING INFORMATION FOR QUESTIONS 1 THROUGH 7

While on a vacation at Ricky Lake, the Youngs had several unfortunate incidents.

- A large pigeon collided into the windshield of their automobile causing $800 worth of damage while driving to the lake.
- David rented a 100 horse power jet ski. While skiing, his wallet was stolen, but he thought he had lost the wallet in the lake, so he did not report the loss to the credit card company until he returned home.
- While David was jet skiing, Susan was taken to the emergency room where she gave birth to twins. Mother and children are doing fine.
- While jet skiing, David saw the ambulance take Susan to the hospital. While he was looking at the ambulance, he skied into a boat causing damage to the jet ski, the boat, and to David. The boat owner had minor medical injuries.
- Upon returning home with the twins and their older child, they discovered that their apartment building had been destroyed by fire.

1. How much will David's insurance company pay to have his windshield repaired?
   a. $0.
   b. $250.
   c. $300.
   d. $550.
   e. $800.

2. When David received his credit card statements, he discovered that the following amounts had been charged to his credit cards by the thief:

   1. Credit card 1 $200.
   2. Credit card 2 $450.
   3. Credit card 3 $35.
   4. Credit card 4 $60.

   How much will David be responsible for?

   a. $0.
   b. $50.
   c. $185.
   d. $200.
   e. $745.

3. The hospital costs for delivery of the twins was $8,000. How much will the insurance company pay?

   a. $8,000.
   b. $6,450.
   c. $6,400.
   d. $6,200.
   e. $6,150.

4. The fire that destroyed the apartment building also destroyed all of the Youngs' personal property. While the depreciated or actual cash value of all their property is $5,000, it would cost the Youngs about $37,000 to replace all of their lost items. How much will the insurance company pay for this loss?

   a. $4,750.
   b. $5,000.
   c. $12,750.
   d. $35,750.
   e. $36,750.

5. David's collision with the boat caused $1,200 of damage to the boat owned by a Mr. George Mitchell. Which of the following is correct?
   a. The HO4 will cover the entire loss if David is found to be responsible.
   b. The HO4 will cover the $1,200 loss less the $250 deductible.
   c. The HO4 will not pay anything, because this situation is excluded under all homeowners policies.
   d. The HO4 will not pay anything, because this is property damage and the liability coverage extends only to bodily injury.

6. The boat owner suffered $200 in emergency medical expense to reset his broken arm caused by the jet ski incident. Which of the following is correct regarding the $200?
   a. The liability section of the HO4 will pay for the full $200.
   b. The medical payments section of the HO4 will pay for the full $200.
   c. The HO4 will not pay for these medical expenses.
   d. The automobile policy will pay these medical expenses.

7. In the jet ski accident, David suffered medical expenses of $1,450. Which of the following is correct?
   1. The HO4 will cover these expenses, but only up to $1,000.
   2. The HO4 will not cover these expenses at all.
   3. The major medical policy will cover 80/20 after the $250 deductible.
   4. The major medical will not cover this situation, because the jet ski is rented.
   a. 1 only.
   b. 1 and 3.
   c. 1 and 4.
   d. 2 only.
   e. 2 and 3.

8. The Youngs want to establish a fund that will provide for each child's college education for a period of four years. Any post-graduate education will be the responsibility of the child. If they can earn an after-tax rate of return equal to the return by the S&P 500 Index, how much do they need to save at the end of each month to be able to fund their children's education by the end of 10 years? Assume that the children will all go to a college on their 18th birthday and tuition is paid at the beginning of each year. (Round to the nearest answer.)

   a. $460.
   b. $435.
   c. $365.
   d. $350.
   e. $300.

9. If David's parents donate the down payment on the house, which of the following is/are correct?

   1. The gift qualifies for the annual exclusion.
   2. The parents, Mike and Kelly, must file a gift tax return.
   3. The parents are liable for a small amount of gift tax.
   4. This donation is a taxable gift.

      a. 1 only.
      b. 1 and 2.
      c. 1, 2, and 3.
      d. 2, 3, and 4.
      e. 1, 2, 3, and 4.

10. Assume Kelly and Mike decide to loan the down payment to Susan and David instead of giving it to them, what are the tax consequences to Kelly and Mike? The federal rate for imputed interest is 9%.

   a. The loan is less than $10,000 and, therefore, excepted.
   b. Kelly and Mike have made a taxable gift of $2,700 to David and Susan.
   c. Susan and David must impute the $2,700 of taxable income.
   d. Kelly and Mike must impute $2,700 of taxable income.
   e. This loan has no adverse tax consequences to Kelly and Mike.

11. Which of the following is/are correct regarding deficiencies in the Youngs' current estate planning?

1. They are subject to probate.
2. They have currently overqualified the estate.
3. They have made no provision for guardianship of children.
4. They have made no provision for a durable power of attorney for health care.

a. 1 and 2.

b. 1, 3, and 4.

c. 1, 2, and 3.

d. 2, 3, and 4.

e. 1, 2, 3, and 4.

THIS PAGE IS INTENTIONALLY LEFT BLANK.

DAVID AND SUSAN YOUNG CASE B SOLUTIONS

DAVID AND SUSAN YOUNG CASE
CASE B

Case B covers the following topics: Fundamentals, Insurance, and Estates)

1.	D	3.	D	5.	C	7.	E	9.	A	11.	B
2.	C	4.	A	6.	C	8.	B	10.	E		

Summary of Question Types

1. Insurance-Comprehensive Insurance
2. Fundamentals-Consumer Protection
3. Insurance-Medical Insurance
4. Insurance-HO4 Policy
5. Insurance-Liability Insurance
6. Insurance-Medical Expenses
7. Insurance-Medical Expenses
8. Fundamentals-College Funding
9. Estates-Gift Tax
10. Estates-Gift Tax
11. Estates-Estate Planning

Insurance-Comprehensive Insurance

1. **D**

Damage	$800
Less Comprehensive Deductible	(250)
Amount Paid by Insurance Company	$550

Fundamentals-Consumer Protection

2. **C**

Credit Card 1	$50
Credit Card 2	50
Credit Card 3	35
Credit Card 4	50
	$185

Insurance-Medical Insurance

3. **D**

Total hospital cost	$8,000
Less deductible	(250)
Net cost	$7,750
Insurance percent	x 80%
Amount insurance company pays	$6,200

Insurance-HO4 Policy

4. **A**

$5,000	
(250)	deductible
$4,750	

Insurance-Liability Insurance

5. C

Rental watercraft over 50 horse power are excluded from all homeowner and renter policies. The coverage will have to be provided by the lessor or David may have to pay personally for any liability.

Insurance-Medical Expenses

6. C

This incident is excluded from coverage under both the HO4 and the auto policy as the jet ski is rented and over 50 horse power.

Insurance-Medical Expenses

7. E

The HO4 will not cover this situation, but the major medical will cover. Rental watercraft over 50 horse power are excluded from all homeowner policies.

Fundamentals-College Funding

8. B

Step 1 = PV of annuity due

	Kim	Twin 1	Twin 2
PMT	$8,000	$8,000	$8,000
N	4	4	4
i	5.714	5.714	5.714
PV_{AD}	$29,497.75	$29,497.75	$29,497.75

Step 2 = PV of future sum

	Kim	Twin 1	Twin 2
FV_{18}	$29,497.75	$29,497.75	$29,497.75
N	17	18	18
i	5.714	5.714	5.714
PV_{AD}	$11,469	$10,849	$10,849

= Determine payment

	=	$33,167 (10,849 x 2 + 11,469)	FV	=	$94,175
	=	10	N	=	120 (10 x 12 months)
	=	11	i	=	11 ÷ 12
FV	=	$94,175	PMT	=	$433.99

Estates-Gift Tax

9. **A**

The gift is from community property. Therefore, it is a joint gift and not a split gift. It qualifies for the annual exclusion as Mike and Kelly are each making a gift of $7,500 to each David and Susan. No gift tax return is required to be filed. This is not a taxable gift.

Estates-Gift Tax

10. **E**

A is incorrect, the loan is $30,000.

B is incorrect, because the loan is not a taxable gift.

C is incorrect, because the borrower does not impute. The lender does.

D is incorrect, because the loan is excepted because it is under $100,000 and David and Susan's portfolio income is also less than $1,000.

Estates-Estate Planning

11. **B**

The estate is so small it could hardly be looked at as currently overqualified. Statements #1, #3, and #4 are deficiencies that the Youngs should correct.